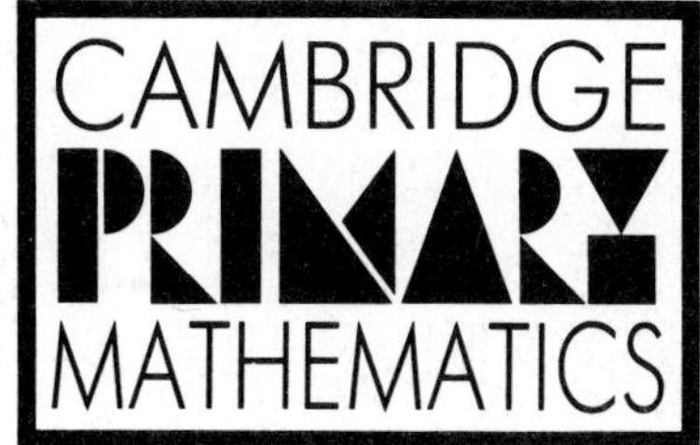

Module 6

Teacher's resource book

Roy Edwards, Mary Edwards
and Alan Ward

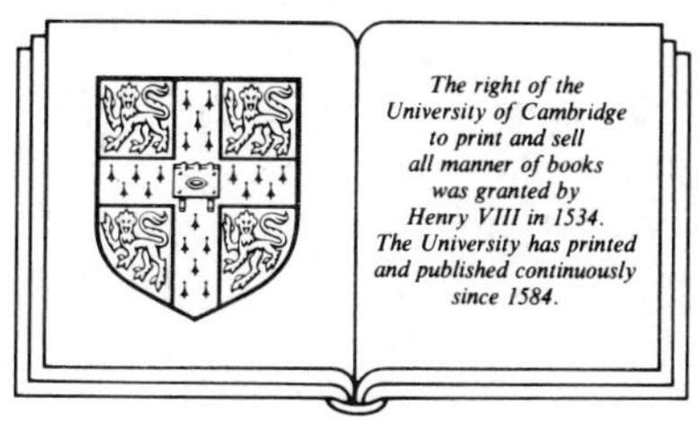

Cambridge University Press
Cambridge
New York Port Chester Melbourne Sydney

Published by the Press Syndicate of the University of Cambridge
The Pitt Building, Trumpington Street, Cambridge CB2 1RP
40 West 20th Street, New York NY 10011, USA
10 Stamford Road, Oakleigh, Melbourne 3166, Australia

First published 1990

Printed in Great Britain by Scotprint, Musselburgh

British Library cataloguing in publication data

Edwards, Roy 1931–
Cambridge primary mathematics
Module 6
Teacher's resource book
1. Mathematics – For schools
I. Title II. Edwards, Mary 1936
III. Ward, Alan 1932
510

ISBN 0 521 35828 0

The authors and publishers would like to thank the many schools and individuals who have commented on draft material for this course. In particular, they would like to thank Ronalyn Hargreaves (Hyndburn Ethnic Minority Support Service), John Hyland, Norma Pearce and Anita Straker, who wrote the chapter on 'Using the computer'.

CONTENTS

Mathematical content of chapters in Module 6

	BOOK 1		
Number (mainly addition and subtraction)	**Number 1** Place value Addition of ThHTU with exchanging from T and U Rounding to nearest 10, 100 Strategy for adding 99	**Number 2** Place value Subtraction of ThHTU with exchanging from H and T Rounding or approximating	
Number (mainly multiplication and division)	**Number 3** Rules for divisibility Number patterns Remainders in context	**Number 7** Multiplication of HTU by 1 digit Linking multiplication and division Multiplication methods	
Number	**Number 4** Negative numbers in context	**Number 6** Function machines	**Number 8** Decimal notation in the context of measurement or money
Number (fractions)	**Number 5** $\frac{1}{6}$, $\frac{1}{12}$, $\frac{1}{5}$, $\frac{1}{10}$ Equivalence of fractions		
Shape	**Shape 1** Lines of symmetry Planes of symmetry	**Shape 2** Properties of triangles Parallel, horizontal, vertical Quadrilaterals Rigidity	
Data	**Data 1** Sorting 2-D and 3-D shapes Classifying and recording	**Data 2** Average (mean) and range	
Probability	**Probability 1** Distinguishing fair and unfair Using the idea of 'evens' Order of likelihood		
Money	**Money 1** Bills and receipts Rounding money	**Money 2** Banking Deposits and withdrawals	
Measurement	**Length 1** Circumference, diameter, radius of a circle	**Weight 1** Reading scales Practical weighing	**Volume and Capacity** Reading scales Notation Practical work
Time	**Time 1** Timing devices Minutes Timing in seconds		
Angles			
Co-ordinates			

	BOOK 2		
Number (mainly addition and subtraction)	**Number 10** Addition of ThHTU with exchanging from H, T and U Rounding or approximating	**Number 11** Subtraction of ThHTU with exchanging from Th, H and T Exploring other number systems	
Number (mainly multiplication and division)	**Number 12** Revision of HTU ÷ 1 digit Using metric units		
Number			
Number (fractions)	**Number 9** Fractions of quantities	**Number 13** Addition of fractions with the same denominator	
Shape	**Shape 3** Constructing 3-D shapes using nets	**Shape 4** Further tessellations	
Data	**Data 3** Line graphs	**Data 4** Equal class intervals Grouping data	**Data 5** Straight line graphs
Probability	**Probability 2** Listing possible outcomes		
Money	**Money 3** Reading and interpreting data Costing holidays		
Measurement	**Area** Finding area using length and width	**Weight 2** Introduction of the tonne	**Length 2** km and m Addition and subtraction Simple networks
Time	**Time 2** The 24-hour clock	**Time 3** Reading and interpreting timetables	
Angles	**Angles 1** Measuring to 10°	**Angles 2** Measuring to 5°	
Co-ordinates	**Co-ordinates** Co-ordinates and direction		

INTRODUCTION

Aims

Cambridge Primary Mathematics is designed for 4–11 year old children. It takes into account current thinking in mathematical education and in particular it provides opportunities for:

- exposition
- discussion
- practical work
- consolidation and practice
- problem-solving
- investigational work

It is also designed to make mathematics relevant for the children and there is considerable emphasis on presenting the mathematics in real situations. Calculator work is incorporated throughout at the discretion of the teacher and ideas are given for using the computer. The materials are for children of all abilities and particular thought has been given to those with special educational needs.

Cambridge Primary Mathematics provides you with a sound foundation for all your mathematics teaching. It is *not* trying to take the place of a teacher, but rather acknowledge your professionalism. All the materials that make up Cambridge Primary Mathematics are giving you, the teacher, a core of valuable resources, so you can teach mathematics in whatever way suits you best. Cambridge Primary Mathematics can be used in its entirety and does not need additional material in order to provide a thorough mathematics curriculum. However you may prefer to teach using a variety of materials and Cambridge Primary Mathematics will give you a rich source of teaching ideas which you can supplement.

The materials

Each topic can be introduced to a class or group with activities and discussion. Ideas for these are given in the teaching notes. The children can then try the relevant chapter in the pupils' book.

Pupils' books

Each chapter in the pupils' books has its concepts developed in three stages.

Section A is intended for all children and care has been taken to make it easily accessible. It consolidates the introduction, discussion and practical work provided by the teacher and finishes with a

Module	For teachers	Pupils' core materials	Reinforcement and enrichment		Software	Assessment
1 4–5 yrs	Module 1 Teacher's resource pack	Module 1 Workbooks	Module 1 Games pack Module 1 Extra cut-up cards and rules Module 1 Rhymes pack			
2 5–6 yrs	Module 2 Teacher's resource pack	Module 2 Workcards	Module 2 Games pack Module 2 Extra cut-up cards and rules			
3 6–7 yrs	Module 3 Teacher's resource pack	Module 3 Workcards	Module 3 Games pack Module 3 Extra cut-up cards and rules			
4 7–8 yrs	Module 4 Teacher's resource book	Module 4 Book 1 Module 4 Book 2 Module 4 Answer book	Module 4 Skill support activities	Module 4 Games pack Module 4 Puzzle pack Module 4 and Module 5 Project booklets	SOFTWARE	Module 4 Assessment pack
5 8–9 yrs	Module 5 Teacher's resource book	Module 5 Book 1 Module 5 Book 2 Module 5 Answer book	Module 5 Skill support activities	Module 5 Games pack Module 5 Puzzle pack		Module 5 Assessment pack
6 9–10 yrs	Module 6 Teacher's resource book	Module 6 Book 1 Module 6 Book 2 Module 6 Answer book	Module 6 Skill support activities	Module 6 Games pack Module 6 Puzzle pack Module 6 and Module 7 Project booklets		Module 6 Assessment pack
7 10–11 yrs	Module 7 Teacher's resource book	Module 7 Book 1 Module 7 Book 2 Module 7 Answer book	Module 7 Skill support activities	Module 7 Games pack Module 7 Puzzle pack		Module 7 Assessment pack

problem or investigation. Children who need further reinforcement can be given work from the skill support masters.

Section B is suitable for the majority of children and covers the same concepts in more breadth, and again includes an investigation.

Section C, which includes a further investigation, can be used as extension work.

The work in these sections is usually based on a theme of interest to children (e.g. school fund-raising, dinosaurs, etc.) in order to give the material more cohesion and to make it relevant to the environment.

This structure ensures that all children can follow a basic course of mathematics, covering all the concepts at whatever stage is appropriate to them. Organisationally this allows the teacher to teach the children as a class or in groups, as all sections cover the same topics but at increasing breadth. Children who complete only section A will not be left behind in the progression. The A, B, C format will provide for problem-solving and investigational skills to be developed across all areas of the mathematics curriculum by all children.

Logos

Throughout the pupils' books, certain logos are used to show children the items they will need or which would be particularly helpful.

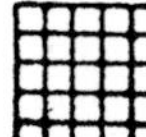 shows that squared paper is needed.

 means a clock face stamp would be useful.

 tells children they can time themselves.

 indicates that a calculator would be useful.

 shows that glue is required.

 indicates that scissors are needed.

The logos are used partly to reduce the language in instructions and partly to give children visual clues for items they need.

Coloured text

Two colours of text are used in the pupils' books in order to help the children. Black text is used for instructions and information. Blue text shows the parts the children will need to record in their books.

Answer books

The answer books contain reduced facsimiles of the pages in the pupils' books. The answers are superimposed.

Games packs

There is a games pack for each module. The games are linked to the mathematical content of the course and are intended to consolidate children's skills and also to encourage children in logical thinking and development of strategies.

Puzzle packs

There is a puzzle pack for each of Modules 4–7. These packs provide extra extension material and additional interest.

Skill support activities

The packs provide extra work for those children who need it. One set consolidates the basic concepts, and another set develops the concepts still further for the more able.

Project booklets

These are written for use by pupils and provide opportunities for project work and the linking of mathematics with the environment and with other areas of the curriculum.

Organisation and management

The materials needed are readily available, but to help you further there is a complete list of all equipment required at the end of this book. Materials can be collected, boxed and labelled so that they are easily accessible to the children. Picture labels will help those with reading problems.

Cambridge Primary Mathematics is not intended as a scheme for children to work at individually, but instead to give you control over how the mathematics is taught. The following ideas have been suggested by teachers who used the early materials.

- Introduce each topic using your own ideas plus the information in the teacher's notes.
- Let children develop the concepts at their own levels using the A, B, C structure and the skill support masters.
- Some of the investigations are particularly suitable for work and discussion in a large group or whole class.
- Overcome a shortage of equipment, like balance scales, by organising groups to work at several different activities.
- Use the games and puzzles to reinforce particular teaching points or skills as part of the normal mathematics lesson.
- Look for the calculator games in the teacher's notes.

Cambridge Primary Mathematics gives you the space to include your own ideas and to develop concepts as part of the whole curriculum.

Using the teacher's resource book

There is a section in the teacher's book for each chapter of the pupils' material. The format for each one is as follows:

Purpose

This outlines the mathematical objectives of the pupils' pages for the particular chapter.

Materials

This lists all the materials required by the pupils as they work through the mathematics.

Vocabulary

This provides you with the essential mathematical vocabulary that is used in the pupils' books. You will know which words the children will be meeting and be able to introduce them during earlier teaching sessions.

Teaching points

This section contains possible teaching approaches and activities for all the mathematics in the pupils' books. Many of these are introductory activities for the concepts. As well as activities, the notes are full of ideas and games to add to your own approach and already successful methods. You will also find ideas for mental skills, such as a quick way to add 2-figure numbers, that will help children master and enjoy mathematics.

The Cockcroft report emphasises the importance of discussion between teacher and child, and between children. These notes give you suggestions for questions to set discussion going, and give children the opportunity to talk, ask questions and develop their mathematics. It also allows you to listen to the children and see how their understanding is developing.

There are also ideas for introducing the practical activities and further suggestions for developing these.

Using the calculator

In this part there are ideas for incorporating a calculator into mathematics. The calculator is to be used at your discretion and there will be occasions when you won't want the children to use one. However, you will probably want to have calculators readily available and there will be times when children will need a calculator to help them complete their work. The calculator is a useful aid for children to develop a particular piece of mathematics. In the pupils' book a logo is used to indicate where a calculator will be especially useful.

Links with the environment

These notes show how the mathematical ideas may be related to the everyday environment or linked to other curriculum areas. You can develop these ideas further and incorporate them into topic work across the curriculum. The project booklets will also be useful in developing many of these ideas.

Notes on investigations

Investigations are essentially open-ended situations where different approaches can be made. The notes are not meant to be used rigidly but to give guidance and suggestions for developing the mathematics. There is an additional section on investigations included in the introduction (pages 10–11).

ISSUES IN MATHEMATICS TEACHING

Language in mathematics

Language gives mathematics context and meaning. It sets the scene, poses problems and gives information. But the way language is used and how children interpret it is crucial to their success and progress. How then does language affect mathematics?

The words used are important. Some are found only in mathematics and have to be learned, like 'parallelogram' and 'right-angle'. Some, like 'add' and 'equal', have the same meaning in or out of mathematics, and some, the ones most likely to cause problems, have different meanings according to their context; 'table' and 'difference' have both mathematical and ordinary English meanings.

Not only are the words important but so is the style of writing. There will be *explanations* of concepts, methods, vocabulary, notation and rules. *Instructions* will tell the reader what to do, and *exercises* will give practice of the skills and set problems or investigations. *Peripheral text* will introduce exercises or give clues to ways of approach, and *signals* give structure to the text with headings, letters, numbers, boxes and logos. Children must be able to see their way through all these forms of writing.

But, in addition to the words and writing, mathematics also involves reading visual information. A good mathematics text should use illustrations effectively to add information. They should not be purely for decoration, or related but not essential to the mathematics. There are also many forms of visual language which children need to understand. These include tables, graphs, diagrams, plans and maps. It is important to teach children to decode this information, interpret and make use of it, and present their answers or conclusions in different forms.

The skills children need for reading mathematics have only been touched on here. An awareness of the complexities involved will help you to overcome any difficulties caused by language and so prevent them becoming mathematical problems too. Useful books to read are *Children Reading Mathematics,* by Hilary Shuard and Andrew Rothery (John Murray) and *Maths Talk,* from The Mathematical Association.

Mathematics and special needs

Many difficulties which children experience with mathematics are not genuinely mathematical. Children with special educational needs, for whatever reasons, may have problems with mathematics because of a wide variety of factors. By looking at possible causes of difficulty many problems can be prevented or at least significantly helped.

In writing Cambridge Primary Mathematics careful attention has been given to making the mathematics accessible to *all* children, particularly in the A sections. The following areas have been looked at carefully.

Mathematical language

- Familiar words
- Words in context
- Repetition of important words and phrases
- Clear and unambiguous instructions
- Clear indication of response expected
- Sentences of a suitable length and structure
- Clear and unambiguous symbols

Presentation

- Appropriate quantity of work
- Interesting and relevant illustrations
- Variety of presentation
- Attractive page layout to encourage a positive attitude

Independence

- Clear indication of apparatus needed
- Materials that will be readily available
- Instructions children will be able to read and understand

Recording

- No unnecessary writing
- Minimum writing to help children with motor-control difficulties
- Word prompts to aid spelling

Practical work

- Plenty of practical activities
- Use of concrete apparatus encouraged
- Practical work encouraged and built in with the maths

Attitude

- Children are given a purpose to their work
- The mathematics is put in meaningful contexts
- Mathematics is related to other curriculum areas

There are some aspects of special needs that can only be dealt with by you in the classroom. For example, children may not be able to get all the equipment they need and so labelling boxes and drawers with pictures can help. Sometimes their handwriting can cause problems through poor letter or number formation, or because they are left-handed, and extra practice in this may be needed.

Skill support masters for section A give extra support and reinforcement for those children needing further practice or consolidation. Where possible, alternative methods of approach have been given but the masters are essentially to strengthen work already done.

Mathematical language, presentation, independence, recording, practical work and, just as important, the attitude children bring to their work are all vital for success. By identifying whether a difficulty is genuinely mathematical you can remove or alleviate many problems. You know your children best, and by looking at all the factors affecting their learning you can meet their special needs. By doing so, you can give them the love and fascination for mathematics so that they achieve to the best of their potential.

English as a second language in mathematics

Research suggests that many children lack a firm grasp of the language of mathematics. In the case of children with English as a second language, this is often compounded by other language difficulties.

All pupils need the opportunity to hear and use the correct mathematical vocabulary. They need to develop concepts and the appropriate language together. You should not assume that because children can perform a mechanical mathematical task that they understand the associated language. You can check this by discussion with the pupil.

Practical activities are the essential starting point for any topic. Every opportunity should be taken to use correct mathematical vocabulary with pupils and to encourage them to use it when talking with other children and teachers. Where possible this vocabulary should be reinforced in other curricular areas, e.g. art and craft, games, PE etc.

Activities which offer opportunities for group work are also very useful for language development since the children are required to cooperate and to discuss the work they are doing. Investigations, calculator and computer work all lend themselves to pair or group activities.

When discussing work or activities with the children you should try to avoid the questioning approach which only requires short or one-word answers. Instead encourage full explanations of pupils' thoughts and actions using the correct vocabulary.

Weaknesses in mathematical language and the comprehension of mathematical texts often only become apparent in the junior school where greater emphasis is placed on reading and recording. Even pupils who can read a mathematical text may well be unable to interpret it. Oral discussion, individually or in groups, will help to develop the skills required.

Special attention should be given to words which sound similar; for example, 'hundred' 'hundredth', and 'seventeen' 'seventy'. Pronunciation is often a problem with second-language learners because certain sounds may not exist in their mother tongue. However, they should be encouraged to attempt to make the distinctions clear.

Words which have a mathematical meaning different from that in normal English – like 'similar', 'difference' and 'table' – also need special attention.

It is important not to skimp on the language aspect of mathematics in order to 'push on' with mechanical exercises and recording. A weak language base will lead to downfalls later.

Mathematics and gender

There is evidence that in the past many girls have under-achieved in mathematics. The reasons for this are complex and only an indication can be given here. Although the problem may only become apparent in the secondary school, the roots of it can often lie in the primary school.

In Cambridge Primary Mathematics there has been an attempt to produce material which will encourage girls as much as boys. As far as is possible, the pupil materials show equal numbers of girls and boys, show them participating equally in all types of activity, and illustrate how mathematics can be used in situations familiar to girls as well as to boys.

However, the written materials are only a part of the mathematics teaching. There is a great deal that you, as a teacher, can do to help the girls in your class.

- Try to encourage girls to use apparatus and toys which encourage spatial awareness, for example, Lego. Girls often have less access to this kind of toy at home, and an intuitive feeling for space is important for later work.
- Try to make sure that you spend as much time interacting with girls as with boys. It is very easy to give more time to a group of demanding boys and to leave a group of quiet girls to get on with their work.
- There has been research which shows that girls in primary schools are less likely than boys to have a calculator, to own a digital watch and to have a microcomputer at home. You may find it useful to do a survey of your class so that you are aware of the children who may need extra help with these items.

If you would like to find out more about encouraging girls to achieve their potential in mathematics, then you may find it useful to read *Girls into Mathematics* by the Open University (published by Cambridge University Press). The book was written mainly for teachers in secondary school, but many of the activities could be adapted easily for use in primary schools.

Using the calculator

Calculators are now widely available and are used extensively in the world of work. It is therefore important that children should learn to use them intelligently. The course has been written on the assumption that children have calculators available, although the extent to which they are used is left to the individual teacher.

In the pupils' books a logo is used to show activities which would particularly benefit from the use of a calculator. The teaching notes contain suggestions to develop use of the calculator including many ideas for games.

A simple four-function calculator is all that is required. Ideally these should be to hand whenever children are doing mathematics and it should be natural for children to turn to them when they are needed. Children with special needs may need to use a calculator to complete section A even in places where the logo is not shown.

The use of the calculator has brought about a shift in the content of the mathematics included in the course. There is less emphasis on straight computation and more on problem-solving. It is also important that children develop mental strategies so that they can check that calculator answers are approximately correct and they have not miskeyed. Ideas for developing these mental skills are given in the teaching notes.

Using the computer

The computer is a useful tool for developing mathematical ideas. It can also be a useful way to get children to discuss their mathematics.

Make the most of any opportunities you have for using the computer during mathematics. Children should work at it in twos or threes as this allows scope for discussion. It is important that within each group, there is no one child dominating and restricting the participation of the others. For this reason it may be necessary to select the groups carefully.

Ideas for using the computer with Module 6 are given in the chapter on using the computer on pages 12–29. This chapter was written by Anita Straker who has a lot of experience in this area. The ideas are not restricted to any particular model of computer.

There is software planned for use alongside the course. The aim of it is to develop problem-solving skills. It is not tied to any particular chapters of the course.

Investigations

Investigations are essentially open-ended activities where children may devise various approaches. They provide an ideal opportunity for children to devise their own pieces of mathematics, to use logical reasoning, and to discuss mathematics between themselves.

Ideally children should work on investigations in small groups. This gives them the chance to talk, think and express their ideas.

When they have worked on an investigation as a group for a while, it can be very beneficial to have the group report to the rest of the class on how they approached the task. This gives an opportunity for the class to see alternative approaches and various problem-solving techniques.

It is important not to make remarks that judge children's contributions and not to become so involved that the investigation ceases to be the child's. The ideal contribution from the teacher is questions such as:

> 'Why did this work?'
> 'Will it work with other shapes or numbers?'
> 'What would happen if . . .?'

The teaching notes include comments on the investigations. These are not meant to be used rigidly but merely to give some indication of where the investigation might lead. Other approaches may be just as good, or better! Children should be encouraged to find their own way of recording and to ask further questions in order to extend their work.

Algorithms

Algorithms are methods for doing calculations. On the whole, these detailed methods are not given in the texts in order to allow freedom of choice. You can introduce your preferred method, or alternatively the children can devise their own. If children do work out their own algorithms then a teaching approach similar to investigations can be used with children sharing their ideas. This approach has the advantage that the method becomes the child's own and they are more likely to remember it.

Use of practical work

Children should be encouraged to use apparatus and concrete materials whenever possible. It is important that children have plenty of experience in practical situations before moving on to doing more abstract activities. They should not be hurried into making this step.

The materials required for this course are widely available. A checklist of what you will need for Module 6 is given at the end of the book.

USING THE COMPUTER

The computer's contribution to children's mathematical work comes through using:

- specific programs in which children can explore mathematical ideas
- adventure games and simulation which support mathematics across the curriculum
- software tools like databases and programming languages which support open-ended problem-solving

In each case, the software can act as a stimulus to children to talk about mathematical ideas. Through their informal discussion with each other and with their teacher children can build sound intuitive ideas about mathematical concepts. Children need to work in small groups at the computer, so that they have a chance to share and to talk about what is happening on the screen.

Specific programs

Although there are many 'drill and practice' mathematics programs, there seems little point in using the computer for practice when there is already an abundance of mathematics practice material in books, on workcards and on worksheets.

Some of the most attractive of the specific programs are in the form of strategic games or puzzles. In these the children need to focus on the strategy which is to be used, and they will often use mental skills in the process. It is important that teachers link the use of these programs to the children's work away from the keyboard: both preliminary and follow-up activities need to be planned in advance.

There are also specific programs which encourage mathematical investigation. The starting point of the investigation should be through practical work away from the computer, but when the diagrams become too complicated, or the calculations too difficult, the computer program can take over.

Adventure games and simulations

Adventure games, based on fantasy, and simulations, based on fact, give children opportunities to solve problems across the curriculum in a context of fact or fantasy. Simulations like *Cars – Maths in Motion* (Cambridge Software House), *Suburban Fox* (Newman College) or *Bike Ride* (Energy Pack, Cambridge University Press) require strategic thinking and planning, and the use of a range of mathematical and other skills. Adventure games, like *The Lost Frog* (ESM), *Dread Dragon Droom* (RESOURCE), *Puff* or *Martello* (A. Straker), all have a series of mathematical puzzles and problems which need to be resolved.

Primary children often lack confidence in problem-solving situations but such programs can provide them with additional opportunities for developing their mathematical thinking and increasing their range of problem-solving strategies. The role of the teacher in encouraging discussion about the possible forms of solution is an important one here. Questions like 'What would happen if instead . . .?', or 'How many different ways could we . . .?', or 'Would it be possible to . . .?', all help to extend the children's thinking about a particular problem.

Databases

Databases support a range of statistical work across the curriculum. Databases can be used to encourage the children to ask questions, to collect, organise and analyse data, and to find patterns and relationships.

There are two kinds of databases which are useful.

Sorting Game (MESU), *Seek* (Longman) and *Branch* (MEP Project Work Pack) are databases based upon a branching-tree structure. They encourage the use of very precise mathematical description in sorting and classifying. Children can set up binary-tree classification systems, using the program alongside the practical sorting activities which take place throughout the primary school.

Databases like *Our Facts* (MESU) or *Factfile* (CUP) work in the same way as a card index system. Graph drawing packages like *Picfile* (CUP), which display the data graphically, are very helpful here.

Programming

Young children begin 'to program' as soon as they start to find ways of recording things like a sequence of moves in a game, the commands to give to a battery-driven robot, or the shapes which are needed to make up a picture. A computer program, like a sheet of music or a knitting pattern, is simply a set of precise, coded instructions arranged in an appropriate order, and programming is another way in which children can use the computer as a tool to explore mathematical ideas.

The programming language which is most often used in primary schools is Logo. The point of introducing young children to programming with Logo is to allow them to feel in control, to give them a way of clarifying their ideas, and to encourage them to order their thoughts logically. Although the children will need to be taught some simple programming techniques, the emphasis needs to be not on learning these techniques, but on the mathematics that can be explored through programming.

Number

Place value

Place value is still one of the most important of the mathematical concepts which need to be developed at this stage. Activities with concrete materials like an abacus or Dienes blocks, and activities with calculators, can be supplemented by the use of place-value games in the form of computer programs. After they have used the computer it is important that children discuss or write about the strategies which they used. Ask them 'How did you know where to place your marker?' or 'Were there any quick ways of winning?'

- *Place Value Activities* (ESM): a set of six different place-value games.
- *Guess* (MicroSMILE): guess a number between 1 and 100 using clues of 'too big' or 'too small'.
- *Minimax* (MicroSMILE): put five numbers in boxes, do a sum, and make a smaller or bigger number than the computer.
- *Zoom* (Shell Centre – Teaching with a Micro 2): zoom in and out on a number line refining the degree of accuracy with which a number's position can be described.

Calculations

There are many different computer games and puzzles which help children to develop strategies for dealing with numbers. Some of these involve the representation of a number as a fraction.

- *Bango* (ESM – Mathematics 9–13): burst a balloon by identifying the point at which it is tied as a fraction of the distance along a line.
- *Hunt* (ESM – Mathematics 9–13): guess a vulgar fraction between 0 and 1.
- *Wall* (SMILE): a fraction wall appears and the bars slide out – the users must reassemble the wall.

Other computer games help the children to develop and practise mental strategies.

- *Number Games* (ESM): a set of ten different number games, each related to National Curriculum attainment targets.
- *Mathematical Games and Activities* (Capital Media): a set of games and other activities requiring the use of mental arithmetic.
- *Number Puzzler* (ESM – Shiva): five number games involving logic and strategy help one or two players to reinforce addition and subtraction skills.
- *Table Adventures* (ESM – Shiva): four stimulating games to help children to understand their tables through factorisation.

A good follow-up activity to the use of strategic number games and puzzles on the computer is to suggest that the children make changes either to the numbers or to the rules and devise their own game or puzzle using A4 card, dice, or other apparatus.

The activities which children have been doing with their calculators can also be done with a computer. By programming the computer, using either Logo or BASIC, the children can explore the effects of typing in some simple statements to see the result on the screen. The advantage of using the computer rather than the calculator is that the entire sequence of operations remains on the screen for counting and comparison. For example,

```
PRINT 336 + 499 − 250
PRINT 458 * 9
PRINT 150 / 2
```

Using the PRINT command, the children can try to solve some problems. For example,

- Which pairs of whole numbers give the result of 10 when one of the numbers is divided by the other?
- 3080 is the product of two consecutive numbers. What are they?
- 1 □ 2 × 8 = 10 □ 6. What are the values of the missing digits?
- What number, when multiplied by itself, gives the answer 64?
- Find the average (mean) of 32, 87 and 49 without using division; without using multiplication or division.

Solving practical problems using number skills

The PRINT command is also useful for investigating the relationship between pairs of numbers which result from a practical experiment. For example, weights which are suspended by a rubber band will produce a table of results:

Weight (g)	Extension of rubber band (cm)
10	2
15	3
20	4

By typing in the first number of the pair divided by the other:

```
PRINT 10 / 2
PRINT 15 / 3
PRINT 20 / 4
```

and so on, the children are helped to an understanding of the underlying relationship. Pairs of measurements of the circumference and diameter of a number of circular objects (lids, hoops, quoits, coins, cake tins, . . .) can be explored in the same way and should result in a conclusion like 'The circumference divided by the diameter is always a little bit more than 3'.

Applying number skills in adventure games and simulations

For many children, one of the most exciting ways of using the computer is participating in an adventure game or simulation in which different mathematical puzzles or problems need to be solved. Adventure games and simulations offer opportunities for cross-curricular work, since they stimulate many different activities away from the keyboard. Programs like these are best used by small groups, so that discussion about strategies can take place. The children will need to keep careful records of their positions, the routes followed and the decisions made.

Some adventure games which provide a series of situations in which number skills and strategic thinking are both developed are:

- *Martello Tower* (ESM): the object is to find your way through a tower and out to sea again solving many puzzles and problems as you do so.
- *Dread Dragon Droom* (ESM): rescue the princess and avoid the dragon by solving the puzzles.
- *Cars – Maths in Motion* (Cambridge Software House): a simulation of a car race on a choice of tracks.
- *The Fun Fair* (Northern Micromedia): with a set sum of money children must decide which attractions to visit. Each visit involves solving a mathematical problem.

Algebra

Number patterns

The use of computer software to support number work can provide opportunities to explore number patterns. Although discovery of a pattern is a first step, children need to be encouraged to do more than this. Patterns can help to identify or to explain relationships, to make predictions or to form generalisations. The programs require the children first to spot a pattern, and then to make use of it in some way. Some of these programs may have been used at earlier levels, but options within them can offer a greater degree of challenge to the children.

- *Ergo* (MEP Microprimer): patterns in a set of two-digit numbers hidden on a square grid must be discovered with the help of clues saying 'too big' or 'too small'.
- *Monty* (ATM): the python called Monty wriggles around on a number grid. The challenge is to discover which numbers he is covering.
- *Counter* (ATM): set a starting number, and a jump size, so that patterns of digits can be explored.
- *Patterns 1* (MEP Primary Mathematics Pack – RESOURCE): choose the width of a grid and investigate the patterns created by one or two multiples.

Programs like *Counter* and *Patterns 1* are open ended – small tools which carry out particular tasks. It is up to the users to decide what they would like to do with them. For this reason, it is best if the teacher works with the children at the computer, helping them to select and to refine suitable ideas.

For example, with *Patterns 1*, you could create the pattern of 7s on a grid with eight columns.

- Would 108 be in the pattern? How do you know?
- What number would be at the top of the column with 157 in it?
- What other grids produce the same pattern for multiples of 7? What do all these grids have in common?
- What would the pattern of 7s look like for a grid with five columns? Can you explain why?

With *Counter* you could decide to start on 564, and jump on in 99s.

- What is the pattern in the sequence of the units digits? In the sequence of tens digits?
- How many digits are there in the tens digits pattern? Can you explain this?
- What would the sequence be if you jumped on in 999s instead? Why?

Counter can also be used to explore the sequence of negative numbers. For example, start on 52 and count backwards in 6s. When the counter reaches 3, stop the count. Ask the children:

- What was the pattern of the units digits?
- What will happen when the counter continues? Will the pattern be different? Why?
- What will happen if the counter starts at 52 and counts backwards in 7s?

Children who have some familiarity with the programming language BASIC will be able to write simple programs and use them to explore number patterns. The lines of a BASIC program are numbered. It is usual to number the lines in multiples of 10 to start with so that intermediate lines can be added at a later stage if necessary. For example, this program will print out the first few multiples of 11.

```
10  FOR NUMBER = 1 TO 10
20  PRINT NUMBER * 11
30  NEXT NUMBER
40  END
```

Once the program has been typed in it can be made to work by typing

```
RUN
```

If there is a mistake, the program will stop and an error message will appear. To correct the 'bug', first examine the list of instructions which have been typed. To do this, type the word

```
LIST
```

so that the lines of the program appear again on the screen. To make the correction, there is no need to type the whole program again, only the line in which the mistake appears. For example, if the mistake is in the line 30, then type the whole of line 30 again, including the line number. If you then type LIST once more, you will see that the new line 30 has replaced the old one. Try out the revised program by typing

```
RUN
```

The program can now be used to investigate the outcome of multiplying a number of any size by 11. By retyping line 10 so that it reads, for example,

```
10  FOR NUMBER = 50 TO 65
```

blocks of numbers can be printed out and examined for patterns to help determine a rule. The program can easily be modified to print, for example, sequences of square numbers or cubic numbers.

Number patterns can also be investigated using a spreadsheet, if one is available. The advantage of the spreadsheet is that tables of data and different sorts of graphs can also be printed out to aid the investigation or to help communicate what has been discovered. Some introductory spreadsheets which include a range of graphs and charts are:

- *PPS* (Cambridge Software House): a spreadsheet for the Nimbus specially written for primary school users.
- *Grasshopper* (Newman College): an introductory spreadsheet for the BBC or Nimbus.

Formulating rules

Some computer programs provide particular situations for investigation. By making generalisations about the patterns which they see, or about the relationships which they discover, and putting these into words, the children start to use algebraic ideas.

It is important to start investigations like these away from the computer using pencil and paper or other apparatus. Encourage the children to predict what will happen before they try something out. Help them to organise in a sensible way the results which they gather and to look for patterns which might help them. When diagrams become too difficult to draw, or when the numbers become too difficult to calculate, move to the computer program. At the end of the investigation, ask the children to tell you in their own words what they have found out.

- *Routes* (ESM – Mathematics 9–13): find a rule for the number of different shortest paths between two points on a rectangular grid.
- *Triangles* (ESM – Mathematics 9–13): discover how many triangles can be formed by intersecting straight lines.
- *Bounce* (MEP Primary Maths Pack – RESOURCE): discover the rule for predicting the number of bounces made by a billiard ball before it lands in a pocket. Alternatively, predict which pocket the ball will land in.

- *Patterns 2* (MEP Primary Maths Pack – RESOURCE): investigate the patterns to be found on a triangular grid.
- *Diagonal* (Mathematical Investigations – Capital Media): investigate the number of unit squares crossed by the diagonal of a rectangular grid.
- *Polygon* (Mathematical Investigations – Capital Media): discover how many diagonals there are in a polygon.
- *Circle* (MicroSMILE): jump round points on a circle and discover the kind of patterns produced.

Function machines

Children who are confident about programming, will have met the idea of a variable, the use of a letter or word to stand in the place of a number. For example, a Logo procedure to draw a square could be written as

```
TO SQUARE
    REPEAT 4 [FORWARD 30 RIGHT 90]
END
```

When the procedure name SQUARE is typed, a square with side 30 units is drawn. To draw squares of any size a variable must be introduced.

```
TO SQUARE :side
    REPEAT 4 [FORWARD :side RIGHT 90]
END
```

When the procedure name is typed, it must now be followed by a number to indicate the length of the side. SQUARE 50 will draw a larger square with a side of 50 units, whereas SQUARE 10 will draw a smaller square with a side of 10 units.

Variables are also useful in procedures which can be used to investigate possible rules. For example, a procedure called, say, TRY that has a variable input can be written and hidden away so it works like a function machine:

```
TO TRY :number
    PRINT 5 * :number + 1
END
```

By typing TRY 5, TRY 2, TRY −3, and so on, a selection of outputs can be generated. Players can use these to help them guess the rule 'hidden' in the machine. Encourage the children to try small negative numbers as inputs, as well as positive numbers, and also to try zero as an input. When the rule has been discovered and tested, the middle line of the procedure can be replaced by a similar line so that the next group of children have a different rule to investigate.

Co-ordinates

There are a number of computer programs which require the children to make use of co-ordinates as part of a game or puzzle.

Some of these programs are computerised versions of well-known board games such as three-dimensional noughts and crosses or Othello. In the computer versions the players need to use co-ordinates in order to tell the computer where they want to place a marker.

- *Co-ordinate Jigsaw* (Maths with a Story 1 – BBC Publications): create a jigsaw by specifying the co-ordinates of the puzzle pieces to be changed over.
- *Pirate Gold* (Maths with a Story 2 – BBC Publications): the aim is to fill a treasure chest with gold by hunting for it on an island or under the sea.
- *Lines* (MicroSMILE): play four in a row on a 9 × 9 board.
- *Rhino* (MicroSMILE): hunt a lost rhinoceros on a 10 × 10 co-ordinate grid making use of clues which give the distances along the grid lines.
- *Locate* (MicroSMILE): a small cross appears within a large blank square. The object is to locate the cross by typing in two numbers to represent co-ordinates.

It is also possible for children to produce line drawings based on co-ordinates by programming the computer in either Logo or BASIC. In Logo, the command to move the turtle to position (X, Y) on the screen is

```
SETPOS [X Y]
```

If the pen is up, the turtle will move to the position (X, Y) without drawing a line. If the pen is down, the turtle draws a line as it moves. The mid-point of the screen is the position (0, 0). Points on the X axis to the left of the centre point are negative with a minus sign; points on the Y axis below the centre point are also negative. You could try experimenting with this set of commands, trying them first with the pen up and then with the pen down. The command CS will clear the screen and either HOME or SETPOS [0 0] will put the turtle back in the centre.

```
SETPOS [100 300]
SETPOS [−100 300]
SETPOS [−100 −300]
SETPOS [100 −300]
```

If you are not sure about the position of the turtle on the screen, typing

```
PRINT POS
```

will produce the co-ordinate position for you.

One game that children enjoy programming for each other starts by one group drawing a small square somewhere on the screen. The turtle is then returned to the centre position. The next group then tries to move the turtle into the square by using the smallest number of SETPOS commands.

Similar ideas can be developed using BBC BASIC, available for the Nimbus as well as for BBC machines, although in BASIC the position (0, 0) is generally the bottom left-hand corner of the screen. Before you begin you must make sure that the screen is ready for drawing. You can do this by typing MODE 1. This command will clear the screen and place the 'pen' in the bottom left-hand corner.

There are then two commands which are useful to use. The command

```
MOVE 100, 300
```

makes the 'pen' move to the co-ordinate position (100, 300) without drawing a line, whereas the command

```
DRAW 300, 500
```

draws a straight line from the existing position to the new position of (300, 500).

Children could try typing this BASIC program to draw a square into the computer.

```
10  MODE 1
20  MOVE 200, 200
30  DRAW 500, 200
40  DRAW 500, 500
50  DRAW 200, 500
60  DRAW 200, 200
70  END
```

Once the program has been run and is working in a satisfactory way, some decoration could be added to the square by adding further lines. For example, try drawing the diagonals.

Whether they are programming in Logo or in BASIC, encourage the children to suggest their own ideas for drawing. Provide them with squared paper on which to make their plans before they go to work at the computer.

Data handling

The computer is capable of producing a wide variety of graphs, charts and tables very quickly and accurately. It makes it possible for children to spend much more of their time on the important skills of handling real information collected by themselves, rather than on the mere drawing of graphs related to information provided by others. These skills involve:

- deciding what data to collect
- deciding how to collect it
- deciding how to record or represent it
- framing questions, and using the data to find answers
- explaining results
- communicating findings

Line graphs

Children at this stage will be starting to construct and interpret a line graph and becoming aware that intermediate values on the graph may have no meaning. For example, if the height of a runner bean plant is measured and plotted at intervals of one week, the mid-weekly reading from the line graph will not necessarily be accurate.

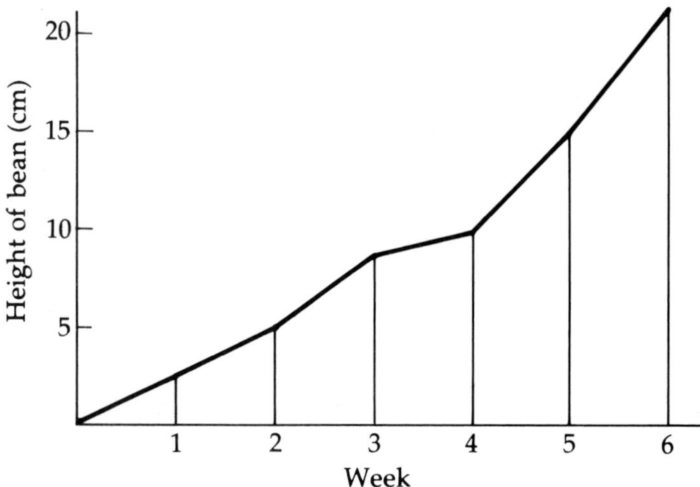

Two programs which can help children to interpret line graphs, and to draw similar graphs to represent 'stories' for friends to read and interpret, are these.

- *Airtemp* (Longman – Micros in the Primary Classroom): a dynamic graph of air temperature appears against the model of a thermometer during a simulated 24 hour period.
- *Eureka* (MEP Microprimer): another dynamic graph, this time of the level of water as a man takes a bath, puts the taps on or off, the plug in or out, and so on.

Bar charts, frequency diagrams and pie charts

There is an easy-to-use program which is still useful at this stage to display and print the data which children have collected.

- *Datashow* (MESU – Information Handling Pack): a group of children, or a teacher working with them, can enter up to eight items of data, sort the items either numerically or alphabetically, and display the data in a table, bar chart or pie chart.

The program is most suitable for displaying counts of various kinds, perhaps made by a whole class, or even the whole school. The data can often be collected very quickly on a 'hands up who . . .' basis. It can be used to represent the results of a simple survey.

Another way of using the computer to handle and display information is by using a database.

Shoe size	Number of children
11	●
12	● ● ●
13	● ● ● ● ●
1	● ● ● ● ● ● ●
2	● ● ● ●
3	● ●

- *Ourfacts* (MESU – Information Handling Pack): an introductory database which is extremely easy to use. It displays information in tables, on Venn diagrams, in pictograms, block graphs, pie charts and scattergrams. Depending on the data being collected, it can handle about 60–80 records.
- *Grass* (Newman College): a more sophisticated database which can handle much larger amounts of information. It displays information in pie charts and count graphs.
- *Key* (ITV Software): an information handling package with search and sort facilities together with a range of graphical representations.

A database can support any cross-curricular work in which children are gathering and using information. For example, if children as part of a food science project are making a study of different packets of crisps then they might want to examine connections between the price of a packet and its stated weight or (if a suitable balance is available) between its stated weight and actual weight. They will need to know what 'average contents' (EEC) and 'minimum contents' (UK) mean. They may also want to see if there is any connection between the freshness of a packet of crisps and the shop from which the packet was purchased. The record for each packet of crisps might look like this.

PACKET NO: a number to identify the packet
MAKER: manufacturer
SHOP: shop from which purchased
STATED WT: stated weight in grams
ACTUAL WT: actual weight in grams
PRICE: cost of the packet
FRESHNESS: days left to 'best before' date
TASTINESS: rating on a five-point scale
APPEARANCE: rating on a five-point scale

Alternatively, children who are making a study of local history may be examining census records for a particular year. The information gathered may help to answer questions such as what kind of jobs people undertook or what proportion of children under the age of 14 were at work. The use of words like 'average' and 'range' will come in quite naturally. What was the average number of domestic servants in a Victorian household in the area? What was the average size of a Victorian family? What was the age range of people at work? What was the range of distances moved by families who came to live in this area?

NAME:	name
SEX:	male, female
AGE:	age
RELATION:	relationship to head of household
JOB:	occupation
BIRTHPLACE:	town in which born
DISTANCE:	distance away

When the children are making interpretations from the graphs and charts which they produce, encourage them to use familiar fractions to make estimates of proportions. When examining pie charts, for example, it is relatively easy to see things like 'about three quarters of the population were born here' or 'about one third of the population were agricultural labourers'. Ask them to suggest reasons for their findings. For example, why were so few of the children still at school at the age of 16? Why did so many families have domestic servants? Why might the people of 1870 move from where they were born in order to live in a different area?

Likelihood

The program *Datashow* can also be used to collect guesses or predictions and then checked with the real result to see how the predicted and actual results compare with each other. Some suggestions are:

Way I will come to school tomorrow:
walk, bus, train, tube, bike, car.

I think I can swim:
10 metres, 20 metres, 100 metres, more.

Tomorrow's wind direction will be:
N, NE, E, SE, S, SW, W, NW

I think I can run 50 metres in:
10–12 s, 13–15 s, 16–18 s, ...

In 60 rolls of a dice, I think the number of 6s will be:
0–10, 11–20, 21–30, 31–40, 41–50, 51–60.

After each display using *Datashow,* it is important to ask the children 'What does the graph show us or tell us?' and 'Why do you think that?' Ask them to place outcomes or events in order of 'likeliness' and to talk about the 'chance' of something happening.

Encourage them to use words like 'unlikely', 'possible', 'likely', 'highly likely', 'highly probable' and to associate these words on a scale from 'impossible' to 'certain'.

Some other programs which simulate experiments with dice or coins, and which can help children to appreciate simple ideas of probability are:

- *Roller* (ESM – Mathematics 9–13): roll a dice to accumulate a score but all is lost if you roll a one.
- *Dicecoin* (ATM – Slimwam 1): simulates throwing dice and tossing coins – useful for gathering lots of data quickly.
- *Digame* (ATM – Slimwam 2): strategic games using dice.

Tree diagrams

Decision tree diagrams are used to sort and identify a collection of objects: for example, some twigs.

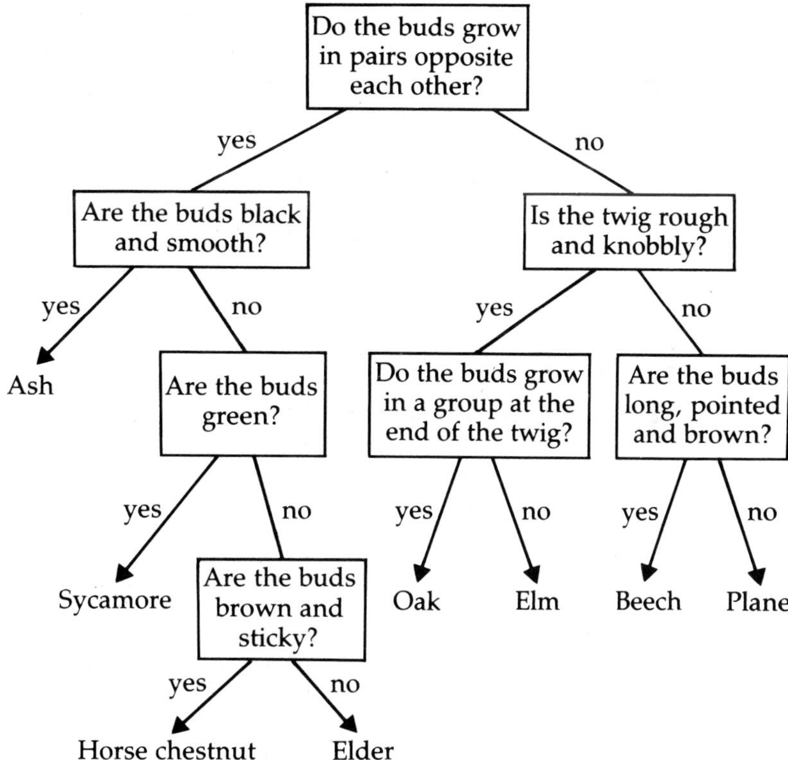

The most well-known decision tree program is *Animal*, included in the Microprimer Pack for each school. This allows children to frame questions in order to identify animals. More flexible programs allow questions to be framed about any set of the children's choice.

- *Sorting Game* (MESU – Information Handling Pack): large text makes the display easy to read by a group of children; records of questions and objects are kept separately for children to refer to.

- *Branch* (MESU – Information Handling Pack): the graphic display of the 'tree' helps children to appreciate that framing questions which divide the sets of objects into two equal halves enables a single object to be identified in the shortest possible time.

Branching tree programs are always best used when they are based upon the children's direct experience, first hand research and/ or practical work. They can be used to classify, represent and identifying properties of objects in many areas of the curriculum: for example

science:	cheeses, mineral objects, fabrics, pond life, . . .
mathematics:	shapes, numbers, coins or stamps, directions to reach local landmarks, . . .
language:	characters in a story, library books, . . .
history:	gravestones, architectural features, old packets and tins, battles, . . .
geography:	holiday regions, railway routes, fruits from overseas, wine labels, . . .

Shape and space

Angles and bearings

Children who have been accustomed to working with Logo should have a firm grasp of angle as a measure of turn. They will be comfortable with the use of degrees as a unit of measurement, although they may not be familiar with the word 'degrees' itself. They will be aware that a right-angled turn of 90 is needed to make the corner of a square and will have used commands like RIGHT 180 or LEFT 180 to make the turtle turn and face the opposite direction.

Words like 'acute' and 'obtuse' and 'reflex' can be introduced as children discuss their Logo drawings. 'Here the turtle turned LEFT 45 so it turned through an acute angle. Where else did you make the turtle turn through an acute angle?'

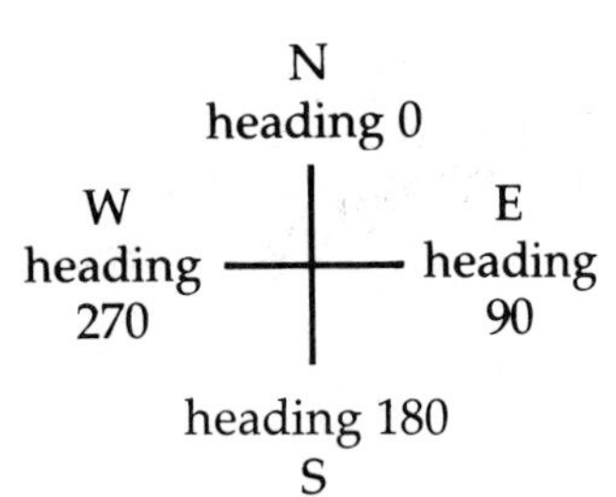

You can also make use of Logo to give children a feel for compass bearings. To do this you will need to make use of a Logo command which sets the turtle's heading, or the direction in which it is pointing. If you set the heading, and then type FORWARD 100, the turtle will set off in the direction of its heading. The turtle measures its heading using bearings measured clockwise from the top of the screen. A heading of 0 is straight up the screen, a heading of 90 is to the right, 180 is straight down, and 270 is to the left.

Try typing a sequence of commands using the abbreviation SETH to set the heading and FD to move forward: for example,

```
SETH 90 FD 50 SETH 135 FD 50 SETH 90 FD 50
```

The children can try tracing a path by using compass bearings and will enjoy planning 'walks' for the turtle in this way. Alternatively, they can use a computer game which requires them to use angles, bearings or compass directions.

- *Angle360* (MicroSMILE): estimate the size of angles drawn on the screen.
- *Pirates* (Longman – Micros in the Primary Classroom): find the treasure by hunting for it by making use of clues which refer to coordinates, compass directions or bearings.
- *Goldhunt* (MicroSMILE): the user is taken on a seven-stage journey which must be completed by using compass directions. There are several levels of difficulty; at the harder levels the north line is unlikely to point to the top of the map!
- *Merlin's Castle* (ESM): avoid Merlin the wizard and his traps as you explore the surroundings of a grassy bank using compass directions.
- *Spanish Main* (MEP Microprimer): hunt the treasure in a Spanish galleon.

Tessellations

Computer software can provide opportunities for building shapes and patterns, and for discovering the relationships which allow shapes to fit together to cover a surface in a tessellating pattern.

- *Picture Maker Plus* (ESM): patterns can be built up using eight colours, five shapes, and four movements, then printed out.
- *Tiles* (MicroSMILE): the screen displays a 10 × 7 array of square tiles. The tiles may be rotated through 90 degrees individually, or in lines (horizontal, vertical, diagonal) to make interesting patterns.
- *Mosaic* (Advisory Unit, Hatfield, Hertfordshire): generate tiling patterns by creating a motif which is then transformed in various ways.
- *Tilekit* (ATM – Slimwam 2): formulate rules for generating patterns to cover a surface using one or more different shapes.

Using programs like these the children could try to fill the screen with

L shapes
T shapes
squares of two different sizes
squares within squares
combinations of squares and oblongs
other shapes of their own choosing

The children can also try these same challenges using Logo, first drawing the shape of their tile and then trying to repeat it to fill the screen.

It is important to discuss with the children the properties of shapes which fit together without leaving any spaces. Why will four squares fit together round a point? Why do certain patterns create an effect of straight lines?

Line symmetry

The computer can also be used to explore line or mirror symmetry. The children can try to make symmetrical pictures or patterns with the same tiling programs that they have used to investigate space filling with simple tessellations. Other programs which can be helpful are:

- *Turnflex* (Maths with a Story 2 – BBC Publications): this is a puzzle in which the aim is to rebuild a picture using mirrors and rotations.
- *Symmetry Patterns* (Maths with a Story 1 – BBC Publications): this program allows children to create patterns using different kinds of symmetry, with one, two or four mirror lines.

Symmetry can also be investigated using Logo. For example, this procedure will draw a squiggle of lines on the right-hand side of the screen.

```
TO SQUIGGLE
    FD 100
    RT 90
    FD 250
    RT 90
    FD 400
    RT 90
    FD 100
END
```

What procedure would draw the reflection of the squiggle in a vertical line down the centre of the screen?

Scale

Logo is also useful for developing ideas of scale to enlarge or reduce a shape. For example, what modifications would need to be made to the SQUIGGLE procedure to produce a similar shape one tenth of the size? Many children find it surprising that all angles remain the same while linear distances are all reduced (or enlarged) by the same factor. Any procedure which children have written to produce a simple pattern or picture can be modified in the same manner. It is often an interesting struggle for them to discover the modifications which can be made to a procedure similar to this one for drawing a circle in order to produce one which is relatively larger or smaller.

```
TO CIRCLE
    REPEAT 36 [FD 5 RT 10]
END
```

Children who are familiar with variables will have used procedures similar to this one for drawing a pentagon. By varying the number used for the input they can explore the effects of changing the scale factor to produce pentagons of various sizes.

```
TO PENTAGON :size
    REPEAT 5 [FD :size RT 72]
END
```

Work on scale developed through Logo can be supplemented by work with other computer programs and complemented by practical work with construction kits, microscopes, maps, aerial photographs, and so on.

- *Tile Stretch* (Maths with a Story 2 – BBC Publications): players take turns to fit square tiles on a board. Tiles can be stretched by a factor of 1, 2 or 3 along either the length or the breadth of the tile.
- *Diagram* (MEP Primary Maths – RESOURCE): sketch a pattern and give commands to see it reflected, rotated or enlarged.
- *Mapping Skills* (ESM): seven related programs locating treasure using coordinates, compass directions and scale to calculate distances.

Number 1

Purpose

- To revise place value of thousands, hundreds, tens and units
- To introduce addition of thousands, hundreds, tens and units with exchanging (or carrying) from both tens and units
- To introduce rounding and approximating numbers to the nearest 10, 100
- To develop a strategy for adding 99

Materials

Structural apparatus, squared paper, calculators, reference books on Olympic Games

Vocabulary

Total, pattern, round, nearest, magic square, magic triangle, approximate total, rounded number, scores

TEACHING POINTS

1 ThHTU numbers

Ask the children to find everyday situations that involve thousands of people or things. Examples might include:

- Crowds at sports meetings such as football, rugby, athletics, tennis
- Fans at a pop concert
- The number of leaves on a tree
- The number of steps to walk home from school
- The number of minutes in a day
- The number of words in a book

2 Revise place value of thousands, hundreds, tens and units

Write a number such as 1243. Ask the children to read it. Can they say what each digit is worth?

3 units = 3
4 tens = 40
2 hundreds = 200
1 thousand = 1000

→ 1243

How many ways can the children find to show a number? Here are a few ideas.

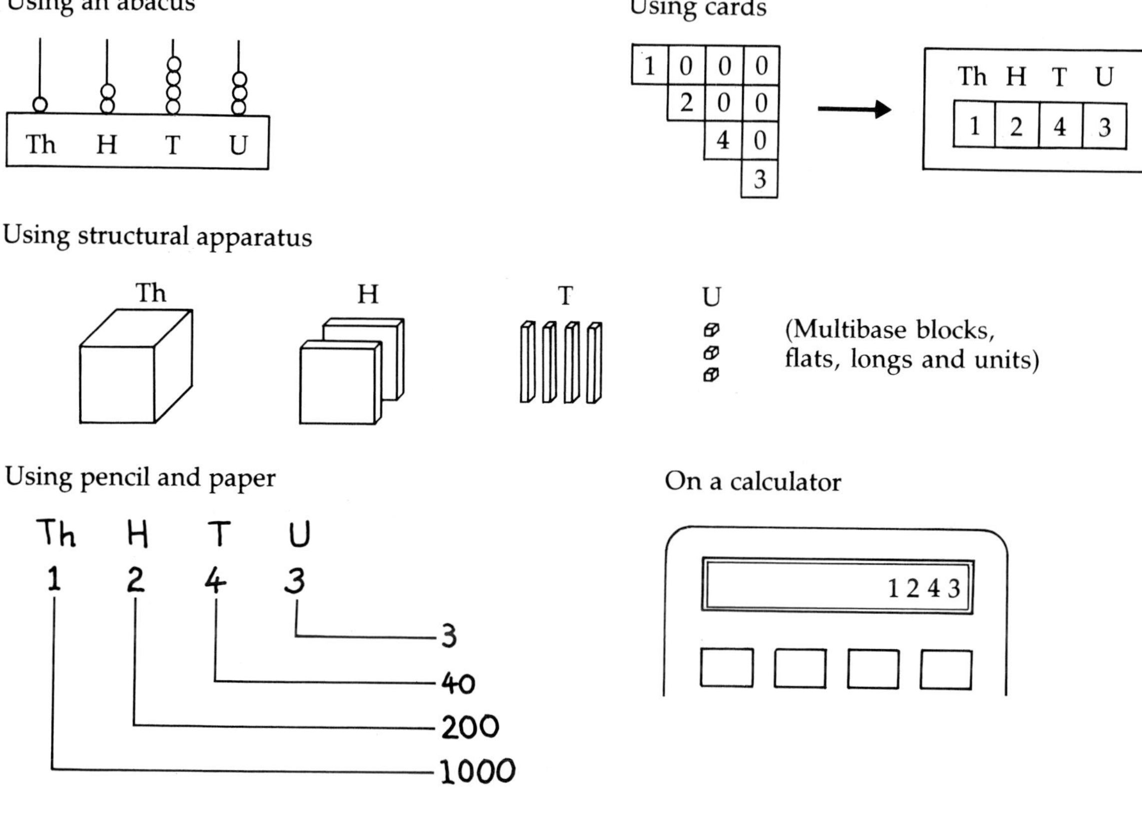

1243 → 1000 + 200 + 40 + 3

Talk about numbers where all the digits are the same such as 4444. Point to two of the 4s (for example the units and the tens 4s) and ask how many times larger the tens 4 is than the units 4. Do this for the other 4s and find a pattern. Practise this with other similar numbers.

Write a number with different digits such as 2649. Ask the children to write numbers that are larger than 2649 but less than 3000. Vary this by asking for an odd number or an even number.

Ask the children to record 3000 as 3 thousands or 30 hundreds or 300 tens or 3000 ones. Can they do this with other numbers?

Ask the children to write 508 and the numbers which follow. Make sure that 510 is not written 5010 – do the children know why 5010 is not the same as 510? Repeat the activity with numbers involving ThHTU, for example 6008, 6009, 6010.

3 Addition of ThHTU with exchanging from both tens and units

This can be introduced practically using structural apparatus. Write two numbers which use **exchanging** from both tens and units, such as 1587 + 1285. One child could add them as a sum and another could add them using structural apparatus. Compare the answers.

	Th	H	T	U
	1	5	8	7
+	1	2	8	5

Let the children work out their own algorithms for recording addition of ThHTU. Talk about them, and give plenty of practice in using them.

4 Rounding numbers

Explain how we can estimate the size of numbers by rounding up or down. For example 99 and 101 are about 100.

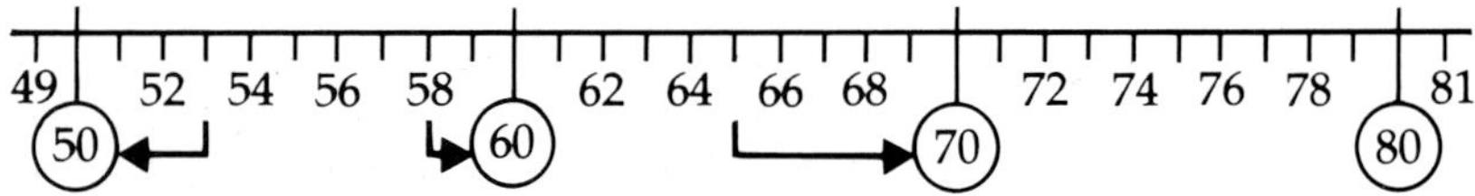

Draw a section of the number line and ring the tens. Talk about rounding numbers to the nearest ten. For example:

'What is the nearest ten to 53?' (53 → 50)
'What is the nearest ten to 58?' (58 → 60)

Explain how we normally round numbers with a units digit of 5 **up** to the nearest ten, e.g. 65 → 70.

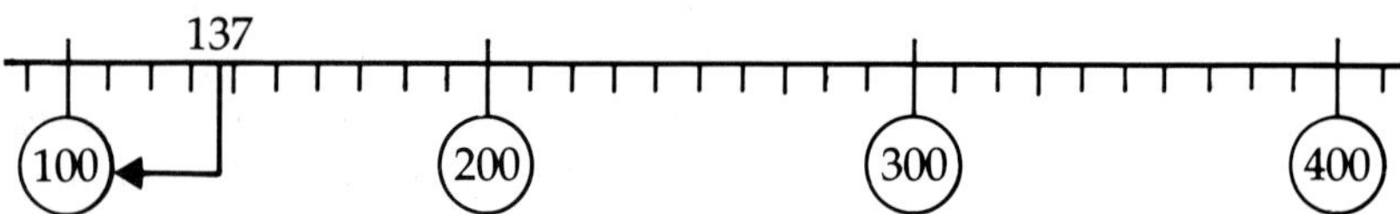

Discuss rounding numbers to the nearest 100. Draw a number line and ring the hundreds. Ask a child to point to where a number such as 137 would be. Ask which is the nearest hundred (137 → 100). Explain that 50 or more rounds up to the next hundred and less than 50 is rounded down. For example,

351 → 400 350 → 400 348 → 300

A game to play

THE NEAREST TEN

Make a set of number cards 50–70 inclusive and three tens cards 50, 60, 70. Place the three tens cards face upwards on the table. Shuffle and deal out all the number cards to the players. The dealer starts by trying to place a card which will round to make 50 underneath the 50 card. The next player tries to place a number card which rounds up or down to make 60. Play continues with each person trying to place a number card underneath the tens cards in sequence 50, 60, 70, 50, 60, 70, 50, . . . If a player is unable to place a card they miss that turn. The winner is the first person to play all their number cards. This game can be adapted to other numbers.

5 Estimation and approximation

Write two numbers such as 198 and 203. Ask the children to round the numbers to the nearest hundred and find the approximate total:

$$198 + 203 \rightarrow 200 + 200 = 400$$

Give the children practice in this. For example,

$$187 + 195 \rightarrow 200 + 200 = 400$$
$$311 + 501 \rightarrow 300 + 500 = 800$$
$$183 + 625 \rightarrow 200 + 600 = 800$$

This could be played as a team game where the first child to answer correctly scores a point for their team. A calculator could be used to compare the approximate answer with the true one. The activity could be extended by using three numbers or larger numbers.

6 Mental work

These examples can be introduced in oral or written form or as word problems.

- Add 99 + 99 + 99 (100 + 100 + 100 − 3)
- Add 357 + 99 (357 + 100 − 1)
- Add 150 + 20 + 40 (by adding the tens digits)
- Add 400 + 300 + 900 (by adding the hundreds digits)
- Add 2000 + 3000 + 4000 (by adding thousands)
- Add 99 + 100 + 101 (100 + 100 + 100)
- What hundred does 653 round to?
- At a cricket match there were 1059 in one stand and 401 in another. How many people were there altogether?

7 Magic squares

4	9	2
3	5	7
8	1	6

Draw a magic square. Discuss how each row, column and diagonal adds up to the same number – the magic number.

Ask the children to complete these squares by turning the first square and putting the numbers in their new positions. Is each square still magic?

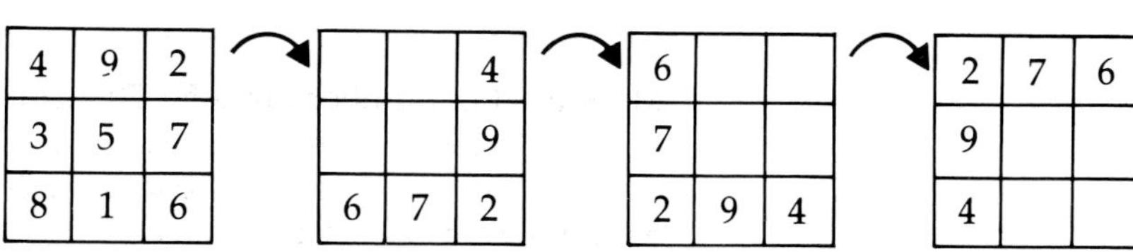

magic number 15

8	1	6
3	5	7
4	9	2

4	9	2
3	5	7
8	1	6

Is the reflection of a magic square still a magic square?

Discuss these magic squares and how they are formed. Ask what they add up to and why.

4	9	2
3	5	7
8	1	6

magic number 15

40	90	20
30	50	70
80	10	60

magic number 150

400	900	200
300	500	700
800	100	600

magic number 1500

The work on magic squares is developed in the pupils' pages.

USING THE CALCULATOR

Ask the children to use the constant function to add in 99s.

99 198 297 396 495 . . .

Can they see the pattern? Does the pattern continue into the thousands?

Ask them to try to find other numbers which give patterns by repeated addition:

101 202 303 . . .
1001 2002 3003 . . .

Give the children plenty of practice in showing thousands numbers on the calculator and observe how these are displayed.

A game to play

MAKE THE NUMBER

One child writes down a four-digit number such as 3674. Another child adds four separate numbers to try to make the four-digit number, for example,

3000 + 4 + 70 + 600

One point is scored for doing it correctly. Then the children can change over. The winner is the player with the most points.

LINKS WITH THE ENVIRONMENT

Explore where we see or use four-digit numbers in everyday life. These might include:

- Dates in history linking well-known events: 1066 and the Battle of Hastings, or 1666 and the Great Fire of London
- Dates on coins
- Populations of small towns and villages

- Distances travelled. Ask the children if any have travelled more than 1000 kilometres or miles.

NOTES ON INVESTIGATIONS

Section A

Calculators will be useful. There are many different sets of four numbers which add up to 34, other than the numbers in each row, column and diagonal. Examples are:

- 13, 1, 4, 16 (the four corner numbers)
- 11, 7, 6, 10 (the centre four)
- 13, 8, 11, 2 and 12, 1, 14, 7 and 6, 15, 4, 9 and 3, 10, 5, 16 (the four quarters)
- 8, 12, 9, 5 and 2, 3, 14, 15 (the middle numbers opposite to each other)

The investigation could be extended by finding whether this works for other 4 by 4 magic squares. It will work by adding any number to each number in the magic square.

Section B

When children have found the magic triangle that adds up to 10, they may use it to make magic triangles that add up to 100 and 1000.

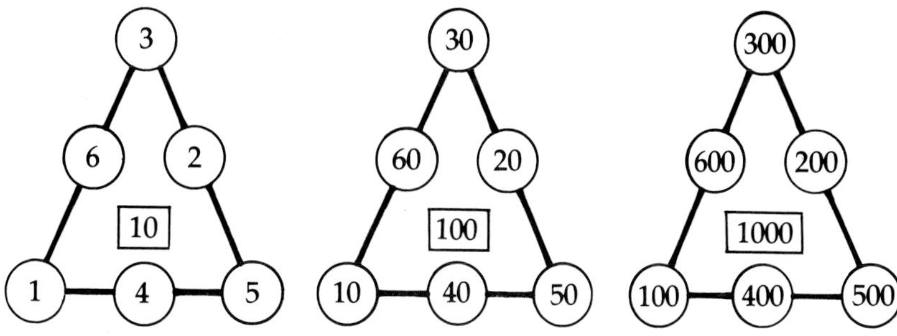

Alternatively, different numbers can be used to make the magic triangles, for example:

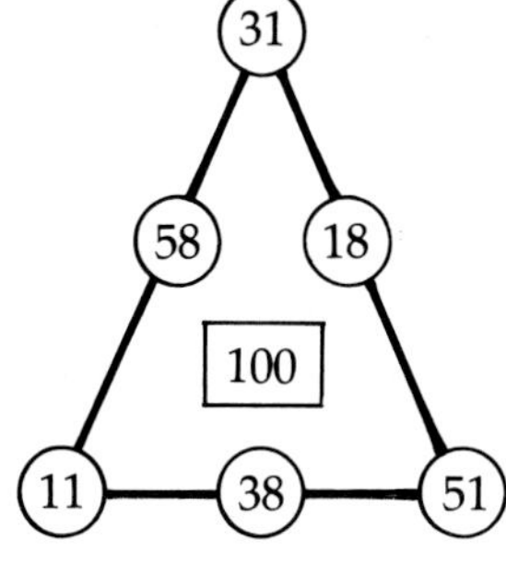

The investigation could be extended by using the numbers 1 to 6 initially to find magic triangles totalling 9, 11, 12; subsequently triangles totalling 90 and 900, 110 and 1100, 120 and 1200 can be made.

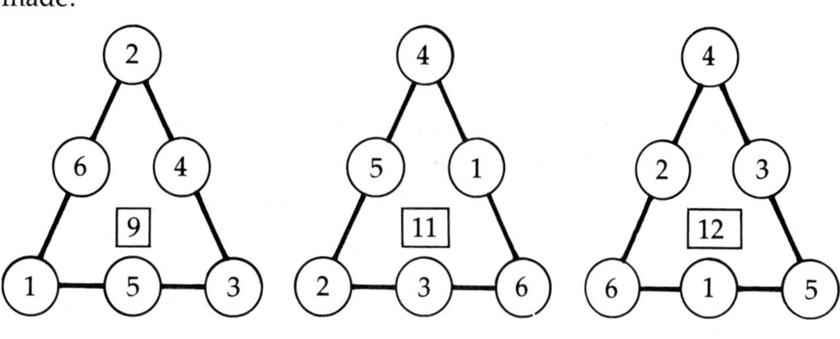

Section C

Reference books on the Olympic Games are needed for this investigation.

The children could write out the pattern of 4 and look for a way of finding numbers that will divide exactly by 4. Some might use the constant function on the calculator.

Do the children realise that the numbers must be even? Do they finally come to the conclusion that the last two digits must divide by 4? For example, 384 will divide by 4, whereas 386 will not. Are their explanations for divisibility by 4 clear? Do they check that other Olympic years divide exactly by 4?

Some children might find the number of medals won in the Olympic Games by different countries. Cross-curricular work involving history, geography, etc. are also possible developments.

Number 2

Purpose

- To revise place value of ThHTU
- To introduce subtraction of ThHTU with exchanging from the hundreds and from the tens
- To give practice in rounding numbers
- To develop subtraction strategies

Materials

Coins, structural apparatus as required

Vocabulary

Thousands, hundreds, tens, units, date, order, oldest, newest, before, difference between, pair, nearest, century, round, ringed, worth, missing numbers, number patterns

TEACHING POINTS

1 Place value

Talk with the children about place value and large numbers. If necessary, revise some of the activities used in the teaching points for Number 1.

2 Numbers on coins

Talk with the children about coins. What does the date on a coin mean? What is meant by 'minted'? Why do coins show a king or queen's head?

Ask the children to put some coins in order of their dates, and to read or write the dates in words.

Ask what the date on a particular coin would have been if it had been minted ten years earlier or later. What would the date have been 100 years earlier? Give the children plenty of practice in answering questions of this type.

A game to play

COINS

Collect old or foreign coins or make card discs with a date written on each one.

Play the game in pairs. Give each pair a collection of coins. At a given signal each pair must arrange the coins in date order. The winning pair is the first to complete the task correctly.

3 Number patterns

Revise number patterns using the date on a coin. Ask the children to keep subtracting 10 years from the date (e.g. 1934) to make a number pattern:

1934 1924 1914 . . .

It might be helpful to use structural apparatus at this point to show the pattern for subtracting tens or hundreds. The children should record the new number as they remove each ten. After removing three or four tens, can they predict what the next number will be without using the structural apparatus?

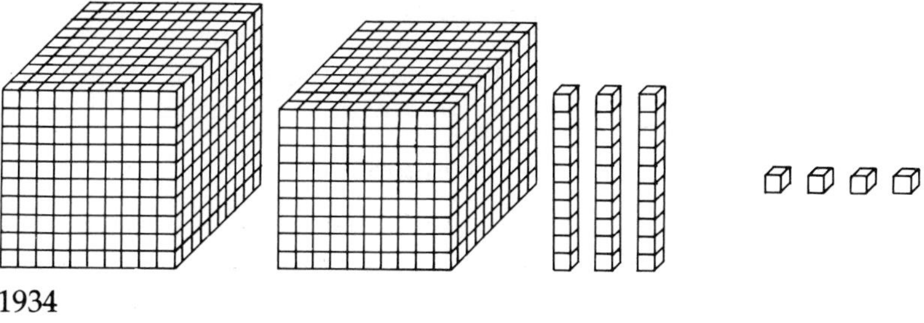

1934

Remove 10

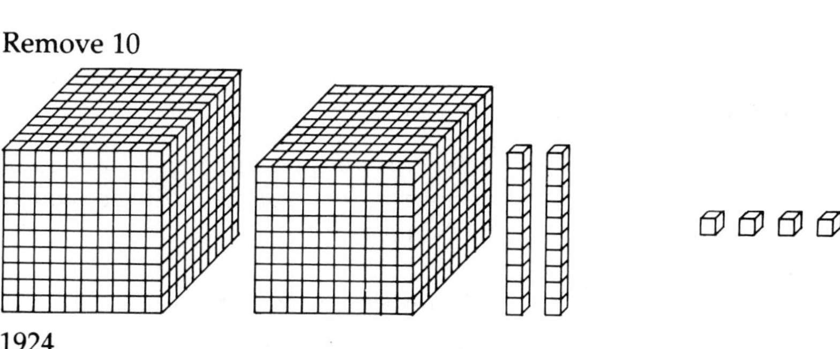

1924

Repeat the activity for other subtraction patterns such as 100. These activities may also be done using a calculator.

Games to play

KEEP THE PATTERN GOING

Any number of children can play. Each child starts with a number of points.

Decide on a subtraction pattern (e.g. subtract 100) and choose a number (e.g. 2860). The first player mentally subtracts 100 and quickly calls out the new number (2760). The second player subtracts from the new number and calls out the result. All players follow suit until it is impossible to go any further (without using negative numbers).

Any player who gives the wrong answer must do it using a calculator and loses a point! The winners are those with most points left.

At first the children may need to write down the numbers.

A development is to make the subtraction pattern more difficult, for example, subtract 50.

JUMBLED NUMBERS

Choose five or six numbers, four of which show a subtraction pattern, and write them on cards:

1942, 1947, 1932, 1934, 1912, 1922

Give the children a time limit to find the pattern and write it down, starting with the largest number.

4 Rounding up and down

Remind the children how to round numbers to the nearest ten, and that 5 or more rounds up to the next ten, while less than 5 is rounded down. For example,

36 → 40 34 → 30

Do the same for rounding to the nearest hundred.

351 → 400 350 → 400 348 → 300

Talk to the children about rounding numbers up or down to the nearest thousand. Give them practice in this

5465 → 5000 5644 → 6000

Explain that 5500 rounds up to 6000.

Talk about how useful the rounding process can be for estimating answers.

5 Subtraction of ThHTU with exchanging

Revise the exchanging method with the children, using your normal method of subtracting. Structural apparatus may be used to show this.

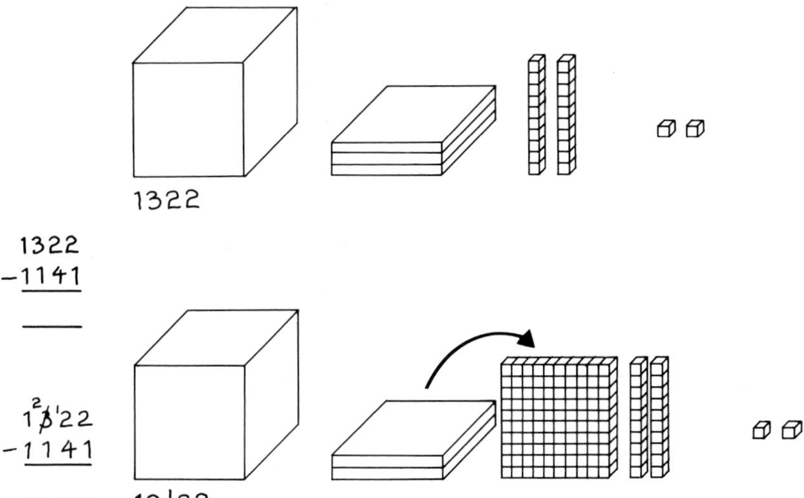

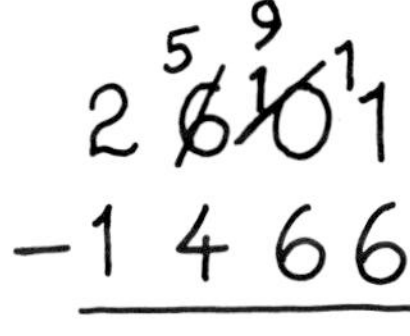

Explain how to subtract numbers such as 2601 – 1466 and talk about the method of recording. Here is one way although you may prefer others.

The children may work out their own methods for recording.

Give the children plenty of practice with subtraction, especially with numbers including a zero digit.

6 Difference between

Revise the concept of finding the difference between two numbers. Do the children remember that it is a subtraction process?

A game to play

FIND THE DIFFERENCE

Make number cards for the hundreds numbers from 100 to 1000.

Play the game in small teams. Call out the 'difference' required, for example, 200. The first player to hold up two number cards with that difference (e.g. 600 and 400) scores a point for their team.

A development of the game is to use numbers greater than 1000 or numbers involving 50.

7 Mental work

Some of the following activities may be introduced in oral or written form, and sometimes as word problems:

- Subtract 9
  $34 - 9 \rightarrow (34 - 10 + 1)$
- Subtract 99
  $134 - 99 \rightarrow (134 - 100 + 1)$

- Subtracting 10, 20, 100, 200 etc.
- Checking subtraction by adding

$$\begin{array}{r} 3453 \\ -\ \underline{1621} \\ \underline{1832} \end{array} \qquad \begin{array}{r} 1621 \\ +\ \underline{1832} \\ \underline{3453} \end{array}$$

This reinforces the link between addition and subtraction.

- Ask word problems involving subtraction

USING THE CALCULATOR

Check that the children are able to use the calculator for the subtraction of ThHTU.

Use the calculator for work on place value. Ask children to enter a number digit by digit (e.g. 2465) and then read it back in words digit by digit.

Ask children to enter numbers such as 499, 999 or 1999. Can they predict what will happen if they add 1 to the number? Ask them to enter 600, 1000 or 3000. Can they predict what will happen if they subtract 1 from each number? They can then check their predictions on the calculator.

Use the calculator to devise subtraction patterns using the constant function.

A game to play

LAND ON ZERO

This is a game for a group of children, each with a calculator. Ask them to show 2000 on the display. Write a number to be subtracted repeatedly (e.g. 200). Each child writes down their prediction of the number of subtractions needed to make the calculator display 0.

At a given signal they do the subtractions on their calculators and record the pattern on paper. The first to show the correct pattern of numbers and prediction is the winner.

LINKS WITH THE ENVIRONMENT

Use everyday situations involving ThHTU numbers and subtraction.

- Coins. Length of reigns of monarchs shown on coins. The history of coins in Britain. Differences in dates. The history of other coins, e.g. Roman coins, how old are they?
- Films and TV programmes. These usually show the date of production (often in Roman numerals) with the captions. How old are the productions?
- Use situations that involve subtraction of numbers. For example, count-downs, subtracting in a darts game, descending a mountain, miles left to go during a journey.

NOTES ON INVESTIGATIONS

Section A

Do the children appreciate that they have to use the thousand, a hundreds number, a tens number and a unit number each time?

Do the children adopt a systematic approach?

Do they find all possibilities (27)?

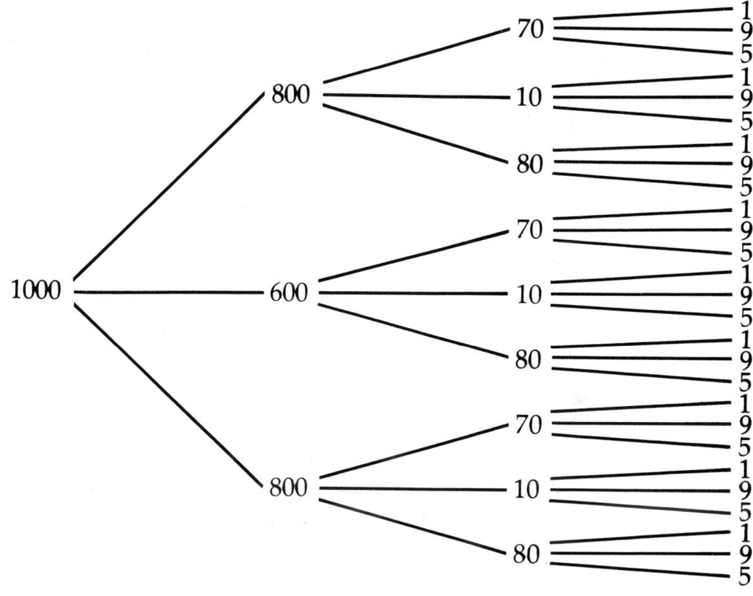

Section B

Do the children give the coins sensible dates?

Do they devise interesting and appropriate questions, possibly based on the type of questions in the pupils' text?

Section C

Do the children make three different patterns for the dates? Did they arrange them in such a way that the pattern is not immediately obvious to their friends?

Purpose

- To investigate lines of symmetry
- To investigate planes of symmetry

Materials

Mirror, paper, scissors, templates for two-dimensional shapes, cubes, binca material, squared paper, paper circles, boxes, cereal packets, plasticine, craft sticks

Vocabulary

Lines of symmetry, planes of symmetry, patterns, reflects, folded, unfolded, cubes, cuboids, polyspheres, circles, halves, quarters, cross stitch patterns

TEACHING POINTS

1 Lines of symmetry

Revise the idea that a symmetrical shape has a line of symmetry and can be divided into two halves which are reflections of one another.

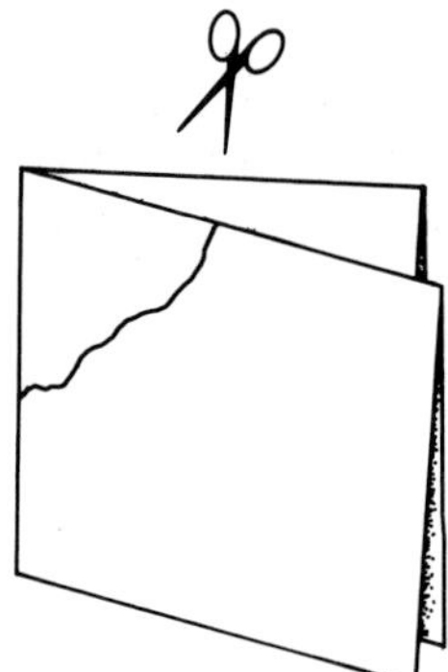

2 More than one line of symmetry

Ask the children to fold a sheet of paper into quarters and cut out a shape. Ask how many lines of symmetry it has.

3 Looking for symmetry

Ask the children to discover shapes that can be seen in the school or classroom that have one or more lines of symmetry.

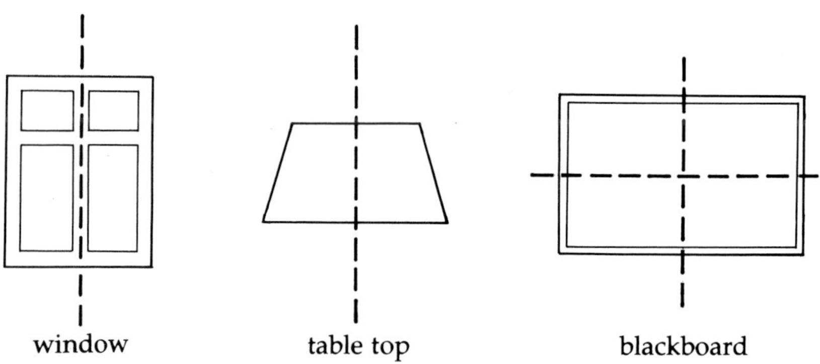

Look outside school for shapes that have one or more lines of symmetry.

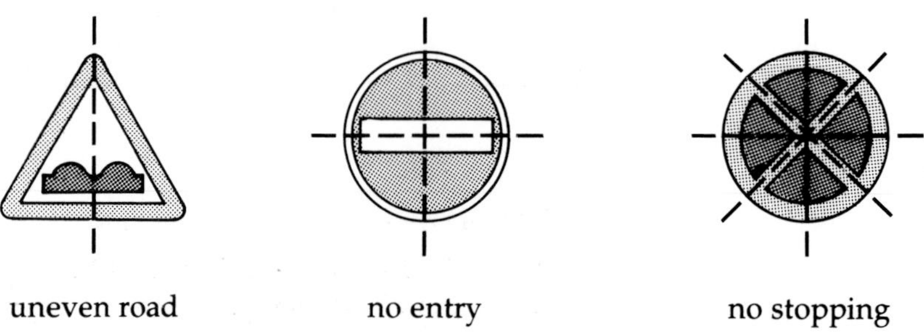

wild animals

A game to play

FIND THE SYMMETRY

Number some cards 1 to 4. Shuffle them and place them face downwards. Pick them up one at a time and show the number to a group of children. Each child has to write down a shape in the classroom (or a shape in a picture such as a road scene) that has that number of lines of symmetry.

The shape of a road sign may have a line of symmetry but the overall picture may not. Discuss and decide with the children whether to allow this.

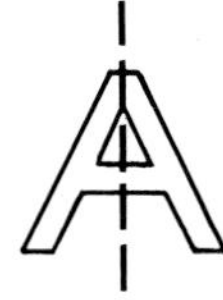

4 Folding paper

Let the children fold and cut paper to make symmetrical shapes.

Ask the children to fold a piece of paper in half and cut out letters of the alphabet. Can the children discover which letters are possible to make and which are not?

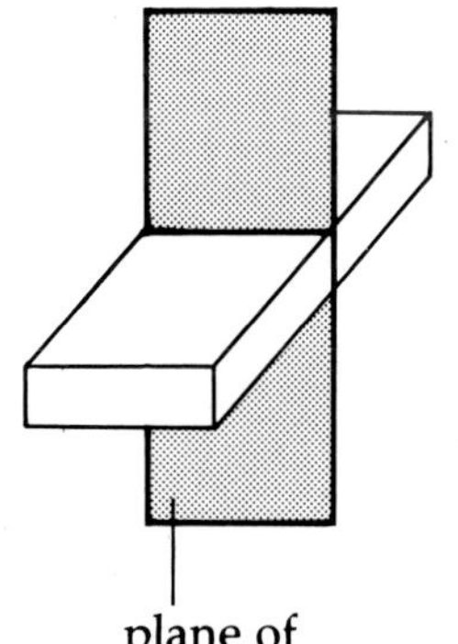

5 Planes of symmetry

Revise the fact that a solid shape can have symmetry about a plane so that one half of the shape reflects the other.

6 Finding planes of symmetry

Ask the children to look at familiar objects, such as cornflake packets, and to suggest where a plane of symmetry might be. These can be drawn on the packets and cut out to demonstrate that one half does reflect the other.

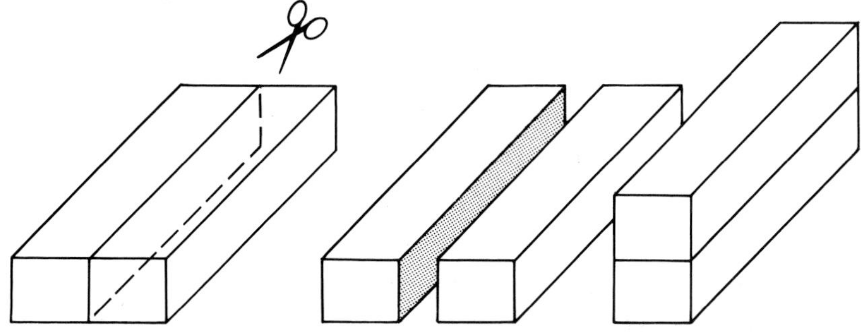

7 Using cubes

Ask the children to use cubes to build shapes that have planes of symmetry. Split the shapes to show the planes.

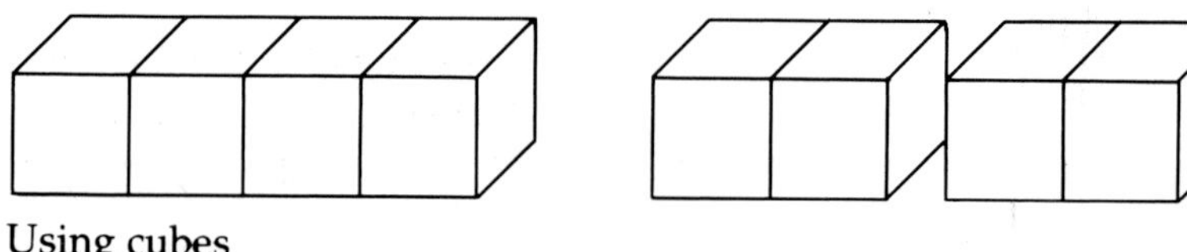

Using cubes

LINKS WITH THE ENVIRONMENT

Look for examples of lines of symmetry and planes of symmetry in pictures and objects.

- Animals. Do they have symmetry of shape? What about symmetry of colour?
- Trees, leaves, flowers and plants. Do they have symmetry?
- Buildings and houses near school. Do they have symmetry?
- Patterns and pictures. The children could make symmetrical patterns using templates. Ask them to show the lines of symmetry
- Reflections in water
- Road signs in the Highway Code
- Boxes, containers, tins and bottles have planes of symmetry. A collection of objects and pictures might be displayed in the classroom.

NOTES ON INVESTIGATIONS

Section A

Do the children understand the meaning of a plane of symmetry? Do they make different cuboid shapes and find different planes of symmetry? Do they appreciate that if they are to make a shape that can be split to show symmetry, they must use an even number of cubes?

Section B

Do the children's shapes have only one plane of symmetry? Do the children appreciate that if they are to split the shape then they must build up an even number of layers?

The investigation might be extended to finding shapes with only one plane of symmetry that cannot be split with a mirror. Can the children explain where the plane of symmetry is?

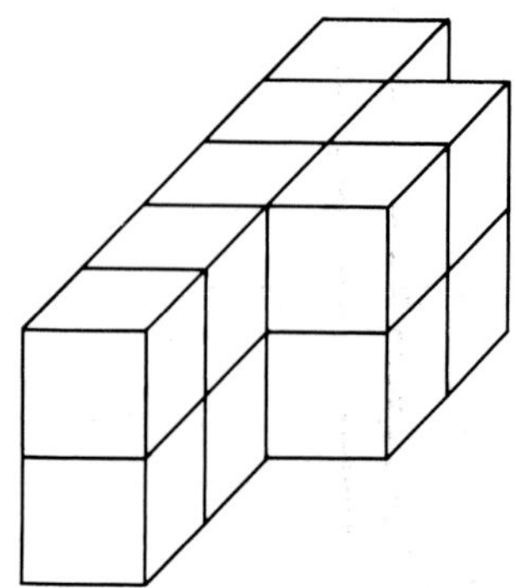

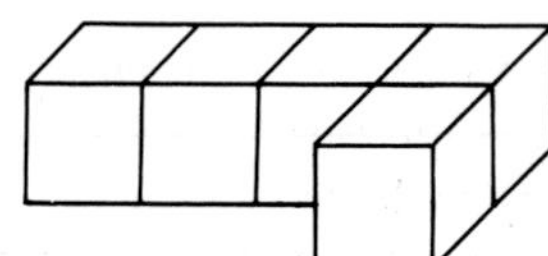

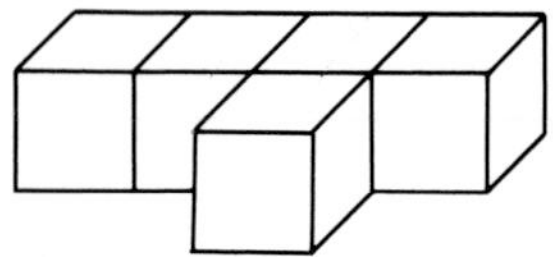

Section C

Do the children consider both lines of symmetry when shown a quarter of the pattern? Do their cross-stitch patterns have complete symmetry of both shape and colour?

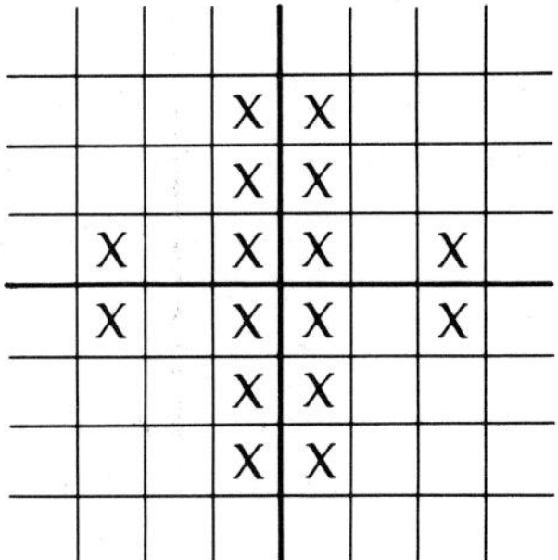

Purpose

- To give practice in choosing criteria to sort and classify objects, and in recording the results
- To sort 2D and 3D shapes, giving reasons for the sorting
- To select the materials and the mathematics to use for a task

Materials

Templates for plane shapes, solid shapes, paper

Vocabulary

Venn diagram, names of plane and solid shapes, tree diagram, Carroll diagram, face, corner

TEACHING POINTS

1 Sorting and classifying

Talk with the children about sorting and classifying objects in everyday life.

- Sorting children by their ages so that they can be put in the appropriate class in school
- Sorting children into those who have school dinners, sandwiches or who go home for dinner
- Sorting children into teams

- Sorting books into reference and fiction for the library
- Sorting clothes into piles (wool, cotton, etc.) to go into the washing machine (discuss the labels that classify garments for a hot, warm or cold wash)
- After shopping, sorting food that goes into the freezer, fridge or cupboard

2 Why do we sort and classify?

Talk to the children about why we often sort and classify – once we have classified an object we know how to treat and act towards it. For example, films are classified so that cinema management know whether or not to let children see the films.

3 Sorting objects

Useful objects for sorting are counters, buttons, beads, plastic shapes, logi-blocks, logic-people.

Use beads of different colours or a set of plastic sorting shapes and ask a child to sort them in some way. Other children can guess how they have been sorted, and then sort them a different way.

Encourage the children to explain precisely how the sets are sorted.

4 Sorting plane shapes

Make a set of four shapes in three colours (red, yellow, blue) and two sizes (large, small). (A set of logi-blocks or attribute blocks may be used if you have them.)

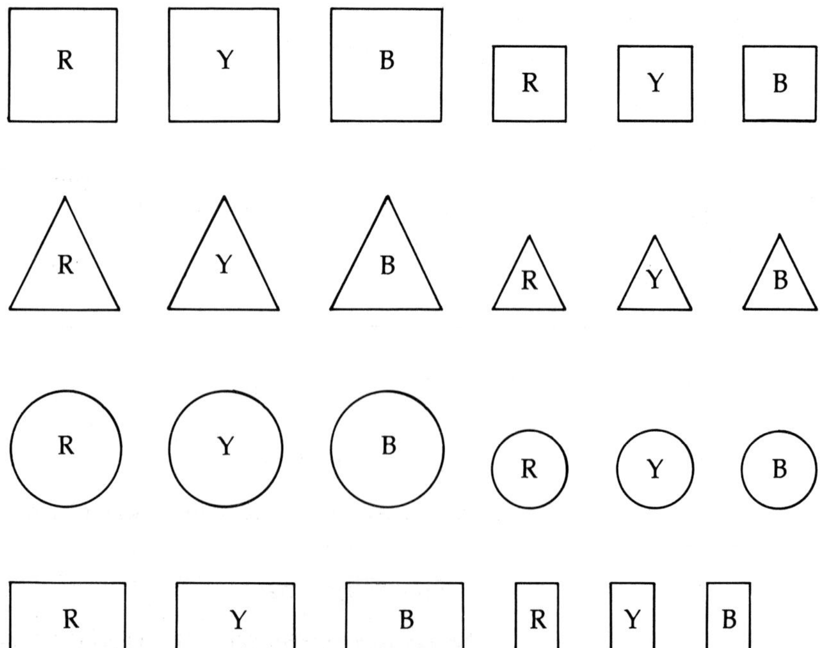

Ask a child to sort the large shapes in some way. Ask another child to guess how they are sorted, and then to sort the shapes in a different way for another child.

A game to play

SHAPE DOMINOES WITH ONE DIFFERENCE

This game is for 2, 3 or 4 players. Use the 24 sorting shapes illustrated above.

One child chooses a shape (e.g. a large red square) as the starting 'domino'. The next child selects another shape from the set with one difference (e.g. a large blue square) and places it in position, stating what the one difference is. Play continues until all the shapes have been used.

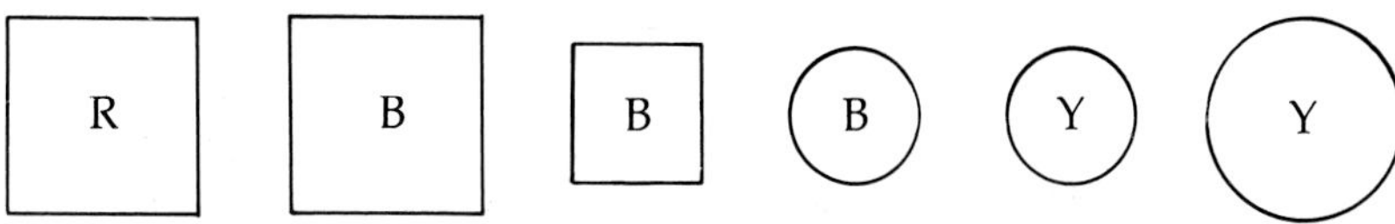

The game can be played with two or three differences.

5 Venn diagrams

Let the children collect data about the colours they are wearing, for example, who is wearing blue. Talk about how they might record this data.

Draw a Venn diagram. Talk about where the data will fit.

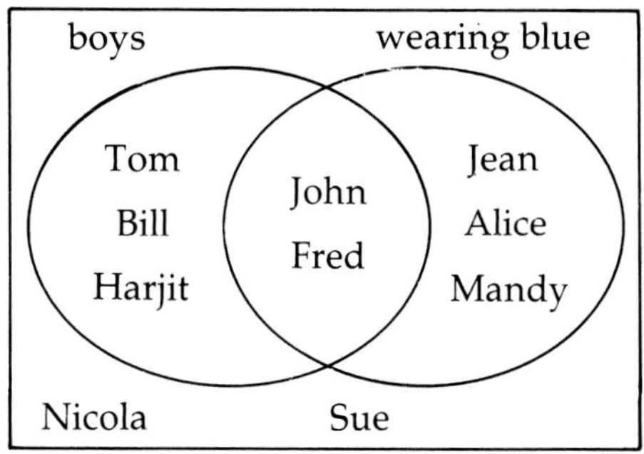

Venn diagram

	wearing blue	not wearing blue
boy	John Fred	Tom Bill Harjit
not boy	Jean Alice Mandy	Nicola Sue

Carroll diagram

6 Carroll diagrams

Repeat the above activities using Carroll diagrams.

7 Tree diagrams

Repeat the activities using tree diagrams.

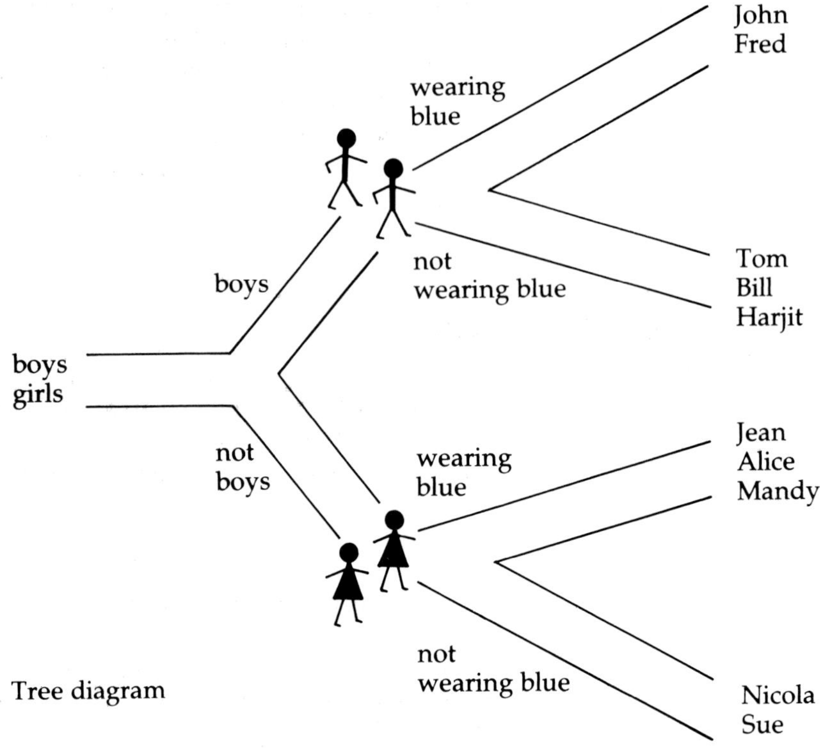

Tree diagram

8 Shape grid

Draw a grid. Can the children put logi-blocks in the correct spaces?

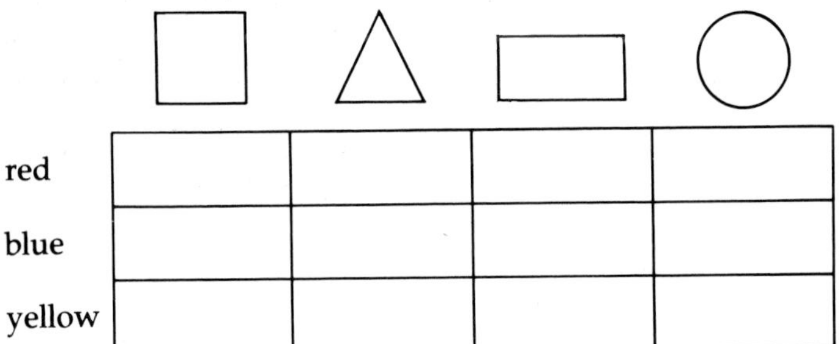

9 Sorting solid shapes

Repeat some of the previous activities, using a set of solid shapes. The children might sort them into shapes with flat faces, shapes that roll, shapes that have a triangular face, etc.

LINKS WITH THE ENVIRONMENT

Talk about everyday situations when we sort or classify and the reasons why we do it.

- We classify clothes and sort them to put them into the correct washing machine programme

- We classify roads as steep, winding, slippery, etc. so we know how fast to drive on them
- We classify people into children and adults for the purpose of travel fares, etc.
- We classify goods in supermarkets into sweets, beverages, spirits, fruit, vegetables, meats, biscuits, etc.

NOTES ON INVESTIGATIONS

Section A

Do the children choose suitable labels for the Venn diagram?

Do they appreciate that the shape where the circles intersect must be related to both labels?

Do they draw five shapes and show them in correct positions?

Section B

Do the children appreciate that each 'fork' of the tree diagram requires a label? Are the labels correct?

Are the shapes in the correct position according to the labels?

Do the children change the labels to produce different tree diagrams?

Section C

Do the children understand Venn diagrams that use three circles?

Do they choose shapes to fit the diagram?

Do they choose different labels for each circle and choose shapes that fit the diagram?

Do any children start from the 'centre' of the diagram and work out shapes that will fit?

Number 3

Purpose

- To introduce rules for divisibility
- To develop an awareness of number patterns
- To understand remainders in the context of calculation

Materials

Structural apparatus

Vocabulary

Patterns, pair, divide exactly, triangle, smallest, digit, sum of the digits, complete sets

TEACHING POINTS

1 Sets of objects

Talk about the numbers involved in sets of everyday objects.

- Clothes: gloves, shoes, socks, trainers (pattern of 2s); handkerchiefs (boxes of 3)
- food: eggs (6s and 12s), packets of crisps (6s), biscuits in packets (3s, 4s, 5s, 6s)

1	2	3
4	**5**	**6**
7	8	9
10	**11**	**12**
13	14	15
16	**17**	**18**
19	20	21
22	**23**	**24**
25	26	27
28	**29**	**30**

2 Number patterns

Talk about number patterns. How many ways can the children think of to show these?

- Using squared paper
- On the number line

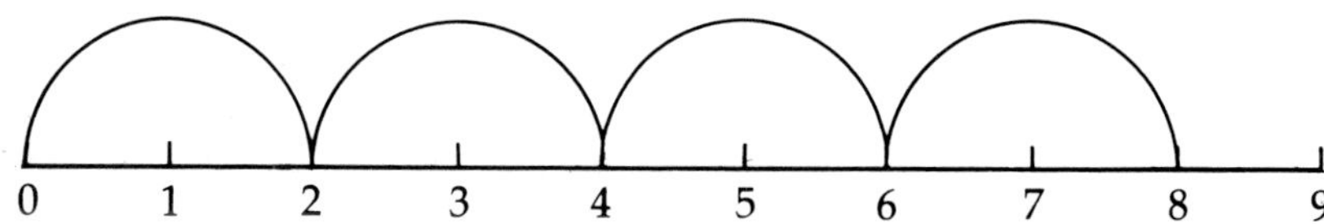

Talk about ways of recording these jumps.

- Using structural apparatus
- On the 100 square
- On the multiplication square

1	**2**	3	**4**	5	**6**	7	**8**	9	**10**
11	**12**	13	**14**	15	**16**	17	**18**	19	**20**
21	**22**	23	**24**	25	**26**	27	**28**	29	**30**
31	**32**	33	**34**	35	**36**	37	**38**	39	**40**
41	**42**	43	**44**	45	**46**	47	**48**	49	**50**
51	**52**	53	**54**	55	**56**	57	**58**	59	**60**
61	**62**	63	**64**	65	**66**	67	**68**	69	**70**
71	**72**	73	**74**	75	**76**	77	**78**	79	**80**
81	**82**	83	**84**	85	**86**	87	**88**	89	**90**
91	**92**	93	**94**	95	**96**	97	**98**	99	**100**

×	1	2	3	4	5	6	7	8	9	10
1	1	2	3	4	5	6	7	8	9	10
2	2	4	6	8	10	12	14	16	18	20
3	3	6	9	12	15	18	21	24	27	30
4	4	8	12	16	20	24	28	32	36	40
5	5	10	15	20	25	30	35	40	45	50
6	6	12	18	24	30	36	42	48	54	60
7	7	14	21	28	35	42	49	56	63	70
8	8	16	24	32	40	48	56	64	72	80
9	9	18	27	36	45	54	63	72	81	90
10	10	20	30	40	50	60	70	80	90	100

- Counting on or using the calculator constant function

2	4	6	8	10	12	. . .
5	10	15	20	25	30	. . .

3 Division into equal sets

Put 12 cubes onto a table. Ask a child to put them into 2s to find the number of sets of 2. Can they record what they have done?

Ask another child to put the 12 cubes into 3s. How many sets of 3 are there?

Repeat this for sets of 4 and 6.

4 Remainders

Put 13 cubes onto a table. Ask a child to put them into 2s. Ask how many complete sets of 2 there are, and how many are left. Can the child record this?

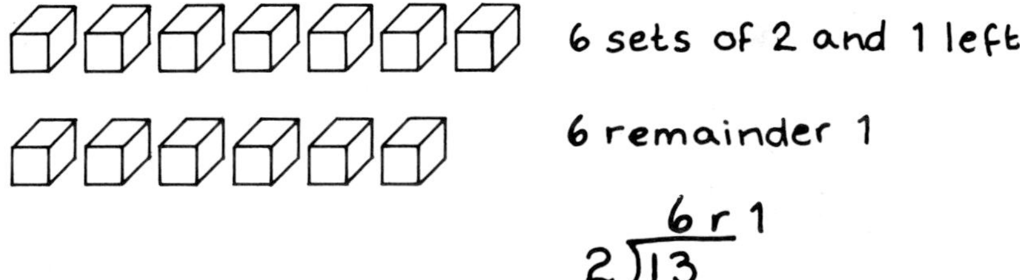

Repeat this for complete sets of 3, 4, 5 or 6.

Do similar activities using other numbers of cubes.

A game to play

EQUAL SETS

Put cubes on a table and ask each child to take a handful. The players then try to divide their cubes into equal sets of 2. If they can do this without a remainder they score 2 points.

Each child then tries to put the same handful of cubes into equal sets of 3, then 4, and then 5. For each successful grouping (without remainders), 3, 4 and 5 points are scored respectively. The winner is the player with the most points.

5 Rules of divisibility

Divisibility by 2

Write some odd and even numbers (e.g. 8, 64, 13, 90, 27, 33). Ask the children which of the numbers will divide exactly by 2, and why. Discuss the pattern of 2s and the even numbers. Do they realise that if the units digit is even then the whole number is divisible by 2?

1	2	3	4	5
6	7	8	9	10
11	12	13	14	15
16	17	18	19	20
21	22	23	24	25
26	27	28	29	30
31	32	33	34	35
36	37	38	39	40
41	42	43	44	45
46	47	48	49	50

Divisibility by 10

Repeat the above activity, including some numbers which are divisible by 10. Do the children realise that numbers which end in 0 are exactly divisible by 10?

Divisibility by 5

Draw the pattern of 5s on a grid and talk about it. Ask the children which pattern of numbers will divide exactly by 5 and why. Are there any numbers in the pattern of 5 which will divide exactly by 10?

Divisibility by 3 and 9

The children are asked to find the rules of divisibility by 3 and 9 in sections B and C of the pupils' book. As this is investigation work, try not to teach here what they are asked to discover.
Divisibility by 3 – the digits add up to 3, 6 or 9.
Divisibility by 9 – the digits add up to 9.

MENTAL WORK

Ask the children division questions in problem form. Remainders sometimes have to be rounded up (e.g. to find the number of egg-boxes needed to pack 27 eggs safely) as well as down.

- There are 12 gloves. How many complete pairs are there?
- There are 17 trainers. How many complete pairs are there?
- Find the next number in the pattern 50, 60, 70, . . .
- Will 65 divide exactly by 5?
- Which numbers divide exactly into 30?
- How many boxes for 6 eggs will 25 eggs fill?

USING THE CALCULATOR

Use the constant function to count on and talk about the patterns.

Test the rule of divisibility for larger numbers. For example, does 2 divide exactly into 3718?

Set the children activities such as:

- Find a number larger than 100 that divides exactly by 2, 3 and 4.
- Find numbers between 500 and 520 that divide exactly by 6. How many are there?

LINKS WITH THE ENVIRONMENT

Use situations in everyday life that involve equal sets or groups.

- Groups in PE lessons
- Team games: soccer and cricket 11 players, netball 7, volleyball 6, basketball 5, rugby league 13, rugby union 15.

- Sports equipment: sets of bowls (2 or 4), pairs of football boots or trainers, sets of darts (3) (see also the pupils' book and section 1 of these notes)

NOTES ON INVESTIGATIONS

Section A

Do the children realise that they are looking for one number that will divide exactly by 2, 5 and 10?

Do they write out the patterns of 2, 5 and 10 before finding that 10 is the smallest number that will divide exactly by all of them?

Do the children realise that multiples of 10 will all divide by 2, 5 and 10?

Can they explain this?

This investigation can be extended by finding numbers that will divide by different combinations of numbers such as 2, 3 and 5.

Section B

Do the children adopt a system of counting on or back in 3s when they have found a number between 100 and 200 that will divide exactly by 3?

Do the children come to realise that the sum of the digits must be 3, 6 or 9 if the number will divide exactly by 3?

Section C

Do the children find the first number by trial and error?

Do they realise that the sum of the digits of the missing number is 9?

Are they systematic in finding all possible ways?

i.e. 405 414 423
450 441 432

This investigation can be extended by using other numbers such as:

$9\overline{)\,2\square\square}$ $9\overline{)\,\square\square 2}$ or $9\overline{)\,\square 2\square}$

Purpose

- To give further practice in working out bills
- To revise the notation for writing money
- To give practice in rounding amounts of money to the nearest pound

Materials

Coins, book and shopping catalogues, calculators, bills and receipts

Vocabulary

Coins, amounts, pence, bill, cheapest, expensive, afford, buy, money left, spent, bought, change, prices, tokens, least, most, difference, price chart, till receipt, items, cost, nearest pound, estimate, total cost, round, exact cost, correct price, catalogue

TEACHING POINTS

1 Coin and note values

Remind the children of the coin values used in everyday life. Show £5 and £10 notes and explain how to write these values.

Make a simple wall shop using pictures of toys and their prices from a catalogue. Ask a child to choose something to buy and to draw the coins or notes needed to pay for it. Can the children find other note and coin values to pay the same amount of money? Can they find a way which uses the smallest number of coins or notes?

2 Notation for pounds and pence

Revise the notation for pounds and pence. Can the children say why it is important to put the point in the correct place?

Write a number, e.g. 315, and ask the children to discover different amounts of money which can be made using all three numbers in the same order. For example

£3·15 £315

Give the children practice in writing pence as pounds and vice versa. For example,

275p → £2·75 £5·46 → 564p

Use prices from catalogues to convert into pence (some children may need help in reading catalogues).

3 Rounding to the nearest pound

Remind the children what we mean by rounding. Explain how it can help us to estimate quickly the total cost of any articles we are buying and to see if we can afford them.

Explain that if the pence amount is below 50p we round down to the nearest pound. For example,

£2·48 → £2

If the pence amount is 50p or more we round up to the nearest pound. For example,

£2·50 → £3   £2·89 → £3

Give the children practice in rounding the prices on the wall shop or on a catalogue page. Let them estimate the cost of two or more articles. They could then work out the exact cost and compare the estimate.

Games to play

ESTIMATE

This game is for two pairs. Make a set of cards showing amounts such as these:

£0·50 £0·99 £1·21 £1·52 £1·98 £2·02
£2·49 £2·50 £2·87 £3·10 £3·64 £4·15

The children shuffle and share out the cards equally between the pairs. Each pair rounds the amounts to the nearest pound and sorts the cards into four groups: £1, £2, £3, £4. The children that sort their cards correctly in the shortest time are the winners.

This game can be developed by using more cards and by extending the range of money used.

HOLD IT UP

Cut out pictures and prices from a catalogue and mount them on stiff paper. Give a selection to each of two groups.

One group calls out an amount in pounds only (for example, £5). The other group holds up an amount that rounds to £5 to score a point. The groups then swop roles.

4 Bills and receipts

Revise the word 'bill' and how to total bills. Use catalogues or wall shops for practice in this. Suggest an amount of money (such as £10) and let the children choose some items from a catalogue page to spend it on. Remind them how to use rounding to estimate how many goods they can buy with £10.

5 What's left?

Remind the children that this means the change after spending some money. Can they suggest ways of working out what's left, such as shopkeeper's addition or subtraction? For example,

'I gave in £1 for an 89p item. The shopkeeper gave me back 11p.' 89p + 1p + 10p

Revise subtraction of money and how to check an answer, using addition.

$$\begin{array}{r} \pounds \\ 5{\cdot}00 \\ -\ 2{\cdot}95 \\ \hline 2{\cdot}05 \\ \hline \end{array} \qquad \begin{array}{r} \pounds \\ 2{\cdot}05 \\ +\ 2{\cdot}95 \\ \hline 5{\cdot}00 \\ \hline \end{array}$$

A game to play

FIND THE CHANGE

Decide upon an amount of money, such as £5 or £10. Make seven or eight pairs of cards for a bill total and the change needed from the agreed amount: for example,

£7·91 and £2·09 to make £10.

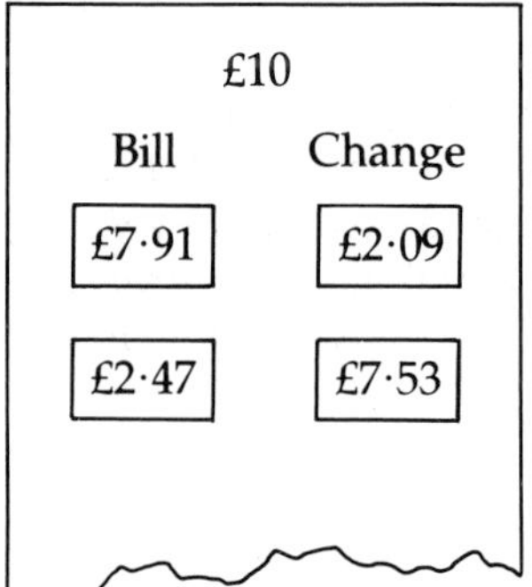

Shuffle the cards and deal them out to a small group of children. The aim of the game is for each player to sort their cards and to match bills with change from £10.

Each correct pair scores a point. The winner is the child with most points.

6 Till receipts

Collect some till receipts from local shops and stores. If they are not very clear it may help to copy them on to larger sheets of paper for display.

Ask the children to look at them carefully and discuss what each amount of money refers to. Do the children think the receipts are clearly presented or can they think of any improvements?

Let them write out some bills as till receipts.

7 Mental work

Give the children mental work involving money.

- Addition. How to total coins quickly by grouping

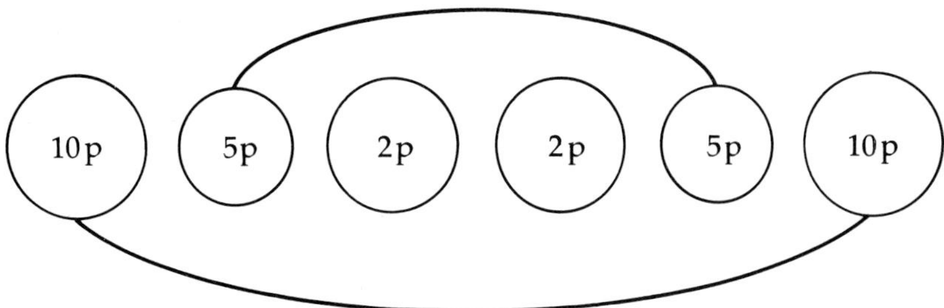

- Coin values. Give practice in making amounts of money using the smallest number of coins
- Rounding. Addition of money using rounding
- What's left? Working change out mentally by whichever method the children find easiest

USING THE CALCULATOR

Remind the children how to enter pounds and pence using the decimal point. Remind them that if the calculator shows 6·7 as an answer then this means £6·70. Give the children practice in using the calculator for bills and change.

Use the constant function for counting down in 20p's, 10p's, 50p's, etc. and to solve such problems as: 'How many 20p's in £2?'

Let the children investigate the possible amounts of money that can be made using 1, 0, 6, 5, and the decimal point, in any order. They must be able to read each amount accurately when they have made it. For example, £106·5 → £106·50.

LINKS WITH THE ENVIRONMENT

- Shopping. Talk about how the things we buy must always be less than or equal to the money we have to spend.
- Catalogues. Talk about family shopping catalogues with a wide variety of goods and how they work, often by mail order. Discuss other specialist catalogues such as book clubs and gardening catalogues.
- Receipts. Discuss and use receipts and till check-outs from local shops. Mention the need to keep them for returning goods or as a guarantee.

NOTES ON INVESTIGATIONS

Section A

Do the children realise that the total bill is £4·90?
Do their three books total this amount each time?
Do they choose sensible and realistic prices for the books?

Section B

Do the children use a book catalogue or look at the prices on some actual books if they are shown?
Do they find a variety of ways of paying?
Do they state which notes and coins they would use?

Section C

Do the children use a book catalogue correctly?
Do they choose different types of books?
Do any children discuss or consider whether to buy a number of cheaper books or a few expensive books in order to spend up to £50?
Do they add up the total cost correctly?
Is the amount of money left over correct?

Number 4

Purpose

- To introduce negative numbers in the familiar context of temperature

Materials

Thermometer, squared paper, reference books or newspapers showing world temperatures

Vocabulary

Temperature, Celsius, minus, freezing point, boiling point, weather, season, thermometer, degrees

TEACHING POINTS

1 Temperature

Talk with the children about the weather. Is it hot or cold? Is it hotter inside than outside? Discuss how we can feel the difference between warm and cold, and how we measure temperature.

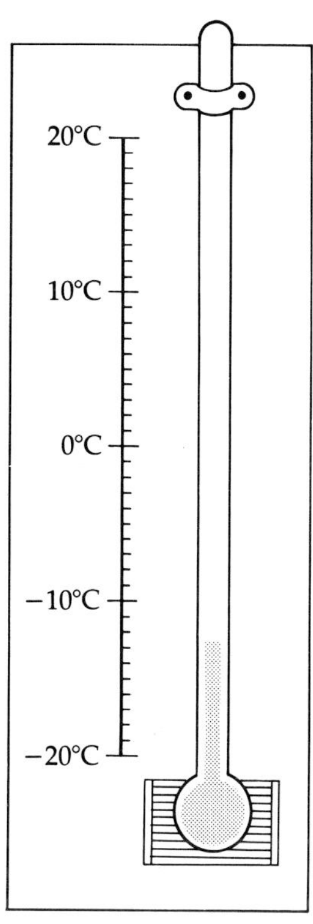

20°C
19°C
2°C
1°C
0
Freezing point
−1°C
−2°C
−19°C
−20°C

2 Using a thermometer

Show the children a thermometer and explain how it works. The liquid in it expands as it grows warmer and contracts as it grows colder and hence moves up or down the tube depending upon the temperature.

Thermometers usually now show the Celsius scale (named after the scientist Celsius). The freezing point of water is taken as 0 degrees Celsius (0 °C) and the boiling point as 100 °C. This scale has also been called the centigrade scale because of the 100 graduations between the freezing and boiling points of water.

3 Below zero

Explain that the temperature can go below zero. Introduce children to the term, for example, 'minus 3' meaning three degrees below zero. Show how it is written:

−3 °C

4 Making a thermometer or temperature scale

The children can make a thermometer or temperature scale using squared paper. Mark 0 °C as a reference point and then show the range, from +20 °C to −20 °C, for example.

Discuss that although 20 is a larger number than 10, −20 is a lower number than −10 because it is further below zero on the scale. Explain that temperatures below zero are shown as negative numbers (e.g. −20 °C) but above zero they are shown as numbers such as 20 °C. We do not usually show them as +20 °C although this is in fact what they are.

5 Games to play

WHICH IS GREATER?

Make a set of cards, say from −20 °C to 20 °C, and play with three or four children.

Shuffle and deal the cards face upwards, one to each child. The child with the hottest temperature card scores a point. The cards are re-shuffled into the pack. The winner is the first to reach 10 points.

COUNT-DOWN

Make a thermometer chart from 20 °C to −20 °C. Start on 20. Throw a die and count down the scale. The first player to arrive exactly on −20 °C is the winner.

6 Looking for temperatures

Encourage the children to check the temperature daily. A record might be kept from the temperature charts in newspapers.

7 Mental work

Ask the children to count up and down using negative numbers:

'8, 5, 2, −1. What are the next two numbers?'

Ask questions such as:
'The temperature was −3 °C and dropped another 2 degrees. What is the temperature now?'

USING THE CALCULATOR

Ask the children to count back in ones from 10 to −10 on the calculator, using the constant function. Talk about what happens.

Repeat the activity, counting back in twos. Talk about the patterns.

Try counting back in other numbers.

LINKS WITH THE ENVIRONMENT

- Frozen foods are stored at temperatures below zero. A freezer is often at a temperature of about −18 °C.
- Look at and keep a chart of the daily temperature both locally and in other parts of the world.
- Look at recipes and temperatures.
- Relate negative numbers to going below sea level.

NOTES ON INVESTIGATIONS

Section A

Do the children appreciate that the pattern is increasing by 3 each time?

−6 −3 0 3 6 9

Do they devise further patterns, using numbers on both sides of zero? For example:

−12 −10 −8 −6 −4 −2 0 2 4 6 8 10 12 14 16 18 20
−12 −8 −4 0 4 8 12 16 20

Section B

Do the children make sensible hypotheses for finding very cold temperatures, such as going towards the Poles or climbing very high mountain ranges? Do they use appropriate reference books? Do they draw an accurate chart to show the temperatures?

Section C

Do the children use the information in the pupils' book that the temperature on a mountain gets colder the higher you climb? Do they draw an accurate chart? Is the temperature at sea level 20 °C or cooler?

Probability 1

Purpose

- To distinguish between 'fair' and 'unfair'
- To introduce the idea of equal or even chances
- To introduce 'likelihood of events' and use appropriate words to identify them

Materials

Coins, counters of different colours, dice, counters (marked 1 on one side and 2 on the other), cubes, stop-watch or timer

Vocabulary

Probability, fair, tally, equal chance, very likely, likely, unlikely, very unlikely, circle, odd, even, die, sum, add, total score, toss, possible, unfair

TEACHING POINTS

1 Equal chances

Talk with the children about situations in everyday life which have equal chances.

- A raffle – each ticket has an equal chance of winning
- Tossing a coin – to decide the choice of 'ends' in a sports match or who starts first. (In the case of the coin because there are only two possibilities (a head or a tail) there is an 'evens' or '50–50' chance of choosing correctly.)

Explore other situations where the outcome may not be equal. For example, does everyone in a race have an equal chance of winning? Do two football teams playing a match always have equal chances of winnning? Suppose one team was top of the First Division and the other was a non-league team as happens sometimes in cup matches.

2 Likelihood

Discuss whether events are very likely, likely, unlikely or very unlikely.

I shall go to school tomorrow.
I shall be awake at 7 a.m. tomorrow.
I shall meet the Prime Minister one day.
I shall meet my favourite television star one day.

A game to play

YOUR CHOICE

Write 'very likely', 'likely', 'unlikely', 'very unlikely' on four equal sized pieces of card. Place them face down and shuffle them. A child picks up one card and chooses a friend to make up an outcome or event to match the word on the card. If it is correct then that child chooses a card and a friend to make up another event. The rest of the children can act as judges.

3 Coin tossing

Ask a child to choose heads or tails on a coin. Toss it and see if they were right. Repeat this several times. Talk about whether the chances of winning are equal.

Games to play

	tally	total
H	II	
T	I	

FIRST TO 5

Two children toss a coin and keep a tally. One child is 'heads', the other is 'tails'. The winner is the first player to reach 5 heads or 5 tails.

THE BEST OF 3

Two children toss a coin 3 times. One child is 'heads', the other is 'tails'. The winner is the player who gets more heads or tails in 3 tosses.

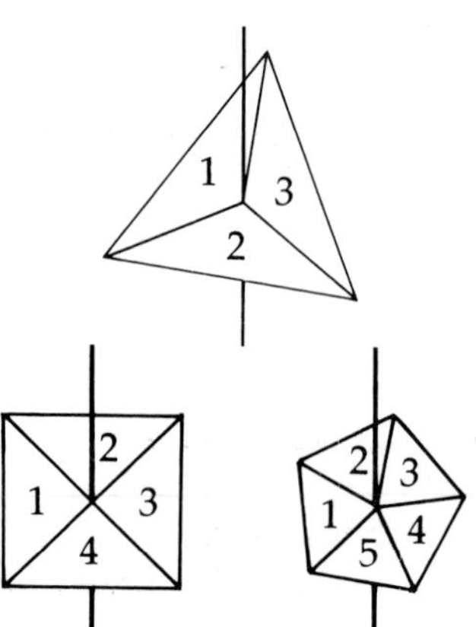

4 Spinners

Use a triangular spinner. Ask three children to be '1', '2' and '3'. Spin the spinner. Discuss whether they have equal chances of it spinning their number. A tally of the spins could be made.

This can be repeated with other spinners. (N.B. Spinners need to be carefully made for accuracy or they may be bought.)

5 Fair and unfair

Use the triangular spinner and ask a child to choose 1, 2 or 3. Spin the spinner. Did they choose correctly?

Games to play

Ask the children to play the following games and talk about whether they are fair or unfair.

TRIANG

Use the triangular spinner and some counters. Three children choose to be '1', '2' or '3'. Each player takes turns to spin the spinner. The person whose number is shown collects a counter. The game stops after 12 spins of the spinner. The winner is the player with the most counters.

The game can be adapted for two players.

SQUARE

1	1	1	1
2	2	2	2
3	3	3	3
4	4	4	4

Use a square spinner, some counters and a board like the one on the left.
Four children choose to be '1', '2', '3' or '4'.
Each player takes it in turns to spin the spinner.
The person whose number is shown covers one of their own numbers on the board with a counter. The winner is the first to complete their row.

The game can be played for two or three players. The board could also be changed in a variety of ways.

1	2	2	1
3	4	4	3
3	4	4	3
1	2	2	1

1	3	3	2
4	1	2	4
4	2	1	4
2	3	3	1

Pentagon spinners could be used for similar activities and games. Activities with a die are suggested in the pupils' book.

LINKS WITH THE ENVIRONMENT

- Board games – they use dice or spinners to give fairness
- Sports events – tossing up at the start to choose ends or who starts. Sports like tennis spin racquets to choose ends
- Raffles – prize draws rely on fairness. Tickets are often drawn from a drum

- Draws – Premium Bonds, cup draws for sports events
- Bingo games often use table tennis balls with numbers on. These are usually chosen by being sucked up a tube

NOTES ON INVESTIGATIONS

Section A

Do the children write sentences for each of the cards?
Are their suggestions related to their own experiences?
Do they relate to the possible outcomes?
Class activities are possible extensions.

Section B

Do the children design a suitable board for the game?
Do they make use of the die? Do they state any rules? Is the game fair, i.e. have they an equal chance of winning? Is their explanation of the game clear?

Section C

Do the children realise that the total scores in the two circles must be

(total score 2 or 4) and (total score 3) i.e. 1, 1 / 2, 2 and 2, 1 / 1, 2

for a fair game? Can they explain why this is?

Do they use the circles and the two counters again to make up an unfair game? Can they explain why it is unfair?

Number 5

Purpose

- To introduce $\frac{1}{6}$, $\frac{1}{12}$, $\frac{1}{5}$, $\frac{1}{10}$
- To understand the equivalence of fractions

Materials

Squared paper, large squared paper

Vocabulary

Fraction chart, whole, half, large squared paper, symmetry, equivalent fraction, fraction pattern, whole strip, label

TEACHING POINTS

1 Sixths and twelfths

Talk about sixths and twelfths, noting that $\frac{1}{6}$ refers to 1 out of 6 equal parts and $\frac{1}{12}$ is 1 out of 12 equal parts.

$\frac{1}{12}$	$\frac{1}{12}$		$\frac{1}{6}$
$\frac{1}{12}$	$\frac{1}{12}$		$\frac{1}{6}$
$\frac{1}{12}$	$\frac{1}{12}$		$\frac{1}{6}$
$\frac{1}{12}$	$\frac{1}{12}$		$\frac{1}{6}$
$\frac{1}{12}$	$\frac{1}{12}$		$\frac{1}{6}$
$\frac{1}{12}$	$\frac{1}{12}$		$\frac{1}{6}$

2 Sixths and twelfths of shapes

Give the children two rectangles of large squared paper, each containing 12 squares. Ask them to colour the first rectangle to show 12 equal parts, labelling each part $\frac{1}{12}$. The second rectangle should be coloured to show 6 equal parts, each labelled $\frac{1}{6}$.

Ask how many sixths there are in the whole rectangle and then how many twelfths there are.

Talk about the equivalence

$\frac{1}{6} = \frac{2}{12}$

and that $\frac{6}{6} = 1$ (whole one) $\quad \frac{12}{12} = 1$ (whole one)

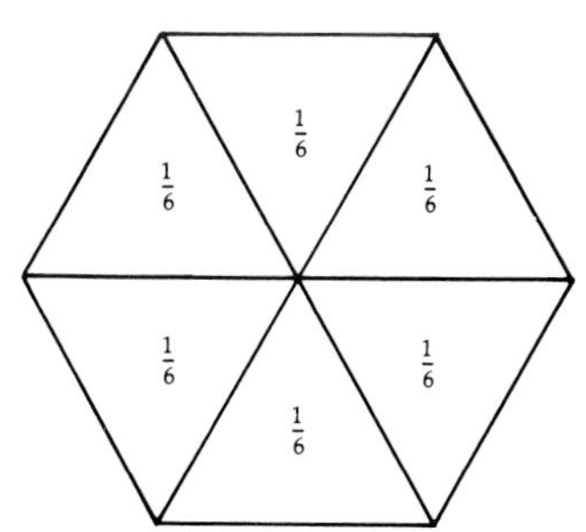

Let the children draw round a hexagon template and divide the shape into six equal parts, labelling each one $\frac{1}{6}$. They can then cut and fold it to show 12 equal parts or twelfths.

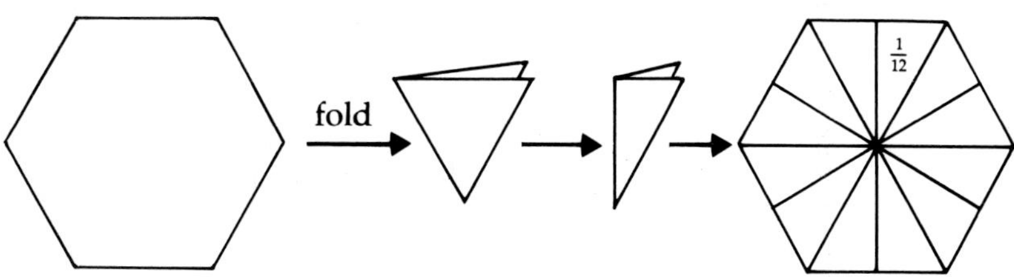

The hexagons could be used for some fraction colouring work, colouring $\frac{4}{12}$ green, $\frac{4}{12}$ pink, $\frac{4}{12}$ yellow, for example. The results might be displayed as mobiles.

3 Equivalence of sixths and twelfths

Draw a fraction wall or equivalence chart for sixths and twelfths.

1 whole											
$\frac{1}{6}$		$\frac{1}{6}$		$\frac{1}{6}$		$\frac{1}{6}$		$\frac{1}{6}$		$\frac{1}{6}$	
$\frac{1}{12}$	$\frac{1}{12}$	$\frac{1}{12}$	$\frac{1}{12}$	$\frac{1}{12}$	$\frac{1}{12}$	$\frac{1}{12}$	$\frac{1}{12}$	$\frac{1}{12}$	$\frac{1}{12}$	$\frac{1}{12}$	$\frac{1}{12}$

Ask the children to make their own walls using three strips of large squared paper, each strip 12 squares long. They should label the fractions, then stick the three strips in their books.

Fraction walls can be used to reinforce children's imagery and understanding of equivalence. Talk about ways of recording fractions and ask questions related to them. For example,

$\frac{6}{6} = 1 \qquad \frac{12}{12} = 1$

'How many sixths equal 1? How many twelfths equal 1?'

The fraction wall or equivalence chart may be extended and equivalence discussed.

$3/6 = \frac{1}{2} \qquad 6/12 = \frac{1}{2}$

'How many sixths equal $\frac{1}{2}$? How many twelfths equal $\frac{1}{2}$?

<table>
<tr><td colspan="12">1 whole</td></tr>
<tr><td colspan="6">$\frac{1}{2}$</td><td colspan="6">$\frac{1}{2}$</td></tr>
<tr><td colspan="2">$\frac{1}{6}$</td><td colspan="2">$\frac{1}{6}$</td><td colspan="2">$\frac{1}{6}$</td><td colspan="2">$\frac{1}{6}$</td><td colspan="2">$\frac{1}{6}$</td><td colspan="2">$\frac{1}{6}$</td></tr>
<tr><td>$\frac{1}{12}$</td><td>$\frac{1}{12}$</td><td>$\frac{1}{12}$</td><td>$\frac{1}{12}$</td><td>$\frac{1}{12}$</td><td>$\frac{1}{12}$</td><td>$\frac{1}{12}$</td><td>$\frac{1}{12}$</td><td>$\frac{1}{12}$</td><td>$\frac{1}{12}$</td><td>$\frac{1}{12}$</td><td>$\frac{1}{12}$</td></tr>
</table>

Let the children use the fraction wall for colouring activities to show they understand equivalence. For example, they could draw a 2×6 rectangle on squared paper and write $\frac{1}{12}$ on each square. They could then colour $\frac{1}{6}$ yellow, $\frac{5}{6}$ green.

4 Fifths and tenths

Talk with the children about fifths and tenths. Discuss how $\frac{1}{5}$ means 1 out of 5 equal parts and $\frac{1}{10}$ means 1 out of 10 equal parts.

Use similar activities to those used for sixths and twelfths to help children's understanding of equivalence.

5 Fractions of numbers

Ask the children to put 10 counters in a row, and then to put them into 5 equal groups.
How many are in each group?

Point out that $\frac{1}{5}$ of 10 is 2.

Give the children plenty of practical experience like this. Discuss their findings each time.

Can they suggest a way of finding $\frac{1}{5}$ of a number without using apparatus? For example, to find $\frac{1}{5}$ we divide by 5.

Do the same for $\frac{1}{10}$, $\frac{1}{6}$, $\frac{1}{12}$.

6 Revision

In preparation for the work in Section B of the pupils' book, it may be helpful to revise the fraction charts for $\frac{1}{2}$, $\frac{1}{4}$, $\frac{1}{8}$ and $\frac{1}{3}$.

7 Games to play

BRING ME A FRACTION

Play the game in two teams or groups.
Give each group an agreed number of counters such as 18.
Ask a player from each team to bring you a fraction of the counters e.g. $\frac{1}{6}$ of 18 counters.
The first player to bring the correct number of counters, scores a point for their team.
The game could be developed to include such numbers as $\frac{2}{6}$, $\frac{1}{3}$ or $\frac{1}{2}$ of 18, depending upon the experience of the children.

HOLD UP

Make two sets of cards showing these fractions: 1, $\frac{1}{2}$, $\frac{1}{6}$, $\frac{2}{6}$, $\frac{3}{6}$, $\frac{4}{6}$, $\frac{5}{6}$, $\frac{6}{6}$, $\frac{2}{12}$, $\frac{4}{12}$, $\frac{6}{12}$, $\frac{8}{12}$, $\frac{10}{12}$, $\frac{12}{12}$.

Play the game with two small groups. Call out a fraction such as $\frac{1}{2}$. The first group to hold up a card showing an equivalent fraction scores one point for the group. Fraction walls may be used for reference.

The game may be used for fifths and tenths or developed further (for example $\frac{1}{3} = \frac{4}{12}$) for those children able to cope with it.

8 Mental work

Ask the children to work out fractions mentally:

- $\frac{1}{2}$ of 6, 10, 12, 20
- $\frac{1}{6}$ of 6, 12, 18, 24
- $\frac{1}{5}$ of 10, 15, 20, 25
- $\frac{1}{10}$ of 10, 20, 30, 40
- $\frac{1}{12}$ of 12, 24

Give simple word problems such as, 'I have 12 marbles and lose one sixth of them. How many have I left?'

USING THE CALCULATOR

- Revise how to find $\frac{1}{2}$, $\frac{1}{3}$ and $\frac{1}{4}$ of numbers using the calculator.
- Talk about how to find $\frac{1}{6}$, $\frac{1}{12}$, $\frac{1}{5}$, $\frac{1}{10}$ of numbers using the calculator. Do the children appreciate that if the answers are to be whole numbers, the original numbers must be multiples of 6, 12, 5 or 10?

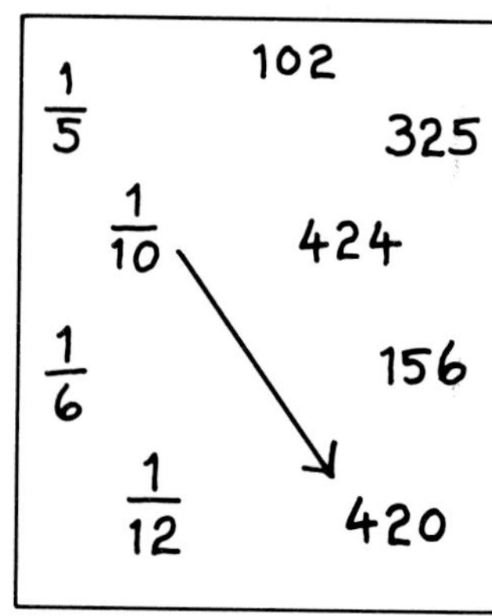

A game to play

MATCH THE FRACTIONS

Write these fractions and numbers:

$\frac{1}{5}$ $\frac{1}{10}$ $\frac{1}{6}$ $\frac{1}{12}$

102 325 424 156 420

Ask the children to match a fraction to a number so that the answer will be a whole number. Which is the odd number out?

LINKS WITH THE ENVIRONMENT

Talk about everyday situations involving fractions.

- Sharing pizza, cakes, pies etc. into equal parts
- Sharing objects such as sweets amongst 5, 10, 6 or 12 people
- A school day is $\frac{1}{5}$ of a school week
- One stamp may be a $\frac{1}{6}$ of a page in a book of stamps

NOTES ON INVESTIGATIONS

Section A

Do the children realise that the number of eggs must be a multiple of 10?

The investigation might be extended by changing the fractions to $\frac{1}{2}$, $\frac{1}{6}$, $\frac{1}{12}$ or $\frac{1}{2}$, $\frac{1}{3}$, $\frac{1}{6}$.

Section B

Do the children copy the pattern correctly? Do they combine ideas of symmetry and equivalent fractions to produce a symmetrical pattern? Are any of the fractions written twice?

Section C

Do the children realise that $\frac{4}{5}$ and $\frac{8}{10}$ are equivalent fractions and so both give an answer of 24? Do they select other pairs of equivalent fractions and then match them with numbers that give whole-number answers? Do they understand that equivalent fractions of the same number will always give the same answer?

Number 6

Purpose

- To investigate inputs and outputs from simple function machines

Materials

Calculators, squared paper

Vocabulary

Machine, chart, table, input, output, fraction chart, double, halve, half, even, instruction, round numbers, nearest, design, label

TEACHING POINTS

1 Machines

Talk with the children about machines. Can they name any? Examples might include: stamp machines, change machines, slot machines (fruit machines), sewing and knitting machines, packing machines, drinks machines.

Explain that machines do a job and that what we put in is called the input and what comes out is the output. Ask what you put into a drinks machine (money) and what comes out (drinks).

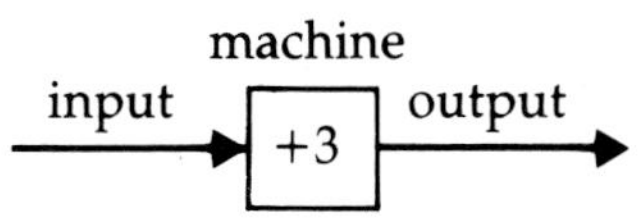

2 Function machines

Draw a machine like this.

Ask a child to input 1 into this machine. What is the output?

Draw tables to show ways of recording what the machine does to numbers.

input	output
1	4
2	5
3	
4	
5	
6	

in	1	2	3	4	5	6
out	4	5				

Draw machines with different designs. Talk about the input and output of each.

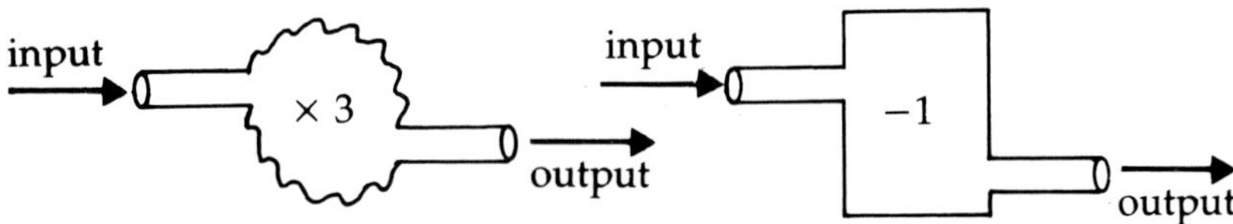

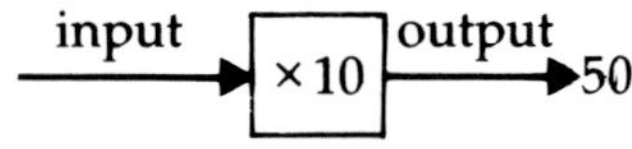

Use machines to multiply by 10. Ask the children to find the input numbers if the output numbers are 50, 70, 90.

Ask the children to input numbers into this machine.

input	output
1	I
	II
5	V
	IX
	X

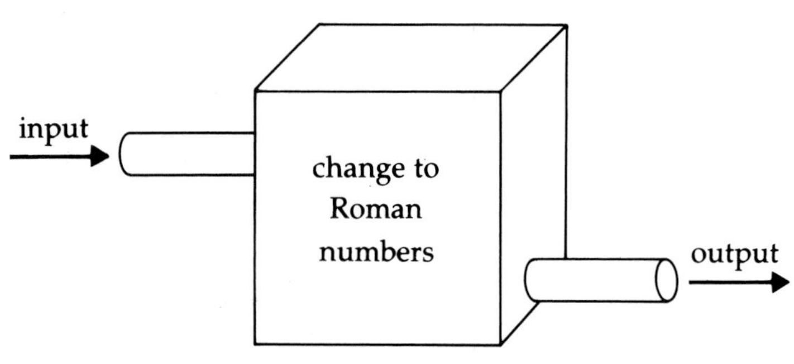

Ask them to work out the missing inputs and outputs in the table.

3 Make a machine

Duplicate some function machines. Let the children make up their own input numbers and function and then find the output.

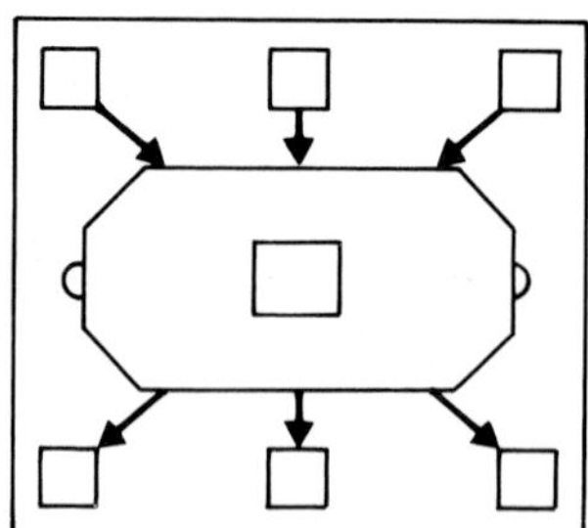

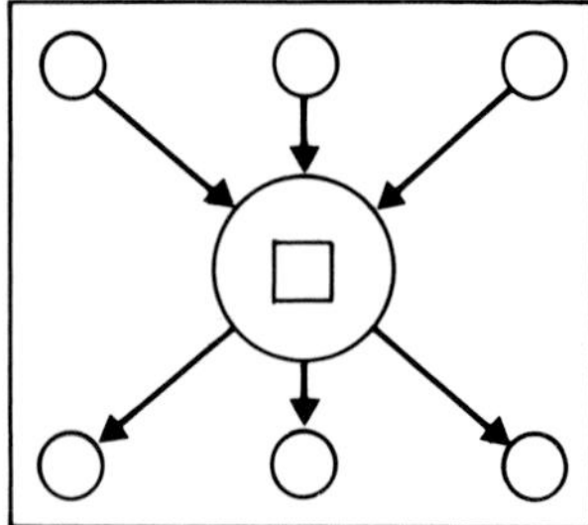

4 Describing machines

Ask the children to describe what this machine is doing to the left-hand numbers (input) to get the right-hand numbers (output). What is the function?

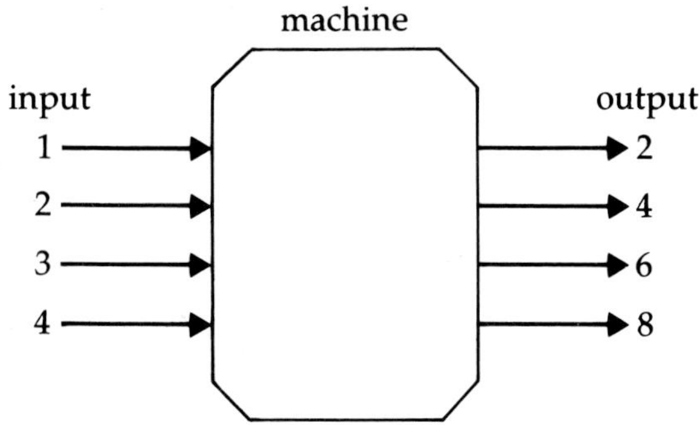

A game to play

I AM A MACHINE

Ask a child to stand at the front as the 'machine'. Give them an instruction card such as '+2' but don't let the rest of the children see it.

Ask the other children to suggest numbers to input. The 'machine' says what the output number is each time. The rest of the children have to guess what the machine does.

5 More complex machines

Machines can be made more complex according to the capability of the children.

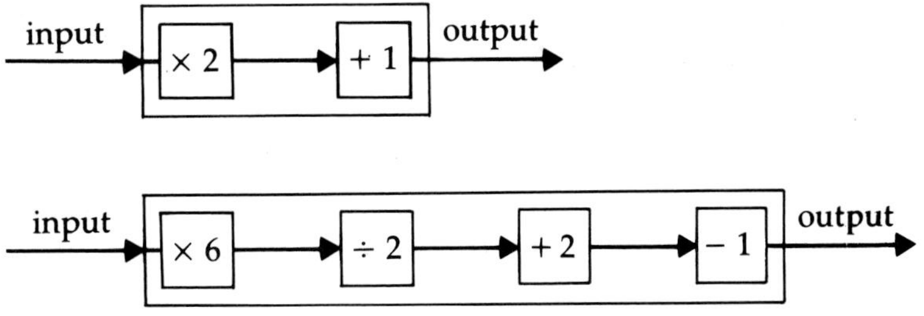

Some of the more complex machines can be reduced.

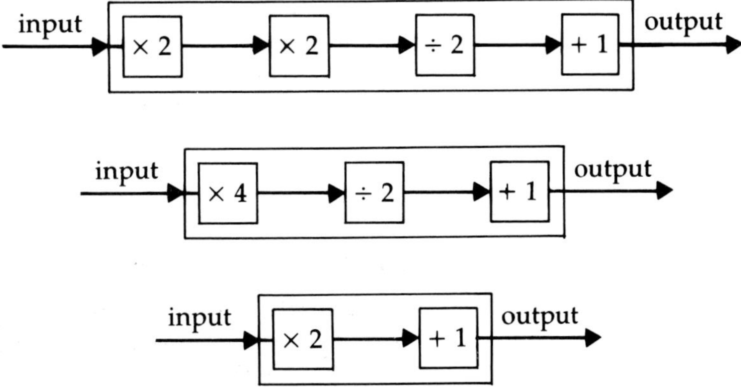

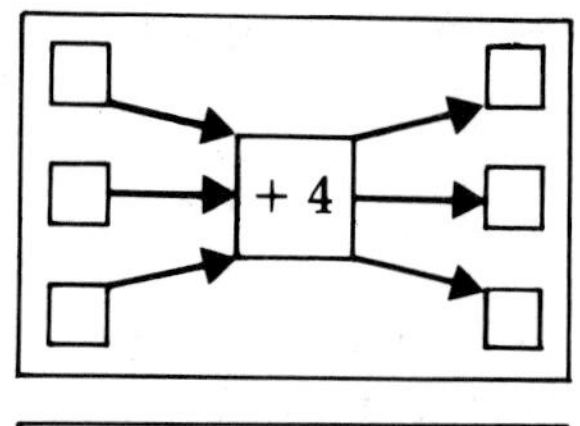

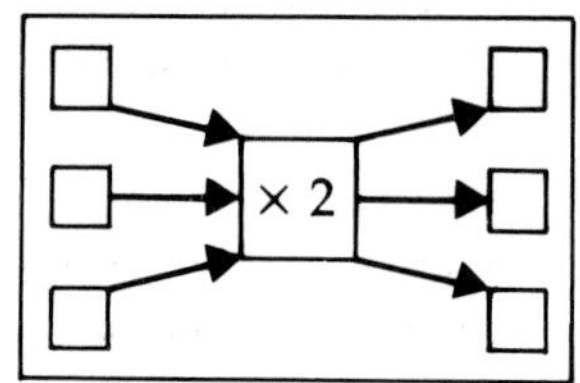

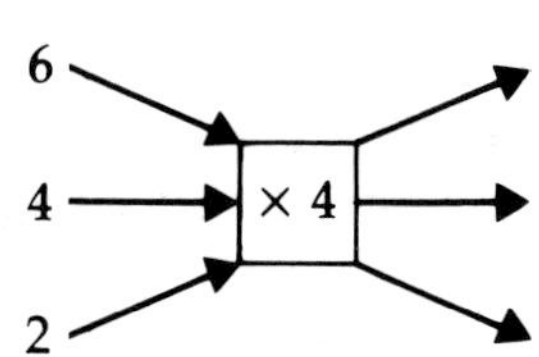

A game to play

BINGO

Make some bingo boards as function machines and a set of input and output number cards from 1 to 20.

Shuffle the cards and place them face downwards in a pile. Each player takes it in turns to turn over a card and then tries to place it onto their board. If a card cannot be placed it is discarded. The winner is the first player to complete their board.

6 Mental work

Ask the children questions about different machines. For example, 'What is the output from a machine which doubles numbers if these numbers are put in: 2, 5, 10?'

Give practice in tables using the function machine idea.

USING THE CALCULATOR

The calculator is a number machine and can be used as an aid to finding input and outputs.

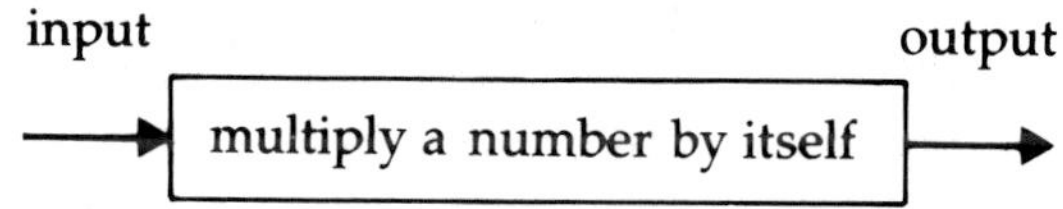

Further work using the calculator is shown in the pupils' book.

LINKS WITH THE ENVIRONMENT

Talk about some of the machines used in everyday life and their function. (See also activity 1.)

- At the post office – franking machines, sorting machines
- At the factory – packing cans, jars, bottles etc. into boxes; putting eggs and chocolates into boxes
- At the bank – counting machines

NOTES ON INVESTIGATIONS

Section A

Do the children design function machines with the functions, inputs and outputs shown? Do their input/output tables relate to their machines?

An extension might be to find two different machines that give the same output.

Section B

Do any children try even numbers in both boxes? If so, do they realise that the division number must be smaller than the multiplication number for the machine to work with all numbers?

Do the children find these machines?

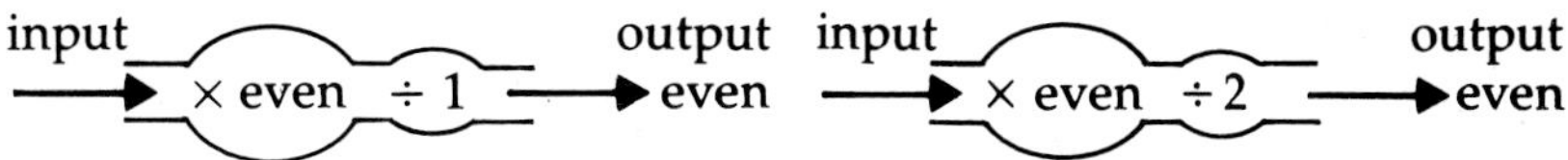

If odd numbers are input other machines will not work.

The investigation could be extended by considering the following machine.

Section C

Do the instructions on the machine match up with the input and output numbers? Can the children explain clearly what each machine does and justify their output numbers?

The investigation could be extended by asking the children to make up their own input numbers as well as the instructions.

Length 1

Purpose

- To introduce circumference, diameter and radius of a circle
- To measure circumference, diameter and radius of circular objects
- To find the relationship between radius and diameter

Materials

Paper circles, card circles (the diameter of some should be twice as large as others), tape measures, trundle wheels, rulers, compasses, cylinders (selection – at least four), circular lids or wheels (selection), string

Vocabulary

Centre, radius, diameter, circumference, circle, fold, half, outside edge, trundle wheel, nearest centimetre, table, different sizes, cylinders, estimate, measure, rings, lengths, pairs, large wheel, penny-farthing, small wheel, metre, faster, longer, slower, turns, distance, larger

TEACHING POINTS

1 Circular objects

Talk with the children about everyday circular objects. Ask them to name them. Some are: balls, rings, dart-boards, wheels, cylindrical tins, coins, some clocks, medals, some bottles, door handles.

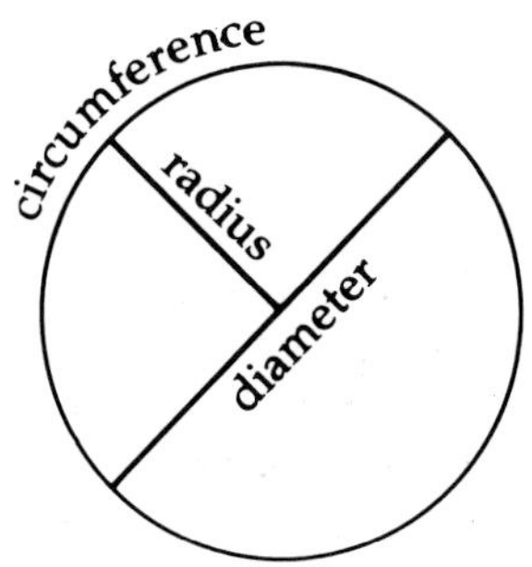

2 Parts of a circle

Draw a circle on the board and talk about the names of some of the parts.

3 Drawing a circle using string

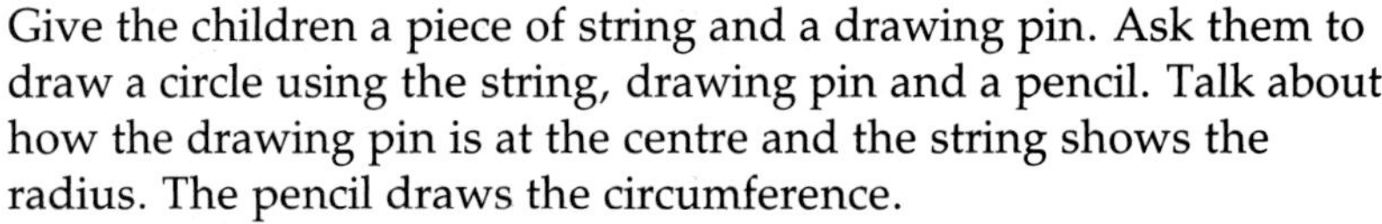

Give the children a piece of string and a drawing pin. Ask them to draw a circle using the string, drawing pin and a pencil. Talk about how the drawing pin is at the centre and the string shows the radius. The pencil draws the circumference.

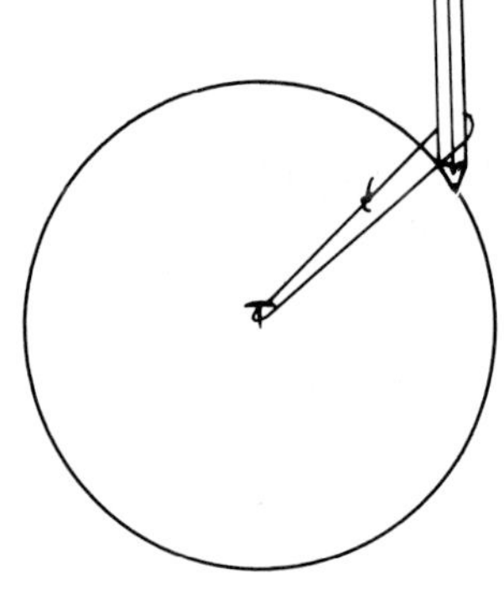

4 Drawing a circle using a ruler

Ask the children to draw a circle using a ruler and pencil. Talk about the different methods.

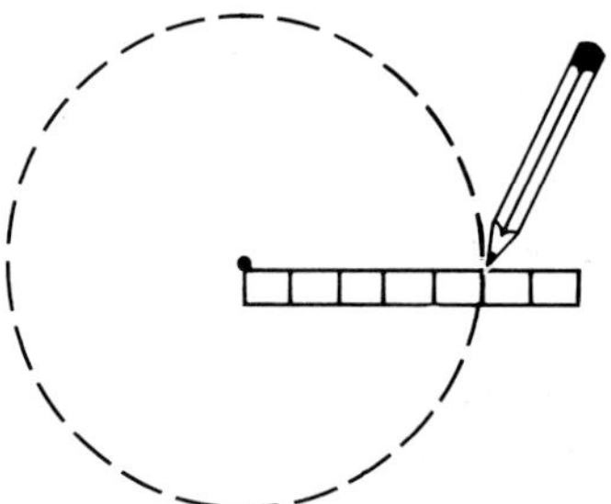

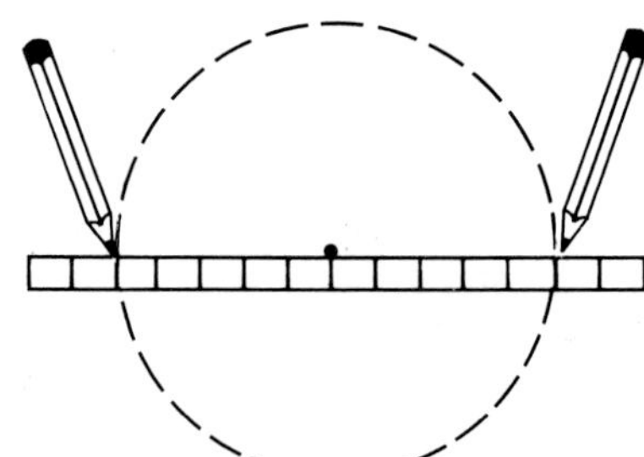

5 Introducing the relationship between radius and diameter

Ask the children to draw a circle of radius 5 cm. Then ask them to measure the diameter of their circle. Can they explain why the diameter is twice the radius?

Ask the children to draw a circle with a diameter of 8 cm. What do they find if they measure the radius?

This work is developed in the pupils' book.

A game to play

FIND THE DIAMETER AND RADIUS

This game is for two children
Make a set of cards giving diameters and radii. For example

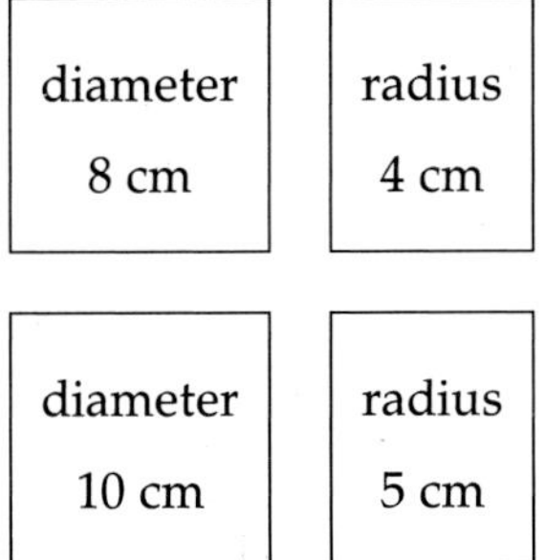

Shuffle and place the cards face down but spread out on the table. Each child in turn picks up two cards. If they make a pair (for example, diameter 12 cm, radius 6 cm), they put the pair in front of them. If the cards do not make a pair, they are placed back on the table face downwards. Players may memorise where particular cards have been placed on the table. When all the cards have been used, the winner is the player with most pairs.

6 Introducing compasses

Show the children how to draw a circle using a pair of large compasses. Write centre, radius, diameter, circumference in a list alongside the circle. Ask some children to point to each of the parts on the circle and explain them.

Show the children how to draw circles using compasses. Ask them to draw a large circle on paper using their compasses and show the centre, radius, diameter and circumference on it.

7 Compass patterns

Ask the children to draw a large circle on paper using compasses and do some compass patterns inside it. Draw different circle patterns for further practice.

8 Concentric circles

Ask the children to draw several circles with the same centre. These are concentric circles. Patterns using rulers and crayons can be made.

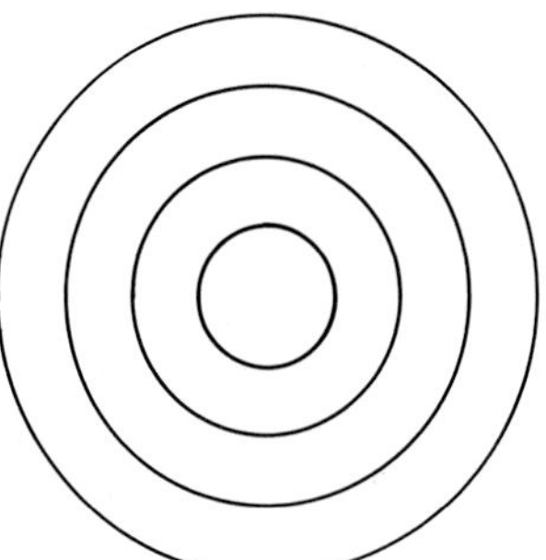

concentric circles

concentric circles and ruler pattern

9 Cylindrical objects

Talk about cylindrical objects being solid shapes (three-dimensional) whereas circles are plane or flat shapes (two-dimensional).

Show the children a cylinder and ask them to point out the circle on it. Ask them to suggest ways of measuring the distance round it, i.e. the circumference. Two methods are by using string, and by rolling. Ask different children to use both of these methods. Do they both obtain the same answer?

10 Spheres

Ask the children to measure the circumference of a sphere using string and by rolling. Do they get the same answer each time? If not, are they measuring accurately with the string?

11 Mental work

Ask the children questions involving circumferences such as:
'If the circumference of a wheel is 3 metres, how far will it have travelled after 4 turns?'
'What is the radius of a circle if the diameter is 16 cm?'

LINKS WITH THE ENVIRONMENT

Talk about situations in everyday life that involve circles, cylinders and spheres.

- Science – wheels, balls, girth of tree trunks and annual rings
- Geography – the earth, equator, tropics, diameter of the planets
- History – story of the wheel, transport (cars, bicycles, carts etc.), clocks

- Sport – discus, shot, putting circle, cricket ball, football, netball ring, etc.
- Art – patterns using circles
- Home economics – cake tins, plates, saucers, bun tins

NOTES ON INVESTIGATIONS

Section A

Do the children record the radius and diameter of the circles in a systematic way? Do they find the relationship that the diameter is twice the radius of a circle? Do they appreciate that this relationship holds for all circles, regardless of size?

Section B

The children need card circles for this investigation. The diameter of some of these should be twice as large as others.

How do the children measure the circumference of the circles – by rolling or by using string? Do they find that the circles whose diameters are twice as large have twice the circumference?

Section C

The children need some lids or wheels for this investigation.

How do the children measure the circumference and diameter of the lids or wheels – using string or by rolling and measuring? Do they record their findings systematically? Do they find that the circumference is just over 3 times longer than the diameter? (This is π, which is about 3.142.) Do any children simply mark the distance of the circumference of each wheel or lid by rolling it and then fitting the diameter of the wheel along it 3 times? Can the children explain their findings?

Purpose

- To give practice in reading and interpreting weight scales
- To give experience in practical weighing situations

Materials

Weighing scales, spring balances, board with cup hook, S hook or paper clip, rubber bands of various thicknesses, key, scissors, plastic bags for hanging on spring balances, ruler, cardboard tube, Blu-tak,

50 g and 100 g weights, newspapers (of various thicknesses, sizes and qualities of paper), magazines and comics, suitable objects for weighing activities

Vocabulary

Weigh, weight, scales, spring balance, stretch, balance, different thicknesses, bar chart, graph, pairs, record, results, see-saw balance, heaviest, lightest, estimate, total weight, readings, estimate

TEACHING POINTS

1 Reading weighing scales

Talk with the children about when and why weighing scales are used. Examples may include in the home, in shops, in supermarkets, in post-offices, in hospitals to weigh new born babies and children, in sport to weigh jockeys before and after races, at airports to check luggage. The children might work in groups to draw pictures of these weighing activities.

Talk about the different types of scales in use: How are new-born babies weighed? Which scales have digital read-outs? (airport luggage scales, supermarkets, etc.) Where do the children see 'pan' scales reading in kg and g? (sweet shops, post offices, home) How often do they get weighed on bathroom scales?

Mention scales that have a pan suspended from them such as in some supermarkets for weighing vegetables.

Have they seen scales for weighing letters, which use very small weights?

Have they any scales at home? What kind are they? What are they used for? Do they all weigh in kilograms and grams or do some still show pounds and ounces?

2 Reading scales

If possible, have two or three sets of scales which show different calibrations, for example, just grams, kg and g, just kg.

Ask the children how many grams there are in a kilogram. Let them weigh the same object on each set of scales. What do they notice?

Can they suggest why scales vary in their calibrations or markings? It is difficult to weigh very small things accurately on the same scales as those designed to weigh heavy objects. Point out that the markings or calibrations on scales vary according to the range of weights they measure.

3 Calibrations

Look at scales with different calibrations or markings. Let the children work in groups. Give them squared paper to record different ways of calibrating or marking a scale from 0 g to 500 g or 1 kg. For example,

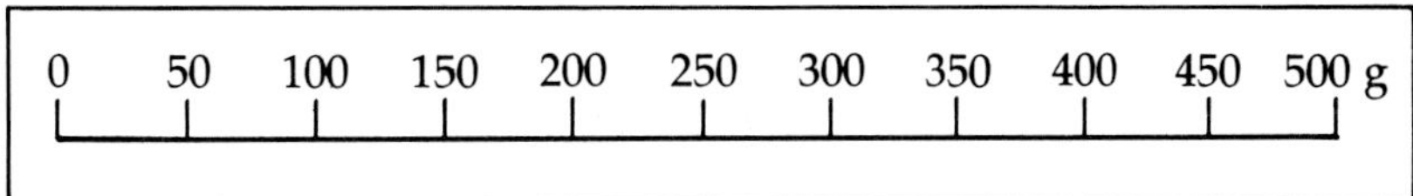

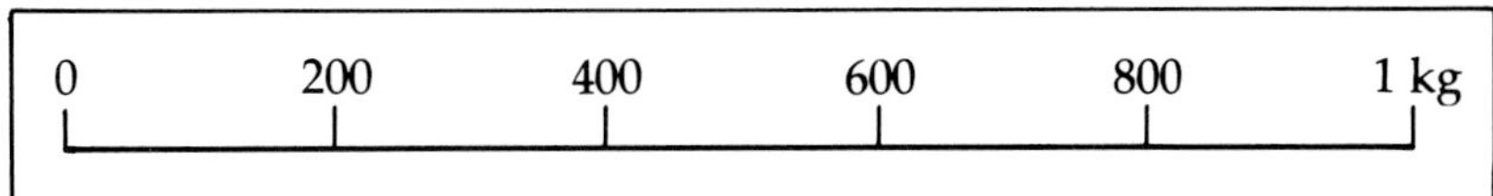

The results from each group might be displayed and discussed.

Look at the different weighing scales. Can the children read the calibrations on the scales? Some scales are labelled to indicate what the calibrations are, for example 3 kg × 100 g. This means that the scales are marked in 100 g intervals up to 3 kg.

A game to play

FIND THE SCALE

Draw a calibrated scale, for example,

1 kg × 100 g

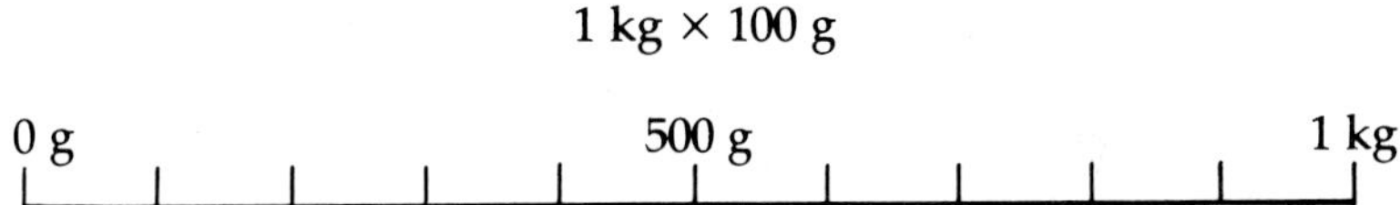

Make a card for each weight on the scale, such as 100 g, 200 g, etc.

The children play in two small groups or teams.

The cards are shuffled. One player from each team chooses a card and Blu-taks it at the correct place on the scale. If the card is placed correctly, the player scores a point for their team.

The game can be developed using more difficult scales as the children become more competent.

4 Using weighing scales

Give the children plenty of practice in using weighing scales and reading the weight accurately. For some children it may be necessary to pre-select the objects in order to give an easy reading on the scale.

When weighing, point out the pointer must initially point to zero. This needs to be set on some scales. Do the children know how to adjust this?

5 Spring balances

Talk about spring balances and how to use them. Can the children suggest ways of weighing objects that will not easily hang from the hooks, such as sand or rice? For example, plastic bags could be used.

Can they suggest how a spring balance works? Have they ever seen one in use?

6 Spring balance calibrations

Look at the calibrations on spring balances. Can the children read the vertical scale? Give them practice in this.

Ask them to plan some vertical scales on squared paper as in activity 3. Can they record the scale they use as, for example, 2 kg × 100 g?

Give the children opportunities to weigh the same object on at least two different spring balances.

7 A game to play

I ESTIMATE

This game is for two or more groups.

Give each group four objects and a card for each object showing its weight. The group has to match the card to the object by estimating and recording their estimates. The objects are then weighed. Each correct estimate scores a point. The winning group is the one with most points.

8 Recording results

Object	Weight

Remind the children of the notation for recording weight, for example, 1800 g = 1·800 kg, and how to make tables to show results. Talk about showing the results as bar graphs and the necessity of devising a scale to cover the range of weights.

The children could think of other ways to record their results – for example, as a scale with the objects drawn on.

A game to play

ON THE GRAPH

Draw two graphs, each using a different scale, such as 100 g and 200 g. Ask a child to come out and show the same weight on both graphs.

9 Mental work

Ask questions about kg and g. For example, how many grams are in 1 kg, 2 kg, 3 kg etc.

Give revision practice on notation. 'Write 4650 g in kg.'
Give the children practice in adding weights. For example, add 750 g and 1200 g.

USING THE CALCULATOR

Use the calculator to show weight patterns as in calibrations, perhaps by starting at 0 g and adding 200 g each time, up to 5000 g.

0 g 200 g 400 g 600 g . . . 5000 g

Reverse the process:

5000 g 4800 g 4600 g . . . 0 g

A game to play

HOW MANY PRESSES?

All players have a calculator and start at 0. Ask them to add 150 g each time using the constant function and stop at, say, 1500. Before they do it, ask them to guess and write how many times they will have to press = . A child who gives the correct answer scores a point. All answers should be discussed.

LINKS WITH THE ENVIRONMENT

Talk about everyday situations involving scales and weighing.

- Weighing ingredients for cooking
- Weighing in shops and supermarkets
- Weighing in pharmacies
- Weighing of babies and children
- Sport – weight of boxers before a fight and jockeys after a race
- Weighing in science experiments
- Travel – weight of luggage for flights.
- Weighing lorries and aeroplanes. Why do they need to be weighed? How are they weighed?

NOTES ON INVESTIGATIONS

Section A

Do the children discover that the greater the weight, the more the rubber band stretches? Do they realise that thicker bands do not stretch as much as thinner ones when the same weight is used?

Section B

Do the children realise that the two 50 g weights need to be equidistant from the fulcrum to balance? Do they discover that a

100 g weight needs to be only half the distance of the 50 g weight from the fulcrum to achieve balance, and that the 150 g weight needs to be only a third of the distance away from the fulcrum as the 50 g weight to balance? Do any children manage to generalise this result in words?

Section C

Do the children make a careful list of the newspapers and magazines delivered in one week? Do they estimate the weight of paper for one week? Do they weigh one paper (or a similar one) from the class collection and use its weight to find the approximate total weight of that paper for a week? Do they repeat this for all types of papers, magazines and comics and then add the weights together? Do they compare their estimate with the total weight? Are the estimates close?

Volume and capacity

Purpose

- To give practice in reading and interpreting scales on measuring cylinders and containers
- To use the notation for writing capacity
- To give practical experience of volume and capacity

Materials

Variety of measuring cylinders and containers, centimetre cubes, plastic straw, plasticine, stones, piece of cloth, balance scales, displacement bucket, water

Vocabulary

Litre, millilitre, measuring cylinder, container, centimetre cubes, water level, estimate, cubic centimetre, volume

TEACHING POINTS

1 Litres

Revise the litre. Ask the children what comes in litre containers. Talk about the amount in bottles, cartons and cans of lemonade, cola, and fruit juice.

2 Millilitres

Revise the millilitre, reminding the children that 1000 ml = 1 litre. Remind them how small a millilitre is, possibly by reference to a medicine spoon which normally holds 5 ml.

3 Recording capacity

Talk about how we write a capacity greater than 1 litre, for example,

1450 ml = 1 l and 450 ml = 1·450 l

Give plenty of practice in this.

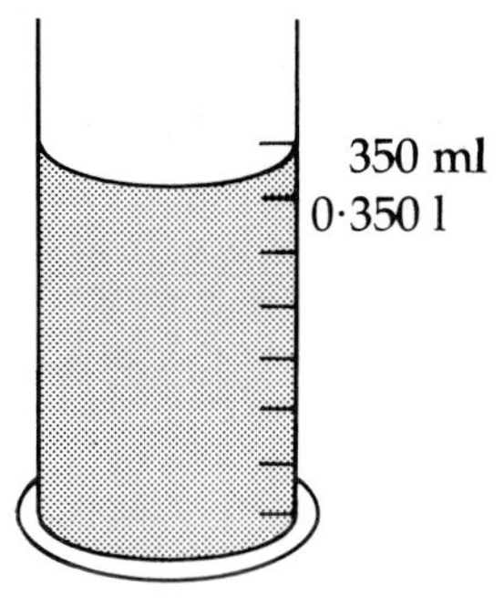

4 Reading scales

Give the children practice in reading scales on measuring cylinders and recording the reading, using the correct notation.

A game to play

READ IT

Pour an amount of water into a measuring cylinder. Ask a child from a team to interpret the reading and write it down. A correct reading scores a point. A second child from the same team then writes the capacity in l and ml. This scores another point.

The turn then passes to the next team, using a different amount of water.

Reading	Litres	Millilitres
0·650 l	0 l	650 ml

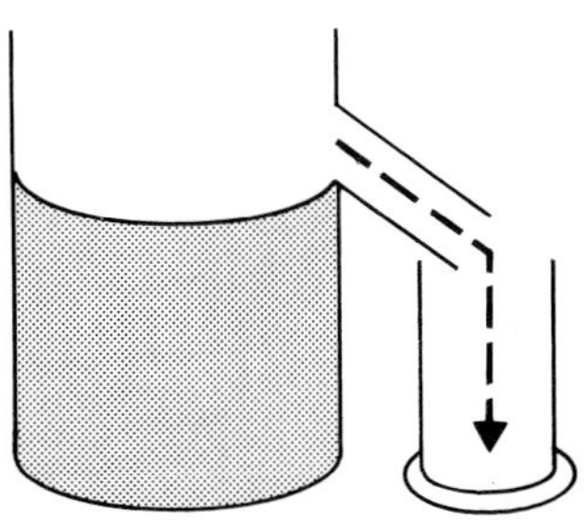

5 Displacement activities

Show the children that when objects are added to the water in a measuring cylinder the water level rises. Discuss why this happens.

Show how a displacement bucket can be used to collect the overflow. This can then be measured to show how much water has been displaced by an object. For example, the object takes up the same space as 300 ml of water.

(This activity leads directly into the activities of Section A.)

6 Mental work

Call out capacities and let the children say or write the amount in l and ml. For example, 1574 ml → 1 l 574 ml

USING THE CALCULATOR

A game to play

SHOW IT IN LITRES

Call out a number of millilitres for the children to show in litres on their calculator. For example, 2476 ml → 2·476

A point is scored for each correct answer.

LINKS WITH THE ENVIRONMENT

Talk about everyday situations which involve capacity and displacement. These might include:

- Buying petrol in litres
- Buying drinks in litres and millilitres
- Using capacity in cooking – for example, making a jelly
- Taking a bath – the water level rises

NOTES ON INVESTIGATIONS

Section A

Do the children devise a way to discover how much space the plasticine takes up? Do they use a measuring cylinder and take readings before and after? Do they use a displacement method? Do they adopt a sensible method of recording their results?

Section B

Do the children discover that the plasticine displaces the same amount of water regardless of its shape? Can they explain this conservation?

Section C

Do the children realise that it would not be sensible to try to weigh an individual millilitre of water? Do they devise a method such as weighing an empty measuring cylinder and then re-weighing it with, say, 100 ml of water in it and then calculating the weight of 1 ml of water?

Do they use a calculator? Do they discover that 1 ml of water weighs 1 gram? Do they use this fact to find how many ml the wet cloth (in question C1) was holding?

Time 1

Purpose

- To introduce telling the time to an exact minute
- To introduce seconds
- To interpret and use different timing devices (sundials, stop-watches) and measuring instruments

Materials

Demonstration clock faces with Roman numbers, seconds stop-watches or clocks, plasticine, string, drawing pins, clock stamps, squared paper

Vocabulary

Sundial, shadow, east, west, Roman numbers, time, watch, botch, accurate, seconds, minute, past, to, digital times, clock face, swinging pendulum, total points, stop-watch, complete swings, pointer, activity, points chart

TEACHING POINTS

1 Introduction

Ask the children about clocks and watches. What kind of watches are there – with faces, or digital? Look at a real clock or a geared teaching clock face. Talk about the hands and their movement around the clock face.

2 Revise telling the time to five-minute intervals

Ask the children to count in fives up to 60. Display charts showing five-minute intervals.

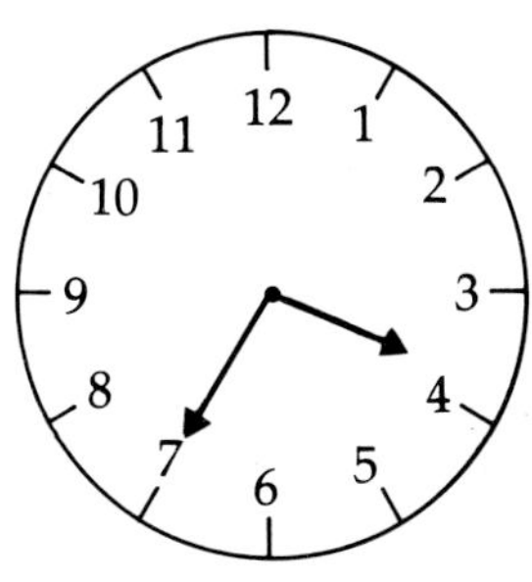

35 minutes past 3
25 minutes to 4
3:35

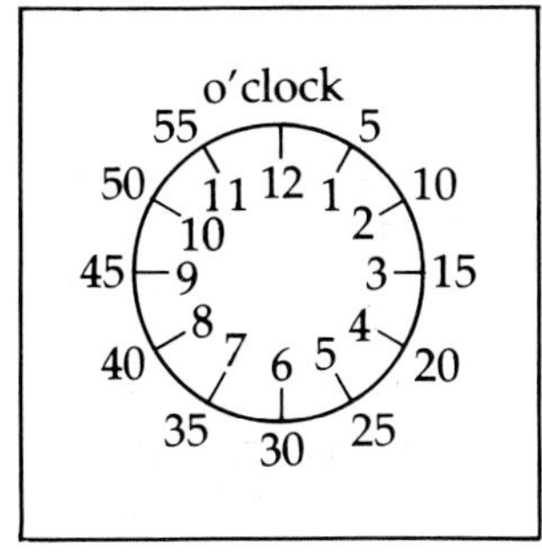

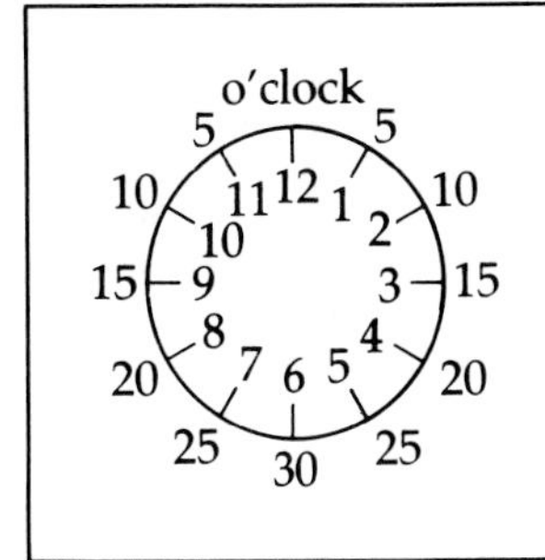

Draw some clock faces and ask children to draw the hands to show various times in five-minute intervals. Ask them to record the time in different ways, including digital times.

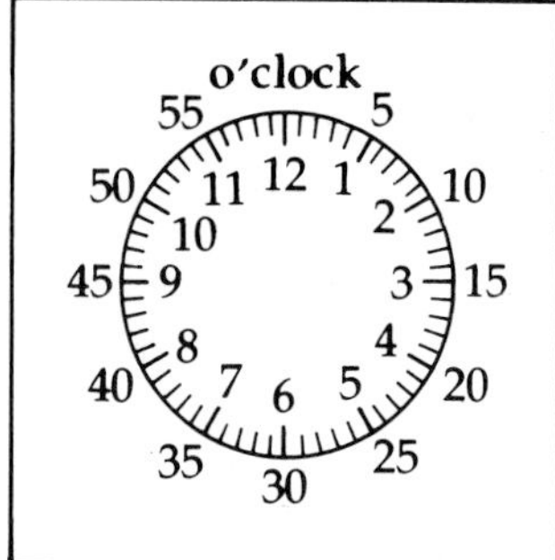

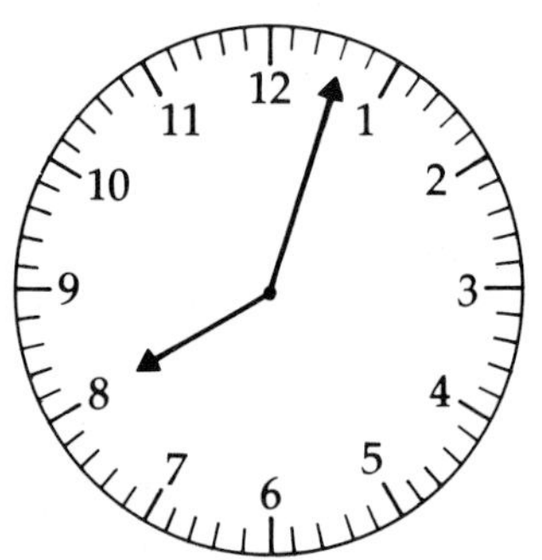

3 minutes past 8
8:03

3 Introduce one-minute intervals

Talk about the minute intervals on the clock face. Explain it also with the aid of a clock chart.

4 Telling the time

Set the hands of a geared clock or real clock to a time such as eight o'clock. Move the hands to three minutes past eight and ask the children the time. Talk about ways of recording it.

Repeat this for other times.

Draw some clock faces and ask children to draw the hands to show certain times and record them in different ways.

Ask the children to stamp some clock faces and to show specified times and to record them in different ways.

A game to play

CLOCK TIMES

Divide the children into two teams. Draw a clock face. Say a time, for example, 'Five fifty-three'.

Ask a child from the first team to draw in the hands on the clock correctly. Ask a child from the other team to record the time in as many ways as possible. A point is scored for each way they write it.

5 Revise a.m. and p.m.

Talk about a.m. and p.m. times and show them on a time line.

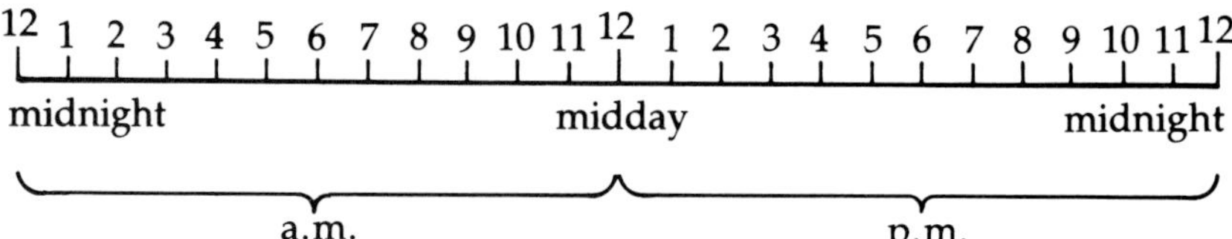

Ask a child to show where times like 8:42 a.m. and 5:27 p.m. are on the time line.

6 Introducing seconds

Talk about seconds, asking the children where seconds are used. An example is timing sporting events like 100 m races in seconds.

Show the children a real clock with a seconds hand and ask them to watch it go once round the clock face. Can they work out how many seconds there are in 1 minute?

Ask a child who has a digital watch or a watch with a second hand to count the seconds out loud. Ask the class to join in with the counting. Show the children a stop-watch or clock and how to use it.

7 Estimating

Explain that some people estimate the length of a second by saying 'one elephant', 'two elephants', 'three elephants', etc. and the 'one', 'two', 'three' represent seconds.

Ask the children to estimate lengths of time – one child times the seconds and the other children put up a hand after they think 30 seconds (or a minute) have passed.

Ask the children what they can do in one minute – for example, write their name 10 times, run round the playground. Make a list of one-minute jobs or activities in the classroom. Try this for 30 seconds time spans.

8 Timing devices

Talk about some of the early clocks and methods used for telling the time, for example, sand clocks, candle clocks, water clocks, sundials. How accurate were these?

- Sundials – explain how sundials work and that most sundials use Roman numbers. (Sundials are shown in the pupils' book.)
- Sand clocks – examples are egg timers and hour glasses. Some children might be asked to make one themselves.
- Water clocks – explain and show how a water clock works. Some children might be asked to design and make one.
- Candle clocks

9 Roman numbers on clocks

Talk with the children about Roman numbers up to 12 and show them on a clock face. Explain that most early clocks used IIII for 4 and only later was IV used.

Draw a circle and ask children to write a Roman number in the correct place to form a clock face.

A game to play

ROMAN MATCH

Make two sets of number cards, one with numbers 1 to 12 and another with I to XII. Shuffle the cards. Lay them face down on the table but spread out. The first player turns over any two cards. If they match, the player keeps the cards. If not, both cards are turned face down again. Play continues in this way until all the cards have been matched. The winner is the player with the most matching cards.

10 Pendulums

Explain that pendulums are used in many old clocks to control the timing. Have the children ever seen a grandfather clock? (The children are asked to make a pendulum in the pupils' book.)

11 Using a stop-watch or clock

Ask a child to time a friend doing various activities such as tying shoelaces, running or hopping across the playground.

12 Mental work

Ask the children to work out mentally the answers to questions like these.

How many seconds are in half a minute?
What is the time 7 minutes after 4:15?
Is 5:23 a.m. morning or afternoon?
What is 7 in Roman numbers?
What is IX in ordinary numbers?

LINKS WITH THE ENVIRONMENT

Talk about the different types of clocks we see in everyday life.

- At home – alarm clocks, cooker clocks, grandfather clock, watch, video clocks
- On the way to school – church clock, clocks and watches in a jeweller's shop window, bus and railway station clocks
- At school – classroom clock, school clock, children's watches

Make a display of clocks and watches from catalogues. Look at the many different faces and sizes. Collect pictures of timing devices such as sundials and water clocks.

Talk about things which are commonly measured in hours, minutes and seconds; for example, journeys (hours), cooking (minutes), 100 m race (seconds).

Talk about estimating the distance a storm is away by seeing the lightning and then counting the seconds to hearing the thunder. This is about 2 km ($1\frac{1}{4}$ miles) for every 5 seconds.

NOTES ON INVESTIGATIONS

Section A

Do the children find practically how far they can run in 10 seconds? Do they ask a friend to help? Can they use a stop-watch or clock correctly? Is the list of activities which they can do in 10 seconds sensible? Do they time them accurately?

Section B

Do the children choose activities that can be timed in seconds? Does their points chart have a range of times? Are there more points awarded to the shorter times? Do they carefully record the times taken by the two children?

Section C

Do the children try changing the length of the string, the height of the swing and the plasticine? Do they make the pendulum swing once in 2 seconds eventually? Do they discover that the length of the string changes the time of the swing?

Purpose

- To introduce multiplication of HTU by 1 digit
- To link multiplication and division
- To introduce different approaches to multiplication

Materials

Calculator, individual multiplication squares, large squared paper. (To avoid wasting pupil time writing out Napier's rods, photocopies of large squared paper with the diagonals marked on (and possibly the numbers as well) could be provided.)

Vocabulary

Multiplication square, diagonal, line pattern, doubling, explain, multiply, Napier's rods, pairs, diagonally, multiplying

TEACHING POINTS

1 Tables

Revise the multiplication tables with the children using a variety of methods.

Count on in 2s, 5s, 10s etc.
Look at patterns on a 100 square.

1	2	3	(4)	5	6	7	(8)	9	10
11	(12)	13	14	15	(16)	17	18	19	(20)
21	22	23	(24)	25	26	27	(28)	29	30
31	(32)	33	34	35	(36)	37	38	39	(40)
41	42	43	(44)	45	46	47	(48)	49	50
51	(52)	53	54	55	(56)	57	58	59	(60)
61	62	63	(64)	65	66	67	(68)	69	70
71	(72)	73	74	75	(76)	77	78	79	(80)
81	82	83	(84)	85	86	87	(88)	89	90
91	(92)	93	94	95	(96)	97	98	99	(100)

the pattern of 4

Talk about number patterns

4 8 12 16 20 . . .

5 10 15 20 25 . . .

9 18 27 36 45

2 Finger tables

Show the children how to use their fingers to show the 9 times table. For example, to find 3 × 9, hold down the third finger and read off 27. This method is shown in the pupils' book.

The children might be interested in another finger method. This can be useful with the harder tables. Number your fingers 6 7 8 9 10. To multiply 7 × 7 put the 7 finger of one hand against the 7 finger of the other (thumbs downwards). Count the number of fingers underneath, including the touching ones. This gives the tens digit. Multiply the others (3 × 3). This gives the units digit.

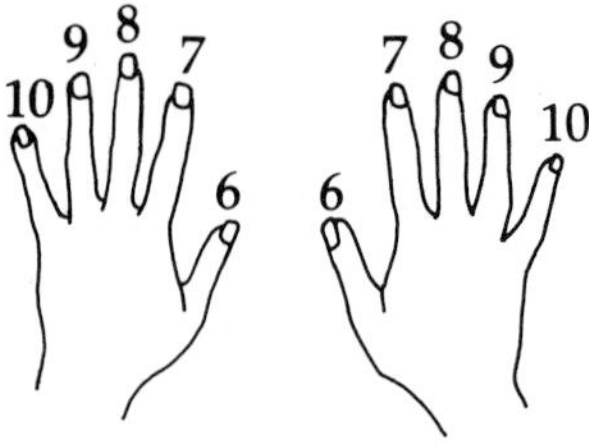

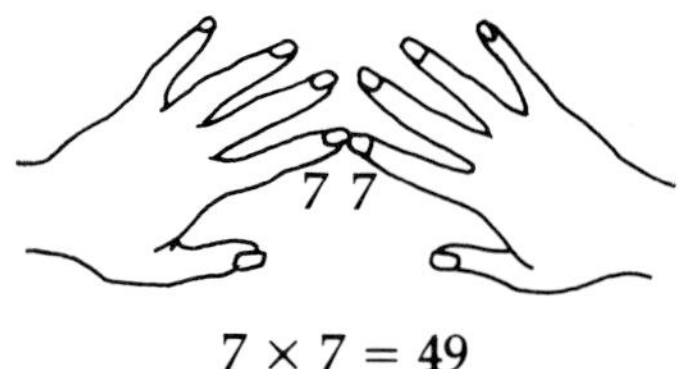

$7 \times 7 = 49$

3 Tables using dice

16	20	24	25	28
30	32	35	36	40
42	45	48	49	54
56	63	64	72	81

A game for practising harder tables uses two dice numbered 4–9, a grid, as shown, and two sets of coloured counters. When the dice are thrown, the numbers are multiplied and the result covered by a counter. The first to cover a line of four in any direction wins.

4 The commutative property

Do the children remember that $2 \times 4 = 4 \times 2$ (i.e. the commutative law)? This is useful when using more difficult tables. Give them practice in it.

5 Doubling

Talk about doubling. Do the children remember that it is multiplication by 2?

A game to play

DOUBLES

A game for 2 groups or teams.

One player from each team throws a die each. They both add the numbers on the two dice and double the total.

The first player to write the correct answer scores a point. The winning team are the ones with most points after all the children have had a turn.

An extension to this game is to put the two dice together to make a TU number and double the number. For example 3 2 doubled is 6 4 or 2 3 doubled is 4 6 .

6 Multiplication squares

Ask the children to complete a multiplication square.

×	1	2	3	4	5	6	7	8	9	10
1	1	2	3	4	5	6	7	8	9	10
2	2	4	6	8	10	12	14	16	18	20
3	3	6	9	12	15	18	21	24	27	30
4	4	8	12	16	20	24	28	32	36	40
5	5	10	15	20	25	30	35	40	45	50
6	6	12	18	24	30	36	42	48	54	60
7	7	14	21	28	35	42	49	56	63	70
8	8	16	24	32	40	48	56	64	72	80
9	9	18	27	36	45	54	63	72	81	90
10	10	20	30	40	50	60	70	80	90	100

Check that they can use this as a ready reckoner.

7 Link multiplication and division

Remind the children of the link between multiplication and division, for example

$3 \times 2 = 6$ $\quad 64 \times 2 = 128$

$2 \times 3 = 6$ $\quad 2 \times 64 = 128$

$6 \div 2 = 3$ $\quad 128 \div 2 = 64$

$6 \div 3 = 2$ $\quad 128 \div 64 = 2$

Give them practice in this.

8 Napier's rods or bones

Talk about Napier's rods and show how they can be used for multiplication. For example

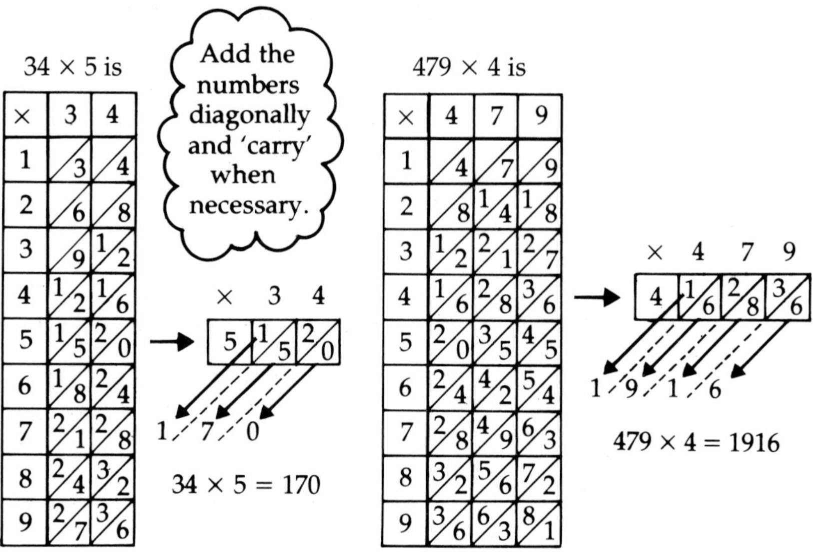

This is shown in the pupils' book.

Although the children are asked to copy and make their own set, it might be advisable to provide copies on large squared paper to cut up. An ideal arrangement is to mount the squares on card. These can be kept for future use.

9 To introduce multiplication of HTU by one digit

Show the children how to record and work out these multiplications. Use your own words and methods.

$$\begin{array}{rccc} & H & T & U \\ & 2 & 4 & 7 \\ \times & & & 3 \\ \hline & & & \\ \hline \end{array}$$

Can the children suggest any methods of their own? Here are some.

$$\begin{array}{rr} & 247 \\ \times & 3 \\ \hline & 741 \\ \hline & {\scriptstyle 1\,2} \end{array} \qquad \begin{array}{rr} & 247 \\ & 247 \\ + & 247 \\ \hline & 741 \\ \hline & {\scriptstyle 1\,2} \end{array} \qquad \begin{array}{rr} & 247 \\ \times & 3 \\ \hline & 21 \\ & 120 \\ & 600 \\ \hline & 741 \\ \hline \end{array}$$

10 Mental work

Ask the children multiplication and division questions using different forms of words.

- What is 8 × 5?
- Multiply 5 × 8.
- Find the product of 5 and 8 etc.
- What is 40 divided by 5?

Ask questions involving observation in the classroom. For example,

- Multiply the number of lights by the number of doors.
- Multiply the numbers of panes of glass in one window by the number of legs on a chair.

USING THE CALCULATOR

Ask the children to use the calculator to do the following:

- Multiplication of HTU by one digit, for example 278 × 4
- To check answers using repeated addition (using constant function)
- To double numbers
- To consider how quickly large numbers can be made by repeatedly doubling 2

A game to play

× 2
× 5
double
× 4
× 3

× 3
× 2
× 5
× 4
double

TABLE LADDERS

This game is for a group of children. Make some table ladders, one for each player. Use the same numbers on each but arrange them in a different order.

Each player in turn throws a die and multiplies the number shown by the bottom number on the ladder. They use their calculator and record the result as their score. On their next turn they multiply the number on the die by the next number up the ladder, and so on. The game continues until they reach the top of the ladder and have had five turns each. The players add their scores. The winner is the one with the highest total.

LINKS WITH THE ENVIRONMENT

Talk with the children about situations using multiplication in everyday life.

- Sport – the number of players in a team multiplied by the number of teams on a pitch, at a tournament or in a league; in relays – the number of lanes on an athletics track or swimming baths multiplied by the number of competitors in each
- Time – the number of days/weeks/months in 1 year, 2 years, etc.
- Early methods of multiplication – Napier's rods

- Equipment for schools – multiply the sets of books or boxes of chalk by the number of classes
- Dozen, score, gross of objects.

NOTES ON INVESTIGATIONS

Section A

Do the children see a pattern when a number is multiplied by 10? For example,

$7 \times 10 = 70$ $\quad$ $9 \times 10 = 90$

$15 \times 10 = 150$ $\quad$ $75 \times 10 = 750$

It should be pointed out that a zero is not added but the number moves one place to the left and becomes 10 times larger each time.

Do they find a similar pattern when multiplying by 100?

$9 \times 100 = 900$ $\quad$ $17 \times 100 = 1700$

Can they explain what is happening?

Section B

Do the children see how the system works? Are they able to apply it to other multiplications of their own? Do they check their multiplying with a calculator?

Section C

Do the children realise that exchanging is involved in the multiplication? Are they systematic in trying to find the missing numbers? For example, do they try ×2, ×3, ×4, . . . , ×9? Do they use the link between multiplication and division to find an answer? For example, is 984 divisible by 2?

Number 8

Purpose

- To understand decimal notation to two decimal places, in the context of money or measurement

Materials

Coins, tape measure

Vocabulary

Pattern, decimal, value, metric, pennies, pounds, amount, metre

TEACHING POINTS

1 Decimal Day, 15 February 1971

Talk to the children about how, before 15 February 1971, there were 12 pennies in a shilling and 240 pence in a pound. Britain changed to a decimal currency to come into line with other 'metric' countries and to make money calculations easier. It was agreed to have £1 = 100p.

2 The 10p coin

Talk with the children about how ten 10p coins make £1, so 10p is $\frac{1}{10}$ of £1. This is written in pounds like this:

10p = £0·10 — no 1p coins

no pounds (0) one 10p coin (1)

Give the children practice in writing multiples of 10p.

10p = £0·10
20p = £0·20

. . .

100p = £1·00
110p = £1·10

3 The 1p coin

Talk about how there are 100 pence in a pound, so 1p is $\frac{1}{100}$ of £1. This is written:

1p = £0·01 — one 1p coin

no pounds (0) no 10p coins (0)

Give the children practice in writing amounts in pence, using decimal notation:

1p = £0·01
2p = £0·02 etc.

Ask them to change fractions of £1 to pence. For example,

$\frac{1}{100}$ of £1 = 1p $\frac{9}{100}$ of £1 = 9p

A game to play

PICK THEM UP

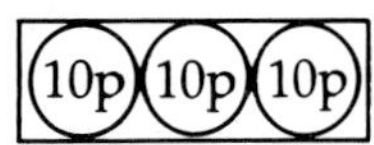

Make a set of flash cards showing amounts of cash and coins. Shuffle the cards and scatter them face down on the table. Children take turns to pick up and turn over a pair of the cards. If they match, the child keeps the pair. If they don't match, they are placed, face down, back on the table. The next child then tries to pick up a pair, using memory to help. The winner is the child with most pairs.

4 Combining 10p and 1p coins

Talk to the children about when we combine the coins to make

10p + 1p = 11p

Children are familiar with writing 11p as £0·11 and might now be asked to explain what each digit represents.

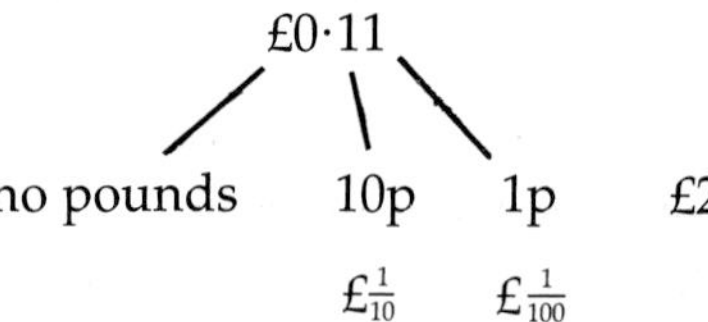

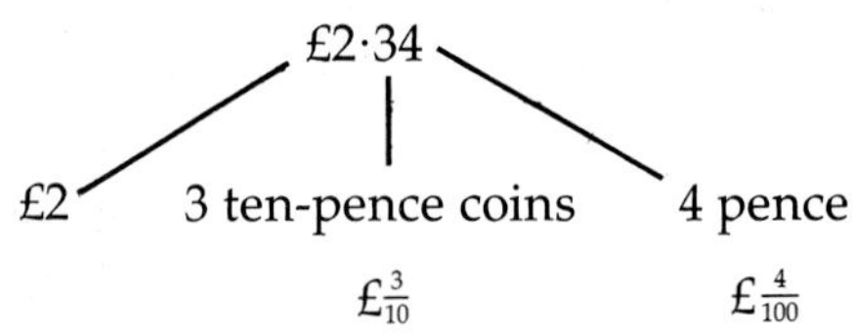

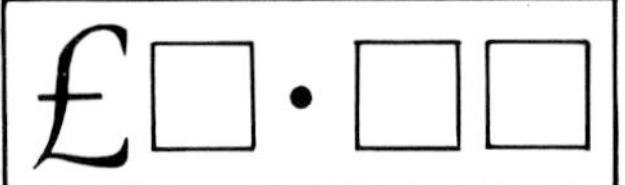

Make a board large enough to place amounts of money on. The children give each other amounts of money which have to be correctly placed on the board and the amount and fraction stated as it is placed in the correct position:

'Four ten-pence coins, that's 40 pence, that's $\frac{4}{10}$ of a pound.'

5 Other units

Discuss how the same notation is used for other measures. For example, children are familiar with writing 1 m 27 cm as 1·27 m. Ask them to give a value to each digit.

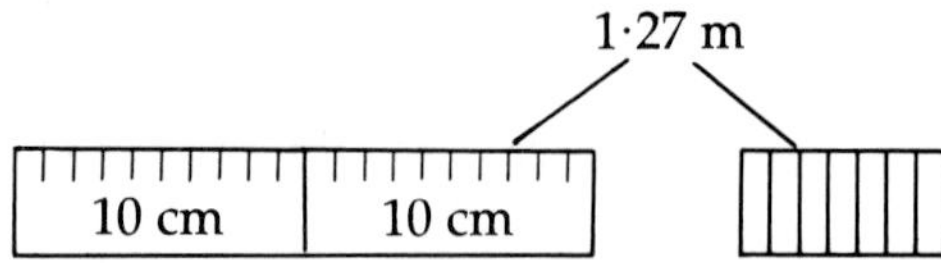

It is useful to have 10 cm strips cut ready to demonstrate.

6 Mental work

Write amounts of money or length on the board. Point to particular digits and ask the value and the fraction.

£3·46 '$\frac{4}{10}$ of £1, that's four 10p coins.'
↑

USING THE CALCULATOR

Show children amounts of money or measurements and ask them to enter the amounts on the calculator, using decimal notation. For extra practice, the children could set each other problems. For example, one child could lay out an amount of money using pound coins, 10p coins and 1p coins and point to one set. The child with the calculator has to show the value of the set of coins (0·30).

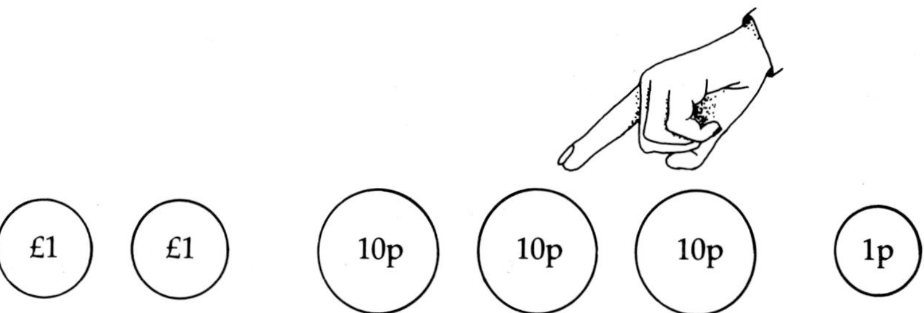

LINKS WITH THE ENVIRONMENT

Talk about everyday situations which use decimal notation for recording.

- Prices in shops and on check-out displays, £2·99 etc.
- Measurements on plans and specifications
- Metric measures in this and other countries
- Catalogue prices

NOTES ON INVESTIGATIONS

Section A

Do the children use the numbers 1, 2, 3 in a systematic way for recording the different amounts of money?

use 1 as the first digit	£ 1 · 2 3
	£ 1 · 3 2
use 2 as the first digit	£ 2 · 1 3
	£ 2 · 3 1
use 3 as the first digit	£ 3 · 1 2
	£ 3 · 2 1

Do they appreciate the different value of the digits each time?

Section B

Do the children appreciate that the machine is showing the value of each digit in fractions of a pound? Do they try different amounts in the machine and show the output correctly?

Section C

Do the children understand that the notation used for money can also be used for m and cm because there are 100 cm to a metre just as there are 100p to a pound? Do some children go on to investigate kg and g and realise that the third decimal place refers to thousandths?

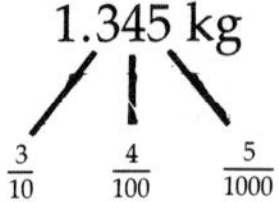

Data 2

Purpose

- To introduce average
- To introduce the terms 'mean' and 'range'

Materials

Counters may be useful for the practical work

Vocabulary

Litter, altogether, average, size, largest, smallest, range, mean, set of numbers, difference between, graph, clutch, twice as big, nearest whole number, similar

TEACHING POINTS

1 Average

Talk with the children about when they have heard the word average. Examples might include football averages, average speeds, average marks or scores in tests, average ages or heights of groups of children. Point out that mean is another name for average.

Explain that to find an average or mean we find the total and share it out equally between the number of people or things. For example, in their last three skittleball matches a team scored 3, 4 and 5 (total 12) goals. If the total is shared equally between the three games the answer is 4. This is the average number of goals scored for the three games.

2 Practical work

Give the children plenty of practical work involving averages. Put some children into four groups (make sure the total is a multiple of 4).

Collect the children into one large group, count the total and split them again into four equal groups.

What is the average group size?

Repeat the activity for other numbers.

3 Other activities

Put counters in each of three yogurt pots and ask the children to find the average number for the pots.

Put some books in two piles for the children to work out the average number for the piles.

The children can do some interesting display work.

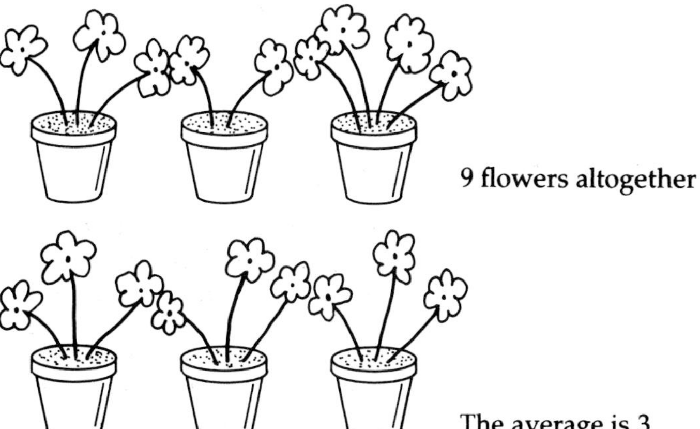

9 flowers altogether

The average is 3

A game to play

PONDS

This game is for two small groups.

Cut out some paper fish and some paper ponds. Give each group about 20 fish and 5 ponds. Call out an average number, e.g. 3. The first group to put fish in ponds (not the same number in every one) to give an average of 3 scores a point.

A development is also to call out the number of ponds. For example, 'The average number of fish in 4 ponds is 3.' The children then have to decide upon the total number of fish.

4 Algorithm

Talk about how to find the average without using apparatus but using a pencil-and-paper method. For example, 'The average of 7, 2, 9, 1 and 6 is 25 ÷ 5 = 5.'

Let the children use their algorithms to find some averages.

5 Range

Talk about what we mean by range and how it is the difference between the greatest and the smallest value in a set. For example, in the set of children in a school the youngest child is four years old and the oldest is eleven years old. The range is 7 years, i.e. 11 – 4 = 7.

6 Averages to the nearest whole number

This work is appropriate for those children going on to tackle Section C.

Talk about what happens when the average does not work out to a whole number but we want the answer to be given as close as possible to the nearest whole number. For example, show 14 bottle tops in three groups.

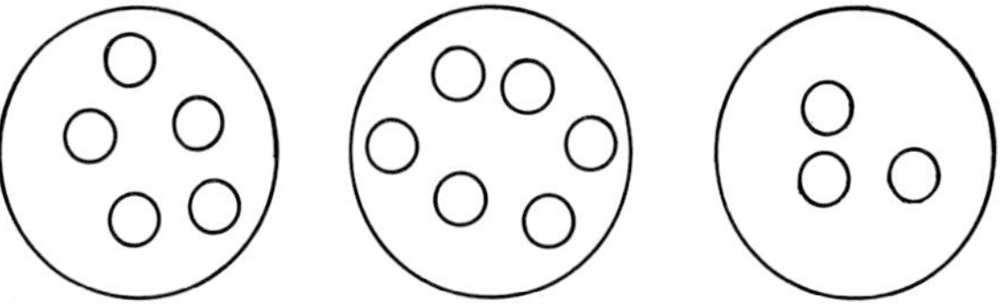

The mean is 14 ÷ 3, which gives 4 in each set and 2 left over. To the nearest whole number the mean must be 4 or 5. If the mean were 4, that would be 3 × 4 = 12 bottle tops, while a mean of 5 gives 3 × 5 = 15 bottle tops. Since 14 (the actual number of bottle tops) is nearer to 15 than to 12 we say the average is 5 to the nearest whole number.

Consider 10 bottle tops in four sets. The mean is 10 ÷ 4, which gives 2 in each set and 2 left over. To the nearest whole number the mean must be 2 or 3. Ask if 10 (the bottle tops) is nearer to 8 (four twos) or 12 (four threes). Explain that it is at the half-way mark and so is rounded up. So the average is 3 to the nearest whole number.

Give plenty of practice in this. Can any children suggest other methods?

7 Mental work

Give revision practice of tables using division. For example, 24 ÷ 3.

Find the averages of sets of numbers such as 1, 3 and 5.

Find missing numbers. For example,
'3, 2, □. The average is 2. What is the missing number?'

Keep the numbers small as the children may find this quite difficult.

Find the range of sets of numbers such as 9, 4, 1 and 3.

A game to play

FIND THE RANGE

This game is for small groups. Give each group a set of cards numbered 1–20. Ask the groups to find sets of three cards with a range of, say, 6. The group that can find the most in a given time are the winners.

USING THE CALCULATOR

Talk with the children about using the calculator to find an average. For example,

3 + 2 + 1 = 6
6 ÷ 3 = 2
The average is 2.

Ensure the answers are whole numbers.

A game to play

AVERAGES

Play this game in pairs or small groups. Call out an average, e.g. 20. The first group to give three different numbers which have that average scores a point.

LINKS WITH THE ENVIRONMENT

Talk about everyday situations involving average (mean) and range.

- Sport – scores in cricket and football, etc.
- Average speeds – what do we mean by this?
- Animals – average numbers of young in litters, etc.
- People – average ages, heights and weights
- Average sizes in clothes
- Financial – average incomes, house prices and pocket money

NOTES ON INVESTIGATIONS

Section A

Do the children realise that the total of puppies is 20? Do they arrange this total into four sets in a variety of ways?

Section B

Do the children realise that they must choose the same number for the average each time? Do they realise that they must multiply by 3 to find the total for the first set and by 4 to find the total for the second set? Do they choose different averages and repeat the activity?

Section C

Do the children design a data collection sheet before collecting the information? Do the children make a careful list of the family sizes and the number of families? Do they realise that they must divide the total by the number of families in order to find the average? Do they devise a way of finding the average to the nearest whole number? Do they compare the result with the Victorian average of between 8 and 12 children? Are their results less than the Victorian average?

Extension work might include finding how many families are above or below the national average.

Purpose

- To introduce banking, deposits and withdrawals
- To add and subtract amounts of money

Materials

Catalogues showing the prices of gardening tools and shrubs, calculators, coins

Vocabulary

Conservation area, pounds, raised altogether, bank account, balance, deposit, deposited, new balance, final balance, spend, total sum, collected, notes, coins, silver, bronze, dates, withdraw, withdrawn, withdrawal, item, different varieties, choices, cost, different amounts

TEACHING POINTS

1 Banking

Talk with the children about banking – what are banks for? Ask the children to name some banks, including the Bank of England and Royal Bank of Scotland. Explain that the Bank of England is in London. It is sometimes called 'The Old Lady of Threadneedle Street'.

Some children may have a building society account. Discuss this also.

If your school has a school bank, talk about that.

2 The Royal Mint

Talk with the children about the Royal Mint. Explain that notes and coins are made there and sent out to all the banks. Old coins and dirty and torn notes are collected and destroyed. The Royal Mint is now based in Wales.

3 Coin values

Ask the children to name all the coin values. Talk about the copper and silver coins. Explain that the copper coins are actually made of bronze. The silver coins are made of copper and nickel and pound coins are made of copper, nickel and zinc.

Explain that banks put different coins in plastic bags and weigh them when exchanging them for notes. Show them some bags and ask how many of each coin they should hold.

Remind the children about recording money in pounds and pence such as £3·27. Give them practice in making up amounts of money using coins.

Games to play

SORTING

This can be played by two children. One child takes a handful of mixed coins and sorts them before counting the amount. They score a point if their total amount is correct. The second child checks the amount.

AMOUNTS

Two children can play this.

Make a set of cards showing amounts that can be made using only silver coins and place them face downwards. A child turns over a card, tries to make the amount using only silver coins, and scores a point if the total is correct. The second child checks the amount. They then change over.

COINS

Make a set of cards showing an amount of money less than £5, for example, £4·83.

Divide the children into two teams. A card is turned over. A child from each team tries to make the amount using coins. The first person to make the amount correctly scores a point for their team. The winners are the team with the most points after all the children have had a turn.

4 Notes

Talk with the children about note values. Show them a real £5 or £10 note. Explain the markings on it, including 'Bank of England', value and pictures front and back. The metallic thread and watermarks make it more difficult to forge. Show them a Scottish bank note and explain the markings.

Games to Play

BANKS

Make a set of cards showing pound note and coin values such as £20, £10, £5, and £1, and another set showing amounts in pounds such as £47 and £65.

Two children can play this game. One is the cashier. The other chooses a card with an amount of money on it and hands it to the cashier who pays the amount in pound cards. The cashier scores one point for every correct amount given. The children change places after several turns.

ADDSUP

This can be a team game.

Make several sets of cards numbered from 3 to 8 and use some pound value cards such as £20, £10, £5 and £1. Place both sets of cards face down. Ask a player from one team to turn over a number card. A child from the other team has to turn over that number of note value cards and add them. A point is scored for each correct total.

5 Deposits

Talk about depositing money into a bank (it could be a school bank). Talk about what 'deposit' means and show them a deposit slip or draw a simplified one (see the pupils' book).

Give them practice in adding up amounts in notes and coins. For example,

	£	p
notes	35	00
£1 coins	14	00
silver	3	55
bronze	1	42
total		

A calculator may be used.

Talk about the meaning of 'balance' and the link between deposit and balance. Explain how to record it.

date	deposit	balance
3 January	–	£100·00
5 January	£20·20	£120·20
10 January	£1·52	

Ask a child to work out and record the new balance on the chart.

6 Withdrawals

Talk with the children about withdrawals from a bank (possibly the school bank again) and how this can be recorded. Show the children a withdrawal slip. Explain what happens to the balance when money is withdrawn. Give the children practice in this.

USING THE CALCULATOR

Remind the children how to enter pounds and pence using the decimal point. Remind them that if the calculator shows 3·5 this means £3·50 (three pounds and fifty pence).

Give them practice in using the calculator for adding and subtracting amounts of money.

Use the constant function to count in 5s, 10s, 20s. This can be used to find how many £5 notes are in £65. The constant function may also be used to count down in 20p coins from £2, say.

LINKS WITH THE ENVIRONMENT

- Collect money bags from banks and discuss how many of each coin they should hold.

- Collect 'savings stacks' designed to hold particular coins and discuss these.
- Talk about pocket money with the children – how they spend it and save it.
- Talk about people buying stamps for electricity, television licence bills.
- Talk about saving money for school camps, holidays, Christmas and depositing and withdrawing the money for these.
- Talk about the cost of going out for the day. What are the costs and what are the bills? Talk about buying petrol, having a snack, buying tickets to get in places, etc. Is there such a thing as a 'cheap day out' for families?

  Discuss major fund-raising events at school, for example, raising money for a conservation area in school grounds.

NOTES ON INVESTIGATIONS

Section A

You need a catalogue showing garden tools and their prices. Do the children choose garden tools which are less than £100 altogether? Do they include a spade, fork and rake among their most useful tools? Can they give reasons for their choices? Do they use a calculator to keep a running total?

Section B

Do the children realise that both withdrawals must add up to £110? Are they systematic in finding possible amounts that might have been withdrawn? For example,

£51 + £59 = £110
£52 + £58 =
£53 + £57
£54 + £56

Do any children use amounts that include pounds and pence such as £50·01 and £59·99?

Section C

You need a gardening catalogue showing the price of shrubs. Do the children choose at least three different sorts of shrubs in finding the cost of 9 shrubs?

Do they use multiplication in preference to only addition to work out the totals?

Purpose

- To revise the properties of the equilateral triangle
- To introduce isosceles and scalene triangles
- To introduce parallel lines
- To introduce vertical and horizontal lines
- To introduce quadrilaterals
- To introduce the concept of rigidity

Materials

Geo-strips and fasteners, squared paper, geo-board, coloured straws and pipe cleaners for joints, newspapers, sellotape (strips of card might be substituted for geo-strips if necessary)

Vocabulary

Geo-strips, equilateral triangle, isosceles triangle, scalene triangle, equal lengths, different lengths, measure, strips, parallel, vertical, horizontal, pattern, chart, rectangle, square, sideways, position, quadrilaterals, diagonal, rigid shape, diagram, templates, results, pennant

TEACHING POINTS

1 The triangle

Talk about the word 'triangle', explaining that 'tri' means 'three' as, for example, in tricycle or tripod.

Are there any triangles in the classroom or in school? Examples might include patterns on jumpers or socks, shelf brackets, display work, etc. Examples of triangles outside school might include road signs, pylons, bridges, etc.

2 Properties of the equilateral, isosceles and scalene triangles

Make three large triangles, for display, from vivelle, card or paper. Ask children to measure the sides of each triangle and to record what they discover.

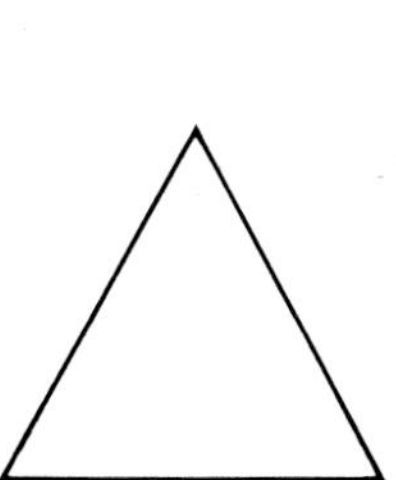

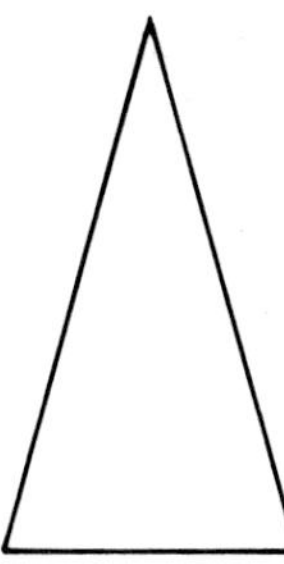

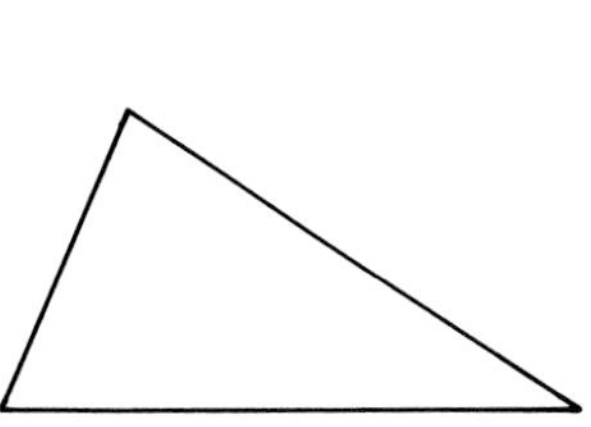

Make three name cards: equilateral triangle, isosceles triangle and scalene triangle. Talk about each kind of triangle and explain the origin of their names:

- Equilateral triangle – from Latin, meaning 'equal sides'.
- Isosceles triangle – from Greek, meaning 'equal legs'.
- Scalene triangle – from Greek, meaning 'uneven'.

Draw some different triangles for the children to measure and match the correct names to. They must explain their choice of name.

Give the children practice in drawing isosceles and scalene triangles, using squared paper if necessary. Point out that isosceles and scalene triangles may also be right-angled triangles. Children could draw equilateral triangles, using templates for accuracy.

A game to play

TRIANGLES

This game is for two groups.

Make a selection of paper triangles – equilateral, isosceles and scalene – in different sizes. Give an assortment to each group. The object of the game is for each group to sort them into three categories as quickly as possible.

3 Parallel lines

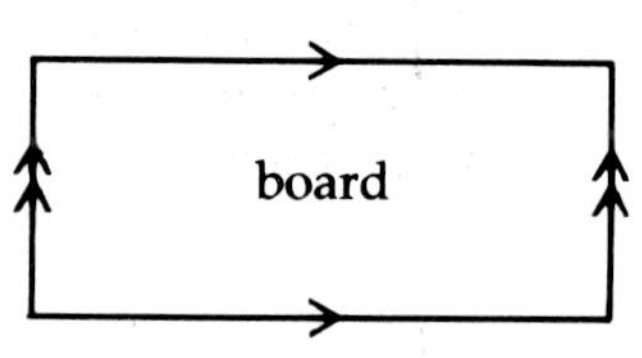

Talk about parallel lines, explaining how they are sets of lines which are the same distance apart for their whole length.

Can the children find any parallel lines in the classroom? Let them make a list and compare findings. Can they think of any parallel lines in the environment? Examples are walls of houses, window frames, fence posts and in structures.

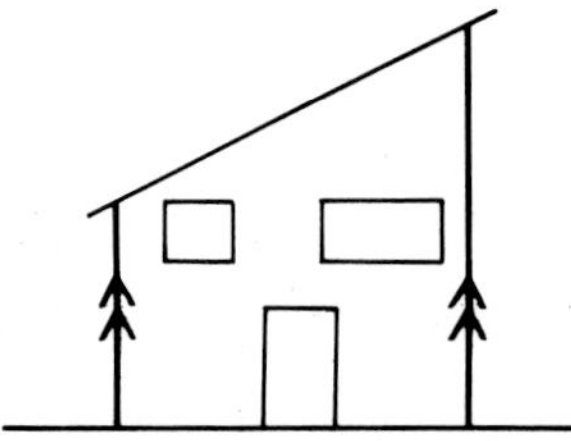

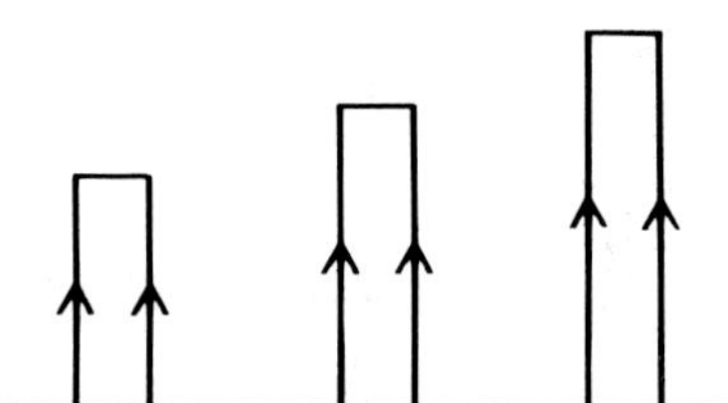

Let the children draw patterns of parallel lines on squared paper or make parallel patterns using a ruler.

A game to play

KEEP IT GOING

This game can be played by the whole class. You may need a referee with a timer or stop-watch.

Each child in turn has to name a pair of parallel lines in the classroom. If they repeat an answer already given or take longer than the stated time (at the discretion of the teacher) they are out.

4 Vertical and horizontal

Ask the children if they have seen, in gymnastics, horizontal bars and vertical rings. Talk about the meaning of each word and point out the relationship of each to the horizon.

Talk about horizontal and vertical lines in houses and buildings and how important they are. What would happen if the floors were not horizontal? Can they think of a famous building which is not vertical? (The Leaning Tower of Pisa).

Can they suggest other things in the environment which are vertical or horizontal?

5 Quadrilaterals

Can the children suggest what a quadrilateral is by hearing or reading the name? (Latin – 4 sides). Let them draw some.

Can the children name any quadrilaterals, like a square or a rectangle? At this point you may wish to extend the work in the chapter by referring to the names and properties of other quadrilaterals such as the kite, rhombus, trapezium and parallelogram. This will obviously depend upon the capabilities of the children.

Let the children make as many quadrilaterals as they can, using a geo-board. Then ask them to make a square and a rectangle and list what they notice about each shape. For example, opposite sides parallel, opposite sides equal, etc.

A game to play

DRAW ME

Make some cards like these:

I am a quadrilateral. I have 2 pairs of parallel lines, all the same length.	I am a quadrilateral I have two right-angles and one pair of parallel lines.

Make up some more, giving properties for particular quadrilaterals. Give the cards to groups of children. A correct drawing scores a point. The correct name of the shape scores another point. The winner is the player with most points.

6 Rigidity

Discuss the meaning of the word 'rigid', explaining that a rigid shape is one that cannot be pushed out of shape (without bending or breaking).

Rigidity in plane shapes and the discovery of the triangle as the basic rigid shape is for the children to explore in the pupils' book so too much preliminary work on this would pre-empt their findings. It would be helpful, however, to remind them what a diagonal is.

LINKS WITH THE ENVIRONMENT

Talk about the different shapes and lines in everyday life. Can they name them?

- Look for triangles in structures such as pylons and bridges. Are there any horizontal, vertical or parallel lines?
- Look for quadrilaterals (and triangles) in designs for fabrics and knitting patterns.
- Look at shapes of buildings and road signs for triangles, quadrilaterals, horizontal lines and parallel lines.
- Look for parallel lines at the railway station, on the road and on maps
- Look for vertical and horizontal lines: bars and rings in gymnastics, lamp-posts and buildings. What do the horizontal and vertical holds on TV sets do to the picture?

NOTES ON INVESTIGATIONS

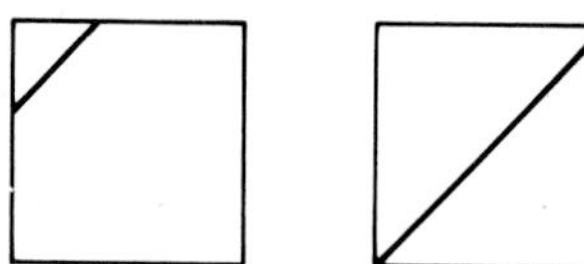

Section A

Do the children discover that the triangle is a rigid shape? Do they discover that the square and the rectangle can be made rigid by putting in one diagonal strip? Do they discover that all squares and rectangles can be made rigid by using one extra strip?

Section B

Various answers are possible. Squared paper may be useful.

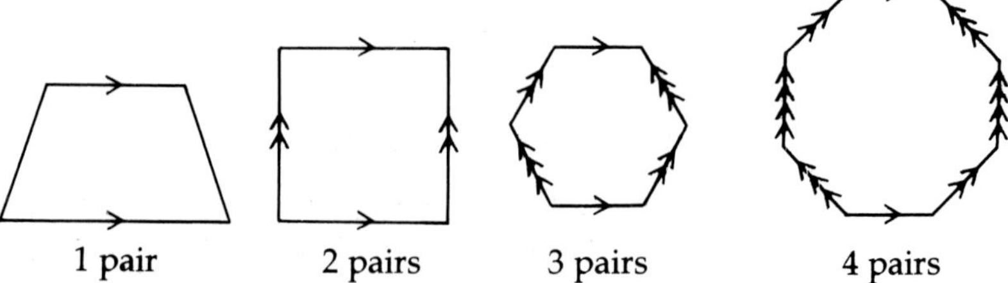

Section C

Do the children find structures that show triangles in them? When making their models, do they use triangles in order to give their shapes rigidity?

Number 9

Purpose

- To give practice in finding fractions of quantities

Materials

Squared paper, crayons

Vocabulary

Section, rows, fraction patterns, record, answers, different, fraction sections, design

TEACHING POINTS

1 Half of quantities

Put 12 counters or cubes in a container. Ask a child to divide them in half and then write the number on the board.

$\frac{1}{2}$ of 12 is 6.

Do the same with other numbers.
Do the children see any relationships between the numbers?

$\frac{1}{2}$ of $12 = 6$
$12 \div 2 = 6$

Can any child suggest an algorithm for finding half of a quantity? For example, to find half, divide by 2.

○ ○ ○	○ ○ ○
○ ○ ○	○ ○ ○
To find half of 12, divide by 2	

2 Other fractions of quantities

Use similar activities to find algorithms for other fractions. Consider, for example, $\frac{1}{4}$, $\frac{1}{8}$, $\frac{1}{3}$, $\frac{1}{5}$, $\frac{1}{10}$, $\frac{1}{6}$. The discoveries could be displayed as mobiles.
Ask the children to show fractions of quantities such as $\frac{1}{3}$ of 9 and record it. For example

○○○|○○○|○○○ or ●●●○○○○○○ or $\frac{1}{3}$ of $9 = 3$

3 More fractions

Talk with the children about how they can find $\frac{3}{4}$ of a number. Ask them to put out 20 counters and group them into quarters.
'How many in a quarter?'
'So how many in three quarters?'
Write the number sentences on the board.

$\frac{1}{4}$ of $20 = 5$
$\frac{3}{4}$ of $20 = 15$

Can the children suggest a way of finding $\frac{3}{4}$ of a number without using counters? For example, divide by 4 and multiply by 3. Do they predict that they could use a similar algorithm for other fractions? For example, $\frac{3}{5}$ of 15 – divide by 5 and multiply by 3. Let them check this by using counters.

Give the children plenty of practice with this.

4 Colouring fractions

Give the children practice in colouring fractions of shapes. For example, draw a shape on squared paper, using 30 squares. Colour $\frac{1}{5}$ purple, $\frac{1}{5}$ green and $\frac{3}{5}$ yellow to make a pattern. Ask, 'What is $\frac{1}{5}$ of 30?' 'What is $\frac{3}{5}$ of 30?'

5 Games to play

BRING THE FRACTION

Put the children in pairs. Ask each pair to count out the same number of counters (e.g. 12). Ask them to show you $\frac{5}{6}$ of 12. The first pair to do so scores a point.

Repeat this for other fractions.

BINGO

This game is for a group of children.
Make four bingo cards with six numbers on each card.

3	5	10
6	2	4

8	3	2
6	12	4

9	2	8
10	5	6

12	5	8
3	9	4

Make fraction cards for these:

$\frac{1}{2}$, $\frac{1}{3}$, $\frac{1}{4}$, $\frac{1}{6}$ of 12
$\frac{1}{3}$, $\frac{1}{5}$ of 15
$\frac{1}{2}$, $\frac{1}{3}$, $\frac{1}{4}$, $\frac{1}{6}$, $\frac{1}{8}$ of 24
$\frac{1}{3}$, $\frac{1}{5}$, $\frac{1}{6}$ of 30
$\frac{1}{3}$, $\frac{1}{4}$, $\frac{1}{6}$ of 36

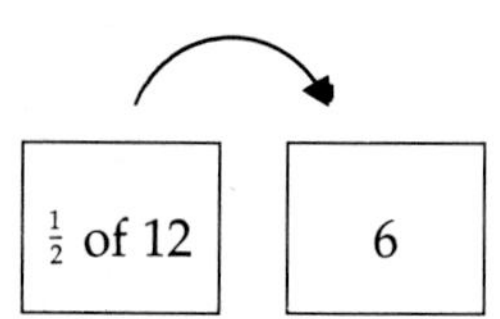

Write the answer on the back of each one.

Put the cards in a box and shake them. A child picks a card out and reads it to the players (e.g. '$\frac{1}{2}$ of 12'). Anyone who has the answer 6 on their card covers it with a counter. The fraction card is placed in a discard pack. The game continues until the winner has covered all the numbers on their card. The caller checks the winner's card by checking the answers in the discard pile.

USING THE CALCULATOR

Talk with the children about how to find fractions of quantities and how to do this using a calculator. For example, to find $\frac{3}{5}$ of 30, we could enter

3 [÷] 5 [×] 30 [=]

or 30 [÷] 5 [×] 3 [=]

or 30 [÷] 5 [=] 6 ($\frac{1}{5}$)

6 [×] 3 [=] 18 ($\frac{3}{5}$)

Give the children plenty of practice in using the calculator to find fractions of quantities. Let them suggest problems for each other.

A game to play

FRACTION RACE

Divide the children into two teams. Call out a fraction for a player from each team to find the answer on their calculator, e.g. $\frac{5}{6}$ of 36, $\frac{7}{8}$ of 56. The first player to show the correct answer on their display scores a point for their team.

LINKS WITH THE ENVIRONMENT

- Talk about fractions of time, e.g. $\frac{3}{4}$ of an hour
- Talk about fractions in sport, such as half time and first quarter in ice hockey.
- Talk about journeys and being half way there and a quarter of the way there. What do we mean by this?
- Knitting – the theme used in the pupils' book.
  History of knitting in Britain and around the world.
  Types of knitting. Arran, Fair Isle.
  Knitting designs and patterns.
  Knitting squares to make blankets for charity organisations.

NOTES ON INVESTIGATIONS

Section A

Do the children work out that there are 2 green rows, 6 blue rows and 4 yellow rows to make up the 12 complete rows? Do they plan different combinations of colours, making 12 each time? Do they state the fractions for the colours each time?

Section B

Do the children realise that in order to divide the sections into fifths and tenths the number of rows in both sections must be multiples of 10?

First section	Second section
10	10
20	20
30	30

Section C

Do the children make the number of rows in the $\frac{1}{5}$ section a multiple of 5 and the number of rows in the $\frac{1}{6}$ section a multiple of 6? Do they design the grey section so that the total number of rows is 100?

Purpose

- To introduce 24 hour clock times

Materials

Clocks, clock stamps, clock showing 24 hour times

Vocabulary

Hour hand, clock, twice, midnight, midday, chart, a.m., p.m., 24 hour clock times, minutes, answers, noon, arrows, time intervals

TEACHING POINTS

1 Vocabulary and discussion

As this chapter is based on the work of the Post Office, the children will need to understand the relevant vocabulary. This includes sorting, postwoman's round, delivery, collection times, Travelling Post Office (or TPO), mail, deliver and maintenance.

2 24 hour clock

Draw a 12 hour clock face. Remind the children about 12 hour clock times and how we write a.m. for the times before midday and p.m. for the times after midday. Talk about the possible confusion if we forget to put the a.m. or p.m.

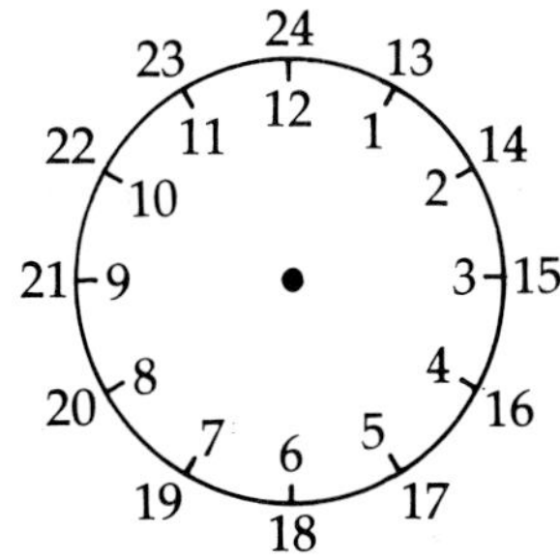

Talk with the children about 24 hour clock times and show them 24 hour clock faces. Explain that with the 24 hour clock it is not necessary to write a.m. or p.m.

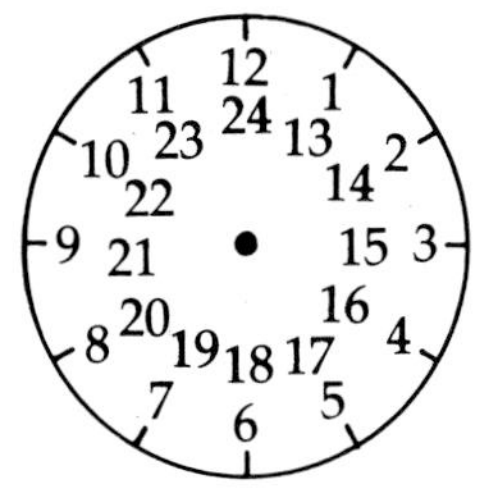

3 Recording

Talk about how we write times using the 24 hour system. Use a geared 24 hour clock or clock face. Set the hands to 1 o'clock and ask the children to predict the hours until noon or midday on the clock. Talk about how, on the 24 hour clock, the hour after 12:00 is 13:00, i.e. 12:00 + 1 hour.

Can the children predict the hours from 12:00 to midnight? Point out that midnight can be written as 24:00 but is often shown as 00:00, and that 24 hour clock times always have four digits so 1 o'clock in the morning is 01:00.

Give the children practice in showing 24 hour times on clocks (to whole hours).

4 Writing times

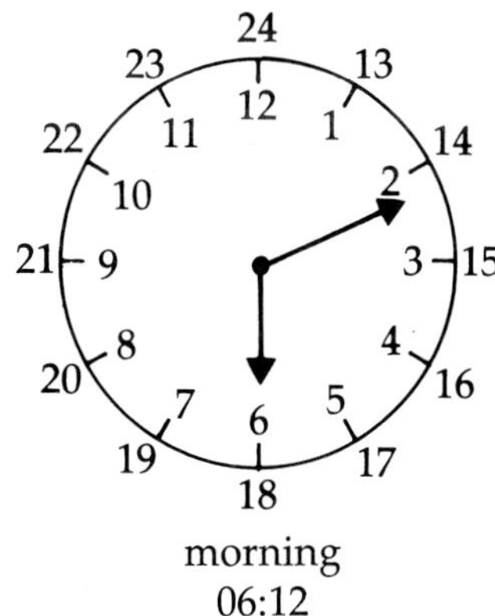

morning
06:12

Talk with the children about how the minutes are written after the hour as in digital times.

Give the children practice in reading times aloud and recording them as 24 hour clock times.

Ask them to write other times as 24 hour clock times. Use different forms of questions. For example,

$\frac{1}{4}$ past 8 (morning) → 08:15
half past ten at night → 22:30
7:00 a.m. → 07:00

Talk about how minutes to the hour are written as minutes past the hour. For example,

$\frac{1}{4}$ to 6 → 05:45

Play a game with the children to give them practice in changing from 12 hour clock times to 24 hour clock times and vice versa. State a time. The children have to record it in as many ways as possible in a given time.

2:15 p.m. → 14:15 → $\frac{1}{4}$ past 2 in the afternoon → 15 minutes past 2 in the afternoon, etc.
16:30 → 4:30 p.m. → half past four in the afternoon, etc.

Can the children suggest how to write 1 minute after midnight, i.e. 00:01?

Talk about the importance of putting the digits in the right place. For example,

01:00, 00:10, 00:01

Can the children say what each time is?
Some digital watches and clocks show times as | 01.00 |

5 Time activities

Let the children write out the school timetable in 24 hour times.

Make some 12 hour clock times and number them.

For example

1	2
3:20 p.m.	11:25 a.m.

Put the cards around the classroom. Give each child a piece of paper and ask them to write each time as a 24 hour clock time. How many do they write correctly?

Games to play

TIME IT

This game is for two groups of eight children.

Make eight pairs of cards for 12 hour and the equivalent 24 hour times. Choose times between 12:00 and 00:00. Each pair must be for a different time.

1:00 p.m.	13:00
4:00 p.m.	16:00

Take four pairs, shuffle them and deal one to each member of the first group, time side down. Do the same for the second group. At a given signal the children turn over the cards and see which group can match up the cards first.

STAND UP

Make one set of time cards in 12 hour times and two sets of matching cards in 24 hour times.

2:30 p.m.	14:30	14:30

Divide the children into two teams and deal out one set of the 24 hour times to each team. Hold up a 12 hour clock time.
The first player to hold up the equivalent 24 hour clock time scores a point for the team. The winning team is the first to score 10 points.

6 Mental work

- Set the hands of a clock to chosen times and ask the children to state the time in 24 hour clock time.
- Say a time for the children to say or write as a 24 hour clock time. For example, 3:30 a.m. → 03:30.
- Give the children practice in calculating time gaps. For example, from 14:00 to 15:30 is how many minutes?
- Count on from a given time such as 14:20 in intervals such as 1 minute, 2 minutes and 5 minutes, recording the answers in 24 hour clock times. Give the stopping time.

LINKS WITH THE ENVIRONMENT

Talk about everyday situations where we see or use 24 hour clock times.

- Railway stations, bus stations, jeweller's windows
- Bus and train timetables
- Post Office collection times
- Look at 24 hour digital clocks.

NOTES ON INVESTIGATIONS

Section A

Do the children plan four collection times for each box? Do they leave a sensible amount of time between each collection? Are the children able to write the times out as both 12 and 24 hour clock times?

Section B

Do the children understand how to write 24 hour clock times that are 12 hours apart? Do they suggest what they might be doing at the times they write? Are their suggestions sensible in terms of the times and activities suggested?

Section C

Do the children realise that the timetable must run from 23:30 to 00:30? Do they realise that, if they work in whole numbers of minutes, the time intervals must be 1, 2, 3, 4, 5, 6, 10, 12, 15, 20, 30 and 60 minutes?

Purpose

- To revise the use of co-ordinates
- To specify location by means of co-ordinates and direction

Materials

Squared paper, atlas or map of the world

Vocabulary

Co-ordinates, direction, reverse, grid, eight points of the compass

TEACHING POINTS

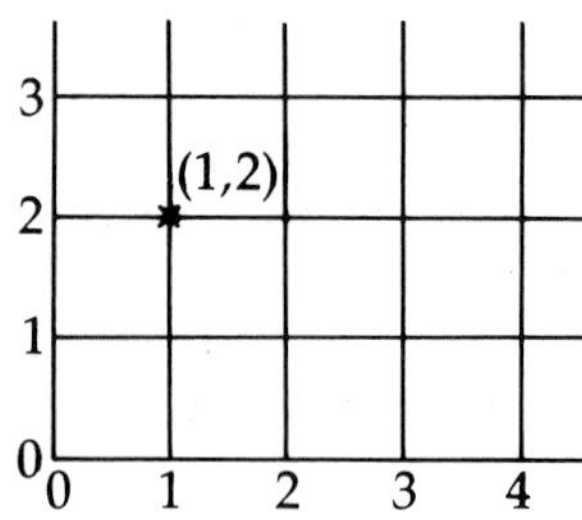

1 Grids and points

Revise with the children how to find positions on grids using co-ordinates.

2 Maps

Draw a simple map for the children and pin-point particular locations. Ask them to state the co-ordinates.

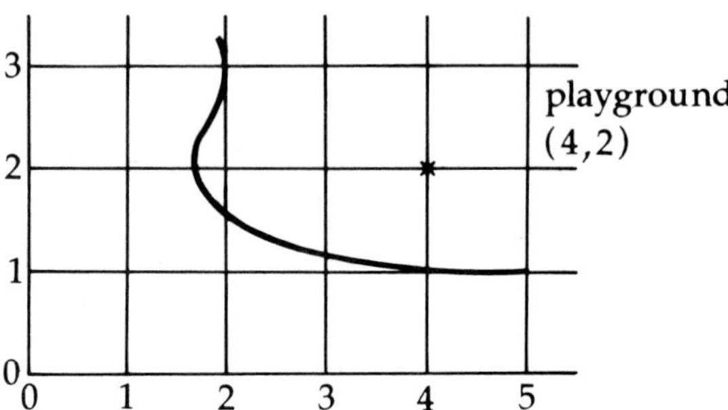

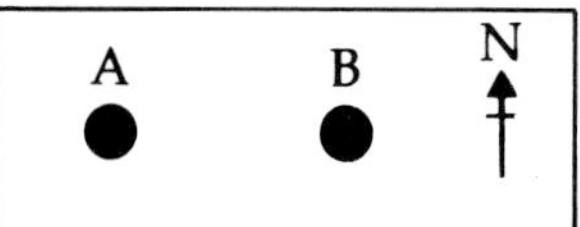

B is due east of A

3 Direction

Revise the eight points of the compass. Talk about locations by asking the children to describe the position of one point from another. Give them practice in this.

A game to play

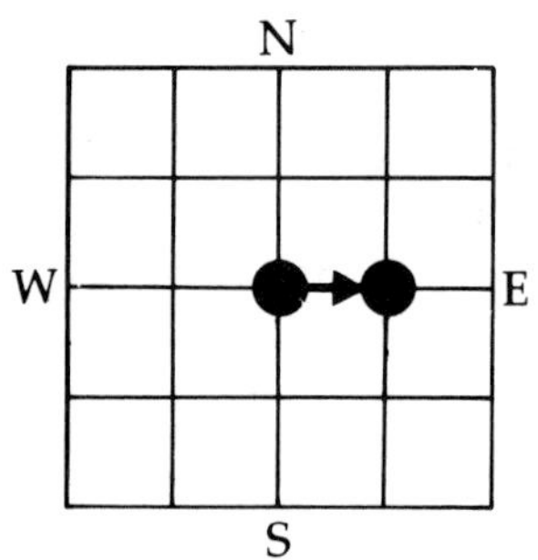

STAY ON THE BOARD

Each child is given a 4 × 4 square grid and a counter. A pack of cards marked N, S, W or E are placed face downwards on the table.

Each child places the counter on the intersection at the centre of the board and then picks up a direction card in turn. The counter is moved one square in the given direction. The winner is the first player to move completely off the board.

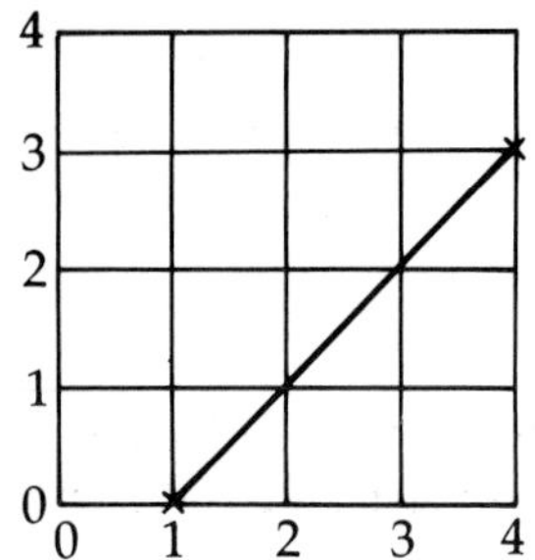

4 Eight points of the compass

Ask the children to follow a route on a grid using co-ordinates and the eight points of the compass.

> 'Start at (1, 0). Go NE across 3 squares. What are your co-ordinates? Now go . . .'

A game to play

MAKE A ROUTE

Make a pack of direction cards (eight points of the compass) and a pack of co-ordinate cards. A number (say four) of each set of cards are dealt to each child. The game is to see who can use their cards to make a continuous route on the board, where the directions follow only the eight points of the compass.

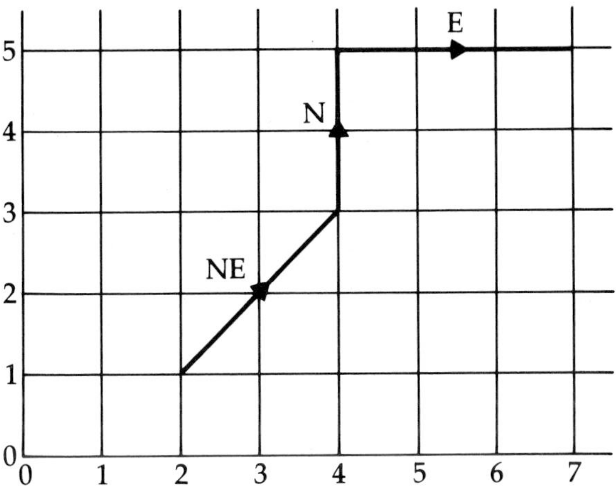

LINKS WITH THE ENVIRONMENT

Talk with the children about using co-ordinates in everyday life.

- Finding places on maps and plans
- Playing join-a-dot puzzles
- Going orienteering
- Look for co-ordinates on Ordnance Survey maps of the local area (This might be linked to a school trip.)
- Make a simple map of an imaginary town or village, showing interesting features

NOTES ON INVESTIGATIONS

Section A

Do the children see the pattern for producing squares? Do they find squares of different sizes?

Section B

Do the children find suitable islands for the word search? Do they draw up an appropriate grid? Do they find the correct co-ordinates for the letters?

Section C

This is likely to be quite a demanding activity for the children.
Do they find that squares that have a corner at the origin (0, 0) work? Do they go on to discover shapes that have a line of symmetry that goes through (0, 0)?

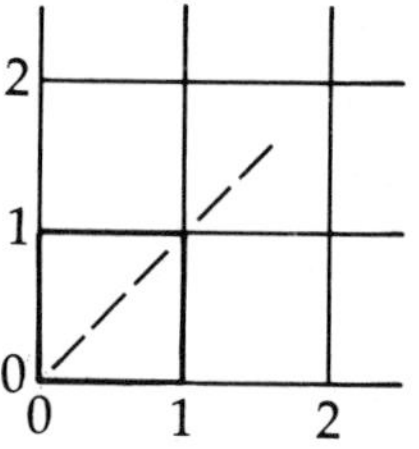
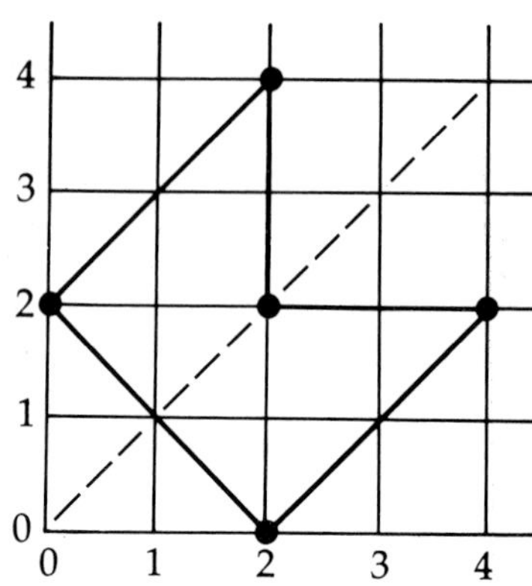

Number 10

Purpose

- Addition of ThHTU with exchanging from the units, tens and hundreds
- To give further practice in rounding and approximating
- To introduce the inequality signs

Materials

Structural apparatus may be useful

Vocabulary

Traffic count, round to the nearest thousand or hundred, total number, pair, closest together, numerals, rounded numbers, totals, traffic survey, record, group, lowest total, highest total, predict, check, approximate, true total, furthest, estimate, total figure, round up, round down

TEACHING POINTS

1 Rounding numbers

Revise rounding numbers to the nearest 10. Show them on a number line. For example, 57 → 60   71 → 70

Revise rounding numbers to the nearest 100.

Remind the children about rounding numbers up or down to the nearest thousand. For example,

4358 → 4000   1947 → 2000

Can they suggest some numbers that round up or down to, for example, 3000? Remind them that 3500 rounds to 4000.

2 Approximating

Talk with the children about using rounded numbers to give approximate answers. This can be useful when deciding if an answer is correct. For example,

$$2890 + 3112 \quad \text{rounds to} \quad 3000 + 3000 = 6000$$

The approximate answer is 6000, so the true total should be close to this.

Do the children understand the difference between an approximate total and a true total?

A game to play

SORT THEM OUT

This game is for two small groups.

Write a selection of numbers on cards, such that half the numbers round to 1000 and the other half to 2000. For example,

1680, 1100, 1470, 987, 1760, 1800, 1920, 1500, 500, 1340, 1035, 2420

Ask one group to find all the numbers which round to 1000 and the other group to find all the numbers which round to 2000. The first group to find all possible numbers wins.

The game may be extended to rounding to other, larger numbers. For example, 3000, 4000, 5000.

3 Inequality signs

Introduce children to the signs for 'is greater than' (>) and 'is less than' (<). It might be helpful to explain that the largest part of the sign goes towards the largest number. Give them practice in using them. For example, put in the missing sign > or <:

32 □ 48 124 □ 111

Can they put in the signs for this? 159 □ 241 □ 374

A game to play

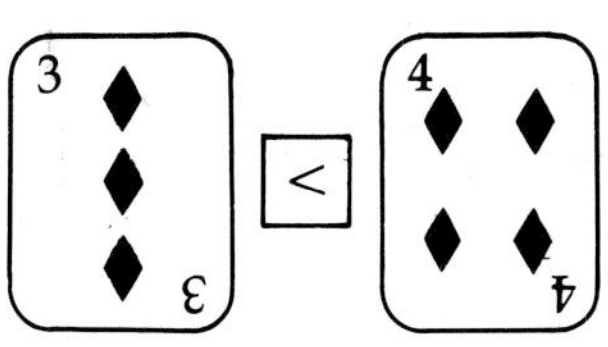

GREATER THAN OR LESS THAN

Divide the children into two groups. Give each group five cards with > on them. Using only the number cards 2 to 10 from a pack of playing cards, shuffle and deal each group 10 cards. The first group to pair their cards, using the signs in the correct way, wins.

Make some cards with larger numbers in order to cater for different ability levels.

4 Numbers in words

Talk about writing ThHTU numbers in words and vice versa. For example,

3574 → three thousand five hundred and seventy-four

Give the children practice in this.

5 Addition of ThHTU

Addition can be shown practically using structural apparatus. Write two numbers on the board which use exchanging in the HTU columns, such as 1567 and 2678. Ask one child to add them as a sum on the board and another to add them using structural apparatus. Do they both get the same answer?

6 Mental work

- Give practice in rounding numbers to the nearest ten, hundred and thousand.
- Give practice in finding an approximate answer. For example, give the approximate answer for 2116 + 2432.
- Give practice in using inequality signs
- Give practice in place value – what is the value of the 9 in 5976?
- Write numbers in words and vice-versa
- Add hundreds to make a number pattern:

1200 1400 1600 . . . 2400

USING THE CALCULATOR

- Use the calculator to find approximate answers to additions of ThHTU and then compare them with the true answers.
- Use the constant function to make number patterns with ThHTU to reinforce place value. For example 4795, 4895, 4995 . . .
- Read numbers in words and then show them on the calculator display.

LINKS WITH THE ENVIRONMENT

Talk about everyday situations that use large numbers.

- Large numbers of vehicles in traffic surveys – discuss road safety and large numbers of road casualties
- Sport – spectators at sporting events
- Populations of small towns and villages

- Nature – birds in flocks, bees in a hive, leaves on a tree, flowers in the park
- Reading – words in a book or newspaper.

NOTES ON INVESTIGATIONS

Section A

Do the children decide upon the purpose of their survey? For example, to find the number of heavy lorries that pass? Do they plan an appropriate data collection chart for the information they intend to collect? Do they consider the length of time their survey would last and the time of day, e.g. busy, quiet? Do they suggest sensible safety rules for their survey?

Section B

Do the children understand when to round up and when to round down? Do they choose one number that rounds up and one that rounds down each time? Does the total of the rounded numbers come to 5000 each time?

Section C

Do the children realise that all four numbers round up rather than down? Do they see that 2910 and 3850 are closest to their rounded up numbers and so will give a total nearest to the true total? Are they able to explain this?

Purpose

- To construct and interpret line graphs

Materials

Squared paper, thermometer, hot tap water, plastic water pot

Vocabulary

Temperature, graph, data, time, increase, noon, hours, record, zero, Celsius, centigrade, winter, summer, average, midnight, month, hotter, colder, coldest, above/below average, estimate.

TEACHING POINTS

1 Data and data collection

Talk with the children about the meaning of the word 'data' and remind them that we often collect data or information and show it as a graph.

Ask the children to suggest what information or data they could collect about themselves. Their suggestions might include hair colour, eye colour, shoe size, number of children in their family, favourite television programmes, football teams, etc.

Ask them to design a data collection sheet for a survey on one of their suggestions (such as favourite ice-cream flavours) and talk about their methods of recording the information. Remind them that tallying is one way of doing this.

ice-creams	tally (or frequency)	total
strawberry	𝍸	5
vanilla	𝍸 𝍸 I	11
chocolate	𝍸 I	6
mint	𝍸 𝍸 II	12

2 Graphs

Ask the children to choose a way of showing the information collected. Talk about the different kinds of graph they could use.

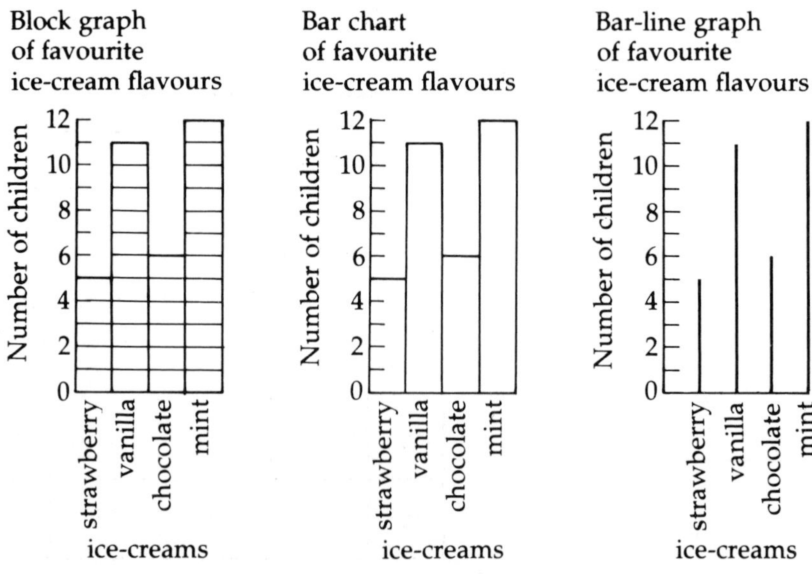

Remind the children about writing the labels, numbers and titles for the graphs.

Give the children practice in interpreting graphs. For example, ask them to suggest suitable questions based on a graph for other children to answer. Ask them what would happen to the graph if it had been made by another class. Would it have the same number and flavours of ice-creams? Ask the children to write some sentences about each graph or explain it to the others.

Can the children write a short story, which contains the information on the graph?

3 Revise scale

Talk about the use of scale on graphs. Draw some bar-line graphs with different scales. For example,

Bar-line graphs of tuck-shop money

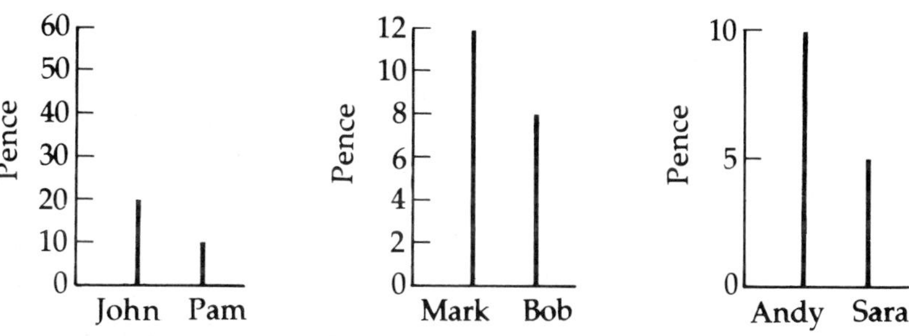

Can the children interpret them?

Remind them that some graphs are drawn horizontally.

Graph of tuck-shop money

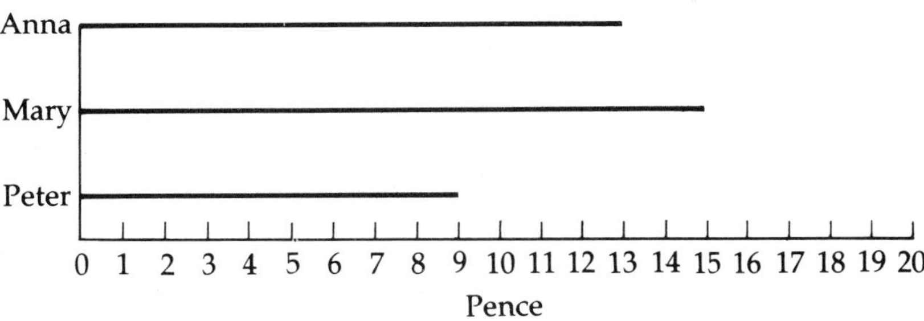

4 Line graphs

Talk with the children about line graphs. Draw a table about temperature and ask them to plot the temperatures at the times shown.

Time	9 a.m.	10 a.m.	11 a.m.	12 noon	1 p.m.	2 p.m.	3 p.m.
°C	12	14	15	17	17	16	15

Explain that the labels do not have to start at zero.

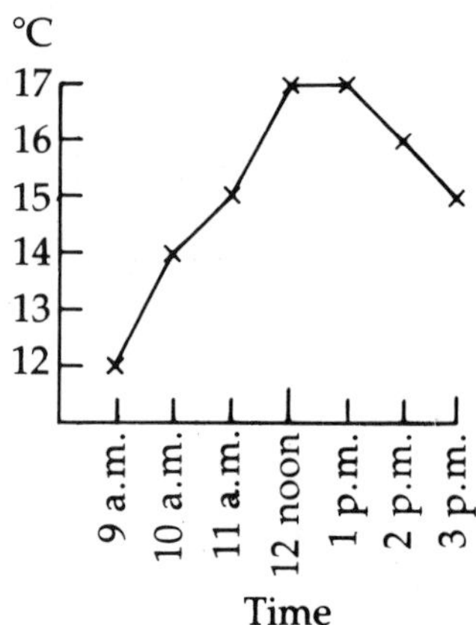

If we want to see the pattern of the weather or to know the approximate temperature between the points, we can join them up. Talk about the shape of this graph. Explain that the lines joining the temperatures only show the approximate temperature. For example, between 12 and 1 o'clock the temperature might really move up

12 noon 1 p.m. or down 12 noon 1 p.m. or both 12 noon 1 p.m. but this is

not shown on the graph.

A game to play

QUESTIONS

Draw a line graph or bar-line graph. Divide the children into two teams. A child from the first team asks a child from the other a question about the graph such as, 'What was the temperature at 10 o'clock?' A correct answer scores a point. Each team takes turns at asking and answering six questions each. The teacher or the other children act as judges. The winner is the team with the most points.

5 Die throwing

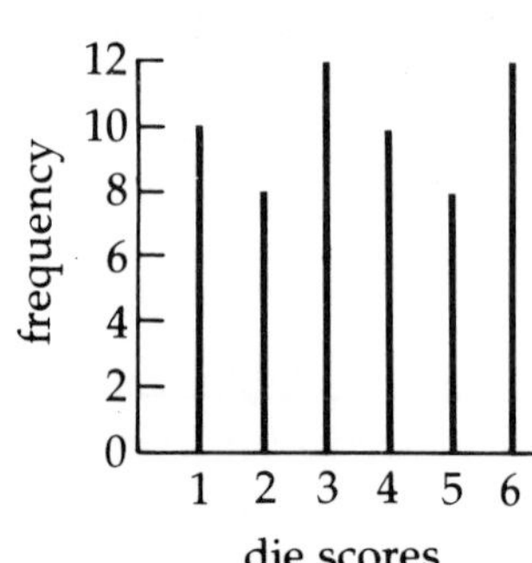

Ask the children to throw a die 60 times and tally the numbers shown. Draw a bar-line graph of the results.

Talk about whether joining the tops of the bar-line or points has meaning. In this case the die cannot have value $1\frac{1}{2}$ so it is not appropriate to join them up. The die scores give separate values (or discrete variables) and should not be joined.

LINKS WITH THE ENVIRONMENT

Use opportunities in schools and elsewhere to produce meaningful line graphs.

- Temperature – record the classroom temperature for a day.
- Growth – record the growth of cress seeds, mustard seeds, plants.
- Look for line graphs in charts or newspapers and magazines.
- Draw graphs to record collection of money for charity.
- Talk about temperature charts in hospitals.

NOTES ON INVESTIGATIONS

Section A

Do the children realise that temperature graphs like this would probably occur during the night at colder times of the year or when something such as water is cooled and then heated up again? Are their suggestions for testing the graph appropriate, for example, recording the night temperature hourly perhaps with the help of a shift worker? Would they record it inside or outside?

Section B

Do the children choose temperatures for each month of the year? Are their chosen temperatures sensible? For example, the summer months should have higher temperatures than the winter months. Do the children draw an appropriate graph for their chosen temperatures? Do any children join the tops of the temperatures (this is not meaningful)? Are the children's explanations for their choice of graphs clear and sensible?

Section C

Do the children think of using hot water from the tap to carry out this investigation? Other ways of heating water include the use of a kettle or pan. Safety factors must be considered carefully and talked through with the children. Do the children plan to collect the data using a thermometer and recording the temperature at fixed time intervals such as 1 minute, 2 minutes, 3 minutes? Do the children draw a graph to show their work? Have they used a line graph and joined the temperatures together which is meaningful in this situation?

Number 11

Purpose

- To introduce subtraction of ThHTU with exchanging from Th, H and T
- To explore other number systems

Materials

Structural apparatus as required

Vocabulary

Numbers, Roman numerals, subtract, dates, twentieth century, Chinese numbers, number system

TEACHING POINTS

1 Number systems

Talk with the children about different number systems. Early humans would probably have counted on their fingers and made marks on cave walls. By about 3000 BC the Babylonians and the Egyptians had a written number system that counted in units of ten. Later, the Romans, too, used a system that counted in units of ten. Although these systems used base ten they did not have a system of place value like the number system we use today.

The children might be interested to look at some of the systems that were used.

2 Roman numbers 1–20 (I–XX)

Ask the children where they might see Roman numbers today – clocks, TV programmes, film production dates, Roman remains, after the names of kings and queens (e.g. Henry VIII). How many of the Roman symbols do they know the value of?

Talk about the different symbols the Romans used when counting up to 20. For example I, V, X.

Let the children build up the numbers 1–20 with you. Can they predict the next number each time? Point out that IIII (the early version of 4) occurs on clocks but in general we use the later version of IV.

A game to play

ROMAN SHUFFLE

Put the children into two groups. Make two sets of number cards 1–20 for each group, one set showing Roman and the other showing ordinary numbers. Ask each group to shuffle their two sets. At a given signal both groups attempt to match ordinary numbers to the Roman. For example,

II → 2

The first group to complete the task is the winner.

The game can be adapted to using only the Roman numerals and arranging them in the order I–XX as quickly as possible.

3 Roman numbers 10–1000 (X–M)

Point out that the Romans counted in units of ten. For example X, XX, XXX. Include L, the symbol for 50. Can the children predict any of the numbers when building up 10, 20, 30 to 100 in Roman numbers?

Next talk about the other numbers up to 100. For example, IV, XXIV, LIV.

Do the children know that C is the Roman symbol for 100? Can they think of any words that are linked with this? For example, century, cent.

Talk about how the Romans used D for 500 and M for 1000. Do they notice the dates at the end of TV programmes? These are usually written in Roman numerals. Can they write the date for this year and their birth year using Roman numbers?

A game to play

MAKE THE NUMBER

Four players can play this game. Make some cards showing the Roman numbers I, V, X, L and C. Make enough for each player to have four or five of them. Deal the cards out between the players. Each player makes the largest number they can, using their cards. The winner is the player with the largest number.

4 Our number system

Ask the children to write one thousand, five hundred and sixty four in our number system and in the Roman number system – which system is easier to use? Why?

Talk about the origins of our present system. Between 200 BC and AD 600 the Hindus in India began to use a system that used the symbols 1 to 9 and zero. It was the use of zero that made possible the place value system that we use today. By AD 800 Indian traders had introduced the system to the Arab world. The Arabs adopted it and from their empire it spread to Europe. Hence it was called the Hindu–Arabic system.

0 1 2 3 4 5 6 7 8 9

Let the children look at the early symbols and how they have changed, although the basic system has not. Point out that a base ten is common to many systems, almost certainly because we have ten fingers.

5 Place value

Ask how many thousands numbers the children can make using only two different symbols. For example,

1000 1001 1010 1100

Try three different symbols. For example, 1012, etc. This can give valuable reinforcement of place value.

6 Subtraction

Revise subtraction of ThHTU with exchanging from the tens and the hundreds.

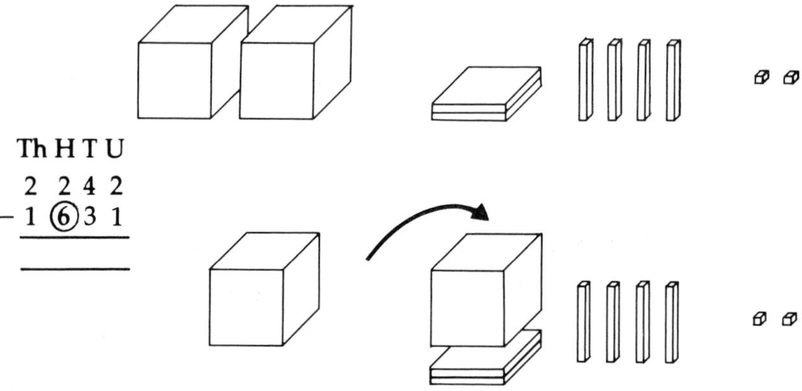

Use structural apparatus to introduce the children to exchanging from the thousands. Give the children plenty of practice in this.

When the children have understood this concept, develop the work to include exchanging from all three columns.

```
  Th H T U
   6 6 3 4
 − 2 8 7 6
 _________
 _________
```

Use your usual method of recording although some children might develop their own algorithms. For example,

```
   1  9  9                  1  9  9  1
   2̸ ¹0̸ ¹0̸ ¹4̸               2̸  0̸  0̸  4
 − 1  4  6  5    or    −    1  4  6  5
 ____________              ___________
 ____________              ___________
```

(Exchanging 1 ten into units from 200 tens leaving 199 tens)

As much of the chapter in the pupils' book is devoted to number systems, you may wish to provide extra computation material of your own. Give plenty of practice in using zeros.

7 Mental work

- Ask the children questions about place value. For example
  2693 = 2000 + 600 + 90 +3
- What is the ringed number worth in 12⑥4?
- How many hundreds in 1000?
  1 thousand = 10 hundreds or 1000
  3 thousand = 30 hundreds or 3000
  13 hundreds = 1300

USING THE CALCULATOR

- Show the children how calculators work in our base 10 system
  units × 10 → tens, e.g. 3 × 10 → 30
  tens × 10 → hundreds
  hundreds × 10 → thousands etc.
- Practise subtraction of ThHTU on the calculator.

LINKS WITH THE ENVIRONMENT

Talk about the development of number and number systems

- History – the Romans and their number system, the Chinese system, the Hindu–Arabic system
- Years – life spans of famous people by subtracting birth from death years, the nineteenth and twentieth centuries
- Sport – centuries in cricket, etc

NOTES ON INVESTIGATIONS

Section A

Do the children find a way to subtract the two Roman numbers? Can they explain what they did? Do they appreciate the difficulties if exchanging is required? Do they see the advantages of our present system?

Section B

Do the children see what the system is? Do they place the units symbol in front of the symbol for ten in order to show multiples of ten? For example,

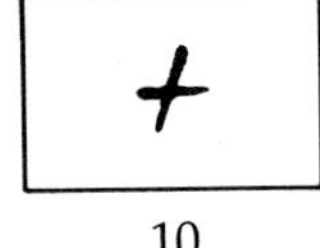

10 20 30 40 etc.

Is their system logical?

Section C

Do the children devise a logical system?
There is potential for valuable discussion work here.

Angles 1

Purpose

- To measure and draw angles to 10°
- To revise and use the language associated with angles

Materials

Protractors, coloured pens, geo-strips, fasteners

Vocabulary

Acute, obtuse, reflex, degrees, circle, seasons, year, angles, angle measurer, protractor, clockwise, anti-clockwise, right angle, dial, straight angle

TEACHING POINTS

1 Acute, obtuse and reflex angles

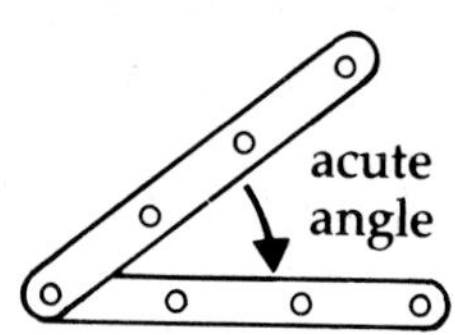

Revise the acute and obtuse angles. Let the children make and display acute and obtuse angles using geo-strips or strips of card joined with a paper fastener.

Talk about angles that are greater than two right angles (but less than four right angles). Let the children think of times when an object is turned through a reflex angle.

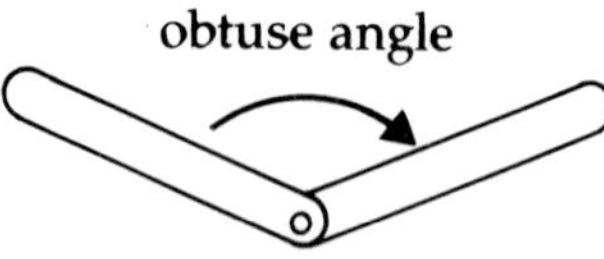

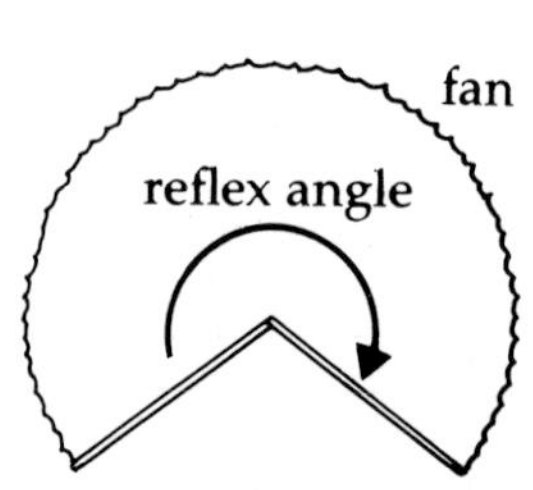

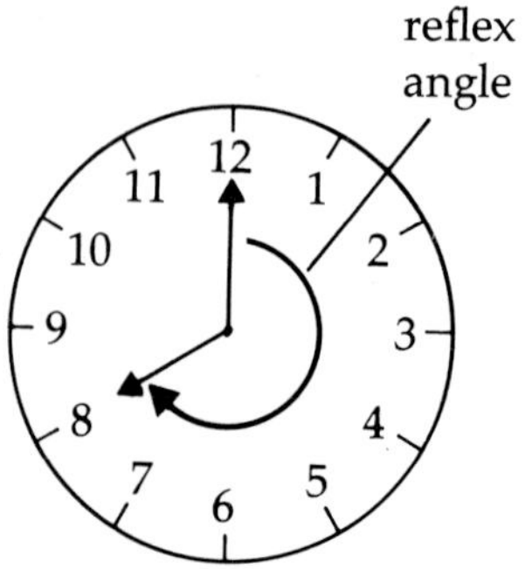

A game to play

MAKE THE ANGLE

Make a set of cards marked acute angle, obtuse angle, reflex angle and right angle. Place them face down on the table, with two geo-strips.

Put the children into two groups. Ask a child from each group to pick up a card and make that type of angle using the geo-strips. A point is given for each correct answer.

2 Angles

Revise with the children that there are 90 degrees in a right angle. Can they see any right angles in the room?

Explain that there are 360° in a circle. How many right angles is this?

A game to play

HUNT THE ANGLE

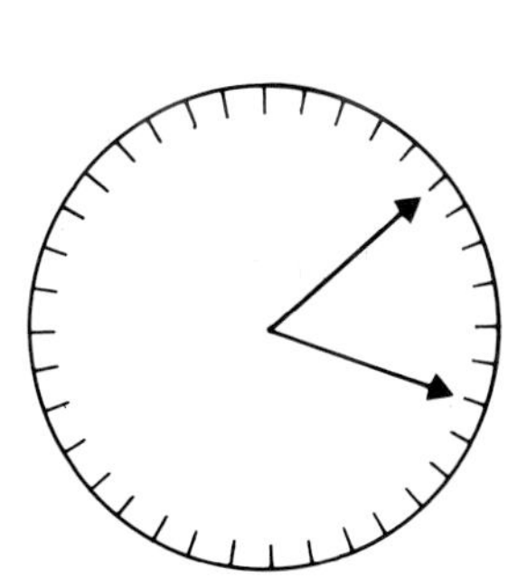

Make a large card circle marked out in 10°, with two pointers.

Put the children into two small teams. Ask a child from one team to state an angle, such as 50°. A child from the other team comes out and sets the angle to score a point. For a bonus point, another child could show the angle in a different position.

You may wish to limit the game to acute angles to begin with.

3 Measuring angles

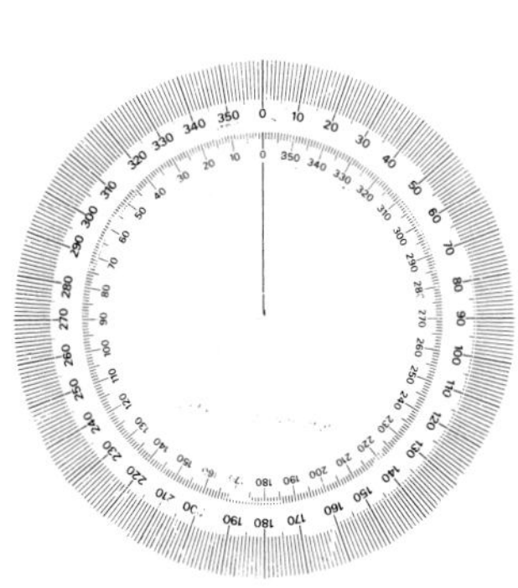

Discuss with the children how to measure angles using a protractor or angle measurer. A variety of protractors are available for school. A useful model is the SMP angle measurer but any simple one is suitable at this stage.

Children will require plenty of practice in both drawing and measuring angles to 10° with the protractor that you use.

A game to play

MATCH THE ANGLES

Make a set of cards showing angles and a set of cards stating angles.

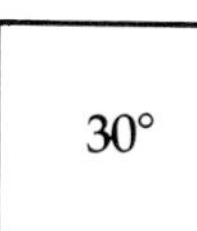

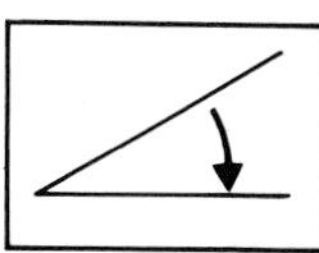

Shuffle and place all the cards face upwards. Ask a child to pick out matching pairs. Answers should be checked with a protractor. A point is awarded for a correct answer.

LINKS WITH THE ENVIRONMENT

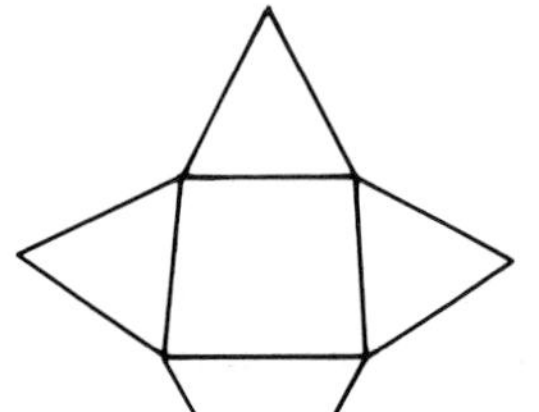

Talk about everyday situations where angles are found.

- Buildings. Look for angles in buildings. What angle do buildings normally make with the ground? What about the Leaning Tower of Pisa? Can the children find out the angle of 'lean'?
- Design and technology. What happens if the corners of the base of a pyramid are not at right angles?
  Make a model to show this.
- Notice the angles between the hands of a clock. For example 2 o'clock → 60° or 300°. Can the children measure and explain this?

NOTES ON INVESTIGATIONS

Section A

Do the children appreciate that a right angle is 90°? Do their two angles add up to 90°? Do they realise that they need to put four right angles together to make a colour spinner?

Section B

Do the children realise that the angles have to come together to make a straight angle or 180°? Do they carefully draw angles, in multiples of 10°, to make this happen?

Section C

Do the children realise that the angles at the centre of the circular selecta-drink dial must add up to 360°? Do they carefully draw another set of angles that add up to 360°? Do they realise that there are always 360° in a circle?

Purpose

- To construct 3D shapes using nets

Materials

Commercially produced packages and boxes, squared paper, stiff paper (or thin card), templates, solid shapes (prisms, pyramids, cubes, cuboids)

Vocabulary

Triangular prism, square prism, hexagonal prism, rectangular prism, octagonal prism, solid shapes, match, label, net, face, flaps, fold, base, template, triangular based pyramid, cube, edge, vertex, vertices, pentagon, equilateral triangle

TEACHING POINTS

1 Plane and solid shapes

Talk with the children about plane (2D) and solid (3D) shapes. Hold up a box and ask for its mathematical name (cuboid). Revise faces, vertices and edges of solids, asking children to describe or name the faces. Look for plane and solid shapes in the classroom.

Ask children to sort shapes in various ways and explain how they did it.

Other children can then try to sort them in other ways.

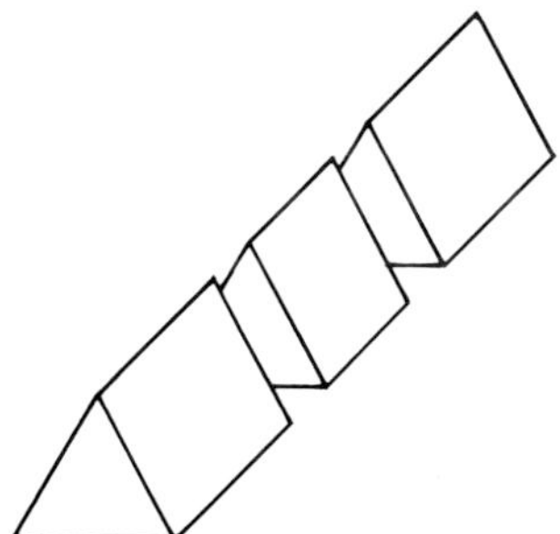

2 Prisms

Remind the children that a prism is a solid shape which is the same shape throughout its length and so has uniform cross-section.

Show the children different types of prisms and talk about their names. Explain to them that some prisms can have more than one name. For example, a cuboid can also be called a rectangular prism

3 Collecting shapes

Ask the children to collect packages and boxes. How many different solid shapes can they find? Can they name and describe them all?

Do they understand the terms vertices (singular: vertex), edges and faces?

The shapes and their properties could be displayed as mobiles or table displays.

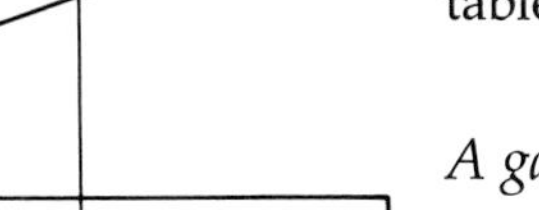

A game to play

MATCH THEM UP

Put the children into small groups. Give one group a selection of solid shapes. Make a card for each shape stating its number of vertices. Do the same for its faces and edges. At a given signal the children have to match the vertices, faces and edges cards to each solid shape. Stop them after a set time. One point is scored for every complete shape matched.

The turn then passes to the next group.

4 Nets

Talk with the children about how solid shapes can be made using nets. Explain that a net is a plane shape that can be folded to make a solid shape.

Demonstrate with an empty cardboard box such as a soap powder or cornflake box. Open it out so that children can see the net. Can they see how the flaps are used to stick it together? When they have looked at the flaps it may be an idea to cut them off so that they can see the basic net. Do the same with other boxes and packets.

Are the children able to predict and draw the nets before the boxes are opened out?

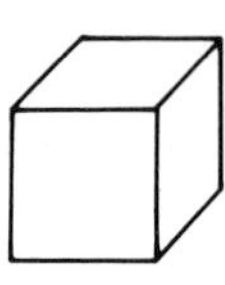

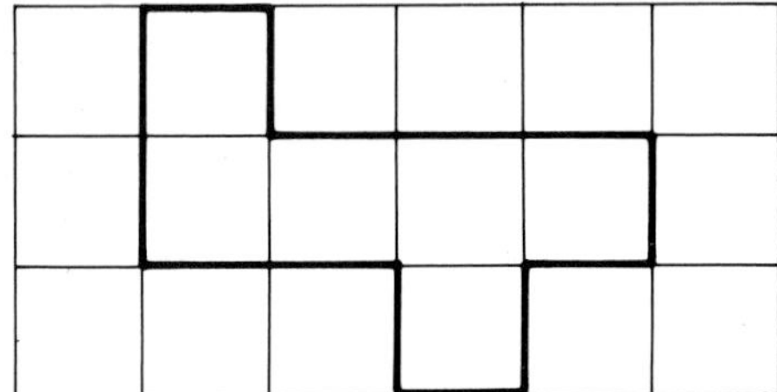

A game to play

FIND THE NETS

Put the children into small groups. Use a selection of cardboard boxes. Don't open them out but draw each of their nets on a piece of squared paper. The first group to match the nets to their boxes wins. Alternatively, each team could be timed.

The boxes should be unfolded at the end of the game to check that the children's predictions were correct.

5 Making a box

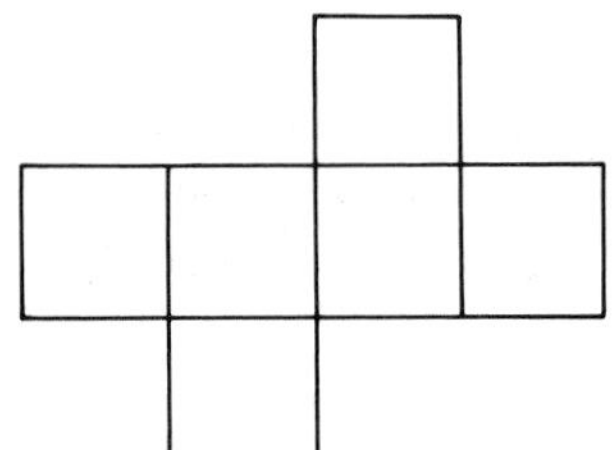

Ask the children to make a cube from a net like the one on the left. Talk about the importance of careful measuring and drawing when planning the net for any solid shape. Remind the children that they need to add flaps for sticking, unless they intend to use sticky tape. Discuss how to fold stiff paper: fold each seam against the edge of a ruler and then run a thumb or finger along the fold.

If possible, look at some decorated gift boxes or fancy chocolate boxes and talk about possible designs for their boxes – for example, a design that is suitable for a gift for a new baby.

6 Apparatus

If commercial apparatus is available in school ask the children to make some pyramids, prisms, cubes and cuboids.

7 A competition

At the end of the work on this chapter the children might hold a 'design a box' competition. They could choose the shape and purpose of their box.

8 Mental work

- Ask questions about properties of shapes. How many sides has a pentagon? How many vertices has a cuboid?
- Ask questions about the names of shapes. What do we call a plane shape with eight sides? What do we call a solid with six square faces?

LINKS WITH THE ENVIRONMENT

- Shopping – look at packaging in shops; open packages and boxes to discover the nets.
- Manufacturing industry – mass production of nets for boxes. Discuss designs to suit particular products, e.g. vacuum cleaners.
- Gifts – look at gift boxes of different shapes and designs. Can the children name them? They could try covering them with wrapping paper.
- Design and technology – design gift boxes or special purpose boxes, e.g. to hold a chocolate egg.

NOTES ON INVESTIGATIONS

Section A

Do the children understand what a prism is?
Do they look for a variety of prisms – not just the triangular prism which is often given as an example? Do they know all the names? Do they show that they realise that cubes and cuboids can also be called prisms? Do the children's lists for home and school differ? Do they find appropriate ways of recording their findings?

Section B

Do the children extend the sides of the regular pentagon to make a pentagram or five-pointed star? This gives a net for a pyramid. Alternatively, do they make the pentagram by joining the vertices of the pentagon?

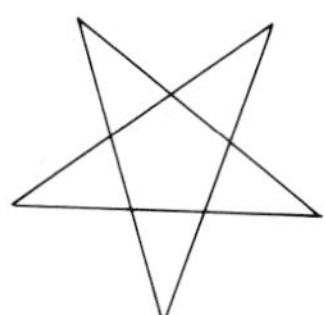

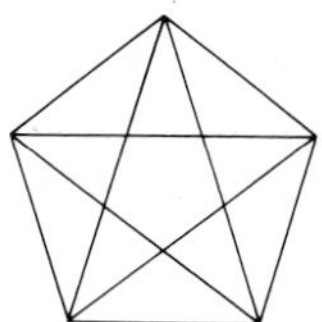

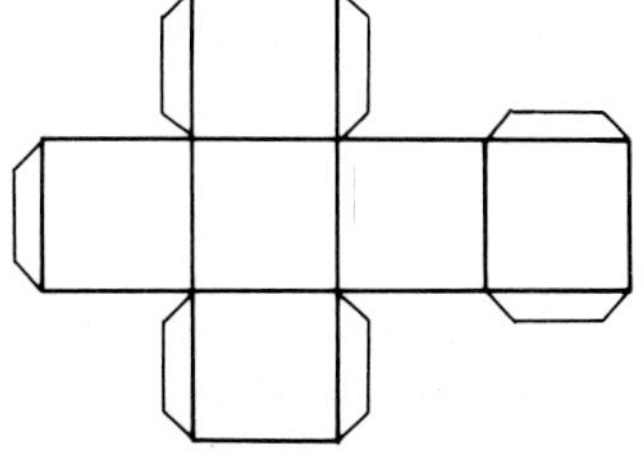

Section C

Do any children put flaps on all edges to make their shapes? Do they discover the technique of placing the flaps on alternate edges to construct the boxes?

Number 12

Purpose

- To revise division of HTU by one digit
- To use a wider range of metric units

Materials

Calendar, structural apparatus

Vocabulary

Days, weeks, quicker, slower, average, kilometre (km), divide exactly, dates, South Pole, return journey, distances, altogether, arrived, set off, leap year, expedition, travelling, calendar

TEACHING POINTS

1 Division patterns

Talk with the children about division and the different ways of recording it. These are some possible ways.

$10 \div 2 = 5 \qquad 2\overline{)10}^{\,5} \qquad \frac{10}{2} = 5$

Remind them that we can show division by grouping the numbers in 5s, 6s etc. Talk about these patterns and draw some of them or ask the children to make them using squared paper.

1	2	3	4	5
6	**7**	**8**	**9**	**10**
11	12	13	14	15
16	**17**	**18**	**19**	**20**
21	22	23	24	25
26	**27**	**28**	**29**	**30**
31	32	33	34	35
36	**37**	**38**	**39**	**40**
41	42	43	44	45
46	**47**	**48**	**49**	**50**

1	2	3	4	5	6
7	**8**	**9**	**10**	**11**	**12**
13	14	15	16	17	18
19	**20**	**21**	**22**	**23**	**24**
25	26	27	28	29	30
31	**32**	**33**	**34**	**35**	**36**
37	38	39	40	41	42
43	**44**	**45**	**46**	**47**	**48**
49	50	51	52	53	54
55	**56**	**57**	**58**	**59**	**60**

Make a display of the patterns and ask questions such as 'How many 6s are in 24?' Use the number patterns to ask the children to count in 5s, 6s, etc.

2 Link multiplication and division

Explain that multiplication and division are related. Write three numbers linked by multiplication and division (for example, 5, 6, 30). Ask the children to write multiplication and division bonds for them.

$5 \times 6 = 30 \qquad 30 \div 6 = 5 \qquad 6 \times 5 = 30 \qquad 30 \div 5 = 6$

Do this for other numbers.

Ask the children to use multiplication and division to check answers. For example, if $42 \div 7 = 6$ then $6 \times 7 = 42$.

3 Revise division of TU by one digit

Use structural apparatus to show what is happening.

4) 52

Use your usual words to explain that we are sharing the number between four equal groups. Talk about the method of recording this. This is one possible way, but the children may prefer to devise their own ways or algorithms.

$$\begin{array}{r} 13 \\ 4\overline{)\,5^{1}2} \end{array}$$

4 Revise division of HTU by one digit

Use structural apparatus for showing this to give the children imagery. Talk about the method of recording.

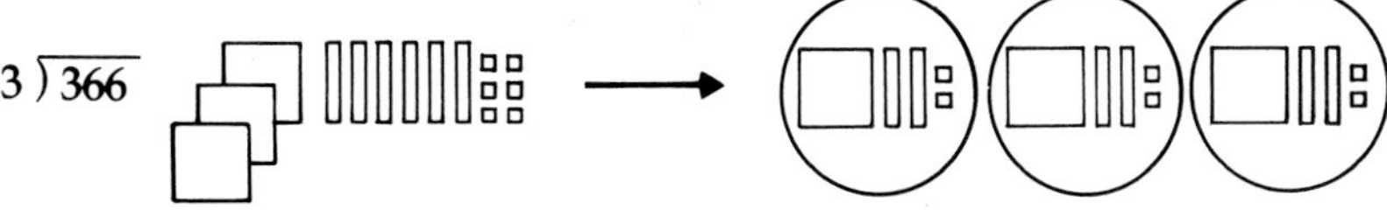

Structural apparatus can also be used to show division with exchanging.

3) 411

5 Division of metric units

Length

Ask the children how many cm there are in 1 m. Talk about division of length in meaningful situations. For example, 'I need to cut three equal lengths of string from a piece 78 cm long. How long is each piece?'
Talk about recording this. Two possible ways are:

78 cm ÷ 3 = or $3\overline{)78}$ cm

The children might find their own way of showing this.

Talk about how we record longer distances in kilometres. Explain that we record kilometres as km and that there are 1000 m in 1 km.

Give the children practice in division of m and km. Explain that they are done in the same way as HTU.
For example

155 m ÷ 5 = or $5\overline{)155}$ m

654 km ÷ 2 = or $2\overline{)654}$ km

Weight

Ask the children how many g there are in 1 kg. Talk about division of weight in meaningful situations. For example, if three identical tins weigh 675 g altogether, how heavy is one tin?

Talk about ways of recording division of weight of both g and kg. Two possible ways are

675 g ÷ 3 = $3\overline{)675}$ g 154 kg ÷ 2 = $2\overline{)154}$ kg

The children might find their own way of doing this.

Capacity

Ask the children how many ml are in 1 litre. Talk about division of capacity. For example, if two equal pots hold 524 ml altogether, how much will one pot hold?

Talk about ways of recording division of capacity, both ml and l. Two possible ways are:

524 ml ÷ 2 = $2\overline{)524}$ ml 352 l ÷ 2 = $2\overline{)352}$ l

The children might find their own way of doing this.

6 Time

Ask the children questions about time facts. For example
How many days are in 1 week? 1 year? 1 leap year?
How many weeks are in 1 fortnight?
How many months are in 1 year?

7 Revise calendars and seasons

Talk about the way we record time using calendars and diaries. Collect some calendars showing the months in the year and talk about the seasons spring, summer, autumn and winter. Which months make up each season?

Show or draw a calendar for any month and ask questions such as: How many Mondays are there? What day is the 23rd?

8 Revise the number of days in the months

Remind the children of the knuckle method for finding the number of days in a month.

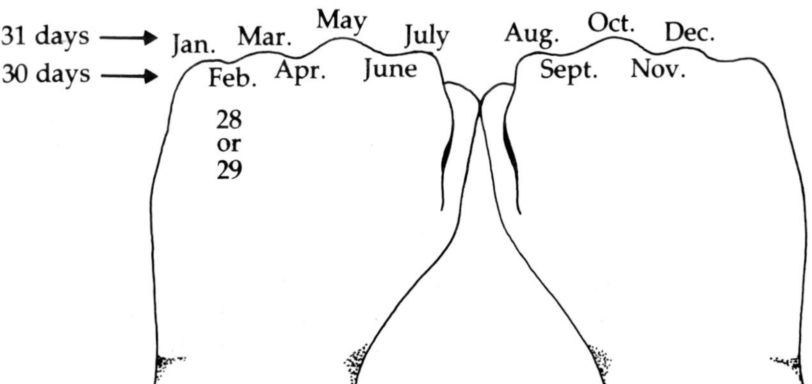

Ask them to use it to find the number of days in particular months.

The traditional rhyme is a good way of remembering how many days in each month.

> 30 days has September
> April, June and November.
> All the rest have 31
> Except February alone
> Which has 28 days clear
> And 29 in each leap year.

Talk about leap years and how they occur every 4 years because there are actually $365\frac{1}{4}$ days in a year so we add an extra day every 4 years. Explain that the year number of a leap year divides exactly by 4. Use a calculator to show that leap years are 1992, 1996, etc.

Talk about the customs of leap year. Mention that the Olympic Games are held every leap year. Does anybody have a birthday on February 29th? How is this celebrated in other years?

A game to play

HOW MANY DAYS?

This is a game for two teams or groups. Make a set of cards showing the months of the year. Shuffle the cards and place them face downwards in a pile. Ask a child from the first team to turn over the top card and write or say how many days are in that month. Set a time limit of 10 seconds to answer in order to score a point. The team with the most points after all the children have had a turn wins.

9 Mental work

Ask the children to work out the average of distances or scores, for example, cricket.

Give the children practice in using both multiplication and division bonds up to 10×10.

$48 \div 6 = \square \qquad 48 \div 8 = \square \qquad 6 \times 8 = \square$

$8 \times 6 = \square \qquad 48 \div \square = 8 \qquad \square \div 6 = 8$

Ask the children division problems involving metric units and time. For example, if a man travelled 100 km in 5 days how many km would he travel in 1 day? How many days are there between 3 January and 3 February? (See also sections 5 and 6 of these notes.)

USING THE CALCULATOR

Let the children practise division by one digit.

544 [÷] 4 [=]

Talk about what happens if the number does not divide exactly and there are numbers after the decimal point. Explain that this shows the answer is not a whole number.

A game to play

GUESS

This is a game for two players. One player enters a three-digit number into the calculator such as 534. The other player tries to guess a number which will divide exactly into it and the calculator is used to check the guess. One point is scored for each correct guess. The players then change over. The first player to score 10 points is the winner.

Ask the children to use the calculator to find whether 1992 or 1994 is a leap year, or to add the number of days in 3 consecutive months of the year.

LINKS WITH THE ENVIRONMENT

Talk about division situations involving large numbers in everyday life.

- At school, 144 children may be put in 6 house teams
- On school journeys, children often divide into smaller groups, each with a leader, or are allocated seats in 2s, 3s, 4s on buses and trains
- We estimate m.p.h. by noting distances travelled and dividing by the number of hours

NOTES ON INVESTIGATIONS

Section A

Do the children choose dates on the calendar which are a whole number of weeks apart, such as Monday 20th March and Monday 10th April? For dates not a whole number of weeks apart, do the children count the number of completed weeks between the date or do they round up or down to the nearest number of weeks? Do the answer cards match up with the questions?

Extension work might include asking such questions as 'Give me two dates with 3 weeks 4 days between them'.

Section B

Do the children find 60 km, 120 km and 180 km by trial and error? Do any of the children realise that the distances must be a multiple of each of the numbers 2, 3, 4, 5 and 6 (i.e. 60 km)? Do they use their table patterns or divisibility rules to find this? Do they find the first distance and then add on in 60s (i.e. 60 → 120 → 180)?

Section C

Do the children try different methods for doing this?

Do the children round 99 days upwards (i.e. 99 → 100) and divide 3500 km by 100, giving an answer of 35 km per day? When finding answers for 49 days and 69 days do they round up (i.e. 49 → 50 and 69 → 70) and divide 3500 km by these?

The different methods and approaches should be discussed with the children.

Data 4

Purpose

- To introduce grouping data and equal class intervals

Materials

Squared paper

Vocabulary

Scores, group together, results, graph, top score, lowest score, grouping, estimate, decide, frequency

TEACHING POINTS

1 A memory game

Talk with the children about collecting data or scores.

Play Kim's game with the children. Ideally it should be played in groups but as a class activity you could stand at the front with a tray of 18 objects. Hold each object up in turn and name it. Cover the objects and ask each child to write a list of all 18 objects (spelling does not count).

Make a table of scores.

Number of objects remembered	1	2	3	4	5	6	7	8	9	10	11	12	13	14	15	16	17	18
Number of children																		

Show the results as a bar chart.

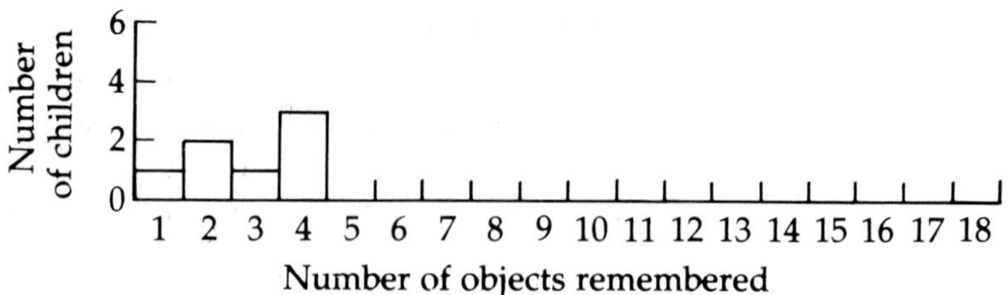

2 Grouping data with equal class intervals

Talk about the problems of recording each individual score, i.e. 1–18. What would be the problem if we had 30, 40, 50 objects? Can the children suggest another way of showing the scores to give a

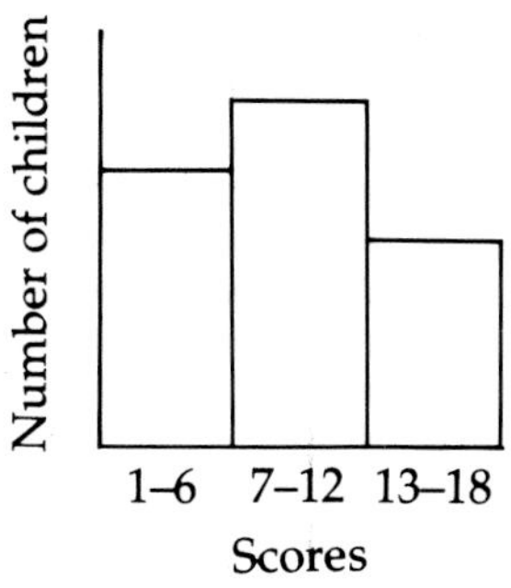

general idea of the pattern of the results? Talk about grouping the scores to show this.

How might we group 1–18? Talk about the possibility of classing the scores into three groups:

1–6 7–12 13–18

Draw a new bar chart for this.

What other intervals could the results be grouped in?

3 Looking at the graphs

Ask the children to look at the bar chart just drawn. Which group do most scores fall into? Can they suggest any reasons for this? Which graph gives a better idea of the pattern of results?

4 Practical work

Let the children work in groups to throw a die and collect and record the results in a table using the intervals 1–2, 3–4, 5–6.

Scores	Frequency
1–2	~~IIII~~ II
3–4	~~IIII~~ I
5–6	~~IIII~~ III

Ask them to draw a bar chart of their results. Remind them about labels on axes. Can the children interpret each other's graphs?

Give the children the opportunity to do similar activities to those given in the pupils' chapter and discuss how to record and group the results. For example, quizzes or spelling tests, etc.

5 Mental work

- Grouping scores. Ask the children to group the scores 1–12 into three equal class intervals (1–4, 5–8, 9–12). Can they group them into four equal class intervals?
- Scores. Give practice in adding scores quickly. For example,

$18 + 17 = 10 + 10 + 8 + 7$

USING THE CALCULATOR Use the calculator to discover ways of grouping larger numbers. For example, 60 into 2s, 3s, . . . , 30s.

A game to play

GROUPING

Children play in pairs. Suggest a number of objects for example, 240. Which pair of children can find the most ways of grouping them into equal class intervals in a given time?

LINKS WITH THE ENVIRONMENT

Talk about everyday situations where results or scores can be grouped equally.

- Sport – recording scores, using equal class intervals
- School – grouping scores to show patterns of achievement
- Newspapers showing statistics – for example, grouped data in opinion polls

NOTES ON INVESTIGATIONS

Section A

Do the children find a variety of ways of grouping 40 into equal class intervals? For example, 1–2, 3–4, etc.; 1–4, 5–8, etc.; 1–5, 6–10, etc.

Extension work might include exploring other numbers for possible groupings.

Section B

Do the children choose a suitable game or activity to give a spread of scores? Could a graph be drawn from the data? When estimating the possible scores, do they choose ones that give a suitable range for both the activity and the grouping?

Section C

Do the children understand that the number of goals must add up to 100? Do they devise a system for working out the answer? Do they work out possible scores for the 5–8 and 9–12 groups first? For example,

let the scores in the 5–8 group be $5 + 6 + 7 = 18$

let the scores in the 9–12 group be $9 + 10 + 11 + 12 = \underline{42}$

Total 60

Then the remaining scores must total 40

That is $4 + 16 + 20 = 40$

Other answers are possible using this system.

Purpose

- To introduce the area of squares, rectangles using length and width ($A = L \times W$)
- To revise perimeters of shapes

Materials

Squared paper, rulers, scissors, glue, plain paper, newspapers containing advertisements

Vocabulary

Area, advertisement, length, width, larger, largest, cost, expensive, cheapest, cm^2, rectangular, measure, perimeter, different shapes, square, smaller rectangle, plan, exactly

TEACHING POINTS

1 Recording area

Remind the children that area is the amount of surface covered by a shape. Draw a rectangular shape and ask them to find its area by counting the squares. Remind them that the standard unit for measuring area is the square centimetre, written as cm^2.

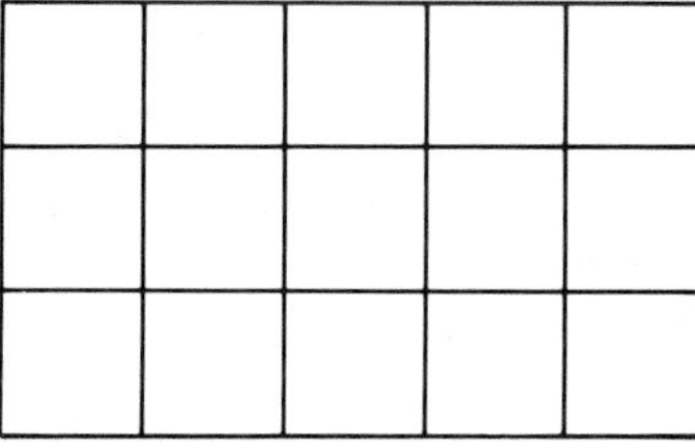

Area = □ cm^2

This shape has an area of 15 cm^2.

2 Area of rectangular shapes

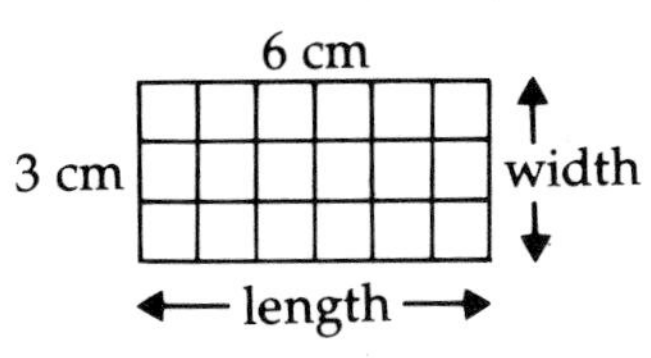

Draw a rectangular shape. Show on it the measurements and squares. Talk with the children about which is the length and width of the rectangle. Ask how many squares there are in the rectangle. Can the children think of a quick way of finding the area? What is the area? Would their method work for any rectangular shape?

Talk about recording the area:

Area = 18 cm^2

This can be repeated with other rectangular shapes.

(The children are asked to find the relationship for the area of a rectangle (Area = Length × Width) in the pupils' book.)

Games to play

DRAW A RECTANGLE

This can be played in two teams. Make a set of area cards, for example, 12 cm^2, 18 cm^2, 24 cm^2. Shuffle the cards and turn one face upwards. A child from one team has to draw a rectangle with this area on squared paper. A child from the other team tries to draw a different rectangle with the same area. One point is scored for each correct rectangle drawn. The turn passes to the first team again and so on. When both teams cannot find any more rectangles with that area another card is turned over and play continues as before. The winning team is the team with the most points.

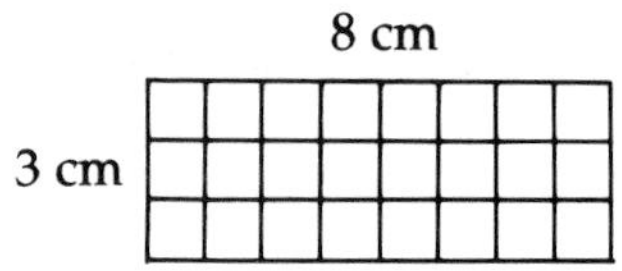

RECTANGLE AND SQUARES

8 cm

3 cm

This can be played in pairs or in two teams. Make a set of 24 area cards like these (i.e. six of each card): 2 cm^2, 3 cm^2, 4 cm^2, 5 cm^2. Draw a 3 cm × 8 cm squared paper grid.

Shuffle the cards and place them face downwards. A child from the first team (team A) turns over a card and draws a rectangle or square with this area anywhere on the squared paper grid and marks the shape with the team letter. A child from team B turns over the next area card and tries to draw a rectangle or square on the grid, marking it B. Play continues in this way with players scoring a point for each correct rectangle or square drawn. If a player is unable to draw a rectangle or square, play passes to the other team. The winner is the team with the most points when no more rectangles or squares can be drawn.

The game can be modified by changing the size or shape of the squared paper grid.

3 Revise perimeters

Remind the children that a perimeter is the distance round the edge or boundary of a shape.

Draw or find some shapes in the school yard or playground. Ask the children to walk round the perimeter. This could be measured using tapes or trundle wheels and the perimeter found to the nearest metre.

Ask the children to measure the perimeter of smaller things such as books, crayon boxes, etc. using their rulers. Measure to the nearest centimetre. Talk about which is the best unit to use in each case, centimetres or metres, and why. Draw some shapes on the board and write their measurements. Ask the children to work out the perimeters.

Ask them to draw some shapes on squared paper and find their perimeters.

4 Linking area and perimeter

Ask the children to draw shapes on squared paper with equal areas but different perimeters. (Geo-boards could also be used.)

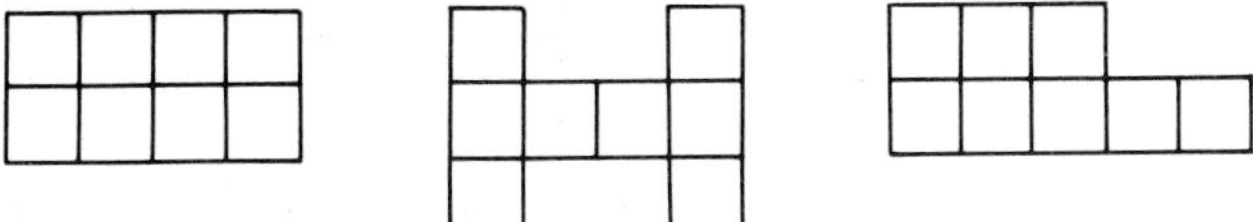

These shapes are equal in area but have different perimeters.

Ask the children to draw shapes with equal perimeters but different areas. For example,

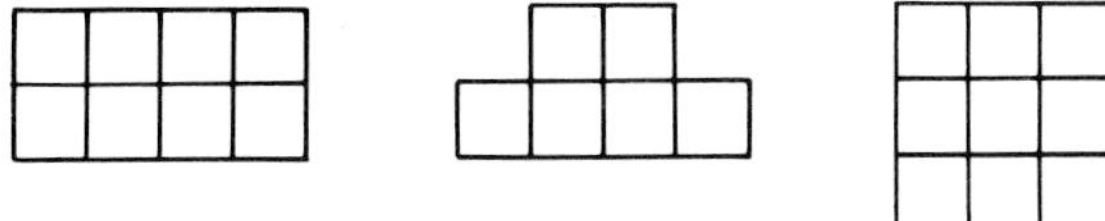

This may help children to distinguish between the two concepts of area and perimeter.

5 Perimeters of regular shapes

Ask the children to draw round some templates of regular shapes and to find their perimeters. Talk about how this might be done for shapes such as the hexagon – either add up the six sides or measure one side and multiply it by six. This gives a good link between addition and multiplication.

6 Mental work

Ask the children questions about the perimeter of some of the regular shapes such as: 'What is the perimeter of a square whose side is 3 cm? If the perimeter of a square is 16 cm, what is the length of a side?'

Can the children think of quick ways of finding perimeters?

- Quick addition – look for easy number bonds first
  (3 cm + 7 cm) + (3 cm + 7 cm) → 10 cm + 10 cm
- Links between addition and multiplication
  8 cm + 8 cm + 8 cm + 8 cm = 4 × 8 cm
- Doubling numbers
  4 cm + 6 cm + 4 cm + 6 cm (2 × 4 cm) + (2 × 6 cm)

LINKS WITH THE ENVIRONMENT

Talk with the children about everyday situations where we might meet areas in square centimetres.

- Graph paper, mosaic pictures and patterns
- The area of book covers or pages – How much of the page area does a picture cover?

- Newspapers and magazines – How much area do different advertisements take up? The cost is usually related to the area. What area of particular pages are taken up by advertisements, cartoons, pictures or articles? An interesting development might be to investigate the cost of commercial advertisements in a local paper.

NOTES ON INVESTIGATIONS

Section A

Do the children draw different rectangular advertisements and record the measurements accurately in a table? Do they realise that the area of any rectangle is Length × Width ($A = L \times W$)?

Section B

Do the children find many different squares or rectangles with an area of 4 cm that will fit the 6 cm × 4 cm grid?

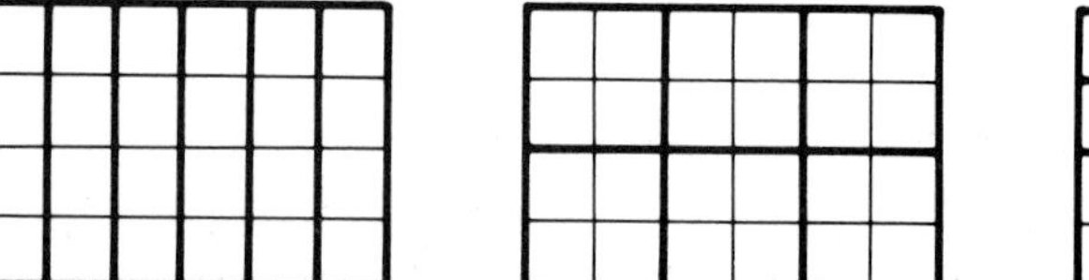

An extension would be to do the same for a rectangle with a larger area.

Section C

Do the children appreciate that for a shape to be a square the areas must be in the pattern of square numbers?

$$1\ \text{cm}^2,\quad 4\ \text{cm}^2,\quad 9\ \text{cm}^2,\quad 16\ \text{cm}^2,\quad 25\ \text{cm}^2,\quad 36\ \text{cm}^2, \ldots$$

Do they draw a rectangle for some of the above areas?

When finding squares and rectangles with the same perimeter, do they realise that the perimeters must be in the pattern

$$4\ \text{cm},\quad 8\ \text{cm},\quad 12\ \text{cm},\quad 16\ \text{cm},\quad 20\ \text{cm}, \ldots$$

in order to make squares? Do they find that when comparing a square and rectangle with the same perimeter the square always has the larger area?

Data 5

Purpose

- To construct and interpret straight line graphs

Materials

Squared paper, phone card (for children to see), road maps from Edinburgh to Oxford

Vocabulary

Data, graph, hours, miles, minutes, first, table, record, time in hours, during, last hour, units on phonecard, cost in pence, line graph, between these times, set off, arrived, how far, how long, further, route, mileage

TEACHING POINTS

1 Data collection

Talk with the children about data and how we can collect it in school. This is usually by putting hands up, individual questioning or survey, or observing and recording as in conducting a traffic survey. Ask the children how they could collect and record data about the way a class of children come to school. Here are three possible data collection sheets. Talk about which is easier to read and why.

	Tally (or frequency)	Total
Car	卌 卌 /	
Walk	卌 卌 卌 //	
Bus	//	

	Frequency	Total
Car	xxxxxx	
Walk	xxxxxxxx xxxxxxxxx	
Bus	xx	

	Frequency	Total
Car	|||||||||||	
Walk	|||||||||||||||||	
Bus	||	

Let them design a data collection sheet for a class survey.

2 Graphs

Talk about the different types of graphs the children have already used and how we interpret them.

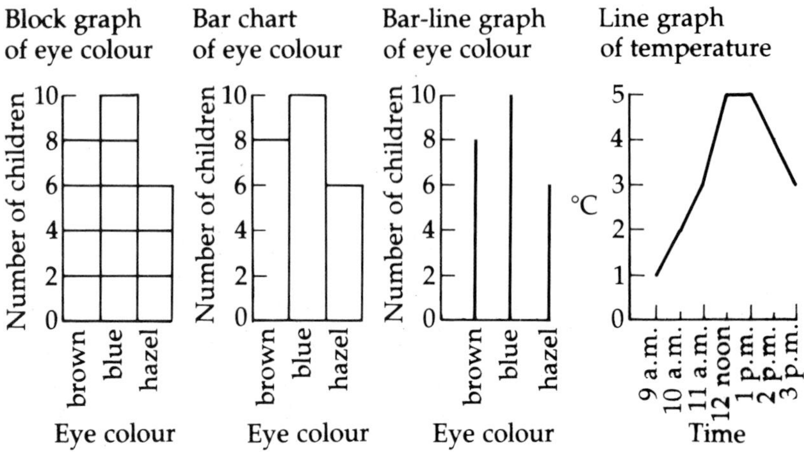

3 Straight line graphs

Ask the children to count in 2s. Draw the table of 2s as a bar line graph. Talk about whether joining the tops of the lines has meaning. Draw the table of 2s as a straight line graph.

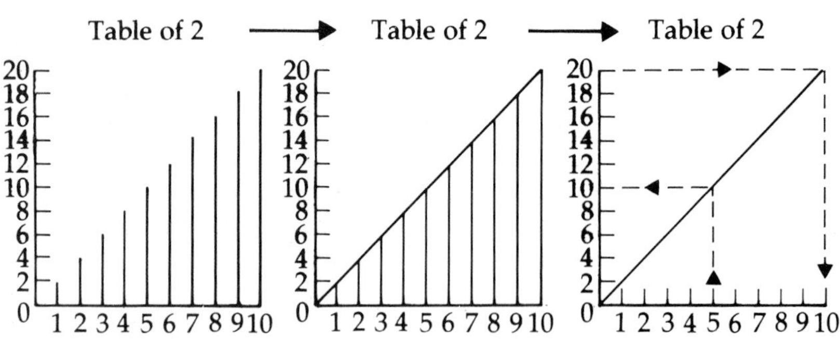

Ask the children questions to answer from the graph such as:

'What is 5×2? Show me 7×2 on the graph.'

Division questions can also be asked, for example,

'How many 2s are there in 18?'

The children might be interested to use the graph to find $3\frac{1}{2} \times 2$ and how many 2s there are in 7.

Other tables can be drawn as straight line graphs and children can be asked to interpret them.

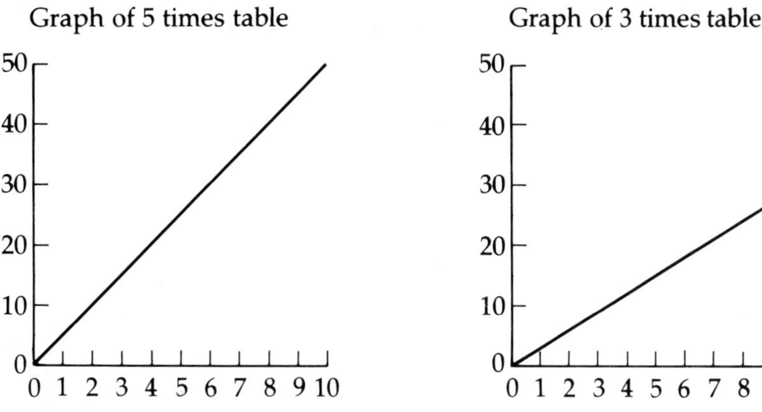

4 Conversion tables

Talk about how straight line graphs can be used to convert currency, for example, pounds to dollars. Draw a partly completed table showing conversion of £ and $. Suppose that £1 is worth $2 (in everyday life, this varies of course). Can the children complete the table?

£	1	2	3	4	5	6	7	8
$	2	4						

5 Conversion graph

Draw two axes and label them. Ask a child to draw the bar-line graph using the conversion table for £ and $. Talk with the children about whether it would be meaningful to join the tops of the bar-lines to produce a straight line graph. Then show how the data can be drawn as a straight line graph.

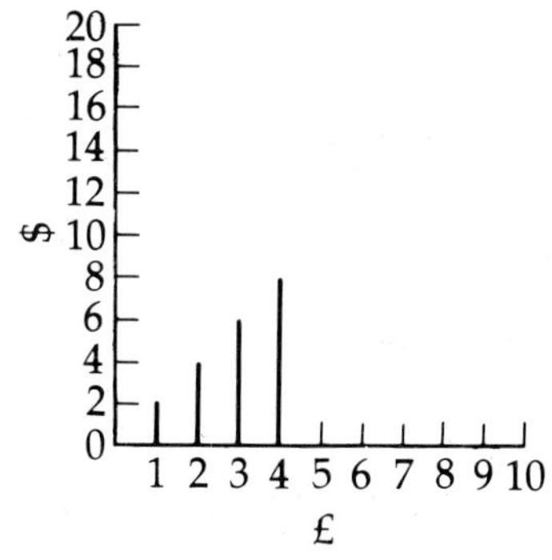

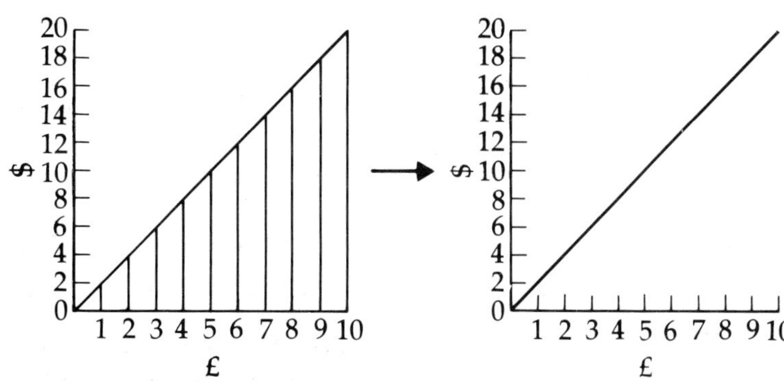

Ask the children questions about the graph such as:

'How many dollars is £4 worth?'
'How many pounds is $10 worth?'

A game to play

LABELS

1 2 3 4 5 6 7 8 9 10
Children

Draw a straight line graph on the board with the axes marked but only one axis labelled. Split the children into two small teams or groups. Each team alternately has to give a label for the other axis and explain what the graph shows. For example, a child might say, 'The vertical axis is £ and the graph is for savings. One child saves £1. Two children save £2.' etc.

One point is scored for each acceptable answer. The teacher or children act as judges. After two answers for each team the graph is changed in some way, as shown on the left, for example.

Graphs can be drawn about such things as eyes, shoes, number of fingers, pocket money, cost of tickets, etc. The winning team is the one with the most correct answers after three different graphs have been shown.

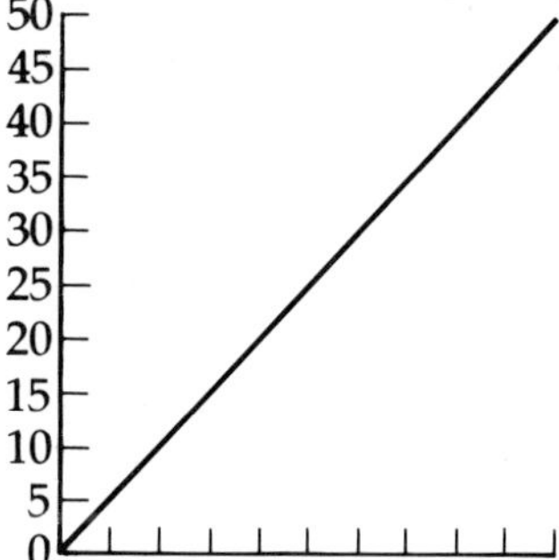

6 Constant speed

Talk about when vehicles might travel at a constant speed: for example, cars on a motorway, express train, aeroplanes.

Ask the children to complete a table for a cyclist travelling at 10 km an hour. (Miles or kilometres can be used at the teacher's discretion.)

hours	1	2	3	4	5	6	7	8
km	10	20	20	30				

Draw the axes for the graph. Ask the children to write the labels, number it correctly and draw the graph. Talk about the graphs which can be drawn. Can the children interpret them? Do they both show the same data?

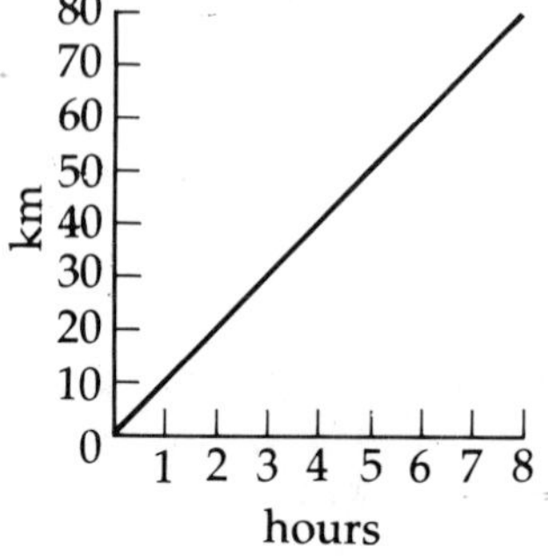

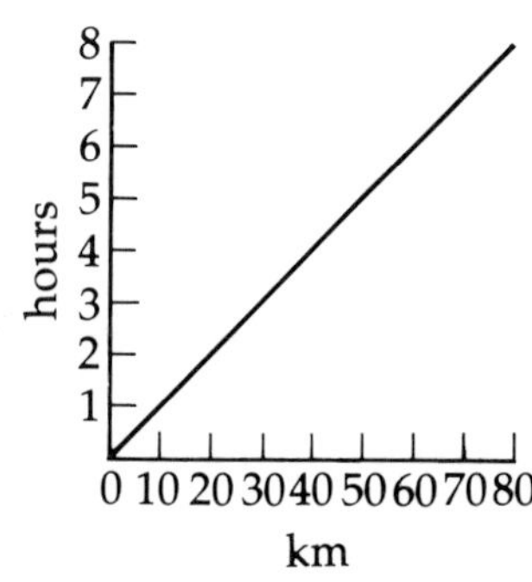

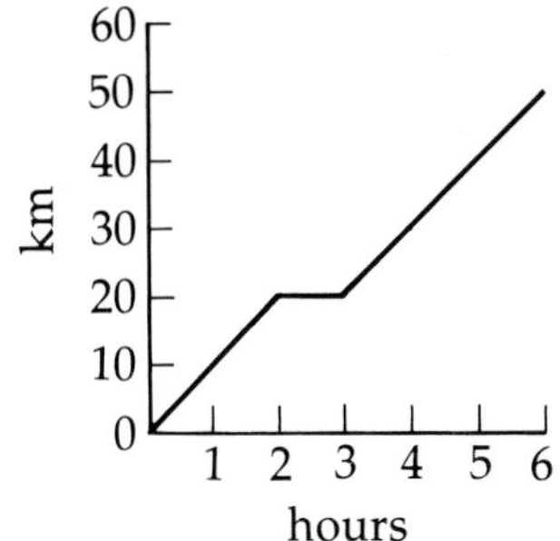

7 Variable speed

Talk with the children about situations where a cyclist may stop for an hour's rest. What happens to the table and graph?

hours	1	2	3	4	5	6
km	10	20	20	30	40	50

8 Mental work

Ask the children questions which could be drawn as a conversion graph. For example,

'If £1 is worth $2, how many dollars are worth £5?'

Ask questions which involve number patterns. For example,

'How many sides are there in 1, 2, 3, 4, 5, 6 squares?

How many sides are there in 1, 2, 3, . . . , 7 hexagons?

If there are 30 children in each class, how many children are there in 5 classes?' (30, 60, 90, 120, 150)

USING THE CALCULATOR Ask the children to use the constant function on the calculator to count in 2s, 5s, 10s etc. These number patterns can then be drawn as straight line graphs.

LINKS WITH THE ENVIRONMENT Talk about everyday situations involving straight line graphs and collect data from newspapers and magazines showing these. For example, look at conversion graphs such as money (£ and $), petrol (litres/gallons), and distance–time graphs.

NOTES ON INVESTIGATIONS

Section A

Do the children realise that when the car is stopped the mileage does not increase? Do the children make realistic mileages between stops such as 1 or 2 hours?

Section B

Do the children give sensible reasons for travelling 10 miles in 60 minutes, such as heavy traffic or a wheel change? Does the graph have correct numbering on the axes? Does the graph show that 10 miles took 60 minutes? Were the children's graphs straight line graphs or did they show changes in speed? For example,

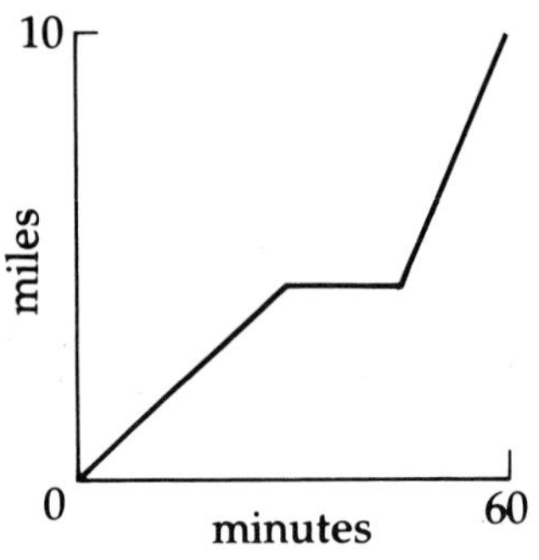

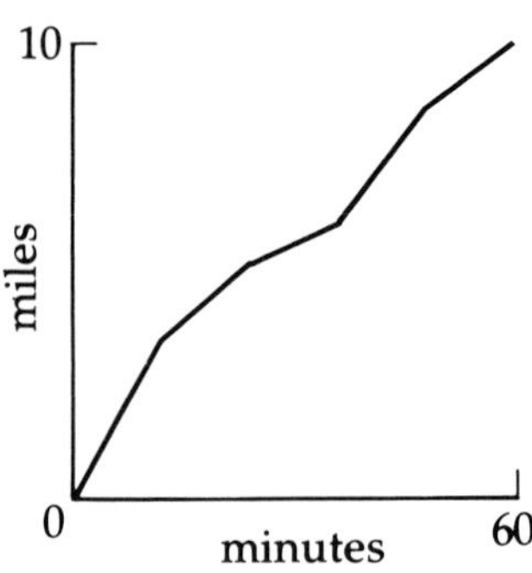

Section C

Do the children's graphs show the two people starting and finishing together? Do they label axes and choose a reasonable length of time for the journey? Do the graphs show the distance of 200 miles for the journey?

Do any of the children's graphs intersect? Can they explain this?

Do the children consider the current speed limit for cars?

Purpose

- To introduce the tonne

Materials

Bathroom scales, reference books on animal weights

Vocabulary

Weights, the names of the dinosaurs mentioned in the pupils' book, kilograms or kg, tonne, heavier, round to the nearest tonne, approximately, balance, order, lightest, difference between, how many times heavier, explain, record your answer, graph, taxi, estimate, simple, basic weight, fat weight, bar chart, compare, findings

TEACHING POINTS

1 The tonne

Talk with the children about objects that are weighed in grams or kilograms and remind them that 1000 g = 1 kg.

Can the children suggest things, such as a lorry, that are very heavy and would weigh a large number of kilograms? Introduce them to the tonne, 1000 kg = 1 tonne. (Take care to make the point that this is the metric unit and not the imperial ton which many children may have heard of.)

2 Kilograms and tonnes

Talk about how to write kg as tonnes, i.e. 1400 kg = 1·400 tonnes. Give the children plenty of practice in converting kg to tonnes and vice versa.

A game to play

MATCH ME

This game is for two teams or groups. Hold up a weight card such as 2468 kg. One player from each team writes it in tonnes (2·468 tonnes). The first player to do so correctly scores a point for their team. The turn then passes to the second pair of players.

3 Understanding the tonne

Can the children suggest things that could be weighed in tonnes? Talk about how the average family car weighs approximately 1 tonne. Some cars will weigh a little under this – can children say which these might be? It might interest the children to collect some car brochures in order to compare the weights of different cars.

Talk about the weight of aeroplanes. What things account for the weight of a plane at take-off? The plane itself, the passengers, luggage, fuel, etc. The maximum taxi weight of a Boeing 757 is mentioned in the pupils' book. The children may be interested to know that the plane is heaviest as it begins to taxi down the runway for take-off. By the time it lifts into the air it is already lighter (having used fuel):

Maximum taxi weight is 100 000 kg or 100 tonnes
Maximum take-off weight is 99 700 kg or 99·700 tonnes

It might also be interesting for the children to try to find out how large objects like planes are weighed, and why.

4 Discussing weight

Talk with the children about how they would find which dinosaur weighed more. What do we mean by 'times heavier'? What do we mean by 'balance'? Discuss ways of recording this.

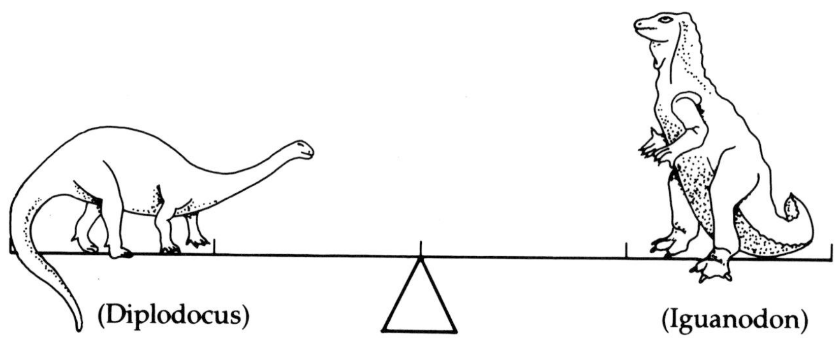

5 Rounding

Remind the children that rounding up or down can give approximate answers which can be helpful. Talk about rounding to the nearest tonne. For example,

2·260 tonnes → 2 tonnes   1·500 tonnes → 2 tonnes

Give the children practice in this.

6 Dinosaur weights

Talk about the weights of the heaviest dinosaurs and how they compare with heavy animals alive today such as the elephant and the whale. Do the children appreciate that the weights of dinosaurs are estimates based on the size of dinosaur skeletons so information in different reference books may vary?

7 Mental work

- Give practice in changing kg to tonnes and vice versa
- Round to the nearest tonne. For example, 2·750 tonnes → 3 tonnes
- Find how many times heavier one weight is than another

USING THE CALCULATOR

- Display kg as tonnes. For example, 4567 (kg) → 4·567 (tonnes)
- Give the children practice in adding, subtracting, multiplying and dividing tonnes

A game to play

MAKE IT HEAVIER

Put the children into two teams. Make a number of cards: 2 times heavier, 3 times heavier, 4 times heavier, 5 times heavier. Shuffle the cards and place them face down on the table. Give one player from each team a weight to display on their calculator, e.g. 2·366 tonnes. Ask a child to take the top card and hold it up, e.g. 3 times heavier. The first player to work it out on the calculator and write the answer in tonnes (and also, perhaps give a rounded weight) scores a point.

LINKS WITH THE ENVIRONMENT

Talk about situations where we might use tonnes.

- Animals – do any animals weigh more than a tonne?
- Transport – weight of cars, trains, lorries, ships, buses, planes
- Take-off weights of planes
- Methods of weighing heavy objects – for example, weigh bridges
- Design and technology – design a machine to weigh a whale

NOTES ON INVESTIGATIONS

Section A

Do the children make sensible estimates of things they see that might weigh more than 1 tonne? Do they, for example, take a family car as their reference for a 1 tonne weight and compare other objects to it?

Section B

Do the children consider a variety of possibilities and consider their accuracy? Do they for example take their own weight and use a calculator to divide their weight into 1 tonne? Do they enter 1000 kg on the calculator and see how many times they need to subtract their weight (using the constant function)? Do they make any attempt to decide upon an average weight for their age?

Section C

Do the children use reference books sensibly to find the weights of heavy animals alive today? Do they include the whale and the elephant? Do they use charts and graphs to display their findings?

Purpose

- To give practice in reading and interpreting data from charts
- To give practice in solving problems involving the costing of holidays

Materials

Calculators, travel brochures

Vocabulary

Total cost, reductions, difference between, cheapest, most expensive, chart, per child, adult, travel, departure

TEACHING POINTS

1 Holiday brochures

Talk about holiday brochures and let the children look at some, particularly at the price of holidays and the charts which show them.

Talk about how charts can contain a lot of information in quite a small space and how they can show seasonal prices, different hotels and different ways of travel. Why does it cost more to travel at certain times of the year and why is this called high or peak season?

Talk about vocabulary associated with travel: for example, departure, hotel, cost per (person, child, adult), rail, air, coach, hovercraft, ferry, bed and breakfast, travel, four-star hotel, reduction, travel brochure, 3, 5, 7 nights. Can the children find references to any of these in their brochures?

2 Reading charts

Make two simple charts for display. For example,

Hotel	Sunset	Bay	Grand
1 night	£20	£30	£40
3 nights	£50	£70	£100
5 nights	£80	£120	£160

	By coach		By rail	
Hotel	5 days	7 days	5 days	7 days
Bay	£140	£170	£150	£180
Grand	£180	£240	£190	£250

Talk about how to find information in the charts and ask questions to give the children practice in reading them.

3 Problem solving

Talk about how to use the charts to work out the cost of holidays for one or more than one person. Ask questions such as the cost for two people for 3 nights at the Sunset hotel. Can the children suggest a way to work this out? Would they use addition or multiplication for 3 nights?

A game to play

TRAVEL AGENTS

Make a basic holiday cost chart. Let two children be travel agents. The other children take it in turn to book a holiday for a number of friends at a hotel of their choice. They will need paper to work this out and a calculator may be helpful for the customers to check that they are being told the correct prices.

An extension of this game would be to give the children varying amounts of money to spend which they must not exceed. The more competent children become at reading brochures, it might be fun and more realistic to introduce commercial brochures, although they might need to be edited to keep them at a simple level. A calculator will be helpful here too.

4 Mental work

- Give the children practice in adding pounds, making the point that the process is the same as adding ThHTU or HTU
- Let them find the difference in prices of holidays
- Make the link between multiplication and addition:

$21 + 21 + 21 = 63$
$3 \times 21 = 63$

USING THE CALCULATOR

- Give the children practice in adding money
- Give them practice in finding the difference between total amounts of money
- Use the constant function to work out bills, for example, the cost for 5 people at £96 each

A game to play

MAKE THE AMOUNT

Write three amounts and three signs on the board, for example,

£3 £10 £4 + − ×

Children work in pairs. One child uses the three numbers and two of the signs to do a calculation, for example,

10 [×] 3 [+] 4 [=] 34 (£34)

The answer is shown to the second child who has to work out which keys were pressed to arrive at that answer.

LINKS WITH THE ENVIRONMENT

Talk about everyday situations where we use money and read charts.

- Holidays – talk about costs and travel brochures
- Travel and fares – work out costs of journeys by bus or by rail
- Sport – read sports charts and tables
- Costing school trips and outings
- Costing sets of books for class use

NOTES ON INVESTIGATIONS

Section A

Do the children realise that the cost per person must be less than £250? Do they look in the chart for appropriate amounts per person? Do they consider the cost of holidays at different hotels, the number of nights and the type of travel?

Section B

Do the children make an appropriate holiday booking form and fill it in correctly? Do they plan a holiday for a family? Is the total cost correct?

Section C

Do the children show an understanding of where an 'exotic place' might be? Do they show an understanding of what 'very expensive' might be? Do they refer to brochures to get an idea of what normal prices are like? Do they work out the cost correctly for two people?

Probability 2

Purpose

- To give practice in listing possible outcomes of events

Materials

Dice, coloured counters, yogurt pots, squared paper

Vocabulary

Total, possible, chess tournament, number pattern, win, lose, draw, probability, die, dice

TEACHING POINTS

1 Different ways

Talk with the children about how there can be different outcomes or results of events.

Talk about a skittleball match. What might the result be? The team can win, lose or draw.

Talk about spinning a coin. We can spin a head or a tail.

2 Throwing dice

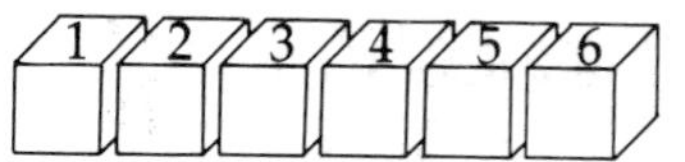

Ask the children how many possible outcomes there can be when throwing a die. Ask them to write them down.

3 Coin spinning

Talk with the children about the possible outcomes of spinning two coins. Discuss how these might be recorded. For example,

1st coin	2nd coin
H	H
H	T
T	H
T	T

```
  H       T
 / \     / \
H   T   H   T
```

(H) (H)
(H) (T)
(T) (H)
(T) (T)

There are four possible outcomes. Talk with the children about HT being a different outcome from TH.

4 Teams

Talk with the children about the possible outcomes of two games played by a school team. Can they think of a way to record the possibilities? For example,

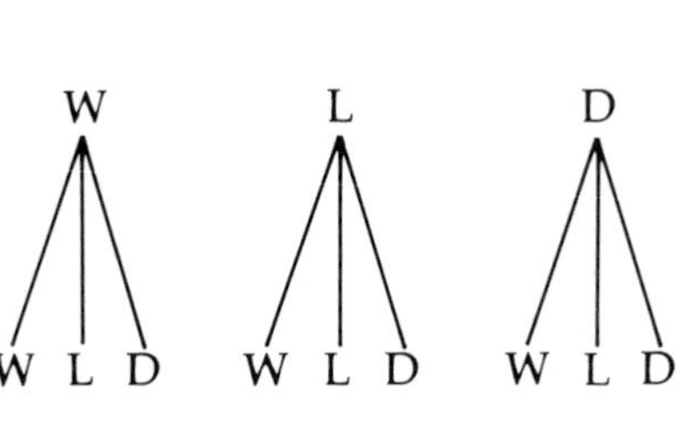

1st game	2nd game
W	W
W	L
W	D
D	W
D	L
D	D
L	W
L	L
L	D

A game to play

COIN AND DIE

Two groups are each given a coin and a die. The winning group is the first to list all possible (12) outcomes.

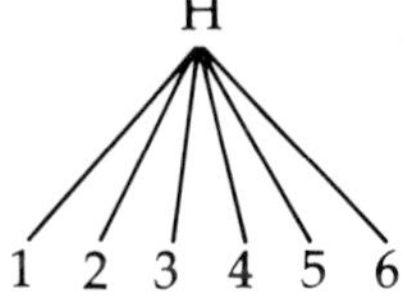

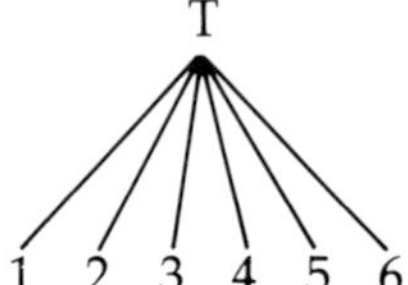

5 Possible scores

Make three counters, each numbered 1 and 2 on either side. Ask how many different scores are possible if all three are tossed? (Four, i.e. 3, 4, 5, 6). Ask the children to think of ways of showing the scores. For example,

1st	2nd	3rd	Total
(1)	(1)	(1)	3
(1)	(1)	(2)	4
(1)	(2)	(1)	4
(1)	(2)	(2)	5
(2)	(1)	(1)	4
(2)	(1)	(2)	5
(2)	(2)	(1)	5
(2)	(2)	(2)	6

(1) (2)

(1) (2) (1) (2)

(1) (2) (1) (2) (1) (2) (1) (2)

3 4 4 5 4 5 5 6

score

Score			
3	(1)	(1)	(1)
4	(1)	(1)	(2)
	(1)	(2)	(1)
	(2)	(1)	(1)
5	(1)	(2)	(2)
	(2)	(1)	(2)
	(2)	(2)	(1)
6	(2)	(2)	(2)

LINKS WITH THE ENVIRONMENT

Talk about everyday situations where outcomes of events are important.

- Sports matches and the possible outcomes
- Games – dice throwing and the possible scores

NOTES ON INVESTIGATIONS

Section A

Do the children approach the investigation in a logical manner?

Do they devise an appropriate way of showing the possible scores?

Do they cover all possibilities?

1st pot	2nd pot	Score
1	1	2
1	2	3
1	3	4
2	1	3
2	2	4
2	3	5
3	1	4
3	2	5
3	3	6

1 2 3

1 2 3 1 2 3 1 2 3

2 3 4 3 4 5 4 5 6

score

Score	1st pot	2nd pot
2	1	1
3	1	2
	2	1
4	1	3
	3	1
	2	2
5	2	3
	3	2
6	3	3

Section B

Do the children adopt a system for working out the number of matches?

For example, do they consider 2 players first, then 3, then 4, etc.?

Do they use charts or diagrams to show the results? For example,

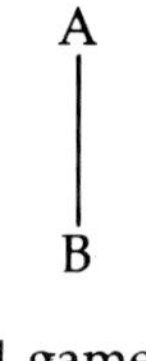

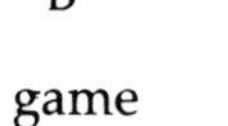
1 game

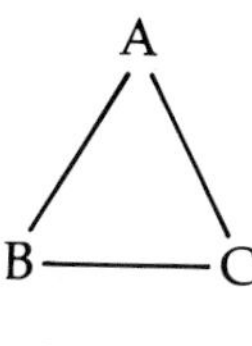

3 games

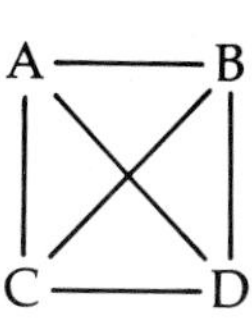

6 games

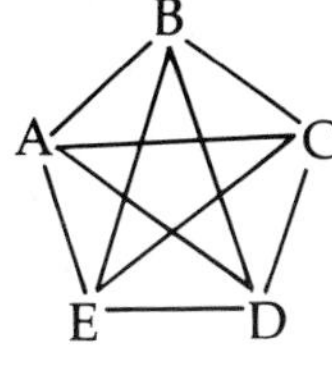

10 games

2 players	3 players
A plays B	A plays B
	A plays C
	B plays C

Do they see the pattern

1 (+2) 3 (+3) 6 (+4) 10 (+5) 15 . . .

and predict the next number of games?

Section C

Do the children allow for each team to win, lose or draw? Do they draw a suitable diagram?

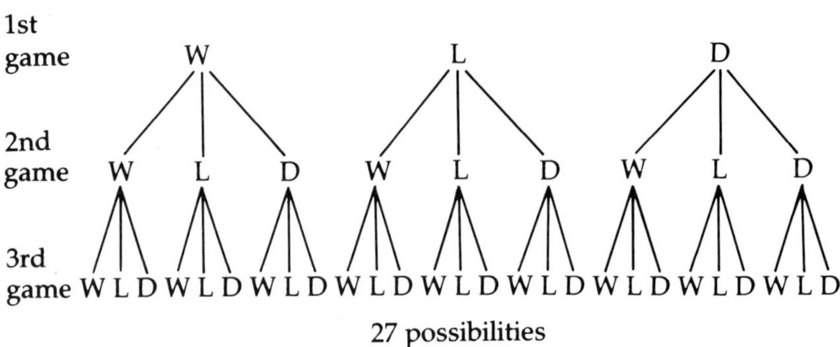

Purpose

- To construct tessellating shapes

Materials

Templates (square, rhombus, rectangle, parallelogram), scissors, card

Vocabulary

Shape, square, template, tessellate, patterns, designs, rhombus, rectangular, parallelogram, different, equal

TEACHING POINTS

1 Revise tessellations

Talk about tessellating shapes.

Can the children see any shapes that tessellate in the classroom or school? Answers might include floor tiles, ceiling tiles, wired glass in doors, brick walls, etc.

Ask the children to name some shapes that tessellate and some that do not tessellate. Record the children's answers in a table.

These shapes tessellate	These shapes do not tessellate
square rectangle equilateral triangle regular hexagon	circle regular pentagon regular octagon

The children can check whether their shapes tessellate or not by drawing round templates or sticking pre-cut shapes together.

2 Combining shapes

Can the children name any shapes which they have seen tessellating together in tiling patterns or patchwork? (See Module 5 Shape 2.) Use templates which are edge matched for size or pre-cut sticky shapes. Ask the children to make tessellating patterns combining two shapes. These are some possibilities. (The shapes must fit together exactly at a vertex.)

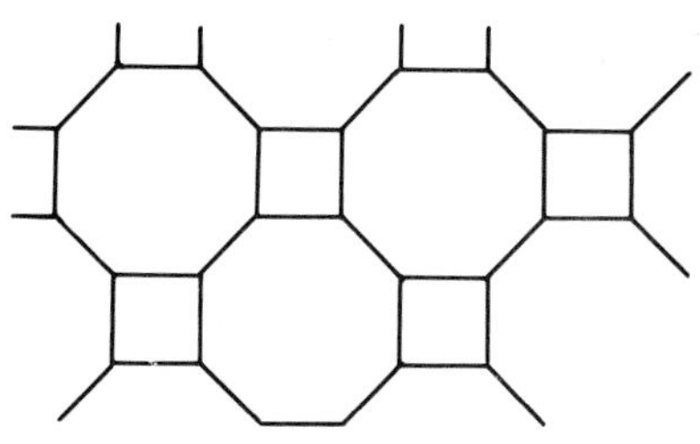
octagon + square

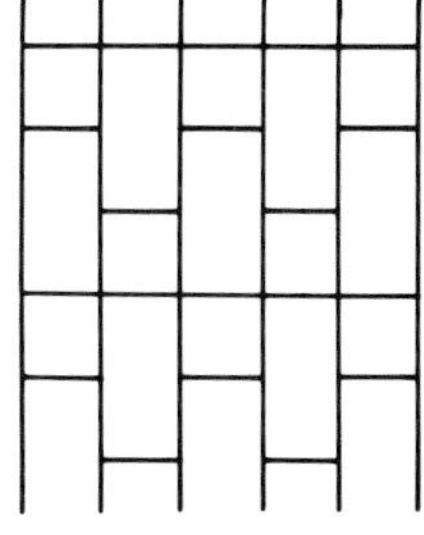
rectangle + square

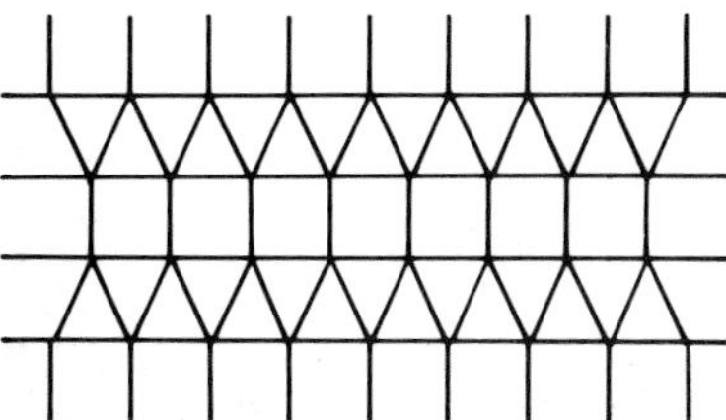
square + equilateral triangle

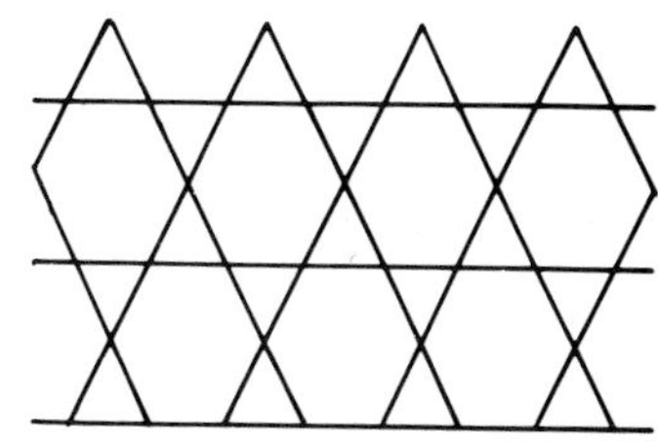
equilateral triangle + hexagon

3 Polyominoes

Talk about the polyomino shapes which are made from edge-matched squares.

Domino – made from two squares,

Tromino – made from three squares,

Tetromino – made from four squares,

Pentomino – made from five squares, e.g.

Hexomino – made from six squares, e.g.

Ask the children to make a squared paper template using a given number of squares such as 4 (i.e. a tetromino). This shape can then be drawn onto squared paper to produce tessellating patterns.

This activity can be repeated using the pentomino or hexomino shapes to make tessellating patterns.

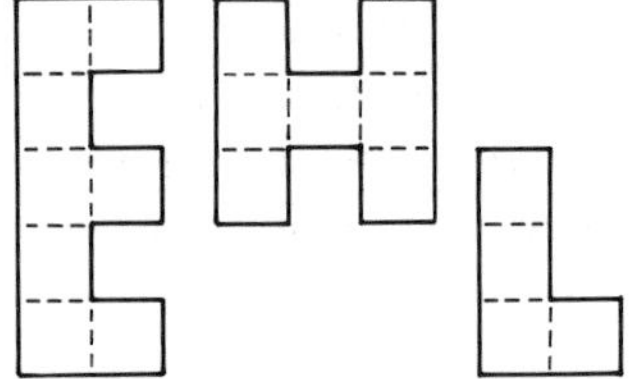

4 Letters of the alphabet

Some of the capital letters can be made as templates and used for tessellating patterns.

5 Parallelograms

Talk about parallelograms and parallel lines. Ask the children to use a parallelogram template to draw a tessellating pattern on plain paper. Squared or dotted paper might also be used.

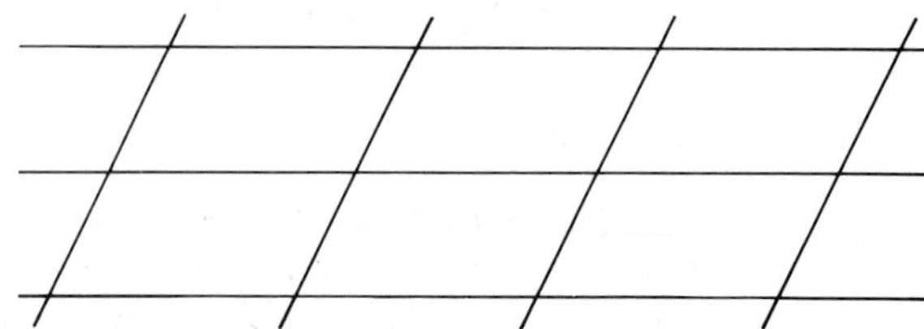

Repeat this using a rhombus template.

6 'Cut and move' tessellations

Ask the children to make a template on card by cutting, moving the cut piece and drawing round it.

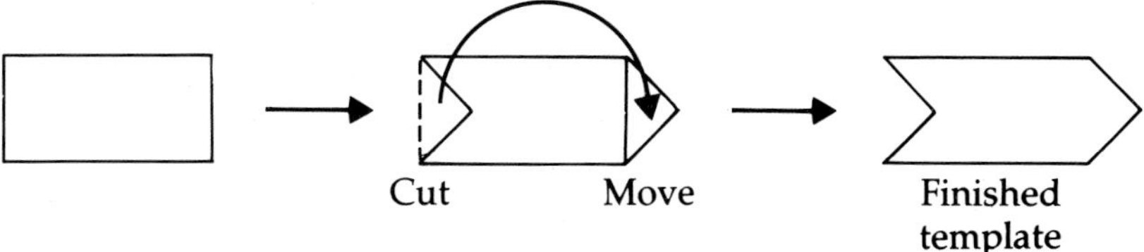

Let the children use their new template to make a tessellating pattern. This work is developed in the pupils' books.

LINKS WITH THE ENVIRONMENT

- Ask the children to look for tessellations as they come to school. Examples of these might include paving stones, zebra crossing, shopping precinct floors
- Some boxes in supermarkets tessellate
- Brick walls have tessellating patterns
- Windows can show tessellations. What other parts of buildings show tessellations – tiles around swimming baths, mosaic pictures, etc?
- Some wallpaper, wrapping paper, tile fabric and knitting designs can show tessellating patterns

NOTES ON INVESTIGATIONS

Section A

Do the children realise that their template can be any shape provided it is a 'cut and move' template (see section 6 above)? Can they suggest why their shape tessellates? Do they appreciate that it is because it is a variation of the rhombus tessellation suggested in the activities above?

Section B

Do the children find that they can make all their templates, which are made from two parallelograms, tessellate?

Section C

Do the children find that all of their templates made from two equal parallelograms will make a tessellating pattern? Do they appreciate that their template is a variation of the 'cut and move' tessellation (see section 6 above)?

Number 13

Purpose

- To introduce the addition of fractions with the same denominator

Materials

Squared paper

Vocabulary

Patterns, fraction sums, coloured parts, whole pattern, fraction sentence, number sentence

TEACHING POINTS

1 Adding fractions

Revise fractions with the children. Ask them to draw shapes and colour the fractions.

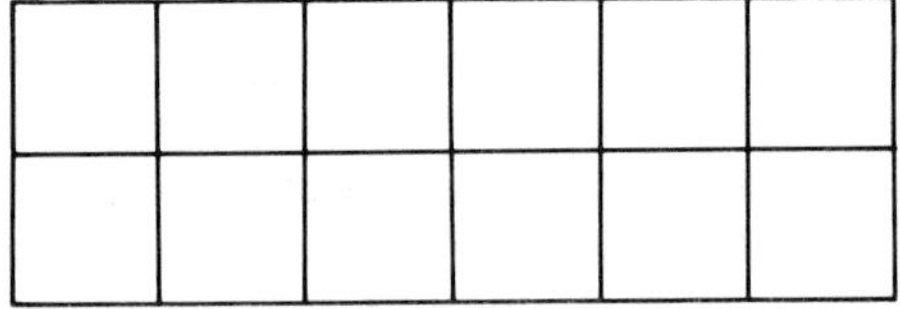

Colour $\frac{7}{12}$ purple, $\frac{4}{12}$ yellow and $\frac{1}{12}$ black.

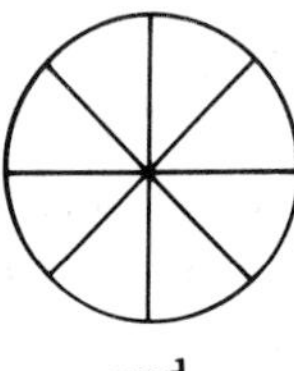

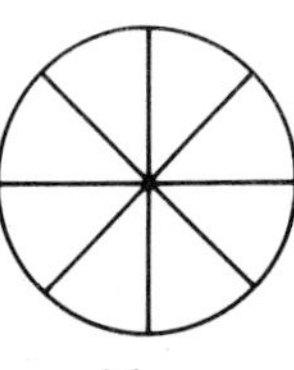

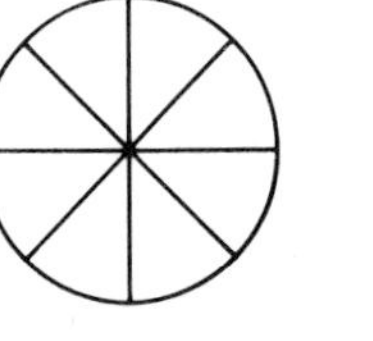

red blue green white

Cut three circles for display from card, poster paper, activity paper or vivelle, each one in a different colour. Cut a fourth white circle and Blu-tak it to the board. Divide and cut the coloured circles into eighths. Use Blu-tak to stick coloured eighths onto the white circle to show addition of fractions.

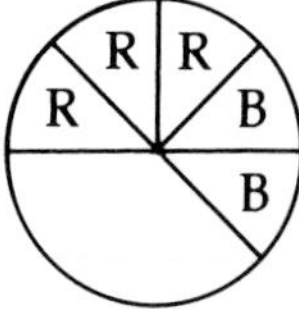

$\frac{3}{8}$ of the circle is red.
$\frac{2}{8}$ is blue.
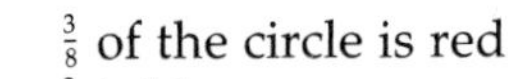
$\frac{3}{8} + \frac{2}{8} = \frac{5}{8}$ of the circle is coloured red and blue.

Give the children plenty of practice in this and also in recording the addition. Point out that you can only do addition like this with fractions of the same family. The terms numerator and denominator might be mentioned if you wish.

Ask the children to show fraction or number sentences on the circle.

'Show: $\frac{1}{8} + \frac{5}{8} = \frac{6}{8}$ is coloured.'

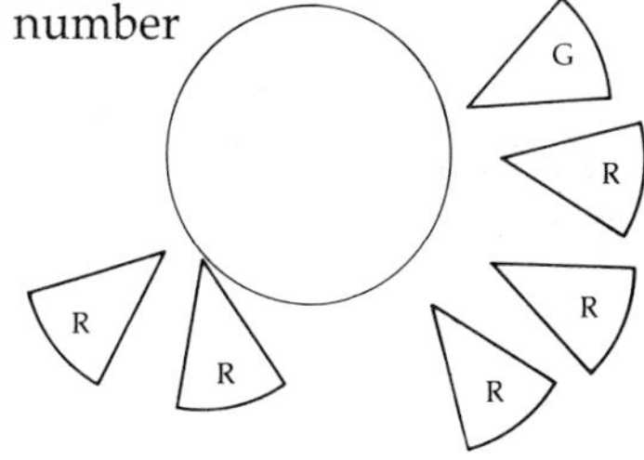

2 Making fraction sentences

Let the children draw shapes on squared paper to show fraction sentences. These can be mounted on stiff paper and displayed or hung as mobiles. The children could work in groups to make further displays.

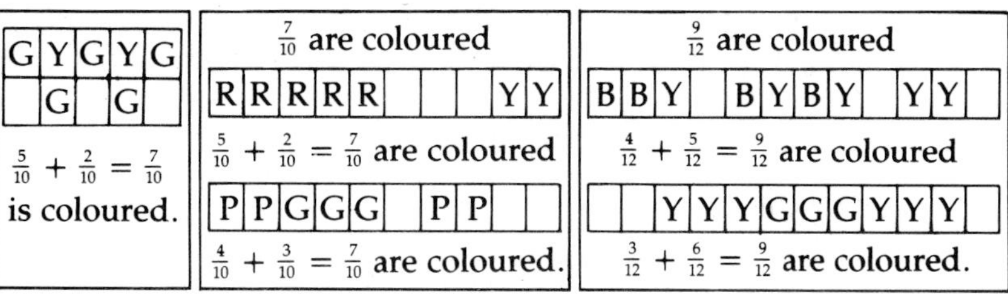

Games to play

MAKE THE FRACTION SENTENCE

Put the children into two teams. Call out a possible answer to a fraction addition, for example, $\frac{11}{12}$. Ask a player from each team to write an addition to match the answer, for example, $\frac{6}{12} + \frac{5}{12}$. The first to do so correctly scores a point for the team.

$\frac{2}{4} + \frac{1}{4} = \frac{3}{4}$
are coloured

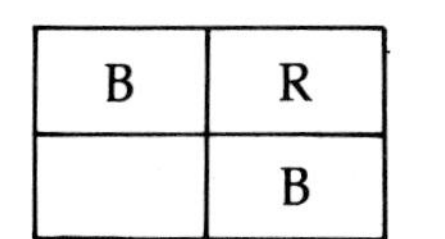

QUICK MATCH

Make sets of cards, some showing pictures and others fraction sentences. Shuffle them up. Give them to a small group of children. Time them to see how quickly they can match the pairs. Try it with another group. Which group is quicker?

3 Mixed numbers

Use the coloured display circles to show simple addition of whole numbers and fractions. Point out that the whole number is written the same size as the fraction.

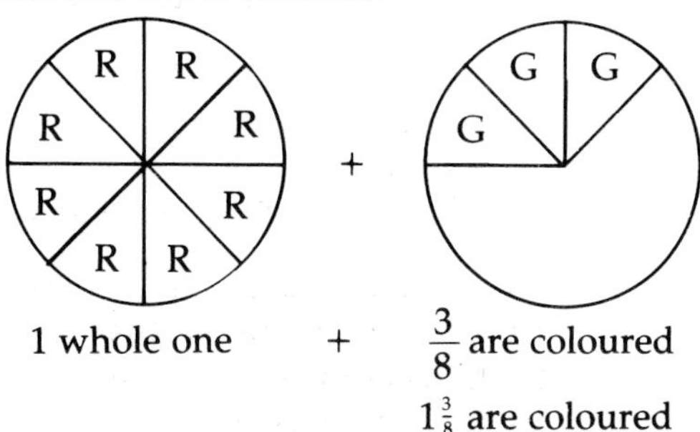

1 whole one + $\frac{3}{8}$ are coloured

$1\frac{3}{8}$ are coloured

Section C work in the pupils' chapter introduces improper fractions (where the numerator is greater than the denominator) and gives children practice in writing these as mixed numbers. However, not too much emphasis should be put on this aspect of fractions at this stage.

4 Mental work

- Revise work finding $\frac{1}{2}$, $\frac{1}{4}$, $\frac{1}{5}$ of quantities such as 20.
- Revise work finding $\frac{3}{4}$, $\frac{4}{5}$, $\frac{3}{8}$ of quantities such as 40.

USING THE CALCULATOR

The activities for mental work, finding fractions of quantities, may also be practised on a calculator, using larger numbers. For example, finding $\frac{1}{4}$ of 368.

LINKS WITH THE ENVIRONMENT

- Sharing activities – sharing pizzas, gateaux, sweets
- Art and craft – making patterns and designs using fractions: for example, seed, lentil and pasta patterns stuck on card or paper or pressed into plasticine like a mosaic

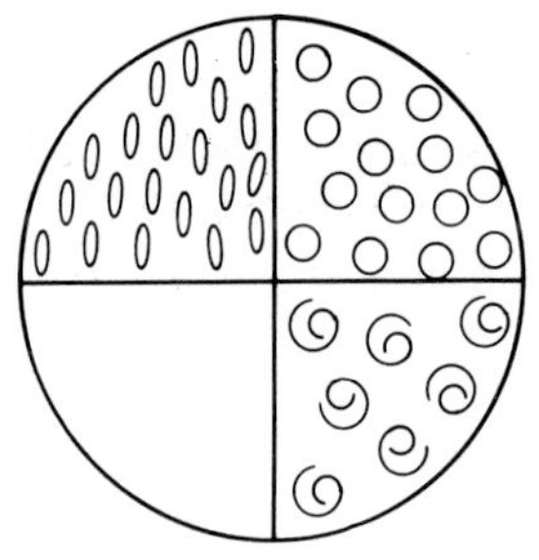

NOTES ON INVESTIGATIONS

Section A

Do the children appreciate that the shape is divided into eight equal parts? Do they understand that each part is $\frac{1}{8}$? Do they make other fraction sentences and match them to the correct drawing?

Section B

Do the children try a variety of additions? Do they include some that involve whole numbers?

Section C

Do the children understand that, in the first fraction, the top number must be greater than the bottom number (but not twice as large)?

Angles 2

Purpose

- To introduce measuring angles to 5°
- To introduce angle sums

Materials

Squared paper, geo-strips, fasteners, scissors, rulers, protractors or angle measurers, plain paper, glue

Vocabulary

Angle, instruction, square, forward, right, paces, squared paper, centimetre (cm), larger, corners, degrees, rectangle, right angles, diagonal line, triangle, measure, together, different sizes, angle measurer, measurement, missing angle, right-angled triangle

TEACHING POINTS

1 Naming angles

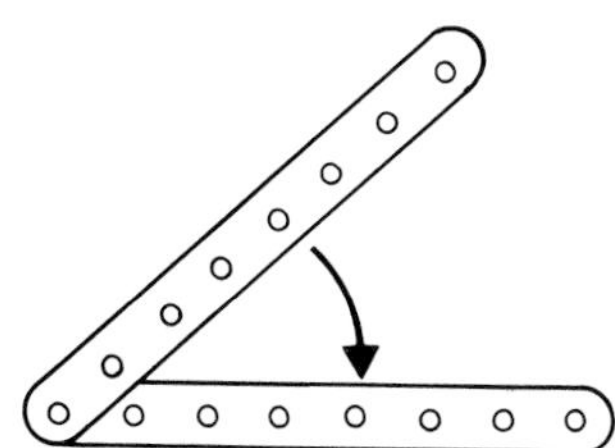

Talk with the children about what an angle is. Use geo-strips or card as an angle maker to show acute, obtuse and straight angles. Can the children name them? Can they find any examples of these in the classroom?

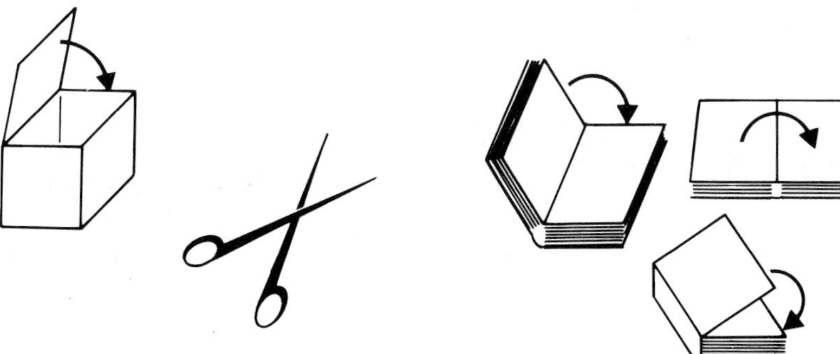

2 Degrees

Talk with the children about measuring angles in degrees and remind them how to write degrees as °. Ask them how many degrees there are in a right angle, a half right angle, a straight angle and a full turn.

3 Following instructions

If possible, chalk a grid on the floor in the classroom, hall or playground. Put a skittle or object somewhere in the grid as the target. Ask a child to stand at the edge of the grid and another child to call out instructions for reaching the skittle. The child moving must keep to the lines of the grid initially.

Instructions

Forward 4 squares
Right 90°
Forward 3 squares

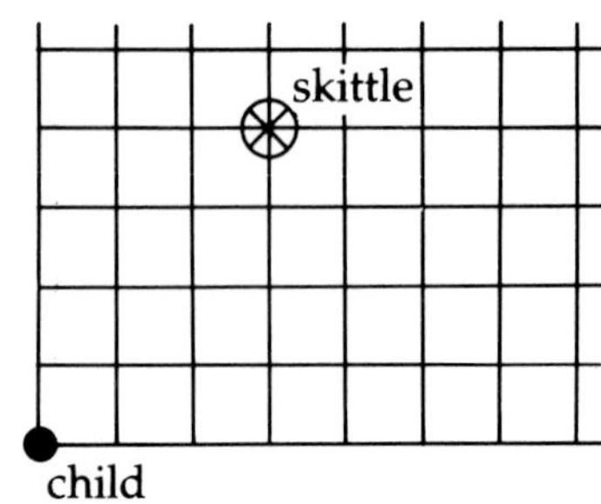

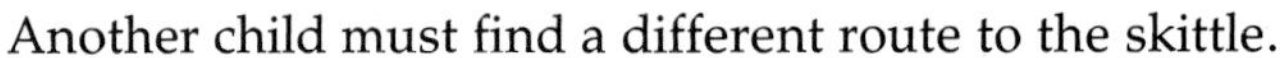

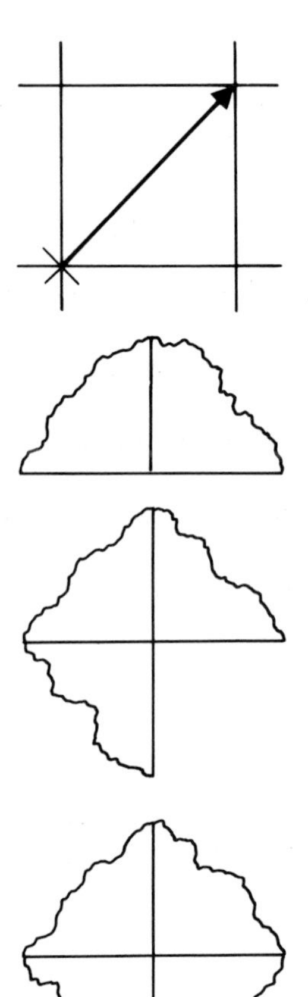

Another child must find a different route to the skittle.

This activity can also be shown on squared paper and played as a team game. Each different successful route scores a point.

A variation could be to move at angles of 45° diagonally across squares.

4 Angle sums

Give the children a rectangle of paper and ask them to name the angles at each corner. Ask them to tear off two of the corners and put them together. Ask what kind of angle they have made and how many degrees do they add up to?

Let them tear off the remaining corners and put all three, then four of them together. Ask each time, 'How many degrees does it add up to?

(The children are asked to find the angle sum of the square and triangle in the pupils' pages.)

5 Measuring angles to 10°

Revise how to use a semi-circular or circular protractor and talk about which set of numbers to use. Give the children plenty of practice in measuring and drawing angles accurately to 10°.

6 Introduce measuring angles to 5°

Talk about measuring angles to 5°. Give the children practice in measuring and drawing angles to 5° accurately.

A game to play

ESTIMATING ANGLES

This can be played in two teams. Ask each child in each team to draw an angle accurately to 5° or 10° on a piece of paper. The first child in one team shows their drawn angle to the first child of the other team who has to call out their estimate of the angle before measuring it. They score 2 points for an accurate estimate, 1 point for a close estimate (e.g. within 10 degrees of the true measurement). The players then change over.

The winning team is the one with the most points after all the children have had a go.

7 Logo

Discuss how angles can be drawn using turtle graphics. Set the children problems to draw using Logo or let them devise their own.

LINKS WITH THE ENVIRONMENT

Talk about everyday situations involving angles.

- Buildings – look for acute, obtuse and straight angles in buildings. Talk about architects and draughtsmen and ask what would happen if they get the angles wrong
- Art and craft – look at pattern work in art and angles in model making
- Clocks – look at the hands of a clock to see the different angles they make. Can the children name them?
- PE – make angles with arms and legs. Look at the large climbing apparatus for angles
- The children's playground in the park – look at the angles made by the fixing poles of swings, roundabouts, climbing frames.
- Walking and hiking – discuss how hikers follow directions using a compass.

NOTES ON INVESTIGATIONS

Section A

Do the children appreciate that the angles of all triangles which are half of a square have angles of 45°, 45°, 90°? Do they appreciate that the angle sum of right angled triangles is 180°?

Section B

Do the children appreciate that the angle sum of all triangles is 180°?

Section C

Do the children draw many different triangles with a 60° angle? Do they realise that it is not possible to draw an isosceles triangle since it will always be an equilateral triangle?

Time 3

Purpose

- To give practice in reading and interpreting timetables

Materials

Train timetables, squared paper, demonstration clocks might be useful

Vocabulary

Timetable, flight, arrival time, leave, often, earliest flight, last flight, take-off, allow, at least, restaurant (car), hour, minute, traveller, change stations, journey, include, 24 hour clock times, destination, departure times

TEACHING POINTS

1 Travel

Talk about some of the vocabulary associated with travel: for example, journey, arrival, departure, intercity, platform, information, booking office, timetable. Explain why some services are called shuttle services.

2 Timetables

Look at some train timetables. Are they written in 24 hour or 12 hour clock times? Remind the children how to write and read 24 hour clock times, and how to read timetables. Copy timetables for one or two journeys and talk about them together.

Do the children appreciate that the time gap between stations on a train timetable is approximately the time it takes to travel between the stations? If no time is stated then the train does not stop at that station.

Talk about how to work out the time a journey takes. Point out that calculating time is not like calculating in ThHTU. Can the children say why and suggest ways of doing it? One method might be:

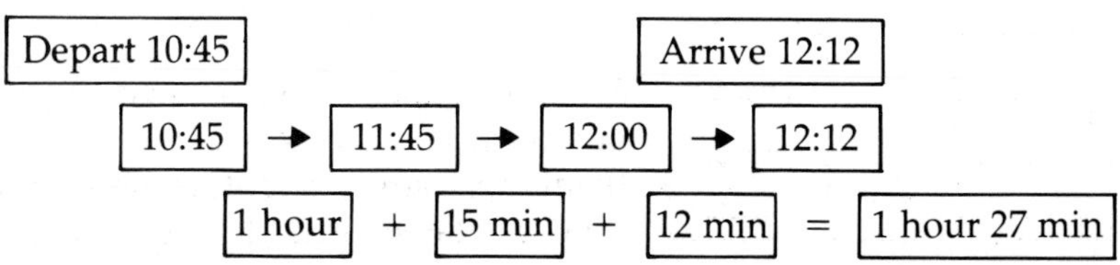

3 Inter-connecting journeys

Talk about journeys the children might have made where they have had to change stations or airlines. Why did they have to?

If possible look at a rail map and talk about the branch lines and the way in which the main lines link up. Can they suggest which might be some of the main stations and why?

Talk about the kind of connections people have to make when travelling by air. For example, flying to major airports when making 'long haul' journeys. Again, map work will be useful.

4 Allowing time

Talk about how important it is to allow adequate time for the change of transport. Can the children suggest things or events that must be allowed for in the change-over time? For example, the possible late arrival of the first train, plane or ship, the time needed to change platforms, terminals or even stations, the airport formalities such as 'checking in'.

Write a timetable on the board and put the possible connection times in a circle at the side with one or two extra times included.

Arrive	Change platform	Depart
09:35		
10:15		
10:50		
11:10		
11:27		

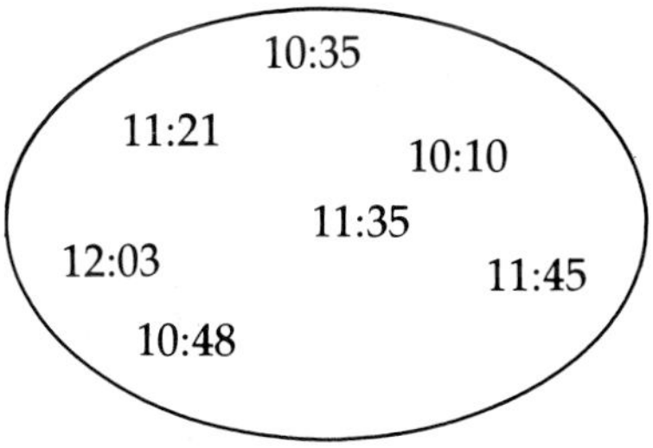

10:35 11:21 10:10 11:35 12:03 11:45 10:48

Discuss with the children how much time to allow to change trains (e.g. at least half an hour) and then ask them to choose the best connections from the times in the circle. A teaching clock might be useful here.

Point out that travel agents often recommend a two-hour time allowance for inter-connecting flights.

A game to play

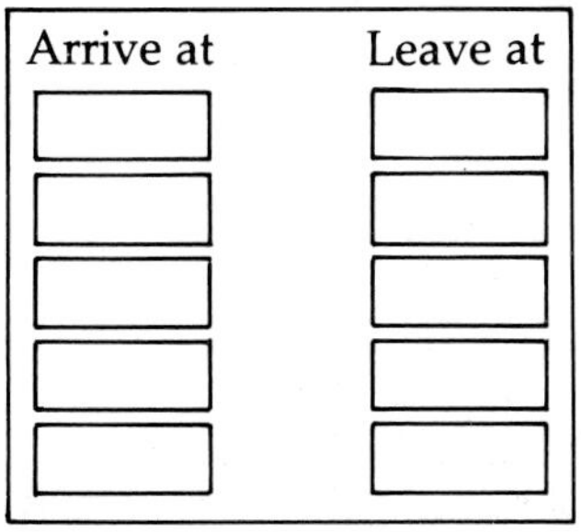

Arrive at	Leave at

CATCH THE TRAIN

Make a card like the one on the left for each group. Make pairs of cards, each with a time difference of half an hour. For example,

12:10, 12:40   13:25, 13:55

Shuffle and deal five pairs to each group. Place the cards face downwards. At a given signal the players turn the cards over, sort them into pairs with half an hour difference and place the pairs on their timetable card. The quickest group is the winner.

The game can be adapted to the capabilities of the children by allowing time differences of, for example, one hour or twenty minutes.

5 Symbols

Ask the children to look carefully at some railway timetables. What symbols can they find? What do they mean? For example,

| IC | Intercity | SO Saturdays only

Ask them to draw some of them, name them and hang them as mobiles in the classroom.

Can they design some of their own for airport or railway station facilities?

A game to play

KNOW THE SYMBOL

Put the children into equal teams. Call out the name of a symbol. The first player to draw a reasonable symbol scores a team point. Continue until all the players have had a turn. The winning team is the one that scores most points.

6 Mental work

- Let the children practise reading and writing 24 hour clock times
- Ask questions such as how long it is from 15:35 to 16:05
- Ask the children to add 20 minutes etc. to 24 hour clock times

LINKS WITH THE ENVIRONMENT

- Travel – by air, sea and land using buses, trains, boats, planes, hovercraft. Discuss the need to read timetables in order to make connections and calculate the lengths of journeys
- Hobbies and interests – reading time schedules to plan visits to theatres, sports fixtures and allowing time to travel to the events
- Everyday life – school timetables, work schedules and appointment systems
- Artwork – studying the design of travel symbols and designing your own
- Safety – rules for travel safety. For example, life jackets, safety drill on aeroplanes and ships, keeping off railway tracks

NOTES ON INVESTIGATIONS

Section A

Do the children plan carefully to make sure there is at least 3 hours between the two take-off times? Do they read the timetables correctly and state the destination each time?

Section B

Do the children ensure that the difference between the departure and arrival times is exactly 1 hour 10 minutes?

Do they take Acton and Espley to start with and fit the other stops in at appropriate times? For example,

Depart Acton	Arrive Espley
14:00	15:10

Do they allow sensible time intervals between the other stops? Do they vary the times?

Section C

Do the children show that they understand how to use train timetables? Do they incorporate changes of train into the journey?

Purpose

- To introduce the notation for kilometres and metres
- To introduce addition and subtraction of km and m
- To introduce simple networks

Materials

Ruler, squared paper, calculator

Vocabulary

Length, distances, metres (m), nearest, furthest, kilometres (km), shorter, difference between, perimeter, square, side, plan, measurements, distance round, straight line distance, less than, start, finish, total distance, twice as long, times as long, half as long, trail

TEACHING POINTS

1 Metres

Revise estimating and measuring in metres. Show the children a metre stick. Ask them how many centimetres there are in 1 metre. Talk about things in the room that are about 1 metre long.

Talk about longer distances and how we measure them using tape measures or a trundle wheel. Remind them of the advantages and disadvantages of each.

- Trundle wheel – It is quick but children have to remember to count the clicks for metres. Also it cannot go right up to walls so the result is approximate
- Long tape measure – This is easy if nothing is in the way to prevent it from being stretched out. It is accurate because it measures in metres and centimetres

Remind the children that when recording longer distances accurately we record in metres, for example, 3·67 m (or 3 m 67 cm).

2 Addition and subtraction of metres

Show the children how to record the addition and subtraction of longer distances in metres. Point out that the addition and subtraction is the same process as for ThHTU.

$$\begin{array}{r} \text{m} \\ 1423 \\ +\ \underline{1384} \\ \underline{} \end{array} \qquad \begin{array}{r} \text{m} \\ 2658 \\ -\ \underline{1472} \\ \underline{} \end{array}$$

3 Kilometres

Talk with the children about how we record long distances in kilometres. For example, distances between towns or cities, fun runs, speeds in kilometres per hour are all used in everyday life. Remind them that we record kilometres as km. For example a fun run could be 10 km long.

Explain that 1000 m = 1 km.

4 Writing m as km

Explain that we can record distances such as 1584 m as 1·584 km. Give the children practice in converting metres to km and vice versa, for example, 2·395 km = 2 km 395 m or 2395 m.

Point out that we record 725 m as 0·725 km and that there must be three digits after the decimal point.

A game to play

EXCHANGING

This can be played in two teams. Call out 1624 m. A point is given to the first member of a team to write 1·624 km.

A variation is to play a snap or domino type game where cards showing, for example, 2459 m and 2·459 km are matched.

5 Addition of kilometres

Talk about how to set out additions involving km and m. Stress how important it is to line up the points, and that the addition is then the same process as for ThHTU.

$$\begin{array}{r} \text{km} \\ 4{\cdot}524 \\ +\ 2{\cdot}149 \\ \hline \\ \hline \end{array}$$

6 Subtraction of kilometres

Talk about finding the difference in kilometres, such as when finding the distance by road and the straight line distance (or 'as the crow flies'). Why can't we travel using the straight line or shortest distance between two places? Again stress the importance of setting down the subtraction carefully. Point out that the working is done in the same way as ThHTU.

$$\begin{array}{r} \text{km} \\ 2{\cdot}582 \\ -\ 1{\cdot}294 \\ \hline \\ \hline \end{array}$$

7 Mental work

Ask the children to change m to km. Let them write distances such as 1925 m or 789 m in kilometres from oral instructions.

Ask the children mental problems involving metres or kilometres. For example,

- Ann cycled $1\frac{1}{2}$ km. How many metres was this?
- John ran 500 metres, 700 metres and 1 kilometre in a day. How far did he run altogether?

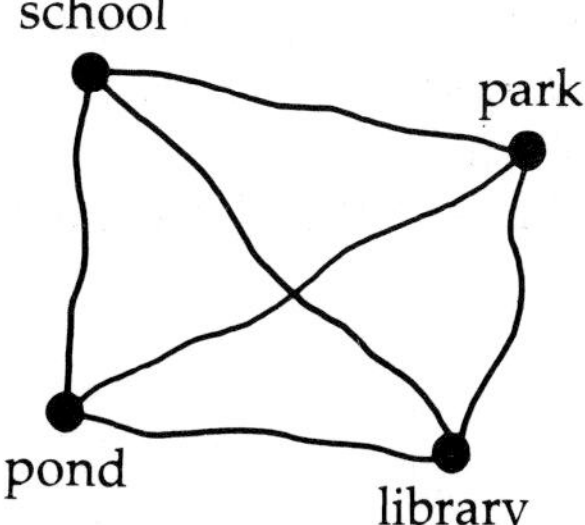

8 Networks

Draw a network diagram of the local area or of local towns. Write on the distances. Talk with the children about finding the shortest route between places, for example school and library.

USING THE CALCULATOR

Ask the children to change metres into kilometres and show it on the calculator display. For example, 5942 m → 5·942.

The calculator can be used to add or subtract lengths in kilometres such as 4·258 km + 1·395 km.

Check that the children can enter the lengths accurately and can read them.

LINKS WITH THE ENVIRONMENT

Talk with the children about distance involving metres or kilometres that we use in everyday life.

- Reading the speedometer on a bike or car – these measure in miles or kilometres
- Sport – what are the world records for high jump, long jump and pole vault? What are the distances of local fun runs?
- Trails – what are the distances around local nature trails? These are often shown in kilometres
- Distances by road – some road charts show the distance between towns or cities in miles and in kilometres. Countries like France use kilometres for distances.

NOTES ON INVESTIGATIONS

Section A

Do the children's plans of the square goat pen show the length of a side to be 15 m (i.e. 60 m ÷ 4)? Do the different shaped goat pens all have a perimeter of 60 m? Do any of the plans of the goat pen have more than four sides?

Section B

Do the children realise that the total distance for the places visited must be less than 5000 m (i.e. 5 km)? Do they find different ways to do it? Do any of the children count the place they start from as one of their places visited?

Section C

Are the children's plans of the trails in the correct proportions? Do they choose distances in m or km that satisfy the information given? Are their answers to their own questions correct?

Module 6 Pupils' book 1
RECORD SHEET

Class .... Pupil ....

Topic	*Section*	*Assessment*	*Comment*
Number 1	A B C		
Number 2	A B C		
Shape 1	A B C		
Data 1	A B C		
Number 3	A B C		
Money 1	A B C		
Number 4	A B C		
Probability 1	A B C		
Number 5	A B C		
Number 6	A B C		
Length 1	A B C		
Weight 1	A B C		
Volume and capacity	A B C		
Time 1	A B C		
Number 7	A B C		
Number 8	A B C		
Data 2	A B C		
Money 2	A B C		
Shape 2	A B C		

General comments:

Module 6 Pupils' book 2
RECORD SHEET

Class .... Pupil ....

Topic	*Section*	*Assessment*	*Comment*
Number 9	A B C		
Time 2	A B C		
Co-ordinates	A B C		
Number 10	A B C		
Data 3	A B C		
Number 11	A B C		
Angles 1	A B C		
Shape 3	A B C		
Number 12	A B C		
Data 4	A B C		
Area	A B C		
Data 5	A B C		
Weight 2	A B C		
Money 3	A B C		
Probability 2	A B C		
Shape 4	A B C		
Number 13	A B C		
Angles 2	A B C		
Time 3	A B C		
Length 2	A B C		

General comments:

MATERIALS REQUIRED FOR MODULE 6

atlas or map of the world
bags (small plastic)
balance scales
bathroom scales
bills
binca material
Blu-tak
board with cup hook
boxes and packages
calculators
calendar
card
card circles and strips
cardboard tubes
catalogues for books, gardening tools and shrubs, shopping etc.
centimetre cubes
circular lids or wheels
clock stamps
clocks (including ones showing 24 hour times)
coins
coloured pens
comics
compasses
containers
counters
craft sticks
crayons
cubes
cylinders
demonstration clock faces with roman numerals
dice
displacement bucket
drawing pins
geo-board
geo-strips and fasteners
glue
key
magazines
measuring cylinders
mirror
multiplication squares for individual use
newspapers
paper
paper circles
phone card
pieces of cloth
pipe cleaners
straws (coloured plastic)
plasticine
protractors or angle measurers
receipts
reference books
road maps
rubber bands of various thicknesses
rulers
S hook or paper clip
scissors
solid shapes (prisms, pyramids, cubes, cuboids, cylinders, cone, spheres)
spring balances
squared paper
sticky tape
stones
stop-watch or timer
string
structural apparatus
suitable objects for weighing activities
tape measures
templates (for two-dimensional shapes; and for making tessellations)
thermometer
train timetables
travel brochures
trundle wheels
water
water pot (plastic)
weighing scales
weights (50 g and 100 g)
yogurt pots

GLOSSARY FOR MODULE 6

acute angle An angle between 0° and 90°.

a.m. Ante meridiem. The time before midday.

angle An angle is the amount of turn or rotation. Angles are measured in degrees with 360° in a whole turn.

angle measurer *See* protractor.

anti-clockwise *See* clockwise.

approximate A number or measurement which is not exact but is accepted as being close enough.

area Area is the size or amount of a surface, and is usually written in units of square measurement.

average (mean) The mean of a set of numbers is the sum of the numbers divided by the number of them in the set. For example, the mean of 1, 4, 5 and 6 is

$$\frac{1+4+5+6}{4} = \frac{16}{4} = 4$$

axis (pl. axes) One of the reference lines on a graph.

balance A balance is a set of scales.

bar-line graph A form of graph where the data is represented by lines.

bilateral symmetry *See* symmetry.

block graph A block graph is a form of pictorial representation where the data is represented by columns.

capacity The capacity of a container is the amount that it will hold.

Carroll diagram A form of diagram for classifying data devised by Lewis Carroll, author of *Alice in Wonderland*. Here is an example.

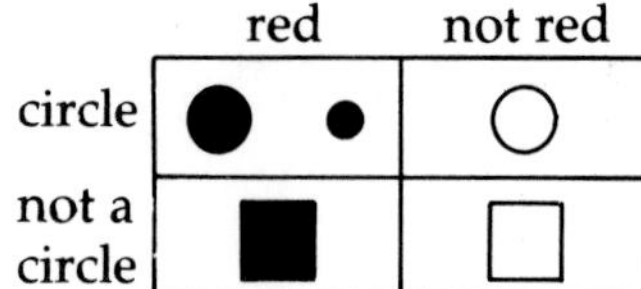

Celsius A temperature scale where 0 °C is the freezing point of water and 100 °C is the boiling point.

Centigrade A temperature scale where 0 °C is the freezing point of water and 100 °C is the boiling point. It is now known as the Celsius scale.

centimetre $\frac{1}{100}$ of a metre (abbreviation: cm).

circle A circle is a set of points, all of which are a fixed distance (the radius) from a fixed point (the centre).

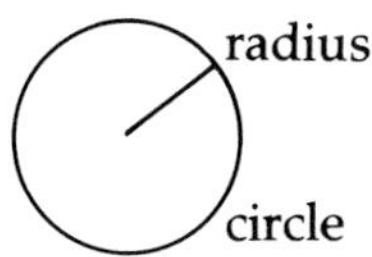

circumference The circumference is the distance around a circle.

class intervals Data is sometimes grouped into classes (usually equal) to give a clearer idea of the distribution.
For example, marks of 1–50 may be grouped as 1–10, 11–20, etc.

clockwise This is the direction in which the hands of a clock turn. Anti-clockwise is the opposite direction.

column A column is a list of numbers (or letters) or squares in a grid going down a page.

commutative An operation, for example +, −, is commutative if numbers can be used with it in any order and still give the same answer. Addition is commutative, since, for example, $3 + 1 = 1 + 3$. Multiplication is commutative, since, for example, $3 \times 2 = 2 \times 3$. Subtraction is **not** commutative, since $3 - 1 \neq 1 - 3$. Division is **not** commutative, since $4 \div 2 \neq 2 \div 4$

compass An instrument for showing direction. The four points of the compass are N, S, E, W. The eight points of the compass are N, S, E, W, NW, NE, SE, SW.

conservation Remaining unchanged even though the position or situation changes. For example, a litre of water is always a litre of water irrespective of the shape of its container.

constant function The use of the constant function on a calculator allows numbers to increase or decrease by a fixed amount. For example, the numbers 2, 5, 8, 11, . . . are increasing by the constant + 3.

co-ordinates An ordered pair of numbers, for example (4, 5), to show a point on a graph or grid.

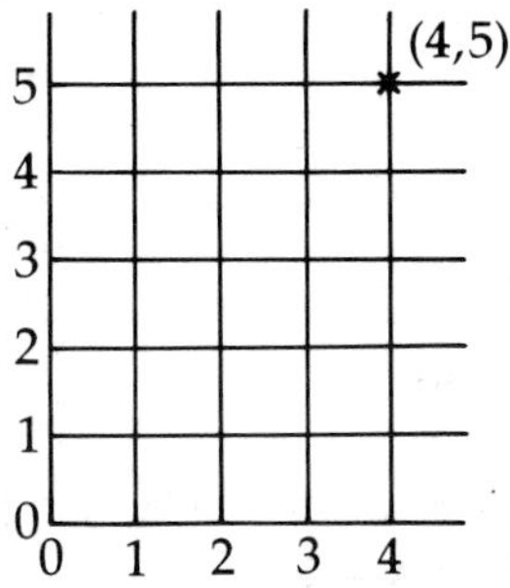

cube A cube is a solid with all its six faces square and all its edges equal in length. For example, a die is a cube.

cubic centimetre A unit of volume (abbreviation: cm^3).

cuboid A cuboid is a solid with six faces that are all rectangles. Opposite faces are the same.

cylinder A cylinder is a solid with the shape of a circle along its length.

data Data is information or facts which have been collected. It is often displayed as a block graph or bar chart.

decimal notation A way of writing numbers that involves a decimal point. For example, a length of 5 metres 23 centimetres can be written in decimal notation as 5.23 m.

decimal places The number of digits after the decimal point.

decomposition Decomposition is a method for subtraction where, for example, a 'ten' is changed into ten units.

$$\begin{array}{r} 5\ {}^{1}\not{7}\ {}^{1}4 \\ -\ 3\ \ 1\ \ 7 \\ \hline 2\ \ 0\ \ 7 \\ \hline \end{array}$$

degree (temperature) A degree is a temperature interval. The most common scales are Celsius and Fahrenheit.

degrees Angles are measured in degrees. There are 360° in a full turn.

diagonal A diagonal is a straight line drawn from one vertex of a shape to another non-adjacent vertex.
For example

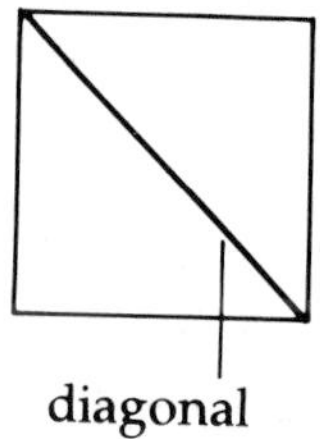

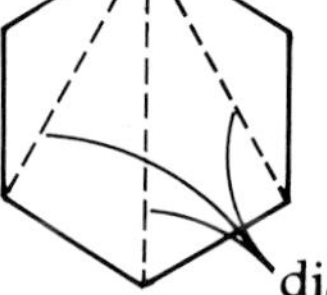

diameter A diameter is any straight line that joins two points of a circle and passes through the centre.

digit A digit is a single figure or symbol in a number system. For example, the digits in 347 are 3, 4 and 7.

edge An edge is the line formed when two faces of a solid meet.

edge

equal chance An equal chance is when every possible outcome has the same chance of happening. For example, there is an equal chance of throwing 1, 2, 3, 4, 5 or 6 on a fair die.

equilateral triangle An equilateral triangle is a triangle with all three sides the same length.

equivalent fractions Fractions are equivalent if they can represent the same fraction. For example, $\frac{1}{2}$, $\frac{2}{4}$, $\frac{3}{6}$, $\frac{4}{8}$, $\frac{5}{10}$, $\frac{6}{12}$ are equivalent.

estimate To estimate is to make an approximate judgement of a number, amount, etc. without measuring it.

even chance	A one in two chance or 50/50 chance of happening.
face	A face is the flat side of a solid shape.
factor	A factor is a number which divides exactly into another number. For example, 3 is a factor of 12.
fair chance	*See* equal chance.
fraction	A number less than 1, written as $\frac{a}{b}$ where a is the numerator and b is the denominator.
function machine	A machine that operates on numbers. For example, machine: INPUT $\xrightarrow{2}$ [+3] $\rightarrow$ 5 OUTPUT
gram	A gram is a unit of weight. It is $\frac{1}{1000}$ of a kilogram. The abbreviation for gram is g.
graph	A graph is a picture or diagram to make information more easily understood. Data is often shown by picture graphs, block graphs or bar charts.
grid	A set of intersecting parallel lines, usually at right angles to one another and the same distance apart.
hexagon	A hexagon is a plane shape with six sides. A regular hexagon has all its sides equal in length and all its angles the same size.
hexagonal prism	A prism with end faces that are hexagons.
horizontal	A line is horizontal when it is parallel to the Earth's horizon. It is at right angles to a vertical line.
irregular shape	A shape that is not regular. All of its sides and angles are not equal.
kilogram	A kilogram is the standard unit of weight (abbreviation: kg). A kilogram is equal to 1000 grams.
kilometre	1000 metres (abbreviation: km).
kite	A quadrilateral that has two pairs of equal and adjacent sides.
leap year	A year with 366 days.
line of symmetry	A line of symmetry on a shape divides the shape into halves so that one half is a mirror image of the other.
litre	A litre is a unit of capacity (abbreviation; l, not to be confused with 1). One litre is a little over $1\frac{3}{4}$ pints.
magic square	A magic square has numbers on a square grid such that each row, column and diagonal add up to the same total. This is a 3 × 3 magic square.

2	7	6
9	5	1
4	3	8

mean *See* average.

measure To measure is to find a size or quantity by comparison with a fixed unit.

metre A metre is the standard unit of length (abbreviation: m).

metric A system of units based on the metre, litre and kilogram and using multiples of 10.

millilitre $\frac{1}{1000}$ of a litre (abbreviation: ml).

minute A minute is 60 seconds.

multiple Multiples of a number are given by that number multiplied by whole numbers. The multiples of 4 are 4, 8, 12, 16, . . . The multiples of 10 are 10, 20, 30, 40, . . .

multiplication square A multiplication square is a square which shows the multiplication table.

×	1	2	3
1	1	2	3
2	2	4	6
3	3	6	9

negative number A number less than zero. For example, −1 is one less than zero.

net A two-dimensional shape that can be folded to make a three-dimensional shape.

For example, is a net for a cube.

notation The way in which symbols are used to represent, for example, quantities. The notation for a length of seven centimetres is 7 cm.

number sentence A number sentence is a mathematical statement or sentence, for example, 2 + 1 = 3.

number system A set of symbols and the rules that they follow.

numeral A word or symbol for a number, for example, VI or 9.

obtuse angle An angle between 90° and 180°.

octagon An eight-sided closed plane shape.

parallel A set of lines are parallel if they never meet.

parallelogram A four-sided shape with opposite sides equal and parallel.

pattern A pattern is an arrangement of numbers, etc. according to a rule. A pattern allows us to predict what might come next. For example, in the sequence 1, 2, 3, –, –, 6, the missing numbers are 4, 5, since the pattern is adding one each time.

pentagon A pentagon is a five-sided closed shape. A regular pentagon has all its sides equal in length and all its angles the same size.

perimeter The distance all the way round a closed shape.

place value Place value is the value of a symbol or digit in a number system due to its position. For example, in the number 22, each 2 has a different value because of its position.

plane of symmetry A three-dimensional shape may possess a plane of symmetry where one half of the shape is a reflection of the other. For example

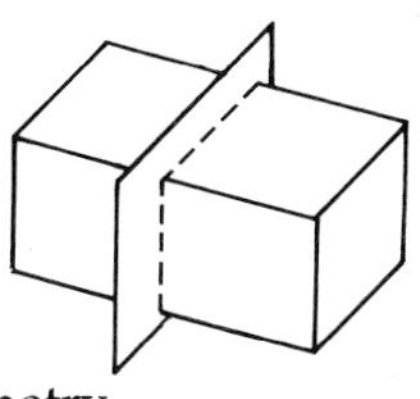

plane of symmetry

plane shape A plane shape is a two-dimensional shape. For example, circles and triangles are plane shapes.

p.m. Post meridiem. The time after midday.

pound (weight) An imperial unit of weight. A pound is a little less than half a kilogram.

prism A prism is a solid with the same shape along its length, so that it has uniform cross-section. Prisms take their name from the end face.

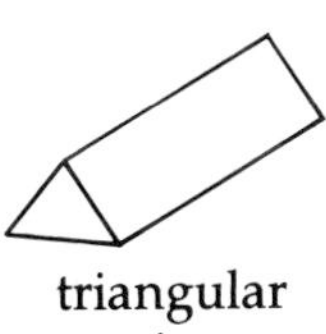

triangular prism

hexagonal prism

probability Probability is the likelihood of an event happening.

protractor An instrument for measuring angles.
An angle measurer.

pyramid A pyramid is a solid shape with a polygon for its base. The other faces are triangles which meet at a vertex called the apex.

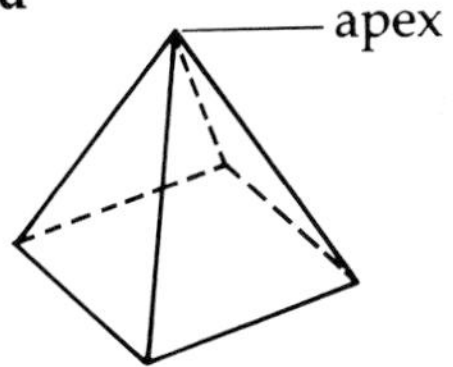

quadrant A fourth part. When drawing a graph the first quadrant is as shown:

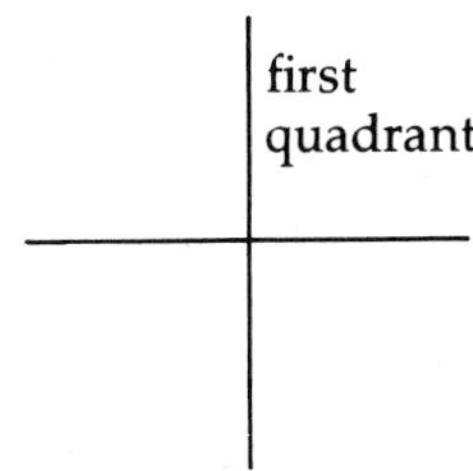

quadrilateral A quadrilateral is a four-sided closed plane shape. For example squares, rectangles, trapeziums, rhombuses are all quadrilaterals.

radius	The radius is the distance from the centre of a circle to a point on the circumference.
range	The range of a set of data is the difference between the greatest and the smallest value in the set.
rectangle	A rectangle is a four-sided closed plane shape with four right-angles and opposite sides equal in length.
reflex angle	An angle greater than 180° but less than 360°. 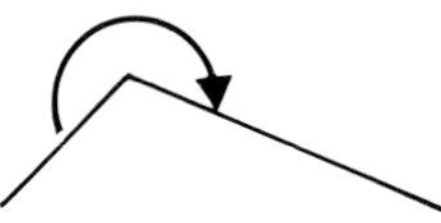
regular shape	A regular shape has all its sides the same length and all its angles the same size, for example, a square.
relationship	A connection between numbers or quantities.
rhombus	A quadrilateral with four equal sides. 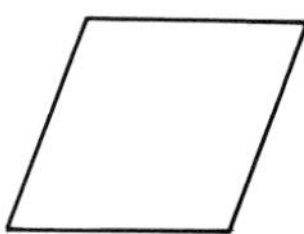
right-angle	A right-angle is a quarter of a complete turn. It is measured as an angle of 90°.
rigid	Not able to be pushed out of shape. A triangle is a rigid shape.
rotate	To turn.
rounding	Writing a number to a required level of accuracy. 126 is written as 130 when rounded (up) to the nearest 10. 124 is written as 120 when rounded (down) to the nearest 10.
row	A row is a list of numbers or letters across the page.
solid	A solid is a three-dimensional shape, for example, a cube.
spring balance	A balance weighing objects by the stretching of a spring.
square	A square has four equal sides and four right-angles.
square corner	A square corner is a right-angle.
square centimetre	A unit of area (abbreviation: cm^2).
straight angle	180°.
straight line graph	A graph which is a straight line. 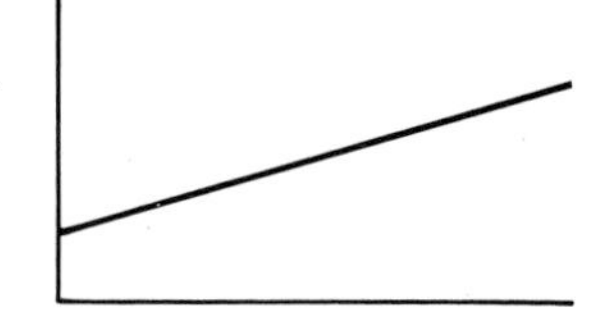
structural apparatus	Structural apparatus is apparatus to show how the number system works.
symmetry	Line symmetry is the exact matching of parts on either side of a straight line. This is sometimes called bilateral or mirror symmetry.

temperature A measure of hotness or coldness.

template A template is an object or shape to draw around.

tessellate A shape or shapes repeat to form a pattern without gaps or overlaps.

tetrahedron A solid shape with four triangular faces.

tonne A metric unit of weight. It is 1000 kilograms.

trapezium A quadrilateral with one pair of parallel sides.

tree diagram A diagram to show possible outcomes of events.

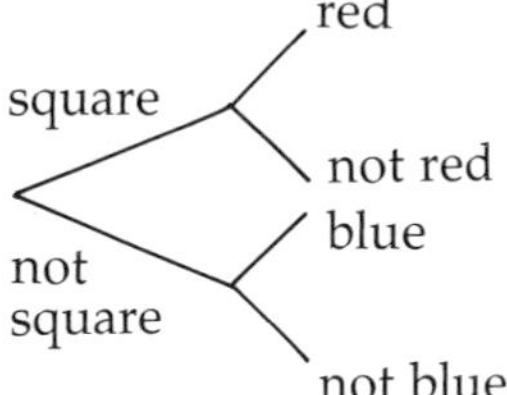

triangle A triangle is a closed plane shape with three straight sides.

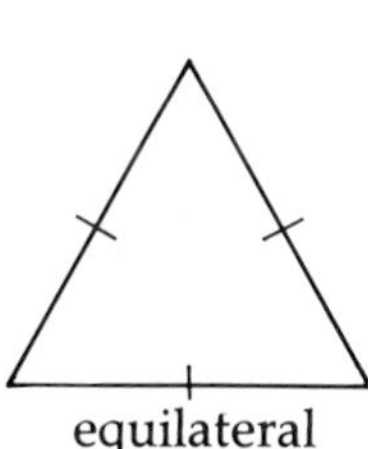

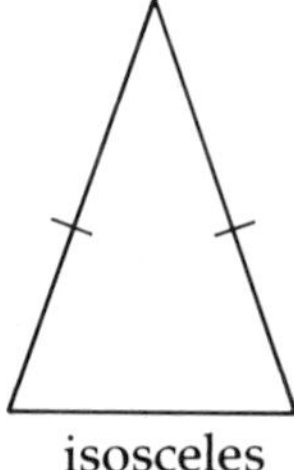

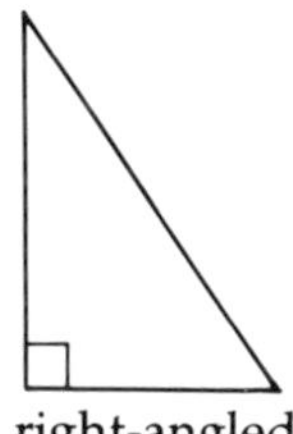

triangular prism A triangular prism is a prism whose end faces are triangles.

Venn diagram A diagram used to show the relationship between sets.

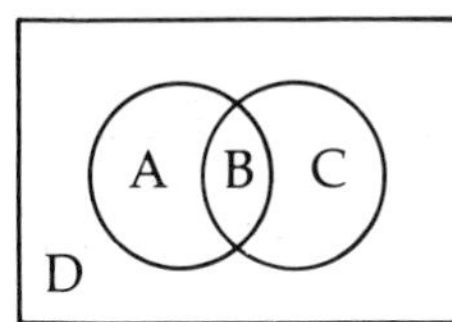

vertex (*plural* vertices) The vertex is a point where lines or edges meet.

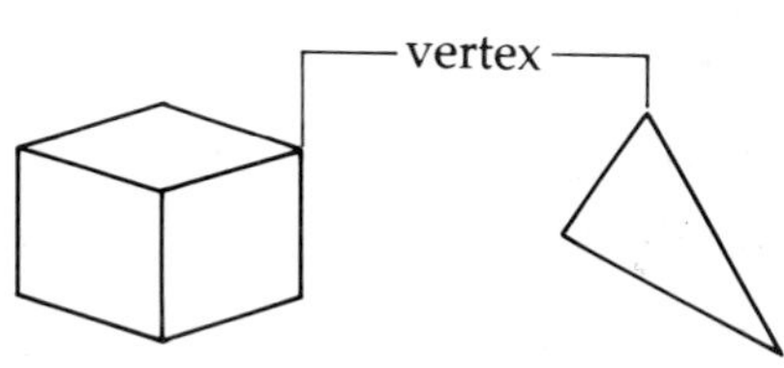

vertical At right angles to the horizontal.

vertices *See* vertex.

volume The volume of a solid is the amount of space it occupies. The units of measurement are usually cubic centimetres or cubic metres.

weight The weight of an object depends on the gravitational force acting on it. An object on the Moon will weigh less than on Earth although its mass will remain the same.

KU-589-628

LEEDS COL OF ART & DESIGN
R49359X0084

portable architecture

-and unpredictable surroundings-

Pilar Echavarria M.

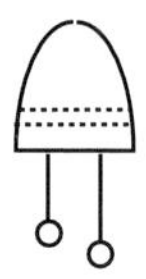

author_ Pilar Echavarría M.

publisher_ Arian Mostaedi

editorial coordination_ Jacobo Krauel

graphic design_ Pilar Echavarría

production_ Jorge Carmona

text_ contributed by the architects-artists-designers
+ edited by Pilar Echavarría

Jonqueres, 10, 1-5 / 08003 Barcelona, España
tel. 34 93 301 21 99, fax. 34 93 301 00 21
info@linksbooks.net www.linksbooks.net

ISBN 84-89861-38-2 / Printed in Spain

portable architecture

-and unpredictable surroundings-

structure

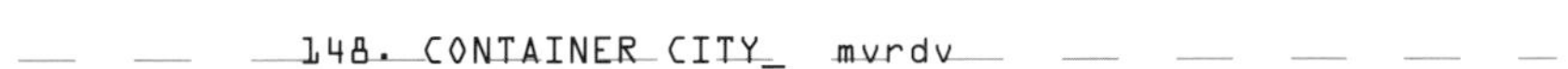

Nomads, journeys, living with the unknown, with the unexpected, daily life filled with surprises, exploring distant worlds on foot, horseback, by car, boat, plane or rocket, while carrying your own house...

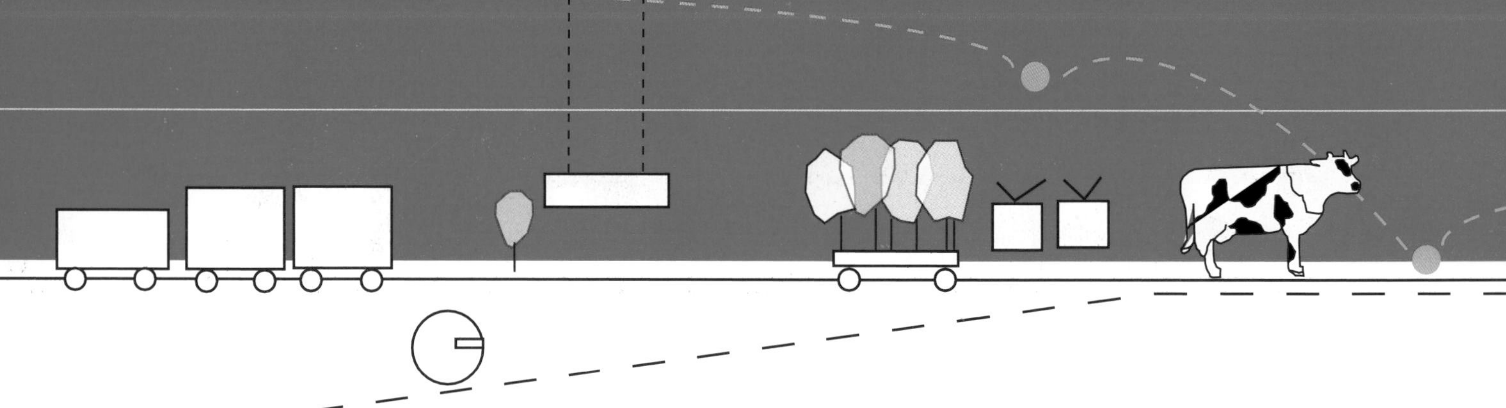

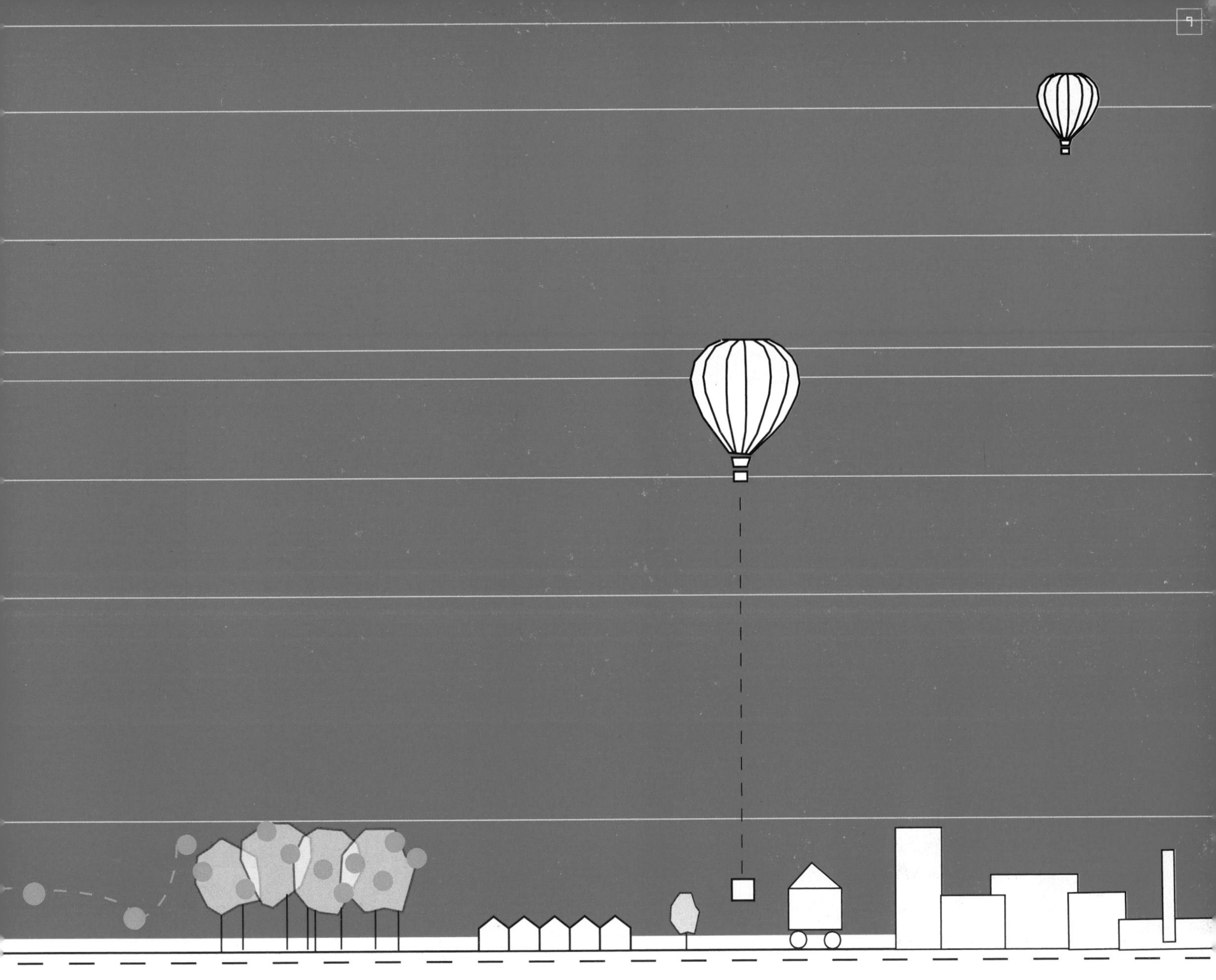

dream, utopia or science fiction?

Portable architecture: "the acknowledgment of unforeseen -and for this very reason almost uncontrolled- circumstances and presences.
Architecture that is fickle, capricious, audacious, unexpected, reactive and 'glocal'.
Architecture that camouflages, floats, flies, rolls, grows and shrinks, appears and disappears within the city, becoming part of the landscape, the terrain, the network; it is invisible yet recognizable and identifiable, giving rise to unpredictable and spontaneous processes, breaking into different levels of reality, searching the city and its present moment, taking it over, invading, re-reading and turning it upside-down.

Mobile architecture is an intelligent way of inhabiting an environment in a given time and place, being able to react and interact with ongoing social and cultural changes, complex cities, uncertain territories, undefined boundaries, changing structures...
All of these multifaceted contemporary phenomena and processes require a more flexible and open architecture.

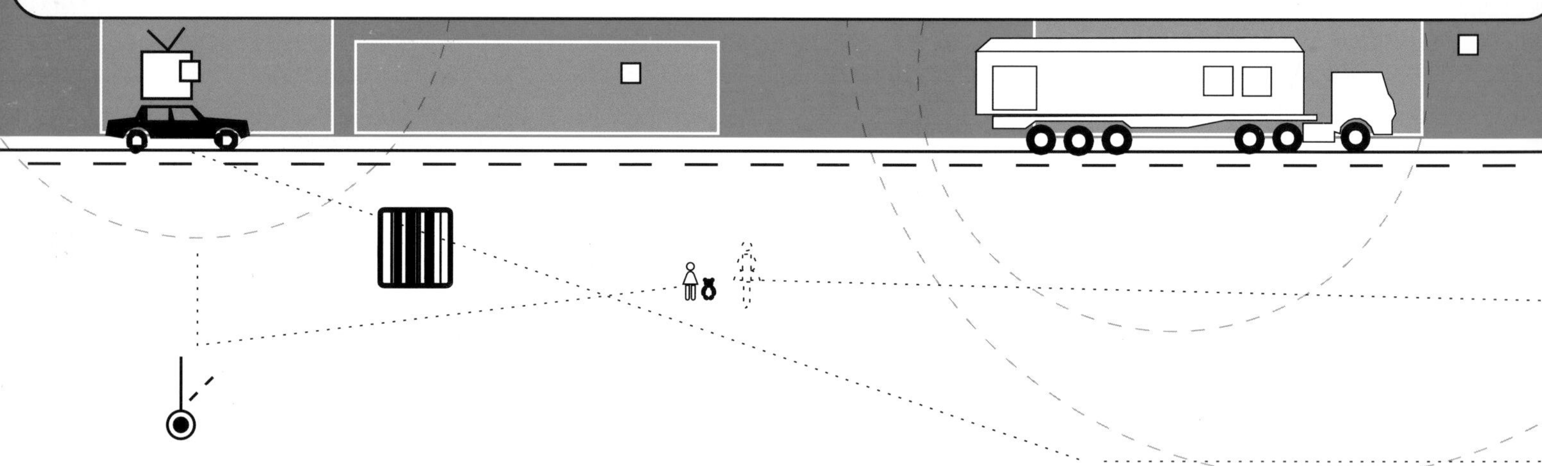

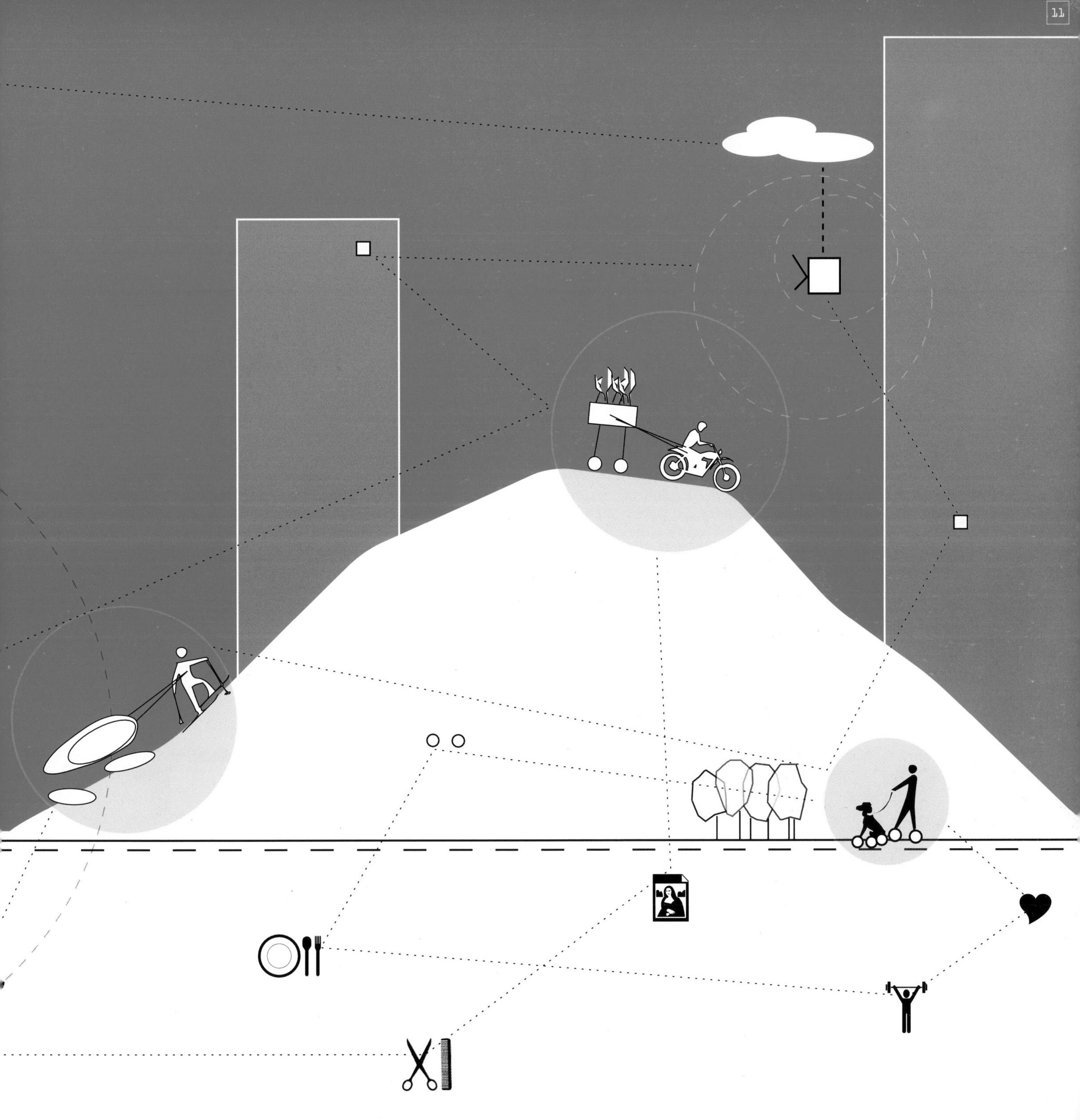

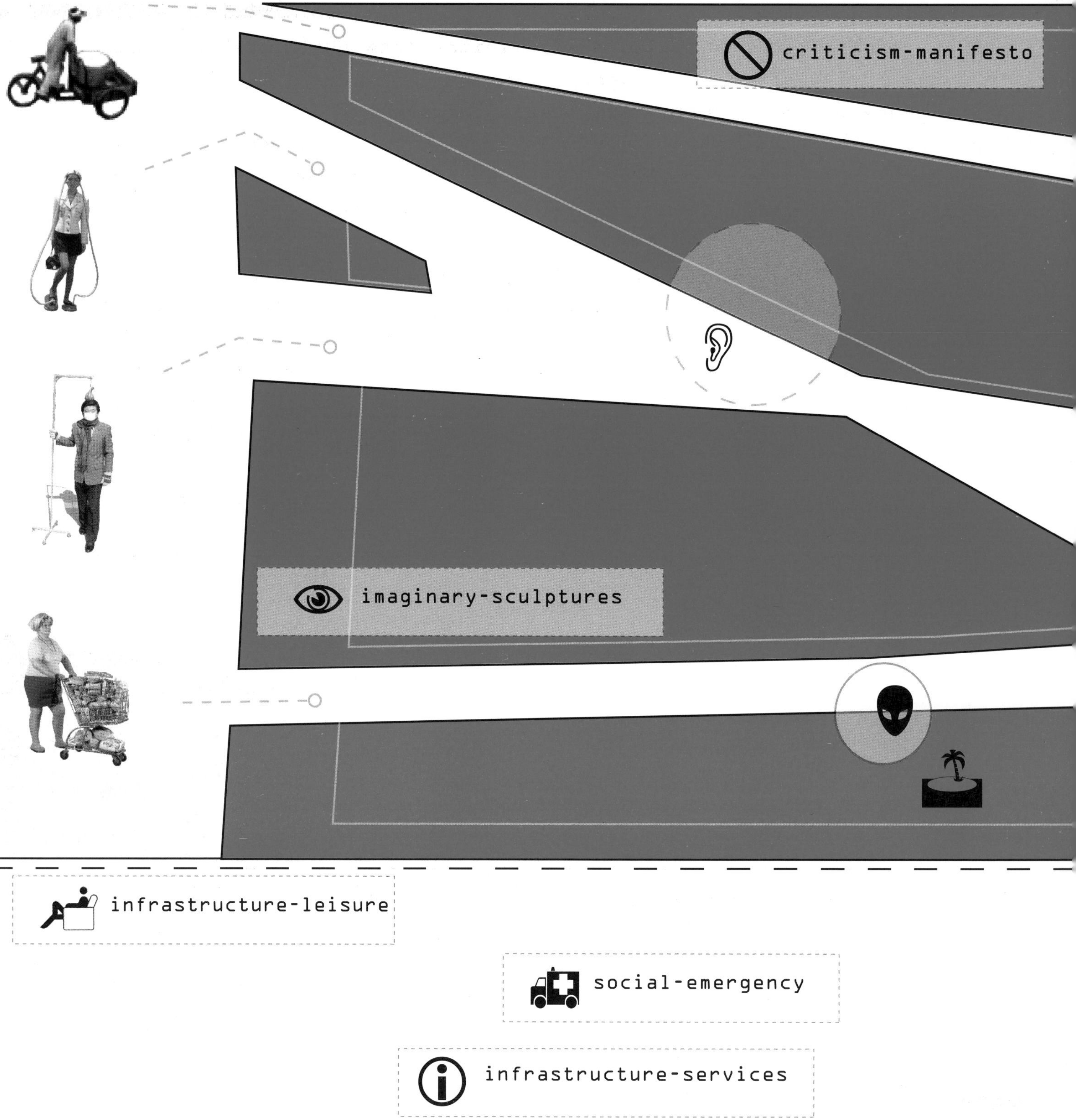
criticism-manifesto
imaginary-sculptures
infrastructure-leisure
social-emergency
infrastructure-services

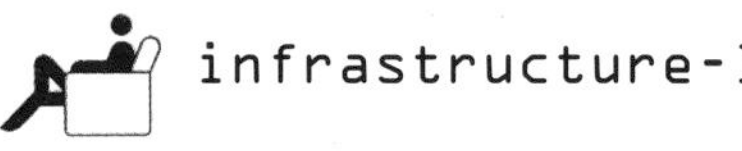

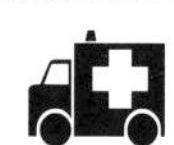

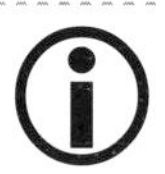

Their applications and uses are infinite, from dwellings for rural communities, emergency situations and infrastructure requirements to much more advanced and sophisticated contexts.
Projects that create the city using independent and mobile units.
Projects that provide the city, taking infrastructure and services to places where there are as yet none; projects that are waiting to be invaded, put to use, brought to life.
Political, critical and social architecture, interested in the inhabitants of the city's spatial leftovers, absent places, complex and extraordinary realities that are not accepted or that are often simply ignored, but that are always present in every urban scene.
Projects that express ideals, that take a stand against some urban event, that make certain realities visible, realities which are tangential, unstable, fragile, realities that survive.
Architecture that isolates, bubbles that protect, minimum room units, a garment, a second skin.

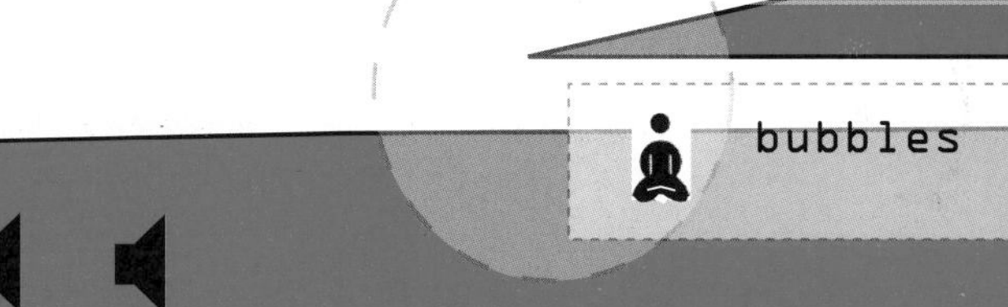

poetic, sculptural, imaginary, utopian projects.

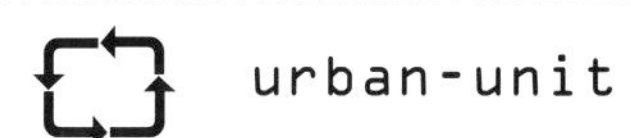

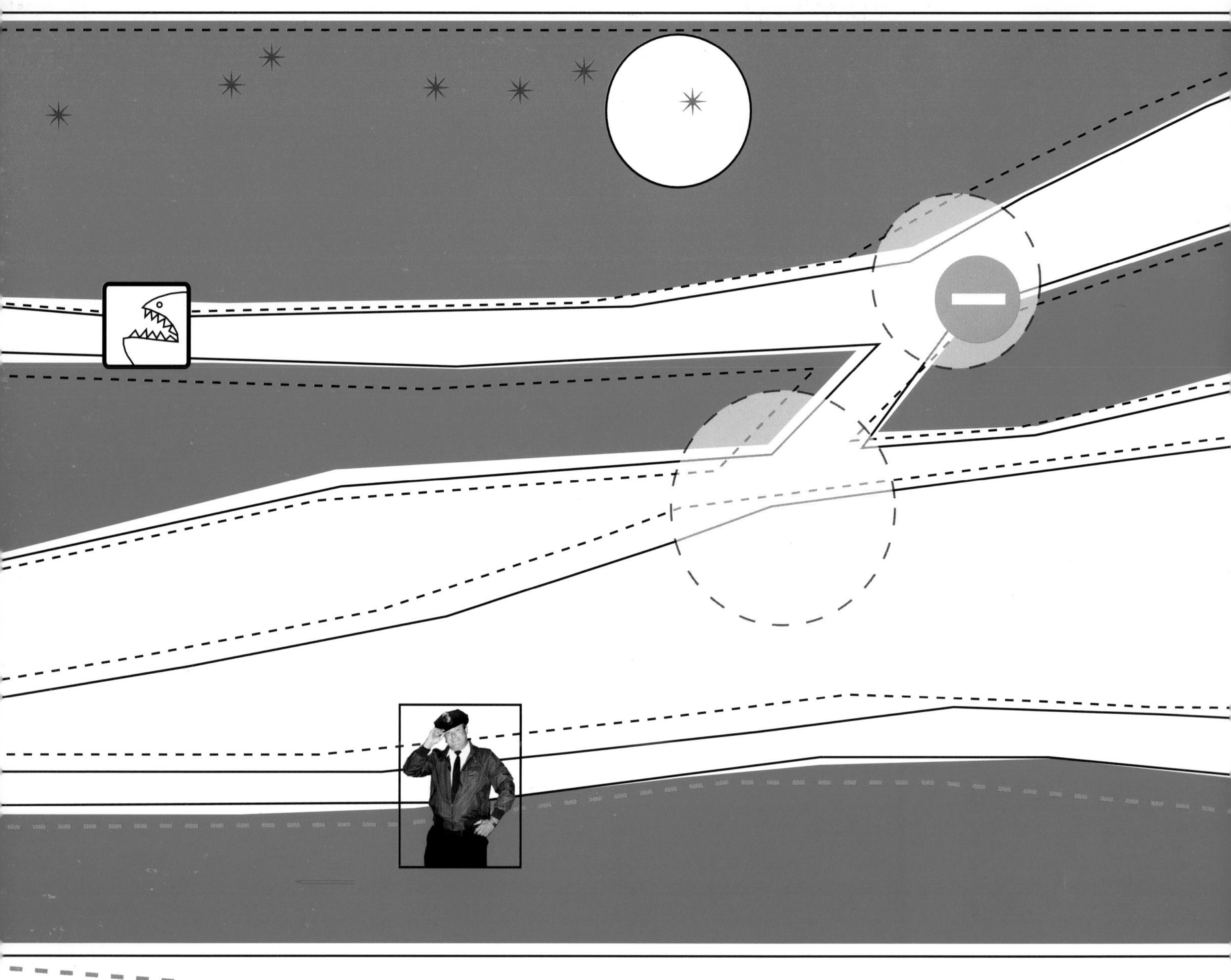

An area —of land, of time, of the imagination— is liberated and then dissolved in order to be built in some other place or time.

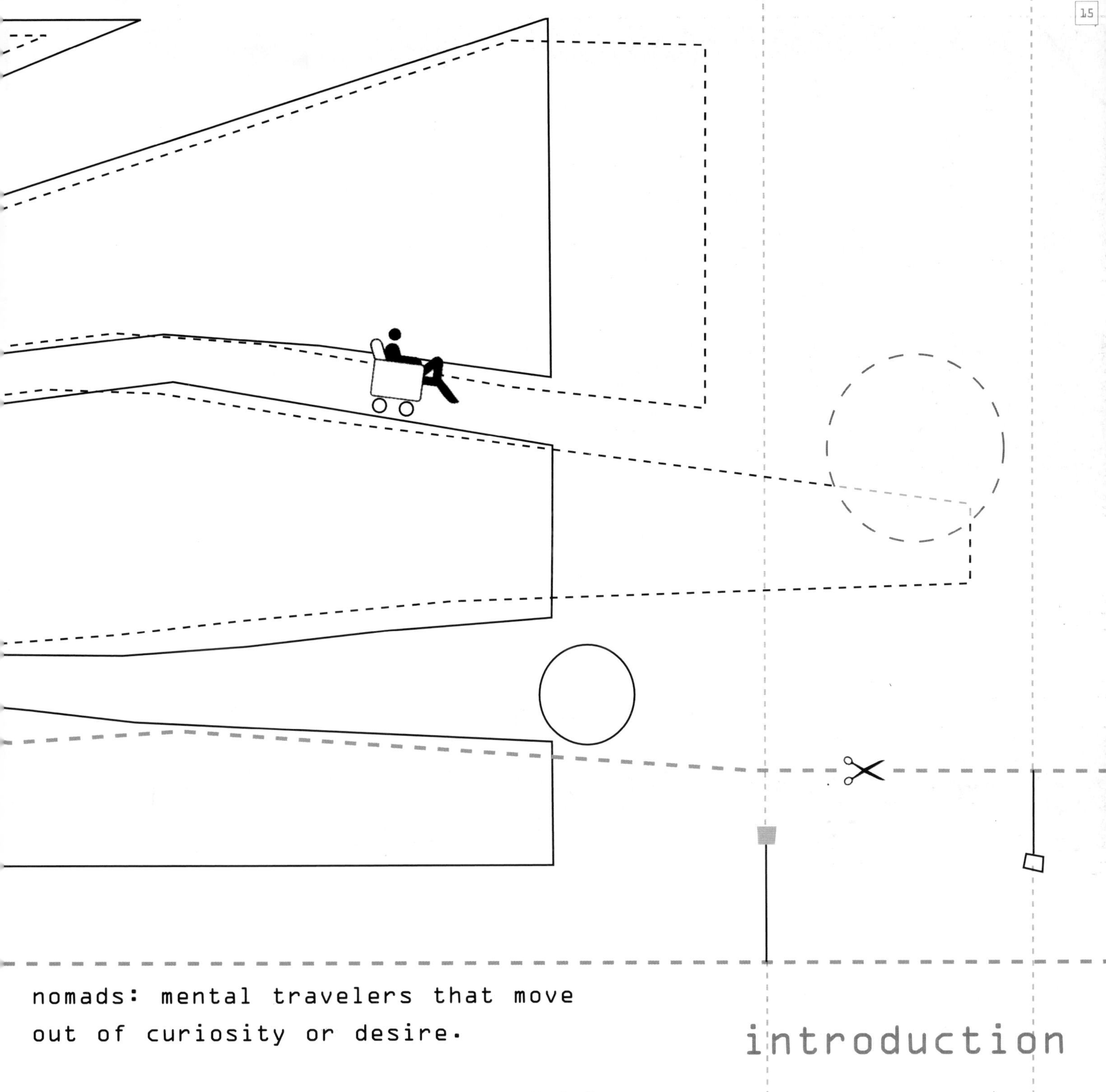

introduction

nomads: mental travelers that move out of curiosity or desire.

*fragments from: TAZ. The temporarily autonomous zone. Hakim Bay

Tipiwakan 2004

Portable Architecture, almost a contradiction.

Where did it begin? How can its history be told?

Thousands of years of tradition, of mobile lives crossing places and situations in a constant state of change, unpredictable landscapes, natural and urban settings, war-torn lands, fictitious and, now, cybernetic-virtual spaces: structures capable of responding, reacting and protecting without leaving a physical trace. Like architecture in stone, they have survived. Today, they still satisfy the demands of a life in motion.

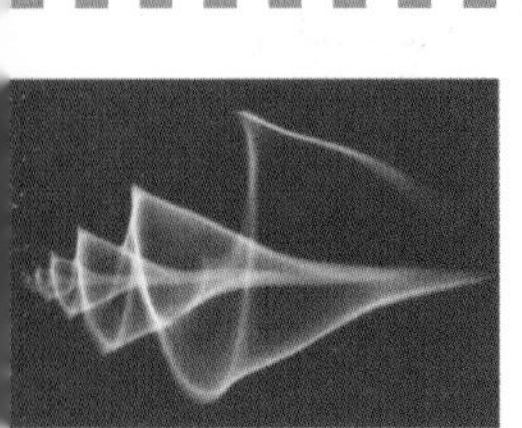

They appear and disappear, because they adapt and inspire.

Easy to move, flexible, single-space structures made from lightweight, resistant materials: construction technology thus merges with that of transportation. Their materials are as light as fabric, branches and leather.

In motion, the concept of permanence is in the repetition, in the recreation of the same spatial order in each new location.

end.

"One Week", Buster Keaton

Nomads of the desert, of water, of work. Mobile, wandering, mutating cities.

'Dymaxion house', designed in 1927 by Buckminster Fuller, was based on aircraft technology and became the universal prototype for low-cost production. It was designed as a new form of domestic living, suggesting the incorporation of mobility and speed into daily life; a prefabricated habitable machine which was independent from urban networks.

Because of its temporary nature, mobile architecture arose with a spirit of playfulness and experimentation in the twentieth century. The wildest dreams and most unimaginable projects took shape as hypotheses, and were made real thanks to advances in construction, transportation, material and information technologies.

Buckminster Fuller

With the automobile industry came a certain fascination for the machine aesthetic.

War and emergencies have always spurred the development of new techniques, minimizing the focus on aesthetics, while generating ingenious and practical designs, new materials, structures which are increasingly more lightweight and easy to assemble, economical and temporary dwellings, inflatable structures: this is the construction of the most precise relationship between form and life.

Airstream, a new form of tourism

mobile cities

They are multi-story, three-dimensional structures set up on pilotis. The inhabitant can freely move about the room according to the layout of the structure.

spatial structures

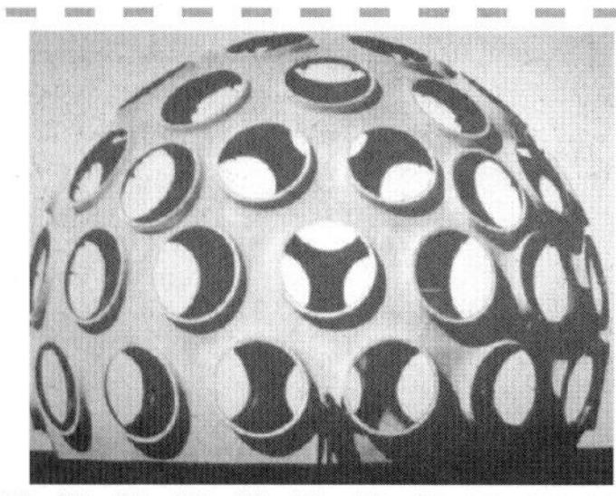

Buckminster Fuller

1959-Ville spaciale, Yona Friedman

Spatial networks: they are structures that allow for the creation of spherical, elliptical, self-supporting and moveable spaces.

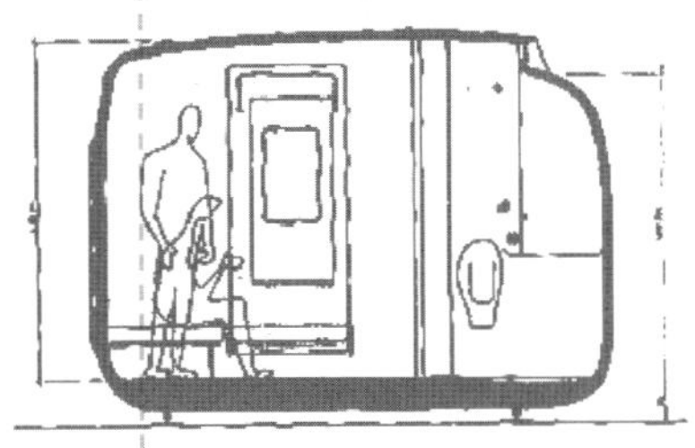

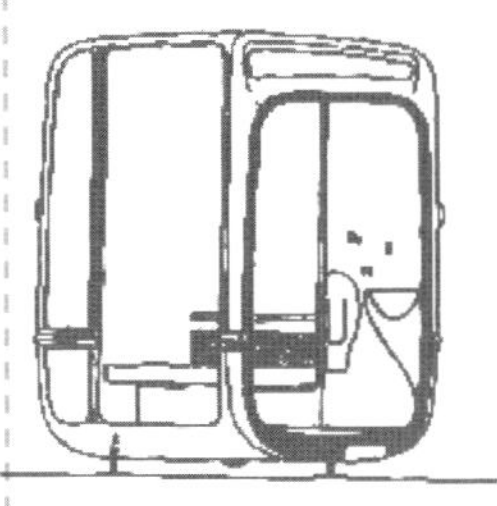

cells

The 1960's exploration of mobility in architecture gave rise to the definition of a new organic and modular space based on the expansion and agglomeration of cells. This stage in the concept of habitat design, with its mobility and economy, gave the inhabitant freedom to adapt by adding on and combining cells.

jean maneval

1956 Ionel Schein

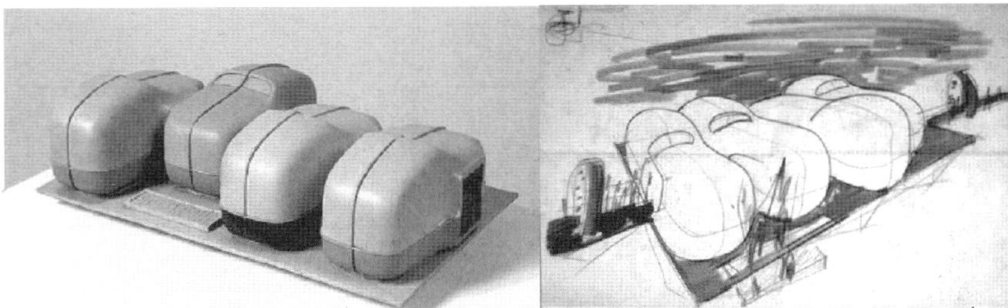

It was the first prototype of a dwelling in plastic.

"What happens if the whole urban environment can be programmed and structured for change?" P.Cook

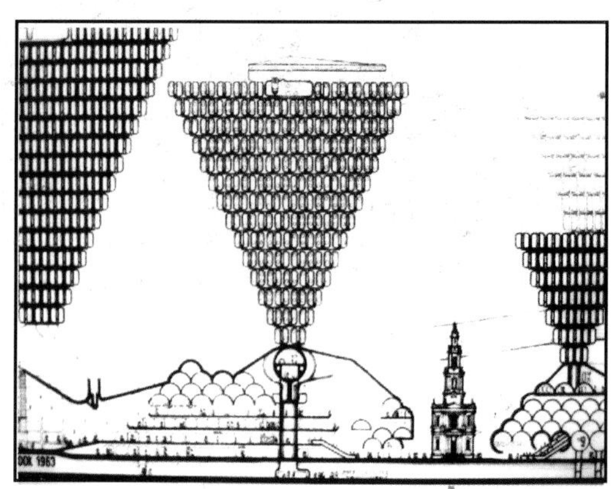

the first global city that was not subject to the logic of location.

Archigram's work focused on an exchange between communication, mobility and the city, foreseeing the major impact that digital technology and global information systems would have on the body, surrounding space and human interaction.
More than proposing a concrete form of architecture, they illustrated relationships and connections within urban life in the desire to provoke the observer and inspire reflection.

Instant city

Walking city, Ron Herron

Plug-in-city, Peter Cook

it moves literally on the landscape

Architectonic, experimental, provocative, psychedelic design

These projects gave the modern nomad the freedom that the materiality of traditional architecture had repressed.

The Plug-in City is set up by applying a large scale, network-structure, containing access routes and essential services, to any terrain. Into this network are placed units which cater to all needs.

Is habitat becoming an ephimeral object to be consumed and thrown away?

Cushicle: inflatable garment featuring food, water, radio and TV.

1966, Cushicle, Michael Webb

Living-pod

1968, Suitaloon, Michael Webb

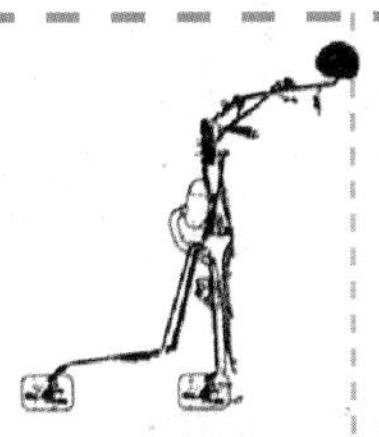

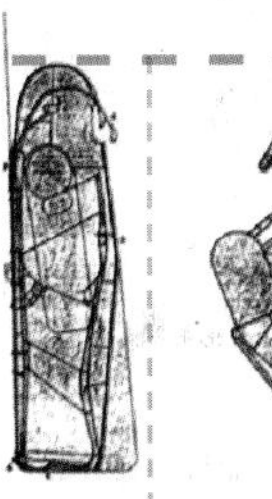

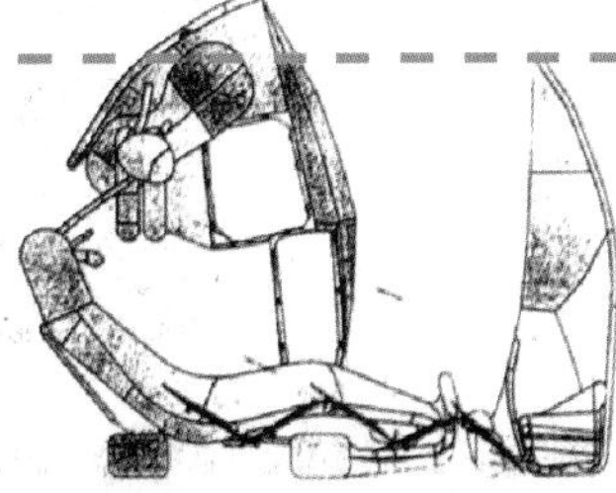

Archigram

mega-structures

Because of the large number of mobile units within each system, they ultimately lose their individual character in the urban context, becoming part of a mass organization.

1964-Wolfgang Doering

Kisho Kurokawa
-Metabolistas

Coop Himmelblau

The philosophy of metabolic design is based on exchangeability, modular buildings, prefabricated parts and capsules. The units move, change or expand according to the needs of the individual, thereby creating organic growth.

Gunther Domenig, Coop Himmelblau and Haus-Rucker-Co explored the potential of pneumatic architecture, a new technology that seemed to offer an immediate, flexible and organic architecture.
The work of Haus-Rucker-Co fluctuated between art and architecture and aspired to shock —a means rather than an end— in order to boost learning processes and experiences.
The construction of lightweight pneumatic structures, of non-physical environments, emerged at the end of the 1960s. Haus-Rucker-Co proposed a provisional, anticipatory architecture that foresaw future changes in the environment, in the territory.

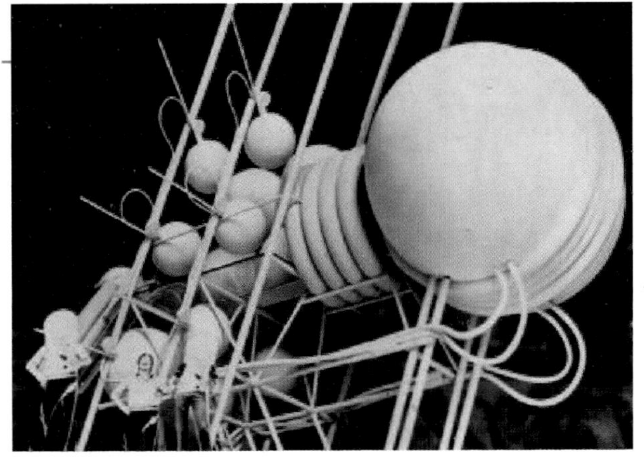

1968 10 x 3.5 x 6 m.

pneumatic architecture

1968-Villa Rosa,
Coop Himmelblau

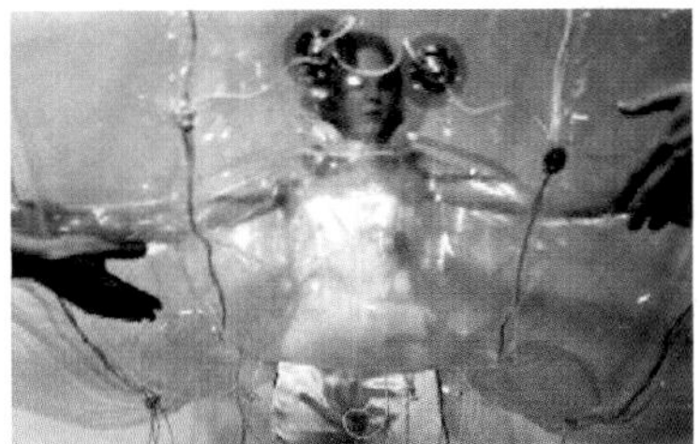

Yellow Heart, Haus-Rucker-Co

For Coop Himmelblau, clouds were symbols of quickly changing states; they come together and mutate according to the interplay of complex and diverse situations.
Rosa II Pneumatic Living Cell.

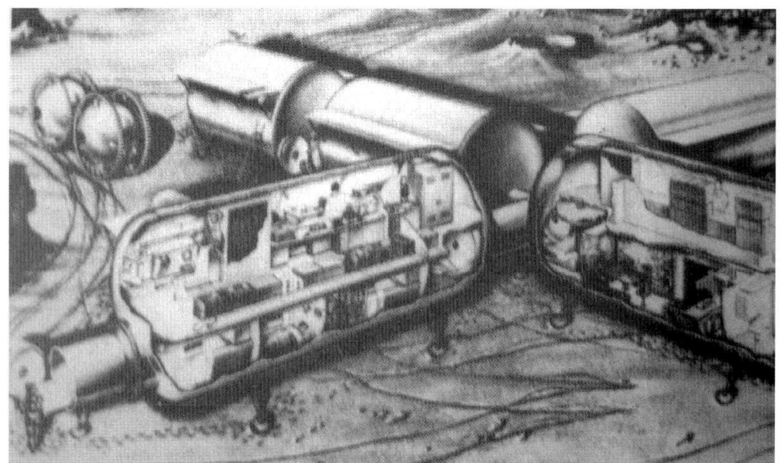

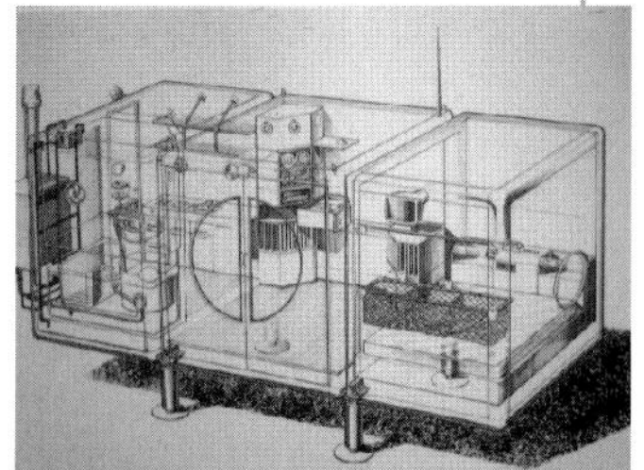

Kurokawa

1960 – The first expedition into space opened new dimensions to architects and urban planners looking toward the city of the future. The technological possibilities and spatial perspectives seemed unlimited at the time. Space architecture shows the need for thinking about self-sustaining, closed systems and survival capsules.

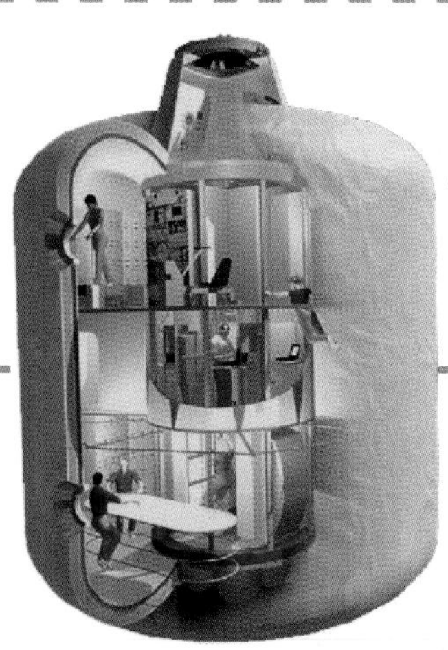

NASA

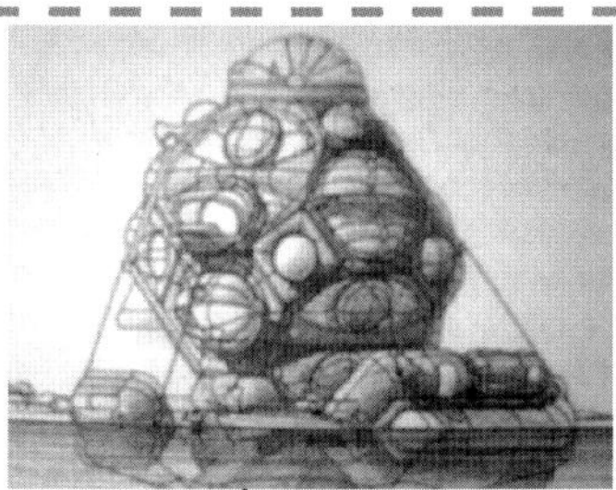

At first, inflatable structures were only used for military purposes.

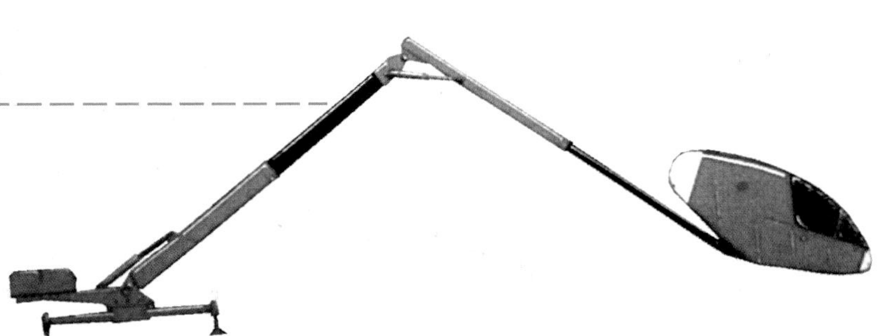

Because of greater migration and increased population density, there was a trend toward reducing the size of the domestic unit, thereby giving way to micro architecture, in which shape is an expression of the body-object relationship. The areas which were at that time uninhabited, such as the poles, the sea and the air, became the stages for fiction and utopia.

Future Systems

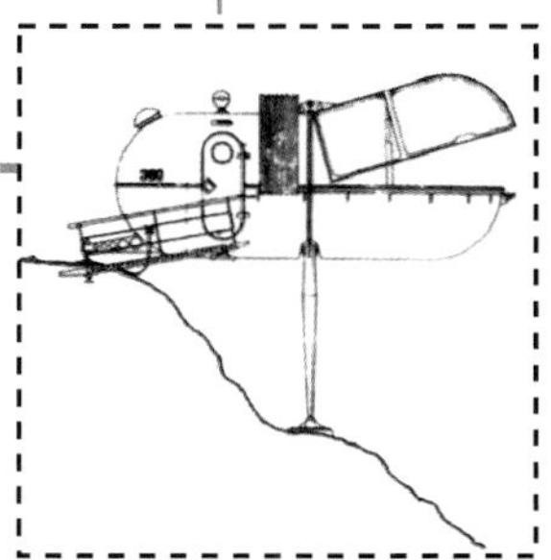

Teatro del Mondo,
Aldo Rossi, 1980

Technology facilitates movement, simultaneousness, communication and information, cutting distances and time, leading us to inhabit a chaos of material and events. If space and time were once universal constants, now it can be said that movement is. Population migrations caused by diverse kinds of political, social, economic and cultural events, natural catastrophes and war — the ratio of population to land has changed dramatically, and the city cannot be planned solely on territories, but rather on behaviors and mechanisms that generate urban life.

'Mobile Home', Peter Garfield

Uprooted homes magically flying over cities, fields, deserts and oceans.

5-17 km/h

All inhabitants build their own constellation of material and immaterial places in order to define multiple personal territories. Intimate and mobile habitats submerged in incomprehensible and uncertain territory and reflecting the contemporary complexity of different lifestyles. A new fragmented and personalized terrain in which the relationship between the local and the global is unpredictable. Bodies in motion, comprising spaces and delocalized urban relations, accentuating changing dynamics, simultaneous experiences, spreading out across the terrain while at the same time being in a fixed location.

More than finished objects, they are processes that make a complex map of relations and tensions more interesting than a physical map of the city or of the territory.

Portable architecture is found and re-found, changing places, constantly altering the city, the landscape, its borders, its mazes, its character.

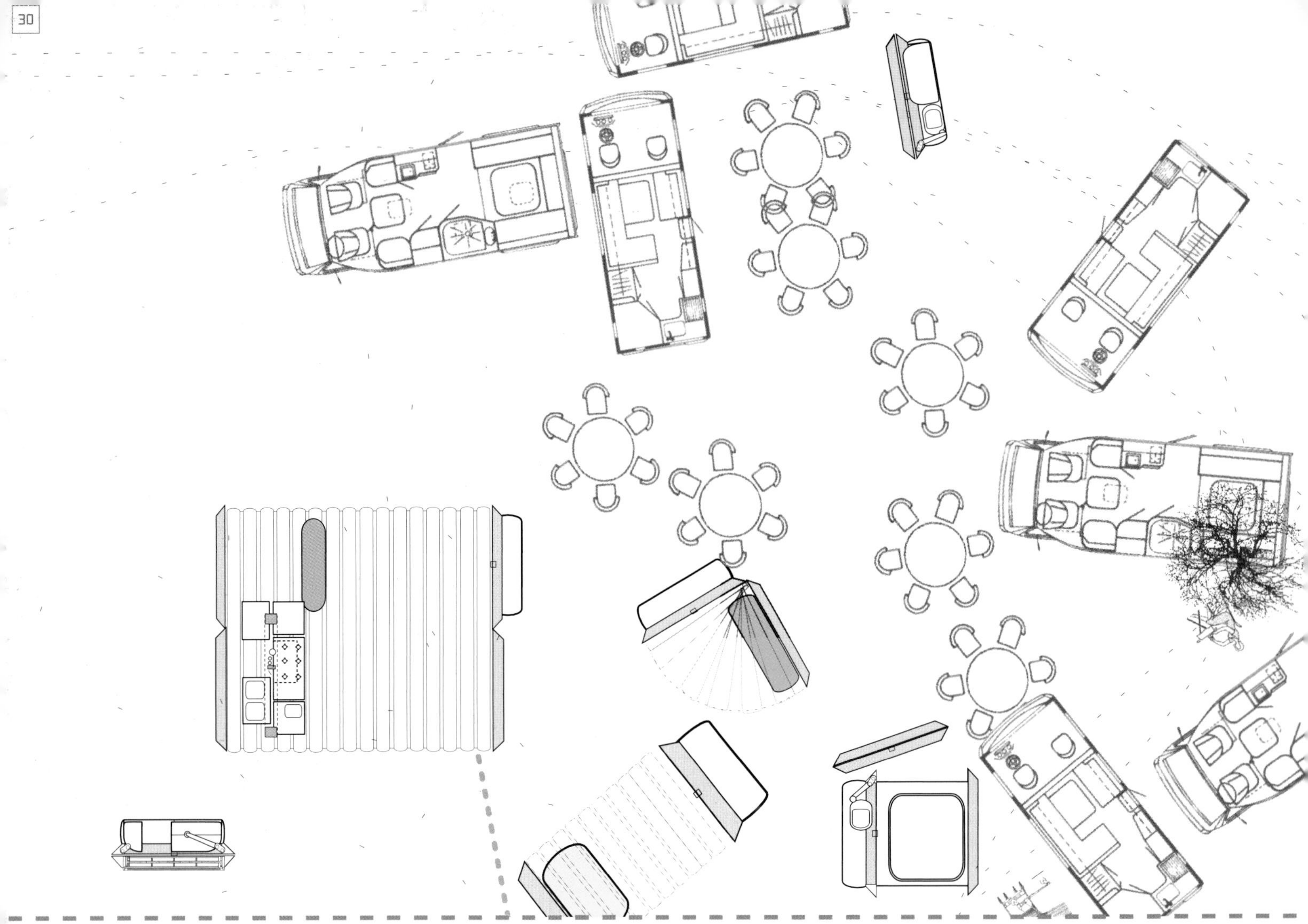

De-materialization is freedom and motion; objects meld with and become the body, portable and light.

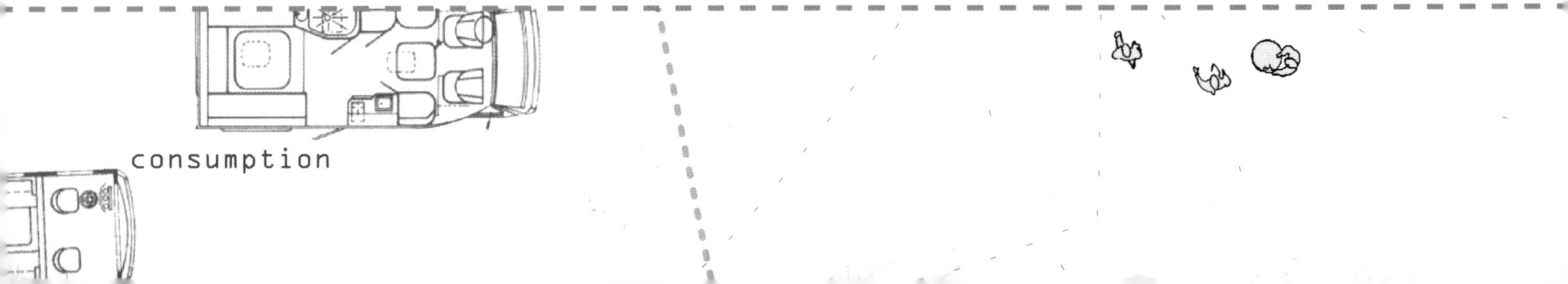

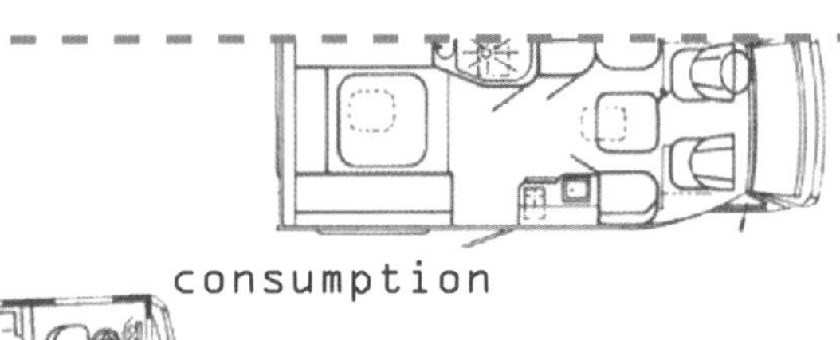

consumption

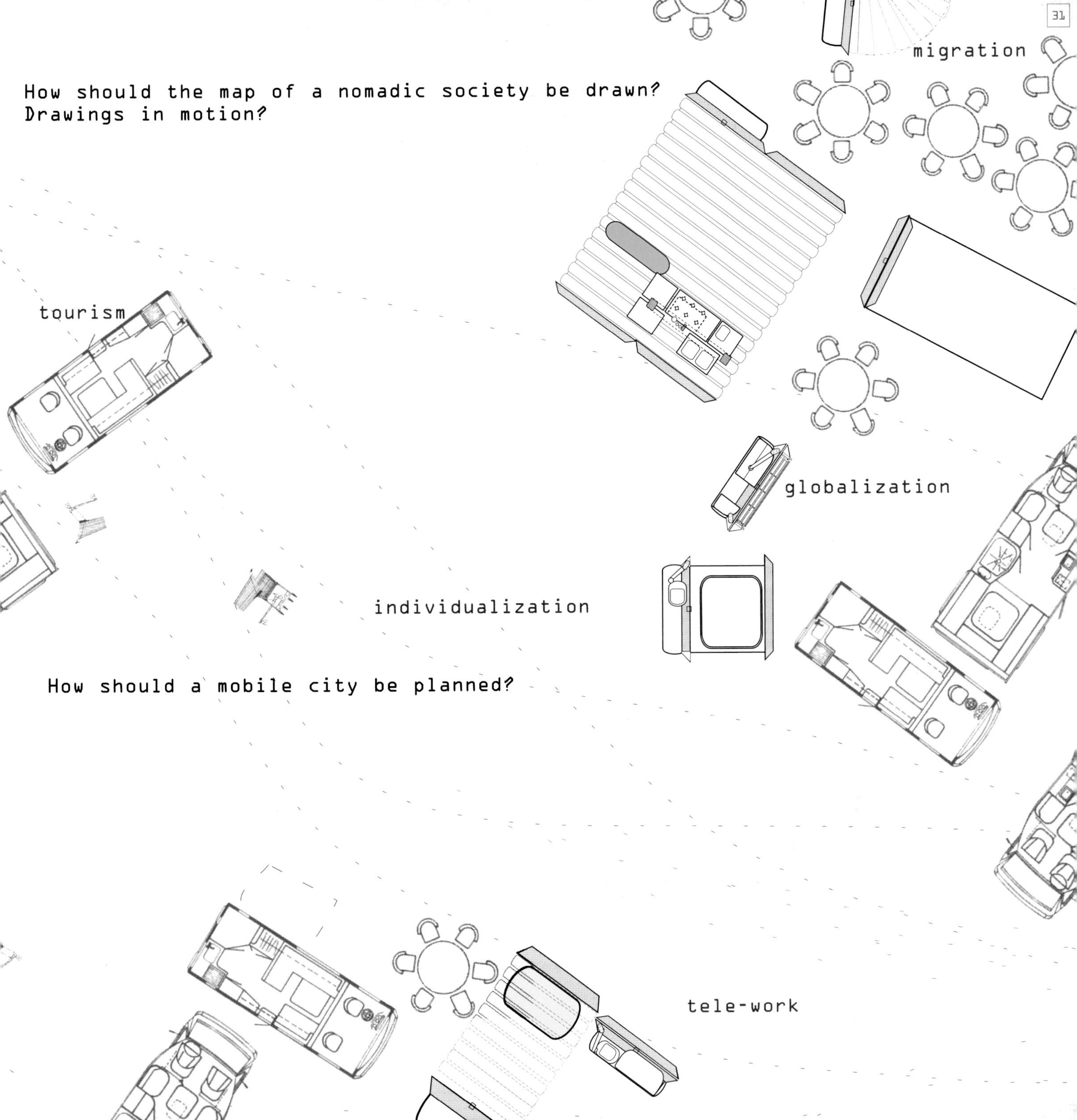
How should the map of a nomadic society be drawn?
Drawings in motion?
migration
tourism
globalization
individualization
How should a mobile city be planned?
tele-work

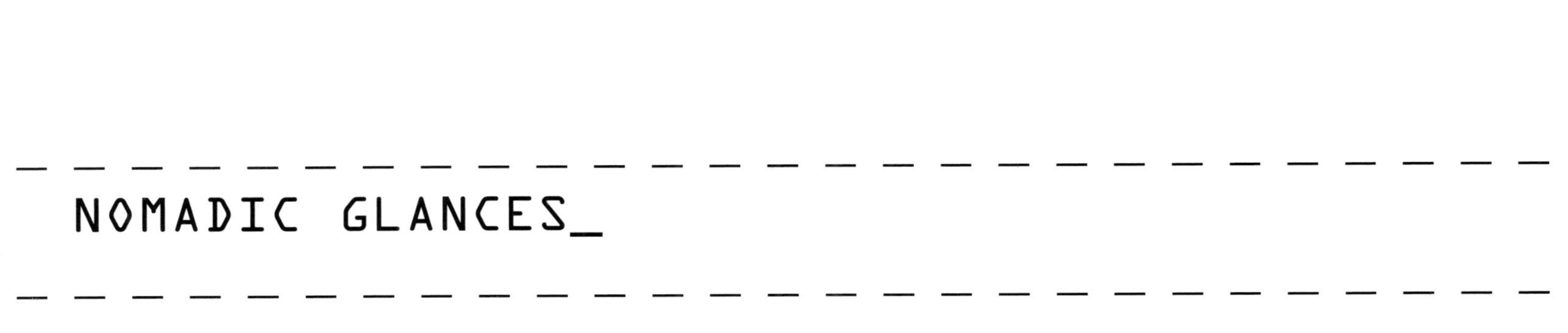
NOMADIC GLANCES_

a portable island

On land, a rowboat is sunk into the ground, its bow filled with soil and grass, with a tree growing out of it. The oars are embedded in the ground, as if rowing on land. You can step down into the boat, and sit inside, as if the land were water. Facing this boat, in the water, is its mirror-image: a rowboat wedged into a circular plane of grass. These dissimilar elements here become one: as in the

PERSONAL ISLAND_ Acconci Studio

rowboat on shore, its bow is filled with soil and grass, a tree growing out of the bow.

You can step out onto the grass plane, and into the boat, and row: the boat takes the circular plane of grass with it, pulling out of a semi-circular cut in the shore as you row your island out to sea.

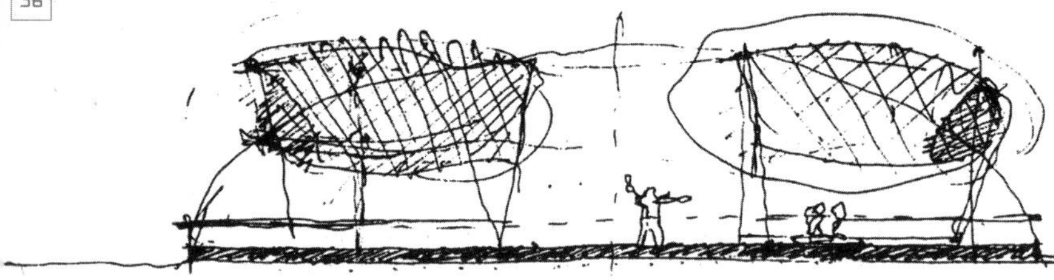

The Floating Pavilion is a multi-use structure that can be used for various creative ventures. Led through canals by a tugboat from the city to the countryside, the pavilion hosts a wide range of activities from festive musical performances to tranquil poetry readings.

Unlike a fixed structure, this pavilion changes location,

space · play · movement · dream · water · change · freedom

FLOATING PAVILION_ Fumihiko Maki +Maki and Associates

evoking different images and, in turn, transforming the image of the place.

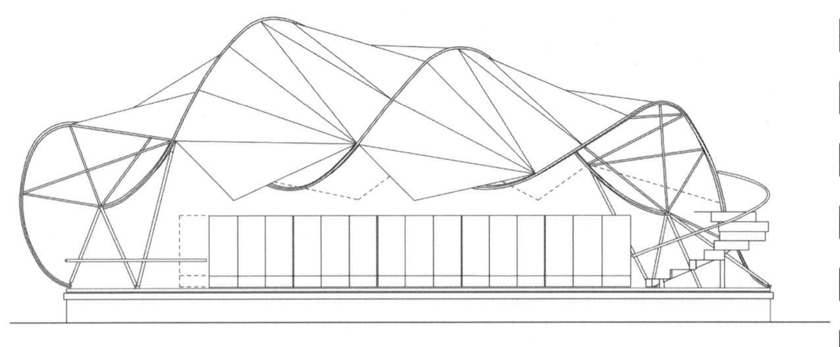

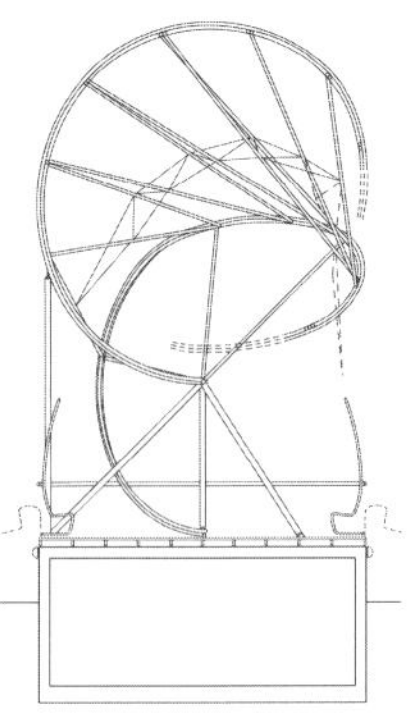

The floating stage enveloped in a white translucent polyester

The canopy rests on a 6 x 25 meter concrete barge that houses dressing rooms,

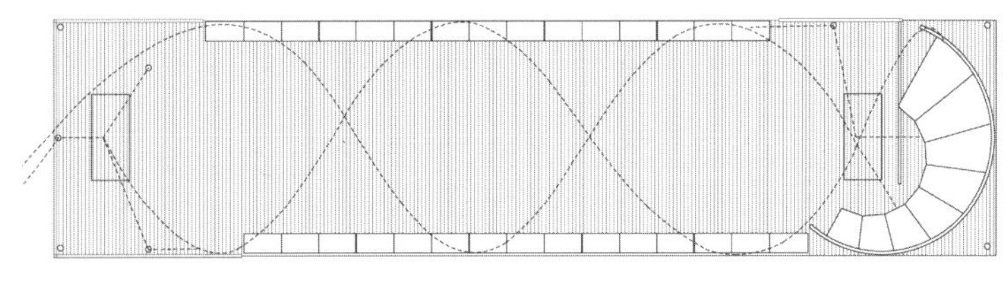

Sailing through the misty countryside, the pavilion's double spiral roof merges with the clouds in the sky. Cast against a dark green forest, the pavilion is transformed itself into a white swan.

canvas is stretched over a double-helical web of light steel tubes and cables.

bathrooms, and storage for the performers.

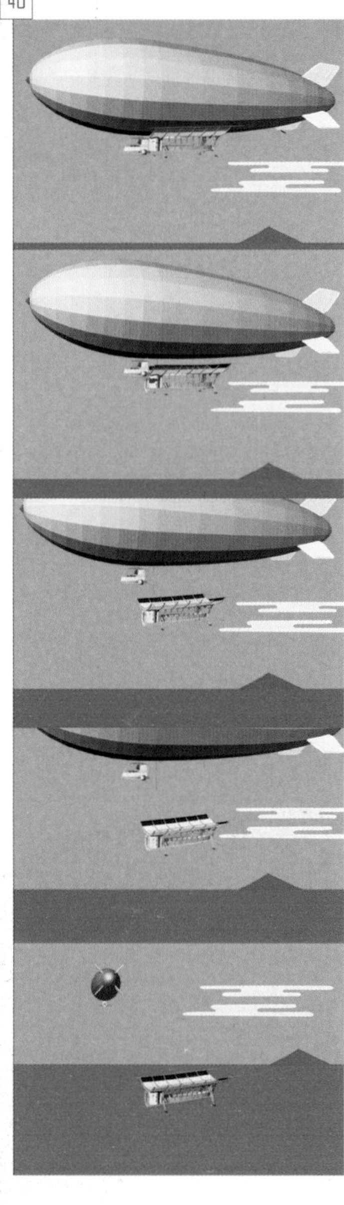

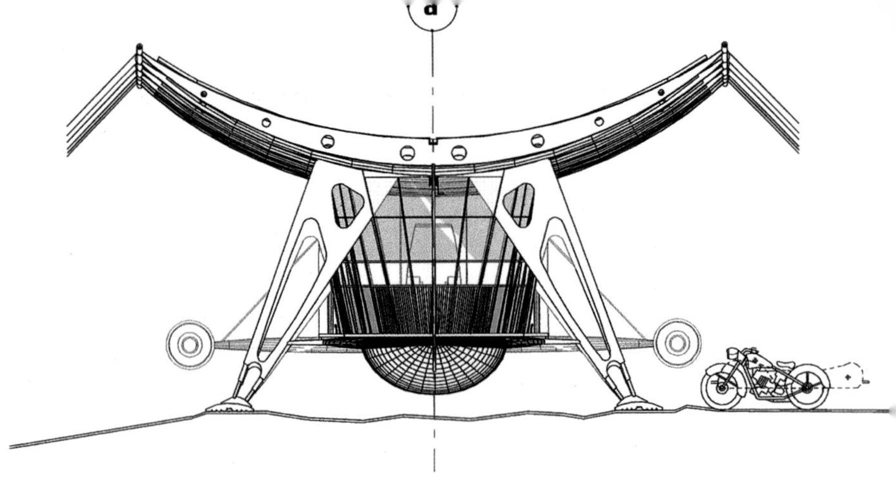

Limitlessly adaptable to terrain, need, and weather; offering patients a degree of comfort and safety, the blimp a symbol of the endless potential and promise of technology, when equipped with the mobile hiv aids clinic, is also a symbol of humanity s benevolence. Modern helium aircraft have been described as the flight of dreams.

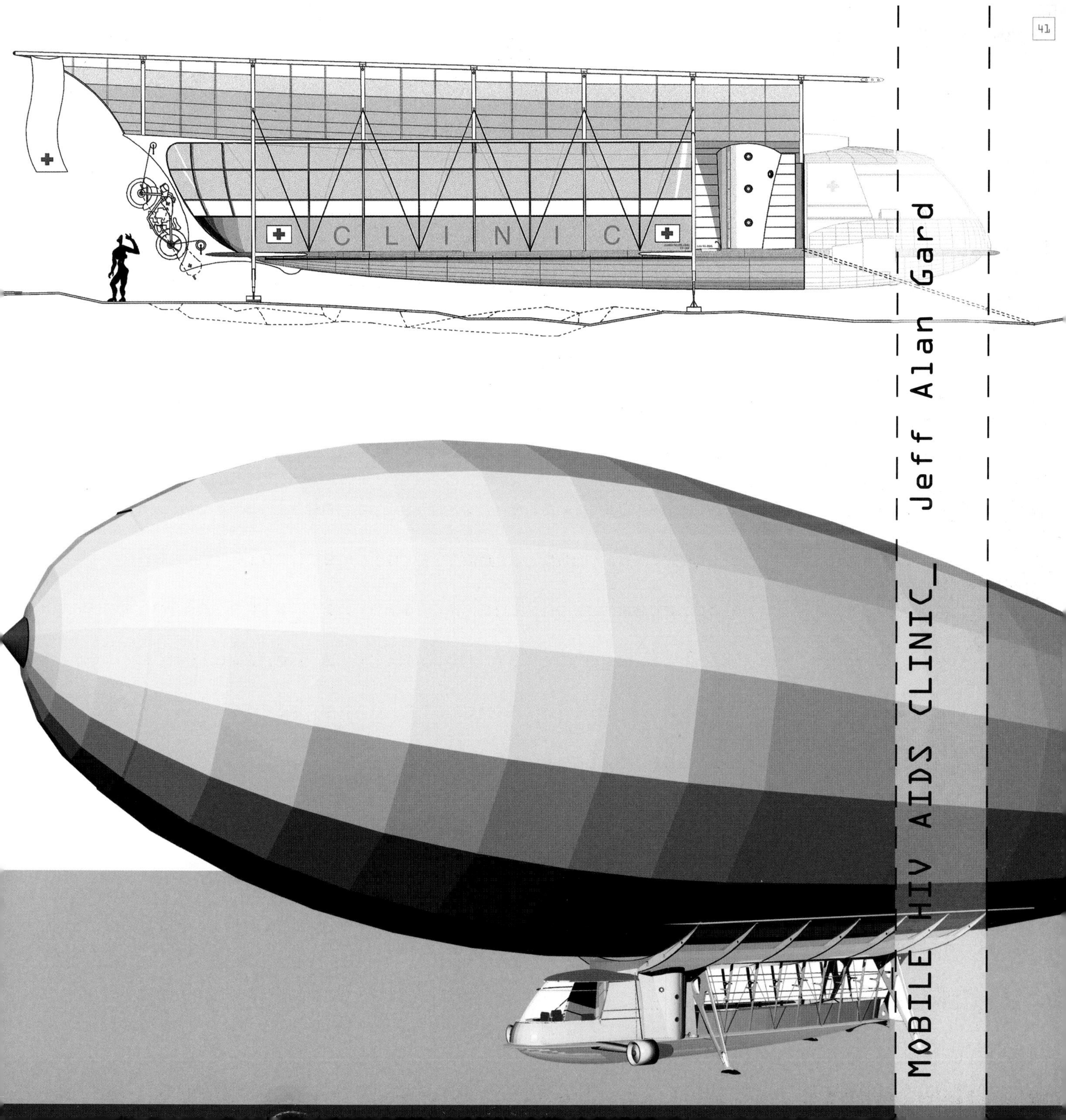
MOBILE HIV AIDS CLINIC
Jeff Alan Gard
CLINIC

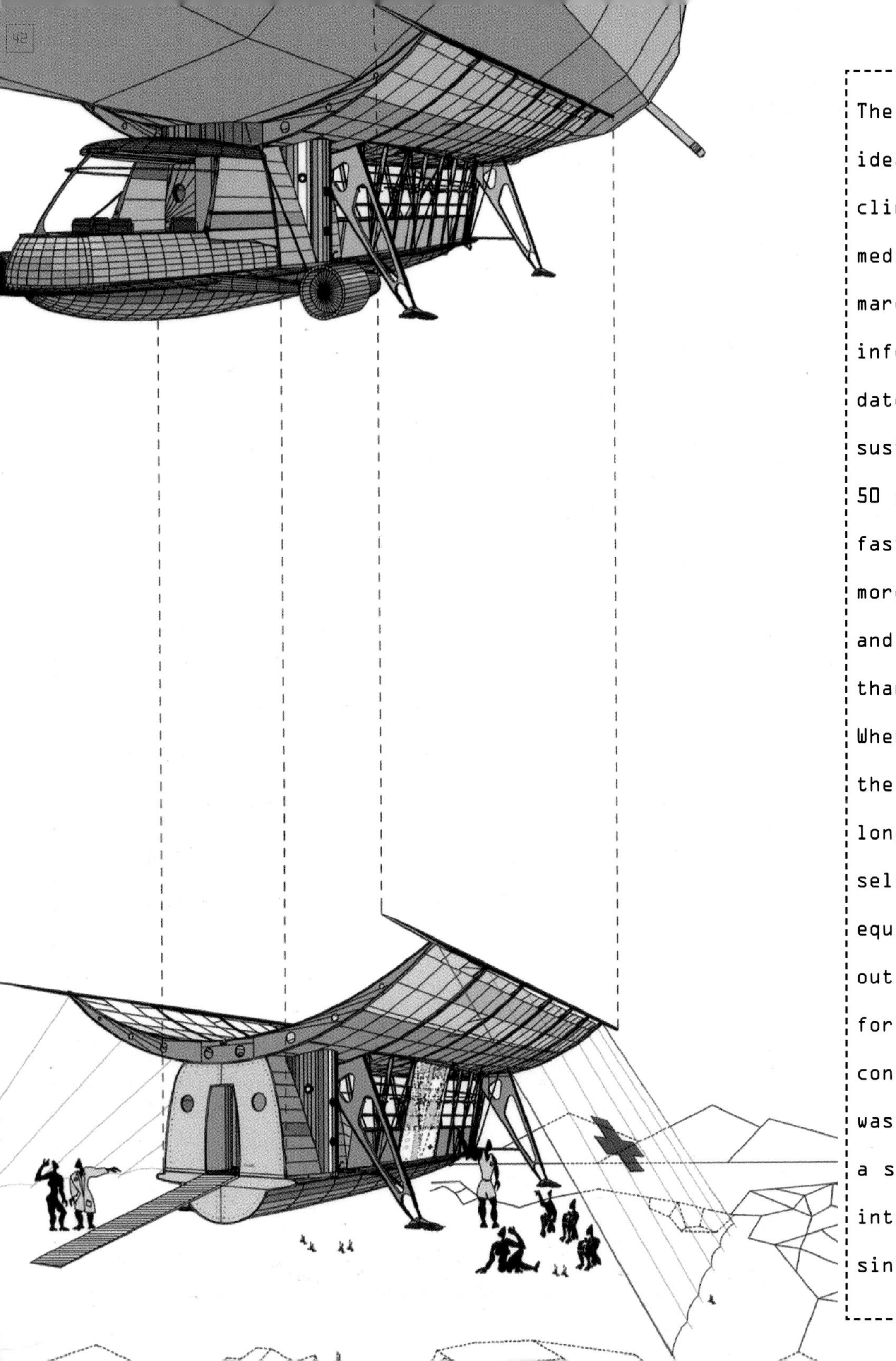

The blimp, besides being an ideal delivery vehicle for a clinic, its staff and sensitive medical equipment, provides a marquee with valuable information, including landing dates and locations. With a sustainable cruising speed of 50 mph, the gentle airship is faster, less restricted, and more reliable over any terrain and over greater distances than a land based vehicle. When isolated from the cockpit, the clinic is roughly 55 feet long, 14 feet wide, and is a self-contained facility equipped with a kitchen, fold out sleeping bunks, storage for supplies, equipment, and containers for water and waste. The clinic includes a shower, bathroom and both interior and exterior scrub sinks.

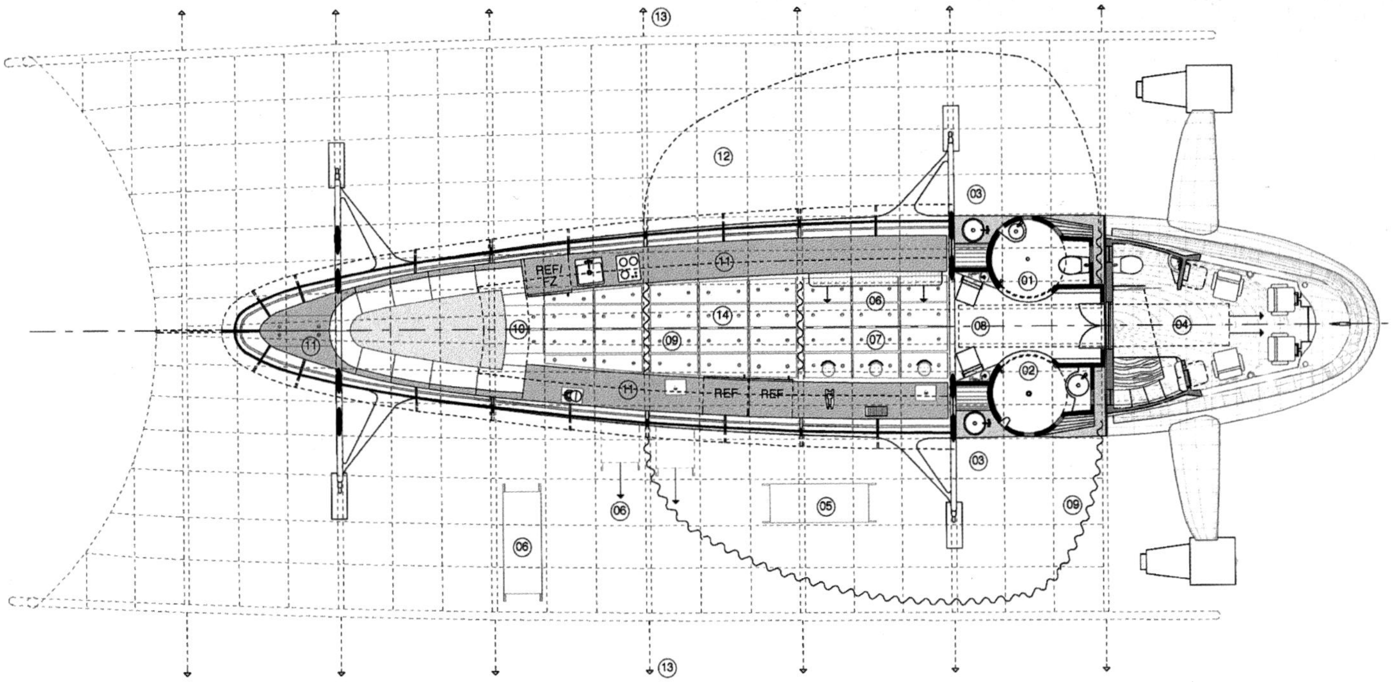

When lowered to the ground adjustable feet and legs level the clinic, and cables coiled at the outriggers of the roof are used to anchor the facility to the site. Tarps strung along the cables create protected areas for classrooms, an outdoor clinic, and camping. Power is provided by a generator and/or solar collectors in the roof. A motorcycle with a stretcher sidecar is mounted to the back of the clinic for local ground transportation. While the clinic is in transit, the smooth ride of the blimp allows the research facilities to remain fully operational and on-line.

The RHINO project seeks to negotiate between the desire to give the reality of HIV a presence through image -a mobile architectural icon- and let the mobile object be a smooth and familiar part of the communities it serves. When arriving at a site, the unit is a distinct object, noticeable in its material difference and shape.

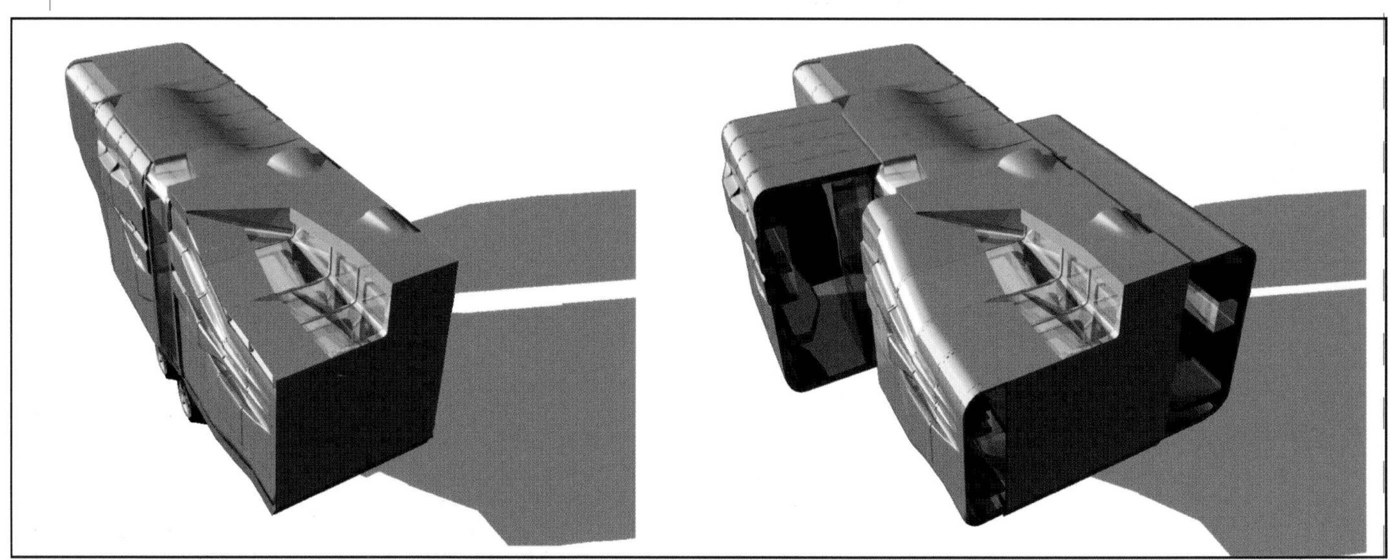

It then begins a transformation which allows it to open up to the community, to take

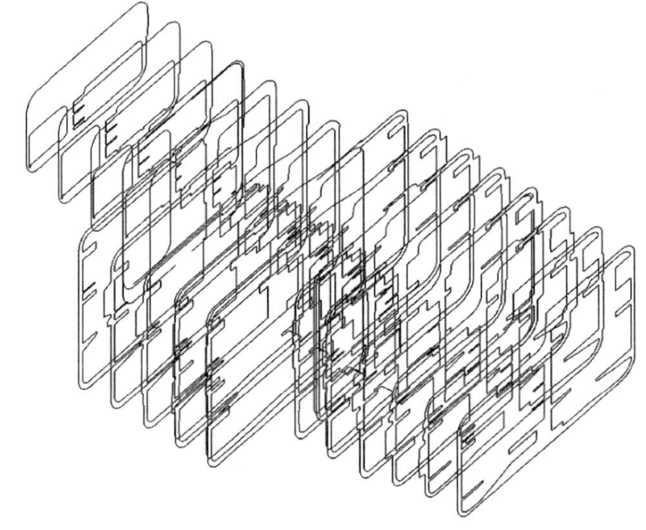

shape and connect to existing familiar networks and pathways.

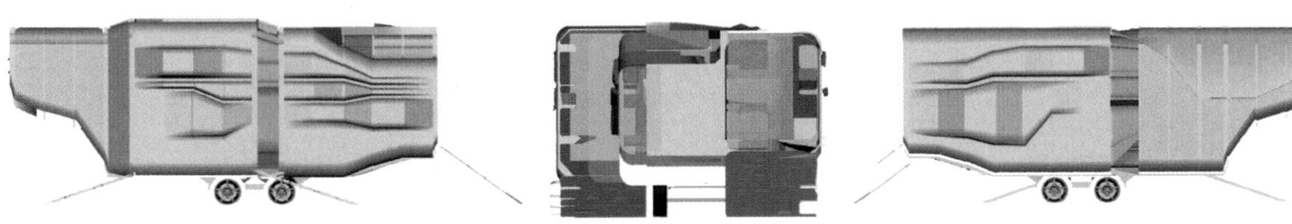

Unpacked, it reveals three areas of engagement: space for education, testing and treatment.

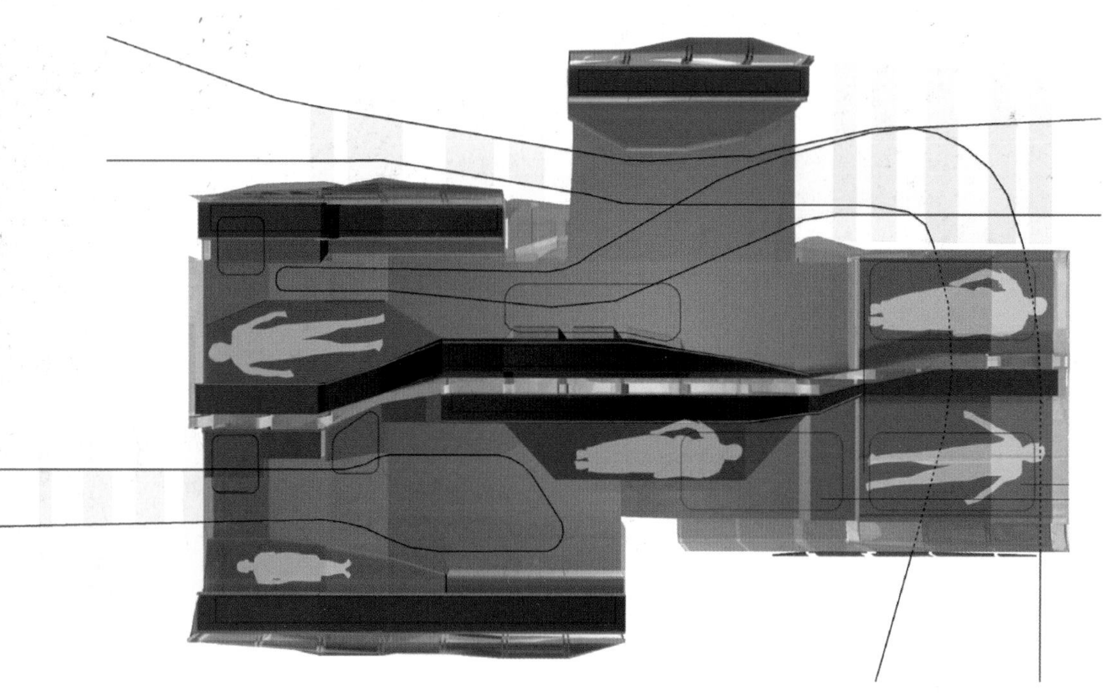

The mobile unit consists of a double-sided spatial configuration that pushes out into its site. The interior is defined by the activities within; specific profiles allow for storage, counter space, seating and bed surfaces to be pushed or pulled from the structural liners. In between the liners lie all of the infrastructure necessary for a medical unit, including water stored in tanks, medical supplies, miscellaneous storage, staff space, rigid structure and electrical systems. These are combined into a central spine in order to increase the area for circulation.

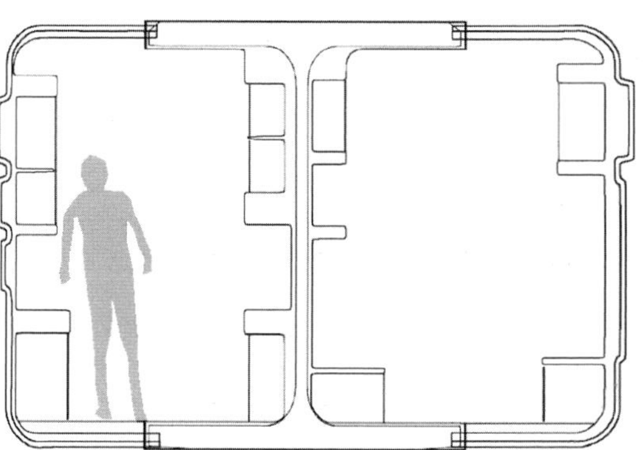

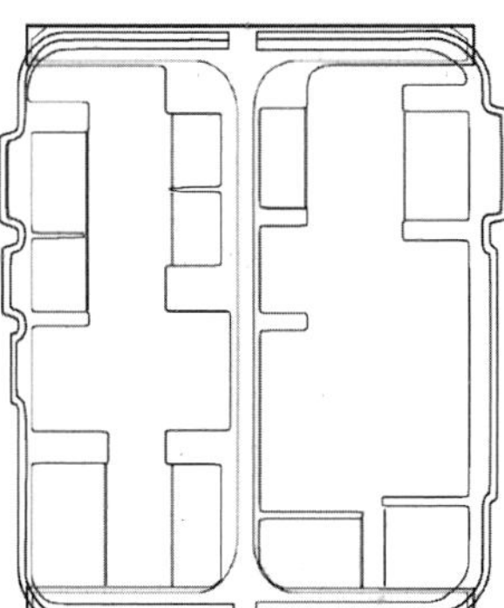

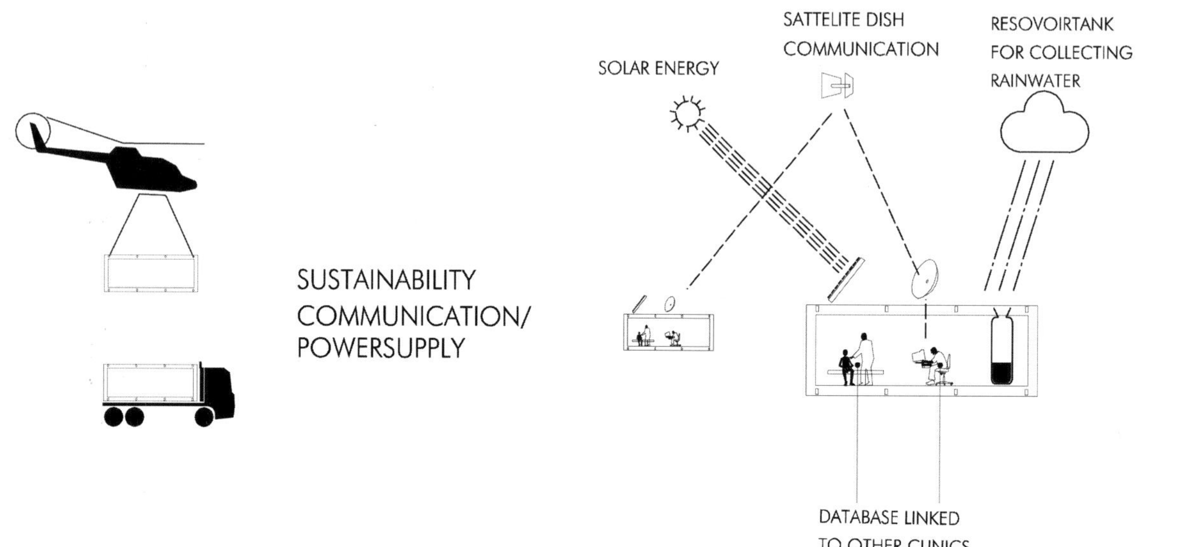

VULNERABLE
CARCASS

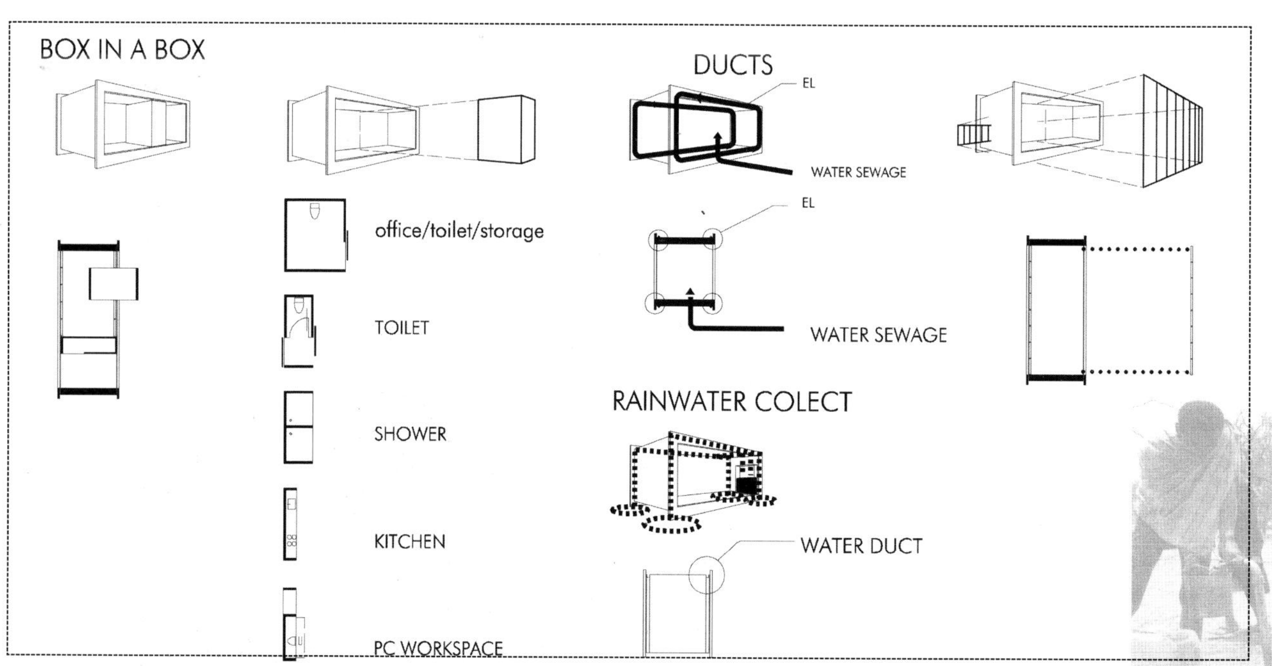

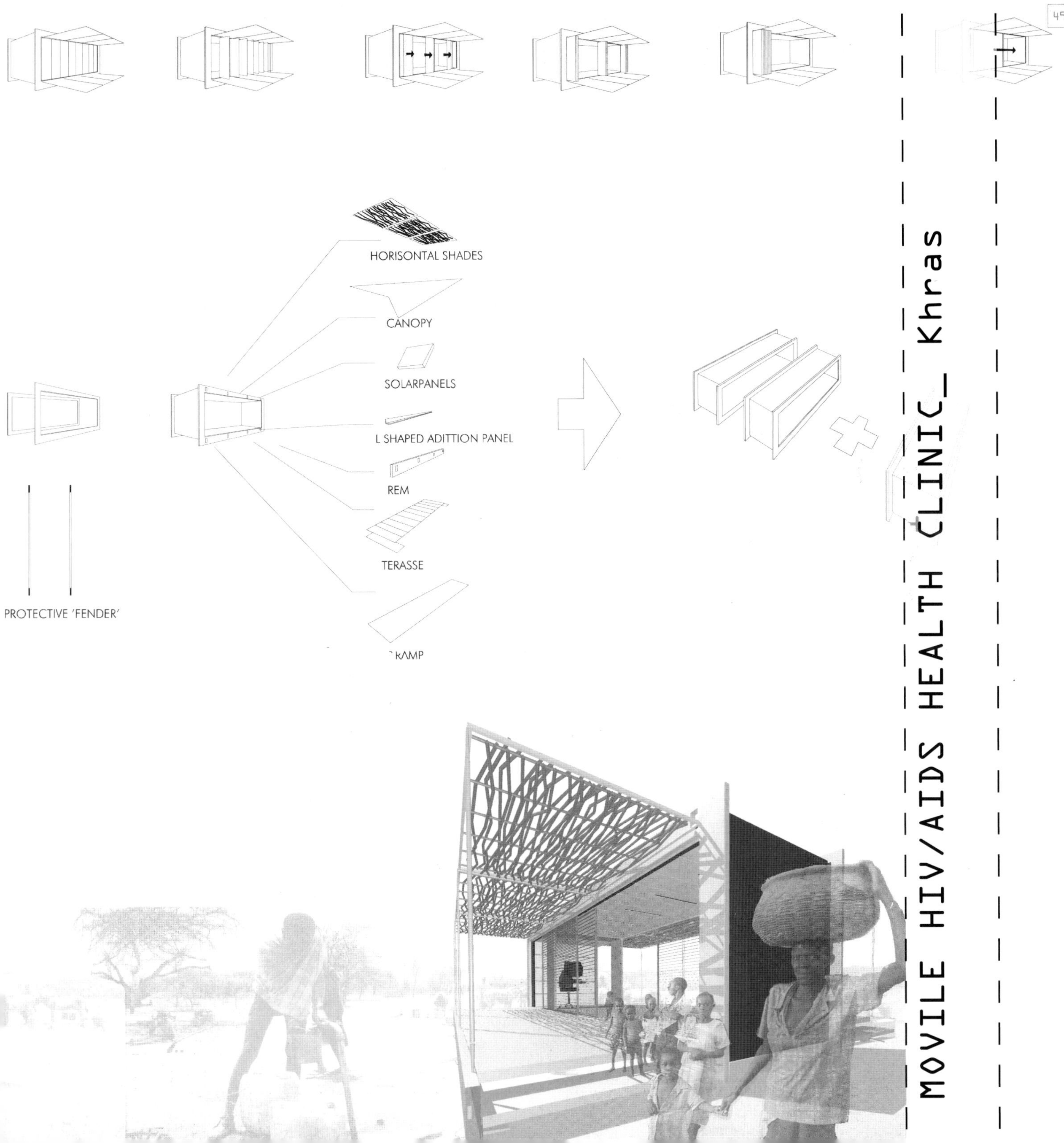
HORISONTAL SHADES
CANOPY
SOLARPANELS
L SHAPED ADITTION PANEL
REM
TERASSE
PROTECTIVE 'FENDER'
RAMP
MOVILE HIV/AIDS HEALTH CLINIC_ Khras

solar panels
satelite dish

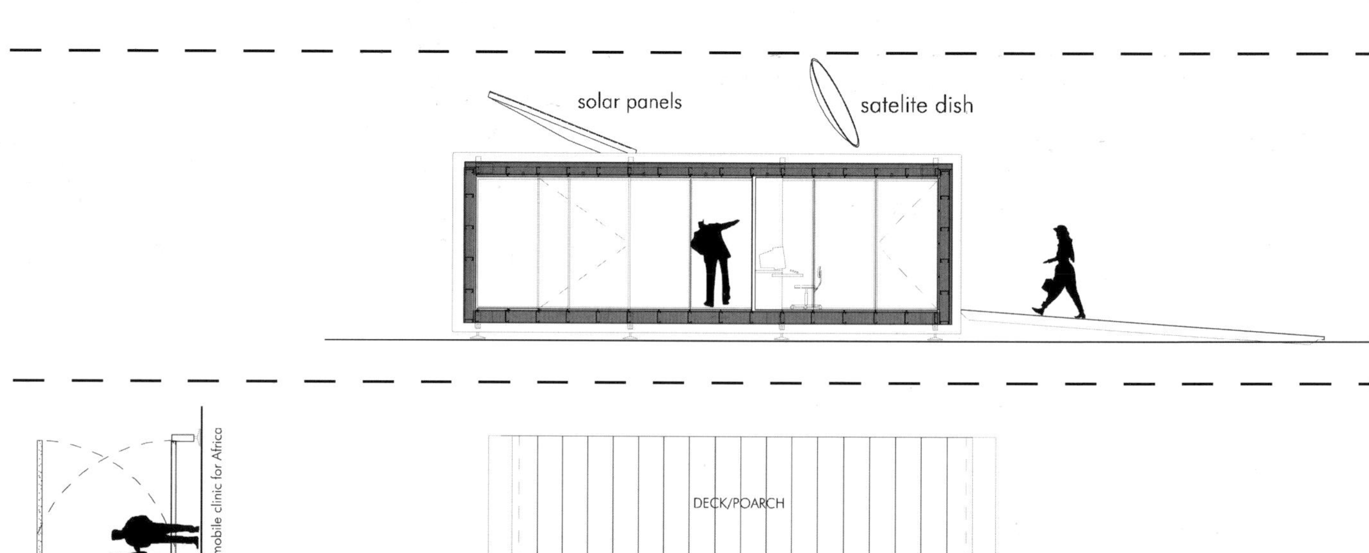

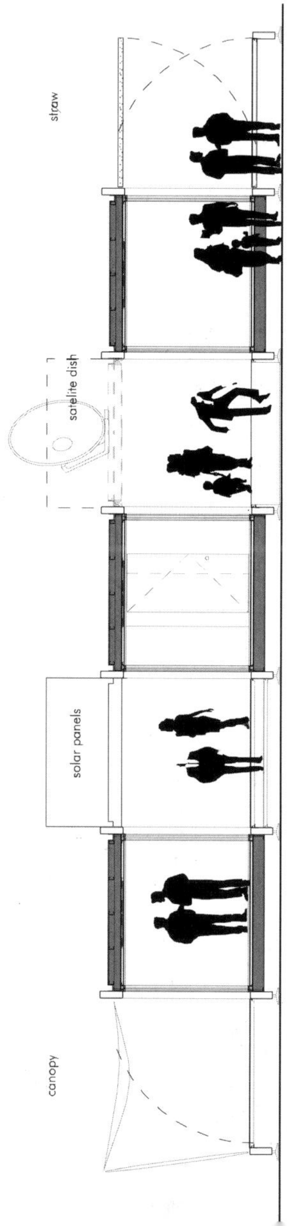

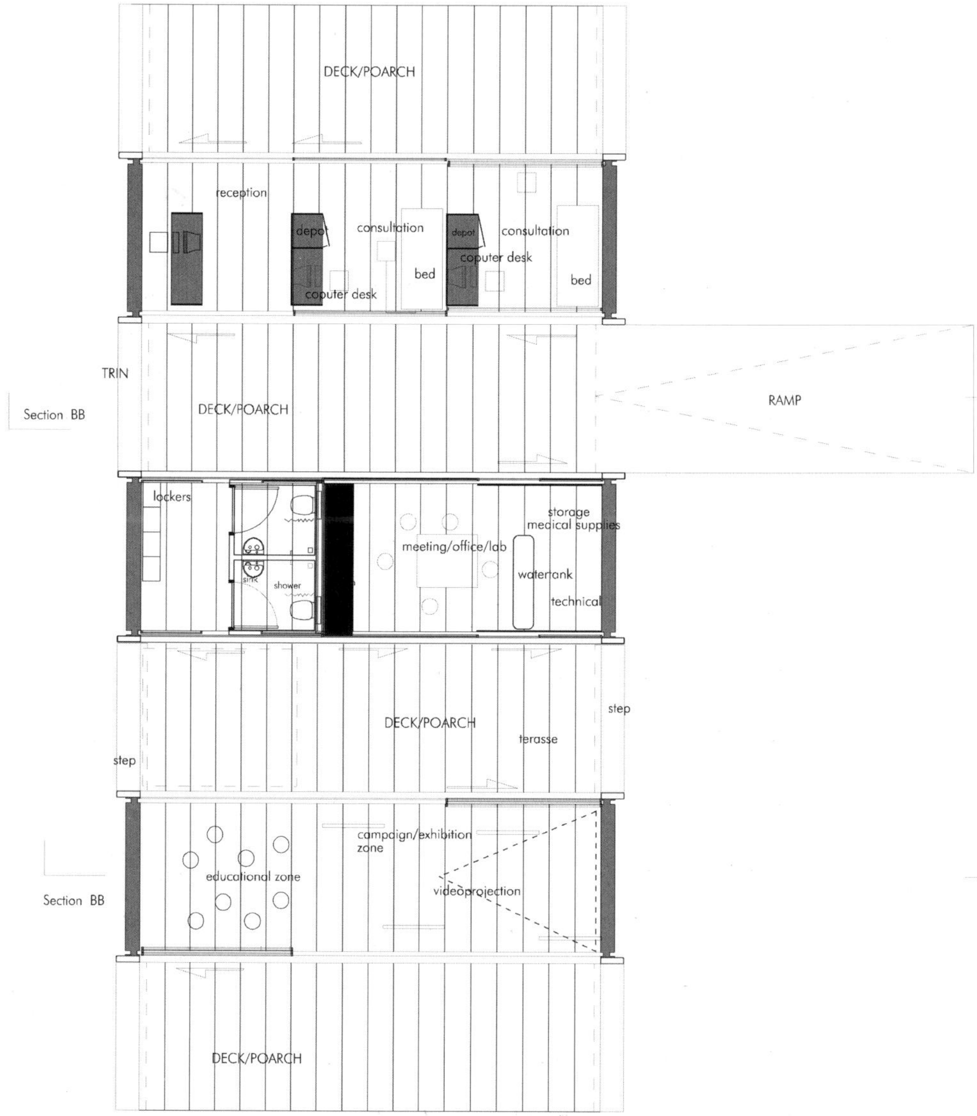

straw
satelite dish
solar panels
canopy

section CC scale 1:100 HIV/AIDS mobile clinic for Africa

DECK/POARCH
reception
depot
consultation
coputer desk
bed
depot
consultation
coputer desk
bed
TRIN
Section BB
DECK/POARCH
RAMP
lockers
sink
shower
meeting/office/lab
storage
medical supplies
watertank
technical
DECK/POARCH
terasse
step
step
campaign/exhibition zone
educational zone
videoprojection
Section BB
DECK/POARCH

In appearance, the clinic aims not to 'Africanize' nor use superficial visual imagery of traditional architecture. Architectural balance and symbolic interaction between the surrounding environment and landscape is achieved through the large steel frames and the nearly nonexistent transparent facade. The simple, open appearance of the clinic invites and encapsulates dialogue between the community and the clinic's medical staff. The building system of the clinic was conceived through close study of other optimized production processes such as the automobile industry. But most importantly, in pursuit of a rational and flexible building system, the designers sought to never lose their focus on keeping the clinic low-tech and easy to operate. The clinic should meet the requirements of both symbolic environmental interaction and isolation from the comfort of any technical support. It's about survival, it's about AIDS.

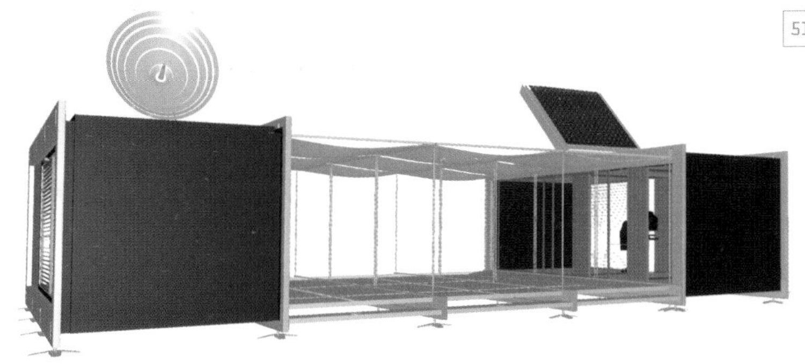

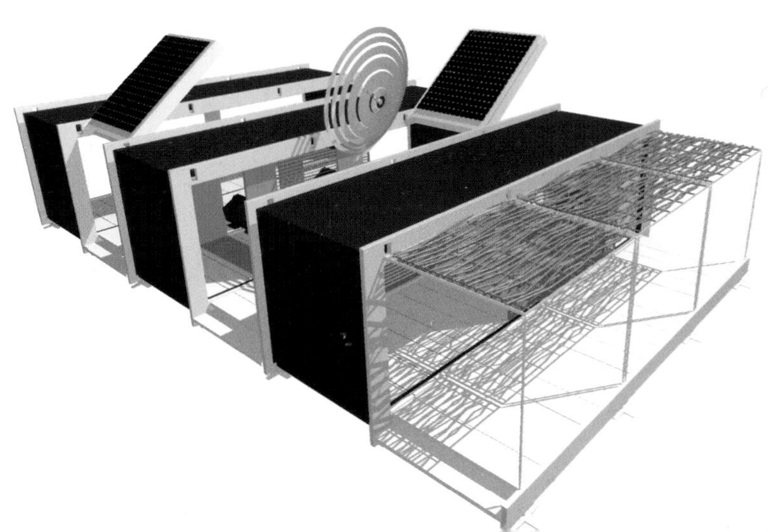

The mobile ECO LAB was built in collaboration with the Hollywood Beautification Team, a grassroots group founded with the mission to restore beauty and integrity to the Hollywood community.

The 8 x 35 foot trailer now travels throughout Los Angeles to inform K-12 schoool children about the importance of saving and protecting our planet.

As a working mobile classroom, the ECO LAB provides a base for a range of exhibits, all of which focus on ecology.

Like a circus tent, this mobile icon arrives at the schoolyard where elevated walkways fold down and slide out of the trailer s body. It is immediately recognizable as a place for interaction, discovery and fun.

MOBILE ECO LAB OMD-Jennifer Siegal

More than just a showroom, not quite a container, situated halfway between an artistic installation and a space cargo, the Voyager is a singular moving object that works like an outlying picket of Experimenta Design, the Portuguese international Biennale dedicated to design, creativity and contemporary culture, which travels across Europe until reaching Lisbon.

This project is a permanent search for new display formats. It works on the notion of movement, displacement, open space, time and speed. It started with the search for an object to exhibit, and it will now be exhibited itself in the urban space.

VOYAGER_ Experimenta Design, Miguel Vieira

Whether the Voyager is parked in the plazas where it is presented,

or on the road on its way to any destination,

it is always visible to the passing public,

it is always communicating.

It is designed on a semi-trailer that will expand itself on public space.

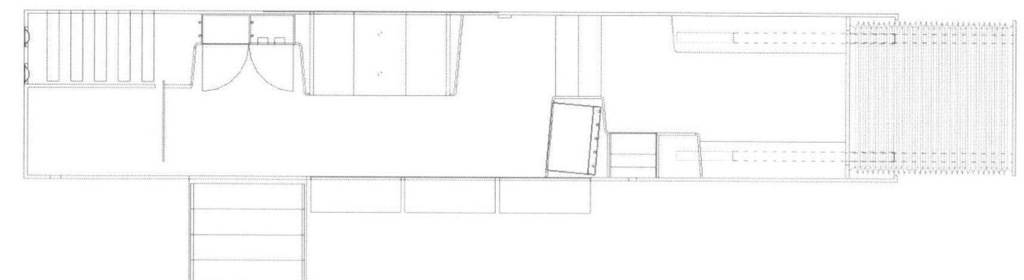

A moving, containing, extendable, habitable object measuring 13x2m.

Compact construction and a minimum amount of space determine exhibition solutions that merge with situations and installations created by artists and designers.
The global soundtrack is distributed throughout interior and exterior, under-lining unexpected uses and multidisciplinary content intersections.

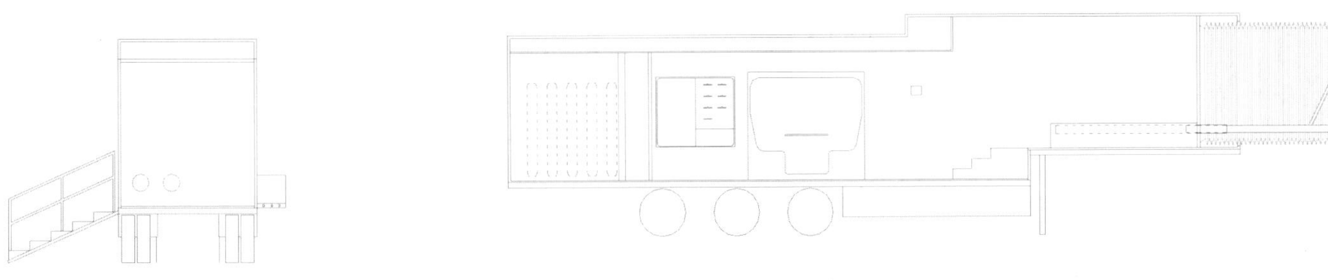

The Voyager is a travelling exhibit for reevaluating the project's nomadic nature.

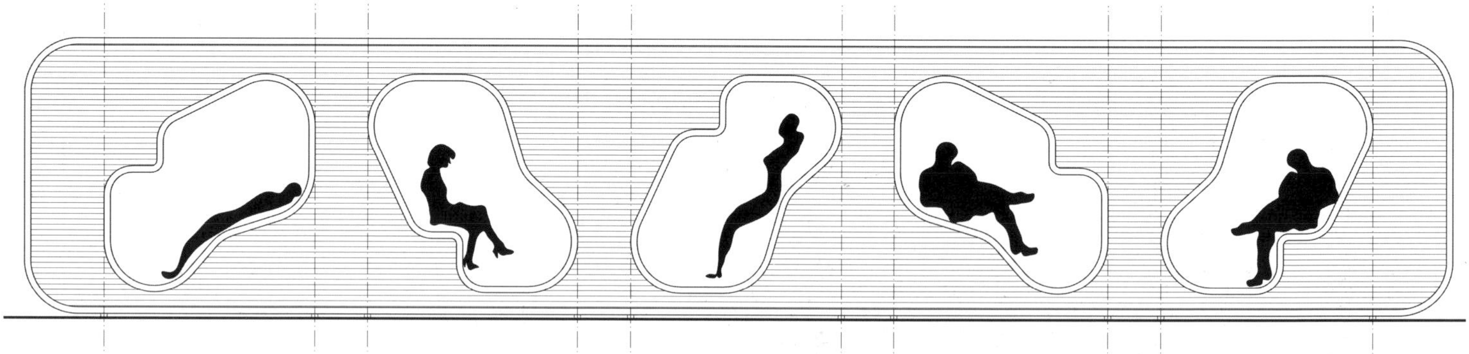

The pavilion Loungin' was presented in Rotterdam for a movable temporary exhibition space for about 20 people.

LOUNGIN'_ SAAS Architecten

Since October 2001, this structure has been used as an information pavilion for the Rotterdam community. Various multimedia presentations are shown in the lounges to inform citizens about new urban developments in Rotterdam.

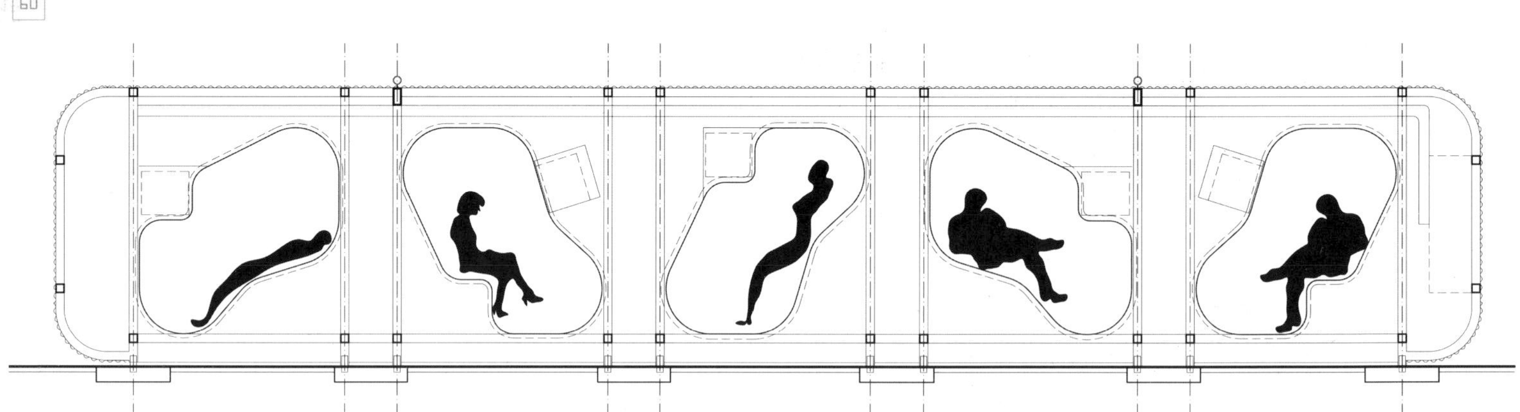

The scheme consists of a steel frame covered with a translucent polycarbonate skin. This frame holds five cabin-like "lounges" clad in red polyester. The deep red is meant to emulate the luxury of a high-end hotel lounge. By rotating the shape, different positions are created in which one can sit or lie down. At the same time, by taking ones position in the pavilion one becomes a part of the exhibit itself.

A translucent skin was chosen so that the aspect of the pavilion changes according to

lighting conditions. Thus, depending on the time of day, the external appearance can range between a stark white to a shadowy gray.

The doors on the exterior are made of stretched metal and are closed at night. The pavilion is one single piece and has been designed with an eye to the maximum length (12 meters) that can be transported on the back of a truck. In this way the structure can be quickly and easily transported, without having to rebuild it at each site.

MOBILE
ECO LAB
THE ART OF
PORTABLE
ARCHITECTURE

STORE HOUSE_ Jennifer Siegal - OMD

Constructed as a mass-customized modular unit, and built from titanium with scrim/fabric clad wings, Storehouse displays architectural models and drawings in an intricate system of hard and soft materials. The wing armature is randomly punctured with shadowbox shelves, creating depth so that each project displayed is uniquely perceived. The base acts both as anchor and bench, unfolding, rolling and adapting to provide comfort for museum visitors.

MOBILE

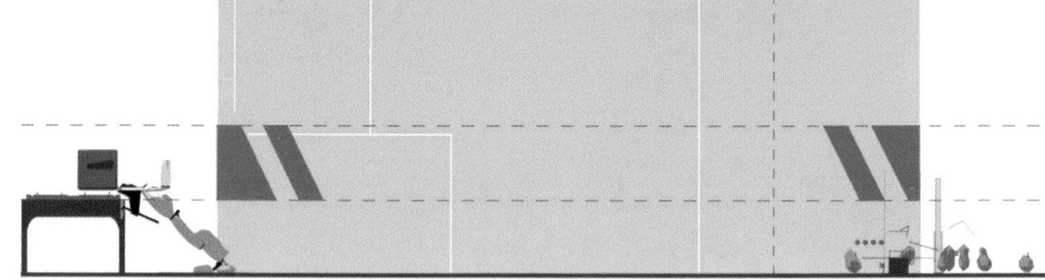

The "El", an elevated train, describes a loop around the center of the city of Chicago. A massive steel construction raises it to the second floor level.

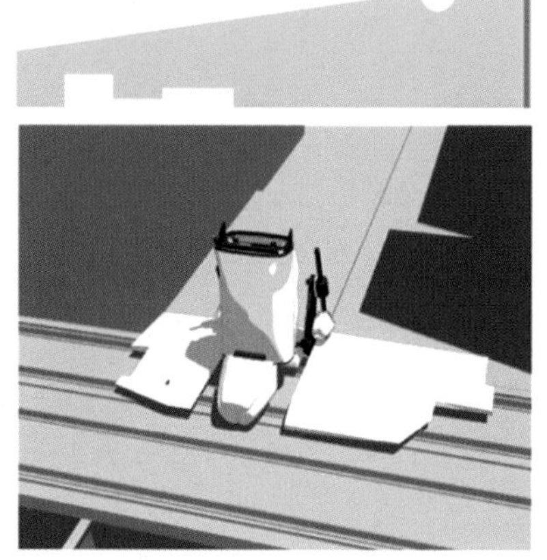

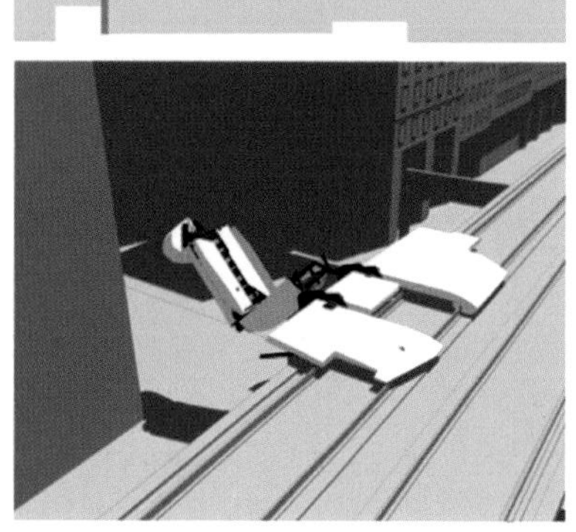

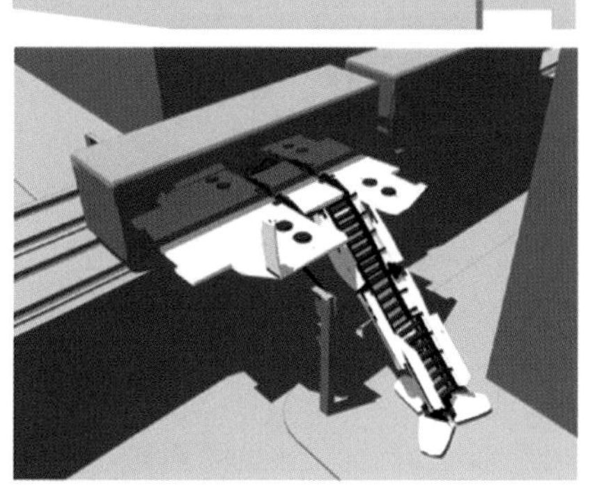

▪ physical ▪▪ ▪▪▪ ▪▪▪▪

▪ ▪▪ ▪▪▪ information ▪▪▪▪

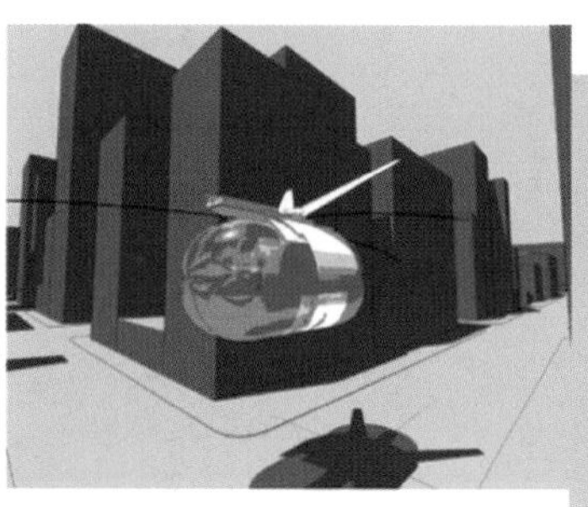

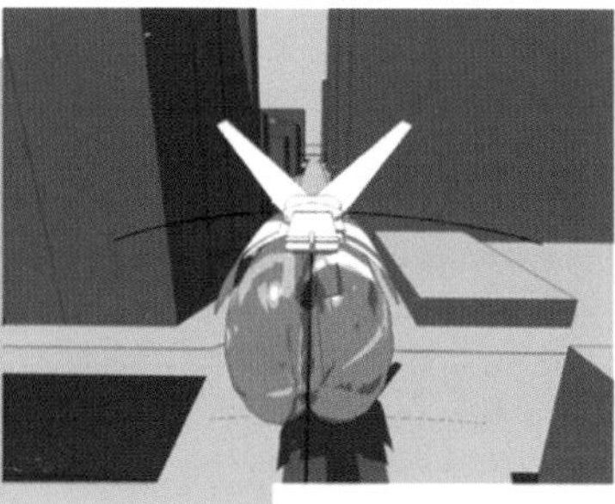

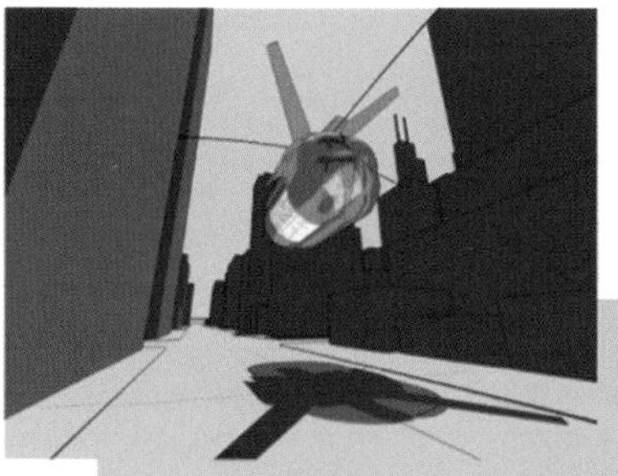

The introduction of a new layer consists of a system of mobile and fixed elements that are interdependently connected by transformation and translocation. They create disturbances in the rigid rituals and procedures by being constantly in unpredictable motion.

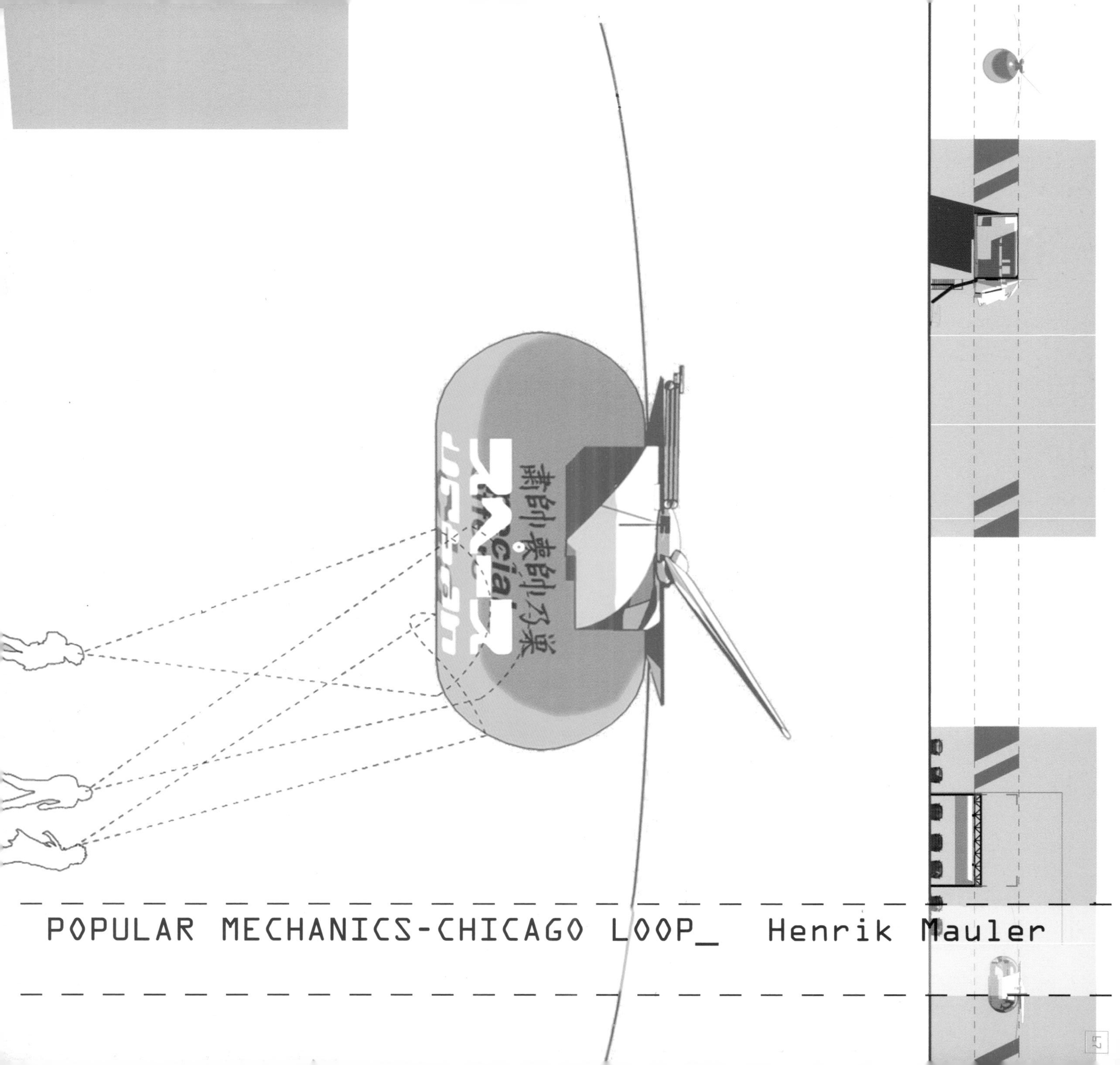
POPULAR MECHANICS-CHICAGO LOOP_
Henrik Mauler
スペース

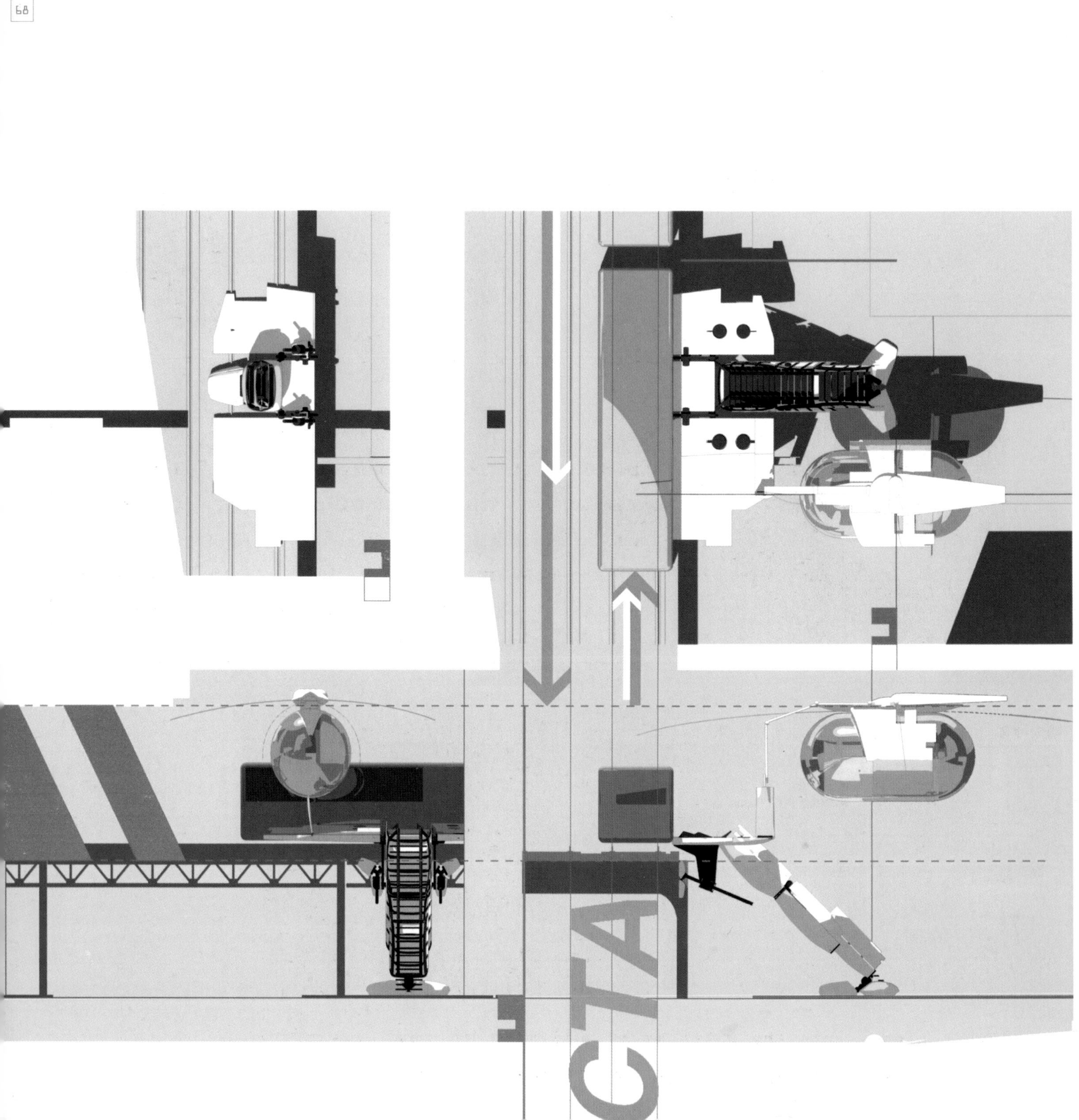
CTA

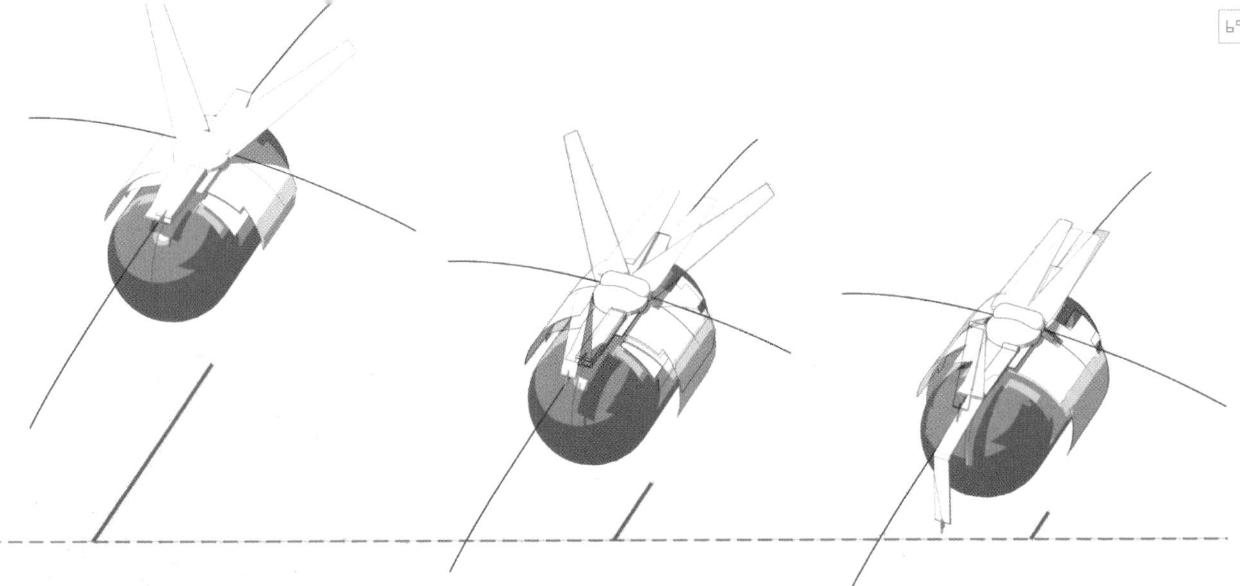

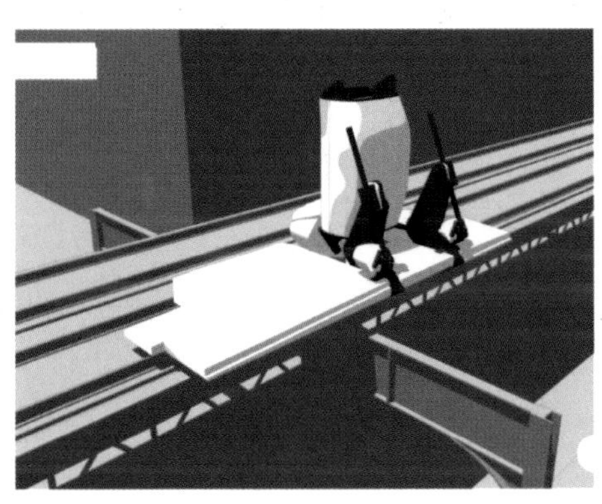

Due to their scale, the single elements seem to be subordinate to the monumentality of the surrounding architecture. Their networking, however, allows them to become present as a mobile, coherent system that directly and readably reacts to the "users" of the city, while undermining the self-righteous aspects of architecture.

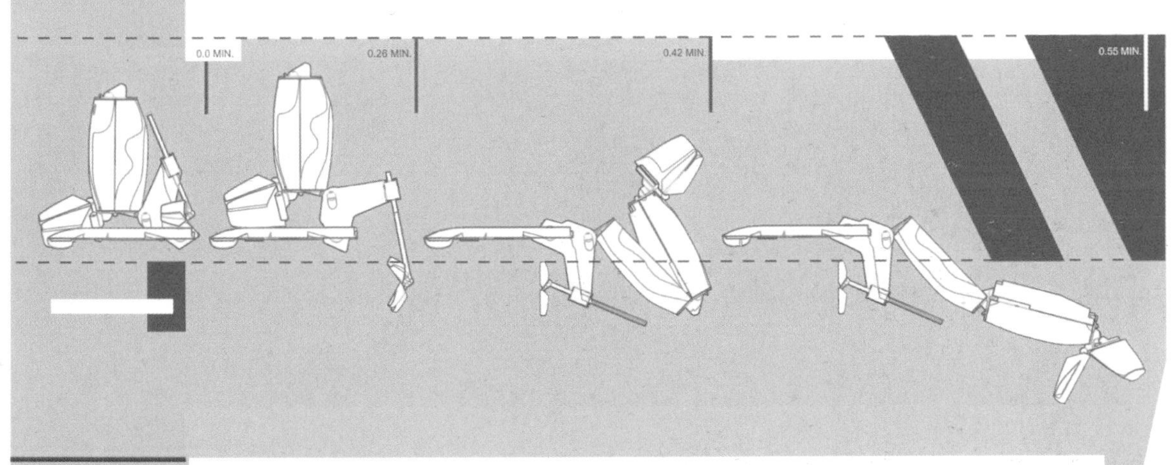

While it blends into the patterns of motion of the Loop, unexpected possibilities of occupying the space are created.

Answer to programmatic voids:

exotic-extra

035_ love in the street:::

Case XIV_	I buy love Wednesday afternoon and I can't go home because my parents are there and I have just the ...
Case XXI_	finding love on a Saturday night in a city far from my house...
Case VII_	I need to unplug in the downtown area now, self/service...
Case XII_	I'm sleepy, think I'll take a dream-break and go on...
Case III_	the girls-boys have to take care of our customers.

Public love::: short-term use for the expression of sexual desire in public areas. Easy access, low cost and privacy ensured.

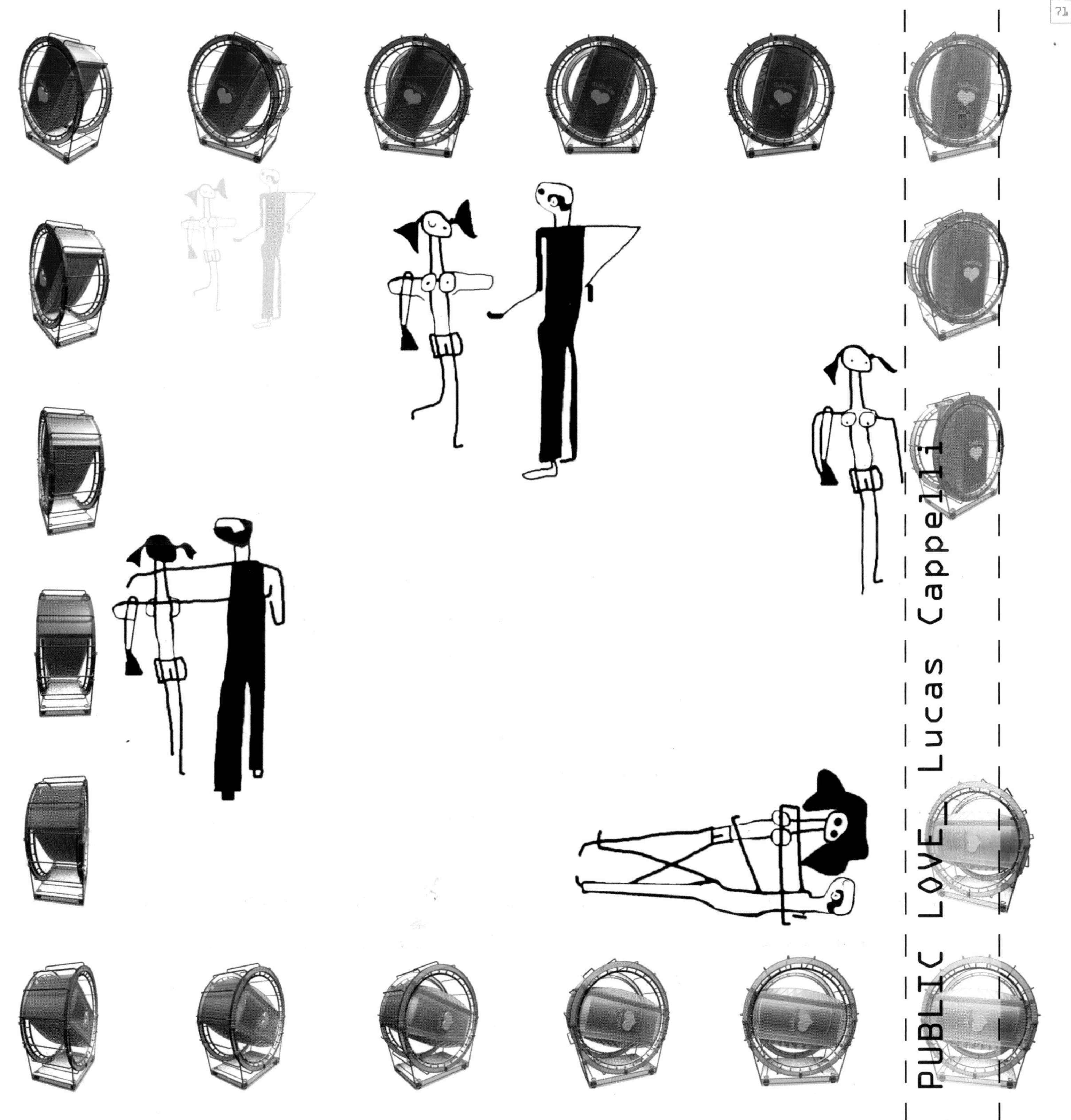
PUBLIC LOVE Lucas Cappelli

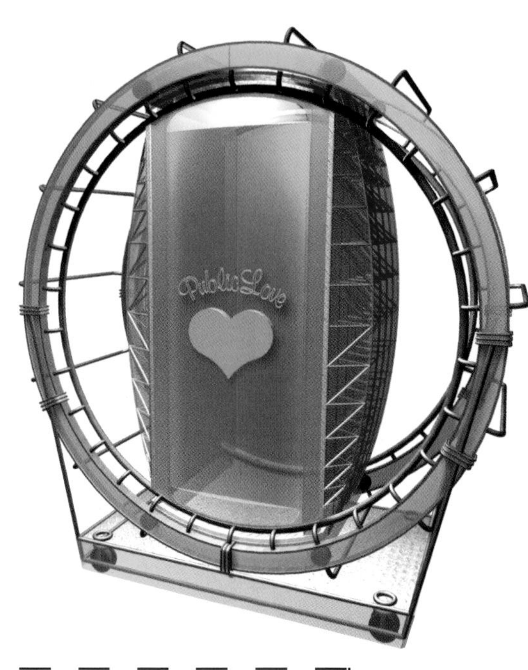
PublicLove

PublicLove

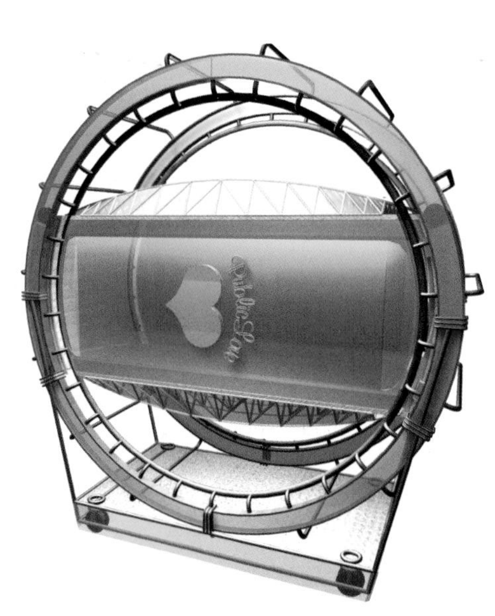
PublicLove

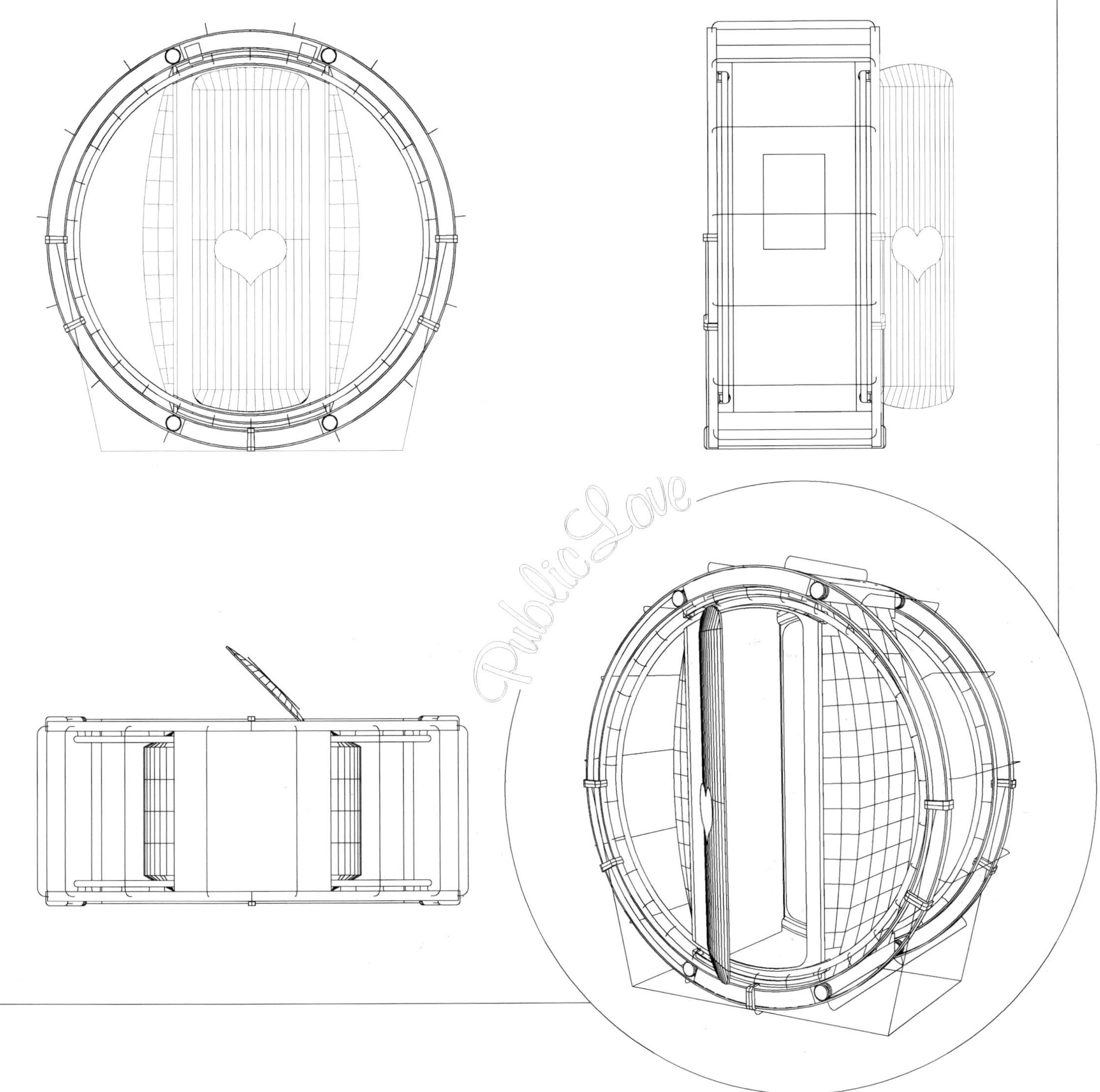
PublicLove

AVL-Ville is the largest work of art by Atelier van Lieshout to date. This "free state" is a pleasing mixture of art, environment and sanctuary, full of well-known and new works by AVL, with the added attraction that everything here is fully operational. Not art to simply look at, but to live with, to live in and to live by.

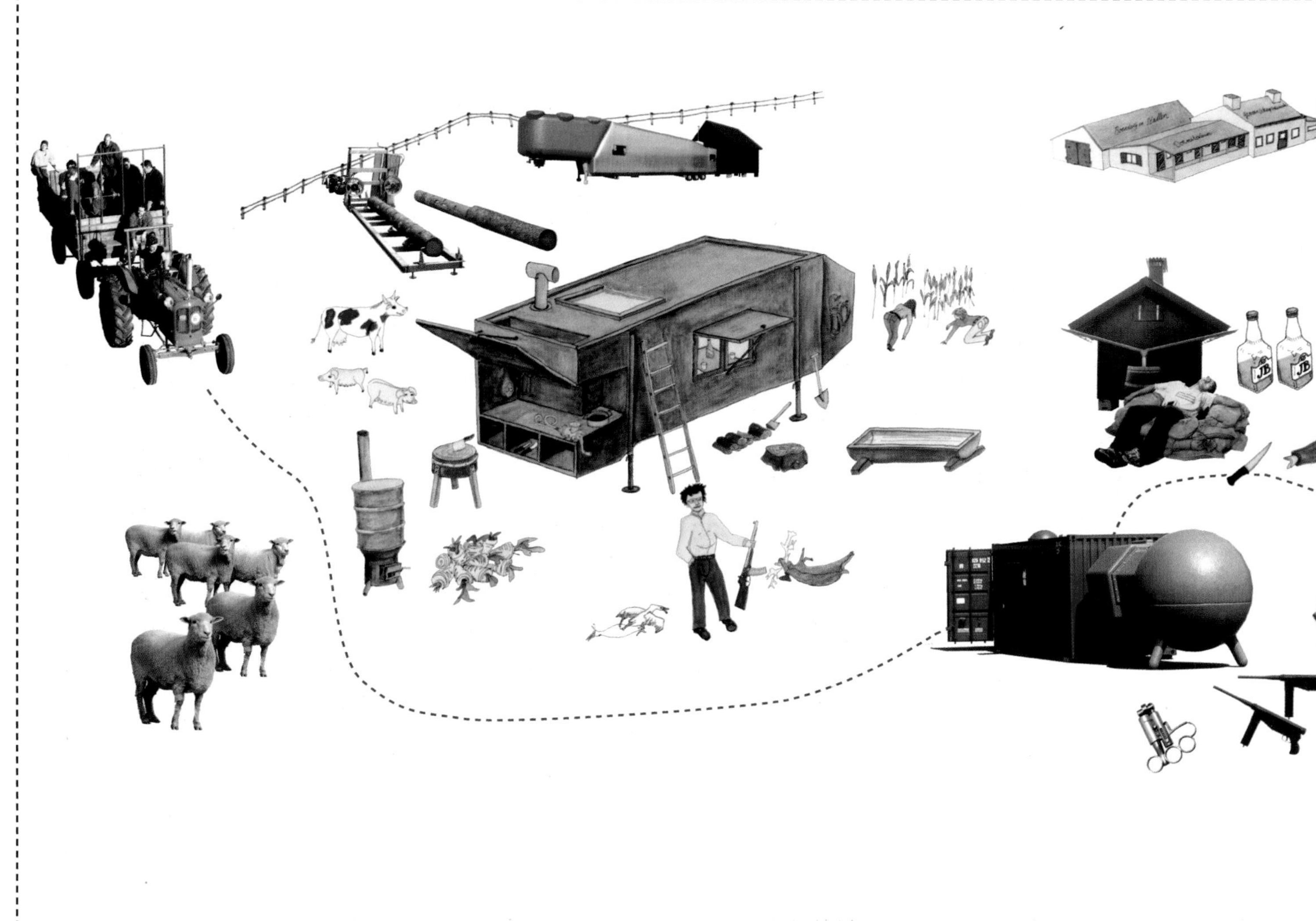

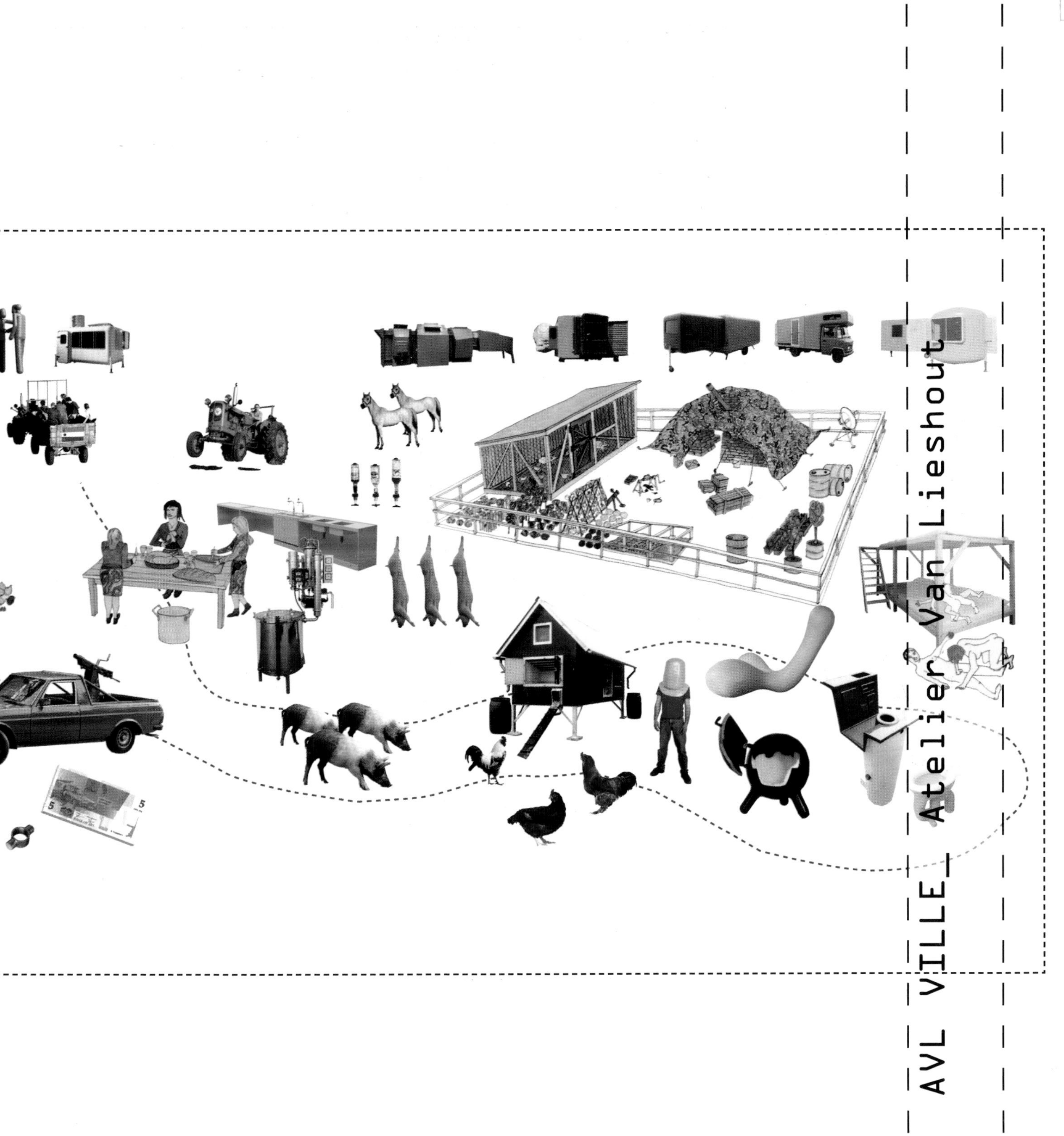
AVL VILLE Atelier Van Lieshout

The goal of the free state is to create an autonomous space where everything is possible within a country that is over-regulated to an increasingly oppressive degree.
AVL-Ville has its own flag, its own constitution and its own money.
It is a harmonious and self-supporting enterprise that is located for the time being in the Rotterdam harbor area and in the future on a contaminated soil dump near Zestienhoven airfield.

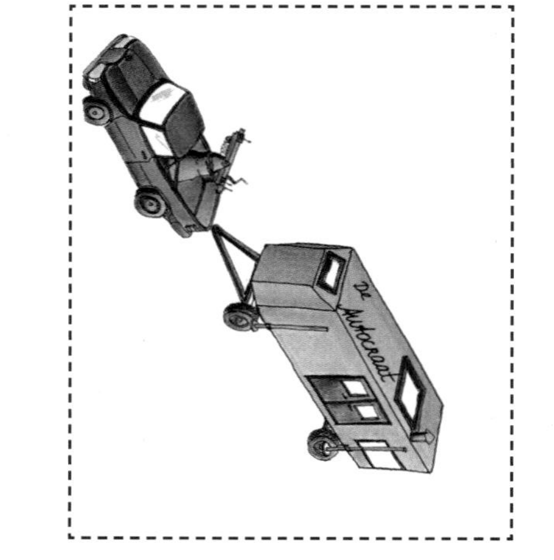

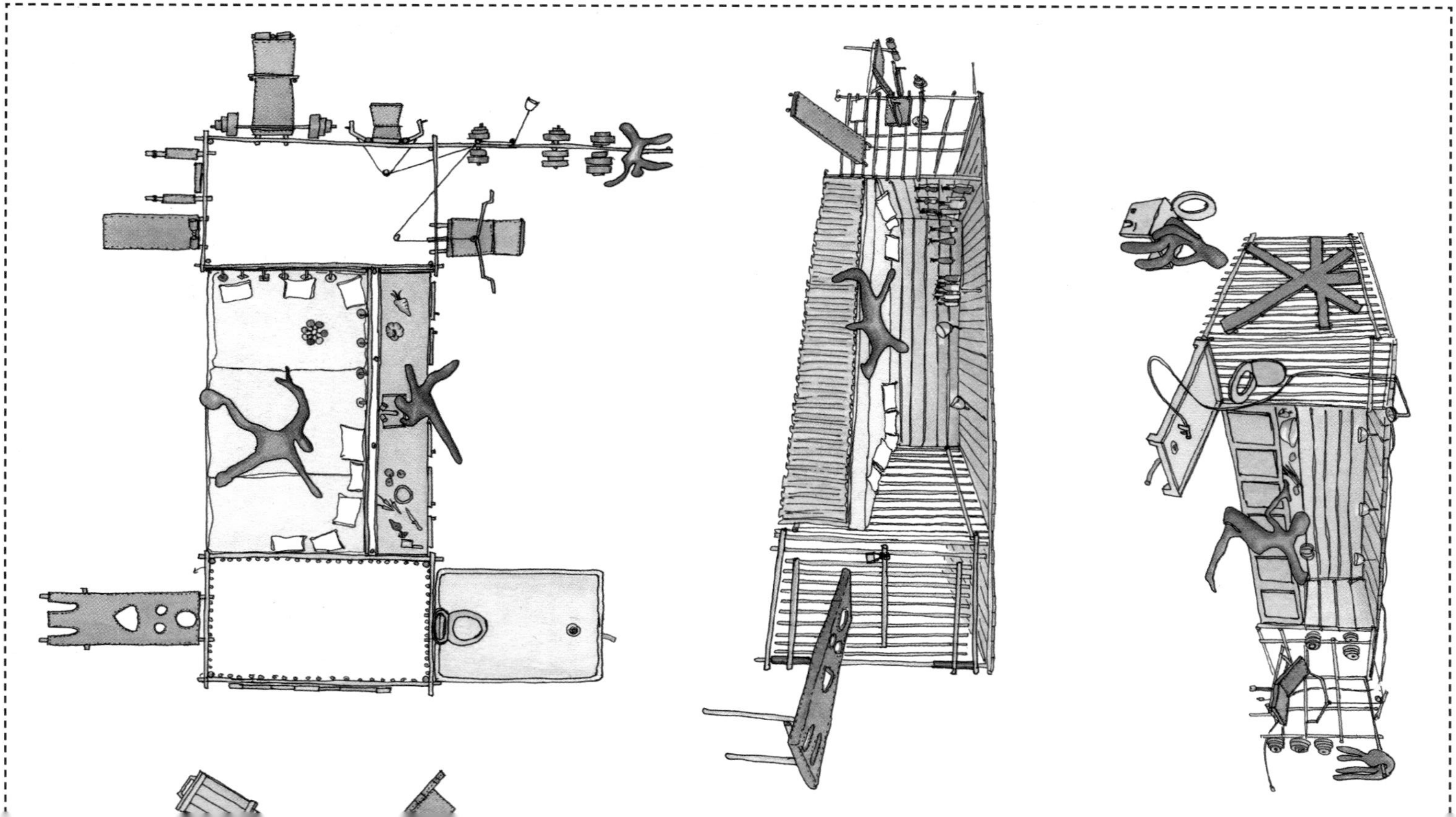

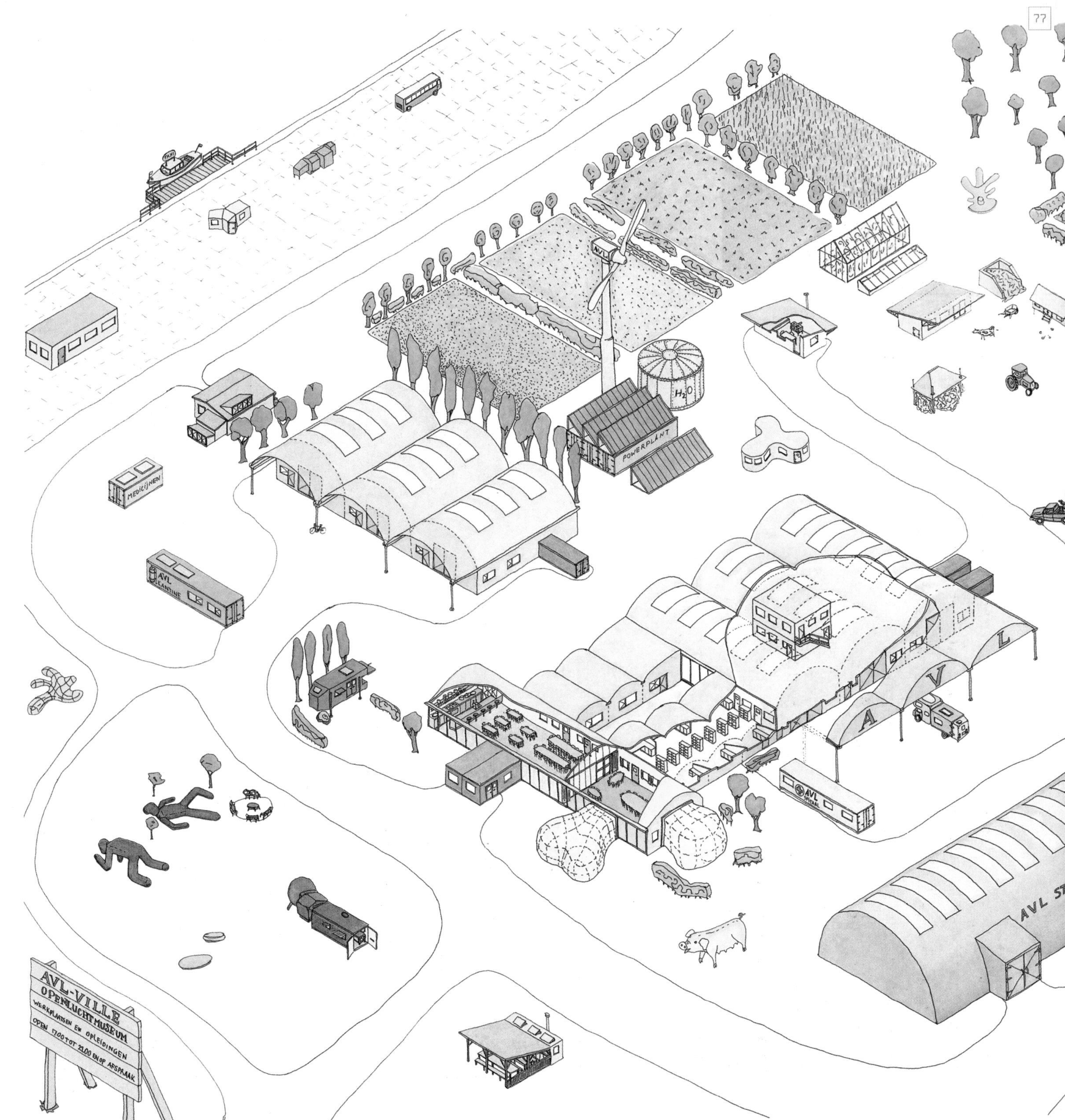
TAXI
MEDICIJNEN
AVL
KANTINE
AVL
POWERPLANT
H_2O
L
V
A
AVL
SPITAAL
AVL ST
AVL-VILLE
OPENLUCHTMUSEUM
WERKPLAATSEN EN OPLEIDINGEN
OPEN 17.00 TOT 21.00 EN OP AFSPRAAK

The motto of AVL-Ville is: as long as it s art, just about anything s possible. AVL-Ville is therefore not a commune or a construction company but an open-air museum bubbling over with enthusiasm, where art is produced on a daily basis: ranging from its own food and energy to its own houses, objects and mobile buildings.

The mega-artwork AVL-Ville is constantly in motion and never finished. Apart from the sections mentioned, there are mobile homes, windmills, a fully operational hospital, a distillery, the AVL energy plant that runs on waste and bio-gas, a biological effluent water purification plant and compost toilets. Watch for satellite developments abroad. (Some of the elements are still under construction).

Mass tourism is based on the concept of giving customers exactly the same services and comforts that they have in their own country, only in a different environment.

"Hitch" tourism, that of campsites and mobile homes, follows similar guidelines. Mobile homes are increasingly larger and better equipped so that the switchover from one's habitual, year-round residence to the new mobile home is as smooth and comfortable as possible.

If the underlying goal behind this type of tourism is to help conserve the surroundings, the environment of the tourist's country of origin, what better way to do so than by bringing the environment along!

Moving Land is a piece of terrain, a bite-sized morsel of the landscape typical of the country, zone or region one is traveling from. Lie down on the lawn and smell the jasmine of your hometown while visiting Lapland in the winter! Journey to the Sahara and contemplate the desert beneath the shade of a cypress tree! Take your desires to their extreme. Why not?

MOVING LAND_barch, Eugeni Bach

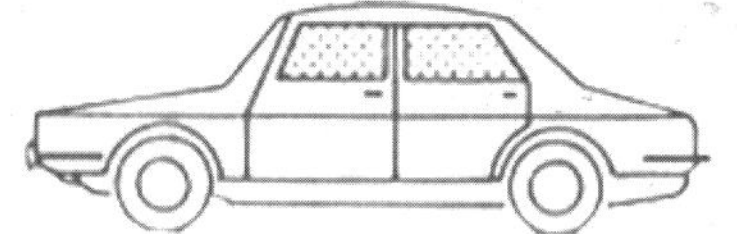

A conventional car, converted from passenger transport to freight storage. The driver's seat remains unencumbered; the rest of the car is filled with equipment and machinery. In the middle of the car is a hydraulic piston, attached to which are stackable bed-&-seat units. A hydraulic pump is stored in the trunk. The shell of the car is separated and hydraulically lifted from the base, subsequently becoming the roof of a four-story hotel. Each floor consists of a bed (made out of rubber for outdoor use), which is formed into a pillow at the head and a seat at the foot. Next to each seat is a television set, which is directed toward the floor below. A chain ladder pulls up from a spool at the floor of the car, allowing access to the stories above.

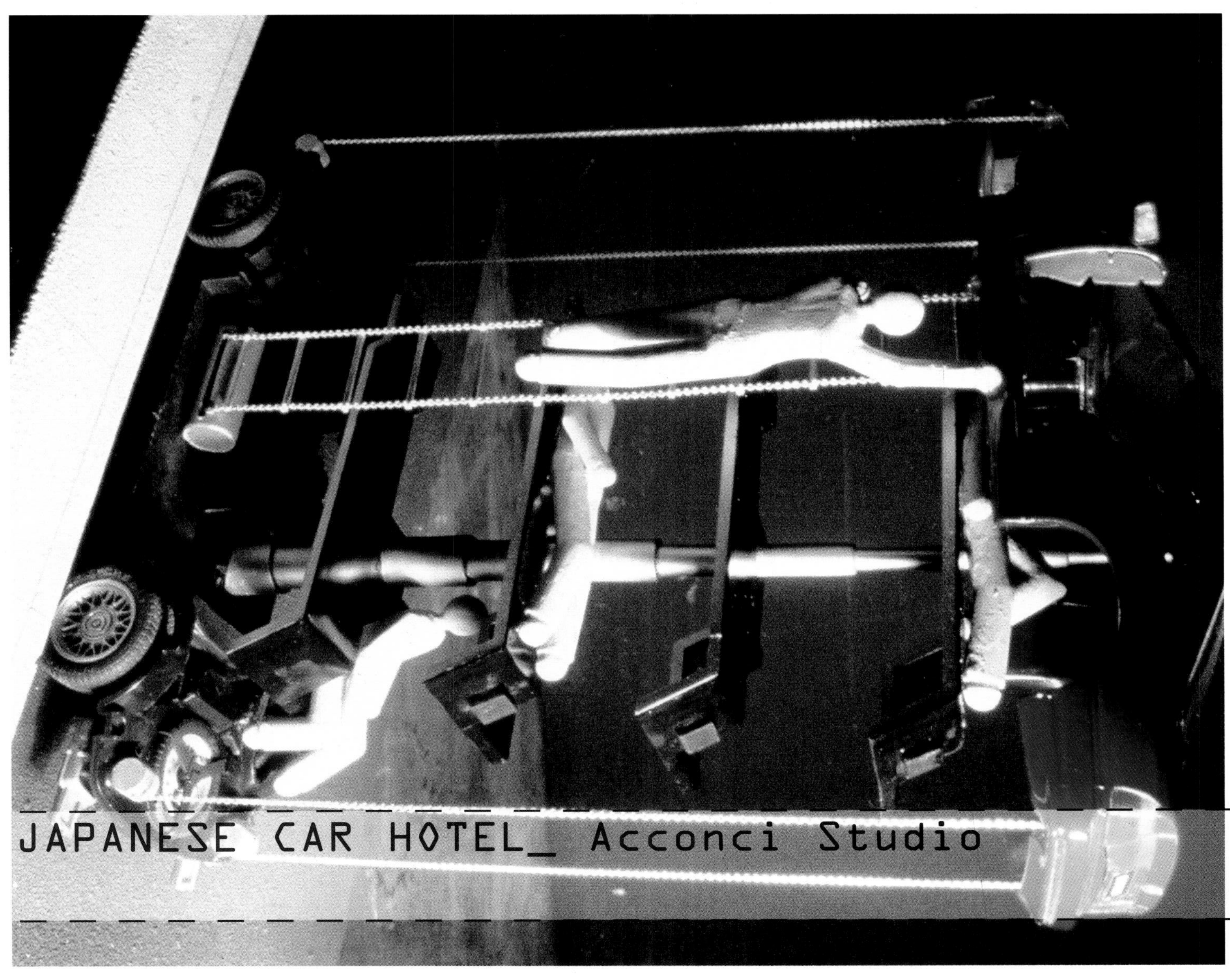

JAPANESE CAR HOTEL_ Acconci Studio

The fisch house's supporting legs can fold down allowing the car to move away.

It is powered from the car's systems
and accessed through the car's sky-light.

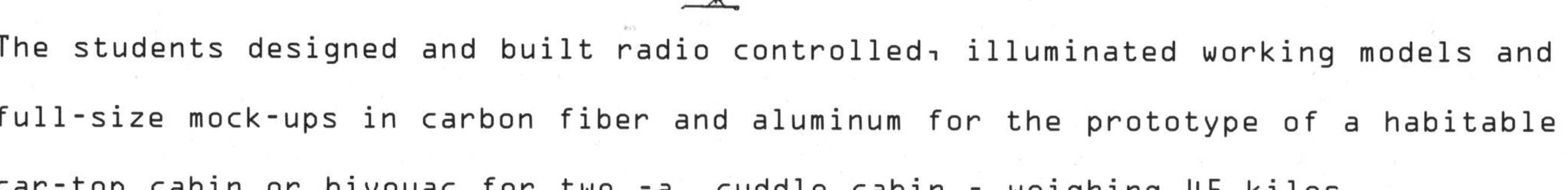

The students designed and built radio controlled, illuminated working models and full-size mock-ups in carbon fiber and aluminum for the prototype of a habitable car-top cabin or bivouac for two -a cuddle cabin - weighing 45 kilos.

The traditional fishing hut was used as a reference for "fisch haus".

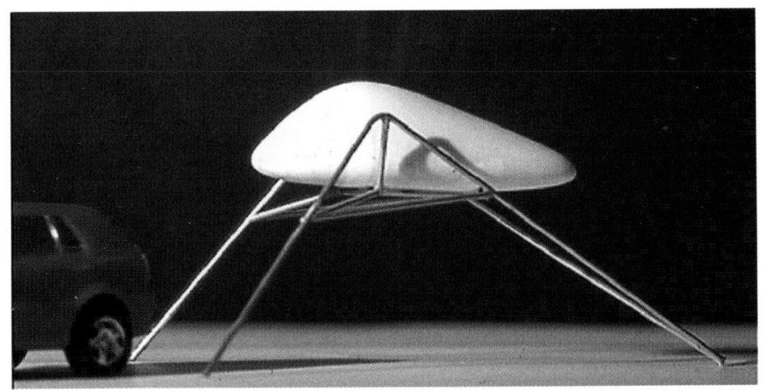

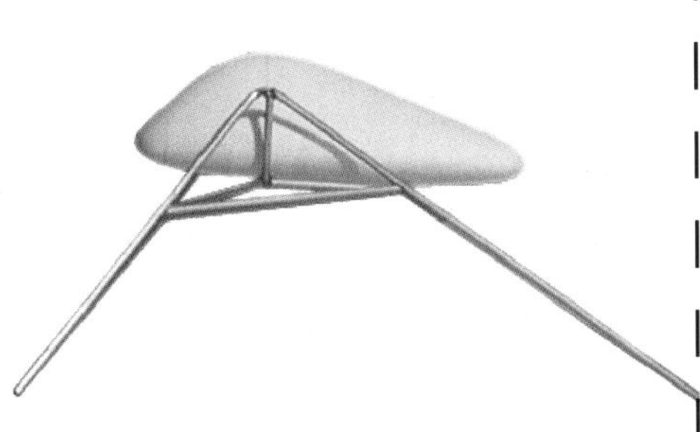

An aerodynamic shape is essential for car top transportation.

FISCH HOUSE_ Richard Horden

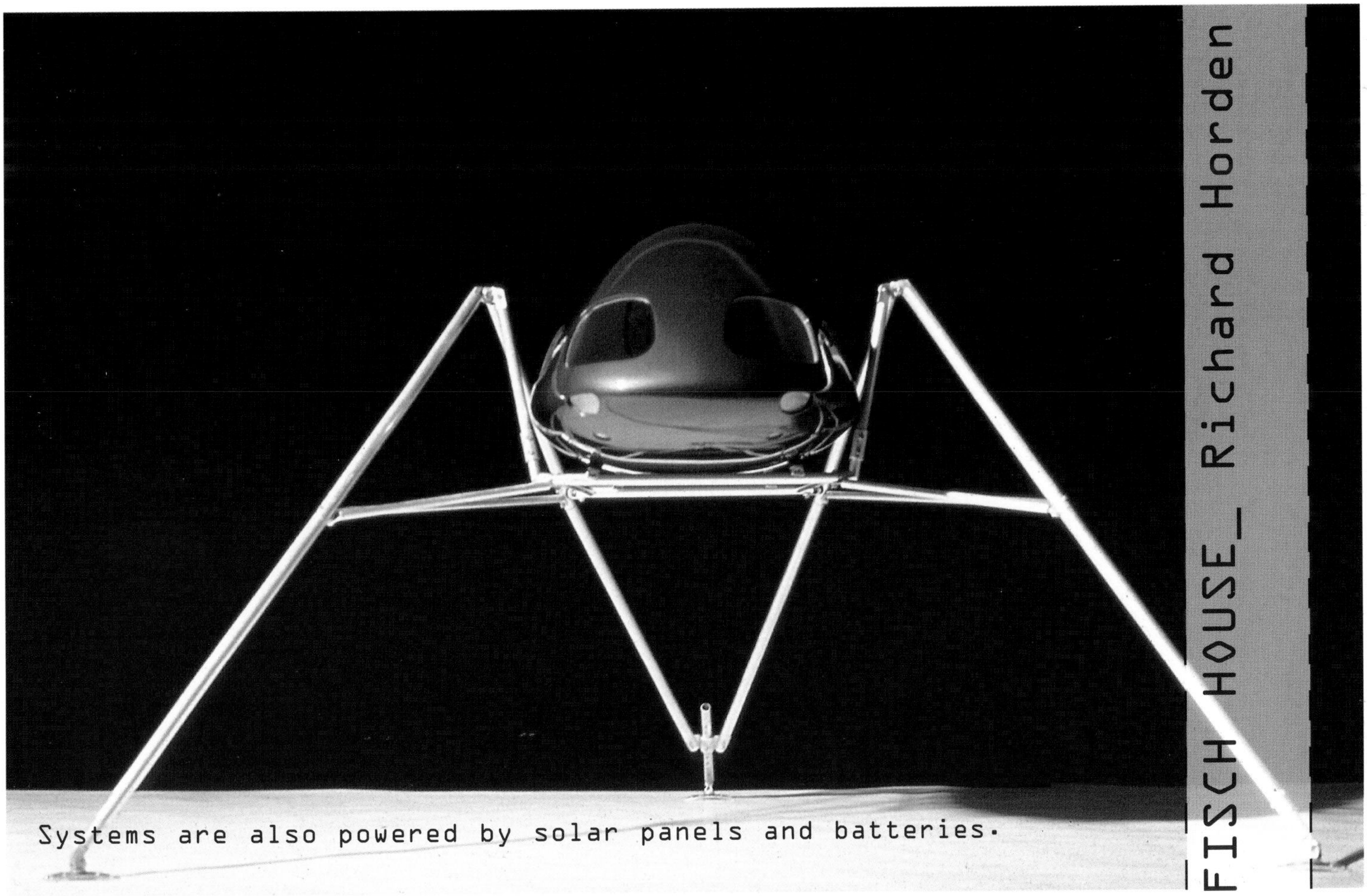

Systems are also powered by solar panels and batteries.

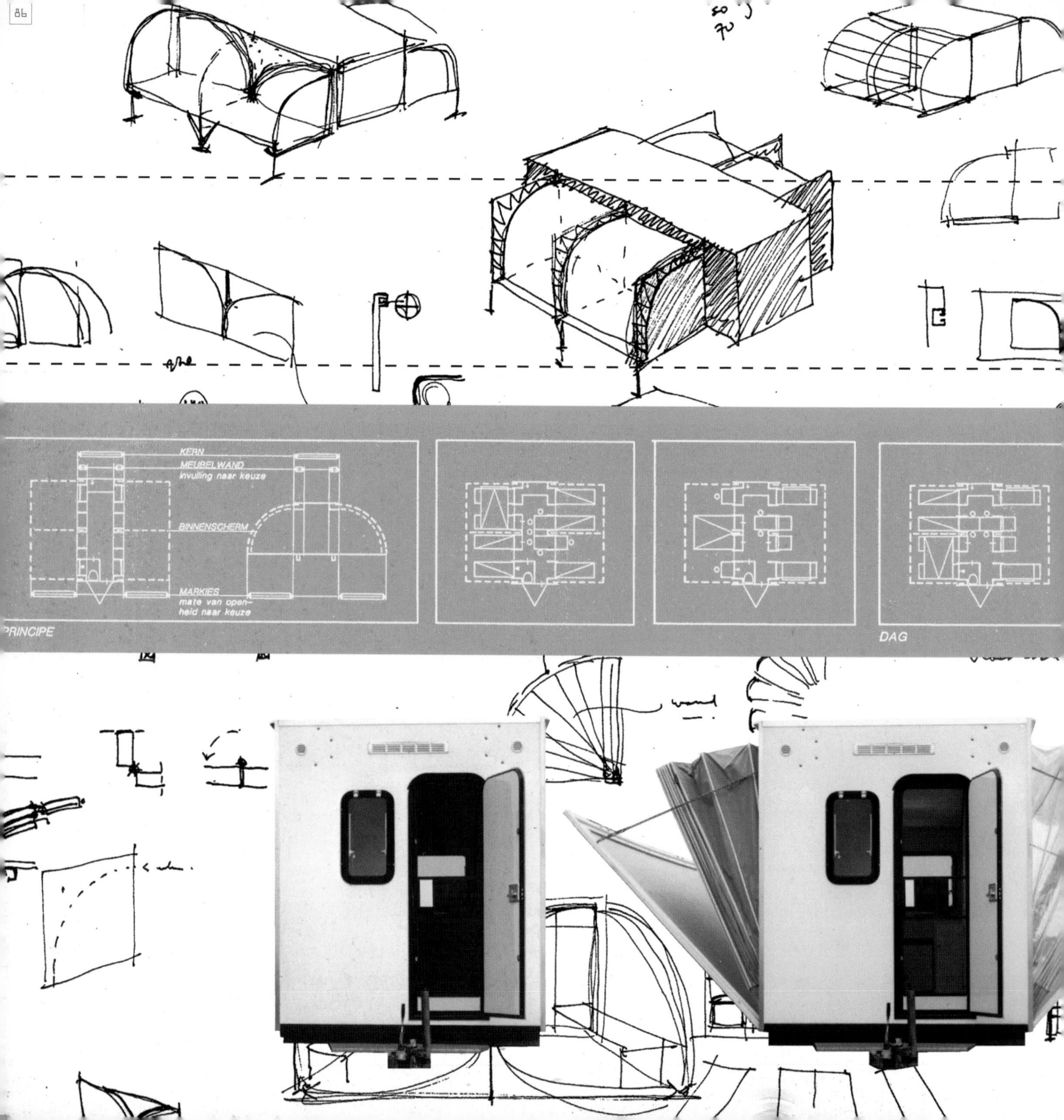
KERN
MEUBELWAND
invulling naar keuze
BINNENSCHERM
MARKIES
mate van open-
heid naar keuze
PRINCIPE
DAG

The Markies is not an ordinary caravan, but it can serve as one since it meets all road transport requirements.
It was an entry for a temporary dwelling competition and was conceived as a mobile holiday home.

MARKIES_ Eduard Böhtlink

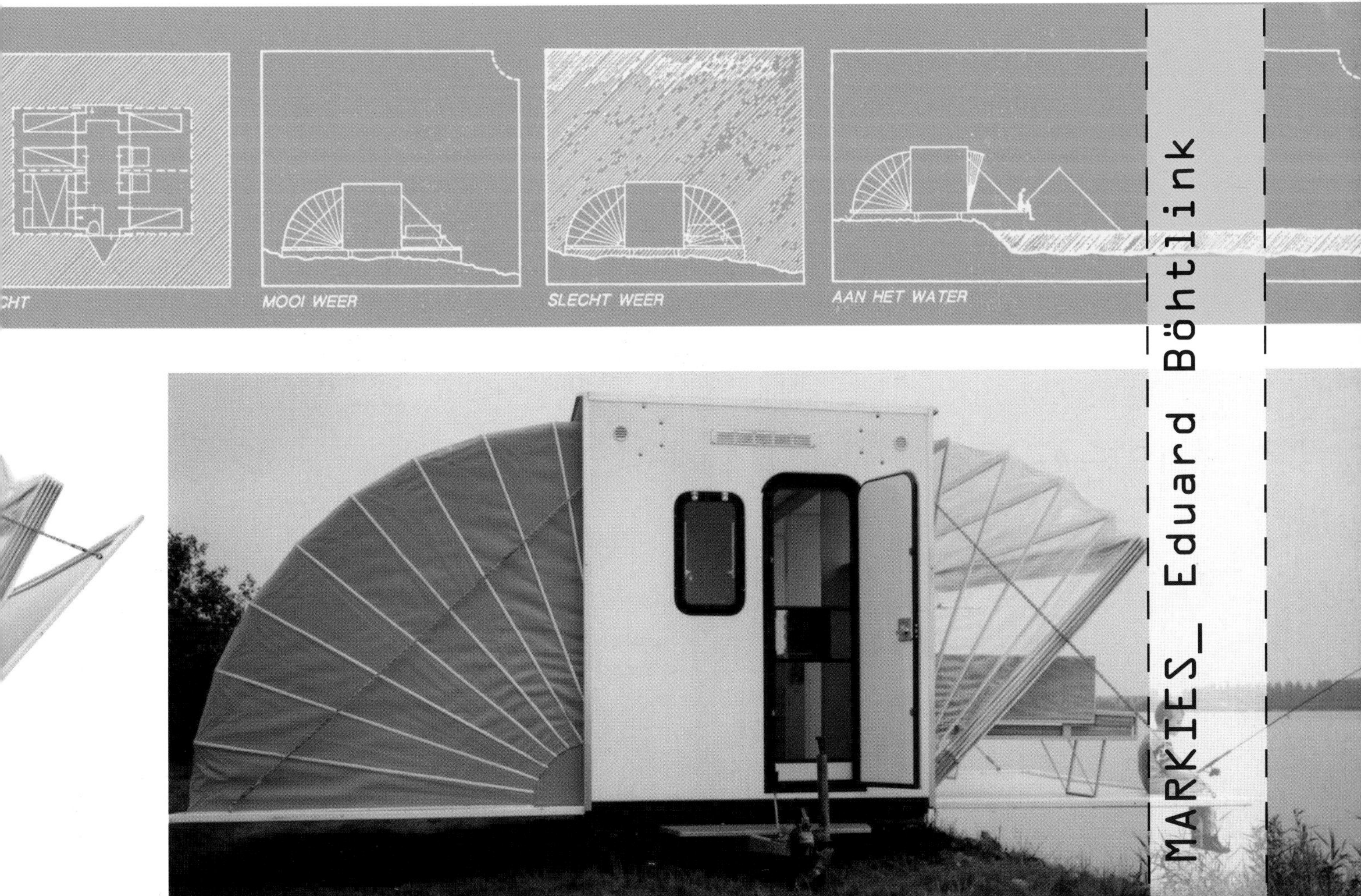

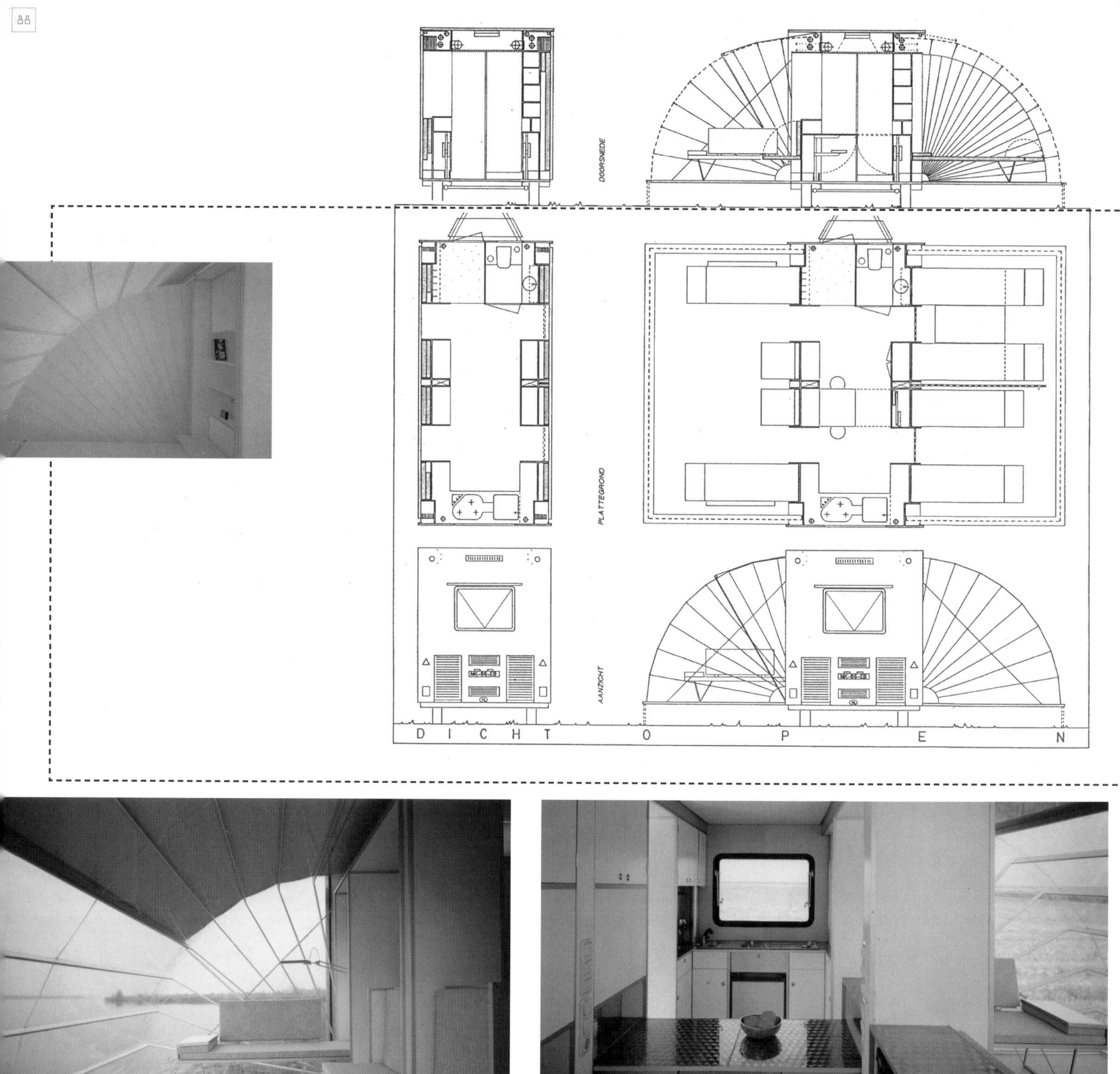
DOORSNEDE
PLATTEGROND
AANZICHT
DICHT
OPEN

When it is on the road, the Markies measures 2.2 x 4.4 meters. Once it arrives at its destination, its floor space can be increased threefold in a matter of seconds. Both side walls can be folded down electronically and the resulting area can then be covered automatically via the concertina-like awnings, which can be lowered to exactly the height desired.

The living space is thus divided into three zones: in the middle there is the kitchen, dining area and wc; and on one side is the living room with its transparent dome, which doubles as a terrace in good weather when the awning is raised. On the other side is the bedroom, which can be split into smaller units and which is covered by an opaque awning.

The space inside has a flexible layout and includes all the essential facilities: built-in cupboards, benches, up to four beds, a refrigerator, a stove and a shower/toilet.

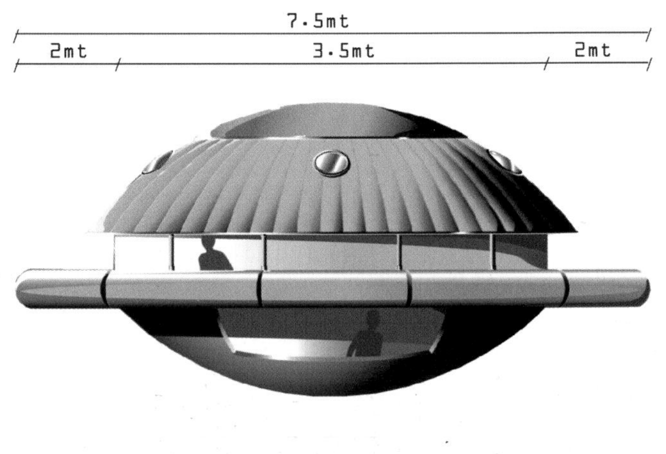
7.5mt
2mt
3.5mt
2mt

LES ANTHENEA_ Jean Michel Ducanelle

A flying saucer has landed. This futuristic pod rests directly on the water, half submerged, while its habitants enjoy spectacular panoramic vistas above and below.

The large underwater window provides a fish-eye view of a magical, mystical world teaming with life.

Half house, half submarine.

This unique floating habitat was conceived and designed so the marine environment could be enjoyed without damaging fragile ecologies. These circular fiberglass pods are anchored to the sea bottom near delicate coral reefs, islands, lakes and bays. Constructed as virtually round spheres with ballast, optional generators, air conditioning, water system and beautifully furnished interiors, Anthenea are very comfortable on the water.

The units are constructed using composite polyester-fiberglas. They are built in sections, which are assembled at their ultimate delivery destinations and easily towed or carried by helicopter.
It has a circular flotation ring around the exterior which is constructed of durable, interlocking roto-molded polyurethane sections. These provide a stable, roomy outdoor terrace for lounge chairs, diving and even equipment storage; providing a protective system against crashes and a landing for windsurfs and boats.

exploration · nature · freedom · anthenea

The versatility of Anthenea enables it to easily become a coursing catamaran. Whether stationary or in motion, the practical Anthenea provides both comfort and serenity.

The Floating Platform is a modular construction which is intended to function as a buoyant foundation for N55 Spaceframe or for other lightweight constructions.

It can also be used for other purposes, for example building land.

The Floating Platform is a space lattice, comprised of small modules, made from stainless steel with built-in buoyant tanks.

The small modules in the platform can all be assembled by hand. The modular system facilitates gradual extensions and makes the platform less vulnerable to damage; for example, leaks have only local impact and can therefore be repaired locally. The platform sinks approximately 1.2 meters when loaded and can float in shallow water. A small boat can be used to tow it.

SPACEFRAME & FLOATING PLATFORM_ N55

The floating system can also be shaped according to the intended usage. The PLATFORM has comparatively low net buoyancy; this is an economic advantage, but limits the amount of weight that can be added to the platform.

It is constructed as an "octet truss" space lattice and is shaped as an equilateral triangle. 189 polyethylene tanks make it buoyant.

Octahedron tanks are fitted into the cavities in the sides of the platform.

They can be attached or removed according to needs. Each tank adds approximately 90 kgs. of buoyancy.

The construction of the spaceframe as a whole is stable and safe in inclement weather and hurricane-strength wind, provided that it is well moored. To secure the construction under these conditions, it should be moored from each corner with a strength of 3.3 tons and an angle of 12°.

Tanks for water and wastewater, toilets, etc., can be integrated in ways that do not overload the construction.

Dimensions: Sides 8.4 meters, approx. area 40 m². Height: 1.5 meters.
Buoyancy in platform: 7500 kg.
Total weight of the construction: 5500 kg.
Net buoyancy: 2000 kg.
Tanks: buoyancy / tank at 20°C: 44.8 liters.
At 0°C: 41.3 liters.

The Hydra House is a mass-customized mobile modular structure that is responsive to environmental issues of global warming, water desalination and recycling.

The structural stalks are separated into chassis (providing internal structure, power, communication, mechanics, and a self-sufficient energy collecting system), and mass-customized elements (for interior build-outs, exterior and interior skins, electronics, and communications).

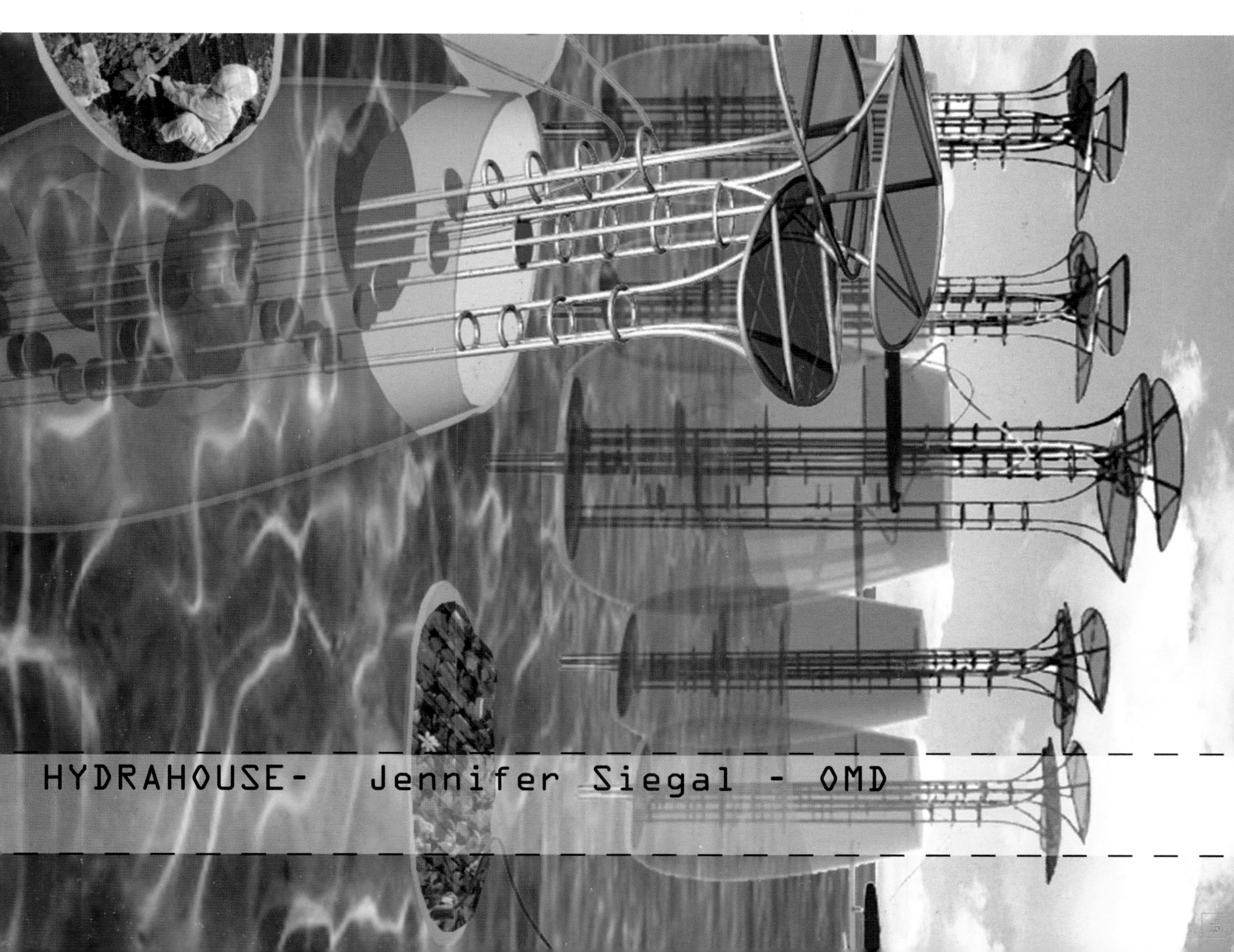

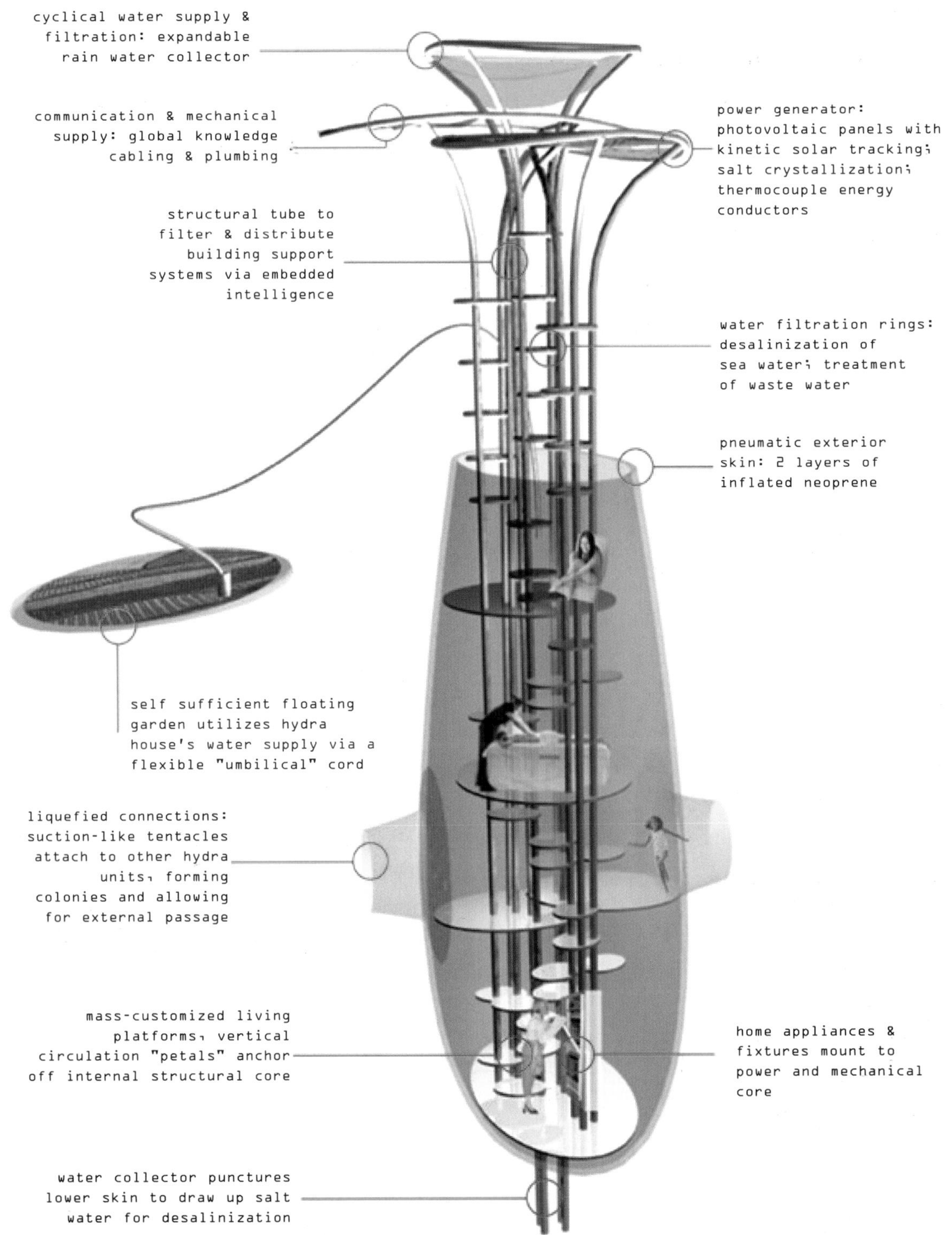

Each independent housing unit has an attached self-sufficient floating garden. These Lily pads stem from Hydra House's structural stalks, using an umbilical cord to provide fresh water and nutrients, give life and feed the floating garden.

Structures + intelligence

- Water: rainwater stored in an expandable bladder, desalination (97% of the planet's water is salt water in the seas and oceans) and treated waste water. Each tube either pulls sea water upward or distributes desalinized water downward to provide drinking and washing water.
- Power: photovoltaics, salt crystalization, and thermocouple energy conductors
- Communication + Mechanical system: global knowledge and plumbing
- Pneumatic Exterior Skin: 2 layers of inflated neoprene

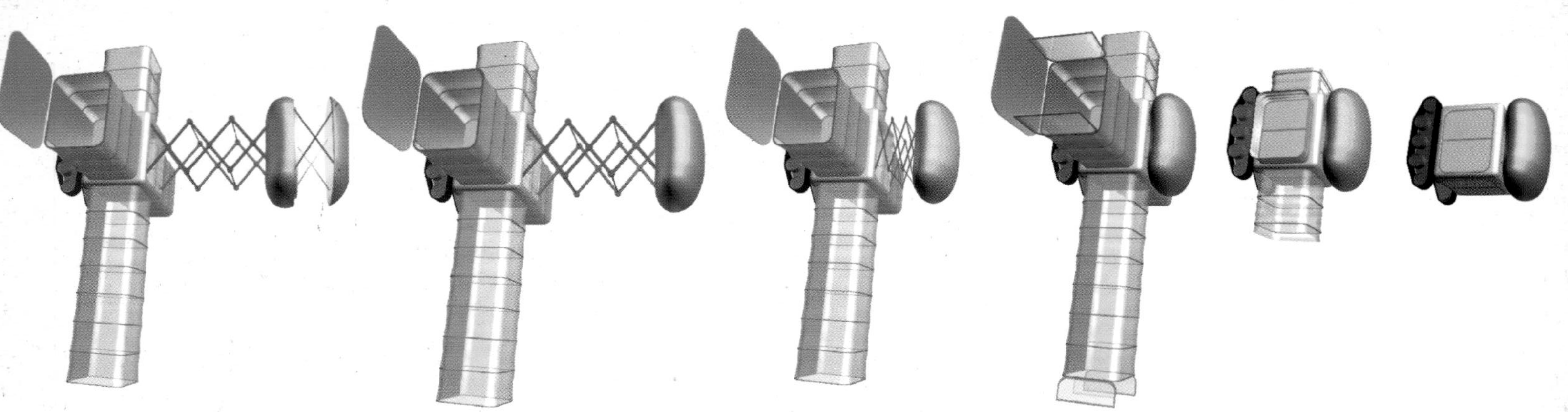

Caravantex is an all-terrain, expanding structure made from high-tech materials. It is flexible and ideal for easy outdoor living. It is built for leisure in uneven landscapes and stepped slopes. Hitch it to any 4WD that can handle a rocky shore, and you're on your way. Caravantex has all the space you need for a modern nomadic lifestyle; a fully-equipped kitchen, generous bathroom, two bedrooms with views and a large translucent living room. On top is the ultimate lounge for lazy summer evenings and crisp dawns.

CARAVANTEX_ mmw
mmw

h-Ouse is more a vision of housing of the future than one of the future of housing: it acknowledges some techincal-constructive and infrastructural potentialities in order to respond to ongoing socio-economic changes, such as the phenomenon of de-territorialization on a global scale which is related to:

- more and more consistent migration streams that break off the culture-territory connection.
- mobility and diffusion of both material and non-material goods.
- radical changes in the pre-industrial ecosystem along with the deprivation of energy and food resources.

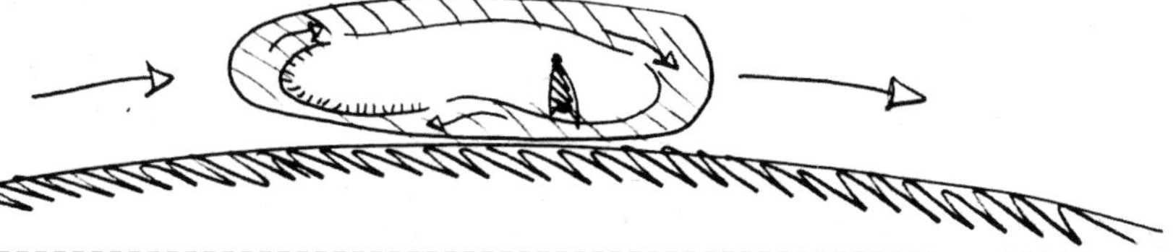

h-Ouse is housing in a future where the condition itself of the currently established rules about housing will no longer count: linking technology and culture to a specific place, that which now defines territory as such.

.....MIGRATING>TRAVELLING>WORKING MULTIMEDIA>BATHING>

H-OUSE_ MaD studio

RELAXING> LIVING>PLAYING>SLEEPING>INTERFACI
>MEETING>ESCAPING>EXPLORING>DRIFTING....

h-Ouse turns the scarcity and need for flexible spaces into an opportunity to imagine an ever-changing interior landscape through the use of ceiling and walls as livable surfaces.

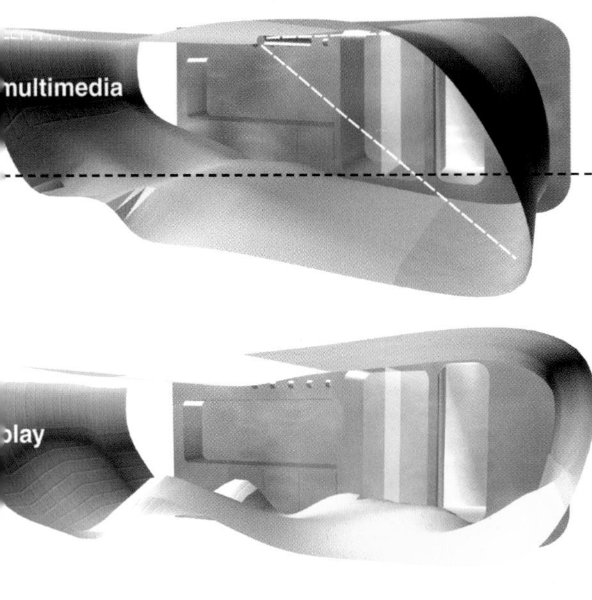

The interior walls, floor and ceiling are part of a continuous surface covered by three different skins (soft, soft/washable, washable/projectable) rotating and morphing following the different uses of the domestic space, while a "technical box" contains all the equipment (closets, cooking deck, multimedia devices, toilets etc.) not compatible with an open and flexible space.

The border between interior and exterior is at the same time the interface with the outside world and the device for moving across it, in conjunction with the immaterial world and moving in the time of the domestic world. The walls and ceiling thereby become informative surfaces.

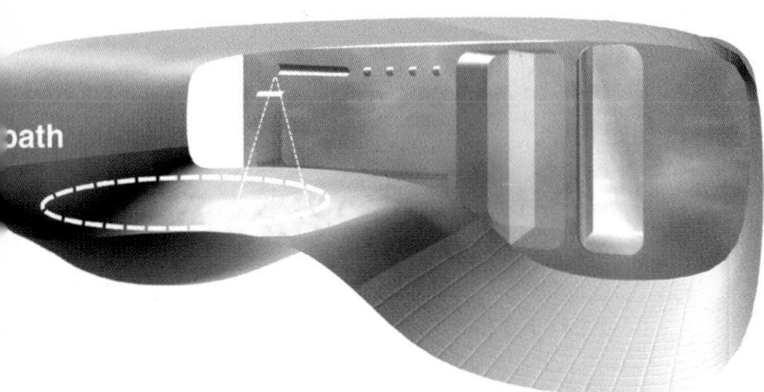

halfway beetween clothing and a house: it becomes an exploring device, a landscape producer.

living space reduced to its minimum

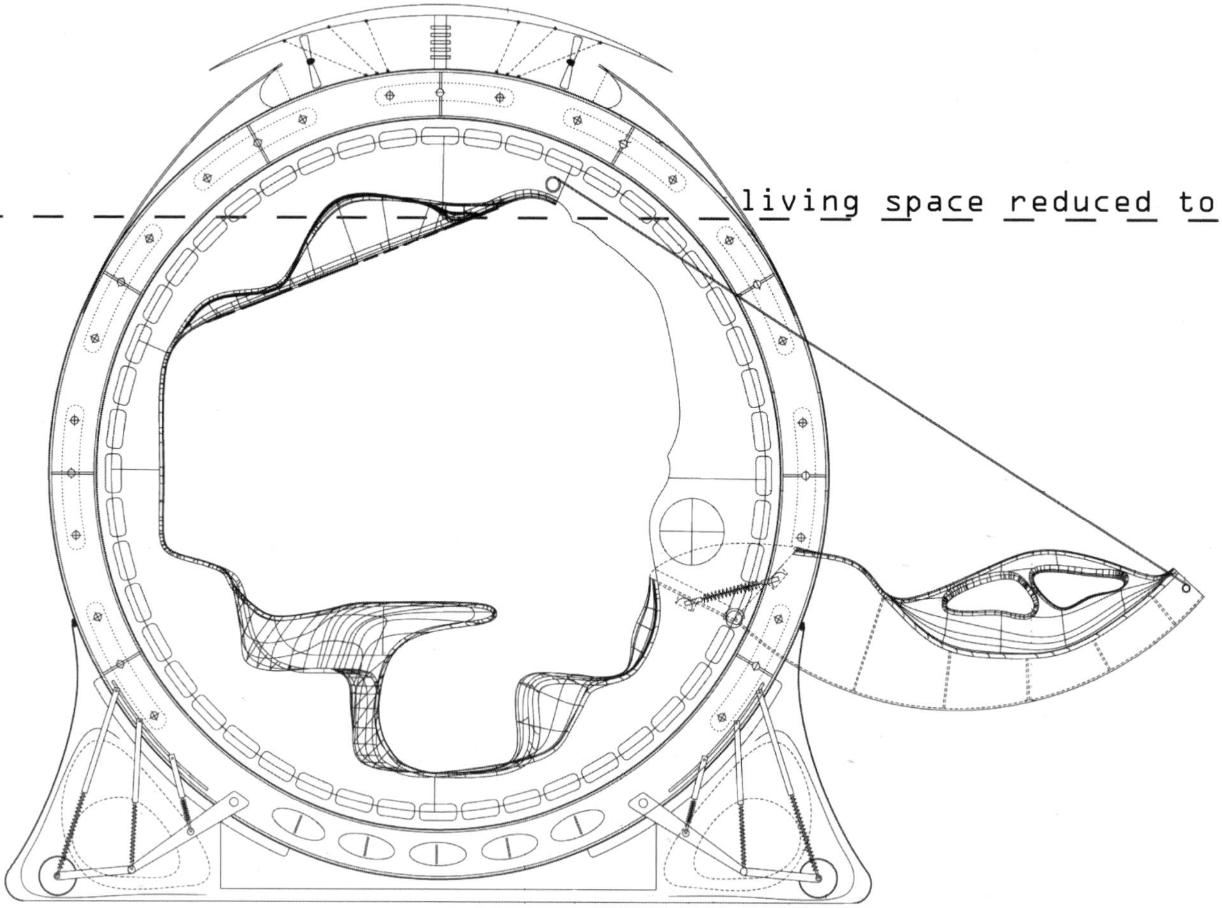

combining the various advantages of the housing and automobile industries

A series of revolving modules, like giant hamster-wheels, contain all living-programs. There is no distinction anymore between wall, floor or ceiling - just one transitional space. A maximum of flexibility and spatial-experience leaving a minimal footprint.

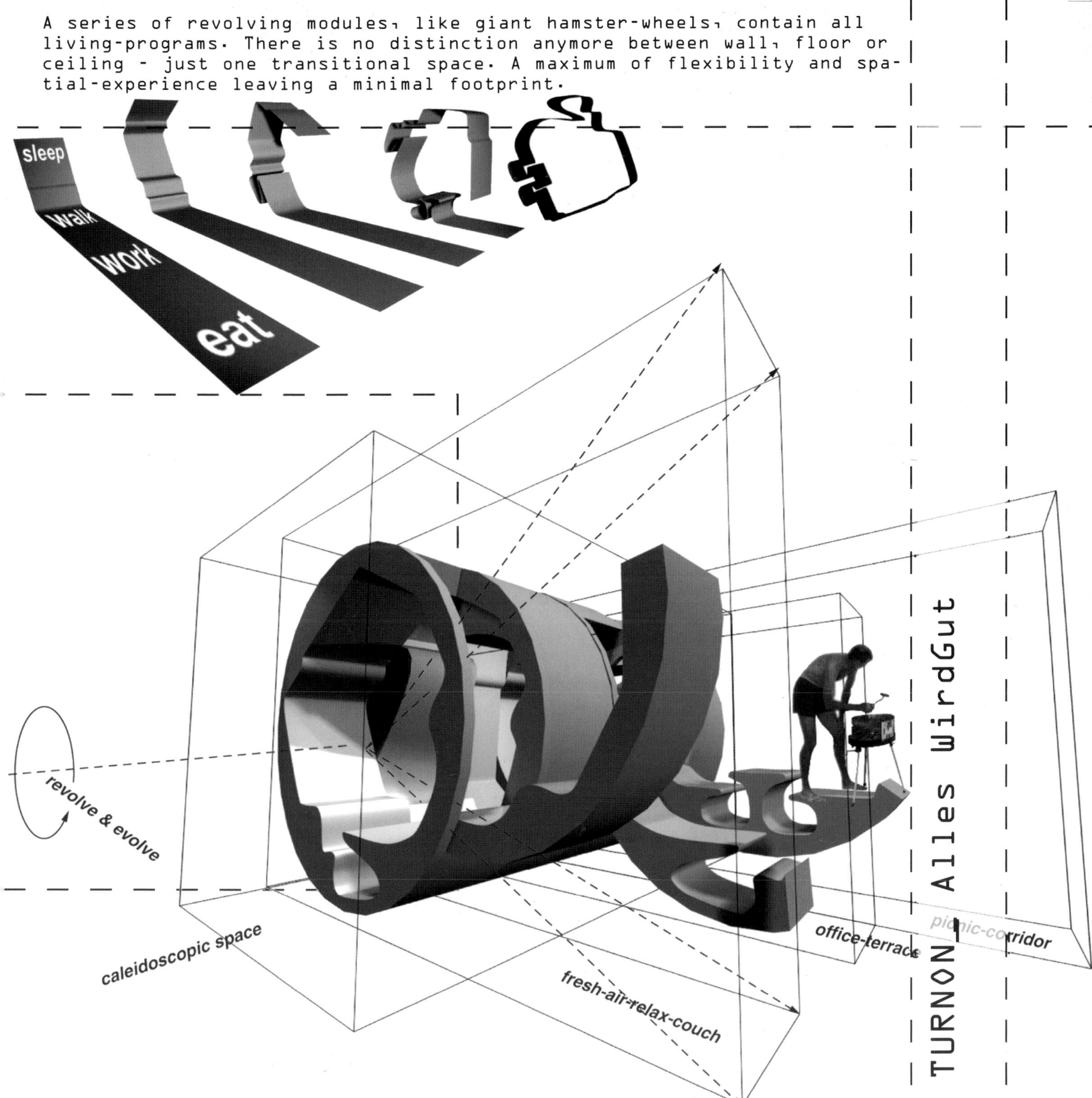

An endless number of different rings - infinite possibilities of combinations. Add as many modules as you want, those which represent your sense of taste, functionality and progress.

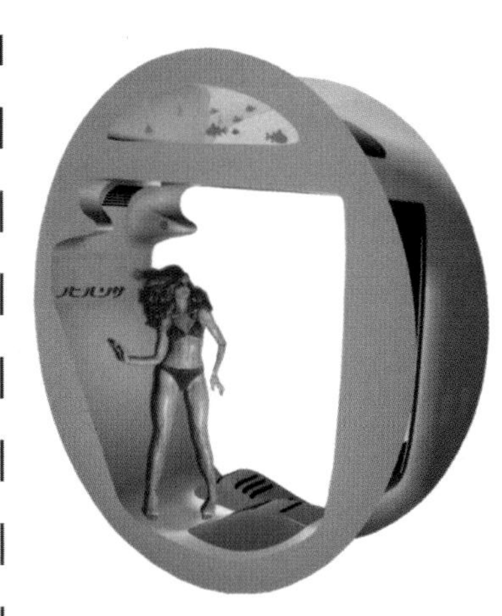

type:	kitch-en	*class:*	A(mini)
group:	avantgarde	*size:*	350 x 100 cm
orderno.:	WQXX789	*weight:*	185 kg

By folding the space, ring-like configurations are created which can be turned on their axes - this creates a continuos inner surface where each point can be rotated 360 degrees.

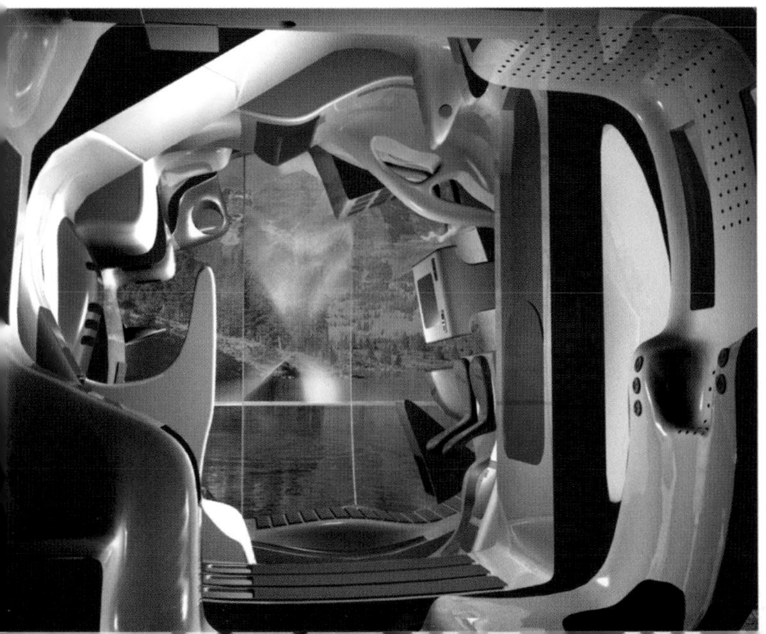

While cooking, the couch becomes the ceiling, the dining table a wall. The interior space changes constantly with the endless positions of each ring. A new flat every day?

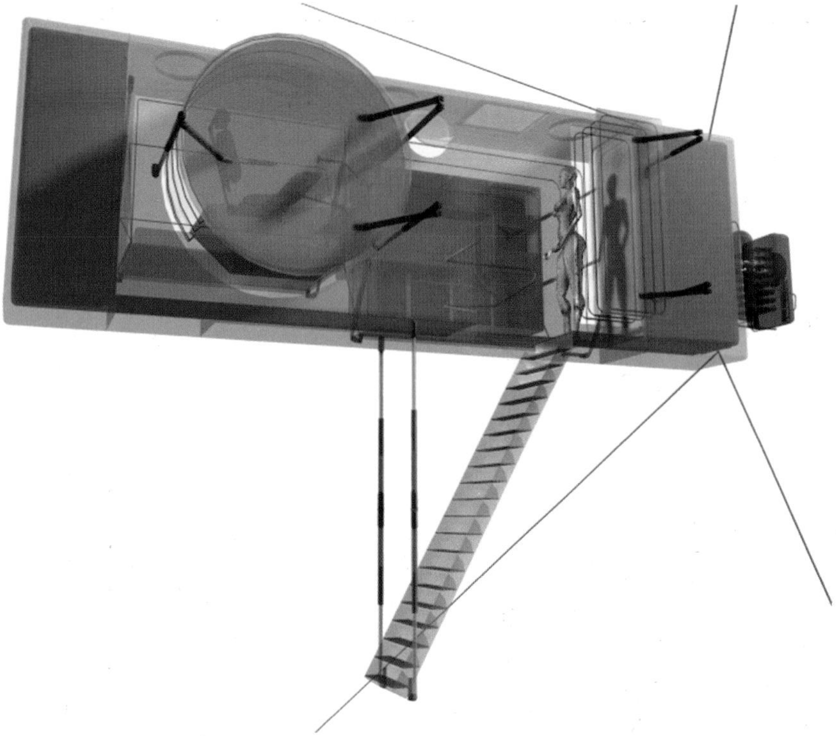

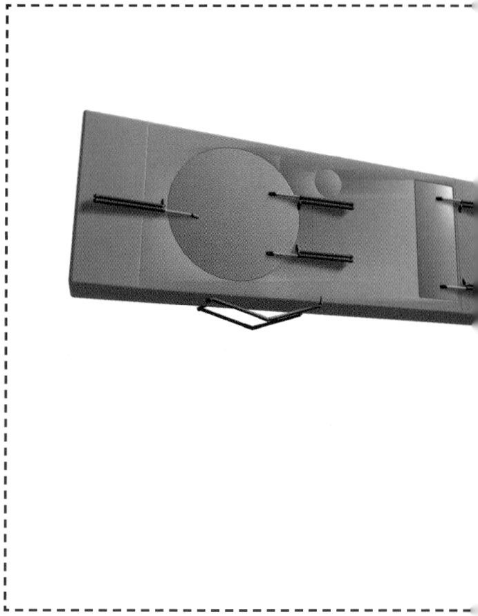

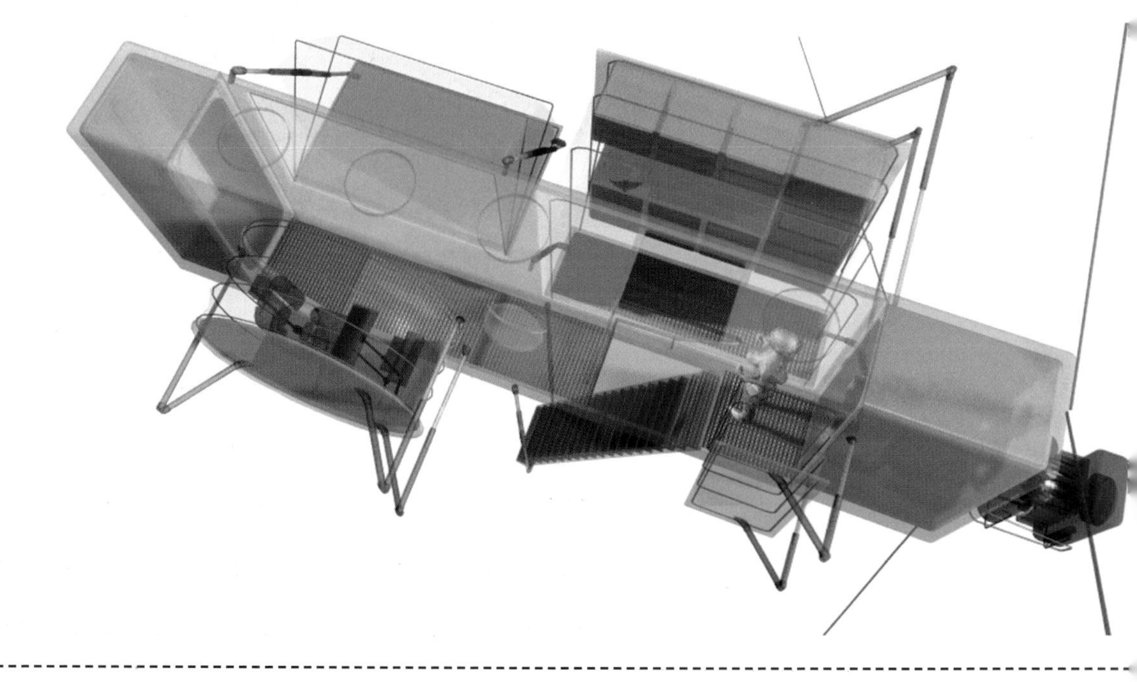

MTI-MOBILE TOURIST INTERFACE_ Urban environments

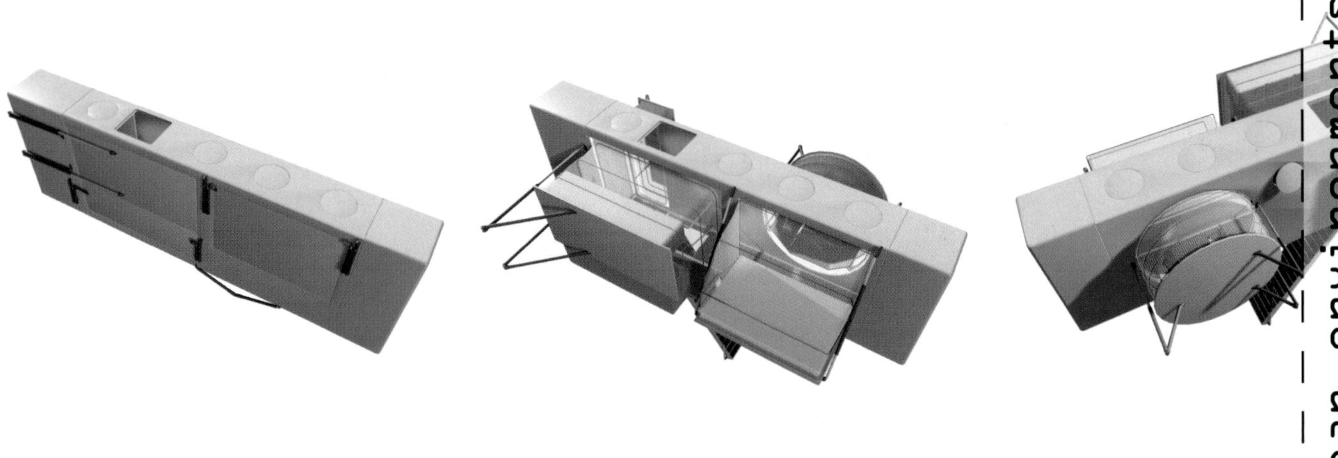

MTI, the "mobile tourist interface" is a high-tech version of the beloved camper van, aiming to address the issue of urban sprawl in areas of tourist activity. MTI is a remedy against unrestricted development. Instead of building more decentralized tourist ghettos, the units are implemented in the streetscapes of local villages.

The extremely lightweight shell of the capsule, consisting of a high-tech composite material, does not require additional structural enforcement when attached to an existing building.

As the interfaces can unfold, their impact is minimized during the off-season, while at peak times they will provide shade and a comforting microclimate in the streets. On the other hand, the mti will enable tourists to live right where they want to be: at an authentic old fishing village on the coast, right in the exciting center of an urban metropolis close to shops, restaurants, bars and clubs or even a few steps away from the beach in a natural environment.

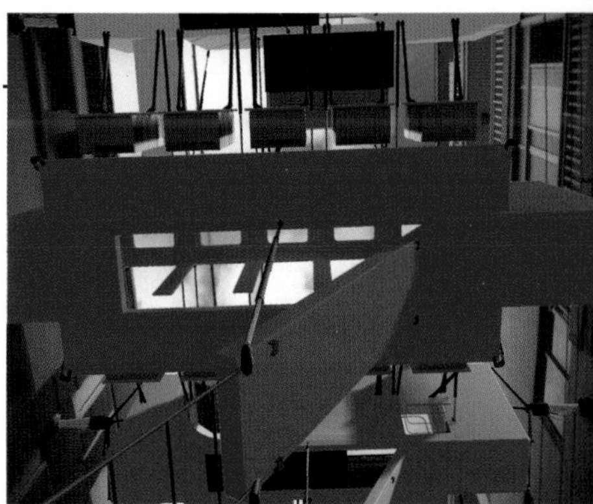

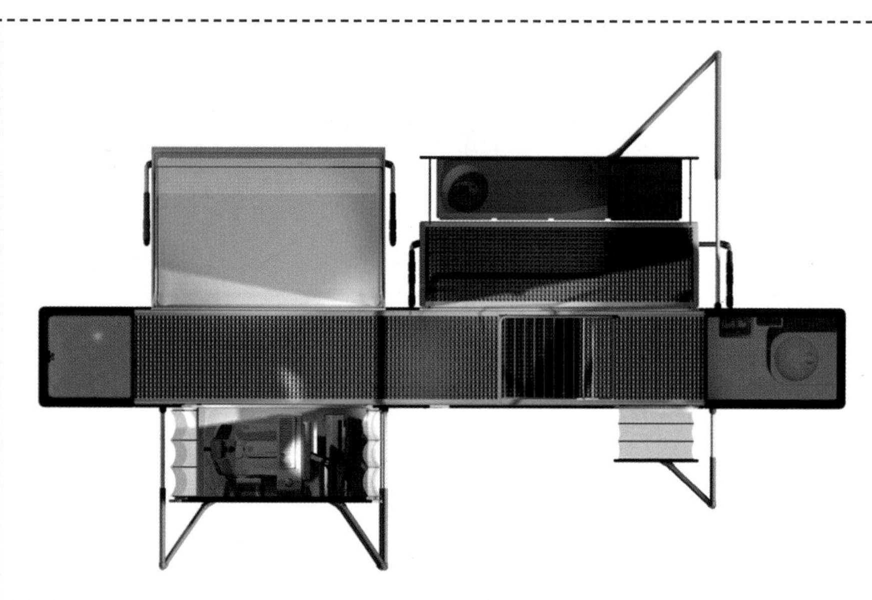

The temporary architecture started out as a site-specific project for the particular problems of Tenerife,
Spain. It was later turned into a more general unit that can be set up anywhere in the world.

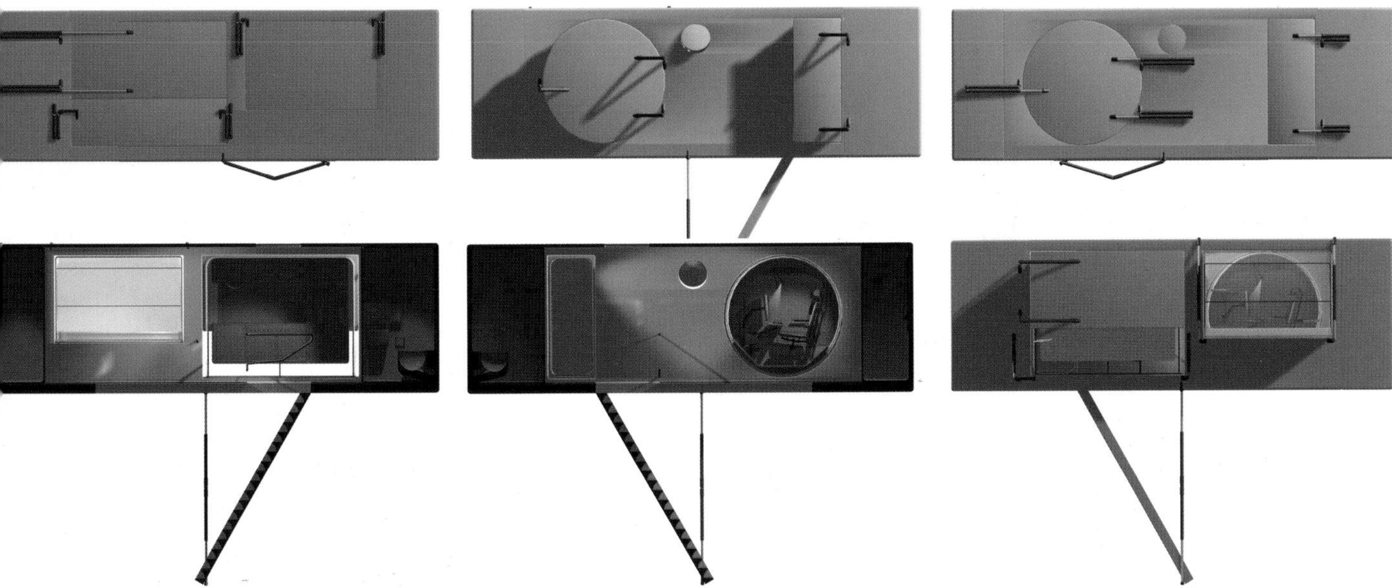

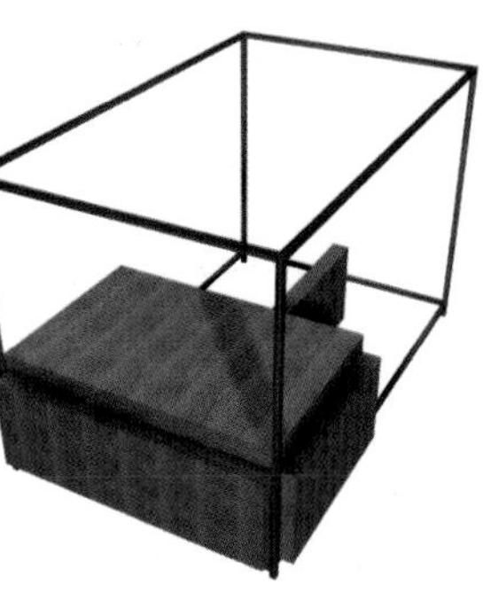

A project dealing with architectural space tailored as an item of clothing; the space encountered between the kayak and the Internet, NhEW is a nomadic dwelling prototype combining economy and comfort. A unit adapted to the needs of the individual, made of lightweight materials for easy transportation, assembly and disassembly. Offering a wide range of possible materials, for different looks, climates and functions, the user specifies the individual needs and desires the structure is to satisfy.

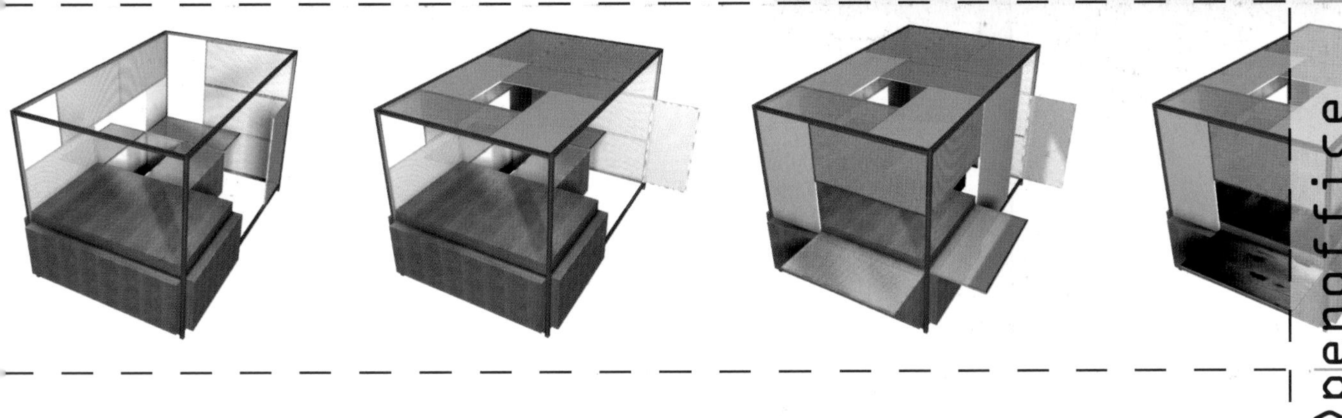

NhEW combines traditional nomadic culture with contemporary culture's latest nomad obsessions, such as wireless technologies and convertible clothing, occupying the space of our future dreams, which are reminiscent of the ancient past.

NhEW PAD_ Copenhagenoffice and Openoffice

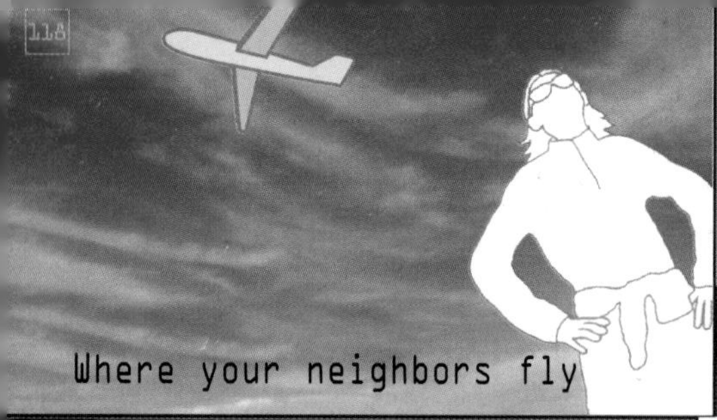
Where your neighbors fly

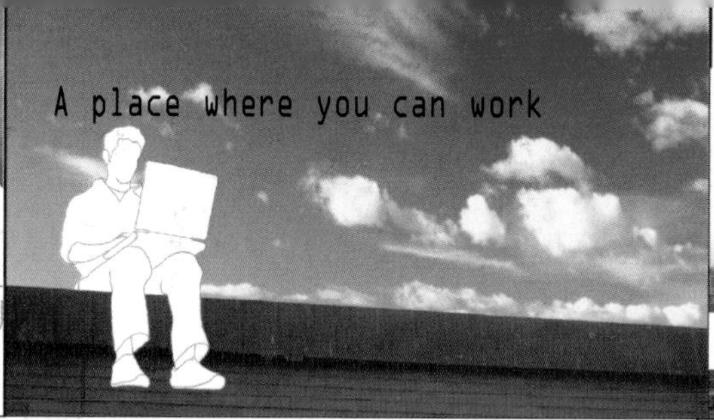
A place where you can work

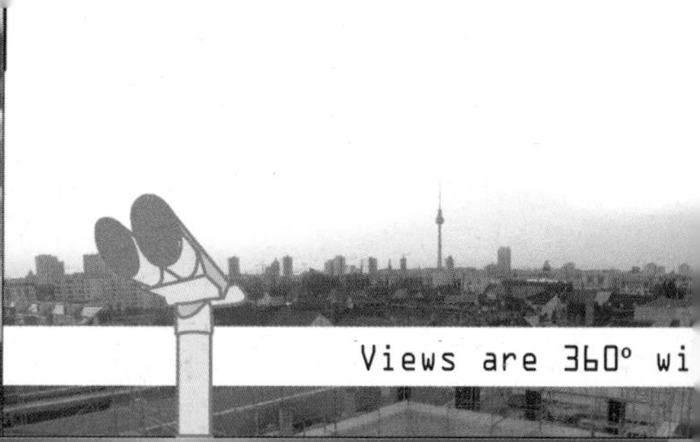
Views are 360° wi

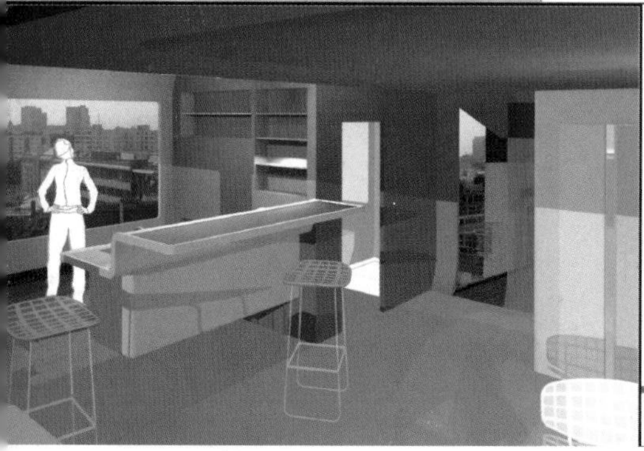

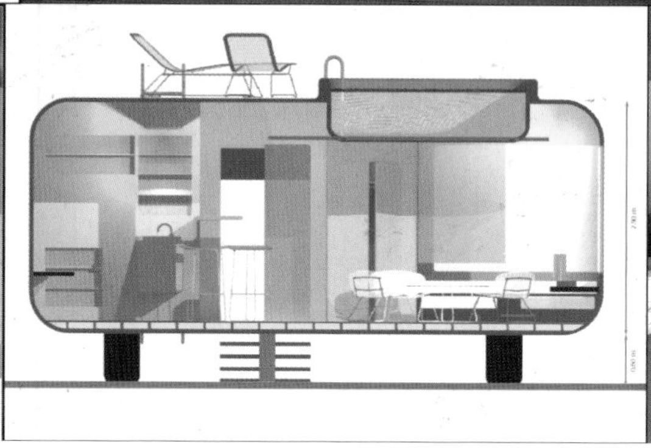

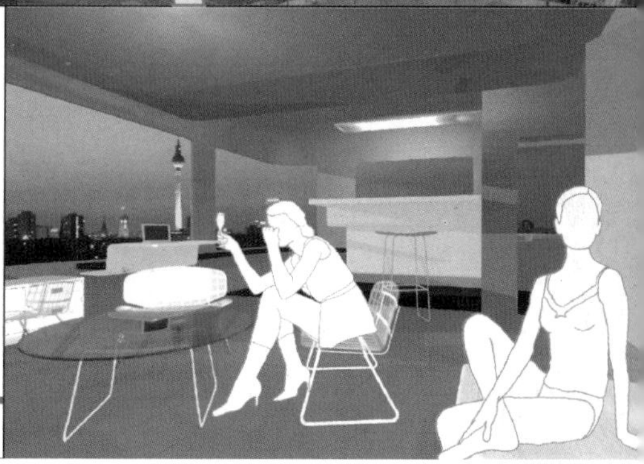

A temporary, minimalistic domicile to suit people of a nomadic lifestyle and living for short periods of time in large cities and dense urban areas, offering both sanctuary and social structure.

Imagine the endless possibilities

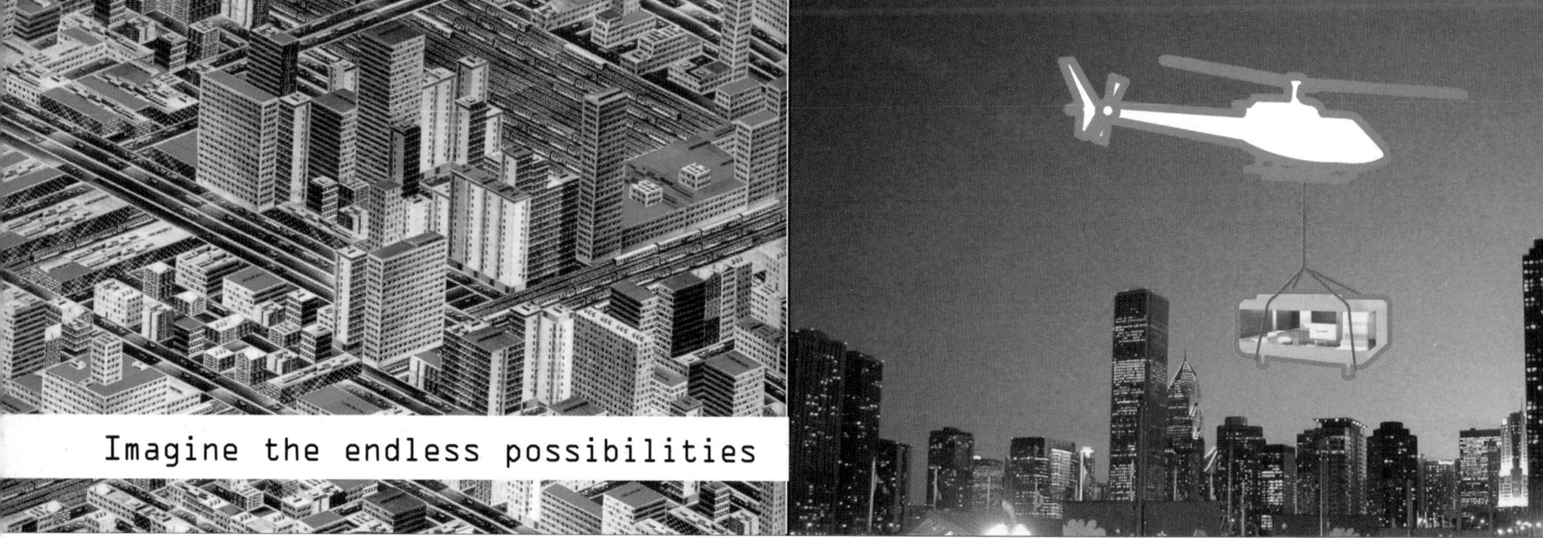

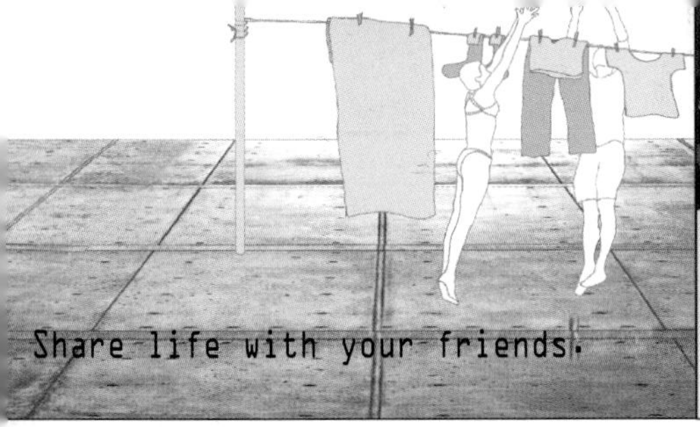

Share life with your friends.

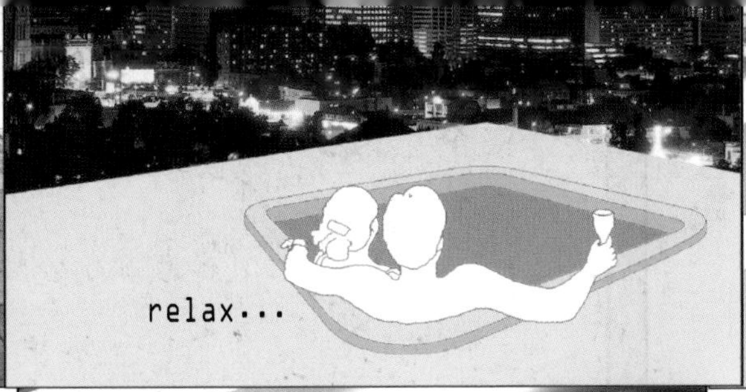

relax...

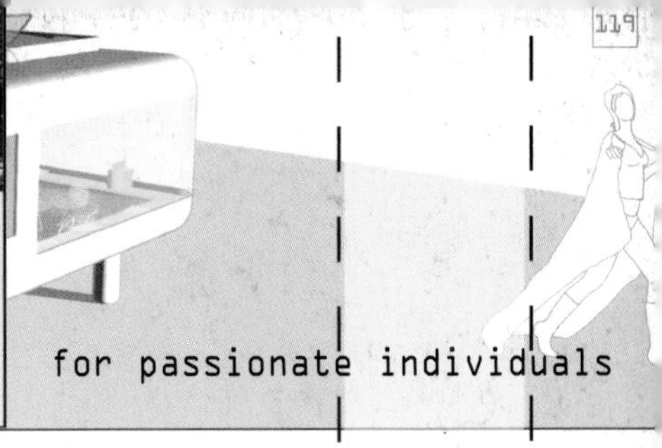

for passionate individuals

LOFTCUBE_ Studio Aisslinger

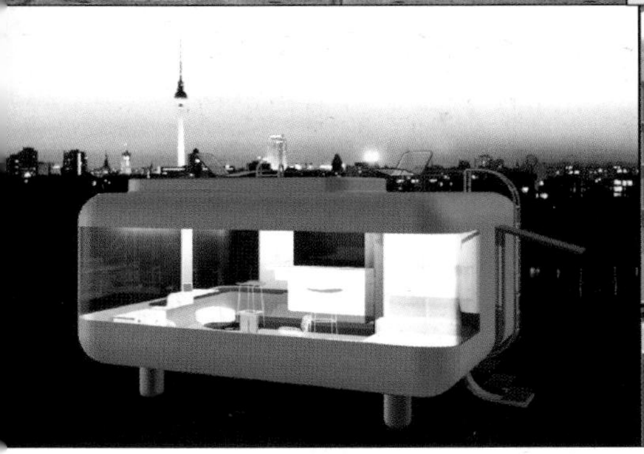

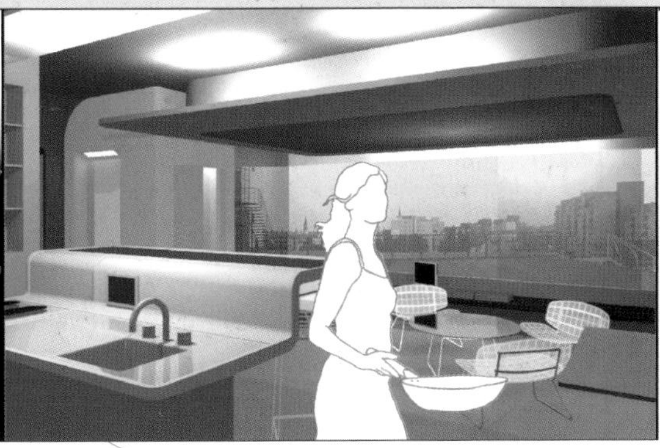

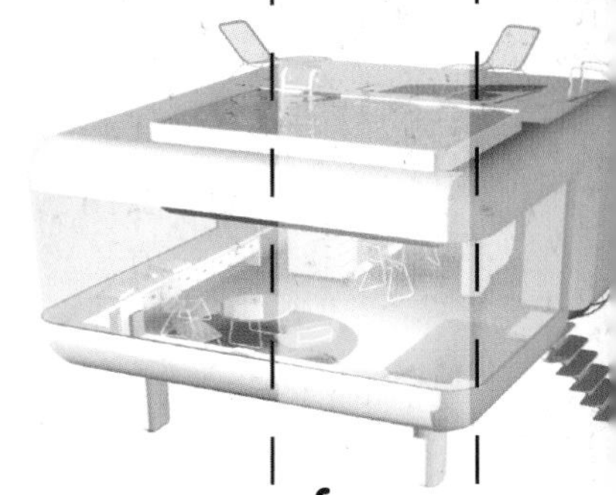

They would be constructed on the roofs of existing architecture, a treasure of sunny sites in prime urban spaces.

Living room
Kitchen
eeping area
Bathroom
an area of 40 m²
Entrance

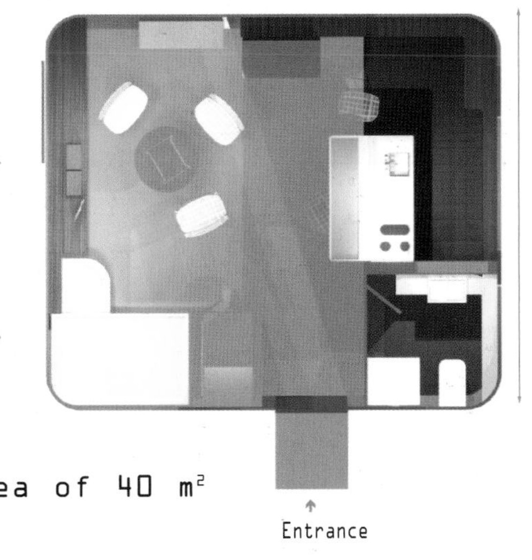

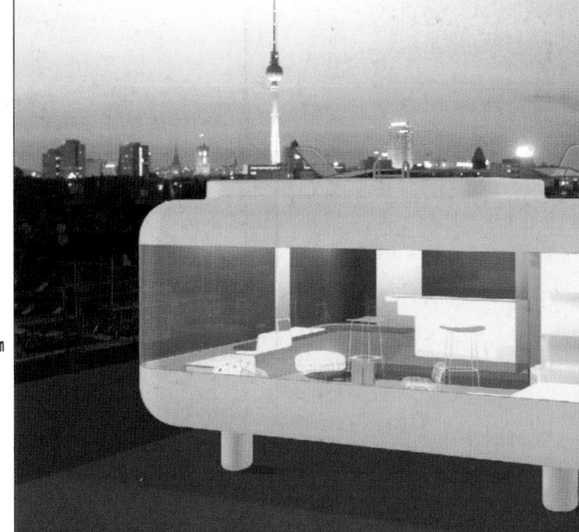

The rooftop communities would first require an extension of the utility lines of the building.

Structural Body: 6.6 m x 6.6 m
Height: 3 m
Space: approx. 40 m^2

The cube's own weight should be able to neutralize maximum wind drag.

Price: Approx. 55,000 Euros

The loftcube has a ground surface of approximately 40 m^2. The organic frame structure consists of four smooth panels. The tenant is free to choose the color, material, and wind resistance of the surfaces. Using movable blinds, glass elements, and either solid or perforated materials.

Container for rent: "Loftcube" permanently located on suitable site, rented through specialized companies.

The real utopia and the big issue is whether investors will venture to rent rooftops on a grand scale and make them inhabitable for "Loftcube" users. Is the colonization of big city "roofscapes" within reach?

For sale: Transport by freight helicopter, relocation by mobile crane, or it could be dismantled, enabling various forms of transport.

FRED s small size makes relocating by truck as quick and uncomplicated as possible.

After arriving at the destination, the user expands FRED by electrical power, connecting it to water and electricity and thus, FRED is ready for operation.

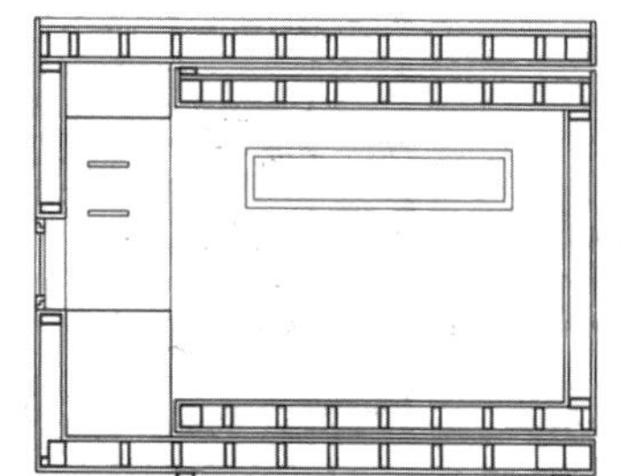

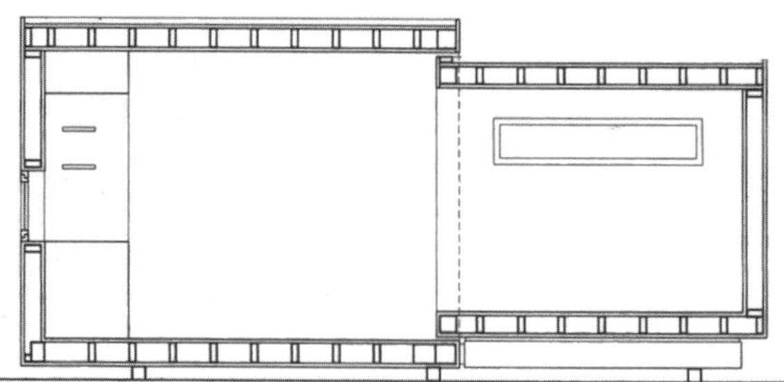

FRED_ Oskar Leo + Johannes Kaufmann

FRED is an expandable room unit measuring $3m^3$ when closed. Electronically controlled sliding wall elements open the unit to provide up to $18m^2$ of floorspace. Included alongside the main interior space are a complete kitchen, toilet and shower.

The project is to develop and construct a sustainable artist-in-residence live/work community. The final objective is to construct and deploy multiple versions of the Portable House (a mass-customized residential building unit), with an emphasis on native Californian drought-resistant plant materials, common gardens, and the use of sustainable building materials.

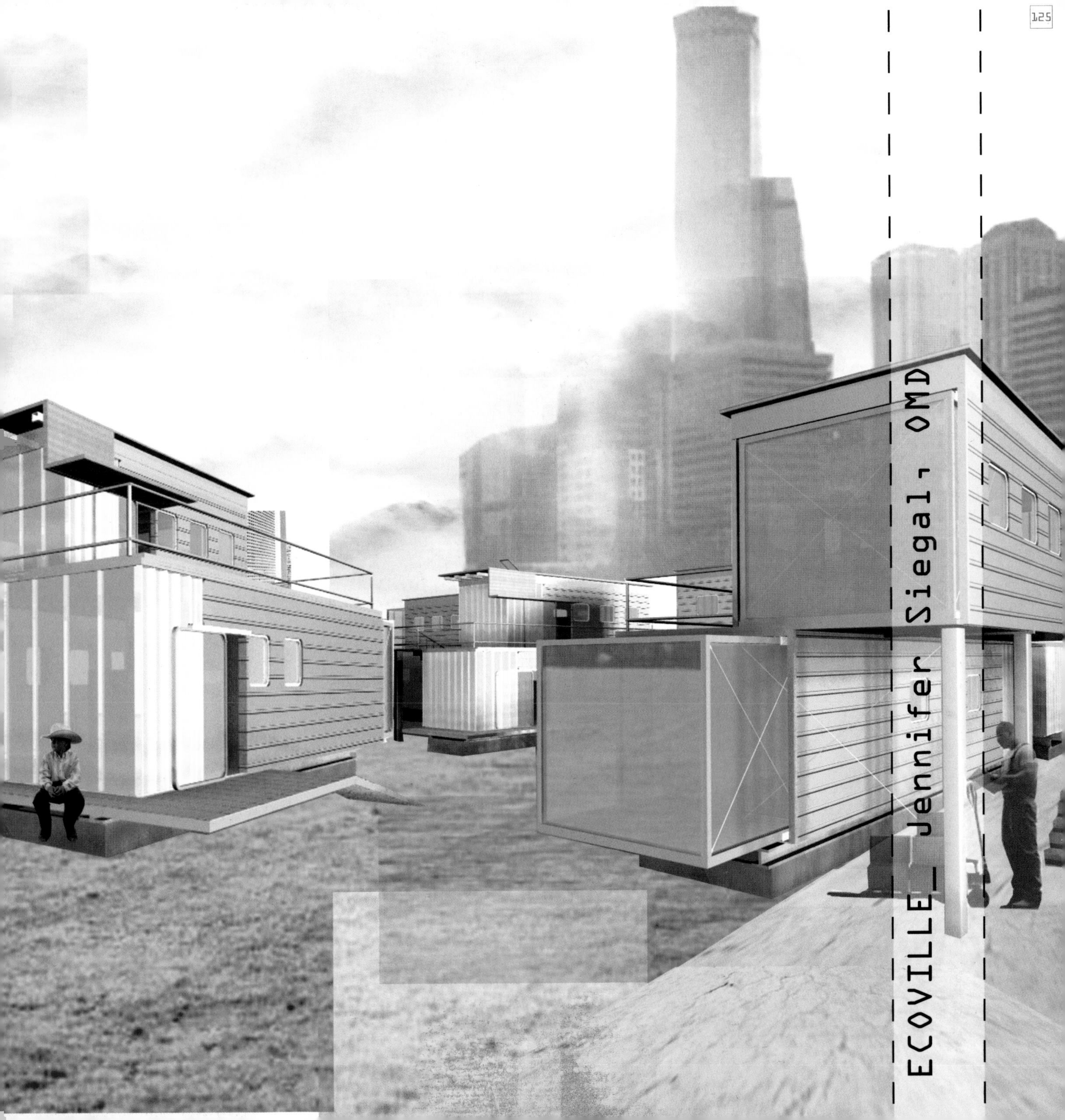
ECOVILLE Jennifer Siegal, OMD

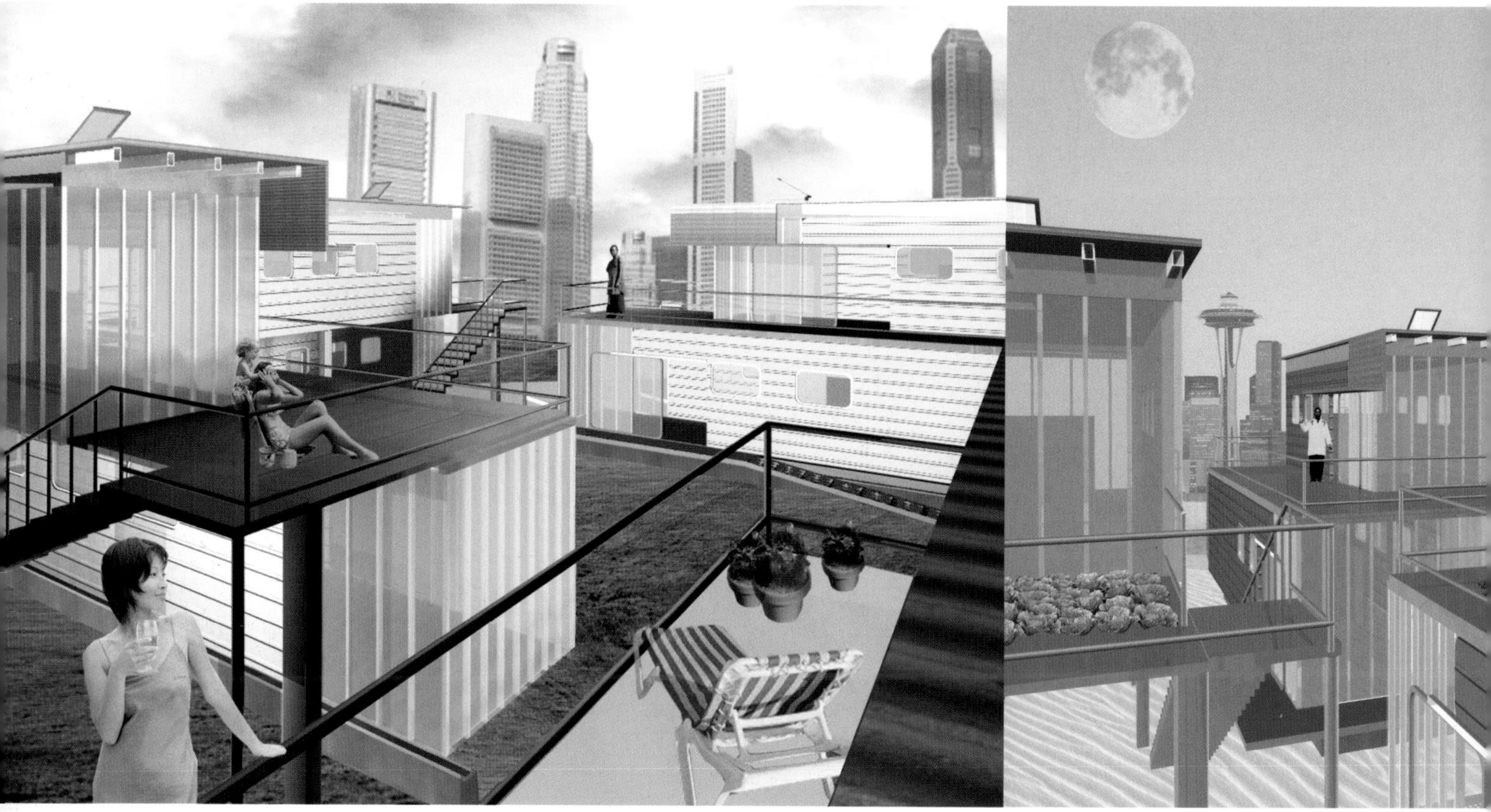

The Eco-Ville Development is comprised of a series of attached and semi-attached buildings in multiple stacked configurations. The bottom unit provides a flexible work space, and the attached upper unit offers a well-lit, open living space with access to a private roof garden.

In an effort to provide affordable artists' residences, the development demonstrates that individual modern design solutions are possible with mass-customization.

The Portable House's expandable/contractible spaces, the varying degrees of translucency of its materials, and its very portability render it uniquely flexible and adaptable.

When additional space is required, the living room structure can be extended outward to increase square footage. By design, the House can be maneuvered and reoriented to take advantage of natural light and airflow.

The Portable House's versatility, the way it moves across and rests lightly upon the landscape, provides a provocative counterpoint to the status quo housing model.

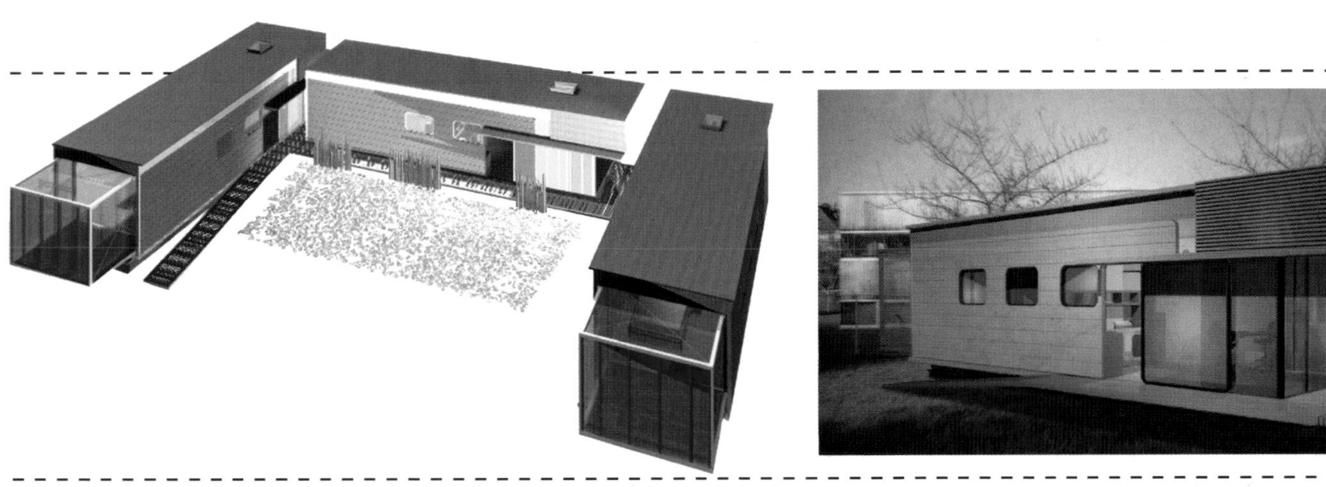

It recalls a time when the elements that constituted shelter were easily manipulated to accommodate innumerable variables and conditions. As an entity unto itself, the Portable House adapts to or creates new social dynamics wherever it goes. Whether momentarily located in the open landscape, briefly situated in an urban space, or positioned for a more lengthy stay, the Portable House accommodates a wide range of economic needs and simple functions.

One shipping container is transformed into a Mobile Dwelling Unit. Cuts in the metal walls of the container generate extruded sub-volumes, each encapsulating one live, work or storage function. When traveling, these sub-volumes are pushed in, filling the entire container, interlocking with each other and leaving the outer skin of the container flush to allow worldwide standardized shipping.

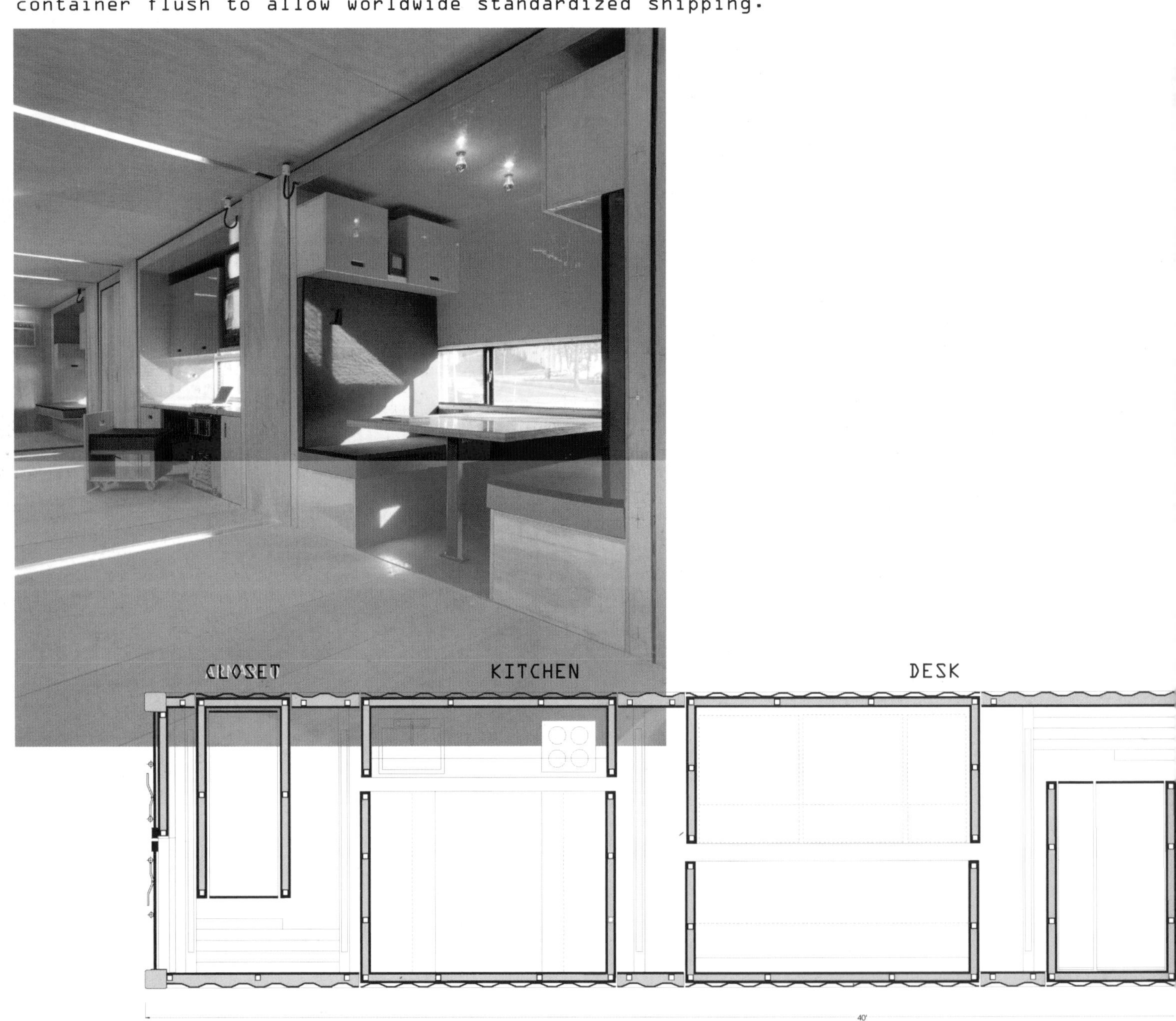

MDUs are conceived for individuals moving around the globe. The MDU travels with its dweller to the next long term destination, fitted with all live/work equipment and filled with the dweller's belongings. Once it reaches its destination, the MDU is loaded in MDU vertical harbors located in all major metropolitan areas.

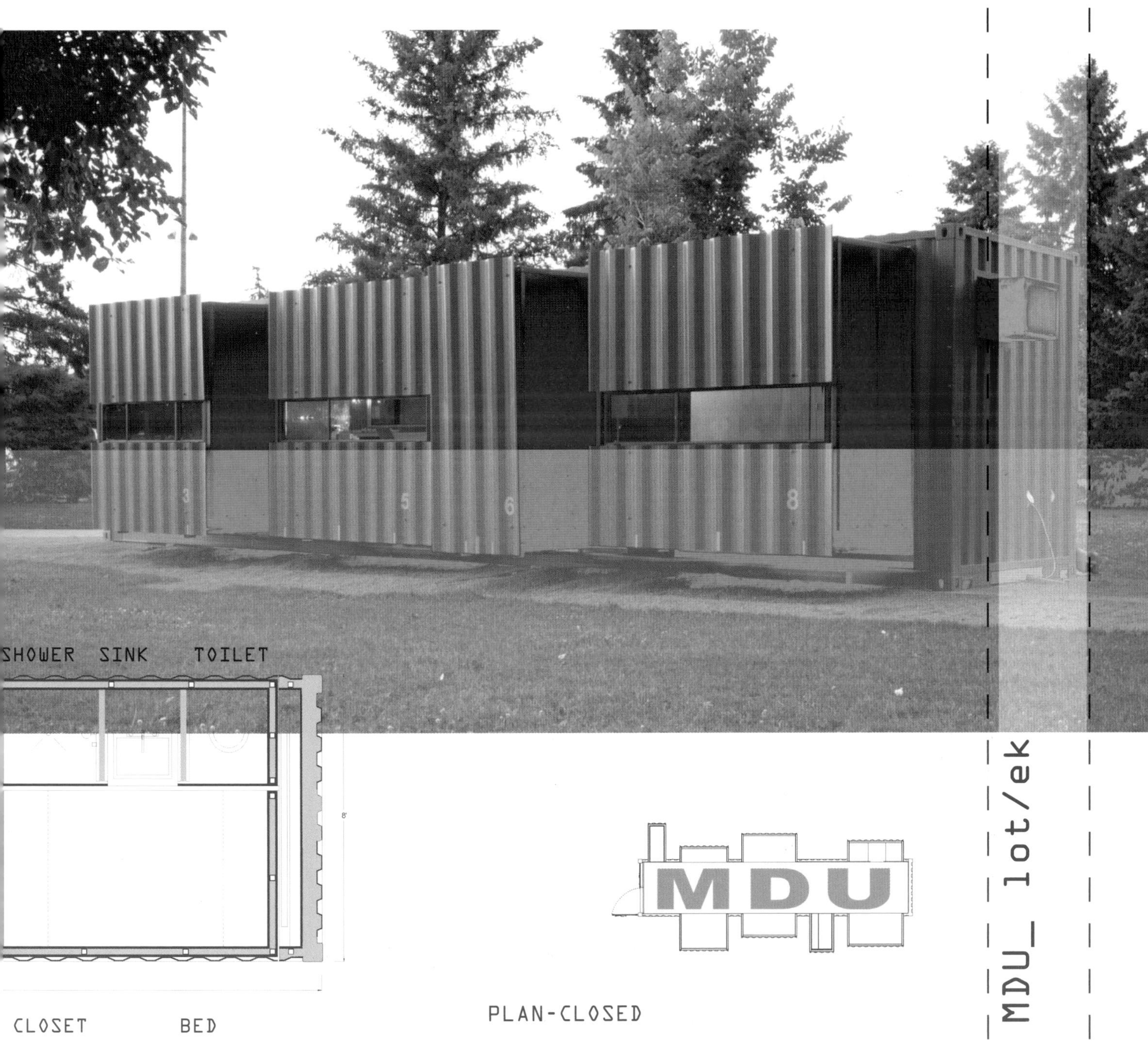

PLAN-CLOSED

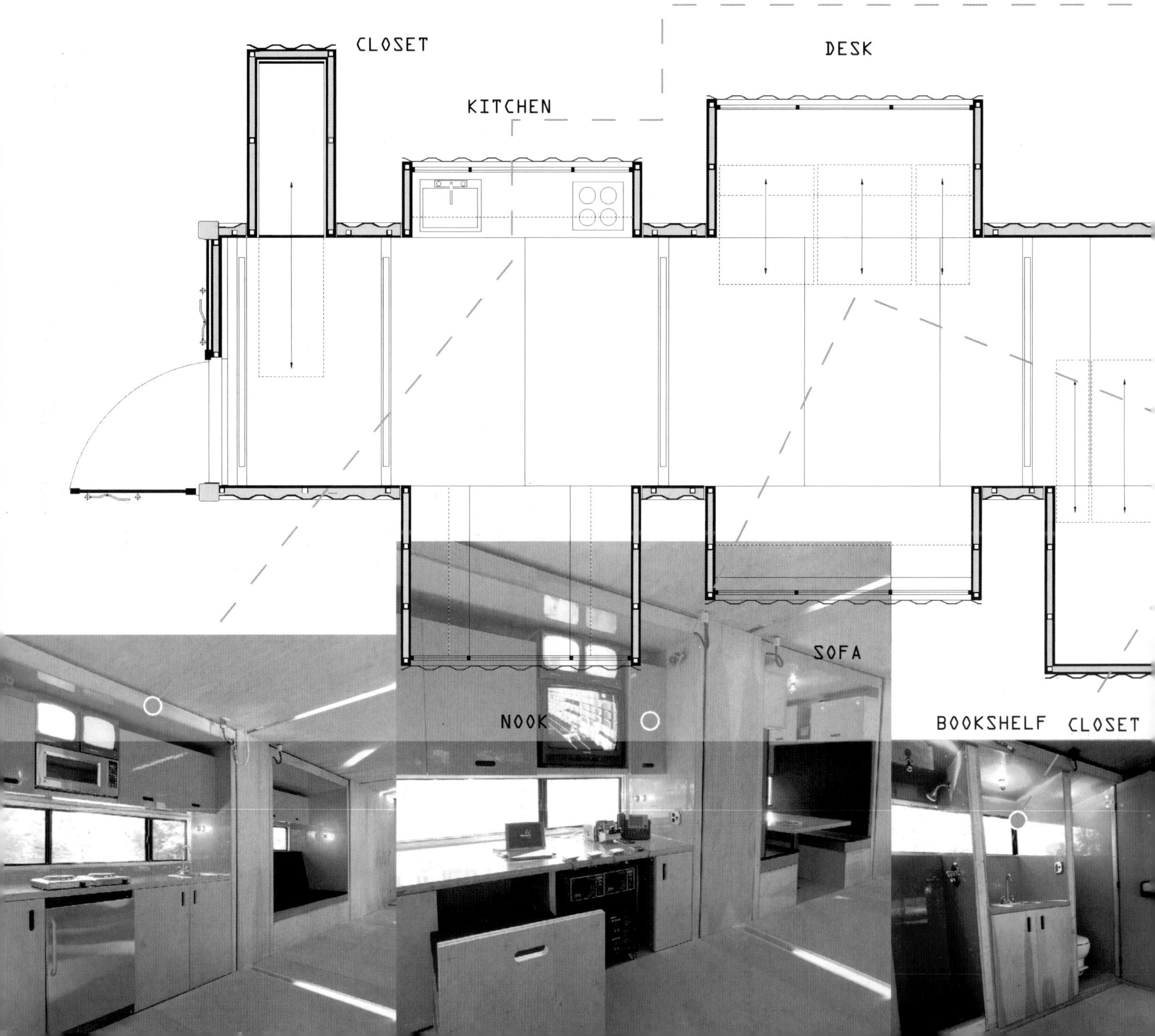

Its stretched linear development is generated by the repetition of MDUs and vertical distribution corridors. Elevators, stairs and all systems (power, data, water, sewage) run vertically along these corridors. A crane slides parallel to the building, along the entire length, on its own tracks. It picks up MDUs as they are driven to the site and loads them onto slots along the rack.

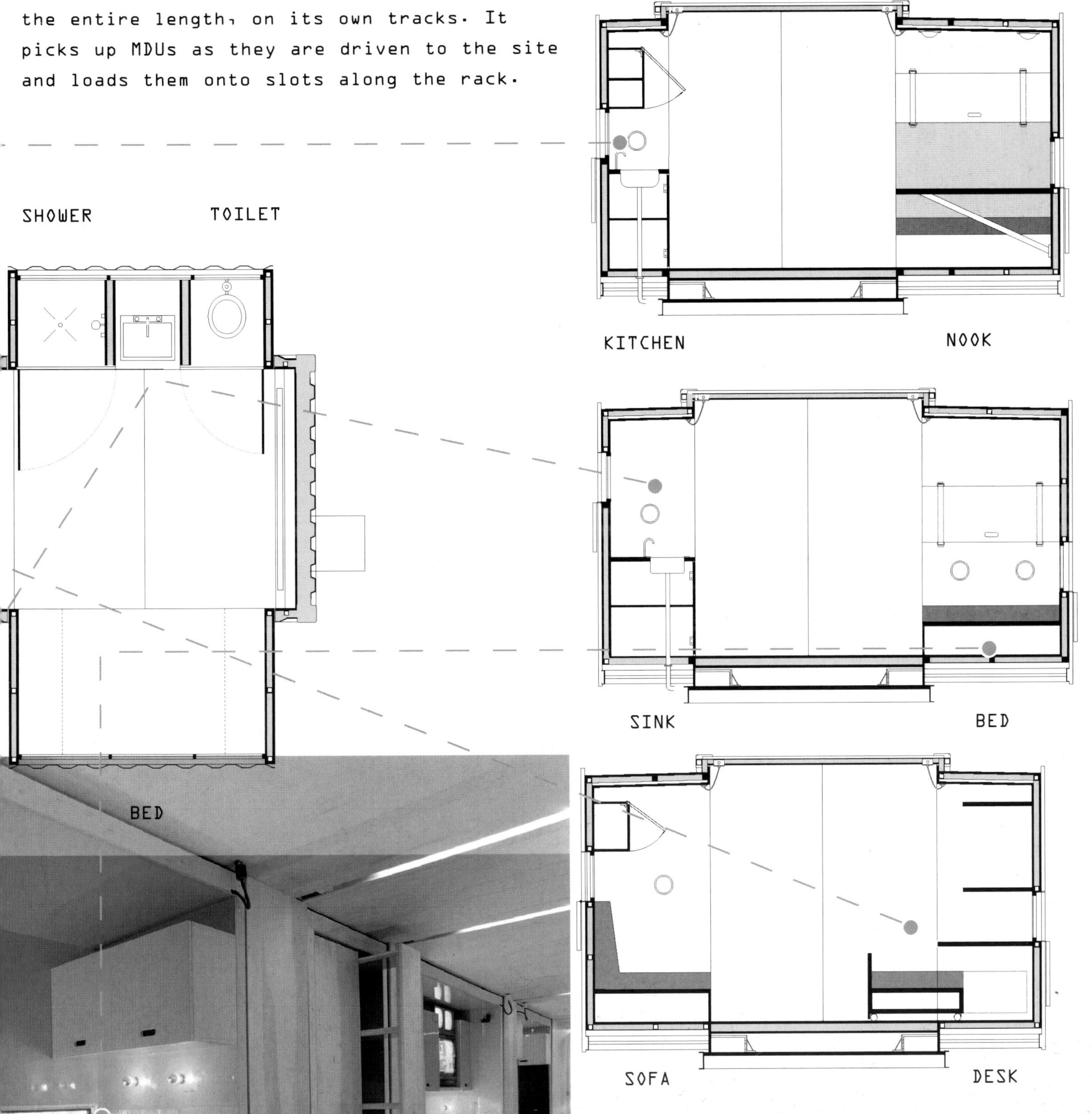

The manufactured housing industry emerged from a convergence of two trends in culture and technology at the beginning of the twentieth century: the desire for travel and mobility, manifest in the travel-trailer industry, and the desire for cost-effective, efficient modes of construction, evident in new models of factory production.

While newness and inventive forms were enthusiastically accepted in trailers or cars, conventional and iconic modes of architecture in homes were still sought. These disciplines could merge to encourage a contemporary practice of manufactured housing that reflects consumer customization and allows architecture to actively participate in a currently inaccessible market. Finally, the proposal seeks to offer a new view of manufactured housing that values strength, durability, emotion and desire, borrowing strategies from the origins of manufactured housing and the automobile industry.

It explores the development of tectonic systems.

TSA Architects have proposed a revised interface with the consumer that encourages the perception of architecture as more than comfortable, but performative and desirable as well. Individuals could therefore customize the options of the house to adapt it to site, climate, materials, function, and wants. These options could be selected and prioritized based on individual purchases and affordability.

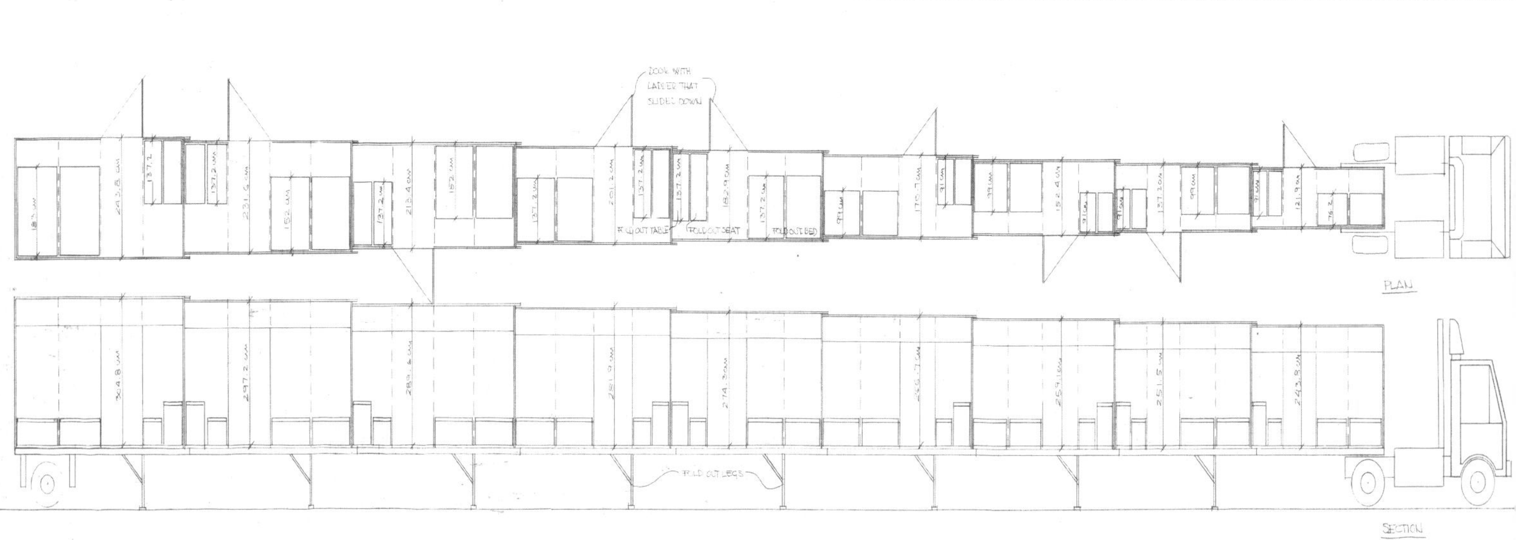

A city stored in a truck: six housing units telescoped into one, a semi-trailer hooked up to a tractor.

When the truck is parked, a line of housing units can be pulled out of the trailer. Each unit slides on a track attached to the walls of the next larger unit. The houses are sheathed in corrugated steel; the sheathing is cut in sections and hinged so that they can be folded down inside and out.

Truck tractor & flat bed, corrugated galvanized steel, grating, chain, fluorescent light

MOBILE LINEAR HOUSE Acconci Studio

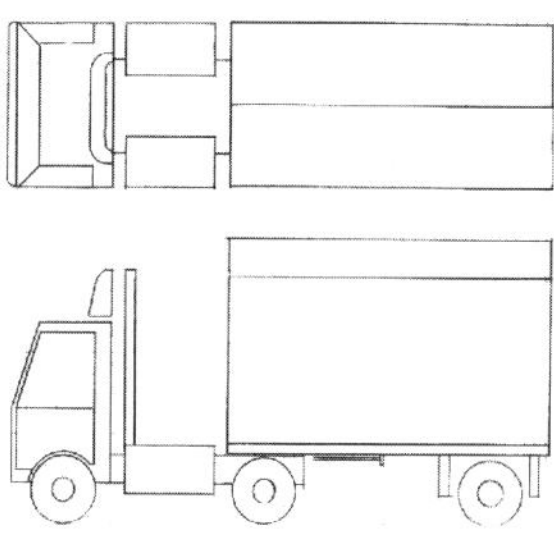

Inside each house, wall panels pivot down to make a table, a bench, a bed, a shelf. The last unit (the smallest) functions as a service module for the entire community of houses. Inside, wall panels fold down on hinges to provide a stove, refrigerator and toilet. Wall panels fold in vertically, forming shower and toilet stalls.

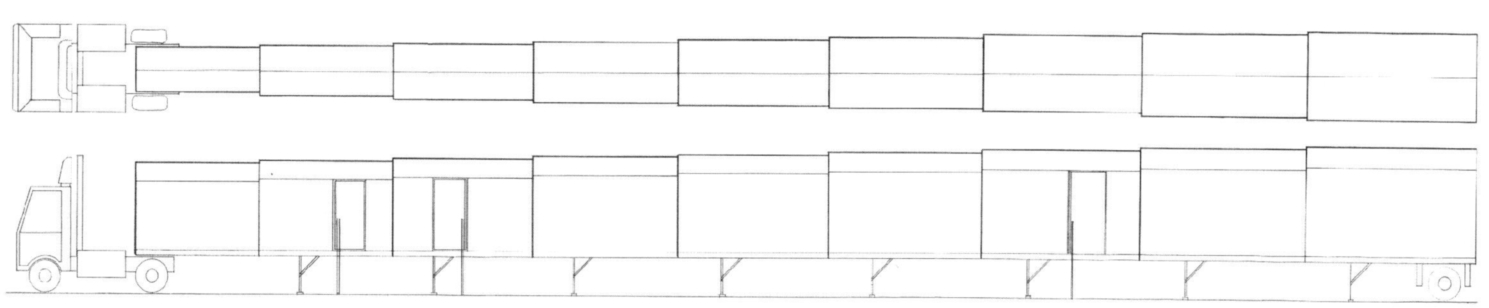

The more you use the service unit, the less private it becomes.

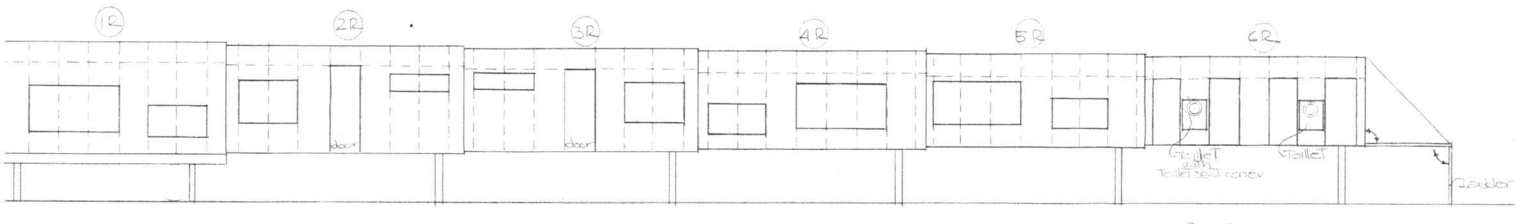

Helly Hansen

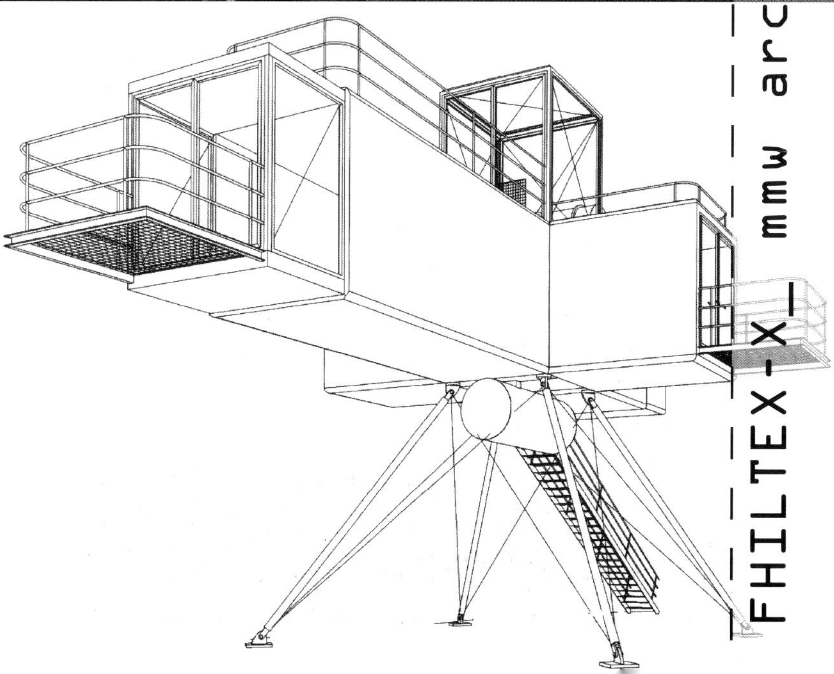

FHILTEX-X— mmw architects

Helly Hansen

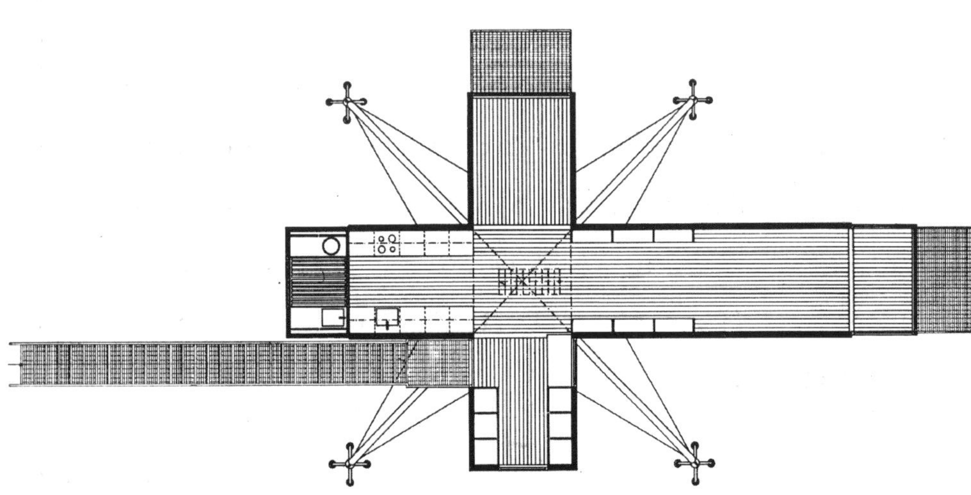

The house is based on two standard 20' x 40' steel containers and requires only four simple support points. It can be totally self-sufficient, with solar panels and tanks for drinking- and waste-water. Its hinged stair, external insulation cloaking and minimal substructure can all be packed away inside the containers for shipment and re-erection anywhere. This is the realization of the dream of an altogether different kind of architecture.

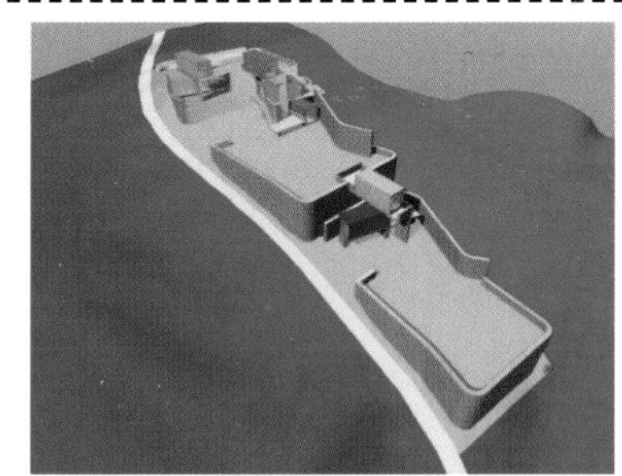

The container project began as research into the limits of habitability. So much of new housing construction - particularly in Asia - is conceived as little more than a conglomeration of minimal containers for maximum volume. Rather than resisting this approach,

the designers were interested in pushing it to the extreme.

The basic principle involves retro-fitting standard shipping containers (cheap and readily-available) with kitchen and bathroom units, then combining the containers themselves into larger units. Some of the early proposals were for student housing, homeless shelters and temporary settlements of all kinds.

In 1995, the city of Kobe, Japan was devastated by an earthquake. Without linkages, the city effectively ceased to exist.

In terms of the buildings that fell, and those that have since replaced them, it was a lesson for architects that there are many issues which transcend style and fashion.

CONTAINMENT_-FOBA/ Katsu Umebayashi

Sometimes, simple containment is enough.

The containers were proposed as emergency disaster relief housing, as they could be quickly and easily assembled. While the newly-homeless lived in containers on public land, concrete foundations would be built on their own personal sites for stability, safety and eventual connection to the city-s power and sewage systems. Once these bases were complete, the containers could be taken home and hooked up.

But an unexpected problem suddenly arose; a terrorist attack changed the public perception of shipping containers, and implementing the project was impossible at that time.

Use of the containers would have avoided an unnecessary rush in the replanning and rebuilding of the city. There would also have been a minimum of waste. If and when the containers were no longer required, they could simply be returned to their original purpose. Kobe is currently looking for ways to dispose of 10,000 abandoned emergency-housing units.

The obvious ease with which they may be transported by ship makes the containers ideal relief housing for disasters anywhere in the world.

3500 containers subtracted temporarily from the worldwide flow of trade are gathered in Rotterdam to form a mega container on the scale of the city: the City Container.

CONTAINER CITY_ mvrdv

The beehive staged the central activities of the first Biennial of Architecture in the Netherlands in 2002. Positioned on the Lloyd Pier in the Rotterdam Harbor, this City Container was the emblematic symbol of the Biennial.

The containers are used as the floor, walls and ceiling of an immense space of unusual dimensions. Cables connect the containers and put them under tension, turning rows of them into hollow 'beams' spanning the hall. Each beam is composed of 6 end-to-end containers. The tension also allows for the stacking of 15 units on top of each other.

The units surround visitors and create a feeling of intimacy within the massive scale of the hall. The effect is like that of a giant 'beehive', with 3500 niches for sleeping, eating, exhibiting, and performing. There is space for hotels, bars, galleries, a spa, conference rooms, shops, business units, ateliers, schools, and day-care centers.

The containers can be accessed by galleries, construction-elevators and stairs. By putting parts of the containers on rails, they can be easily removed in order to create giant openings for exterior views.

SCENE people living in the street people occupying public space unused urban areas, water, air (pressure), parking for free immigration cramped conditions

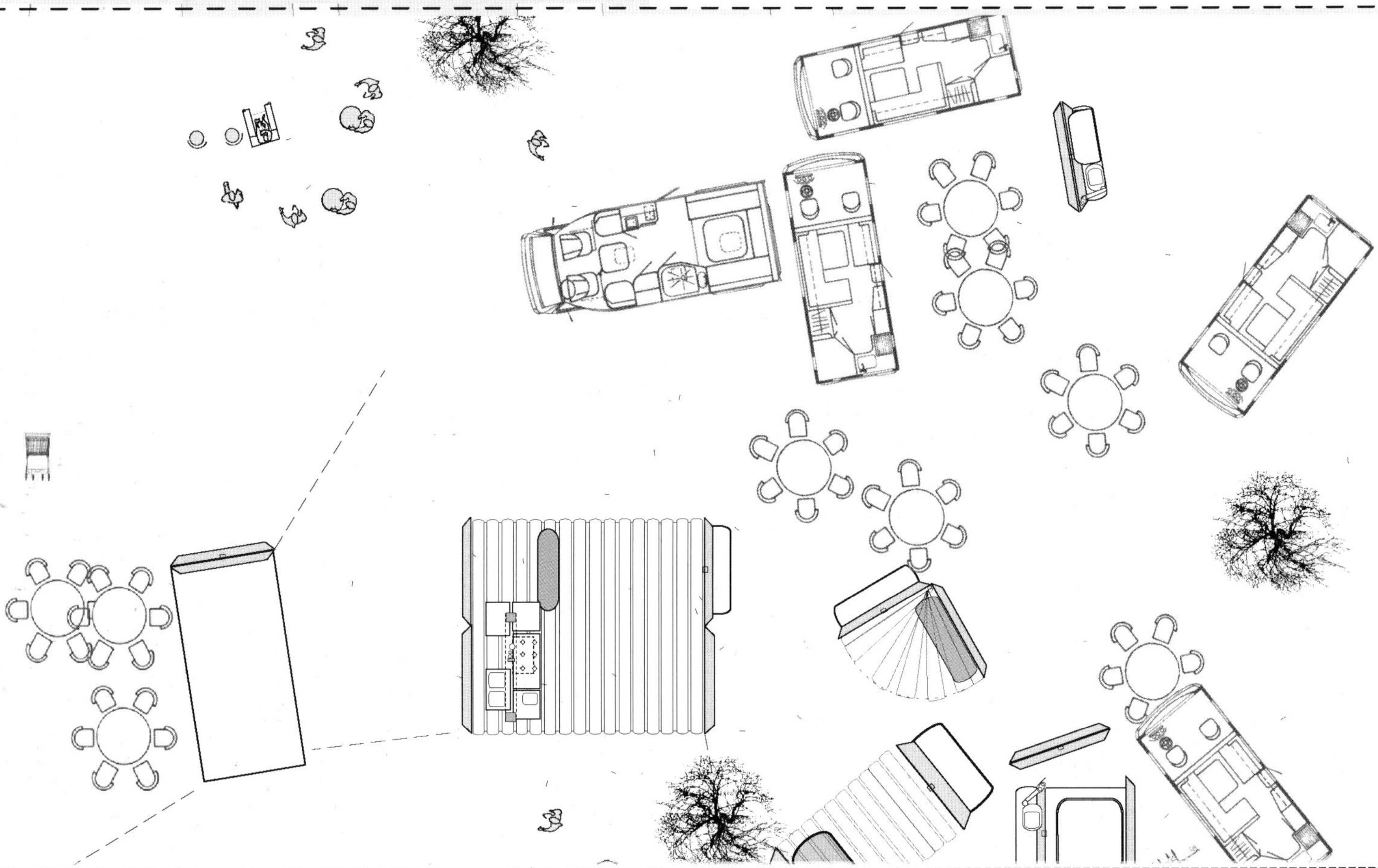

+++Urban Domestic Space System

The uds is a system for mobile and temporal inhabiting. It switch spaces in the city, putting together public and domestic uses in a bizarre relation of interdependence and collaboration. The uds system opens new city areas and activates wasted space.

DOMESTIC URBAN SPACES_ Pilar Echavarria & Chris Kemper

territories wasted space ... rooftops, between houses, parking places, under bridges, and all possible urban rest areas...

domesticate the city.

unit example No.3 domestic public bathroom -

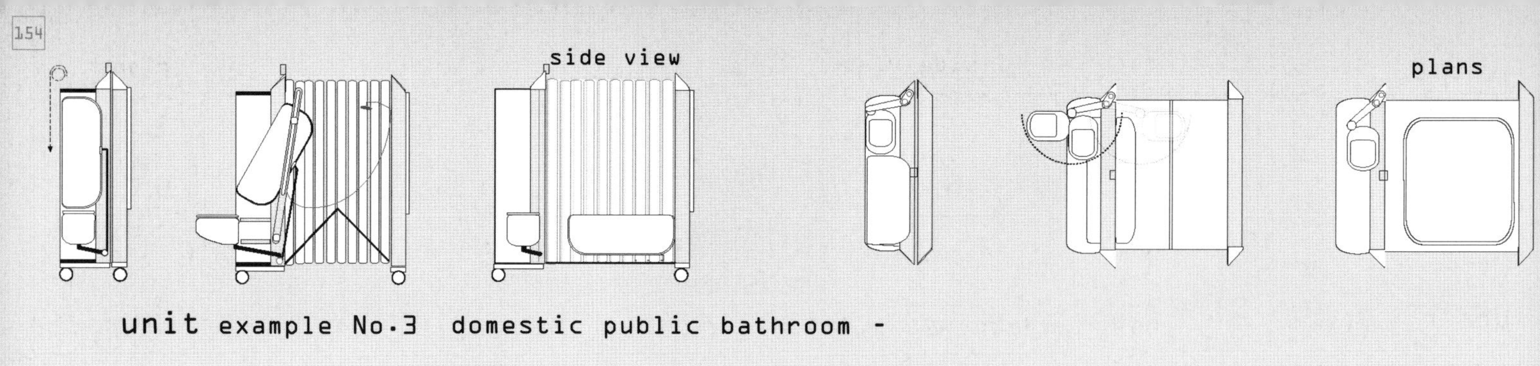

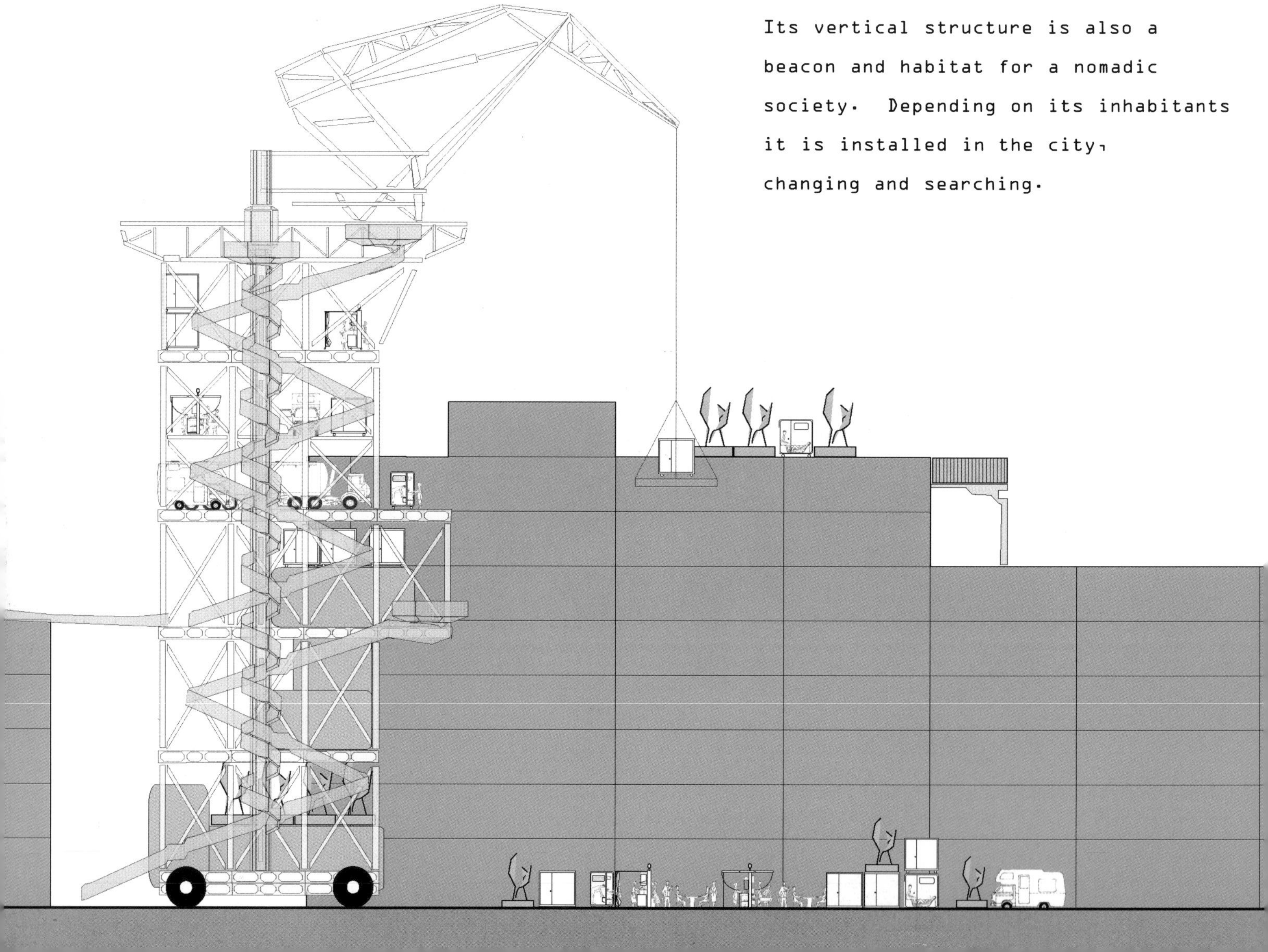

Its vertical structure is also a beacon and habitat for a nomadic society. Depending on its inhabitants it is installed in the city, changing and searching.

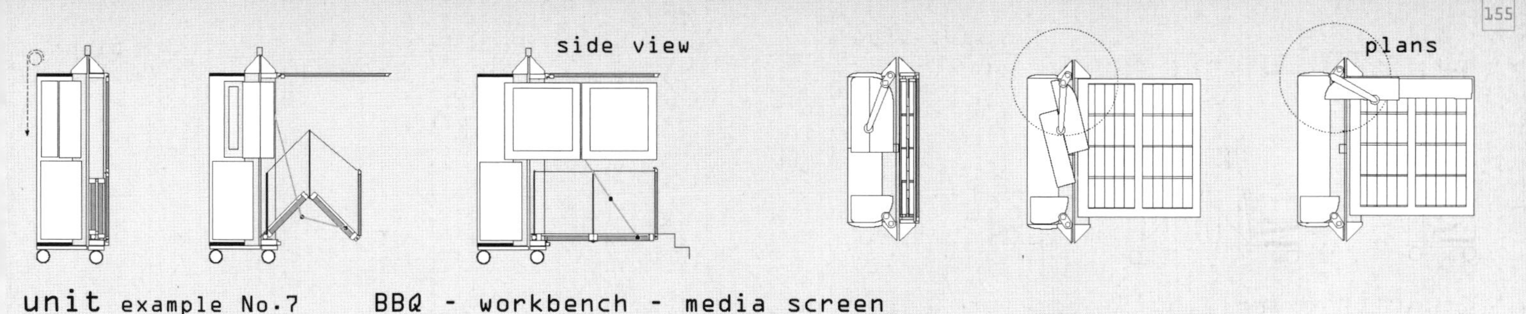

unit example No.7 BBQ - workbench - media screen

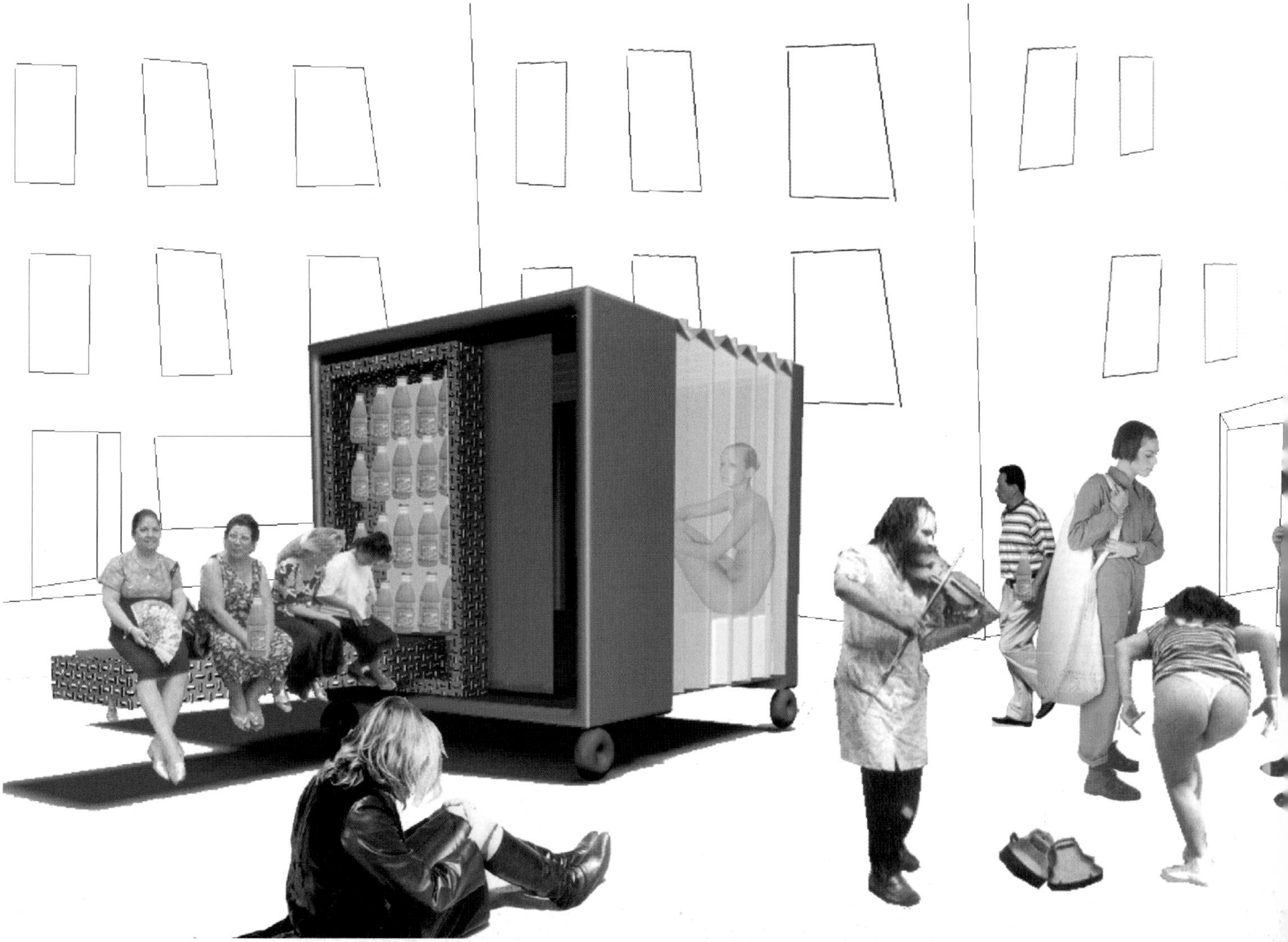

The project explores a way of using the un-used and its potential for activating and extending domestic space in the public domain, creating new situations and new ways of livng. Hazy geografies creating relations between city, landscape and home. Incomplete spaces.

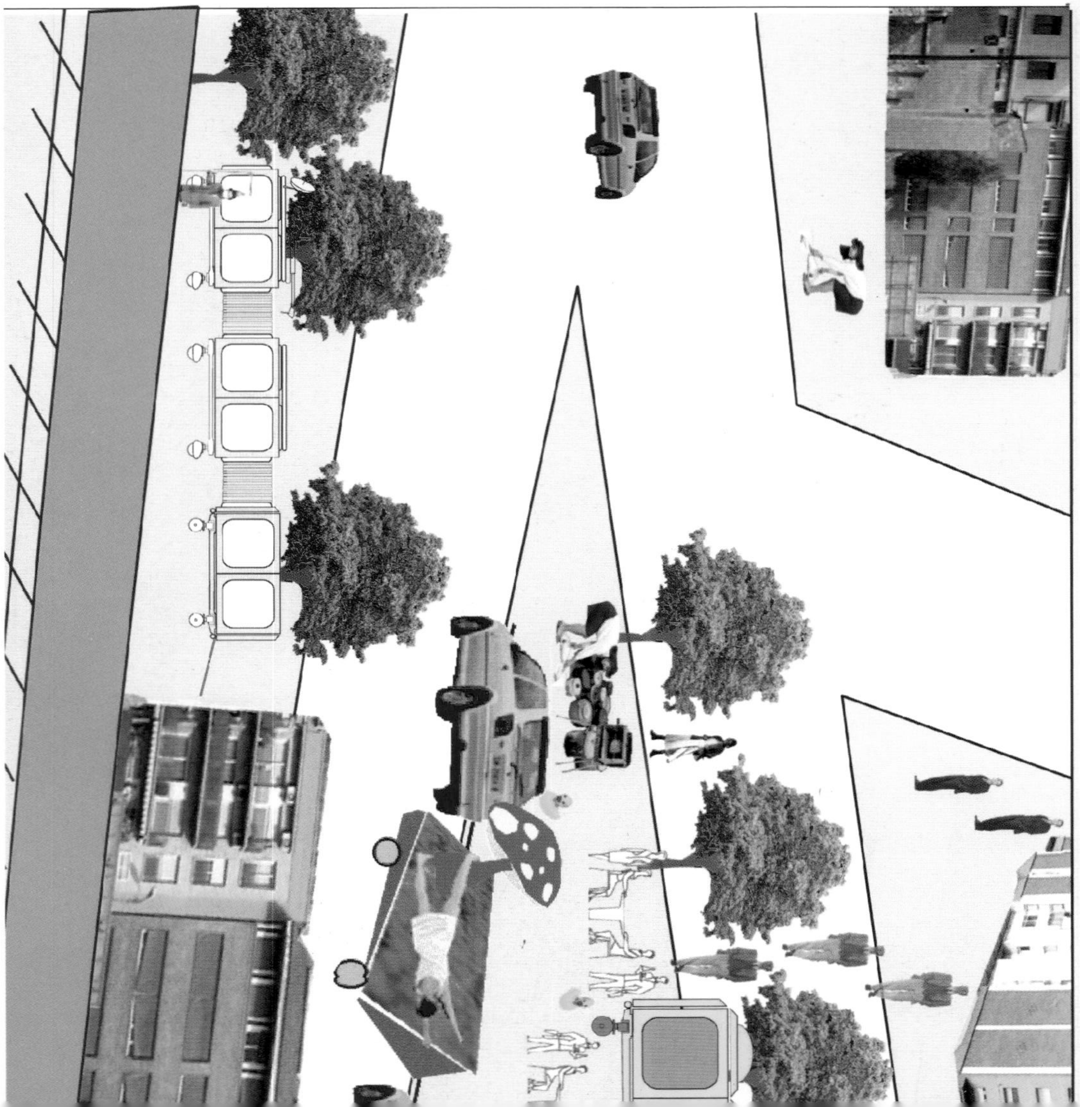

The unit...

as an extension of the house

as an urban fixture

as a basic module for housing

and in case of emergency as a provisional house

157

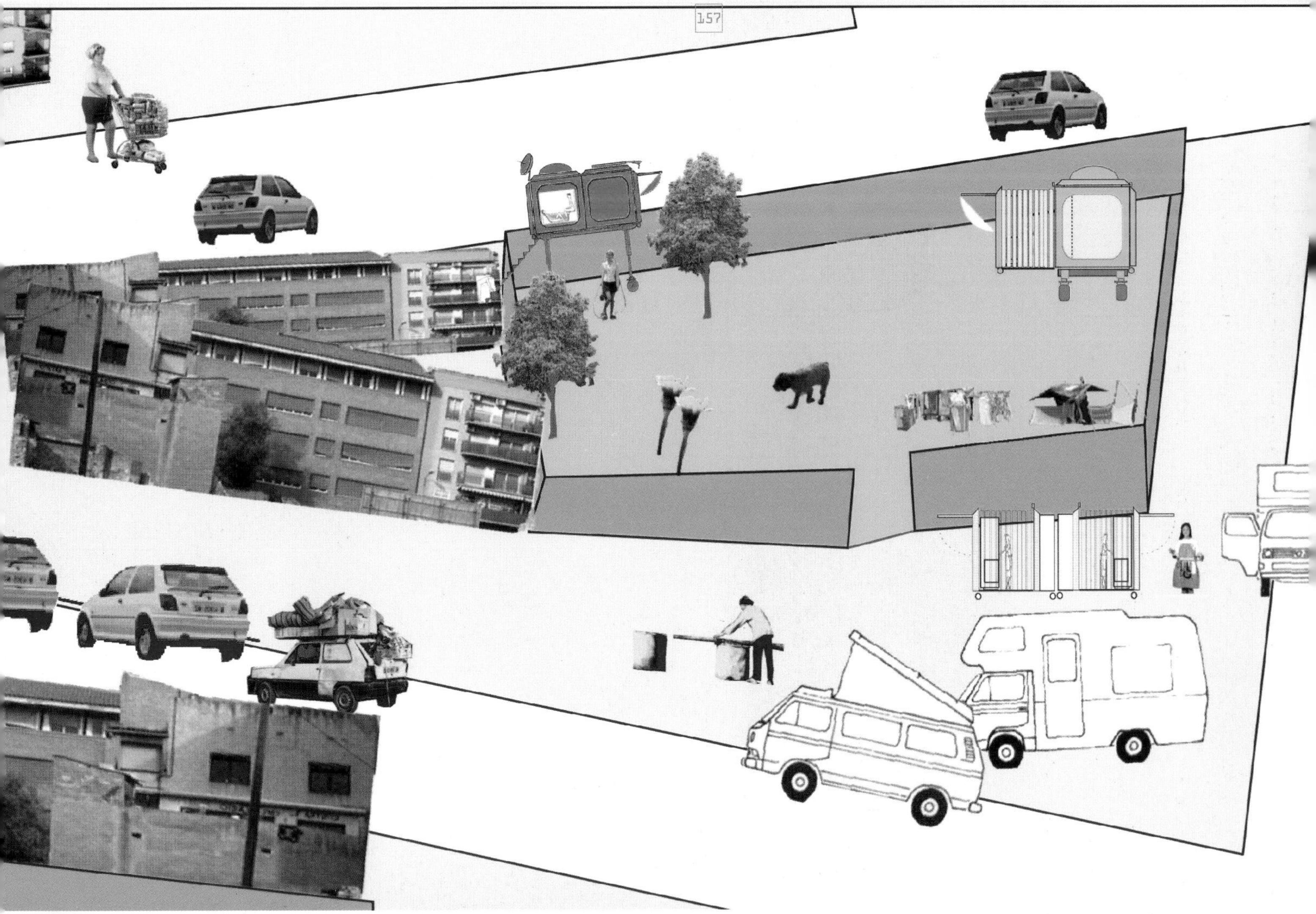

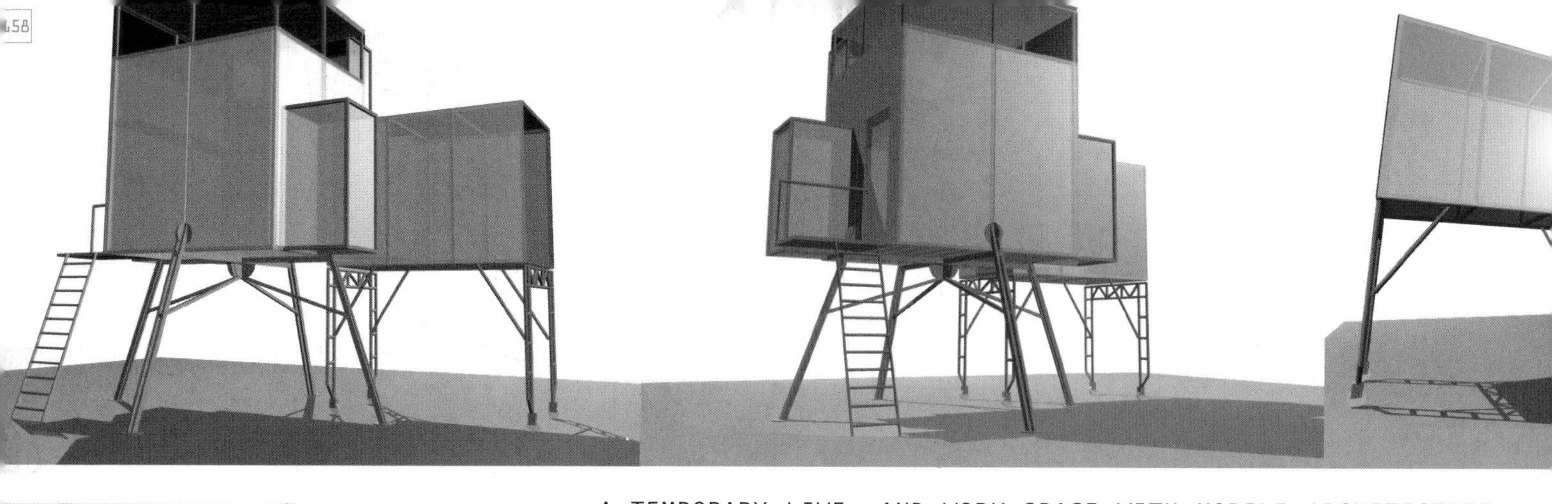

A TEMPORARY LIVE- AND WORK-SPACE WITH MOBILE ARCHITECTURE

The city of Seville is a park of urban plots full of trash and debris concealed behind walls covered in placards and graffiti. Many of them remain in this state of paralysis and for years.

The recycling of defunct plots of land, possibly through legal avenues, will allow for anyone who so desires, for the use of versatile habitable structures, the enjoyment of different temporary locations – all of which will gradually be domesticated in each specific situation..

SOLARES_ Santiago Cirugeda

A position on the fringe of legality, an intellectual embezzlement, freed from that which urban planning proposes as the heritage of papier mache, or that which the historic district begins to resemble: an inhabited theme park. Using the prototype of a collapsible house and its different possible configurations, squatters will gradually occupy various plots of land in the old quarter for up to two years per stay, thus achieving a nomadic lifestyle in an urban setting that tends toward mummification.

A pause in the construction of the urban reality.

A contract for an electrical connection from a private home near the site and a number of portable toilets (which work by chemical processes), along with the collection of rainwater on the roof, are all options that make this form of urban wandering more comfortable and livable.

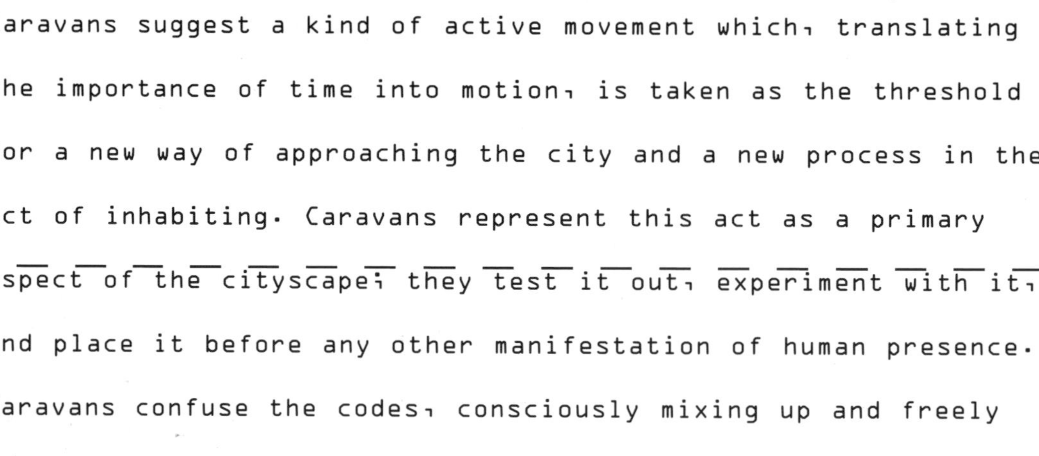

Caravans suggest a kind of active movement which, translating the importance of time into motion, is taken as the threshold for a new way of approaching the city and a new process in the act of inhabiting. Caravans represent this act as a primary aspect of the cityscape; they test it out, experiment with it, and place it before any other manifestation of human presence. Caravans confuse the codes, consciously mixing up and freely interpreting traditional ideas of what constitutes public and private space. Their territory is "everyman's land"; they inhabit spaces without qualities, places abandoned by the city and even ignored by building speculators.

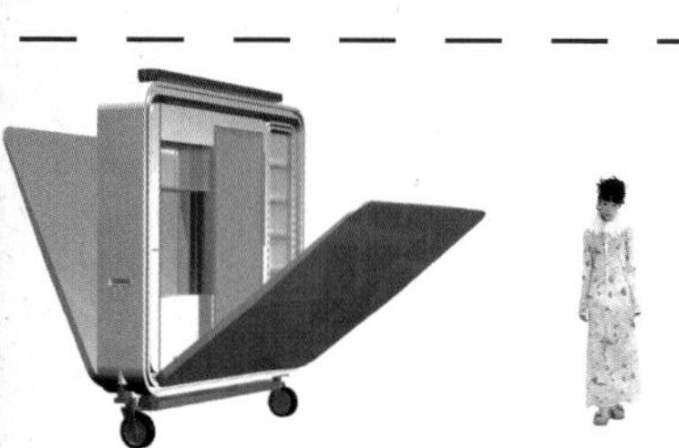

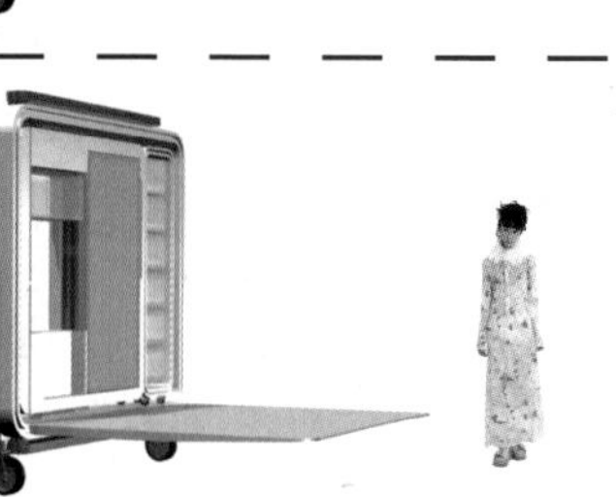

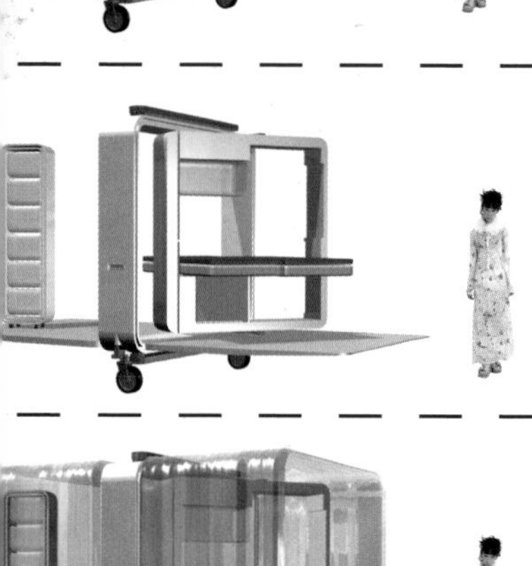

MAISON VALISE

Grègoire & Petetin

FIT YOUR SECOND SKIN

Close to the individual's body, this habitat plays the part of a sort of second skin.

+++Territories as collections of signs that we have set in motion; spaces which determine the identity of a metropolis more than any other territory.

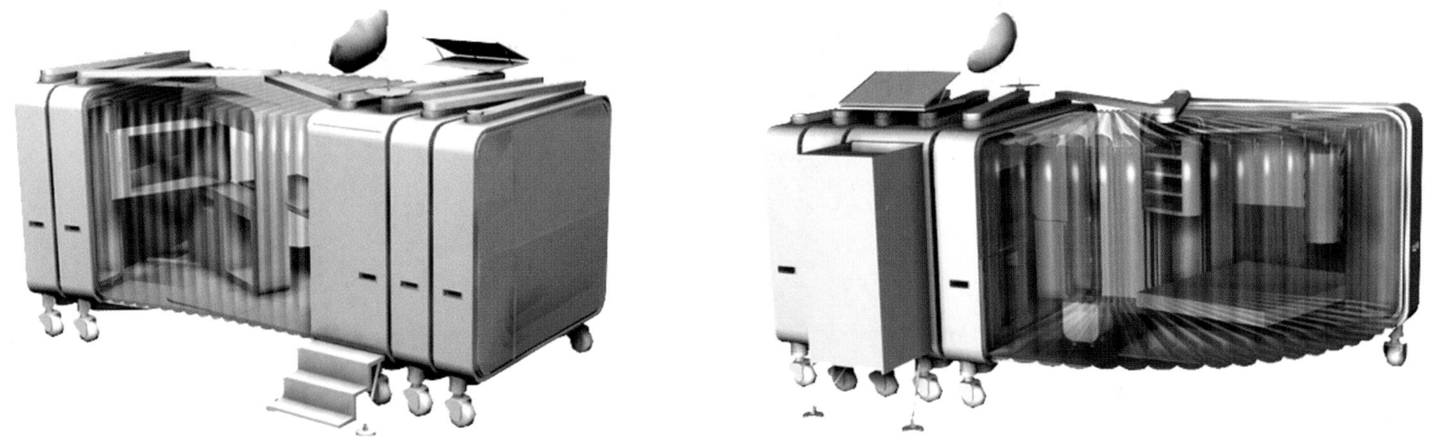

Caravans - fleeting symbols on our landscape and momentary presences in our path.

Their dispersing action combats the methods and actions of the city; they take hold of the cityscape in all its details. They show that other alternatives are possible, that other ways of injecting life into the city are required. They introduce the idea of instability in city planning - the fleeting essence of objects and acts in relation to the passage of time.

+++The approach is to abandon the careful separation of the domestic space of the home from the public space of the road.

BUILDING URBAN REFUGES,

All realities manifest themselves with a gradient of variable factors.
If we want to talk about urban phenomena, we have to do so in terms of complexity and difference. The paths we have to pursue to understand them cannot reproduce the paths of conventional urban planning, as the invisible, mutant structures which interact in the urban space create a complex fabric.
We get the impression that the various levels of complexity grow and die.
The production system, and the political and economic variables and mechanisms which predominate in architecture make the idea of global, closed planning inconceivable.
The speed at which changes take place in urban space suggests specific places and given epochs, so the design and construction of this space constantly require regenerating mechanisms which address the particular factors of the various places and their interaction with global changes and systems.
For institutions, the idea of a global process is an attempt to simplify and control all possible forms of behavior and action. This proposal consists of perpetually redefining global systems (urban planning and legislation), looking out for possible loopholes and uncertainties which allow the various human groups freedom of action.

ARQUITECTURAS SILENCIOSAS_ Santiago Cirugeda

SCAFFOLDING

1. Apply in your local Urban Planning office (or similar) for the license for a minor alteration or to paint the facade of the building to which you want to affix yourself, in which you want to inlay, against which you want to lean, or simply which you want to enlarge. If the facade does not need a coat of paint you can make a few loud paintings on it to justify the re-painting of it.

2. Ask a friend or relative (an architect if possible) to sign the scaffolding project.

3. With the paid minor alteration license and the local authority's permit for the project, you can now apply for the license for placing the scaffold.

4. Design your own urban refuge using your favorite material and style.

5. Once you have the license, install the scaffolding, as well as the refuge.

TAKING THE STREET. "Reserves"

How and Why to construct an urban reserve.

HOW:

Apply to the Urban Planning Department of your town for a permit to install on the chosen site. Your application should include a detailed sketch (pavement, road, position, etc.), along with the costs.

With the permit in hand, proceed immeditely to installation. Ideally, you should build the reserve yourself, thus avoiding possible misunderstandings with a hired firm.

There is also the option of applying, free of charge, for the KUVA SC. 670-794409 reserve, which will be loaned by friendly agreement to the people or groups of people wishing to create reserves of urban land.

The functions and uses which can be created by these urban reserves are open to the imagination of those inhabiting them; they can be filled with the elements suggested or required by given functional and intellectual intentions: a children's playground, information booth, reading room, exhibition space, performance venue, giant flowerpot, or any number of imaginative uses.

Reasons for building an urban reserve can be equal to the number of people that contribute ideas, that dare doing so. What can certainly be said is that this personal and intimate action takes place outside everything politicians and professionals may plan, it follows ways that are labelled by difference, by independence, and it makes it obvious that citizens play a very important role in the development and construction of the environment they live in.

The para-architecture proposed in the action is bred with temporary intentions. With non-inheritable forms, finally, the idea is to silently evoke the incapacity of public institutions to set bounds to the complexities of human reality (once more).

Mobile Artifact_ Minimal Intruder

project for the recuperation of urban space

GREEN MA-MI L. Cappelli, P. Echavarria, C. Kemper

remove a car and insert a bit of green, a square...

The city center is invaded by cars, which take up more than 40% of the width of the streets.

This object moves through the city in areas where individual transportation degrades the quality of the urban space. The “Green-MAMI”occupies the space of a car with the aim of reclaiming urban space for the neighborhood.

The creation of new scenes in the city via "green artifacts" that activate and expand public space. Objects, environments, moving landscapes that occupy a space in the city for a short while and move on, depending on the inhabitants, searching and changing.

Simply a garden, a micro meeting place, where dreaming is not forbiden.

The designer was working on new urban concepts that would reflect modern humanity's living conditions when she struck upon the idea of a portable home as a perfect reflection of, and ideal companion for, constantly on-the-move people.

Made from vinyl, Instant Home is easy to assemble and disassemble. With it, Peschke creates a brash new form of private life assertively inserted into public space.

This is no stale museum piece, but rather a $12m^2$ inflatable, portable installation that she has set up in various environments all across California: at the foot of steel and glass high-rises, in the midst of barren, wind-swept natural landscapes or in the heart of middle-class suburbia.

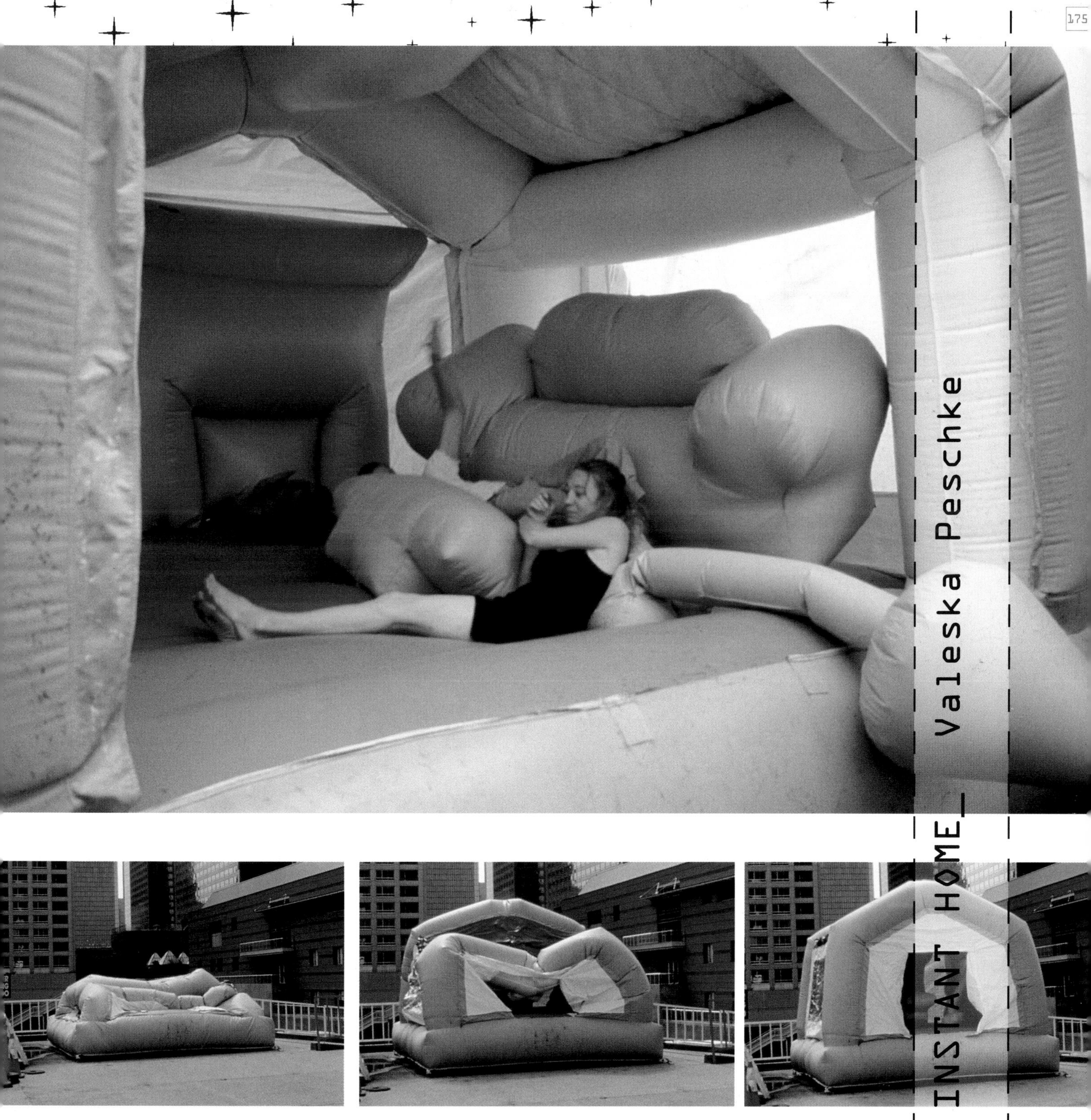
INSTANT HOME_
Valeska Peschke

In so doing, the structure stands as a statement about the thin line separating endless mobility from the processes of social decline, as seen most starkly in the city landscapes of cardboard shelters erected by the homeless.

expert
Ihr Elektrofachmarkt
GRUNDIG

ROBBE

Take a look at the informal work being done in the countryside and in urban territory. Habitats more often than not sustained by their very precariousness.

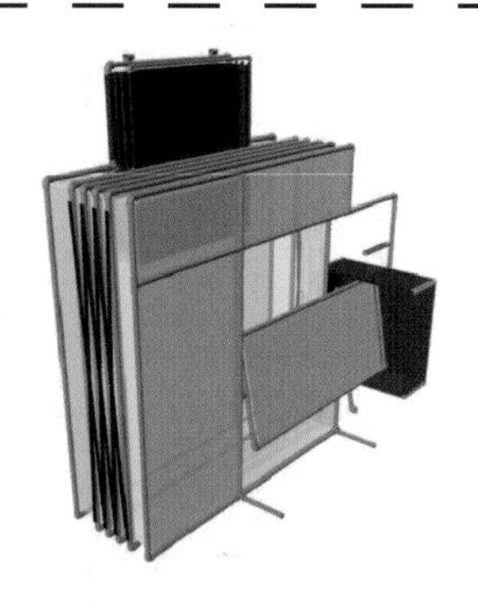

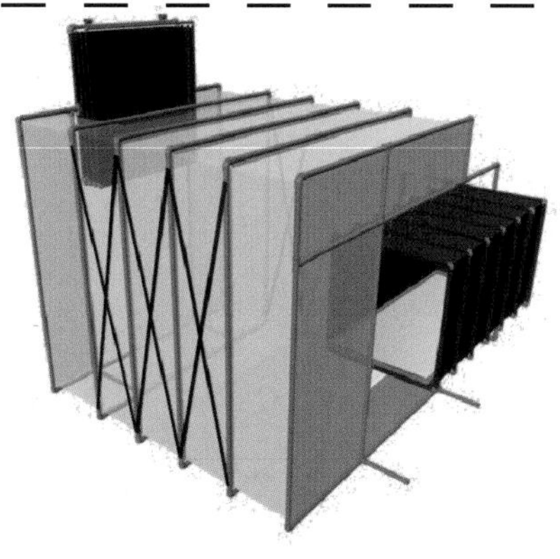

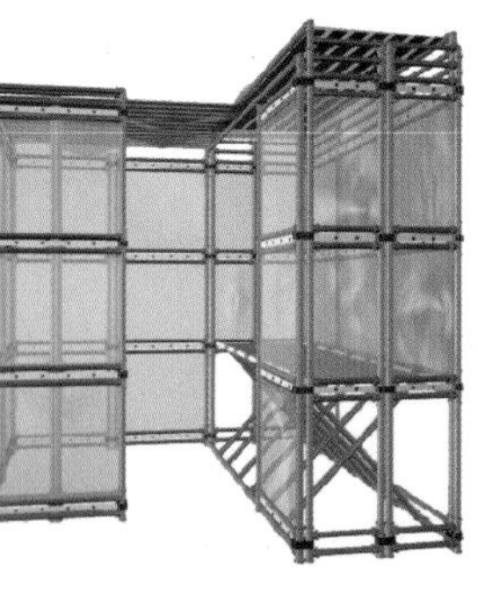

MODULO DE EMERGENCIA_ Univeridad central de Chile

C. Ugarte + J.G. Brugnoli

APPROXIMATIONS OF AN ACADEMIC EXERCISE

The students' work centered on establishing a dialogue on the topic of contemporary habitats. The result: five emergency modules based on a uniform prism measuring 2.1 m^3. This is an exploration of cheap and easily-accessed construction foundations that do not pertain directly to the tenets of formal architecture.

The term "emergency" can have any number of connotations — natural, artificial, social, cultural, political or any of their derivatives: land takeovers, shantytowns, urban nomadism, strikes, and so forth, all of which represent the substratum and constant flux peculiar to human conglomeration.

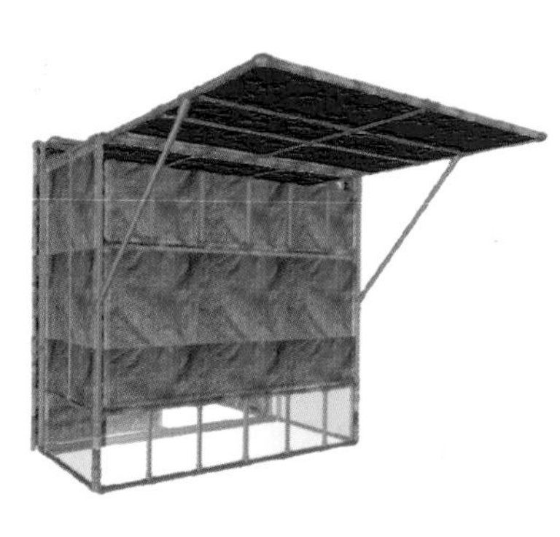

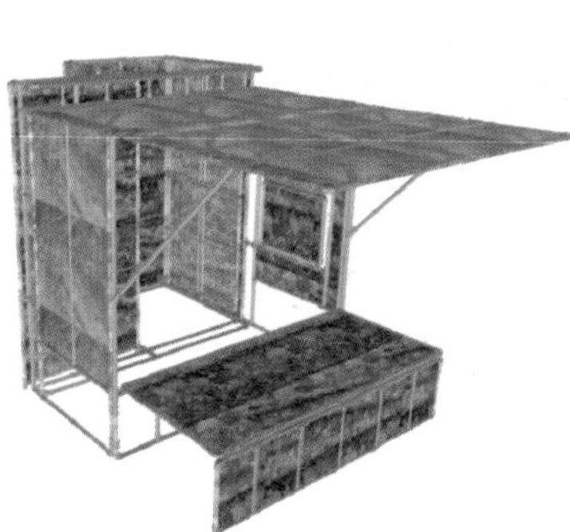

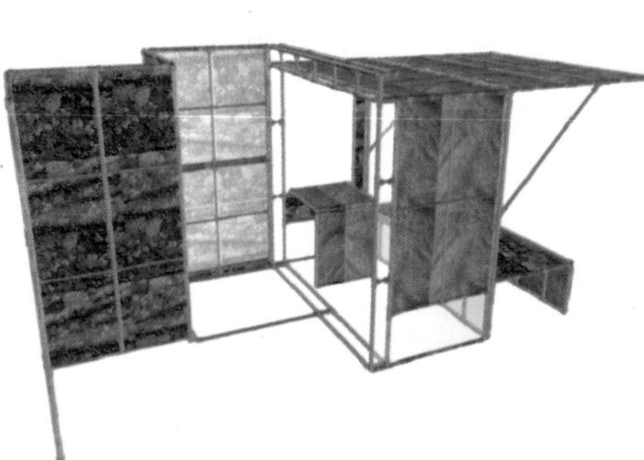

Finally, the modules are meant to provoke a reexamination of space, directing the attention of both user and spectator to the very conditions of different habitats by exploring the means at hand for directly becoming movers and mediators of some of the realities that underlie human activity.

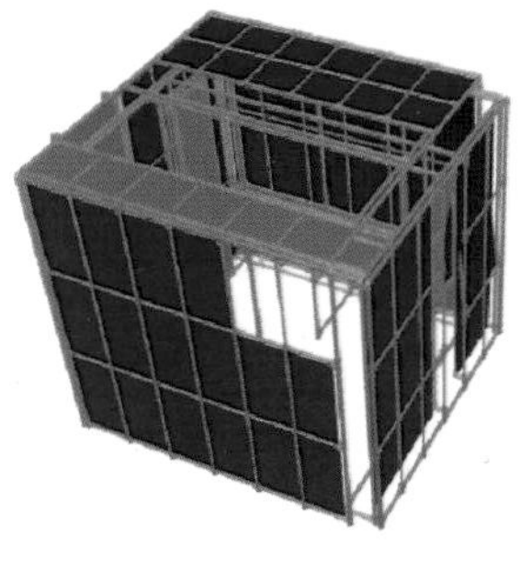

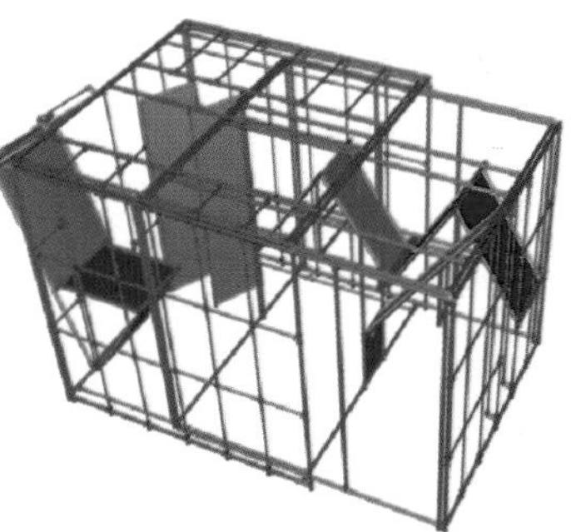

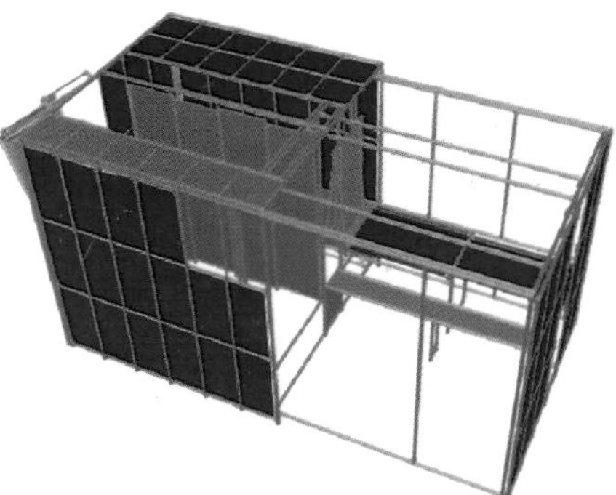

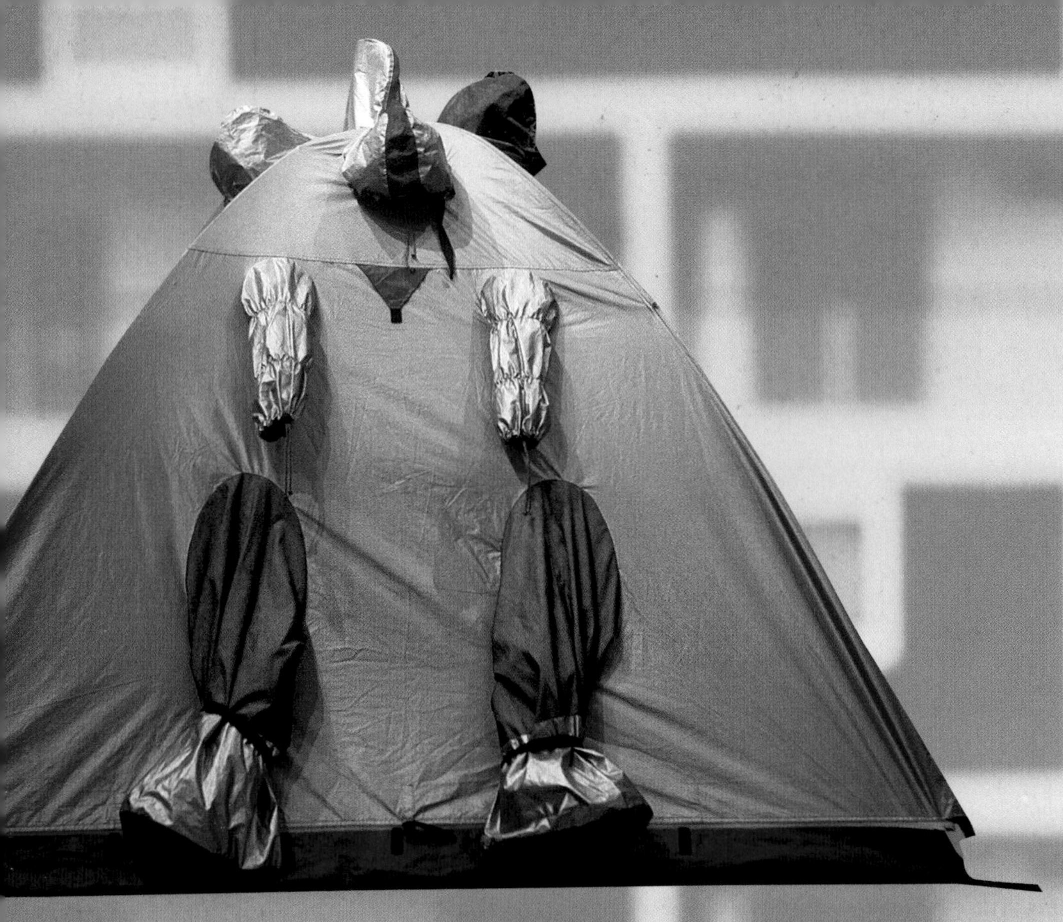

Lucy Orta has used her training as a fashion designer in the creation of Collective Wear, pieces of flexible, modular architecture which serve as genuine individual or collective survival shelters. These textile structures, instantly erected into corporal architecture using a system of pockets and zips, combine various synthetic fibers, technical weaves and natural materials on lightweight carbon fiber armatures.

Her creations cater to the urban homeless as well as to adventurous nature lovers with a taste for extreme conditions. Her shelter-wear projects are designed to enable spontaneous interactive communication. Using the whole range of shelter wear sensitizes one physically and emotionally to the problems of survival in under-privileged zones of the metropolitan jungle.

LIFE NEXUS VILLAGE & REFUGE WEAR_ Studio Orta

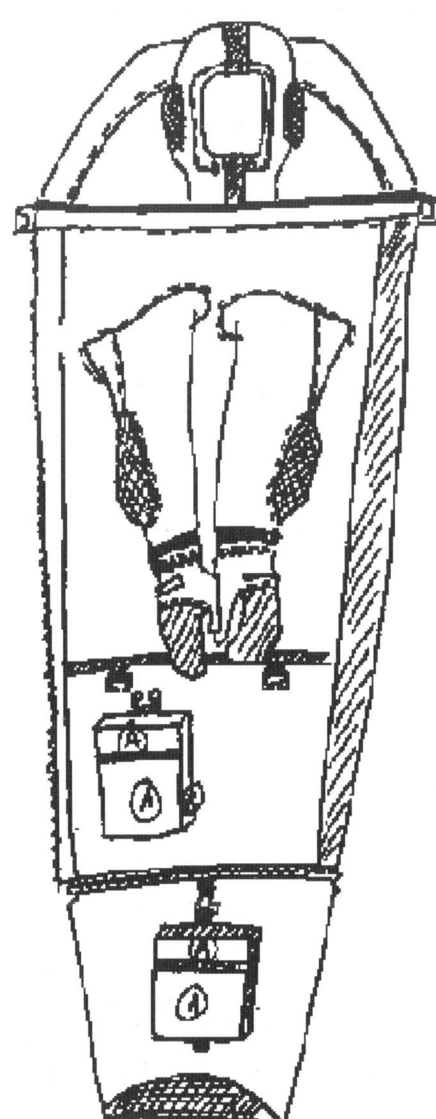

Prototypes were fabricated as personal environments, as portable habitat catering to minimum personal comfort and mobility.

By 1994, she had moved from individual isolation to the concern of the collective and started to construct "Collective Wear".

Nexus Architecture/Collective Wear is one of the most emblematic designs of Lucy Orta's ongoing projects. More symbolic than potentially "useful", Collective Wear is made up of outfits that are linked together by detachable "umbilical" structures and can be worn, hypothetically, by hundreds or thousands of people joined together in a row. It is protective, hinting at physical and psychological refuge within the full-body, somewhat high-tech and at times nearly sci-fi clothing.

It is an eloquent manifestation of the philosophy behind Orta's entire practice because it simply recognizes the interdependency of all people in society. It represents, quite literally, the Social Link.

...fabric as the membrane or a second-skin around our bodies, fabric that forms the walls of our own architecture.

PARASITISM IS DESCRIBED AS A RELATIONSHIP IN WHICH A PARASITE TEMPORARILY OR PERMANENTLY EXPLOITS THE ENERGY OF A HOST.

paraSITE proposes the appropriation of the exterior ventilation systems on existing architecture as a means for providing temporary shelter for homeless people.

PARASITES LIVE ON THE OUTER SURFACE OF A HOST OR INSIDE ITS BODY IN RESPIRATORY ORGANS, DIGESTIVE ORGANS, VENOUS SYSTEMS, AS WELL AS OTHER ORGANS AND TISSUES.

The paraSITE units in their idle state exist as small, collapsible packages with handles for transport by hand or on one s back. In employing this device, the user must locate the outtake ducts of a building s HVAC (Heating, Ventilation, Air Conditioning) system.

FREQUENTLY A HOST PROVIDES A PARASITE NOT ONLY WITH FOOD, BUT ALSO WITH ENZYMES AND OXYGEN, AND OFFERS FAVORABLE TEMPERATURE CONDITIONS.

The intake tube of the collapsed structure is then attached to the vent. The warm air leaving the building simultaneously inflates and heats the double membrane structure.

BUT A HOST IS CERTAINLY NOT INACTIVE AGAINST A PARASITE, AND IT HINDERS THE DEVELOPMENT AND POPULATION GROWTH OF PARASITES WITH DIFFERENT DEFENSE MECHANISMS, SUCH AS THE CLEANING OF SKIN, PERISTALTIC CONTRACTION OF THE DIGESTIVE APARATUS, AND THE DEVELOPMENT OF ANTIBODIES.

In April of 1997, I proposed my concept and first prototype to a homeless person, who regarded the project as a tactical response. At the time, the city of Cambridge had made a series of vents in Harvard Square homeless-proof by tilting the metal grates, making them virtually impossible to sleep on.

In his book, City of Quartz, Mike Davis describes a similar war on homelessness in Los Angeles. He lists a series of these hindrances throughout the city.

Another invention is the aggressive deployment of outdoor sprinklers. To ensure that the park was not used for sleeping, the city installed an elaborate overhead sprinkler system programmed to drench unsuspecting sleepers at random during the night. The system was immediately copied by some local businessmen in order to drive the homeless away from adjacent public sidewalks. Meanwhile restaurants and markets have responded to the homeless by building ornate enclosures to protect their refuse. Although no one in Los Angeles has yet proposed adding cyanide to the garbage, as happened in Phoenix a few years back, one popular seafood restaurant has spent $12,000 to build the ultimate bag-lady-proof trash cage: made of three-quarter inchsteel rod with alloy locks and vicious outturned *spikes to safeguard trash.*

THERE IS TENSION BETWEEN A HOST AND ITS PARASITE, SINCE THE HOST ENDEAVOURS TO GET RID OF THE FOREIGN BODY, WHILE THE PARASITE EMPLOYS NEW WAYS TO MAINTAIN THE CONNECTION WITH THE HOST.

The connection of the inflatable structure to the building becomes the critical moment of this project.

From February 1998 until April 1998, I built seven prototypes of the paraSITE shelter and distributed them to several homeless people in Cambridge, who worked closely with me on the design and production of these units. Most were built using temporary materials that were readily available on the streets (plastic bags, tape).

For the pedestrian, paraSITE functioned as an agitational device. The visibly parasitic relationship of these devices to the buildings, appropriating a readily available situation with readily available materials elicited immediate speculation as to the future of the city: would these things completely take over, given the enormous number of homeless in our society? Could we wake up one morning to find these encampments engulfing buildings like ivy?

The issue of homelessness is of global proportions and it is foolish to think that any one proposition will address all the issues associated with this problem. There are many different types of homeless people. The mentally ill, the chemically dependent, those who are unable to afford housing, men, women, families, even those who prefer this way of life are included among the vast cross section of homeless people in every urban instance. Each group of homeless has subjective needs based on circumstance and location. This project does not make reference to handbooks of statistics. Nor should this intervention be associated with the various municipal attempts at solving the homeless issue. This is a project that was shaped by my interaction as a citizen and artist with those who live on the streets.

This project does not present itself as a solution. It is not a proposal for affordable housing. Its point of departure is to present a symbolic strategy of survival for homeless existence within the city, amplifying the problematic relationship between those who have homes and those who do not have homes. While these shelters were being used, they functioned not only as a temporary place of retreat, but also as a station of dissent and empowerment; many of the homeless users regarded their shelters as a protest device. The shelters communicated a refusal to surrender, and made their situation more visible.

"I would like to believe that my work in design or night projections all can be understood as interventions in the city, intended to provide a critical dimension to the urban experience. Work done in the city, if it's going to be critical and effective, has to question and challenge the way the city operates for most of its inhabitants as an alienating environment in which social and individual concerns and experiences do not correspond to the state and real-estate spatial symbolism."

Rosalyn Deutsche, 'Uneven Development: Public Art in New York City',1988

Survival compels mobility.

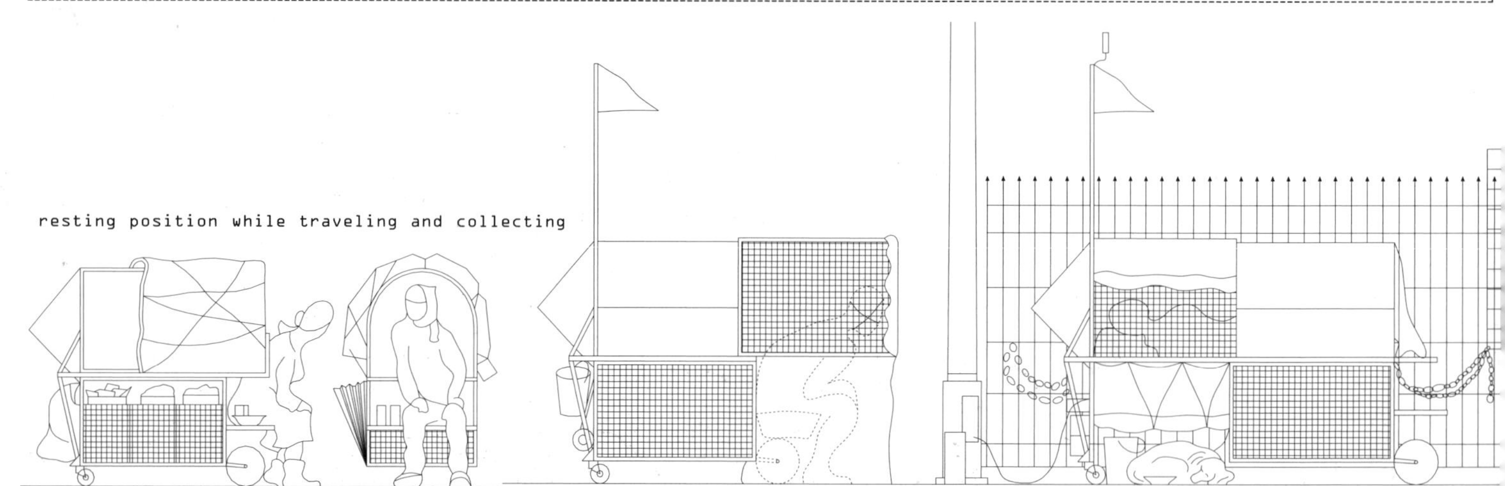

HOMELESS VEHICLE PROJECT_ Krzysztof Wodiczko

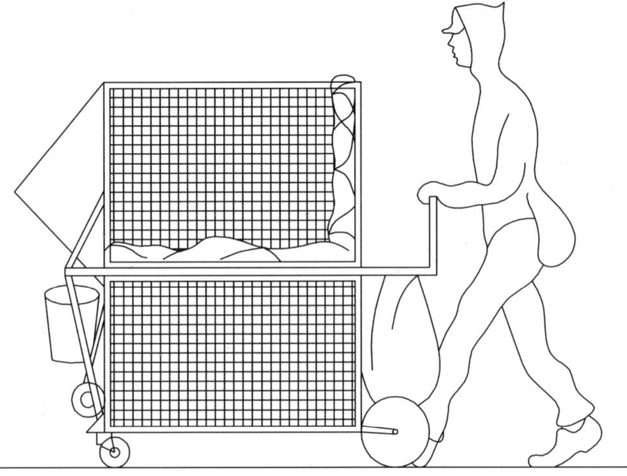

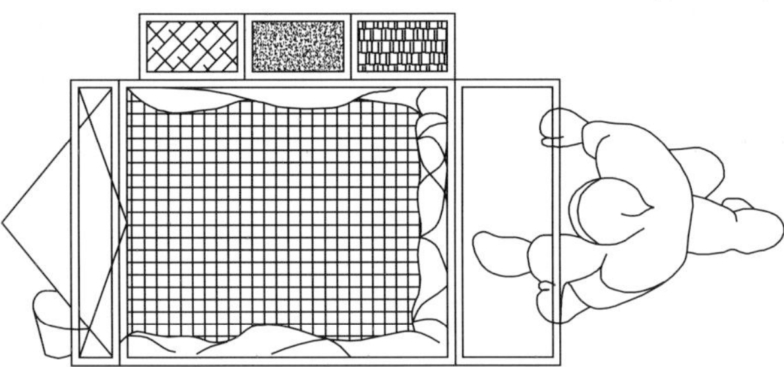

The Homeless Vehicle Project was conceived in response to the immediate needs of a nomadic life in the urban environment of New York. Four specific individuals, known as scavengers, spend their days collecting, sorting and returning cans to supermarkets for economic sustenance.

The vehicle should fill their needs for a means of transportation and shelter, including sleeping, washing, and cooking. It is not a finished product; it is conceived as a starting point for further collaboration between skilled designers and potential users.

Their homelessness appears as a natural condition; the cause is displaced from its consequence and the status of the homeless as legitimate members of the urban community is unrecognized.

The Homeless Vehicle Project represents the resistance of evicted architecture against evicting architecture. It is designed to break through the boundaries between economically segregated urban communities. As it penetrates space, it also establishes a provocative medium of communication between the homeless and non-homeless.

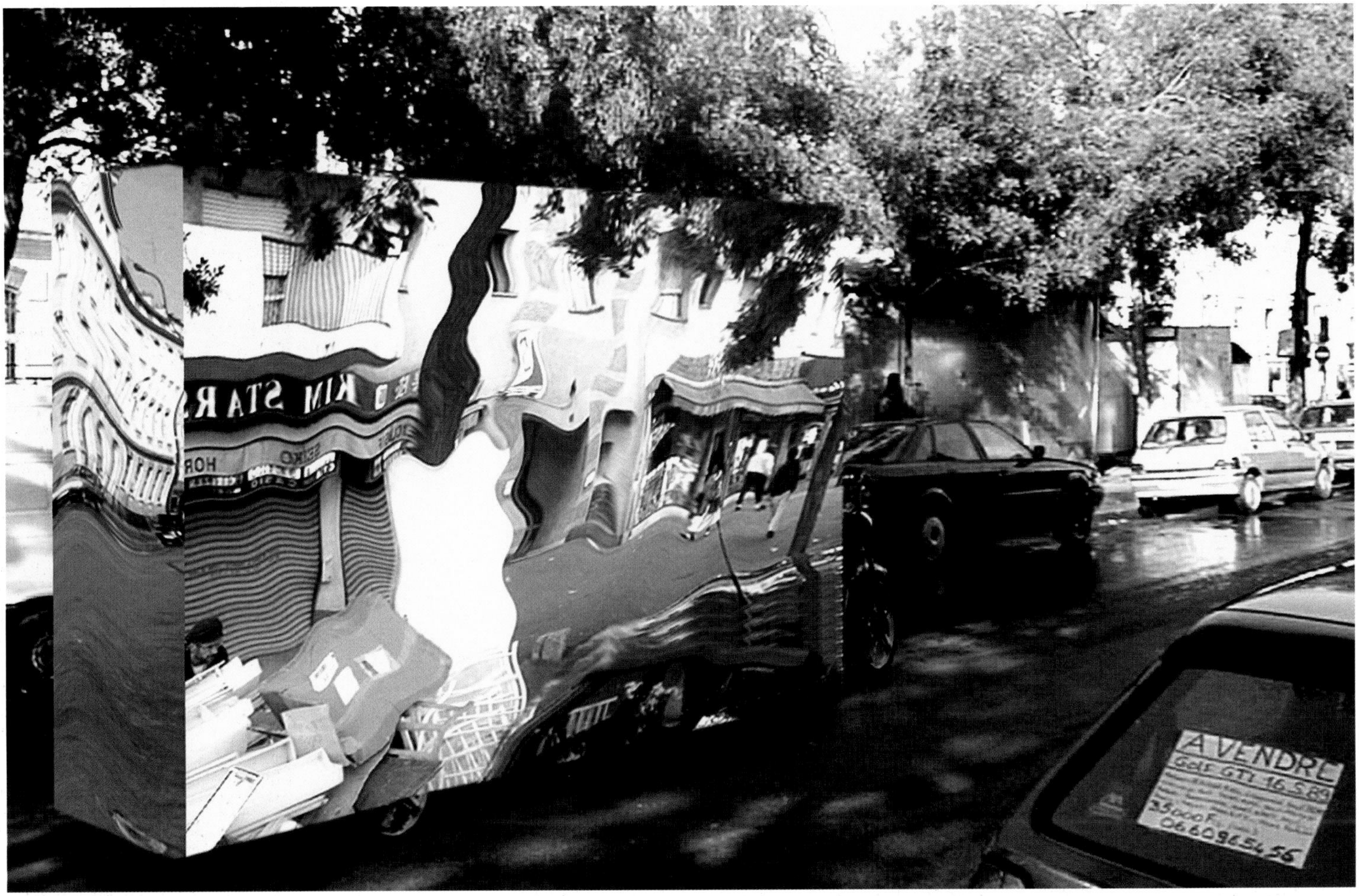
A VENDRE
Golf GTI 16 S 89
35000 F
06 60 96 54 56

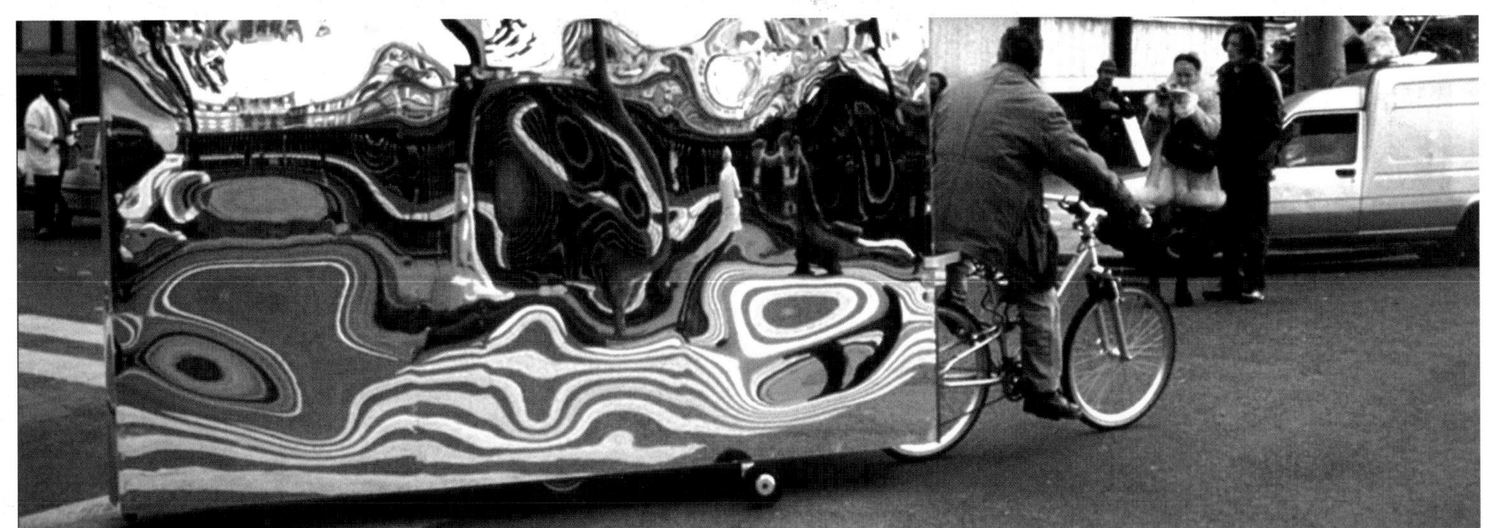

Scenario:

1) Construction of a distorting-mirror vehicle.

2) Driving and parking this distortion in the streets of Paris.

3) Living and sleeping inside.

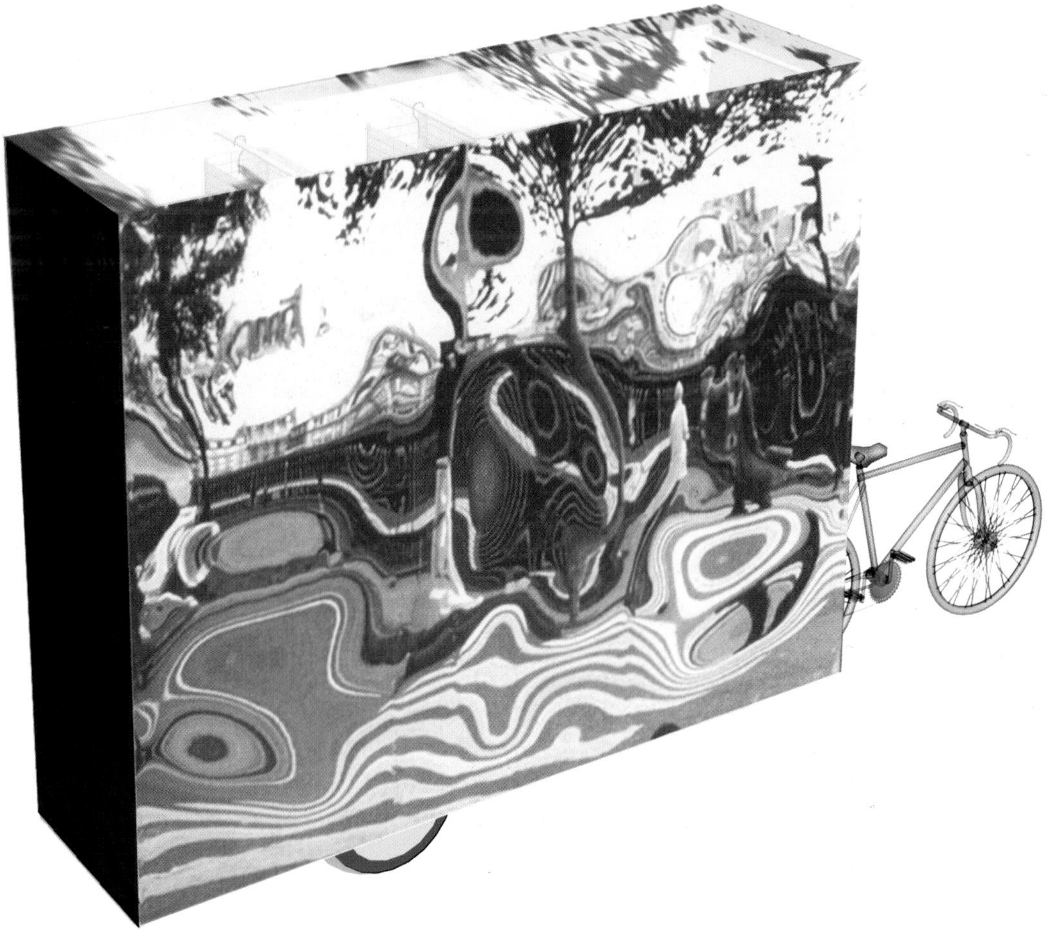

FURTIVE_ R&Sie François Roche

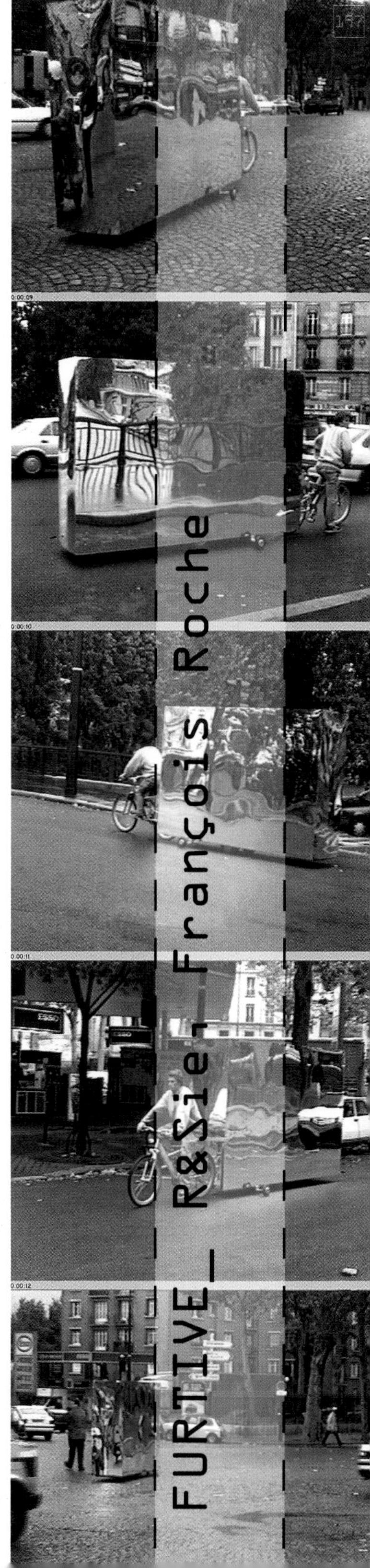

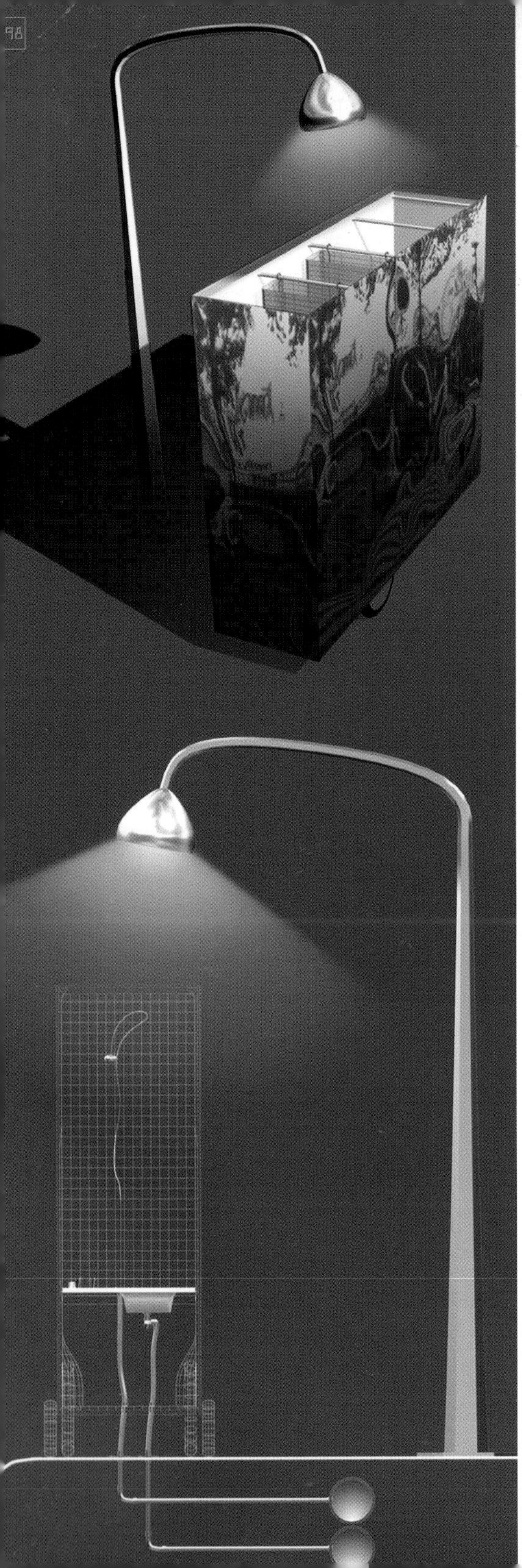

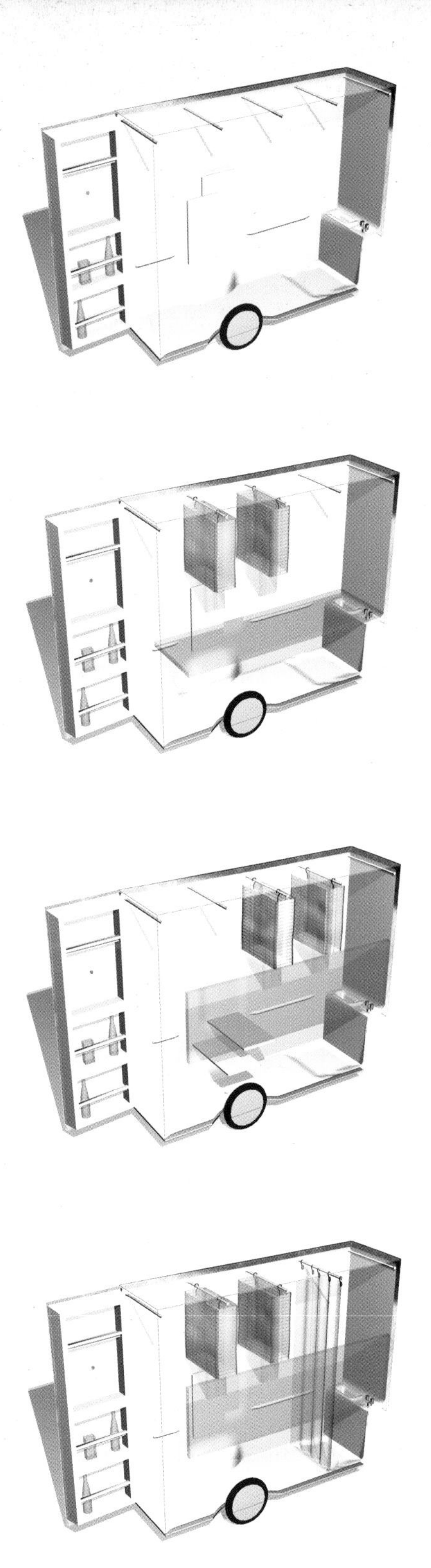

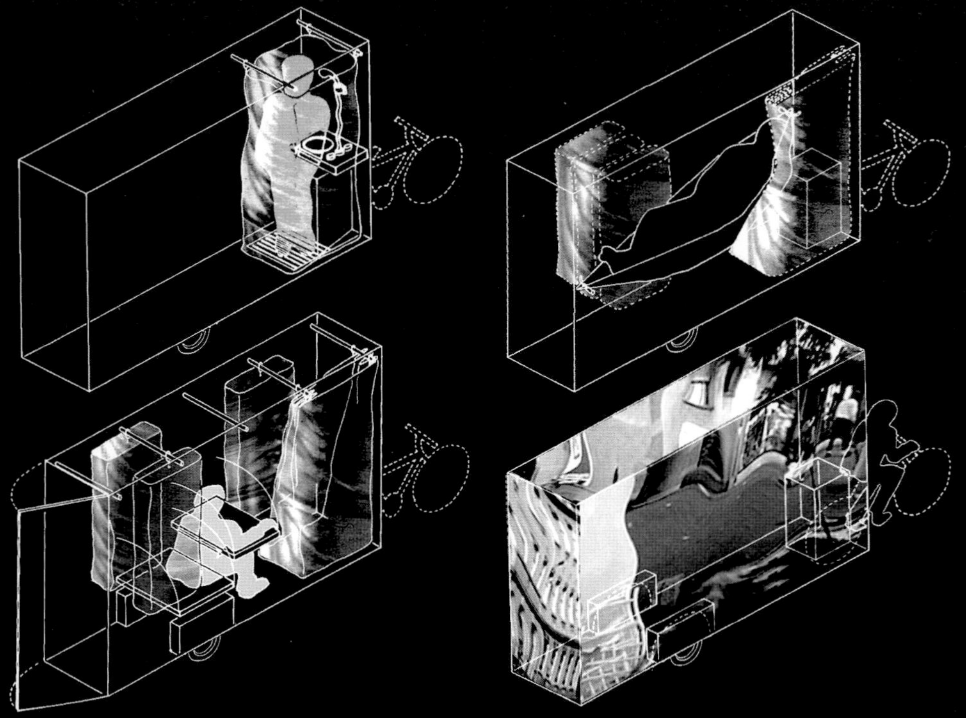

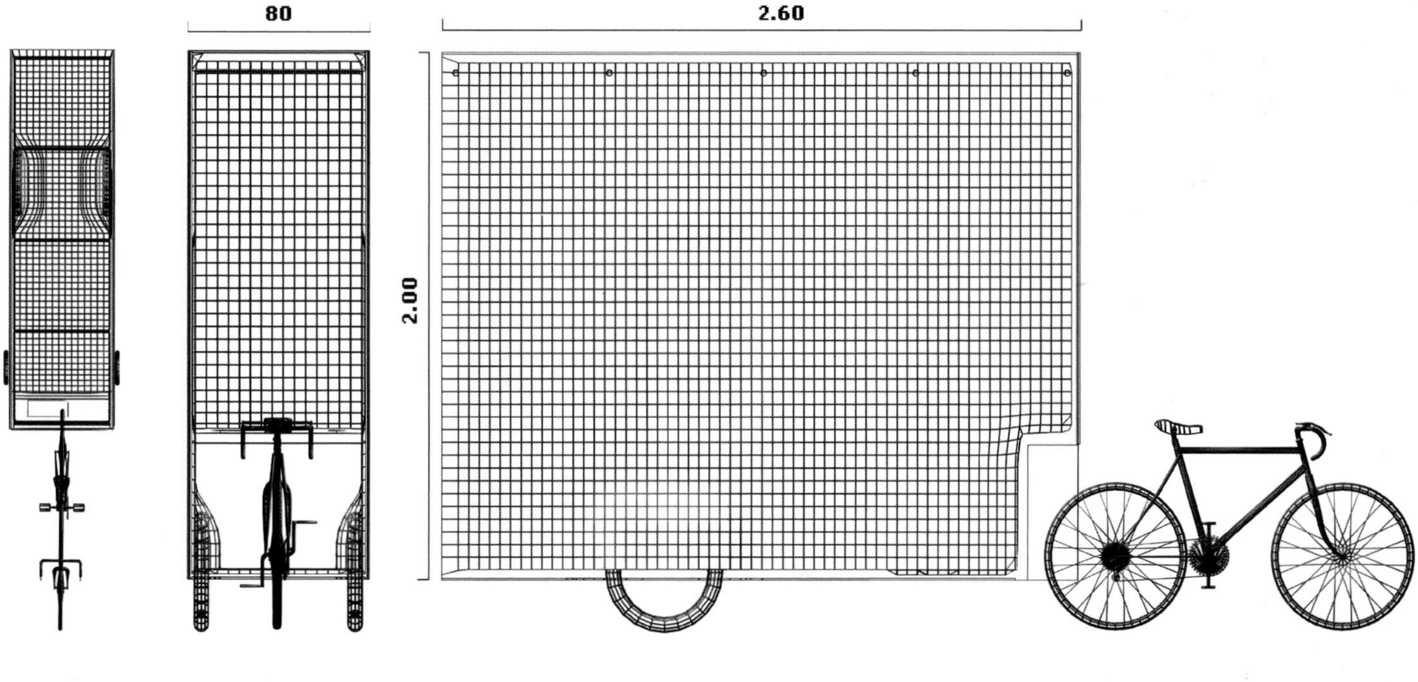

80

2.60

2.00

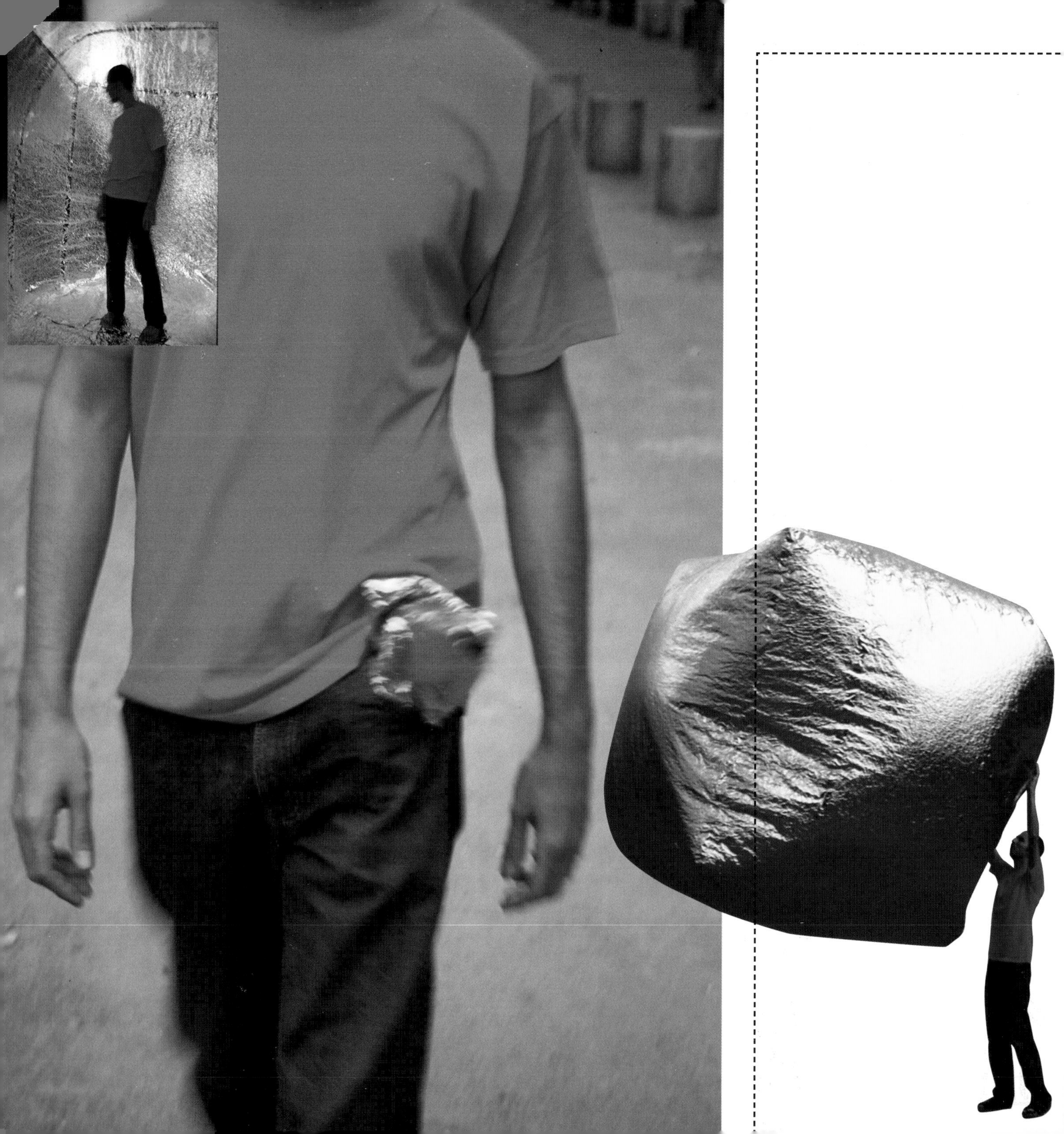

THE BASIC HOUSE_ Martín Ruiz de Azúa

"Our habitat has become a stage for consumption in which an unlimited amount of products satisfy a range of needs stemming from complex relationships that are difficult to control. Cultures that maintain a more direct relationship with their environment show us that habitat can be understood in a more essential and reasonable manner. Having learned from these attitudes, and using the most advanced technology, I propose an almost immaterial house that expands when triggered by body or solar heat. A house so versatile that, by turning it on one side or the other, it protects from the cold or heat, so light that it floats and, moreover, that can be folded and stored in a pocket. A life of transit without material ties. Having it all while hardly having anything."

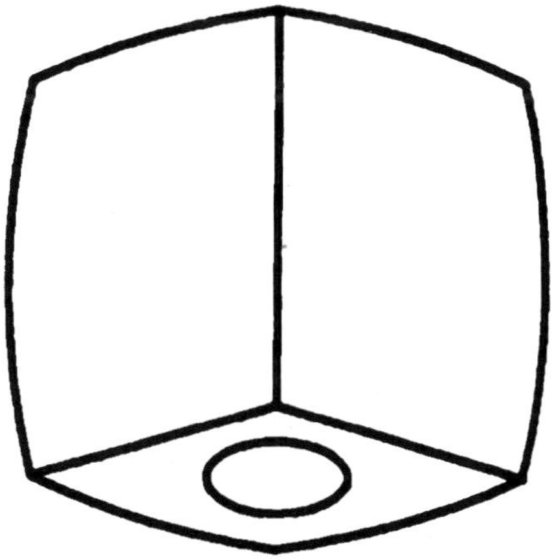

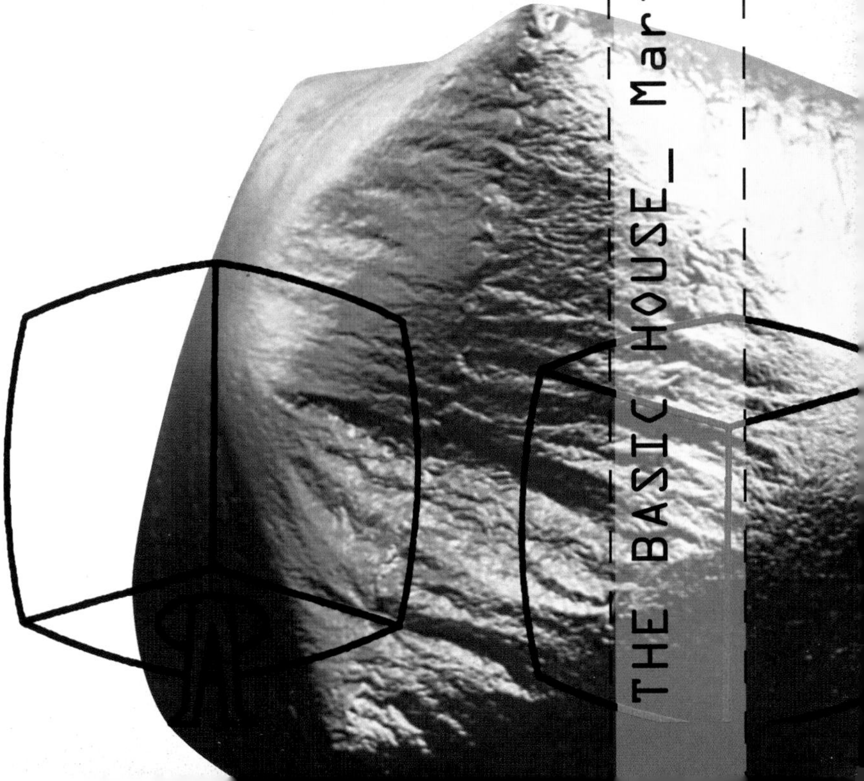

time to build: approximately 3 minutes

It is made of cardboard and coated with a water-resistant foil. Materials are cheap and recyclable.

Consequently it is easy to handle and to carry. One adult can sleep comfortably in it.

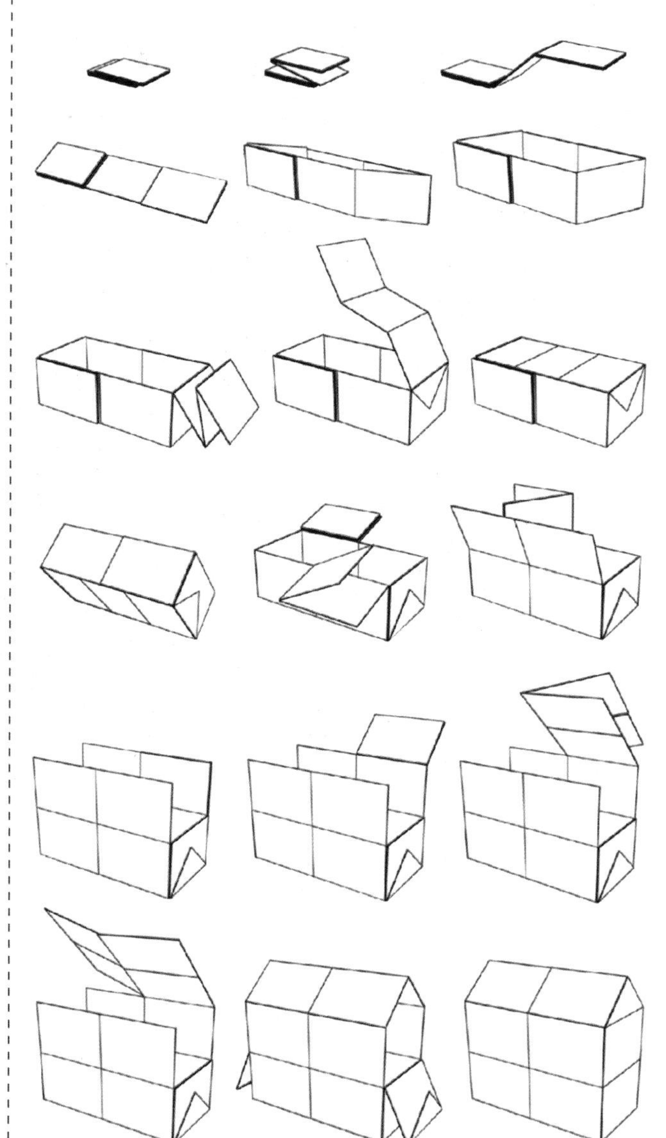

Size unfolded: 2 x 1 x 1.75 m, / size folded: 1 x 0.66 x 0.20 m / Weight: 12 kg.

CARTONHOUSE_ Oskar Leo Kaufmann

Sponsors pay the production costs for one cartonhouse to be given to a homeless person; in return they are able to advertise their product on its surface.

At the same time it offers the possibility to use it as a playhouse for children. People who have a home should pay for it, to support homeless people.

This project gives the most basic form of housing architectural appeal.

CLOUD_ Monica Förster

CLOUD is a portable room for rest, meeting or concentration. A space of its own that can be used within any surroundings, cloud instantly defines an area and a mood apart. Easily transported from place to place, when it is unpacked a silent fan inflates the chamber and keeps it inflated as long as required. The room inflates in three minutes, and it folds away into a bag. CLOUD is entered and exited through a self-closing slit door.

MATERIAL

Rip-stop nylon.

Fan and bag included.

DIMENSIONS:

H230 W530 D400 cm

WEIGHT

12 kg when packed.

COLORS

White. Green-gray floor.

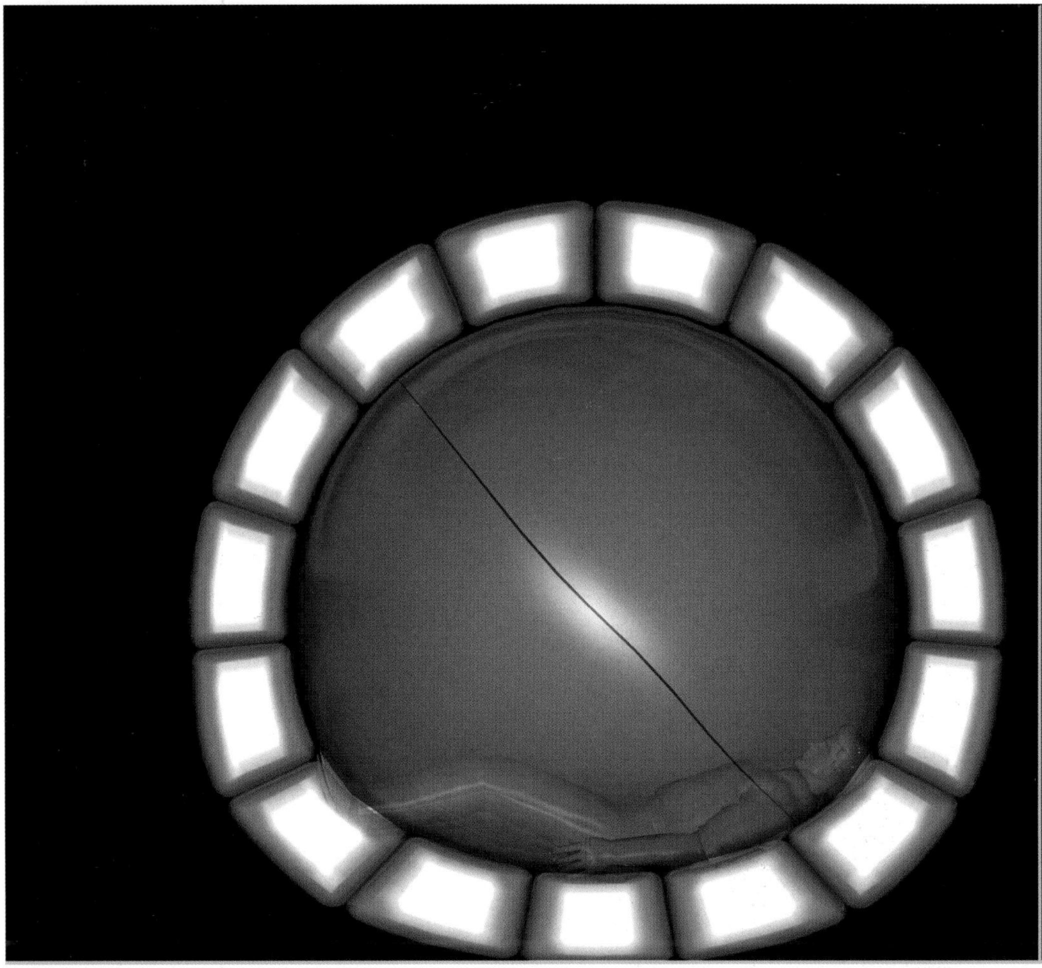

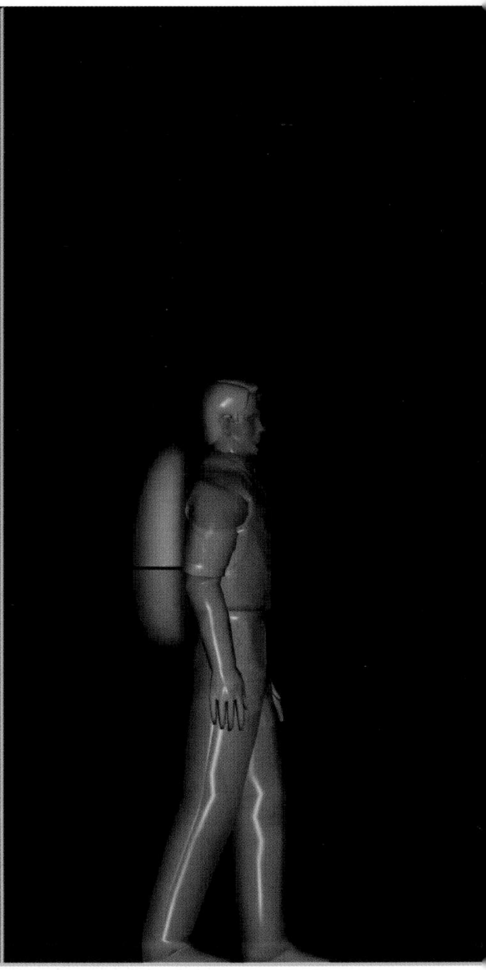

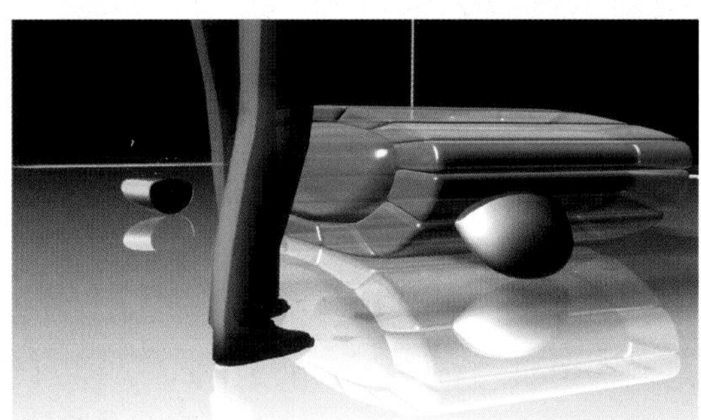

Life today in the urban territory is accelerating at an ever-increasing speed. Interruption time, non-time is thus multiplied and made inevitable. INSTANT eGO and NOMAMBULE are nomadic spaces as a result of these interstitial durations of time, allowing intimacy in the midst of urban public space.

Architecture as a tool grafted onto the immediate surroundings.

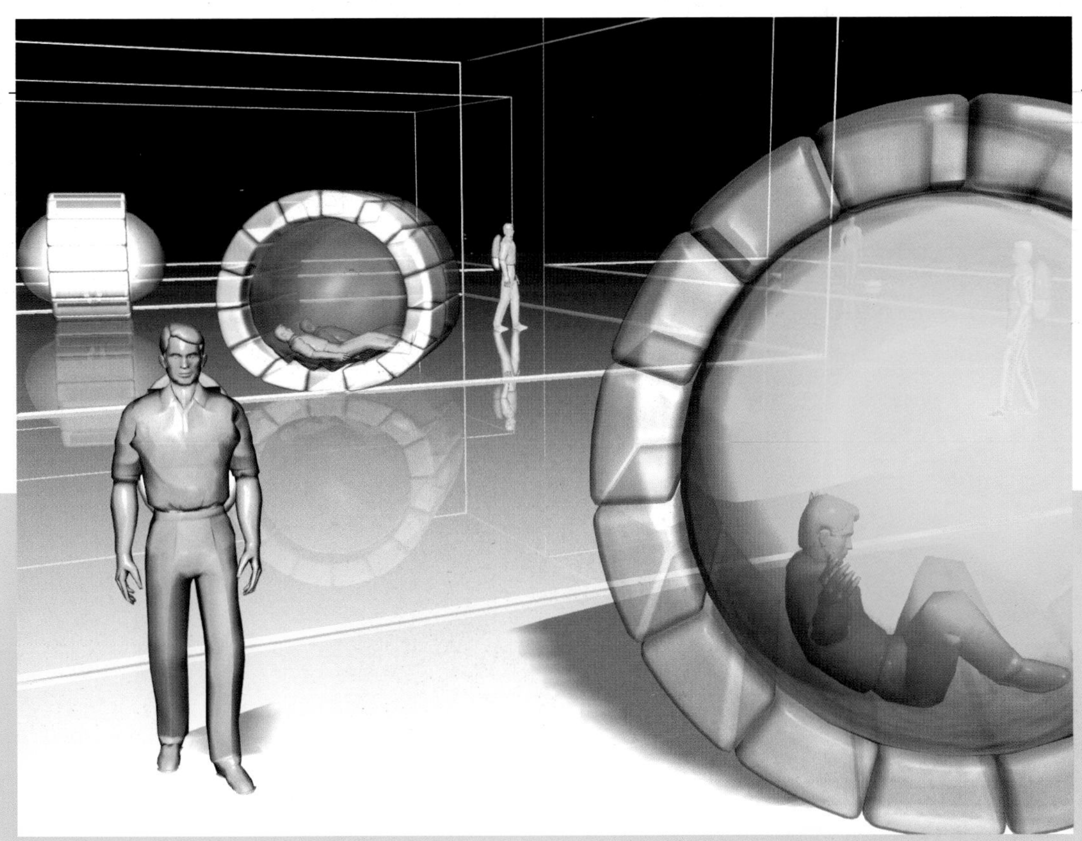

Comfort and intimacy for urban nomads.

INSTANT eGO & NOMAMBULE- Po.D

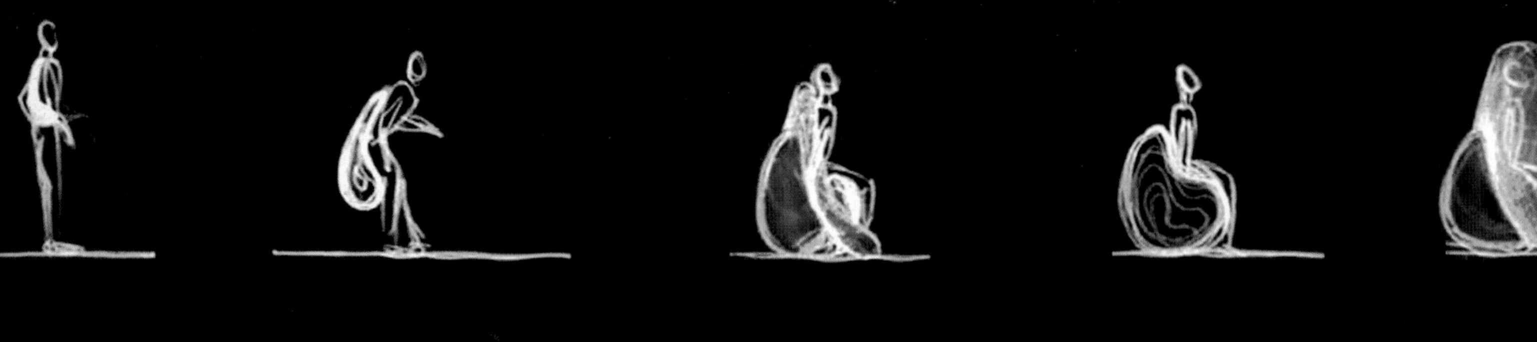

In INSTANT eGO the user is plunged into the realm of cyber space through projections on its inner skin that follow the movements of the user via a series of electronic sensors.

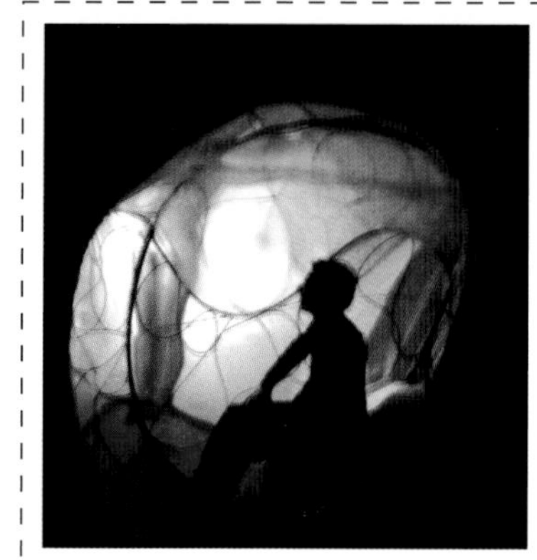

Unfolded, INSTANT eGO is plugged into the clothing and ready for use: INTERFACE, SHELTER, RESTING, THINKING, WASHING, WORKING, SURFING...

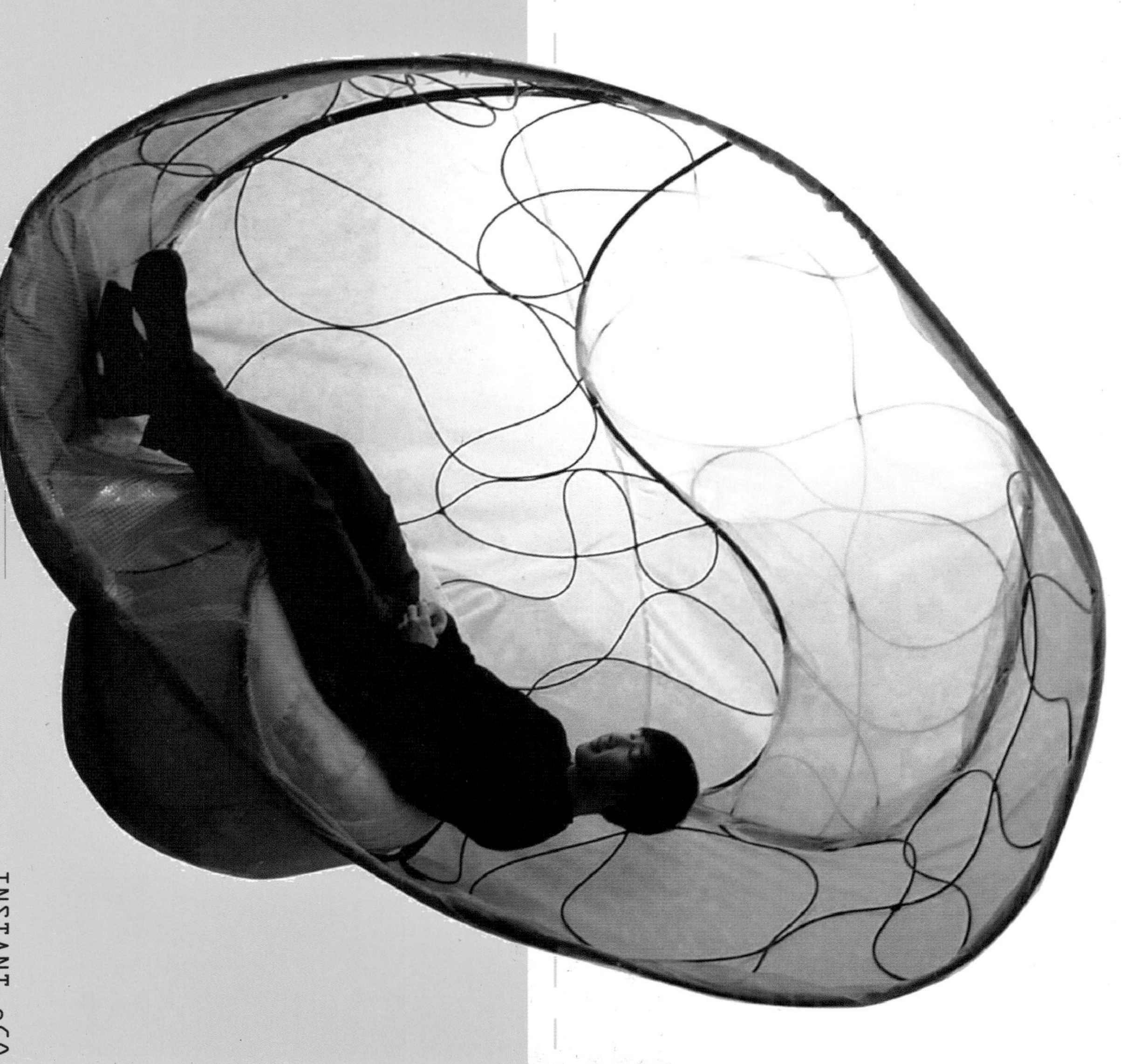

INSTANT eGO

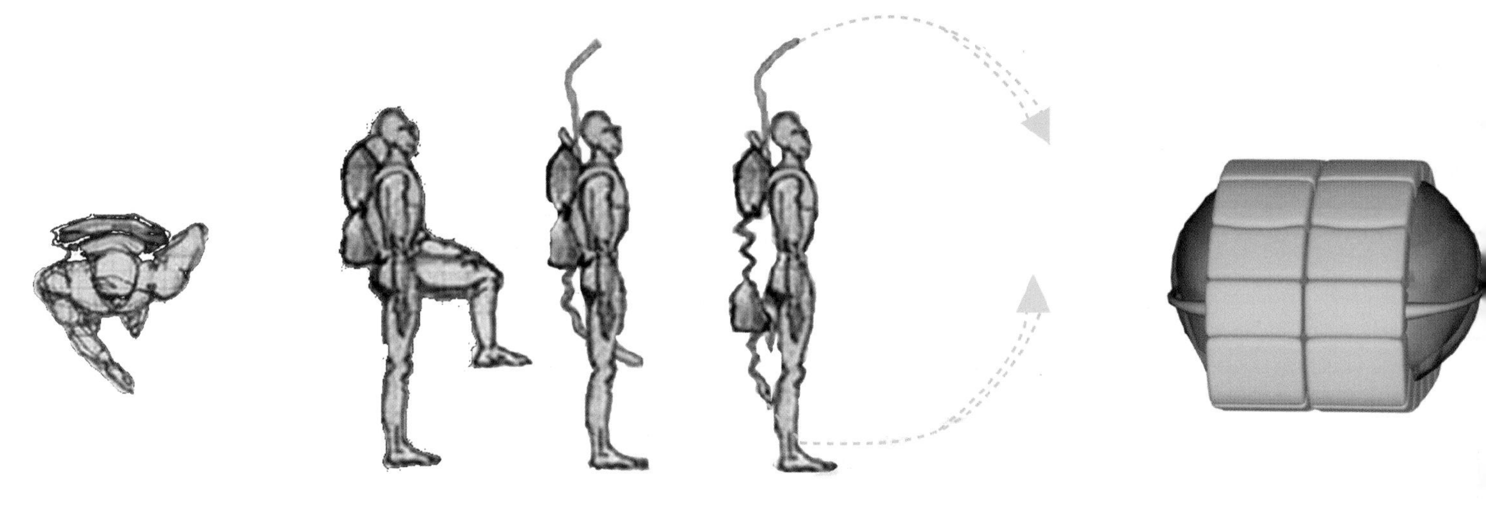

The two projects Nomambule and INSTANT eGO are architecture to go; they are extensions of the body materialized from a backpack.

NOMAMBU

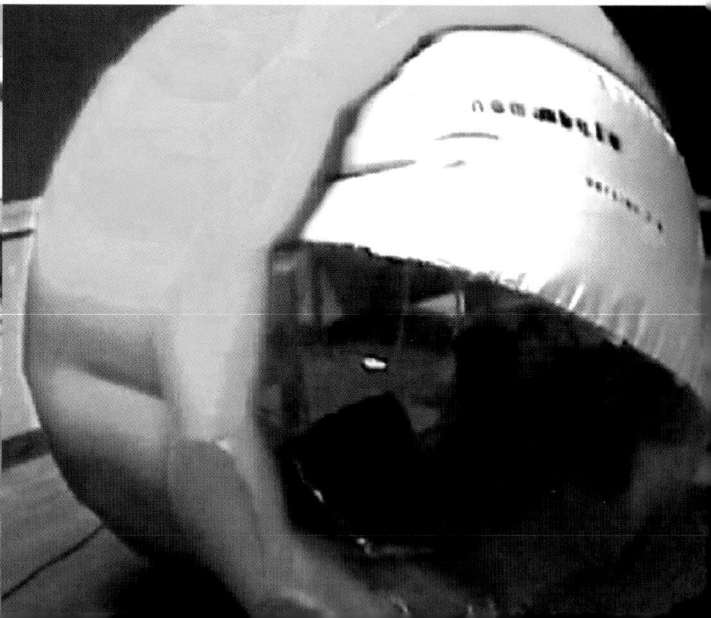

Nomambule is a chain of inflatable compartments possessing the same qualities as our personal effects (clothing, wallet, cellular telephone). It is a part of daily life and contributes to the construction of a personal space.

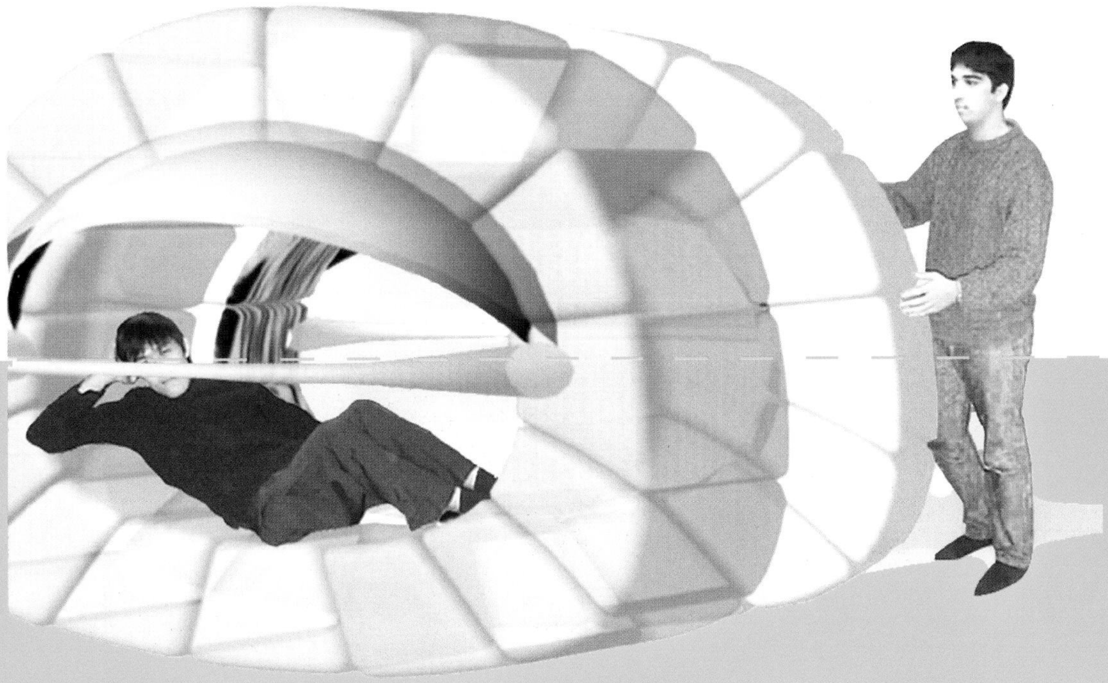

Mobile on land and water.

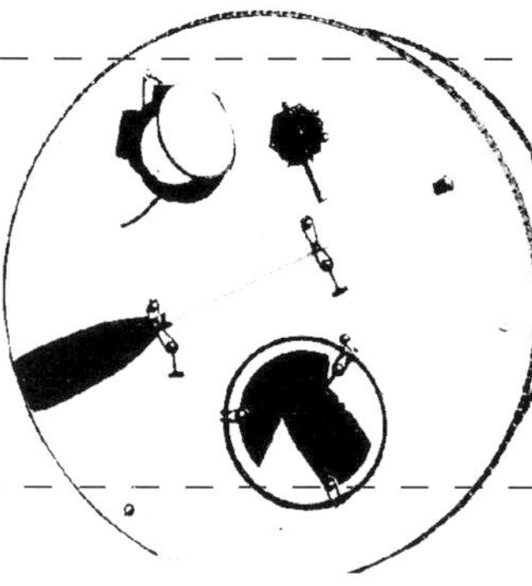

One unit provides space for one person.

The Snail Shell System is a low cost system that enables persons to move around, change their whereabouts and live in various environments. The unit can be hooked up to an existing infrastructure, such as telecommunication lines and electricity cables. With the addition of special devices, the unit can even supply its own energy.

SNAIL SHELL SYSTEM_ N55

Rubber caterpillar tracks protect the tank during transportati

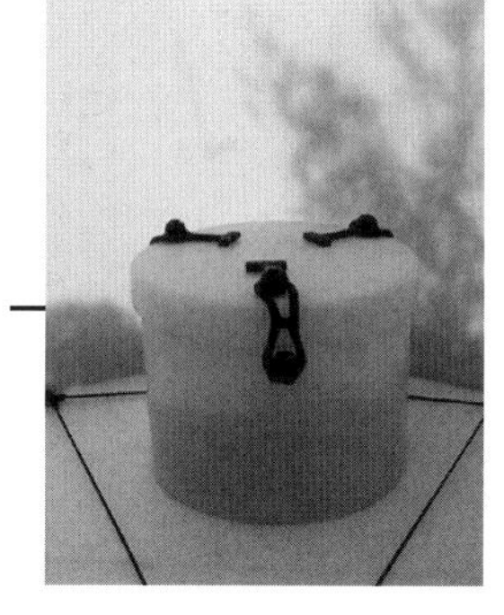

An air intake and the entrance

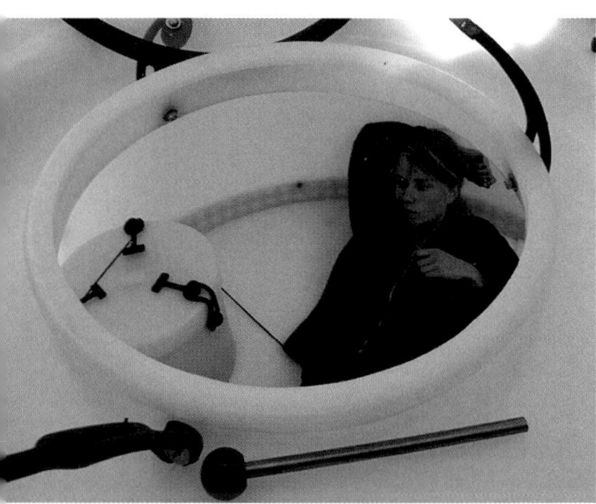

The Snail Shell System is based on a cylindrical polyethylene tank. The tank was chosen for its non-toxic material, low weight and its ability to roll.

Weight: 90 kg

Dimensions: diameter 153 cm, height 105 cm

Displayed in different urban sites, the unit links and confronts it design with the city.

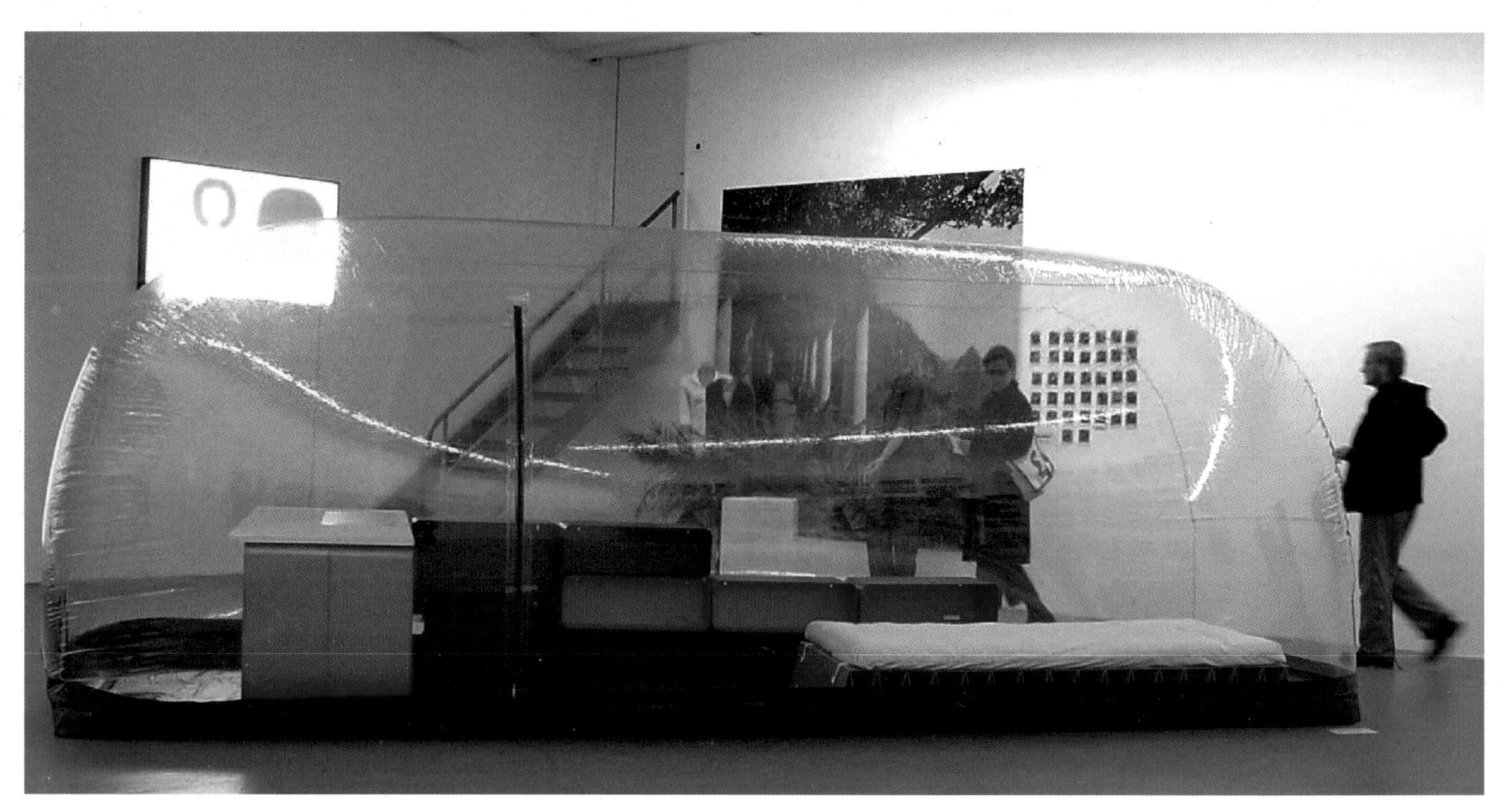

IT LIVING UNIT_ it design

The IT exhibit space is a transparent, mobile dwelling unit displaying the minimum living space concentrated down to a bed, storage space and a desk. The unit reflects IT's design philosophy: compact, light and mobile, it suggests a possible vision of tomorrow's dwelling.

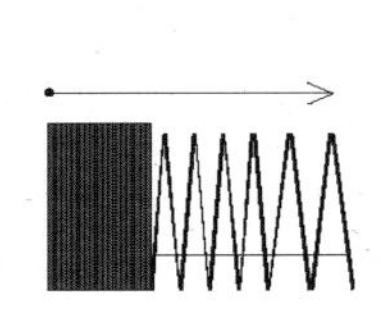

collapsible cardboard bed

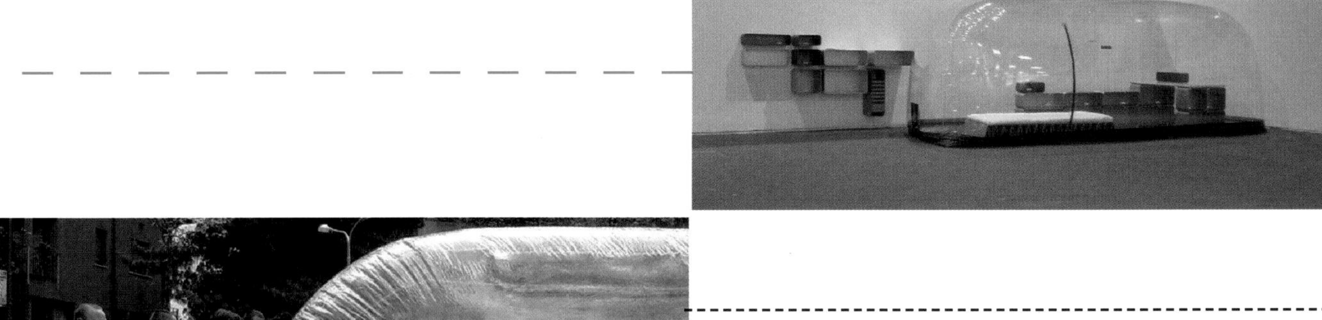

An unusual client brief called for a house that "provides the least privacy so that the family members are not secluded from one another, a house that gives everyone the freedom to have individual activities in a shared atmosphere, in the middle of a unified family". The result is an airy, double-height space with complete visibility from end-to-end. Instead of separating walls enclosing individual rooms, the "private" spaces are open-ended volumes set on coasters for complete mobility within this hangar-like space.

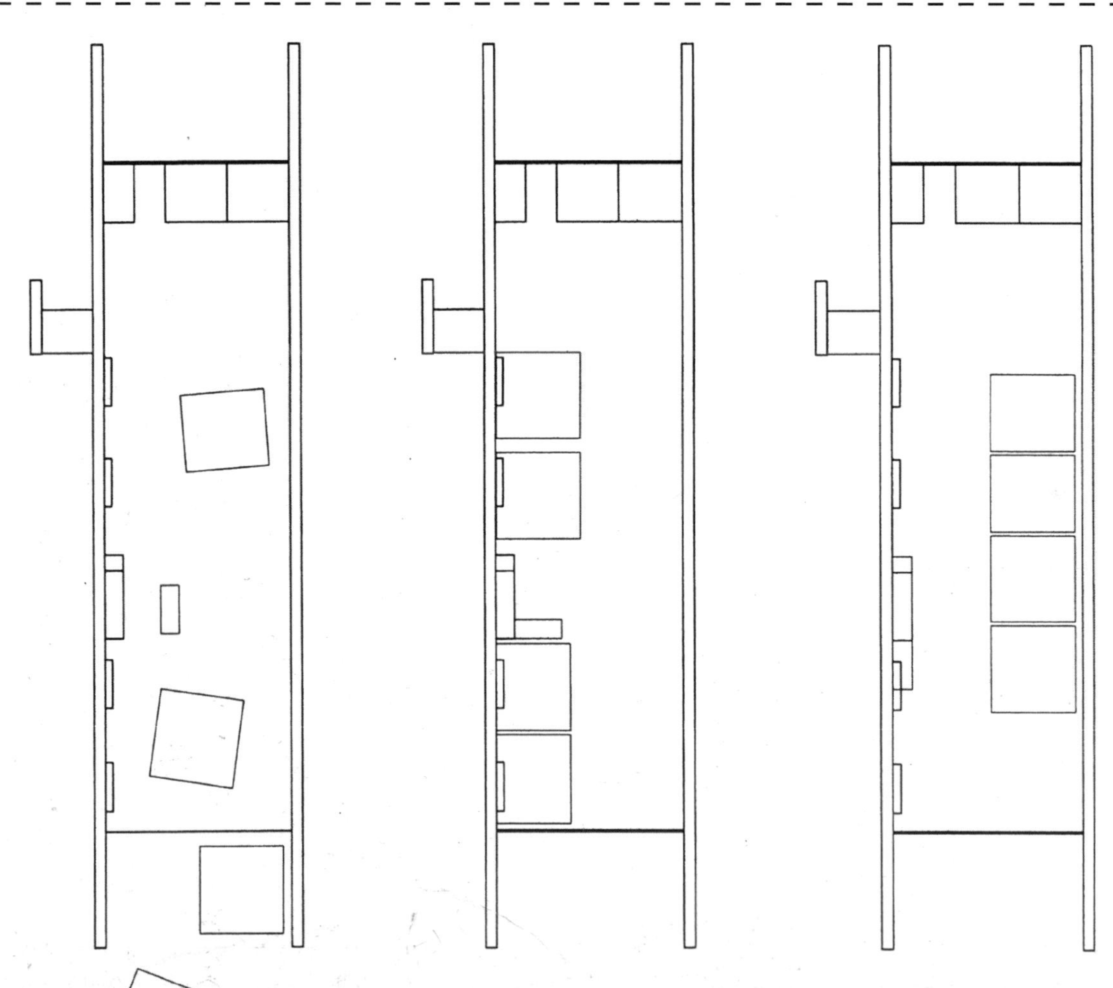

An unusual client brief called for a house that "provides the least privacy so that the family members are not secluded from one another, a house that gives everyone the freedom to have individual activities in a shared atmosphere, in the middle of a unified family". The result is an airy, double-height space with complete visibility from end-to-end. Instead of separating walls enclosing individual rooms, the "private" spaces are open-ended volumes set on coasters for complete mobility within this hangar-like space.

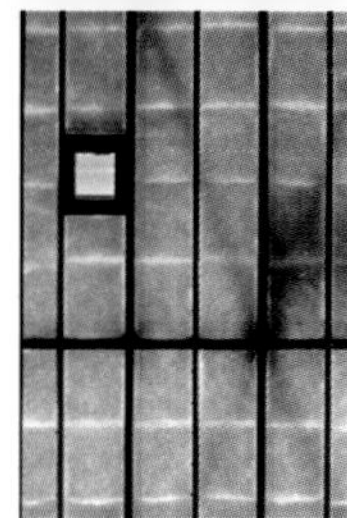

The interior configuration can be changed on a daily basis, if desired; larger "rooms" can be quickly created by removing their sliding doors and setting them side by side. As they are lightweight, these volumes can even be wheeled outside to make maximum use of all the available space. They can be used as an extra "floor", with plenty of sturdy, flat space on top where the children can play or objects can be stored.

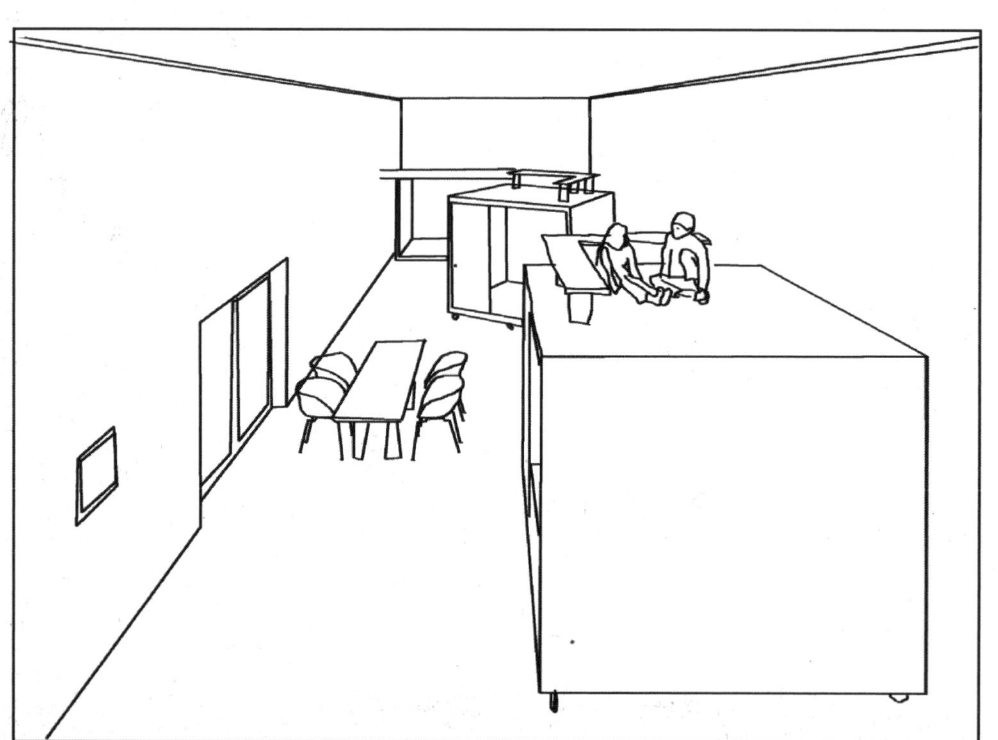

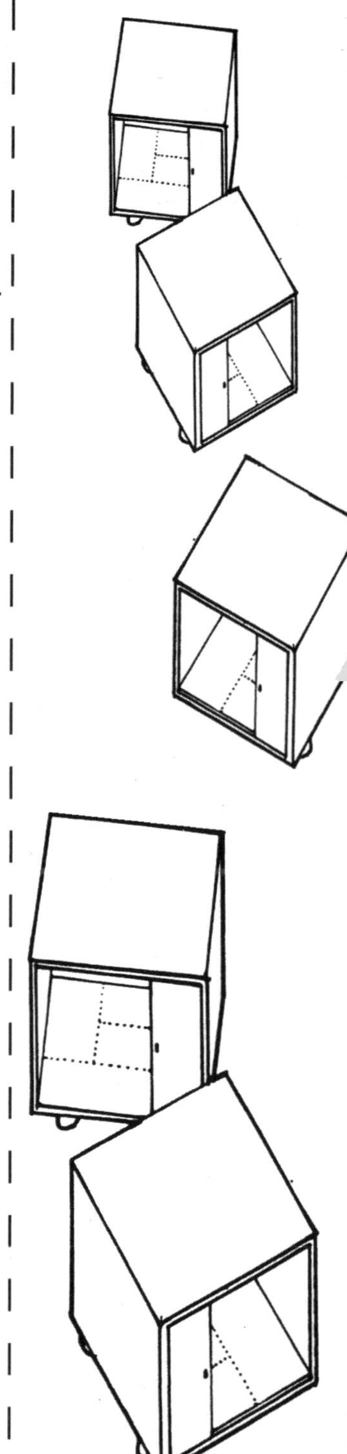

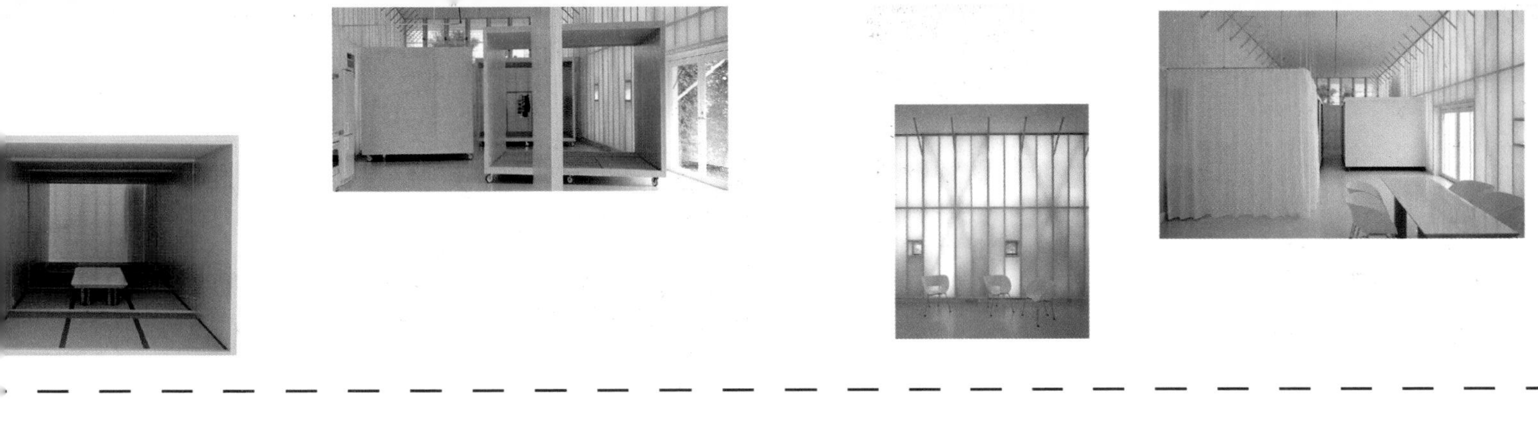

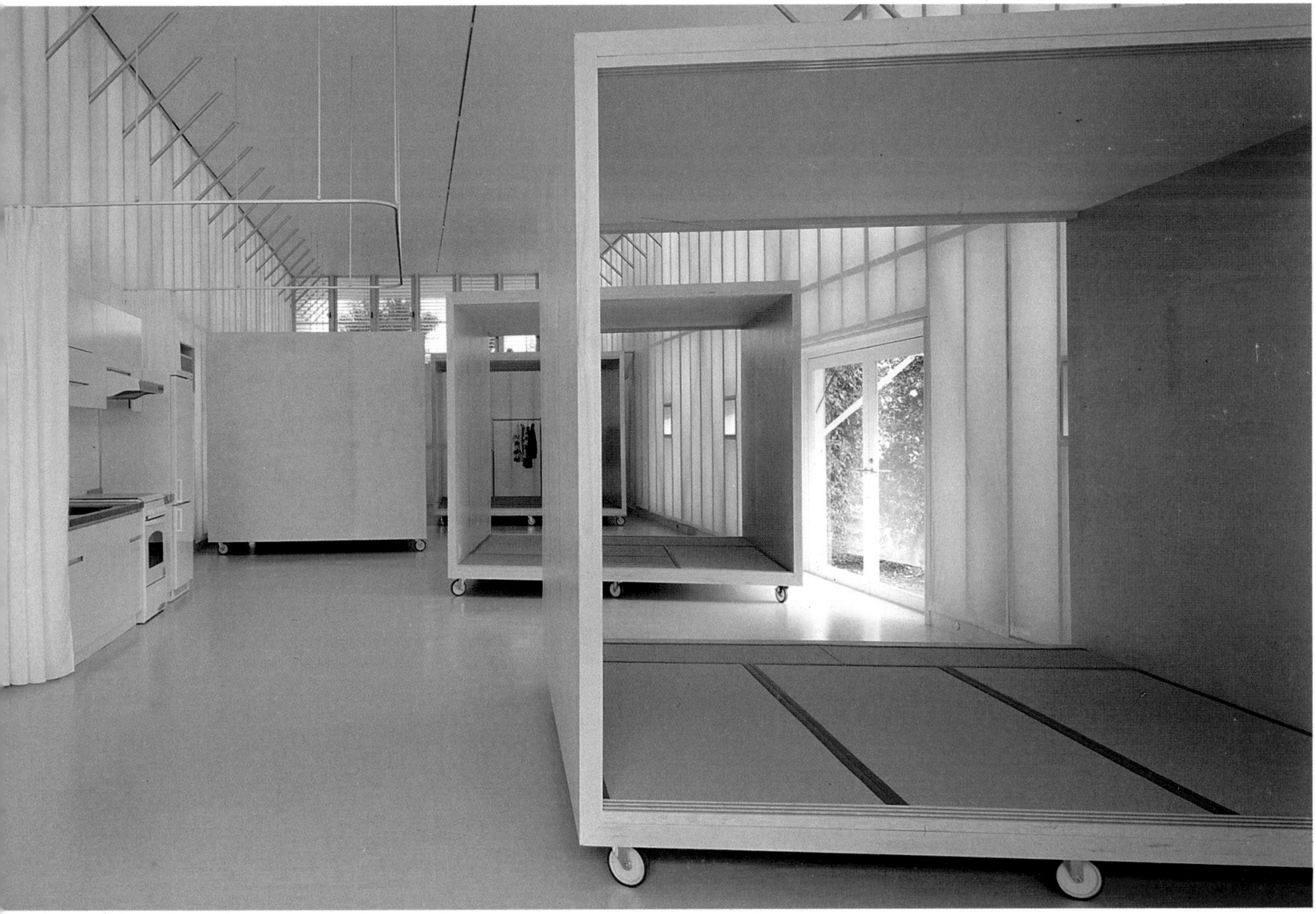

This is a compact, portable piece of furniture that satisfies all of the requirements of day to day living. It contains built in areas for eating, sleeping, cooking and working. But the ambition of this unit goes far beyond the desire to satisfy practical necessities, it also strives to reconcile a human craving for security, stability, freedom and autonomy.

inhabitable sculptures

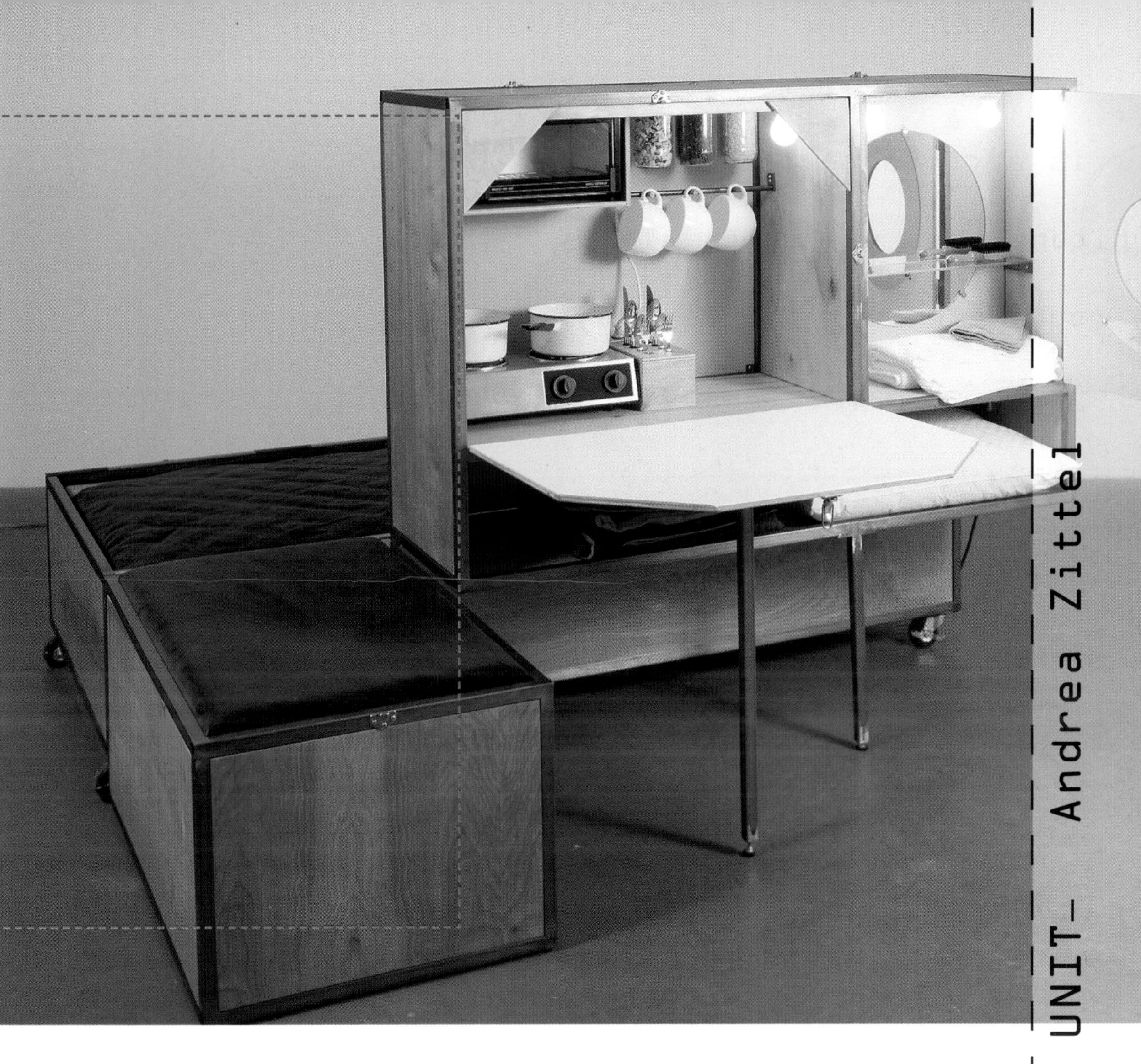

A - Z LIVING UNIT- Andrea Zittel

pillow refrigerator coffee maker

microwave telephone

toothbrush radio

sponge cups

closed: 36 3/4 x 84 x 38 ins/ open: 57 x 84 x 82 ins

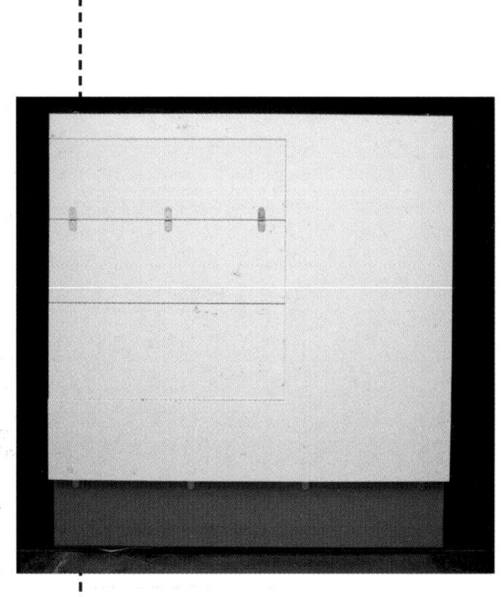

THE LIVINGROOM PROJECT_ Pablo Molestina/ Gruppe MDK + Aysin

This moveable red exhibition box was designed as an exhibit piece to present three architectural projects about architecture and dwelling in the archilab exhibition. The box opens into a miniaturized living-room: a sofa unfolds from the flat cover, complete with a shag carpet, a foot-light and an aquarium, and reveals a typical living room cupboard with shelves and drawers where the architectural models are found.

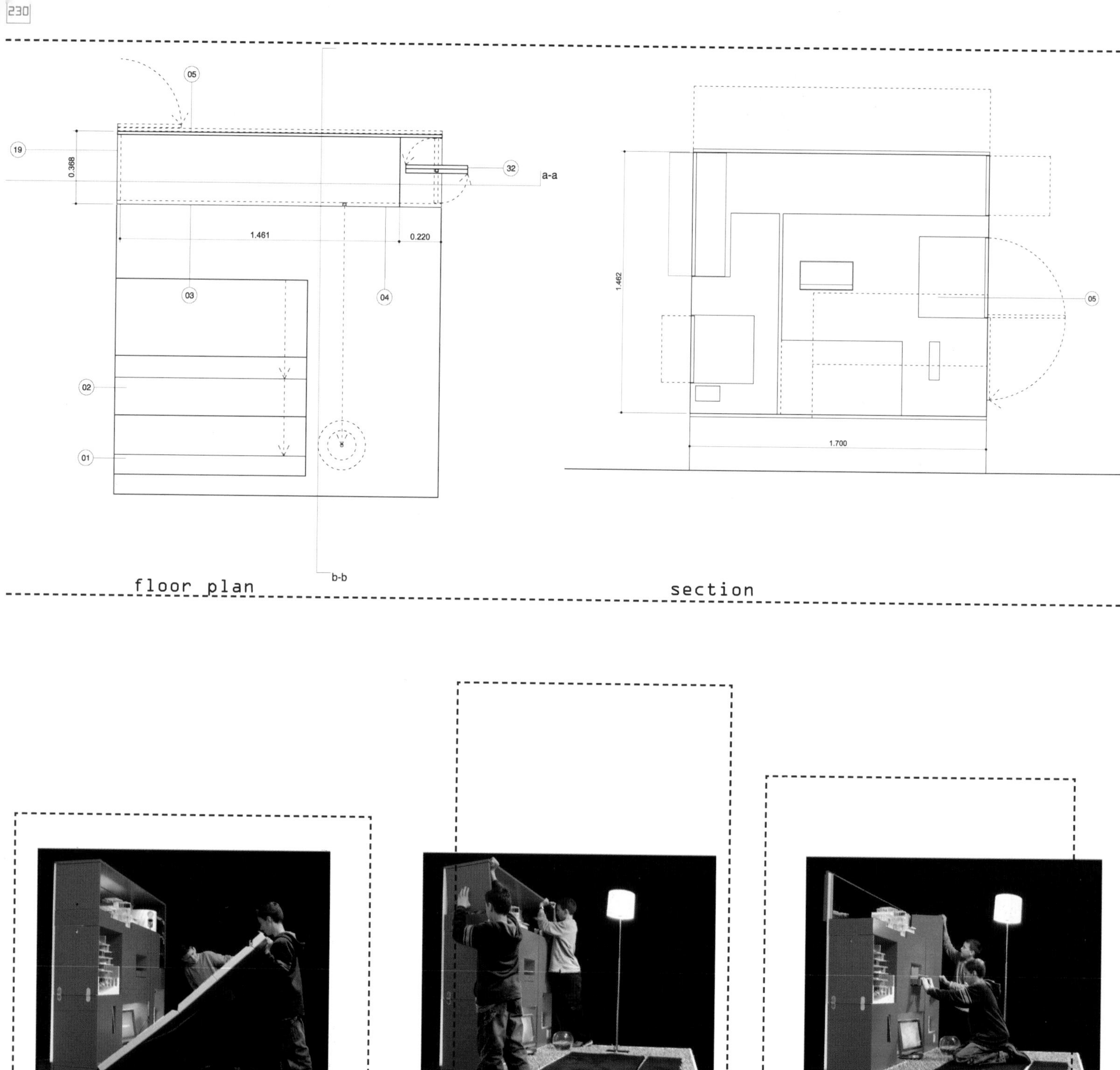
05
19
0.368
32
a-a
1.461
0.220
03
04
02
01
b-b
floor plan
1.462
05
1.700
section

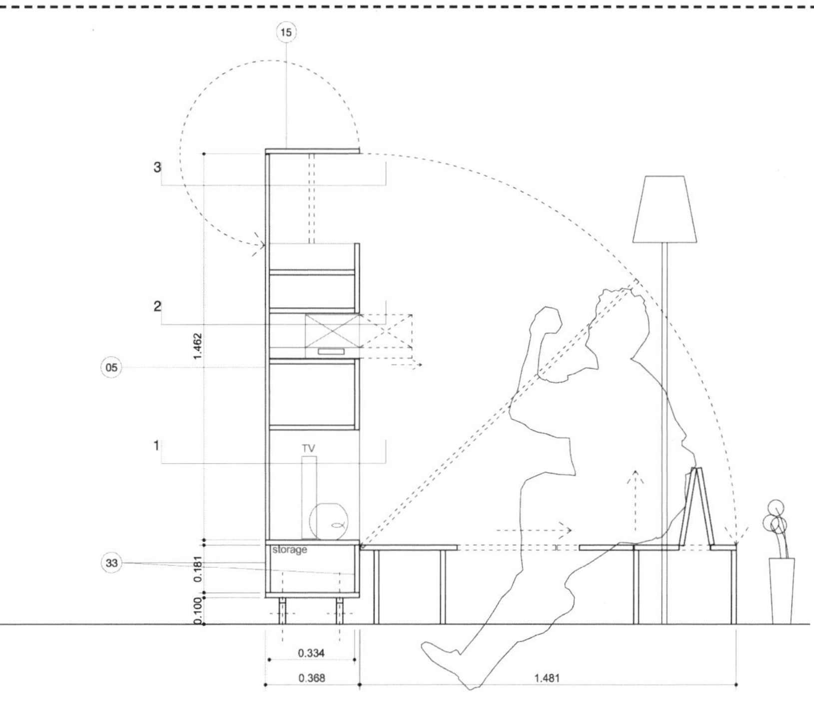

section

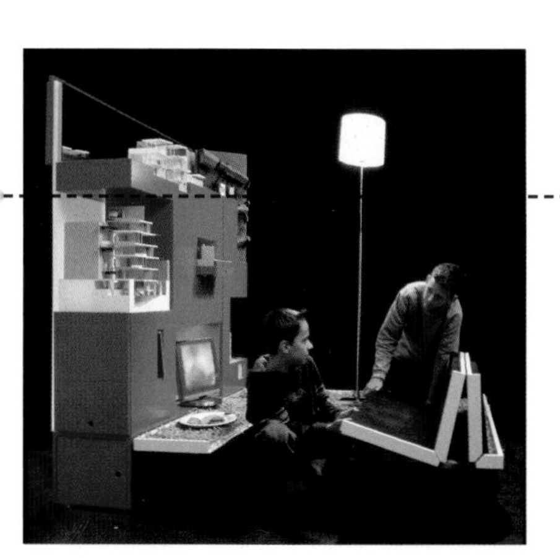

CORN FLAKES
Brillo

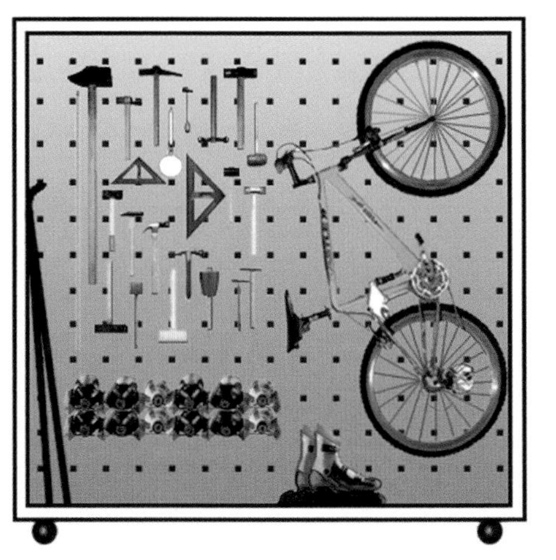

DISAPPEARING ACTS_

Dante Donegani

Giovanni Lauda

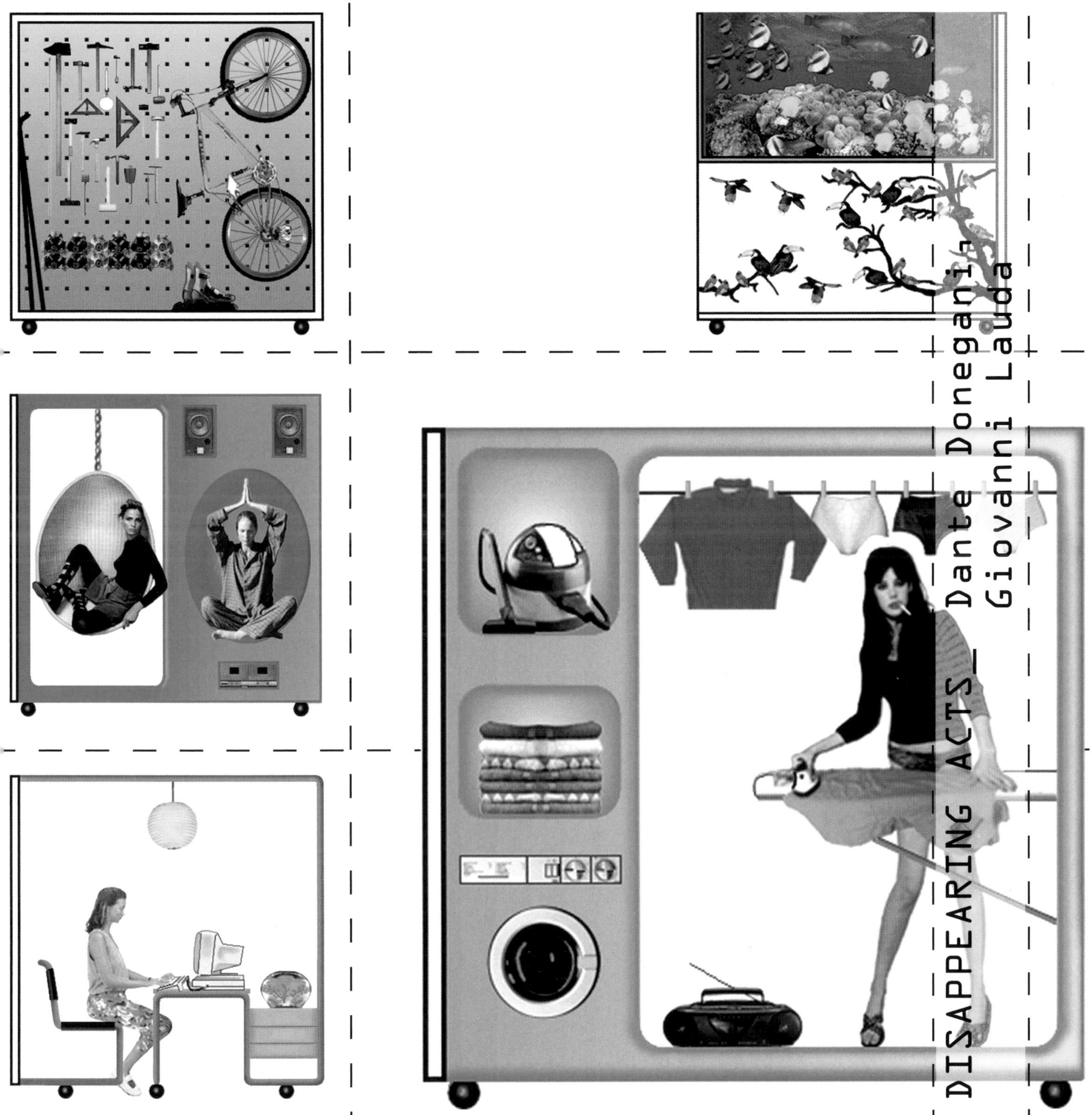

Freeing up spaces is related to indulging in consumption. One should concentrate resources and functions to obtain greater domestic mobility and more freedom in the undesigned space. By combining furniture and fixtures and by using service-furniture, the home ought to be more autobiographical and free individual consumption from owning costly, definitive hardware. Storage unit walls free the home s spaces.
Domestic activities are enclosed inside pull-out components with standard dimensions: custom-made fully equipped boxes.
In this way empty space does not exclude a customer s pleasure.
The complexity and richness of the house finds a new temporary order.
Furniture disappears, reduced to its negative, molds or cavaties, shaped considering the forms of their inhabitants; or else they are integrated by electrical appliances in vanishing wall closets. Nature, boxed in and compacted (greenhouse, aviary, aquarium) becomes an environmental tent, an artificial landscape that mediates home and city.

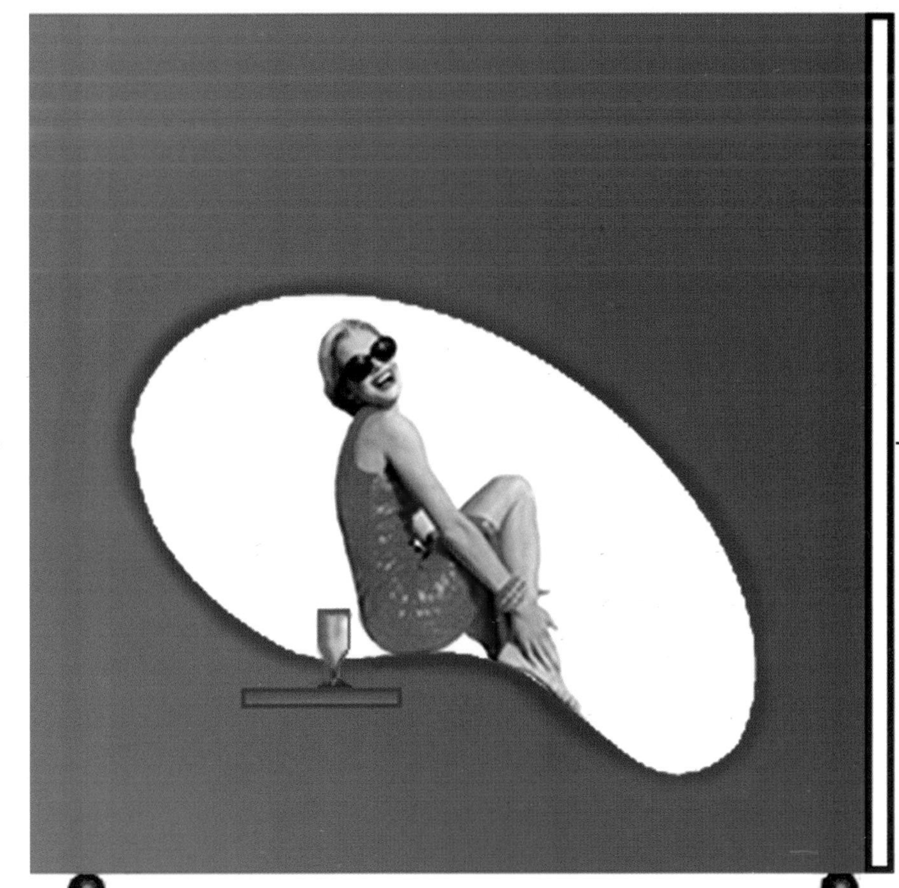

Architecture insulates us from the cold, air-conditions the heat, provides lots of ceiling height, even offers automatic coffee makers programmed to prepare coffee when we awake. Wexler is more interested in discomfort.

An 8 foot white cube is a home. Bedroom, bathroom, kitchen, and living room, each contained in its own crate on wheels. Each function is isolated and studied. The basic activities that take place in the home are pared down to the essential needed and desired objects. What defines a kitchen or a bedroom? Which objects do we choose for function and what actions do these objects imply?

When one function is needed, that crate is rolled inside. When the occupant is tired the entire house becomes a bedroom and when the occupant is hungry it becomes a kitchen.

Crate house examines our present lives as history. Each crate is a diorama in a natural history museum: the pillow, the spoon, the flashlight, the pot, the salt.

Isolated, they are sculpture, their use becomes theater.

CRATE HOUSE_ Allan Wexler

Our perception of home ownership is changing. Hugely inflated house prices and changing work patterns are forcing us to reconsider how we occupy and use our homes.

Shufl·e house redefines the concept of the traditional home by liberating us from the cellular approach to space planning. Fully integrated mobile pods provide us with the items essential for modern living, leaving a generous space for the occupants to design and re-design as they wish.

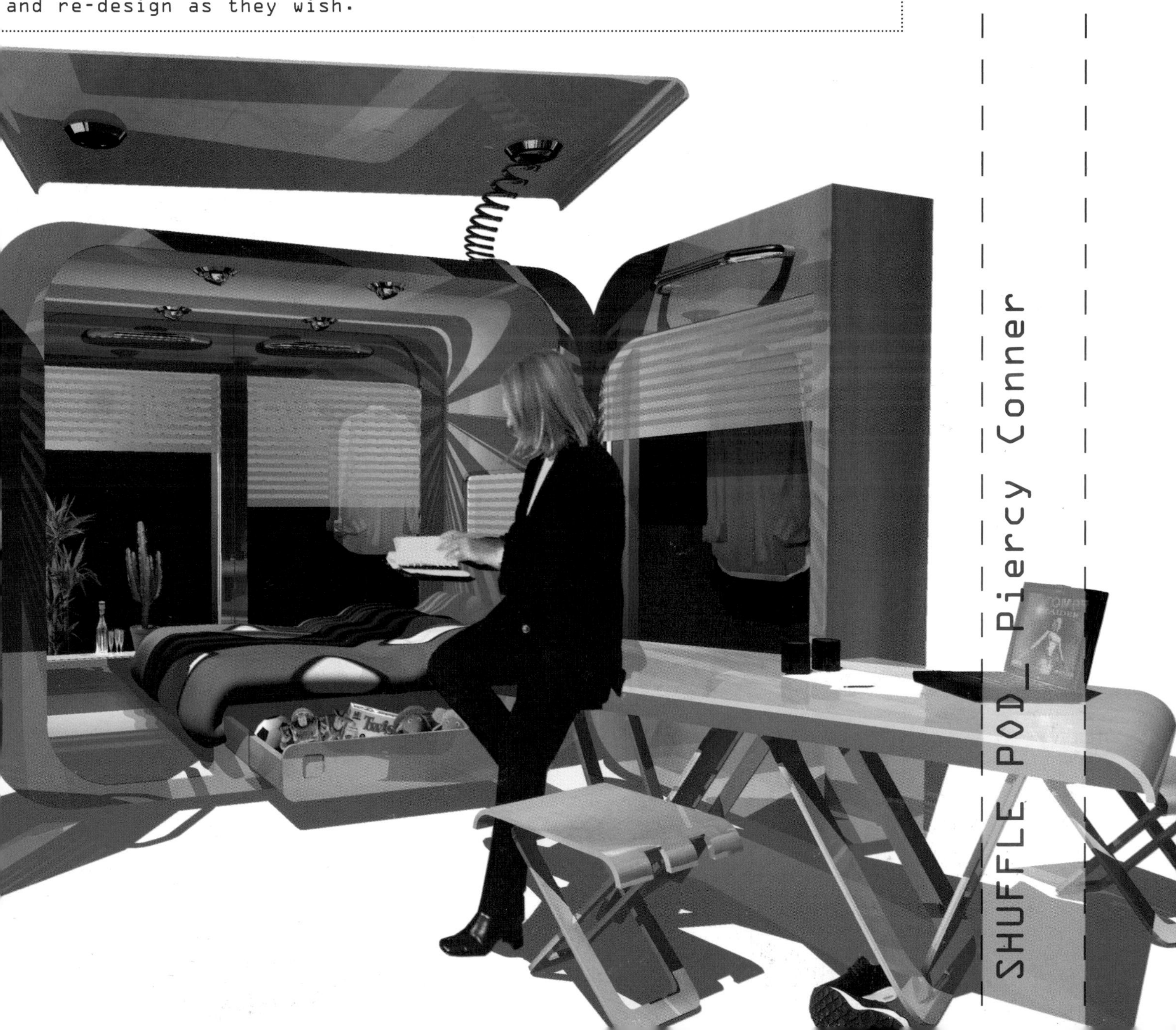

SHUFFLE POD_ Piercy Conner

Relax in the privacy of your own deluxe shufl.e pod. Neatly packed away in the door panels of the pod are all the essential items for work, rest and play. Recline and watch TV, surf the net or have a chat on the videophone. Working or having guests for dinner, pull out the table and chairs and throw a mini-disc into the home entertainment system. Throwing a large party in your one bed flat? No problem! Push your shufl.e pod into the balcony space provided and shut the doors. You now have all the space you need. Care to wake up on a summer morning with fresh air wafting through your bedroom? Simply make sure to position your shufl.e pod the night before.

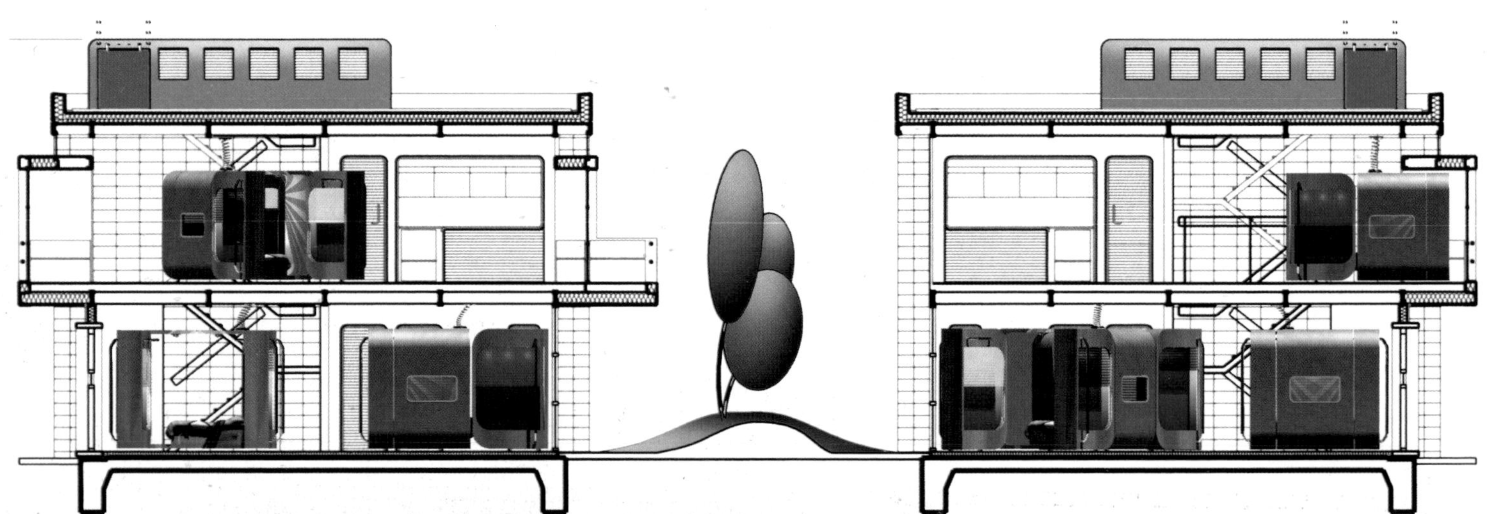

As the space around us become increasingly "universal," there are in reality fewer places left to "escape" to. The designers believe that, as a result of this, people are beginning more and more to turn inward, creating our own intimate personal realms. The A-Z Escape Vehicle allows us to create and access those realms whenever we want, without even ever having to leave home. It could be parked in a back yard, or in the corner of a living room.

In 1995 A-Z fabricated ten small stainless steel EVs. Each one was identical on the outside, but ready for customization on the inside. As they were sold, the inside of each one was detailed with their new owners' ideal escape fantasy - Cinderella's carriage (complete with a stereo system and wet bar) or an interior with a writing desk and custom cladding.

A TO Z ESCAPE VEHICLES- Andrea Zittel

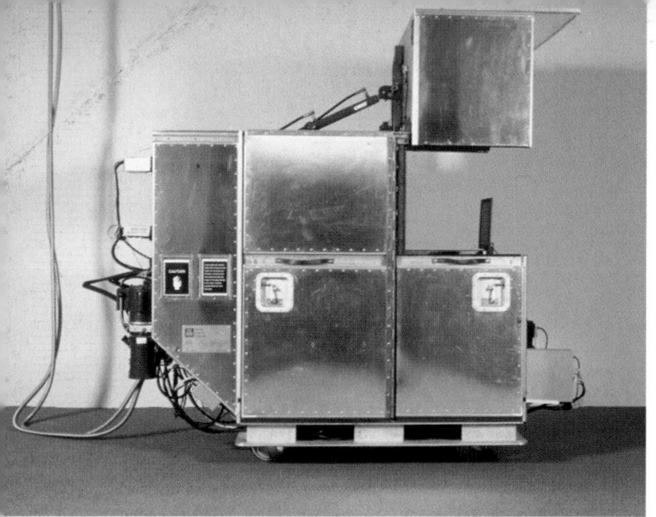

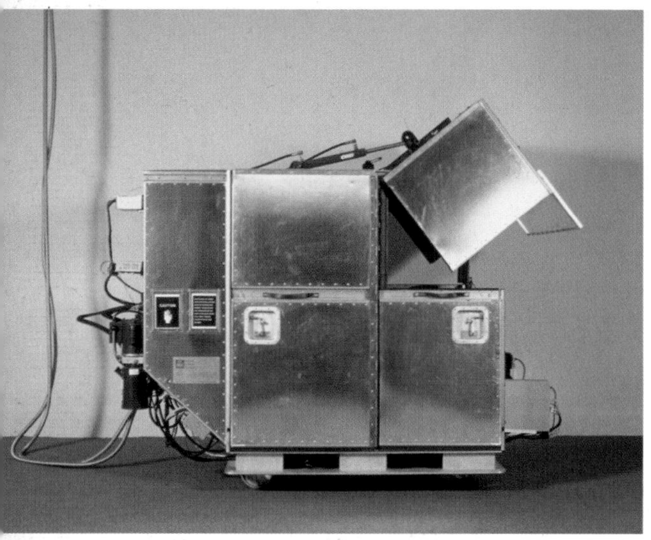

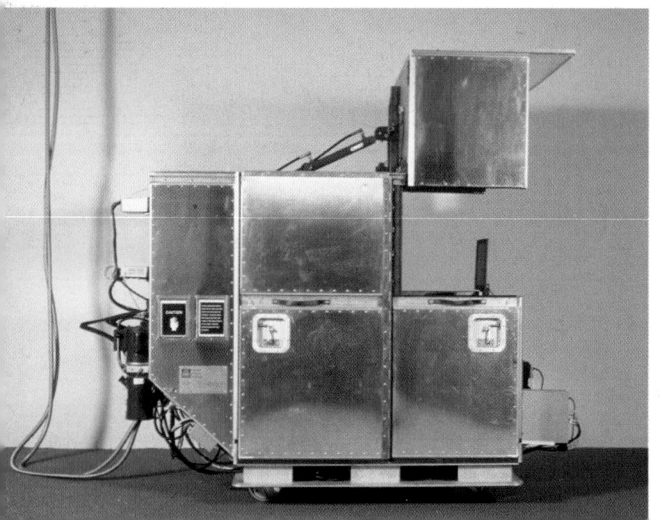

An airplane cargo container (LD3) is transformed into an individual workstation that blurs the boundaries between work/play, activity/relaxation, isolation/communication, meditation/entertainment. The container is conceived as a modular and mobile unit that can provide complete isolation or be combined to allow team work.

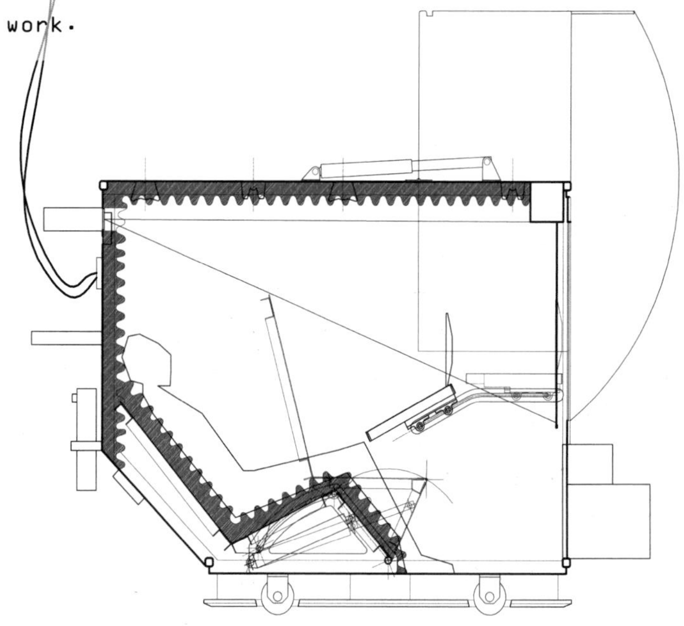

Its top/front portion opens up to connect to more Inspiro-Tainers and create a meeting room. Inside, the container is fitted with a moveable seat and desk that allow the user's body to go from a lounging/reclining position to sitting upright. Both seat and top are operated by hydraulic pistons connected to two separate hydraulic pumps installed on the back of the container. The Inspiro-Tainer is an incubator for ideas. It is equipped with computer, flat screen monitor, stereo DVD/CD player, surround-sound speakers, CD projector and retractable screen, reading lights and ventilation

fans. All inside surfaces are lined with convoluted foam, used both as padding and acoustic insulation. All technology and mechanisms are operated by a touch screen panel through which the user can easily activate and select preferred configurations.

"I was invited to show my support for a group demonstrating civil resistance by occupying the trees of La Alameda, in Seville. By following the fundamental premises of effective urban guerrilla tactics, I designed the shelters with parts that allow for immediate construction. The outside shell would provide protection from possible aggressors using rubber bullets and water hoses. The nocturnal assembly of the shelter requires about 4 people and takes two hours at most. The bottom part of the shelter is usually 4.5 meters off the ground and serves as a storage space; the top part has a sliding shell for protection. These volumes, along with the parts that affix and hold the shelter to the tree, comprise a body whose interior is completely clad in a peculiar insect-ventilation. This feature allows for a pleasant habitation in the summer months, which is when our temporary occupations tend to take place."

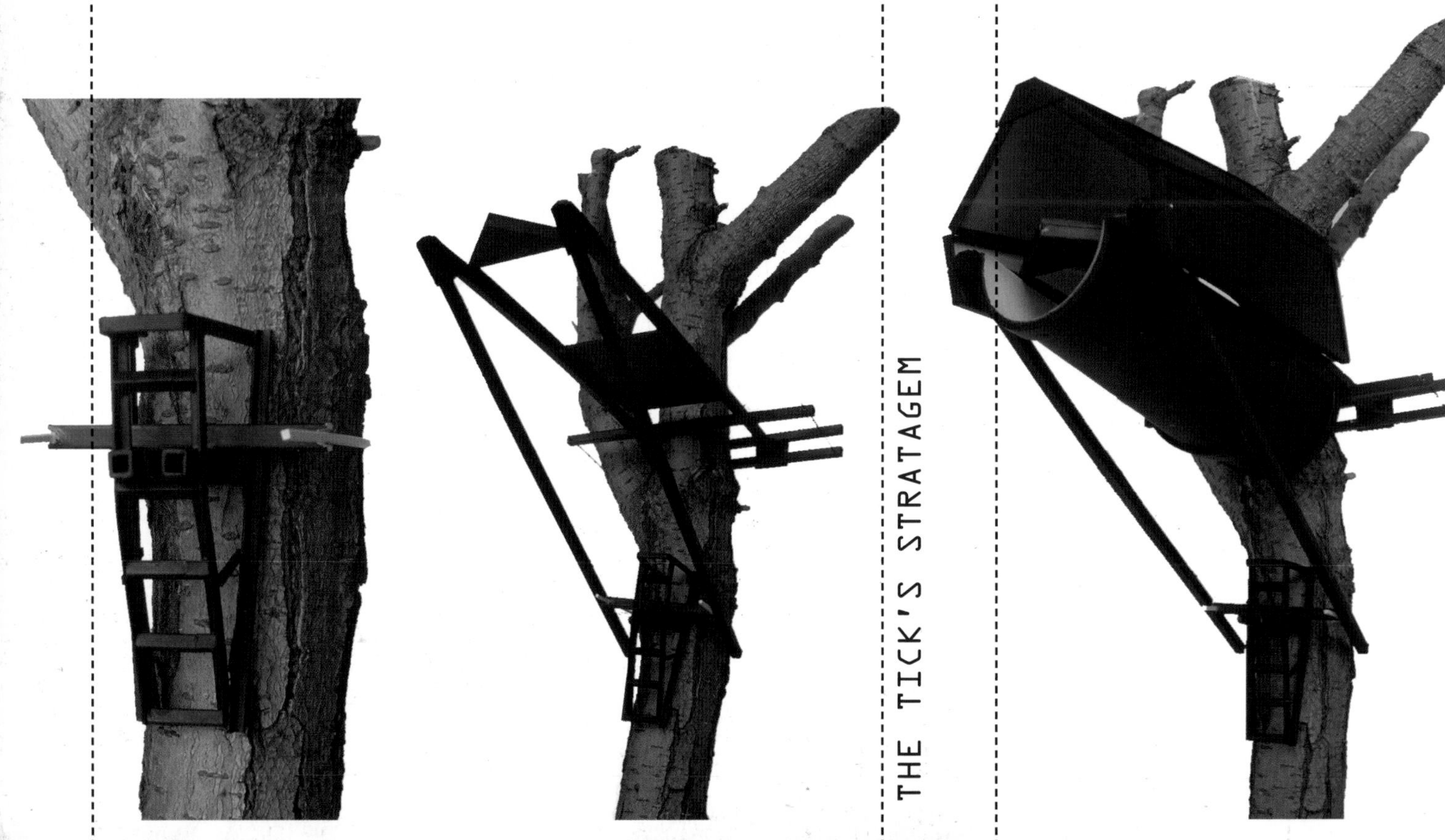

Occupation of a tree with provisional shelter.

Resistance to urban politics.

Lightweight construction systems.

Reversible colonization strategy.

Dynamics of social adhesion.

Instantaneous temporal sequence.

Lucid, but destabilizing, action.

INSECT-HOUSE_ Santiago Cirugeda

"It is not necessary to justify what should be obvious concerning the inability of urban planning to define the development and growth of a city that finds itself incapable of action given the changes in political attitudes, which means an absolute submission to the demands of the market and real estate speculation."

"The implicit goal of the action, and my personal ambition along with that of colleagues with a similar attitude, was to remind people and groups that, even if their voices have been strenuously suppressed, they are still able to act and decide, that they have a say in the development of the city and on how this development will be carried out."

"Beyond a mere ecological attitude concerning the protection of trees to be cut down, this is a strategy of opposition to plans that affect, and are often imposed upon, the population and its urban lifestyle. Such plans affect not only the inhabitants of the neighborhood, but also the vast and diverse groups of visitors who frequent the area of La Alameda."

Spiders have conquered every corner of our planet. Tremendously adaptable, they find a foothold everywhere, whether on their own legs or suspended in their self-built webs. This inspired the concept of the silva spider. The aluminum structure, with three fully movable legs, is resolved into compression and tension members, in accordance with the principle of tensegrity.
Silva spider can, therefore, be accommodated to any topography and will find a firm footing even in gorges and in gaps between buildings.

weight: 130 kg

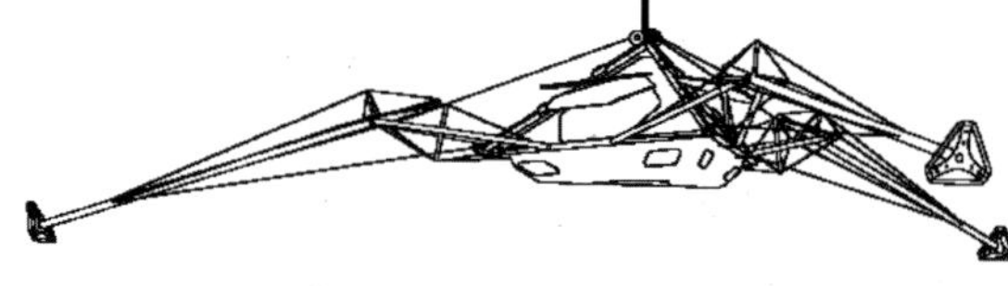

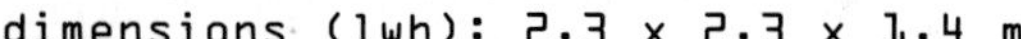

dimensions (lwh): 2.3 x 2.3 x 1.4 m

SILVA SPIDER_ Richard Horden

materials: aluminium, glass-reinforced plastic (grp)

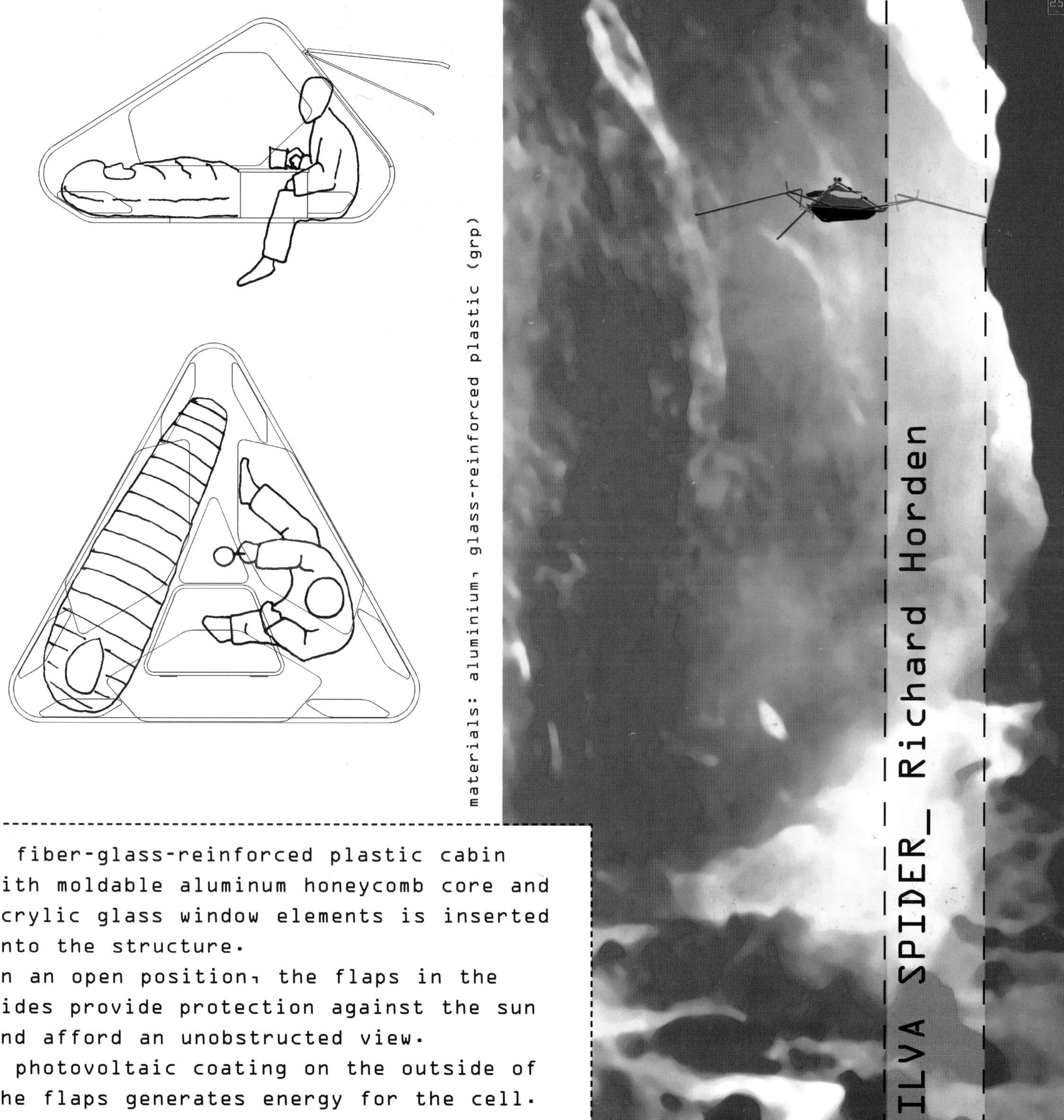

A fiber-glass-reinforced plastic cabin with moldable aluminum honeycomb core and acrylic glass window elements is inserted into the structure.
In an open position, the flaps in the sides provide protection against the sun and afford an unobstructed view.
A photovoltaic coating on the outside of the flaps generates energy for the cell.

a lightweight structure that could be attached to a large tree with minimal impact on its host.

***Like a spider spinning its web, the cradle can travel over to neighboring trees or hang suspended in mid-air high above the forest floor. *** A translucent inflatable mattress and roll-back enclosure allow for panoramic views while the motor is recharged via solar collectors on the canopy. *** The framework has a non-slip surface, but elastic webbing is stretched around the perimeter between the structural booms to catch you, just in case. *** Seated on the treehouse frame, diners around the table may dangle their legs freely. *** The treehouse is reached by climbing a ladder, the lower section of which, like that on a fire escape, can be retracted for security. *** Water drawn from the mains, or a nearby brook or lake, is pumped up to the treehouse via a hose running down the tree-trunk. When the bed is away, its catch-net doubles up as an oversized hammock.

a variety of drop-in living components, such as a picnic table and fly-away bed.

an exercise of the imagination

TREEHOUSE_ Softroom

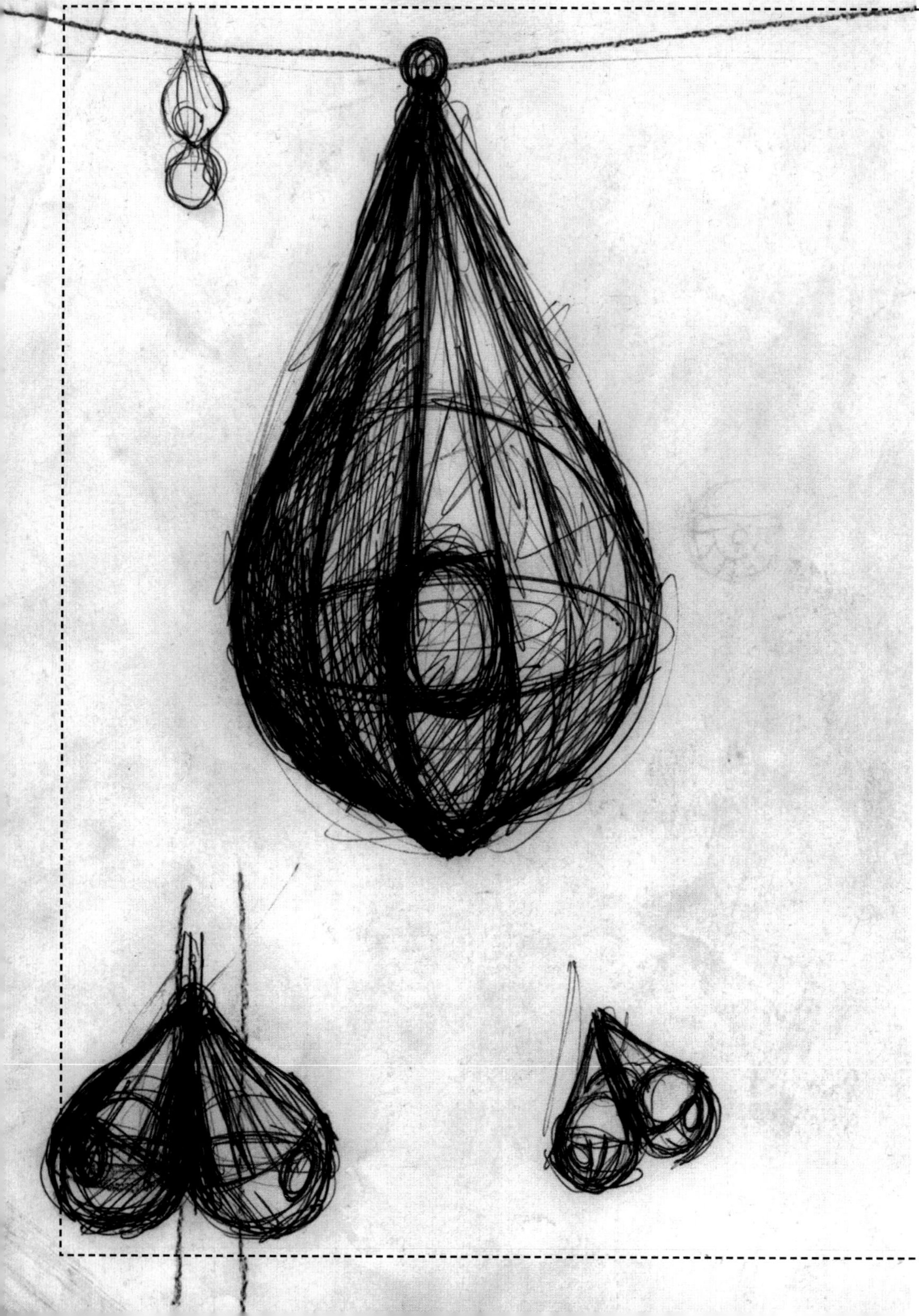

TREETENTS_ Dré Wapenaar

"The story of my tents as they relate to campsites," says Dre Wapenaar, "started with the Treetents, which were originally designed for the Road Alert Group in England. This group of activists fight against the over-construction of highways through forests. During their protest they cover themselves and hide and live in the trees to fight as long as possible against the rushing violence of the chain saws. The Treetents would provide a comfortable place for them to stay during their habitation of the forest and prevent the trees from being cut down. "Even though I designed the tents for use by the Road Alert Group, the project never happened. Before I finished it, a representative from a campsite saw the drawings of the Treetents and convinced me to sell them this project. It was a huge success; and is still in use today. They are rented 5 months out of the year. Two adults and two children can sleep on the main floor, which is about 9 feet in diameter."

"The form for these tents arose naturally when I hung a circular platform with a rope on the side of a tree. My inspiration for the shape was not the dewdrop. Form followed function."

Different techniques for accessing and studying the forest canopy were researched for an international project for the study of insect diversity.

With a holding capacity of three people, they are lightwieght structures which are easy to transport and set up.

The Treetop Raft brings mobility. Ikos, the ability to stay and observe.

Two structures that make a dream of science into reality.

IKOS & TREETOP RAFT_ Gilles Ebersolt

treetop raft

Looking for a completely open structure which would be light enough to rest on a crown of forest trees.

Ebersolt came up with this mobile, twenty-sided, air-filled structure, dubbed Ikos. Transported via hot-air balloon, Ikos is the materialization of the dream of being able to observe the forest s canopy.

The sphere, measuring 3.2 meters in diameter, can be easily taken apart and reassembled for ease of transport and on-site assembly. Once in place, its inhabitant can reach the ground, if necessary, via a fixed line. Aside from its invaluable use as a scientific observation post for an ordinarily very hard to reach habitat.

Ikos can be put to use in eco-tourism, as a temporary dwelling or portable construction site shack.

The mobile spatial composition "Gisant/ Transi" in the Sezon Museum of Modern Art, Japan, occupies a place between architecture and art. This work was inspired by a late-medieval form of tomb in which the dead are depicted in a living state (gisant) or in a state of decay (transi). Translated into a mobile, geometric form, this representation of life and death manifests itself as two "vectors" (memory and foresight) which cross each other. The four elements that make up this object are on rollers and are connected by hinges. By rotating the individual parts, the spatial arrangement can be changed.

Physical space assumes the function of sensitive nostrils that inhale the surroundings. With the bending movement, the mouth vanishes at the maximum point of opening, and another set of beds line up for a night of half-sleep.

"Two objects are set next to each other, with half-open, half-closed spaces. One is too transparent to be called a 'cage'. The other has a light well and is too bright to be called a 'cell'. Be that as it may, they are sleeping platforms on which the human body can lie down.

BLACK MARIA_ Hiroshi Nakao
It breathes in and exhales space. A mouth, in other words. And if so,
can the its body be reduced to a resonant voice or a quivering breath?

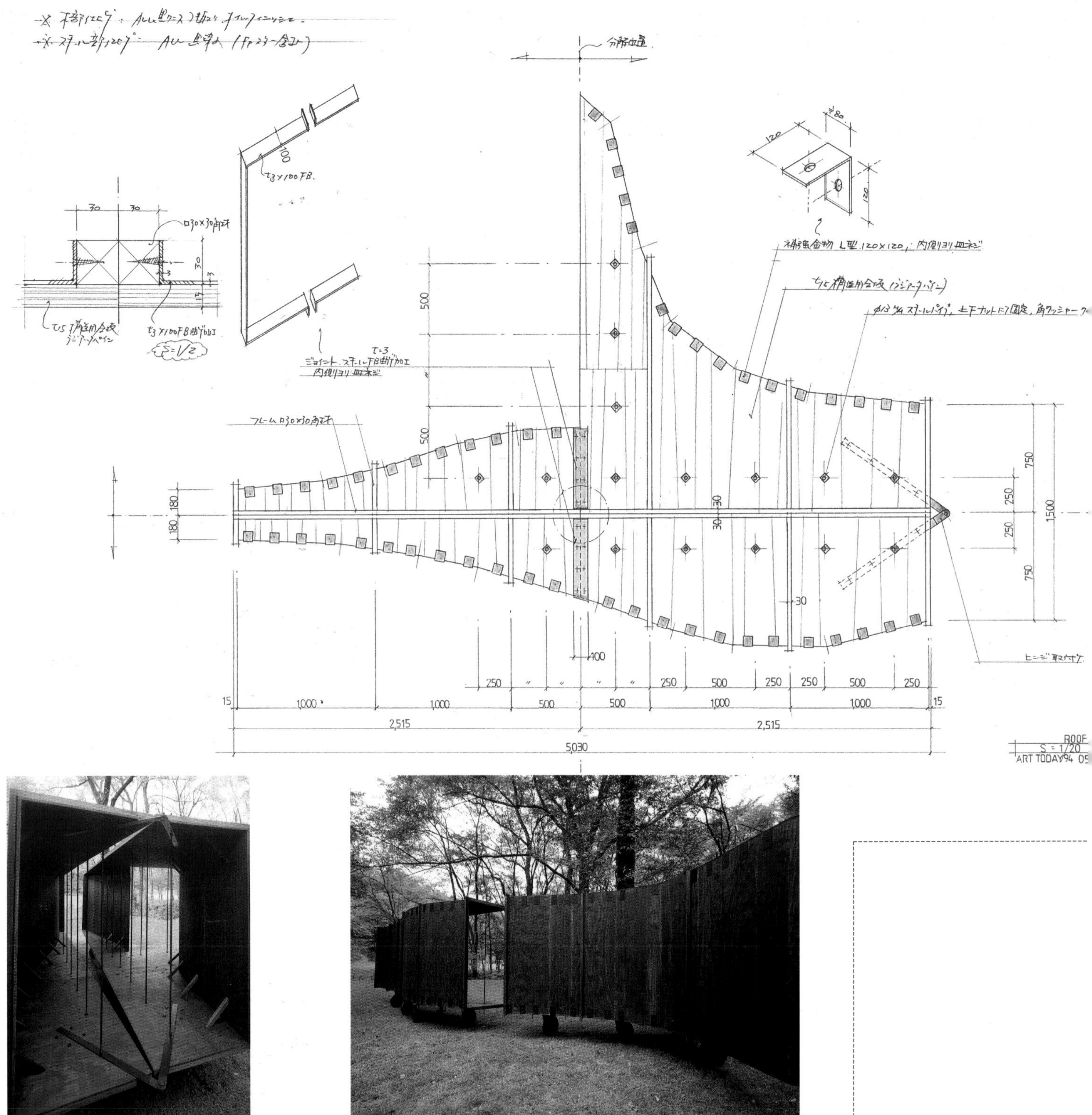
ROOF
S = 1/20
ART TODAY94 05

It is not only a frame, but also a landscape container. It delineates, then renders ambiguous the distinction between interior and exterior. As a hinged device, a manifold in the landscape, it informs many permutations and fluxes between interior and exterior.

In Pink Flamingos, John Waters shows a family of degenerate criminal travellers who live in a caravan. The title of the film refers to a deflated life-belt in the shape of a pink flamingo placed near the vehicle. "I like this kind of reversal by which, through a magnifying effect, an insignificant detail suddenly becomes determining and revealing for a context," says architect Franck Scurti. In Mobilis in Mobile, the caravan takes on the form of a carton of fruit juice.

It is a negative version of Cinderella's pumpkin carriage, which is no longer associated with a fabulous palace or with an art center but with the nearby housing development. The exterior aspect of the mobile living unit resembles commercial packaging. The interior was subsequently altered by covering it from ground to ceiling with a layer of asphalt.

MOBILIS IN MOBILE_ Frank Scurti

'Mobilis in Mobile', this movement in motion, is a response to the new features introduced by travel technology. Here, speed is present in its very shape, which refers to the speed of gesture and the accelerated circulation of goods.

The caravan is open; the door and window frames are empty. It is therefore freely accessible.

KIELDER BELVEDERE_ Softroom

Having previously focused on purely sculptural work, Kielder Water have commissioned the design for a shelter structure for the north side of this reservoir.

The Kielder Belvedere makes use of the vast panoramas of the man-made landscape in three ways:

First, the sides of the shelter reflect a partial image of the forest, screened by the acid etching of their stainless steel panels.

Then, the mirror-polished convex surface at the front draws views in toward a curved slot, which in turn frames the panorama of Kielder Water when viewed from the golden top-lit drum within.

Local climatic conditions demanded robust, hard-wearing materials, which are expected to last for at least a decade. The seats are made from a virtually indestructible man-made resinwhile the screen-like walls are of stainless steel to make the Belvedere less solid in appearance. A feeling of warmth and comfort was created by cladding the interior in gold colored, powder-coated steel and by installing a yellow glass skylight.
Softroom made the Belvedere sit clear of the ground by allowing its outer edges to cantilever a short distance over the sloping grade.

A sculptural artwork to complement the vastness of the extraordinary landscape at Kielder

E100VS 1

2/01 – KIELDER BELVEDERE : VIEW FROM KIELDER RESERVOIR ARCHITECTURE : SOFTROOM CREDIT ESSENTIAL FOR PUBLICATION PHOTOGRAPHY : KEITH PAISLEY

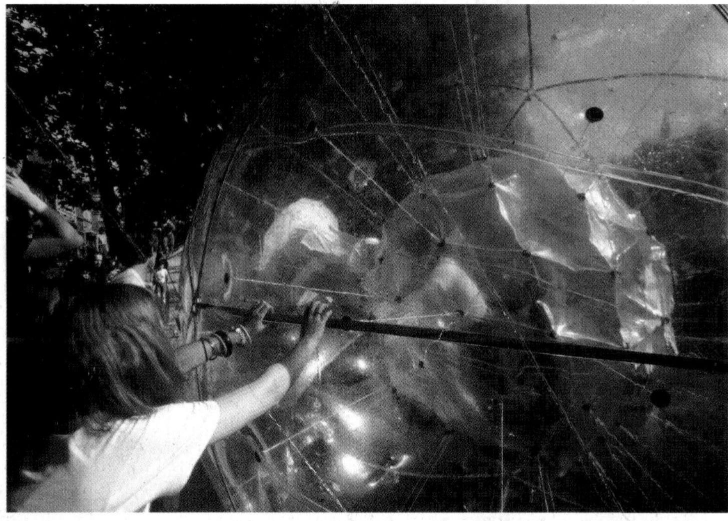

LA BALLULE_ Gilles Ebersolt

This transparent inflatable plastic sphere with a double skin was originally designed as a play object. It has a habitable interior space and it can roll down hills, sand dunes, ski slopes or float on a river or waterfall.

By distributing one's weight, the occupant directly controls the movement of the sphere.

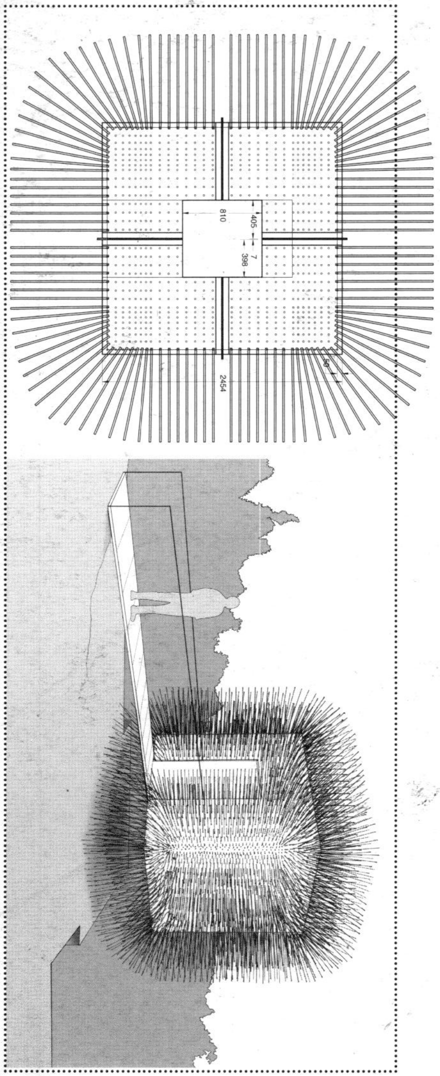

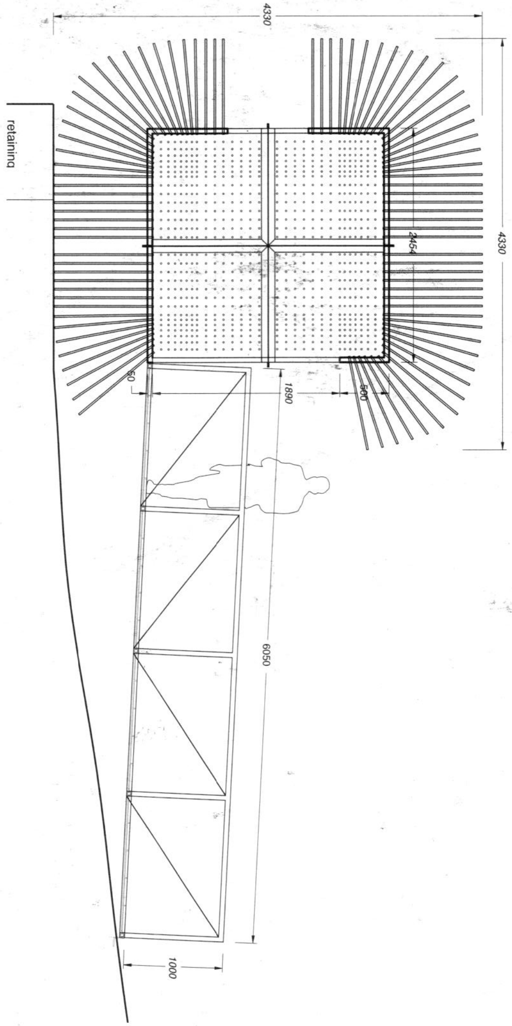

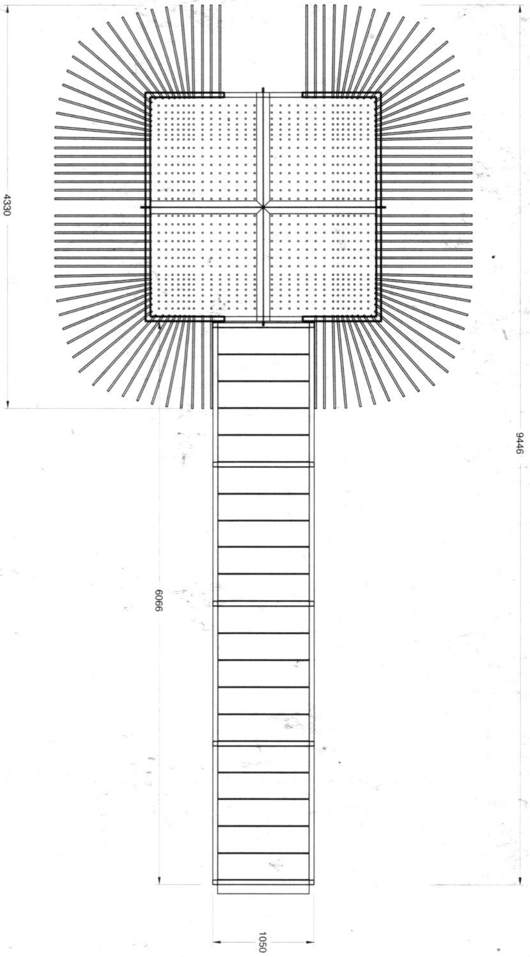

'Sitooterie' is a Scottish derivation meaning summer house - literally, a small building in which to 'sit oot'. The sitooterie is a 2.4 x 2.4 m cube with a window and a door, the enirety of which has perforated with five thousand pre-drilled holes, into which have been pushed five thousand identical staves (one meter long and 18 mm square). The staves are both functional and textural: outside, the projecting staves hold the structure off the ground and create extraordinary texture on an architectural scale.

SITOOTERIE_ Thomas Heatherwick Studio

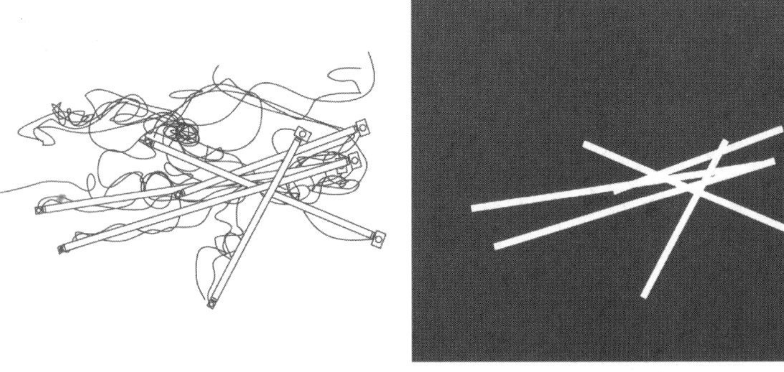
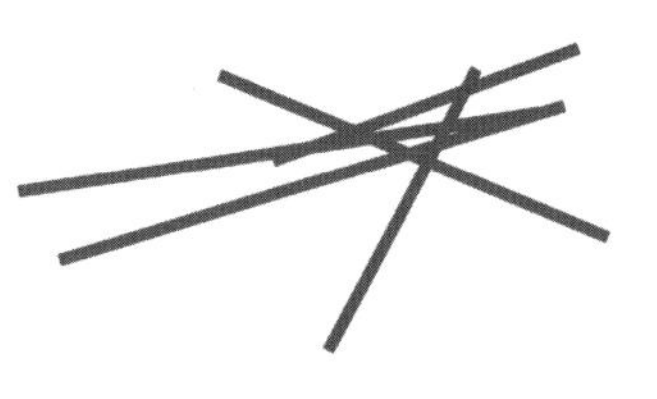
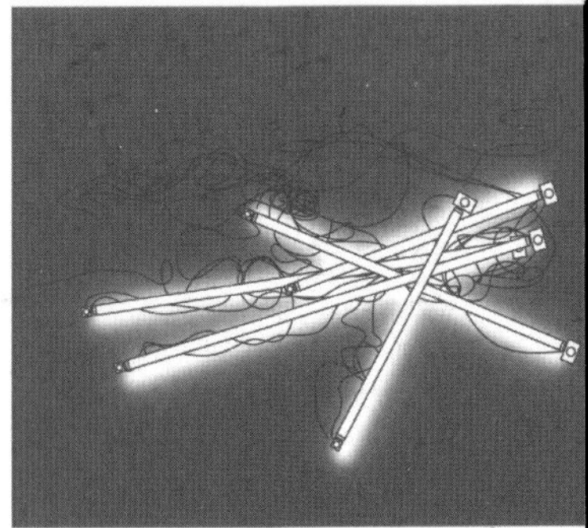

The electromagnetic field is an architecture of expenditure that acts on space itself, on the air as a physical, although invisible, materiality. An architecture that dissipates, that radiates and transforms the electrical, physical and chemical composition of the air, rather than fashioning spatial boundaries by defining an enclosure, building an architectonic structure, organizing the physical delimitation of space. It is a space that dissipates, that has no stated end, no measurable limits, a space that cools to infinity, that is endlessly unfurling. On contact with the body, this electronic radiation stirs the cells in the skin, penetrates deeper within, and heats thebody. Basic combustion, a simple expenditure of energy, transient, without consequences, to be inhabited and abandoned.

The electromagnetic field is a space with no duty of representation. Here, architecture enters a field of physical action, with no decorative or formal function vis-a-vis the boundaries of space. Architecture becomes pure expenditure, a violent act, that touches the eyes and the skin. Physiological, unmediated, formless, unharnessed, acting in the corporeality of the air and the body, the invisible architecture of the field is an immediate force that unfurls, liberated, that conquers the void. This architecture puts a source of energy in place, heat, light and wavelengths that are invisible but necessary to the metabolism of the human body.

an opening to a hormonal relationship between man and architecture, stimulation of the endocrine system, regulation of the neurovegetative system.

ELECTROMAGNETIC CAMP_ Décosterd & Rahm, associés

The source is composed of five fluorescent tubes and five specialized daylight tubes. An open-air architecture, a physical, corporeal, hormonal architecture that acts on the skin and eyes, that affects the endocrine

Nomadic residences for artists in the territories of the Conservatoire du Littoral, Languedoc-Roussillon, France.

RESIDENCES NOMADES_ Décosterd & Rahm-
associes

Inspired by the leather we wear and the meat we eat, this habitat is made from cow-hide, removed by knife, duly cleaned of flesh, immediately salted and folded, and subsequently stretched over a tensile structure. The fur side faces inward, forming an insulating climactic thickness between the grain of the leather and the flax of the interior finish. The flesh is turned to face outward.

The hides are constantly in a precarious state of equilibrium between what may or may not rot. Salt, against which people have fought on these seashores in order to introduce farming, now becomes an ally in the maintenance of this habitable space in the form of temporary tanning. As with the food chain, the ceaseless energy exchange between humankind and its environment through architecture as parasitism and symbiosis is revealed. The habitat or dwelling has been placed in fields of Salicornia, like a link in the carbon cycle, bearing up under the salty winds by frequent additional inputs of salt. Thus, it becomes a possible source of nutrition for wildlife and micro-organisms, which pounce on it as soon as the inhabitant has left.

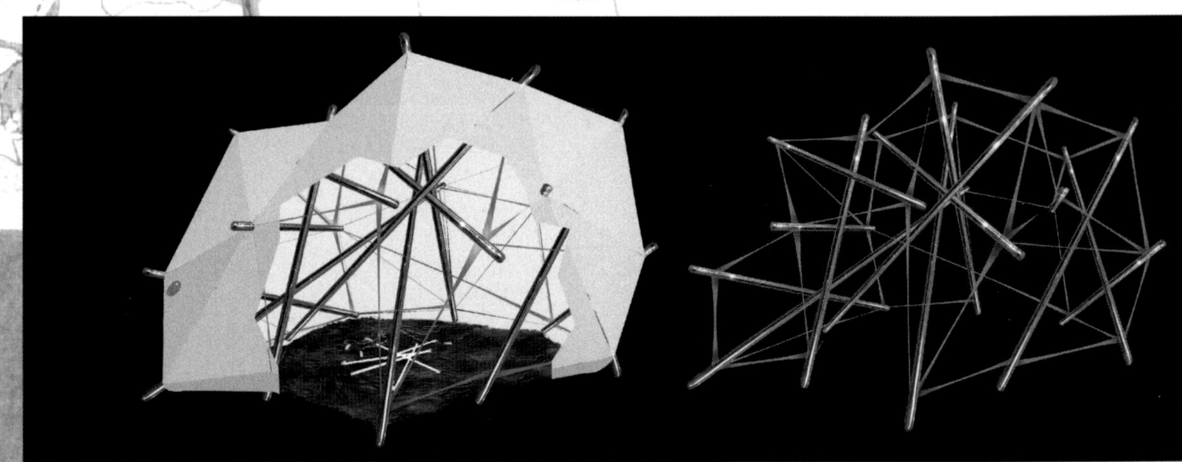

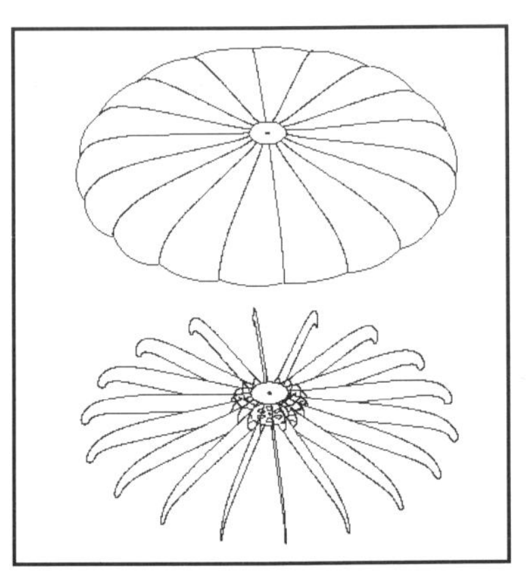

ROTATION PNEU_ Dominik Baumüller

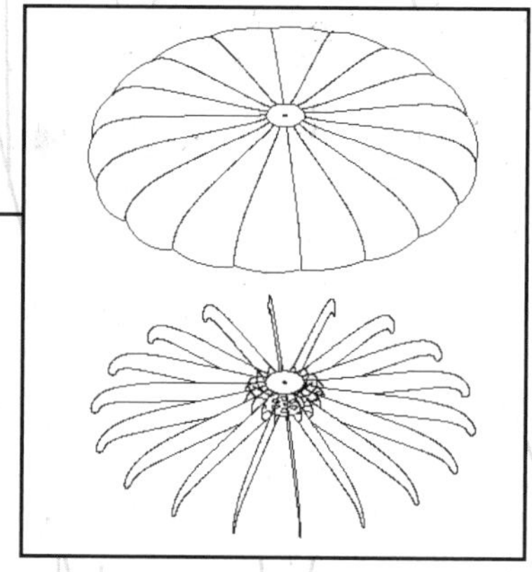

The Rotation Pneu is a building reduced to the very minimum; only the outer shell remains, all rigid structural elements have vanished. Its non-solid behavior is symbolized by the dynamic forces keeping the pneu alive. But it cannot be a real shelter against strong elements, being weak itself. This weakness is the basis for many different, and even contrary, associations. Depending on the speed it looks something like a mushroom, a jelly-fish or even something from outer space.

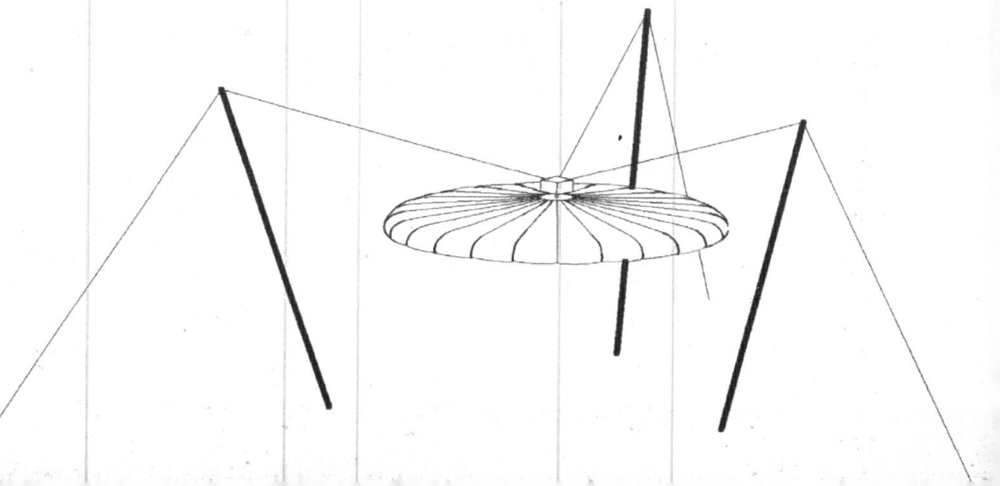

contacts

ACCONCI STUDIO
Tel. +1 (718) 852.6591
studio@acconci.com
www.acconci.com

AWL_ AllesWirdGut
Tel. +43 (01) 961 04 37
awg@alleswirdgut.cc
www.alleswirdgut.cc

AVL- Atelier Van Lieshout
Tel. +31 10 244 09 71
info@ateliervanlieshout.com
www.avl-ville.com

Shigeru Ban Architects
5-2-4 Matsubara, Setagaya
Tokyo 156-0043
sba@tokyo.email.ne.jp

BARCH - Eugeni Bach
Tel. +34 93 301 21 99
barch@coac.net

Dominik Baumüller
Tel. +49-89-555 411
Dominik.Baumueller@beyond-gravity.co
www.beyond-gravity.com

Eduard Böhtlingk
Tel. +31 (010) 591 48 07
mail@bohtlingk.nl
www.bohtlingk.nl

Lucas Cappelli
info@uoku.com

Santiago Cirugeda
archgamessc@ya.com

Piercy Conner Architects
info@piercyconner.co.uk
www.piercyconner.co.uk

Copenhagen-office
info@copenhagenoffice.dk
www.copenhagenoffice.dk

Dante Donegani & Giovanni Lauda
Tel. +39 02 48 02 20 85
degarch@iol.it

Decosterd & Rahm
Tel. +41 (0) 21 320 97 85
info@low-architecture.com
www.low-architecture.com

Jean Michel Ducanelle
Tel. +1 949 723 92 22
sales@anthenea.com
www.anthenea.com

Gilles Ebersolt
Tel. +33 1 42 29 39 74
gilles.ebersolt@wanadoo.fr
www.radeau-des-cimes.org

P. Echavarria + C. Kemper
pechava@yahoo.com
chris.kemper@gmx.net

Experimenta Design
Tel. +351 218 510 283
info@experimentadesign.pt
www.experimentadesign.pt

F.O.B.A
Tel. +81 (77) 42 00 787
foba@fob-web.co.jp
www.fob-web.co.jp

Monica Förster, SNOWCRASH
press@snowcrash.se
www.snowcrash.se

Grégoire & Petetin
Tel. +33 (1) 40 37 20 35
petetin_gregoire@compuserve.com

Thomas Heatherwick Studio
mail@thomasheatherwick.com
www.thomasheatherwick.com

RICHARD HORDEN
info@hcla.co.uk
www.hcla.co.uk

it-Design
Tel. +41 (34) 422 88 96
mail@it-happens.ch
www.it-happens.ch

JAG Design-Jeff Alan Gard
Tel. +1 (415) 776 2939
jeffgardesign@earthlink.net

Oscar Leo Kaufmann
office@olk.cc
www.olk.cc

Kaufmann 96
office@jkarch.at
www.jkarch.at

KHRAS Arkitekten
Tel. +45 (8240) 7000
khr@khras.dk
www.khras.dk

LOT-EK Architecture
Tel. +1 212 255 9326
info@lot-ek.com
www.lot-ek.com

Maki & Associates
Tel. +81 3 3780 38 80
contact@maki-and-associates.co.jp
www.maki-and-associates.co.jp

Henrik Mauler
hello@zeitguised.com
www.zeitguised.com

MaO Studio
+39 0 657 448 29
ma0@libero.it
www.ma0.it

Gruppe MDK-
Pablo Molestina + Aysin Ipekci
Fax. +49 (221) 344 084
molestina@gmx.net

MMW Architects
magne@mmw.no
www.mmw.no

MVRDV
www.mvrdv.nl

N55
n55@n55.dk
www.n55.dk

Hiroshi Nakao
nakaoserizawaarchitectsplus@yahoo.co.jp

OMD- Jennifer Siegal
jennifer@designmobile.com
www.designmobile.com

Valeska Peschke
valeskape@gmx.net
valeskapeschke.com

PO.D
pod@podarchitecture.com
www.podarchitecture.com

Michael Rakowitz
mrakowitz@mica.edu

ROCHE, DSV & SIE
www.new-territories.com
rochedsvsie@wanadoo.fr

Martín Ruíz de Ázua
Tel. +43 93 414 65 82
mrazua@teleline.es

SAAS Architecten
info@saas.nl
www.saas.nl

Franck Scurti
info@franckscurti.net
www.franckscurti.net

SOFTROOM
+44 (20) 74 08 08 64
softroom@softroom.com
www.softroom.com

STUDIO AISSLINGER
werner@aisslinger.de
www.aisslinger.de

Studio Orta. Lucy Orta
Tel. +33 (01) 44 75 51 12
studio-orta@wanadoo.fr
studioorta.free.fr

TSA Architects
contact@thurlowsmall.com
www.thurlowsmall.com

Universidad Central de Chile
Jose Gregorio Brugnoli:
brugnoli@aaschool.ac.uk
Universidad de Chile:
www.fau.cl

Urban Environments
mail@urban-environments.net

Dré Wapenaar
Tel. +31 (6) 53438394
Drewapenaar@zonnet.nl

Wexler Design Studio
Tel. +1 (212) 807 1974
aewexler@aol.com
www.allanwexlerstudio.com

Krzysztof Wodiczko
wodiczko@mit.edu

Andrea Zittel
andrea@zittel.org
www.zittel.org

p.182: Royal College of Art Galleries,
FDAC Seine Saint Denis
John Akehurst

p.184: JJ Crance
Musee d'art et d'histoire de Cholet
Galerie Anne de Villepoix
Art Gallery of Western Australia, Perth
John Akehurst
Lucy Orta

p.186: Michael Rakowitz

p.192: Krzysztof Wodiczko

p.196: R&Sie, Francois Roche

p.200: Martín Ruiz de Ázua

p.202: Oskar Leo Kaufmann

p.204: Bengt O Petersson

p.208: Po.D

p.214: N55

p.218: it design

p.222: Shigeru Ban

p.226: Andrea Zittel

p.228: Gruppe MDK

p.232: Roberto Baldessari

p.236: Ben Barnhart & James Dee

p.238: Piercy Conner Architects / Smoothe

p.242: Andrea Rosen Gallery, Andrea Zittel

p.244: Danny Bright

p.246: Santiago Cirugeda

p.250: Richard Horden

p.252: images were originally published in Wallpaper magazine.

p.254: Robert Roos

p.258: Gilles Ebersolt

p.262: Nacása & Partners

p.266: Marc Domage/ Franck Scurti/ Cortex Athletico

p.270: Keith Paisley

p.274: Gellie, Lison, Lemsky

p.276: Thomas Heatherwick Studio

p.278: Décosterd & Rahm

p.284: Robert Roos

photo credits

end

end

end

end end

end

end

nd

end

end

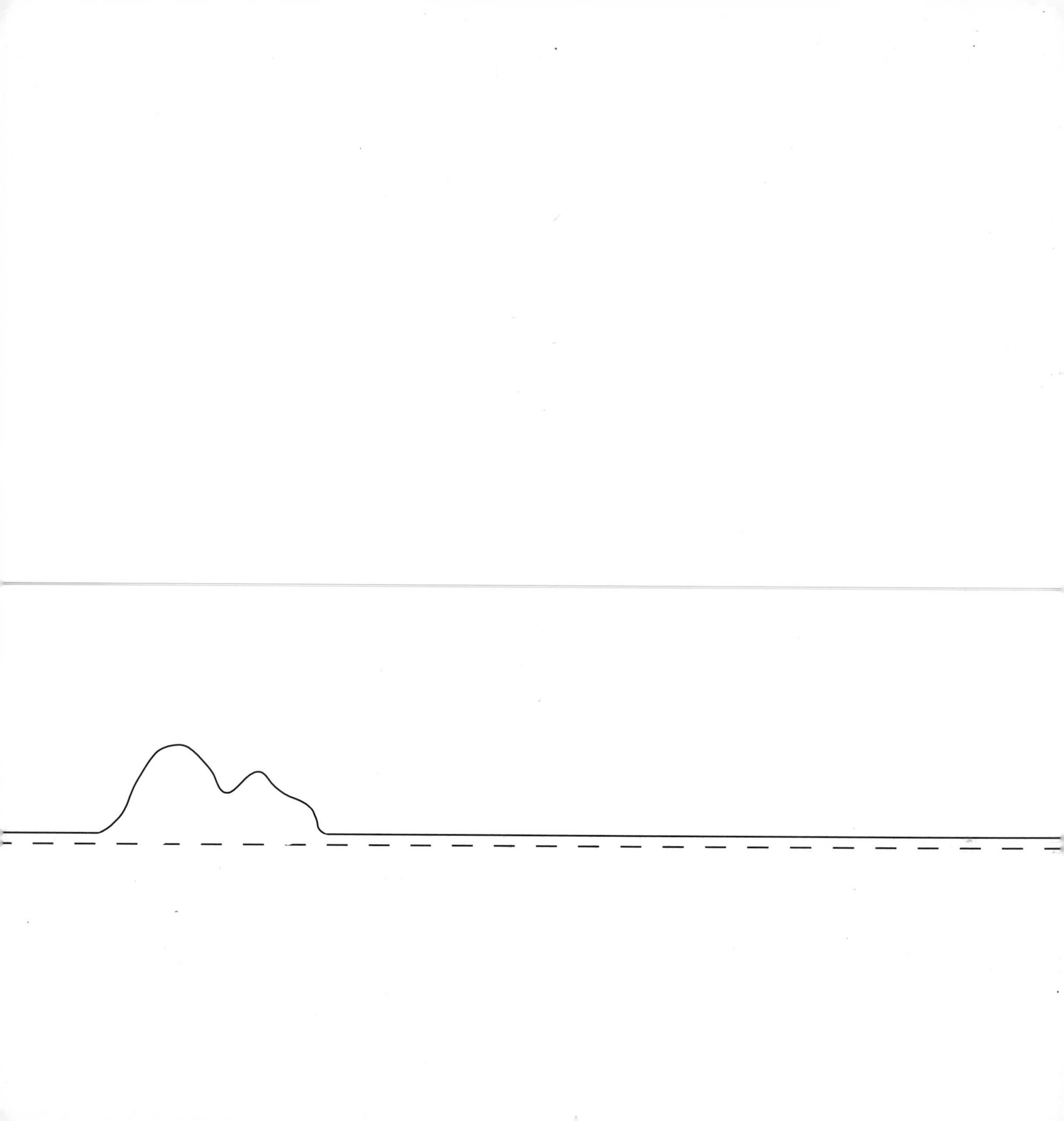